Teacher Presentation Book 1

SRA

Corrective Reading

Decoding C

A Direct Instruction Program

Skill Applications

Siegfried Engelmann

Gary Johnson

Linda Carnine

Linda Meyer

Education Resource Center
University of Delaware
Newark, DE 19716-2940

26633

READ
5r11d
2008
3-12
tr
VC1

Cover Photo: © Chairat/RooM the Agency/Corbis

MHEonline.com

Copyright © McGraw-Hill Education

All rights reserved. No part of this publication may be reproduced or distributed in any form or by any means, or stored in a database or retrieval system, without the prior written consent of McGraw-Hill Education, including, but not limited to, network storage or transmission, or broadcast for distance learning.

Send all inquiries to:
McGraw-Hill Education
8787 Orion Place
Columbus, OH 43240

ISBN: 978-0-07-611236-4
MHID: 0-07-611236-5

Printed in the United States of America.

16 17 LMN 19 18

Contents

Contents

Lesson Objectives	LESSON 1 Exercise	LESSON 2 Exercise	LESSON 3 Exercise	LESSON 4 Exercise	LESSON 5 Exercise
Word Attack					
Decoding and Word Analysis					
Sound Combination: *ai*	3	2	3		
Sound Combination: *ou*	4	4	5		
Sound Combinations: *ir, ur, er*	6	3	4		
Sound Combinations: *ar*				2	2
Visual Discrimination	2, 5	1	1, 2	1	1
Letter Combinations/Letter Sounds				3	3
Word Recognition	1–8	1–6	1–7	1–5	1–5
High-Frequency/Sight Words	6	6	7	5	5
Vocabulary					
Definitions	7	5	3, 6	3–5	3, 4
Usage	7	5	6	4	4
Assessment					
Ongoing: Individual Tests	9	7	8	6	6
Group Reading					
Decoding and Word Analysis					
Read Decodable Text	10	8	9	7	7
Comprehension					
Access Prior Knowledge		8	9		7
Draw Inferences	10	8	9	7	7
Note Details	10	8	9	7	7
Predict		8	9	7	7
Assessment					
Ongoing: Comprehension Check	10	8	9	7	7
Ongoing: Decoding Accuracy	10	8	9	7	7
Fluency Assessment					
Fluency					
Reread Decodable Text	11	9	10	8	8
Assessment					
Ongoing: Teacher-Monitored Fluency	11	9	10	8	8
Ongoing: Peer-Monitored Fluency	11	9	10	8	8
Workbook Exercises					
Decoding and Word Analysis					
Multisyllabic Word Parts	14	12	Ind. Work		Ind. Work
Comprehension					
Note Details	12	10	Ind. Work	Ind. Work	Ind. Work
Vocabulary					
Usage	13	11	Ind. Work	Ind. Work	Ind. Work
Assessment					
Ongoing: Workcheck	Workcheck	Workcheck	Workcheck	Workcheck	Workcheck

Lesson 1

Note: Please read the ***Decoding C Teacher's Guide*** before presenting this program.

Note: NEW indicates the introduction of a new skill or new procedure.

WORD-ATTACK SKILLS

EXERCISE 1

NEW RULES FOR WORD-ATTACK SKILLS

For the first part of every lesson, you'll read words. Some will be on the board, and some will be in your Student Book. Here are the rules for the Word-Attack exercises:

One: Follow my instructions.
Two: Answer when I give you the signal.
Three: Work hard.

To correct word-identification errors:

a. The word is _____.
b. What word? (Signal.)
c. Spell _____. (Signal for each letter.)
- What word? (Signal.)

d. Go back to the first word in the (row/column). ✓
- (Present the words in order.)

Board Work

EXERCISE 2

NEW BUILDUP

1. (Print on the board:)

never

2. (Point to **never.** Pause.) What word? (Signal.) *Never.*
3. (Erase **n:**)

ever

- What word now? (Signal.) *Ever.*

4. (Add **y:**)

every

- What word now? (Signal.) *Every.*

5. (Erase **e:**)

very

- What word now? (Signal.) *Very.*

6. (Change to the original word:)

never

- (Repeat steps 2–5 until firm.)

Student Book

1. Open your Student Book to Lesson 1. ✓
- Everybody in the group can earn 5 points for doing well on reading these words.

2. Here's how this works. First, everybody will read all these words together. If you make a mistake, I'll tell you the right answer, and we'll repeat the row or column. After the group has read all the rows and columns, I'll call on individuals. If the individuals read well, everybody in the group will earn 5 points.

EXERCISE 3

NEW SOUND COMBINATION: ai

Task A

1. Touch the letters **A–I** in part 1. ✓

1

ai

A	B
sailed	bailing
painting	remain
pail	sailor
strain	nails
chain	wait

- The letters **A–I** go together and make the sound **āāā.** What sound? (Signal.) *āāā.*

2. You're going to read words that have the letters **A–I** in them. You're going to say the sound for the underlined part and then read the word.
3. Touch the first word in column A. ✓
   - What sound? (Signal.) *āāā.*
   - What word? (Signal.) *Sailed.*
4. Touch the next word. ✓
   - What sound? (Signal.) *āāā.*
   - What word? (Signal.) *Painting.*
5. (Repeat step 4 for **pail, strain, chain.**)

Task B

1. Touch the first word in column B. ✓
   - What word? (Signal.) *Bailing.*
2. Touch the next word. ✓
   - What word? (Signal.) *Remain.*
3. (Repeat step 2 for **sailor, nails, wait.**)
4. (Repeat steps 1–3 until firm.)

EXERCISE 4

NEW **SOUND COMBINATION: ou**

Task A

1. Touch the letters **O–U** in part 2. ✓

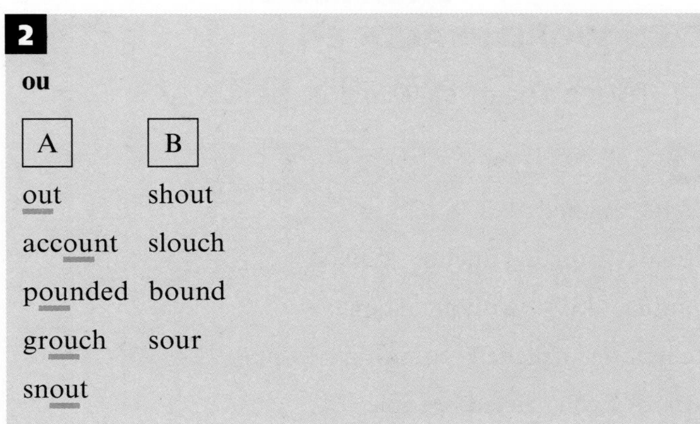

2

ou

A	B
out	shout
account	slouch
pounded	bound
grouch	sour
snout	

- The letters **O–U** go together and usually make the sound **ow,** as in **out.**
- What sound? (Signal.) *ow.*

2. You're going to read words that have the letters **O–U** in them. You're going to say the sound for the underlined part and then read the word.
3. Touch the first word in column A. ✓
   - What sound? (Signal.) *ow.*
   - What word? (Signal.) *Out.*
4. Touch the next word. ✓
   - What sound? (Signal.) *ow.*
   - What word? (Signal.) *Account.*
5. (Repeat step 4 for each remaining word in column A.)

Task B

1. Touch the first word in column B. ✓
   - What word? (Signal.) *Shout.*
2. Touch the next word. ✓
   - What word? (Signal.) *Slouch.*
3. (Repeat step 2 for **bound, sour.**)
4. (Repeat steps 1–3 until firm.)

EXERCISE 5

NEW **BUILDUP**

1. Touch the first word in part 3. ✓
   - What word? (Signal.) *Count.*
2. Next word. ✓
   - What word? (Signal.) *Counter.*
3. (Repeat step 2 for **counting, counted.**)
4. (Repeat steps 1–3 until firm.)

3

count
counter
counting
counted

EXERCISE 6

NEW **SOUND COMBINATIONS: ir, ur, er**

Task A

1. Touch column A in part 4. ✓

4

A	B	C
ir	Bert	turn
ur	clerk	jerked
er	Shirley	third
	buster	dirty
	thirst	shirt
	first	surf

- All those sound combinations make the sound **er.** The sound combination is spelled **I–R, U–R,** or **E–R.**

2. Touch the first sound combination in column A. ✓
- Spell the first combination that makes the sound **er.** (Signal.) *I–R.*
3. Spell the next combination that makes the sound **er.** (Signal.) *U–R.*
4. Spell the last combination that makes the sound **er.** (Signal.) *E–R.*

Task B

1. You're going to read words that have the sound **er.** You're going to say the sound for the underlined part and then read the word.
2. Touch the first word in column B. ✓
- What sound? (Signal.) *er.*
- What word? (Signal.) *Bert.*
3. Touch the next word. ✓
- What sound? (Signal.) *er.*
- What word? (Signal.) *Clerk.*
4. (Repeat step 3 for **Shirley, buster, thirst, first.**)
5. (Repeat steps 2–4 until firm.)

Task C

1. Touch the first word in column C. ✓
- What word? (Signal.) *Turn.*
2. Touch the next word. ✓
- What word? (Signal.) *Jerked.*
3. (Repeat step 2 for **third, dirty, shirt, surf.**)
4. (Repeat steps 1–3 until firm.)

EXERCISE 7

NEW VOCABULARY

1. Touch part 5. ✓
- We're going to talk about what those words mean.
2. Touch word 1. ✓
- What word? (Signal.) *Stout.*
- **Stout** is another way of saying **strong and heavy.** A **strong and heavy** branch is a **stout** branch. What's another way of saying "a **strong and heavy** man"? (Call on a student.) *A stout man.*

5

1. stout
2. churn
3. perch
4. ail
5. strain

3. Everybody, touch word 2. ✓
- What word? (Signal.) *Churn.*
- When something is **stirred up very hard,** it is **churned.** What's another way of saying "He **stirred up** the milk very hard"? (Call on a student.) *He churned the milk.*
4. Everybody, touch word 3. ✓
- What word? (Signal.) *Perch.*
- One meaning for the word **perch** is a small fish. What is one meaning of the word **perch?** (Call on a student.) *A small fish.*
5. Everybody, touch word 4. ✓
- What word? (Signal.) *Ail.*
- Things that **ail you** make you feel bad. If your foot **ails you,** your foot **makes you feel bad.** How would you say "My uncle's back **makes him feel bad**"? (Call on a student.) *My uncle's back ails him.*
6. Everybody, touch word 5. ✓
- What word? (Signal.) *Strain.*
- When you **put forth too much effort,** you **strain** yourself. Everybody, what's another way of saying "The lion **put forth too much effort**"? (Signal.) *The lion strained itself.*

EXERCISE 8

NEW WORD PRACTICE

1. Touch the first word in part 6. ✓

6

felt laughed left sticking
boats woman anchor dollars
didn't don't without sooner
catching dragged thinking
tired can't asked people

- What word? (Signal.) *Felt.*
2. Next word. ✓
- What word? (Signal.) *Laughed.*
3. (Repeat step 2 for each remaining word.)
4. (Repeat each row of words until firm.)

EXERCISE 9

NEW WORD-ATTACK SKILLS: Individual tests

1. Now I'm going to call on individuals. Each person will read a row or column. There are 14 rows and columns. If we can read 11 of them without making a mistake, everybody in the group earns 5 points. So read carefully.
2. (Call on a student.) Read the words in column A in part 1. (Correct any mistakes.)
3. (If the student reads the column without an error, tell the group:) That's one column without a mistake. (Make a tally mark on the board or in your book.)
4. (Call on another student to read the next column. Correct any mistakes.)
5. (Repeat step 4 for all rows and columns.)
6. (If the group reads at least 11 rows and columns without making errors, direct all students to record 5 points in Box A of their Point Chart for Lesson 1.)

The Point Chart is in the back of the Workbook.

7. (If the group did not read at least 11 rows and columns without errors, do not award any points for Word-Attack Skills.)

SELECTION READING

EXERCISE 10

NEW STORY READING

1. Everybody, touch part 7. ✓
   - You're going to read this story. I'll call on individual students to read.
2. Here are the rules that you are to follow.
   - One: Follow along when others are reading.
   - Two: When I call on you, read loudly enough for everyone to hear you.
   - Three: Pause at the end of each sentence.
3. The error limit for this story is 12. If the group reads the story with 12 errors or less, you earn 5 points.

7 **Bert Meets Shirley**

4. (Call on a student to read the title.) *Bert Meets Shirley.*
   - What do you think this story is about? (Accept reasonable responses.)
5. (Call on individual students. Each is to read two to four sentences.)

To correct word-reading errors:
(As soon as a student misidentifies a word, say:)
a. The word is _____.
b. Touch under that word. ✓
c. What word?
d. Go back to the beginning of the sentence and read that sentence again.

6. (Call on individual students to answer the specified questions during the story reading. Numbers in the story indicate at what point you ask each question.)

To correct comprehension errors:
a. (Call on a student to reread the passage that answers the question.)
b. (Repeat the question for the student who made the error.)
c. (Require that student to give an appropriate answer before proceeding with the story reading.)

Bert had a job in a sailing shop. He was a clerk, and he didn't like his job. ❶

1. What does a clerk do? (Ideas: *Works in a store; works as a salesperson.*)
1. Where did Bert work? *In a sailing shop.*

Every day without fail, he went to the shop and waited for people to buy things. Then people came to the shop. They picked up paint and nails and containers for bailing. But every day Bert said to himself, "I'm tired of this job."

Then one day a big sailor came into the sail shop. This sailor was a woman who spoke loudly. "Hello, buster," she said to Bert. "My name is Shirley. I am the best sailor you will ever see. And I need a long anchor chain." ❷

2. What did Shirley do for a living? (Idea: *She was a sailor.*)
2. What did Shirley need? *A long anchor chain.*

"Do you have to shout?" Bert asked.

"Shout?" she shouted. "Don't be such a grouch." She pounded the table. "Get that chain. The sooner I sail, the sooner I will catch perch." ❸

3. What did she want to go catch? *Perch.*

"The chain is upstairs," Bert said. "Wait here, and I will get it for you."

"No," Shirley shouted. "You don't look very stout. I'll go with you and carry the chain down."

So Shirley and Bert went upstairs. She grabbed the chain and gave it a jerk. Then she turned to Bert and said, "How much for this anchor chain?"

"Ten dollars," Bert said.

Shirley said, "That sounds fair. I'll take that chain on account." ❹

4. What does **on account** mean? (Idea: *Buying on credit.*)
4. How much did the chain cost? *Ten dollars.*

"You haven't opened an account here," Bert said. "How can you take it on account?"

The sailor said, "I'll take it on account of I don't have any cash." She laughed and laughed. Then she turned with a jerk. "That's a joke," she said. "You'll get paid without fail. Don't stand there with that sour look."

Shirley dragged the chain down the stairs. When she was at the bottom of the stairs, she said, "You're out of shape. Get out of this sail shop. Go fish for perch."

"I can't do that," Bert said. "I must remain here and do my job."

"Don't you thirst for the sound of the surf? ❺

5. What did she mean by "thirst for the sound of the surf"? (Idea: *The desire to be near the sea.*)

Don't you want to see the waves churn around your feet? Didn't you ever get out under the clouds and the birds?"

"Oh, yes," Bert said. "But—"

"Don't but me," she said. "Get rid of your slouch and fish for perch. It will fix what ails you." ❻

6. What did Shirley think would fix what ailed Bert? (Ideas: *Being a sailor; fishing for perch.*)

Bert found himself thinking of the birds and the waves. Then he said, "When can we go?"

"Now," she said. She pounded the counter. Then she slapped Bert on the back. "Pick up the anchor chain and follow me."

When Bert tried to lift the chain, he said to himself, "This is a strain. I don't know if I will be much of a sailor." 7

7. What did Bert mean by "This is a strain"? (Idea: *This is difficult.*)
7. Was Bert stout? *No.*
7. In this selection, Shirley said that something would **cause** Bert to enjoy life more. What was that? (Idea: *Bert should become a sailor and fish for perch.*)
7. (If the group reads the story with no more than 12 errors, say:) Everybody earns 5 points for the story reading. Write a **5** in Box B of your Point Chart. ✓
8. (If the group makes more than 12 errors, tell them that they earn no points for the story reading. Then do one of the following:)
   a. (If time allows, repeat the story reading immediately. If the group now succeeds, complete the lesson and do the next lesson the following day.)
   b. (If there isn't enough time, repeat the story reading the following day.)

FLUENCY ASSESSMENT

EXERCISE 11

NEW TIMED READING CHECKOUTS

1. (Assign pairs of students to work together during the checkout.)
   - (If one student does not have a checkout partner, arrange another time when you can give the checkout, possibly during the time other students are completing their independent work. Follow the same procedure for students who miss a checkout because they are absent when the checkout is presented.)
2. You're going to do timed reading checkouts. You'll work in pairs. One person in the pair reads for 2 minutes; the other person checks. If the reader makes a mistake or doesn't know a word, the checker makes a tally mark on a piece of paper for each mistake.
3. I'll tell you when to start and when to stop. The reader starts with the first sentence of the story and keeps reading for the entire 2 minutes. If the reader reads at least 200 words without making more than 4 errors, the reader earns 5 points. The 200th word is underlined in the reading selection.
   - While the rest of you are doing your checkout, I'll watch two pairs of students and make sure the checkers are giving good feedback on errors.
   - (During each timed checkout, observe one pair of students for two minutes. Make notes on any mistakes the reader makes. Give the checker feedback on any mistakes that were not caught. Praise checkers who provide good feedback. Praise readers who read accurately.)
4. This is not a race. Just read like you talk.
5. First set of readers, get ready. ✓
   - Go.
   - (After 2 minutes, say:) Stop.

6. (Show students the blue word counts on the Student Book page.) Use the word counts to figure out the number of words that the reader read.
7. Checkers, raise your hand if your reader made no more than 4 errors.
- (Direct students who read 200 words or more and made no more than 4 errors to record 5 points in Box C of their Point Chart.)
8. (Direct all readers to plot their reading rate—the number of words they read in 2 minutes—on the Individual Reading Progress Chart at the end of their Workbook.)
- (Next, direct students to circle the number of errors they made during the timed reading.)
9. Second set of readers, from the beginning of the story. Get ready. ✓
- Go.
- (After 2 minutes, say:) Stop.
10. (Repeat steps 7 and 8 for second set of readers.)
11. (Record the timed reading checkout performance for each student you observed on the Fluency Assessment Summary form. A blackline master of this form is in the back of the Teacher's Guide. Make a copy of this form for each group you teach.)

WORKBOOK EXERCISES

Workbook: Teacher Directed

- Open your Workbook to Lesson 1. ✓
- You're going to do exercises in your Workbook. If you make no errors, you'll earn 5 points.

EXERCISE 12

NEW STORY QUESTIONS

1. Find part 1. ✓
- These questions are about today's story.
2. (Call on a student.) Read item 1. *Where did Bert work?*
- What's the answer? *In a sailing shop.*
3. Later, you'll write answers to all these items.

EXERCISE 13

NEW VOCABULARY REVIEW

1. Find part 2. ✓
- The words in the box are words you've learned.
2. Touch the first word. ✓
- What word? (Signal.) *Churned.*
3. Touch the next word. ✓
- What word? (Signal.) *Stout.*
4. (Repeat step 3 for **ail, perch, grouch, strain.**)
5. (Repeat steps 2–4 until firm.)
6. I'll read the items. When I come to a blank, everybody say the word that goes in the blank.
7. Look over item 1. (Pause.) Listen. **Gina was very big and . . .** (Signal.) *Stout.*
8. (Repeat step 7 for items 2 and 3:)
- 2. He *churned* his soup until it was all stirred.
- 3. The pond had some *perch* swimming in it.
9. You'll write the answers for part 2 later.

EXERCISE 14

NEW WRITING WORD PARTS

1. Find part 3. ✓
- I'll read the instructions: **Write the parts for each word.**
2. The first word is already done for you. The whole word is **sailed.** The first part is **sail.** The ending part is **E-D.** Everybody, spell the word **sailed.** (Signal.) *S–A–I–L–E–D.*
3. (Call on a student.) What's the next word? *Painting.*
- What's the first part of the word? *Paint.*
- What's the ending part of the word? *I–N–G.*
4. Later, you'll write the first part and the ending part for each word in part 3.

NEW Independent Student Work

Task A

Complete all parts of your Workbook lesson using a pencil. If you make no errors, you will earn 5 points.

Task B

1. (Before presenting Lesson 2, check student Workbooks for Lesson 1.)
- Now we're going to check the answers you've written. I'll call on individual students to answer each item. You're going to mark any errors using a pen, not a pencil. Put an X next to any item that is wrong.
2. (Call on a student.) Read question 1 and the answer.
3. (Repeat step 2 for the remaining questions in part 1.)
4. (Call on individual students to read the items and answers in parts 2 and 3.)
5. (Direct the students to count the number of errors and write the number in the Errors box at the top of the Workbook page.)
6. (Award points and direct students to record points in Box D of their Point Chart.)

   0 errors................................5 points
   1 error ....3 points
   2 or 3 errors ....1 point
   more than 3 errors ....0 points

NEW Point schedule for Lesson 1

Box	Lesson part	Points
A	Word Attack	0 or 5
B	Selection Reading	0 or 5
C	Timed Reading Checkout	0 or 5
D	Workbook	0, 1, 3, or 5
Bonus	(Teacher option)	—

END OF LESSON 1

Lesson
1

Errors

1

1. Where did Bert work? (in a sailing shop)
2. a. Was Bert happy at work? No.
   b. How would you know? (He said to himself, "I'm tired of this job." He was a grouch.)
3. Who came to the shop for an anchor chain? (a big sailor; Shirley)
4. What did Shirley do for a living? (fished for perch)
5. How much did the chain cost? ten dollars
6. Did Shirley pay for the chain or take the chain on account? on account
7. What does "on account" mean? (charge it; use credit instead of cash)
8. Where was Shirley taking Bert? (to fish for perch)
9. Was Bert stout? No.
10. **Here are three things that happened in the story.**
    Put the number 1 next to the first thing that happened.
    Put the number 2 next to the second thing that happened.
    Put the number 3 next to the third thing that happened.
    3 Bert tried to pick up the chain.
    1 People came to the shop to buy things.
    2 Shirley took the chain down the stairs.

Copyright © SRA/McGraw-Hill. All rights reserved. *Lesson 1* 1

Lesson
1

2 **Fill in each blank using a word in the box.**

churned	stout	ail
perch	grouch	strain

1. Gina was very big and stout.
2. He churned his soup until it was all stirred.
3. The pond had some perch swimming in it.

3 **Write the parts for each word.**

1. sailed = sail + ed
2. painting = paint + ing
3. brightness = bright + ness
4. slowest = slow + est

2 *Lesson 1* Copyright © SRA/McGraw-Hill. All rights reserved.

Lesson 2

WORD-ATTACK SKILLS

To correct word-identification errors:
a. The word is ______.
b. What word? (Signal.)
c. Spell ______. (Signal for each letter.)
• What word? (Signal.)
d. Go back to the first word in the [row/column]. ✓
• (Present the words in order.)

Board Work

EXERCISE 1

BUILDUP

1. (Print on the board:)

well

2. (Point to **well.** Pause.) What word? (Signal.) *Well.*
3. (Add **s:**)

swell

• What word now? (Signal.) *Swell.*

4. (Erase **w:**)

s ell

• What word now? (Signal.) *Sell.*

5. (Add **ing:**)

s elling

• What word now? (Signal.) *Selling.*

6. (Erase **ing,** add **er:**)

s eller

• What word now? (Signal.) *Seller.*

7. (Change to the original word:)

well

• (Repeat steps 2–6 until firm.)

Student Book

EXERCISE 2

NEW **SOUND COMBINATION: ai**

Task A

1. Open your Student Book to Lesson 2. ✓
• Touch the letters **A-I** in part 1. ✓

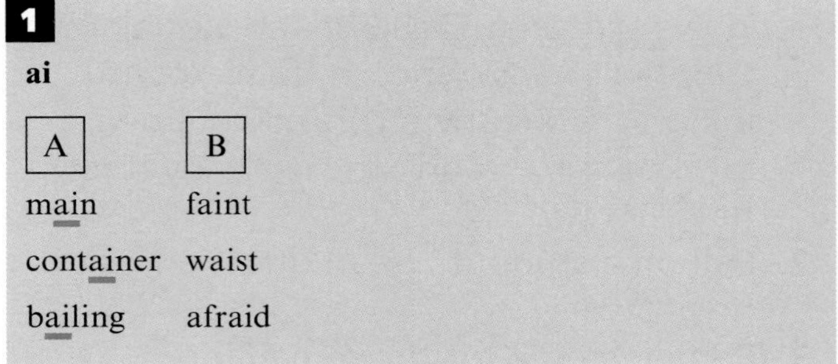

1

ai

A	B
main	faint
container	waist
bailing	afraid

• What sound do the letters **A–I** make? (Signal.) *āāā.*

2. You're going to say the sound for the underlined part and then read the word.
3. Touch the first word in column A. ✓
• What sound? (Signal.) *āāā.*
• What word? (Signal.) *Main.*
4. Touch the next word. ✓
• What sound? (Signal.) *āāā.*
• What word? (Signal.) *Container.*
5. (Repeat step 4 for **bailing.**)

Task B

1. Touch the first word in column B. ✓
• What word? (Signal.) *Faint.*
2. Touch the next word. ✓
• What word? (Signal.) *Waist.*
3. (Repeat step 2 for **afraid.**)
4. (Repeat steps 1–3 until firm.)

EXERCISE 3

SOUND COMBINATIONS: ir, er, ur

Task A

1. Touch column A in part 2. ✓

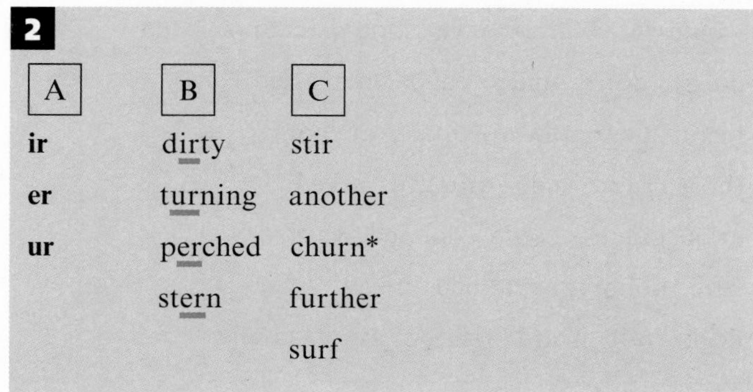

2

A	B	C
ir	dirty	stir
er	turning	another
ur	perched	churn*
	stern	further
		surf

- All those sound combinations make the sound **er.** The sound combination is spelled I–**R, E–R,** or **U–R.**

2. Touch the first sound combination in column A. ✓

- Spell the first combination that makes the sound **er.** (Signal.) *I–R.*

3. Spell the next combination that makes the sound **er.** (Signal.) *E–R.*
4. Spell the last combination that makes the sound **er.** (Signal.) *U–R.*

Task B

1. You're going to read words that have the sound **er.** You're going to say the sound for the underlined part and then read the word.
2. Touch the first word in column B. ✓

- What sound? (Signal.) *er.*
- What word? (Signal.) *Dirty.*

3. Touch the next word. ✓

- What sound? (Signal.) *er.*
- What word? (Signal.) *Turning.*

4. (Repeat step 3 for each remaining word in column B.)

Task C

> *__Note:__ The definitions for starred words appear in the Glossary at the back of this book, the Student Book, and the Teacher's Guide.

1. Touch the first word in column C. ✓

- What word? (Signal.) *Stir.*

2. Touch the next word. ✓

- What word? (Signal.) *Another.*

3. (Repeat step 2 for each remaining word in column C.)
4. (Repeat steps 1–3 until firm.)
5. What does **churn** mean? (Call on a student.)

EXERCISE 4

SOUND COMBINATION: ou

Task A

1. Touch the letters **O-U** in part 3. ✓

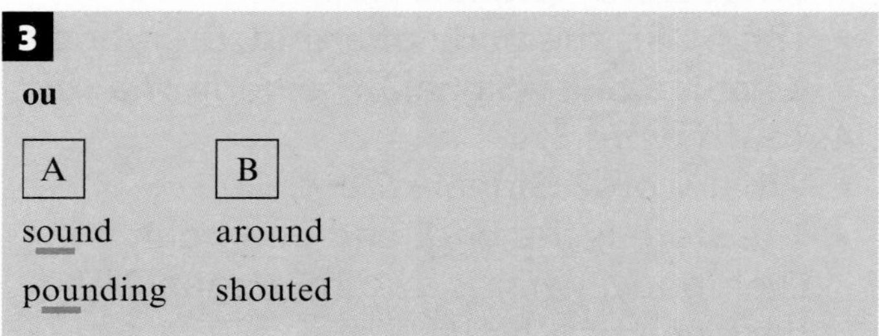

3

ou

A	B
sound	around
pounding	shouted

- What sound do the letters **O-U** make? (Signal.) *ow.*

2. You're going to say the sound for the underlined part and then read the word.
3. Touch the first word in column A. ✓

- What sound? (Signal.) *ow.*
- What word? (Signal.) *Sound.*

4. Touch the next word. ✓

- What sound? (Signal.) *ow.*
- What word? (Signal.) *Pounding.*

Task B

1. Touch the first word in column B. ✓

- What word? (Signal.) *Around.*

2. Touch the next word. ✓

- What word? (Signal.) *Shouted.*

3. (Repeat steps 1 and 2 until firm.)

Lesson 2

EXERCISE 5

VOCABULARY

1. Touch part 4. ✓

4

1. sound
2. hull
3. stern
4. flounder
5. faint
6. waist

- We're going to talk about what those words mean.

2. Touch word 1. ✓
- What word? (Signal.) *Sound.*
- Something that is in **good condition** is **sound.** A boat in **good condition** is a **sound** boat.

3. Touch word 2. ✓
- What word? (Signal.) *Hull.*
- The **hull** is the **body of a ship.** Everybody, what is a **hull?** (Signal.) *The body of a ship.*

4. Touch word 3. ✓
- What word? (Signal.) *Stern.*
- The **stern** is the **back end of a boat.** Everybody, what is a **stern?** (Signal.) *The back end of a boat.*

5. Touch word 4. ✓
- What word? (Signal.) *Flounder.*
- One meaning for the word **flounder** is **flop around.** Everybody, what's another way of saying "The girl **flopped around** in the ocean"? (Signal.) *The girl floundered in the ocean.*

6. Touch word 5. ✓
- What word? (Signal.) *Faint.*
- Something that is **faint** is **very weak.** Everybody, what's another way of saying "The smell is **very weak**"? (Signal.) *The smell is faint.*

7. Touch word 6. ✓
- What word? (Signal) *Waist.*
- Where is your waist? (Call on a student.) (Idea: *Around the middle of the body.*)

EXERCISE 6

WORD PRACTICE

1. Touch the first word in part 5. ✓

5

wouldn't you'll you've should cannot
didn't don't that's can't tried tied
begin hear toward mast anchor
those these side dragged asked
asks grapes could slapped yourself
sure bobbing grabbed below knee
deck hull heard fishing away farther

- What word? (Signal.) *Wouldn't.*

2. Next word. ✓
- What word? (Signal.) *You'll.*

3. (Repeat step 2 for each remaining word.)
4. (Repeat each row of words until firm.)

EXERCISE 7

NEW WORD-ATTACK SKILLS: Individual tests

1. (Call on individual students. Each student reads a row or column. Tally the rows and columns read without error. If the group reads at least 12 rows and columns without making errors, direct all students to record 5 points in Box A of their Point Chart. Criterion is 80 percent of rows and columns read without error.)
2. (If the group did not read at least 12 rows and columns without errors, do not award any points for the Word-Attack Skills exercises.)

SELECTION READING

EXERCISE 8

STORY READING

1. (Call on individual students to answer these questions.)
- What are the names of the two main characters in the last selection? *Bert and Shirley.*
- What jobs did they have? (Idea: *Bert was a clerk in a sailing shop, and Shirley was a sailor.*)
- What happened? (Idea: *Shirley convinced Bert to leave his job and go fishing with her for perch.*)
2. Everybody, touch part 6. ✓
- You're going to read this story. I'll call on individual students to read.
3. Here are the rules that you are to follow.
- One: Follow along when others are reading.
- Two: When I call on you, read loudly enough for everyone to hear you.
- Three: Pause at the end of each sentence.
4. The error limit for this story is 12. If the group reads the story with 12 errors or less, you earn 5 points.

6 **On the Open Sea**

5. (Call on a student to read the title.) *On the Open Sea.*
- What do you think this story is about? (Accept reasonable responses.)
6. (Call on individual students. Each is to read two to four sentences.)

To correct word-reading errors:
(As soon as a student misidentifies a word, say:)
a. The word is _____.
b. Touch under that word. ✓
c. What word?
d. Go back to the beginning of the sentence and read that sentence again.

7. (Call on individual students to answer the specified questions during the story reading. Numbers in the story indicate at what point you ask each question.)

To correct comprehension errors:
a. (Call on a student to reread the passage that answers the question.)
b. (Repeat the question for the student who made the error.)
c. (Require that student to give an appropriate answer before proceeding with the story reading.)

Bert had left the sail shop to go fishing for perch with Shirley. They went to the dock. Bert counted six sound boats at the dock. ❶

1. What does the word **sound** mean in "six sound boats at the dock"? (Ideas: *In good condition; safe.*)

The third boat didn't look sound. It needed paint. Nails were sticking out of the side of the boat. The deck was dirty. "This is my house," Shirley said loudly. "I can't wait to get it under sail."

"This boat is a turkey," Bert said. ❷

2. What three things were wrong with Shirley's boat? (Idea: *It needed paint, nails were sticking out, and it had a dirty deck.*)

Shirley said, "Be fair, Bert. This is a swell home."

Bert dragged the chain on board. "Some boat," he said.

"It's time to sail," Shirley said. "Run up the main sail."

"Where is the main sail?" Bert asked.

Shirley slapped a big mast. "Here it is," she said.

"I can't run up that thing," Bert said. "I can't even climb up that thing."

"You don't run yourself up that mast," Shirley said. "You run the sail up that mast. I'll show you how." ❸

3. Did Bert know what Shirley meant when she said, "Run up the main sail?" *No.*
3. What did Shirley mean when she said, "Run up the main sail?" (Idea: *For him to put the sail up the mast.*)
3. What is a mast? (Ideas: *Where the sail goes; support for the sail.*)

So she did. And then, as Bert stood there, not sure what he was doing or why he was doing it, the boat began to turn and go out to sea.

Soon the boat was in the open sea, bobbing up and down in the surf. Bert began to feel sick. But Shirley was singing. She was perched in a chair under the main sail. ❹

4. What does **perched** mean in this sentence? (Ideas: *Seated, sitting.*)
4. How did Bert feel? *Sick.*
4. Why did he feel sick? (Idea: *Because of the motion of the boat.*)

And the boat churned a path in the surf. At last Shirley shouted, "Bert, grab a container, go below, and start bailing. Our hold must be filled with water."

Bert went below. The water was up to his waist. ❺

5. What's a hold? (Idea: *The part of the boat below the deck.*)
5. How deep was the water in the hold? (Idea: *Up to Bert's waist.*)

He felt faint as the boat pounded this way and that way. He bailed and bailed and bailed. At last the water was only knee-deep. Then Bert went back to the deck. ❻

6. How deep was the water in the hold when Bert finished bailing? (Idea: *Knee-deep.*)

"What ails you?" Shirley shouted. "You look like you just ate sour grapes."

"I'm sick," Bert said.

"Take a turn around the deck," Shirley said. "The sea air will take care of what ails you."

Bert went to the stern of the boat. Just then the boat began to flounder as a big wave slapped the side of the hull. Bert fell into the water. ❼

7. How did Bert fall into the water? (Idea: *A big wave hit the boat.*)

He came up just in time to see another big wave churn toward him. Before he could shout, the wave hit him like a train of water. He came up and tried to shout, but he had water in his mouth. "Blurp," he said. The old boat and Shirley were farther away.

"Help," he yelled, but his shout was faint over the sound of the pounding sea. ❽

8. Did Shirley hear Bert call? *No.*
8. Why was his call faint? (Idea: *Because the pounding of the ocean was too loud.)*

Suddenly Bert was very afraid. But just then he heard somebody say, "Hello." ❾

9. Who do you think said, "Hello"? (Accept reasonable responses.)
8. (If the group reads the story with no more than 12 errors, say:) Everybody earns 5 points for the story reading. Write a **5** in Box B of your Point Chart. ✓
9. (If the group makes more than 12 errors, tell them that they earn no points for the story reading. Then do one of the following:)
   a. (If time allows, repeat the story reading immediately. If the group now succeeds, complete the lesson and do the next lesson the following day.)
   b. (If there isn't enough time, repeat the story reading the following day.)

FLUENCY ASSESSMENT

EXERCISE 9

TIMED READING CHECKOUTS

1. (Assign pairs of students to work together during the checkout.)
   - (If one student does not have a checkout partner, arrange another time when you can give the checkout, possibly during the time other students are completing their independent work. Follow the same procedure for students who miss a checkout because they are absent when the checkout is presented.)
2. You're going to do timed reading checkouts. You'll work in pairs. One person in the pair reads for 2 minutes; the other person checks. If the reader makes a mistake or doesn't know a word, the checker makes a tally mark on a piece of paper for each mistake.
3. I'll tell you when to start and when to stop. The reader starts with the first sentence of the story and keeps reading for the entire 2 minutes. If the reader reads at least 200 words without making more than 4 errors, the reader earns 5 points. The 200th word is underlined in the reading selection.
   - While the rest of you are doing your checkout, I'll watch two pairs of students and make sure the checkers are giving good feedback on errors.
   - (During each timed checkout, observe one pair of students for 2 minutes. Make notes on any mistakes the reader makes. Give the checker feedback on any mistakes that were not caught. Praise checkers who provide good feedback. Praise readers who read accurately.)
4. This is not a race. Just read like you talk.
5. First set of readers, get ready. ✓
   - Go.
   - (After 2 minutes, say:) Stop.
6. (Show students the blue word counts on the Student Book page.) Use the word counts to figure out the number of words that the reader read.
7. Checkers, raise your hand if your reader made no more than 4 errors.
   - (Direct students who read 200 words or more and made no more than 4 errors to record 5 points in Box C of their Point Chart.)

8. (Direct all readers to plot their reading rate—the number of words they read in 2 minutes—on the Individual Reading Progress Chart at the end of their Workbook.)
- (Next, direct students to circle the number of errors they made during the timed reading.)
9. Second set of readers, from the beginning of the story. Get ready. ✓
- Go.
- (After 2 minutes, say:) Stop.
10. (Repeat steps 7 and 8 for second set of readers.)
11. (Record the timed reading checkout performance for each student you observed on the Fluency Assessment Summary form. A blackline master of this form is in the back of the Teacher's Guide. Make a copy of this form for each group you teach.)

WORKBOOK EXERCISES

Workbook: Teacher Directed

- Open your Workbook to Lesson 2. ✓
- You're going to do exercises in your Workbook. If you make no errors, you'll earn 5 points.

EXERCISE 10

STORY QUESTIONS

1. Find part 1. ✓
- These questions are about today's story.
2. (Call on a student.) Read item 1. *Name two things wrong with Shirley's boat.*
- What's the answer? (Ideas [any two]: *It needed paint; nails were sticking out of it; the deck was dirty.*)
3. Later, you'll write answers to all these items.

EXERCISE 11

VOCABULARY REVIEW

1. Find part 2. ✓
- The words in the box are words you've learned.
2. Touch the first word. ✓
- What word? (Signal.) *Sound.*
3. Touch the next word. ✓
- What word? (Signal.) *Stern.*
4. (Repeat step 3 for **faint, hull, floundered, ail.**)
5. (Repeat steps 2–4 until firm.)
6. I'll read the items. When I come to a blank, everybody say the word that goes in the blank.
7. Look over item 1. (Pause.) Listen. **The boat was . . .** (Signal.) *Sound.* It didn't leak.
8. (Repeat step 7 for items 2 and 3:)
- 2. The dog *floundered* on the slippery ice.
- 3. The writing was too *faint* to read.
9. You'll write the answers for part 2 later.

EXERCISE 12

WRITING WORD PARTS

1. Find part 3. ✓
- I'll read the instructions: **Write the parts for each word.**
2. The first word is already done for you. The whole word is **soundest.** The first part is **sound.** The ending part is **E–S–T.** Everybody, spell the word **soundest.** (Signal.) *S–O–U–N–D–E–S–T.*
3. (Call on a student.) What's the next word? *Floundering.*
- What's the first part of the word? *Flounder.*
- What's the ending part of the word? *I–N–G.*
4. Later, you'll write the first part and the ending part for each word in part 3.

Independent Student Work

Task A

Complete all parts of your Workbook lesson using a pencil. If you make no errors, you will earn 5 points.

Task B

1. (Before presenting Lesson 3, check student Workbooks for Lesson 2.)
   - Now we're going to check the answers you've written. I'll call on individual students to answer each item. You're going to mark any errors using a pen, not a pencil. Put an X next to any item that is wrong.
2. (Call on a student.) Read question 1 and the answer.
3. (Repeat step 2 for the remaining questions in part 1.)
4. (Call on individual students to read the items and answers in parts 2 and 3.)
5. (Direct the students to count the number of errors and write the number in the Errors box at the top of the Workbook page.)
6. (Award points and direct students to record points in Box D of their Point Chart.)

   0 errors ....5 points
   1 error ....3 points
   2 or 3 errors ....1 point
   more than 3 errors ....0 points

Point schedule for Lesson 2

Box	Lesson part	Points
A	Word Attack	0 or 5
B	Selection Reading	0 or 5
C	Timed Reading Checkout	0 or 5
D	Workbook	0, 1, 3, or 5
Bonus	(Teacher option)	—

END OF LESSON 2

Lesson 2

Errors

1

1. Name two things wrong with Shirley's boat. (Any two: it needed paint; nails were sticking out of it; the deck was dirty.)
2. What did Bert think of Shirley's boat? (that it was a turkey)
3. Did Bert know what Shirley meant when she said, "Run up the main sail"? No.
4. What did Shirley mean when she said, "Run up the main sail"? (to make the sail go up the mast)
5. Why did Bert feel sick? (The boat was bobbing up and down.)
6. How high did the water get in the hold? (up to Bert's waist)
7. How deep was the water in the hold when Bert stopped bailing? (knee-deep)
8. What happened to make the boat begin to flounder? (A big wave slapped the side of the hull.)
9. Did Shirley hear Bert's call? No.
10. Why was Bert's call faint? (The sea was so loud; he had water in his mouth.)

Copyright © SRA/McGraw-Hill. All rights reserved.
Lesson 2 3

Lesson 2

2 Fill in each blank using a word in the box.

sound	stern	faint
hull	floundered	ail

1. The boat was sound. It didn't leak.
2. The dog floundered on the slippery ice.
3. The writing was too faint to read.

3 Write the parts for each word.

1. soundest = sound + est
2. floundering = flounder + ing
3. remained = remain + ed
4. stoutness = stout + ness

4 Lesson 2
Copyright © SRA/McGraw-Hill. All rights reserved.

Lesson 3

WORD-ATTACK SKILLS

To correct word-identification errors:

a. The word is ______.
b. What word? (Signal.)
c. Spell ______. (Signal for each letter.)
- What word? (Signal.)

d. Go back to the first word in the (row/column). ✓
- (Present the words in order.)

Board Work

EXERCISE 1

BUILDUP

1. (Print on the board:)

ail

2. (Point to **ail.** Pause.) What word? (Signal.) *Ail.*
3. (Add **f:**)

f ail

- What word now? (Signal.) *Fail.*

4. (Add **l:**)

flail

- What word now? (Signal.) *Flail.*

5. (Add **ing:**)

flailing

- What word now? (Signal.) *Flailing.*

6. (Erase **ing,** add **ed:**)

flailed

- What word now? (Signal.) *Flailed.*

7. (Change to the original word:)

ail

- (Repeat steps 2–6 until firm.)

EXERCISE 2

BUILDUP

1. (Print on the board:)

rush

2. (Point to **rush.** Pause.) What word? (Signal.) *Rush.*
3. (Add **b:**)

brush

- What word now? (Signal.) *Brush.*

4. (Add **ing:**)

brushing

- What word now? (Signal.) *Brushing.*

5. (Erase **ing,** add **ed:**)

brushed

- What word now? (Signal.) *Brushed.*

6. (Erase **d,** add **s:**)

brushes

- What word now? (Signal.) *Brushes.*

7. (Change to the original word:)

rush

- (Repeat steps 2–6 until firm.)

Student Book 

EXERCISE 3

SOUND COMBINATION: ai

Task A

1. Open your Student Book to Lesson 3. ✓

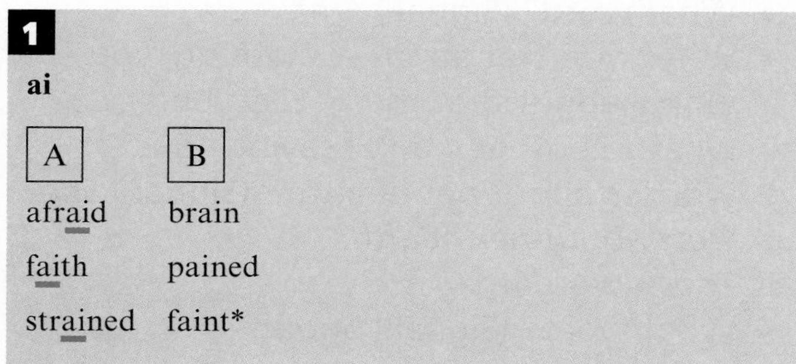

1

ai

A	B
afraid	brain
faith	pained
strained	faint*

- Touch the letters **A–I** in part 1. ✓
- What sound do the letters **A–I** make? (Signal.) *āāā.*

2. You're going to say the sound for the underlined part and then read the word.
3. Touch the first word in column A. ✓
   - What sound? (Signal.) *āāā.*
   - What word? (Signal.) *Afraid.*
4. Touch the next word. ✓
   - What sound? (Signal.) *āāā.*
   - What word? (Signal.) *Faith.*
5. (Repeat step 4 for **strained.**)

Task B

> ***Note:** The definitions for starred words appear in the Glossary at the back of this book, the Student Book, and the Teacher's Guide.

1. Touch the first word in column B. ✓
   - What word? (Signal.) *Brain.*
2. Touch the next word. ✓
   - What word? (Signal.) *Pained.*
3. (Repeat step 2 for **faint.**)
4. (Repeat steps 1–3 until firm.)
5. What does **faint** mean? (Call on a student.)

EXERCISE 4

NEW **SOUND COMBINATIONS: ir, ur, er**

Task A

1. Touch column A in part 2. ✓

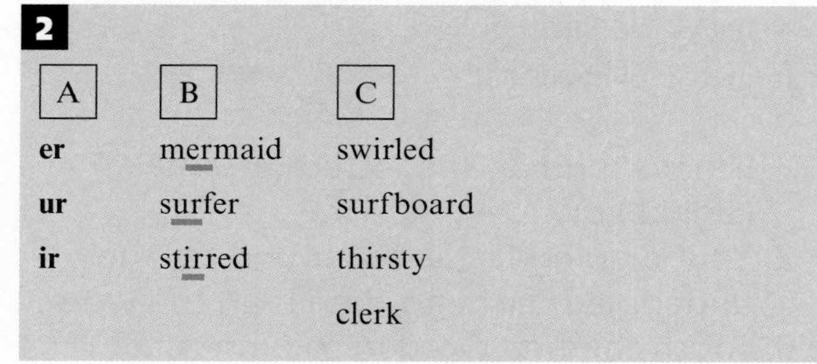

2

A	B	C
er	mermaid	swirled
ur	surfer	surfboard
ir	stirred	thirsty
		clerk

- All those sound combinations make the same sound. What sound? (Signal.) *er.*

2. Spell the first combination that makes the sound **er.** (Signal.) *E–R.*
3. Spell the next combination that makes the sound **er.** (Signal.) *U–R.*
4. Spell the last combination that makes the sound **er.** (Signal.) *I–R.*

Task B

1. You're going to say the sound for the underlined part and then read the word.
2. Touch the first word in column B. ✓
   - What sound? (Signal.) *er.*
   - What word? (Signal.) *Mermaid.*
3. Touch the next word. ✓
   - What sound? (Signal.) *er.*
   - What word? (Signal.) *Surfer.*
4. (Repeat step 3 for **stirred.**)

Task C

1. Touch the first word in column C. ✓
   - What word? (Signal.) *Swirled.*
2. Touch the next word. ✓
   - What word? (Signal.) *Surfboard.*
3. (Repeat step 2 for **thirsty, clerk.**)
4. (Repeat steps 1–3 until firm.)

EXERCISE 5

SOUND COMBINATION: ou

Task A

1. Touch the letters **O–U** in part 3. ✓

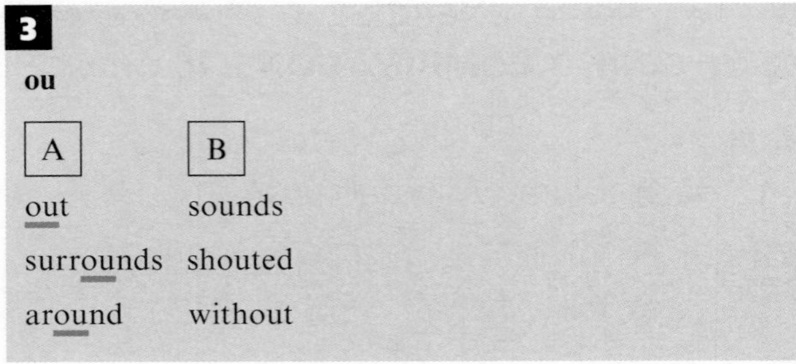
3

ou

A	B
out	sounds
surrounds	shouted
around	without

- What sound do the letters **O-U** make? (Signal.) *ow.*

2. You're going to say the sound for the underlined part and then read the word.
3. Touch the first word in column A. ✓
   - What sound? (Signal.) *ow.*
   - What word? (Signal.) *Out.*
4. Touch the next word. ✓
   - What sound? (Signal.) *ow.*
   - What word? (Signal.) *Surrounds.*
5. (Repeat step 4 for **around.**)

Task B

1. Touch the first word in column B. ✓
   - What word? (Signal.) *Sounds.*
2. Touch the next word. ✓
   - What word? (Signal.) *Shouted.*
3. (Repeat step 2 for **without.**)
4. (Repeat steps 1–3 until firm.)

EXERCISE 6

VOCABULARY

1. Touch part 4. ✓

4

1. flounder
2. flail
3. fret
4. snout
5. swirl
6. surfer

- We're going to talk about what those words mean.

2. Touch word 1. ✓
   - What word? (Signal.) *Flounder.*
   - What's one meaning you learned for **flounder?** (Call on a student.) (Idea: *Flop around.*)
   - **Flounder** is also the name of a fish.
3. Everybody, touch word 2. ✓
   - What word? (Signal.) *Flail.*
   - When people **swing their arms around like crazy,** they **flail** their arms. What's another way of saying "She **swung her arms around like crazy**"? (Signal.) *She flailed her arms.*
4. Touch word 3. ✓
   - What word? (Signal.) *Fret.*
   - When you **fret** about something, you **worry** about that thing. Everybody, what's another way of saying "She **worries** about her health"? (Signal.) *She frets about her health.*
5. Touch word 4. ✓
   - What word? (Signal.) *Snout.*
   - Who knows what a **snout** is? (Call on a student.) (Idea: *The nose of an animal.*)
6. Everybody, touch word 5. ✓
   - What word? (Signal.) *Swirl.*
   - When things such as liquids **twist around,** they **swirl.** Everybody, what's another way of saying "the wave **twisted around** "? (Signal.) *The wave swirled.*
7. Touch word 6. ✓
   - What word? (Signal.) *Surfer.*
   - Who knows what a **surfer** is? (Call on a student.) (Idea: *A person who rides a surfboard.*)

EXERCISE 7

WORD PRACTICE

1. Touch the first word in part 5. ✓

5

won't don't didn't wasn't staring
weren't wouldn't starting swim
swam middle paddled yourself worry
shark anybody rather floating
talking head reached submarine
attack while hungry brushed

- What word? (Signal.) *Won't.*

2. Next word. ✓
   - What word? (Signal.) *Don't.*
3. (Repeat step 2 for each remaining word.)
4. (Repeat each row of words until firm.)

EXERCISE 8

WORD-ATTACK SKILLS: Individual tests

1. (Call on individual students. Each student reads a row or column. Tally the rows and columns read without error. If the group reads at least 11 rows and columns without making errors, direct all students to record 5 points in Box A of their Point Chart. Criterion is 80 percent of rows and columns read without error.)
2. (If the group did not read at least 11 rows and columns without errors, do not award any points for the Word-Attack Skills exercises.)

SELECTION READING

EXERCISE 9

NEW **STORY READING**

1. (Call on individual students to answer these questions.)
   - In the last selection, Bert had a serious problem. What was that? (Idea: *He fell into the water.*)
   - Why did he end up in the water? (Idea: *A big wave hit the boat.*)
2. Everybody, touch part 6. ✓
   - You're going to read this story.
3. The error limit for this story is 12. If the group reads the story with 12 errors or less, you earn 5 points.

6 **The Merman**

4. (Call on a student to read the title.) *The Merman.*
   - What do you think this story is about? (Accept reasonable responses.)
5. (Call on individual students. Each is to read two to four sentences.)

To correct word-reading errors:
(As soon as a student misidentifies a word, say:)
a. The word is _____.
b. Touch under that word. ✓
c. What word?
d. Go back to the beginning of the sentence and read that sentence again.

6. (Call on individual students to answer the specified questions during the story reading. Numbers in the story indicate at what point you ask each question.)

To correct comprehension errors:
a. (Call on a student to reread the passage that answers the question.)
b. (Repeat the question for the student who made the error.)
c. (Require that student to give an appropriate answer before proceeding with the story reading.)

Bert was flailing in the surf, but he was failing to get close to the old boat. ❶

1. What was Bert doing in the surf? *Flailing.*
1. How do you flail? (Idea: *You wave your arms around.*)

Then suddenly somebody said, "Hello."
Bert turned around and saw a head bobbing in the water. "You must be a mermaid," Bert said. ❷

2. Who did Bert first think said, "Hello"? *A mermaid.*
2. What's a mermaid? (Idea: *A female sea creature that is part human, part fish.*)

"Don't be a jerk," the head said. "Do I look like a maid?"

"No, no," Bert said. "You look like a man. So you must be a merman." ❸

3. Now who did Bert think he was talking to? *A merman.*
3. What's a merman? (Idea: *A male sea creature that is part human, part fish.*)

"Don't be a jerk," the head said again. "I am a surfer. I took the wrong turn, and here I am, out in the middle of the sea." ❹

4. What's a surfer? (Idea: *Someone who rides a surfboard on the waves.*)

The surfer paddled over to Bert. Bert said, "I am afraid we won't be able to get back to the beach."

"Don't get yourself stirred up," the surfer said. "Things will take a turn for the better if you just keep the faith."

"How do you do that?" Bert asked just as a big wave swirled over his head.

"Grab hold of my surfboard and play it cool. Don't strain your brain. Somebody will come by if you just wait." ❺

5. How do you "keep the faith"? (Ideas: *Relax; don't worry; hope for the best.*)

"How long will we have to wait?" Bert said as he reached for the surfboard.

"Don't be a pain, man," the surfer said. "<u>Don't</u> worry about how long it will be. Don't start thinking about how we are shark bait sitting out here. Don't think about how thirsty you are. Think of how much fun this is. Like what would you be doing if you weren't out here?" ❻

6. What did the surfer want Bert to think about? (Ideas: *About how much fun he was having; what he would be doing if he weren't at sea.*)

"I would be working as a clerk in a sail shop," Bert said.

"See what I mean?" the surfer said. "Anybody would rather be out here floating around like a flounder."

Bert said, "I don't know about that. I think I would rather—" Bert stopped talking. He was staring at a fin that was cutting a path in the water. Bert said, "Isn't that a shark fin?" ❼

7. What did Bert see? (Idea: *A shark fin.*)

"That's not a submarine," the surfer said. "Look at how that shark can swim. Wouldn't it be neat to swim that well?"

"But—but—won't that shark attack us?" Bert said.

"I'll tell you in a while," the surfer said. "But don't fret about it. If that shark is hungry, we will be its supper."

"But I don't want to be a shark's supper," Bert moaned.

"Well," the surfer said, "if you don't dig it here, why don't you just take the next bus home?" ❽

8. What didn't Bert want to be? (Idea: *Shark food.*)
8. What did the surfer tell Bert to do? (Idea: *Take the next bus home.*)
8. Why couldn't Bert do that? (Idea: *There's no bus in the ocean.*)

> Just then the shark swam under the surfboard. The shark's snout brushed against Bert's foot. "I think I'm going to faint," Bert said.
>
> "That's cool," the surfer said. "You'll feel better after a little nap." ⑨

9. What did the surfer think would make Bert feel better? *A nap.*

> Bert felt sick. He wished he were back in the sail shop.

7. (Award points quickly at the end of the story reading.)
8. (If the group makes more than 12 errors, tell them that they earn no points for the story reading. Then do one of the following:)
   a. (If time allows, repeat the story reading immediately. If the group now succeeds, complete the lesson and do the next lesson the following day.)
   b. (If there isn't enough time, repeat the story reading the following day.)

FLUENCY ASSESSMENT

EXERCISE 10

NEW TIMED READING CHECKOUTS

1. (For this part of the lesson, assigned pairs of students work together during the checkouts.)
- (If one student does not have a checkout partner, arrange another time when you can give the checkout, possibly during the time other students are completing their independent work. Follow the same procedure for students who miss a checkout because they are absent when the checkout is presented.)

2. Now you'll do the timed checkout on the first part of story 3. If you read at least 200 words and make no more than 4 errors, you earn 5 points.
- While the rest of you are doing your checkout, I'll watch two pairs of students and make sure the checkers are giving good feedback on errors.

3. This is not a race. Just read like you talk.
4. First set of readers, get ready. ✓
- Go.
- (After 2 minutes, say:) Stop.

5. (During each timed checkout, observe one pair of students for 2 minutes. Make notes on any mistakes the reader makes. Give the checker feedback on any mistakes that were not caught. Praise checkers who provide good feedback. Praise readers who read accurately.)
6. (Direct checkers to count the number of words read. Students who read at least 200 words and made no more than 4 errors record 5 points in Box C of their Point Chart.)
7. (Direct students to record their reading rate and number of errors on the Individual Reading Progress Chart.)
8. (Repeat steps 4–7 for the second set of readers.)
9. (Record the timed reading checkout performance for each student you observed on the Fluency Assessment Summary form.)

Lesson
3

WORKBOOK EXERCISES

NEW Independent Student Work

Task A

- Open your Workbook to Lesson 3. ✓
- Complete all parts of your Workbook lesson using a pencil. If you make no errors, you will earn 5 points.

Task B

1. (Before presenting Lesson 4, check student Workbooks for Lesson 3.)
   - Now we're going to check the answers you've written. I'll call on individual students to answer each item. You're going to mark any errors using a pen, not a pencil. Put an X next to any item that is wrong.
2. (Call on a student.) Read question 1 and the answer.
3. (Repeat step 2 for the remaining questions in part 1.)
4. (Call on individual students to read the items and answers in parts 2 and 3.)
5. (Direct the students to count the number of errors and write the number in the Errors box at the top of the Workbook page.)
6. (Award points and direct students to record points in Box D of their Point Chart.)

   0 errors.................................5 points
   1 error ....3 points
   2 or 3 errors ....1 point
   more than 3 errors ....0 points

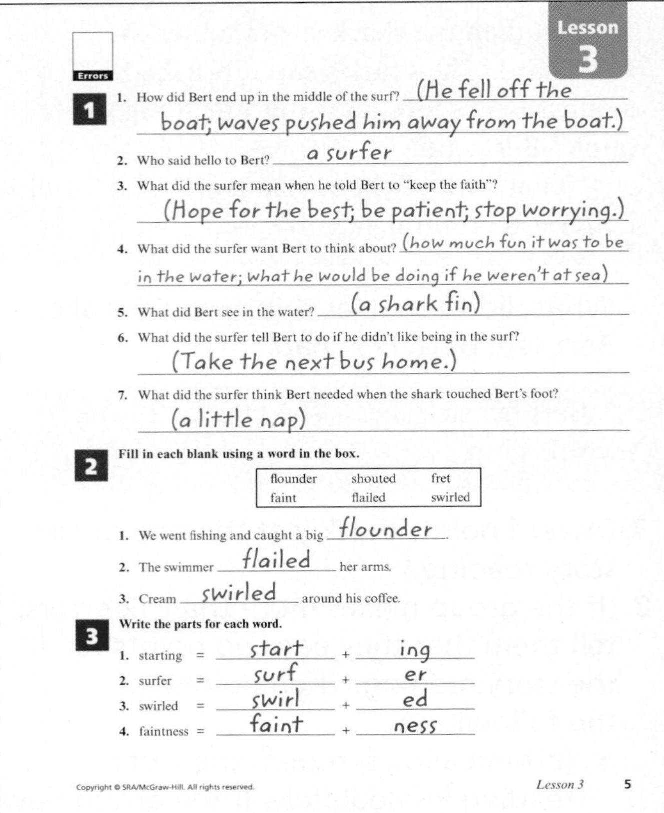

Lesson 3

Errors

1

1. How did Bert end up in the middle of the surf? (He fell off the boat; waves pushed him away from the boat.)
2. Who said hello to Bert? a surfer
3. What did the surfer mean when he told Bert to "keep the faith"? (Hope for the best; be patient; stop worrying.)
4. What did the surfer want Bert to think about? (how much fun it was to be in the water; what he would be doing if he weren't at sea)
5. What did Bert see in the water? (a shark fin)
6. What did the surfer tell Bert to do if he didn't like being in the surf? (Take the next bus home.)
7. What did the surfer think Bert needed when the shark touched Bert's foot? (a little nap)

2 Fill in each blank using a word in the box.

flounder	shouted	fret
faint	flailed	swirled

1. We went fishing and caught a big flounder.
2. The swimmer flailed her arms.
3. Cream swirled around his coffee.

3 Write the parts for each word.

1. starting = start + ing
2. surfer = surf + er
3. swirled = swirl + ed
4. faintness = faint + ness

Copyright © SRA/McGraw-Hill. All rights reserved.

Lesson 3 5

Point schedule for Lesson 3

Box	Lesson part	Points
A	Word Attack	0 or 5
B	Selection Reading	0 or 5
C	Timed Reading Checkout	0 or 5
D	Workbook	0, 1, 3, or 5
Bonus	(Teacher option)	—

END OF LESSON 3

WORD-ATTACK SKILLS

To correct word-identification errors:
a. The word is _____.
b. What word? (Signal.)
c. Spell _____. (Signal for each letter.)
- What word? (Signal.)
d. Go back to the first word in the [row/column]. ✓
- (Present the words in order.)

Board Work

EXERCISE 1

BUILDUP

1. (Print on the board:)

found

2. (Point to **found.** Pause.) What word? (Signal.) *Found.*
3. (Change the word to:)

round

- What word now? (Signal.) *Round.*

4. (Change the word to:)

ground

- What word now? (Signal.) *Ground.*

5. (Change the word to:)

grounded

- What word now? (Signal.) *Grounded.*

6. (Change the word to:)

grounds

- What word now? (Signal.) *Grounds.*

7. (Change the word to:)

grounding

- What word now? (Signal.) *Grounding.*

8. (Change to the original word:)

found

- (Repeat steps 2–7 until firm.)

Student Book

EXERCISE 2

NEW **SOUND COMBINATION: ar**

Task A

1. Open your Student Book to Lesson 4. ✓

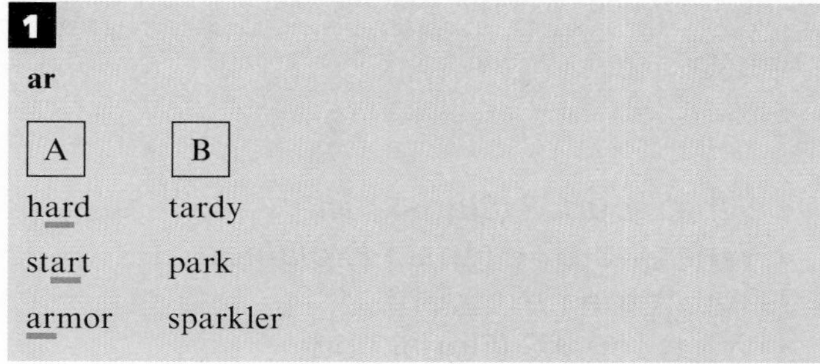

- Touch the letters **A–R** in part 1. ✓
- The letters **A–R** go together and usually make the sound **ar,** as in **hard.** What sound? (Signal.) *ar.*

2. You're going to read words that have the letters **A–R** in them. You're going to say the sound for the underlined part and then read the word.
3. Touch the first word in column A. ✓
- What sound? (Signal.) *ar.*
- What word? (Signal.) *Hard.*
4. Touch the next word. ✓
- What sound? (Signal.) *ar.*
- What word? (Signal.) *Start.*
5. (Repeat step 4 for **armor.**)

Task B

1. Touch the first word in column B. ✓
- What word? (Signal.) *Tardy.*
2. Touch the next word. ✓
- What word? (Signal.) *Park.*
3. (Repeat step 2 for **sparkler.**)
4. (Repeat steps 1–3 until firm.)

Lesson 4

EXERCISE 3

NEW WORD PRACTICE

*Note: The definitions for starred words appear in the Glossary at the back of this book, the Student Book, and the Teacher's Guide.

1. Touch the first word in part 2. ✓

2

explained countless faint* clerk hours
wailed ground painful pouting aid
surround serve bounding surfer* snail
perched complain around flounder*

- What sound? (Signal.) *āāā.*
- What word? (Signal.) *Explained.*

2. Touch the next word. ✓

- What sound? (Signal.) *ow.*
- What word? (Signal.) *Countless.*

3. (Repeat step 2 for each remaining word.)
4. (Repeat each row of words until firm.)
5. What does **faint** mean? (Call on a student.)

- (Repeat for **surfer, flounder.**)

EXERCISE 4

VOCABULARY

1. Touch part 3. ✓

3

1. perch
2. wail
3. survive

- We're going to talk about what those words mean.

2. Touch word 1. ✓

- What word? (Signal.) *Perch.*
- One meaning you learned for the word **perch** is a small fish. Another meaning for **perch** is to stand on something that is unsteady or high.

3. Everybody touch word 2. ✓

- What word? (Signal.) *Wail.*
- The **wail** that is spelled **W–A–I–L** means **cry out in pain.** Everybody, what does **wail** mean? (Signal.) *Cry out in pain.*

4. Touch word 3. ✓

- What word? (Signal.) *Survive.*
- When you **live through** something, you **survive** it. Everybody, what's another way of saying "The man **lived through** the storm"? (Signal.) *The man survived the storm.*

EXERCISE 5

WORD PRACTICE

1. Touch the first word in part 4. ✓

4

slipped climbed bucket strain*
anchor tripped yawned simply
hanging hunger away mount
spotted craft ahoy morning
line move ready

- What word? (Signal.) *Slipped.*

2. Next word. ✓

- What word? (Signal.) *Climbed.*

3. (Repeat step 2 for each remaining word.)
4. (Repeat each row of words until firm.)
5. What does **strain** mean? (Call on a student.)

EXERCISE 6

WORD-ATTACK SKILLS: Individual tests

1. (Call on individual students. Each student reads a row or column. Tally the rows and columns read without error. If the group reads at least 10 rows and columns without making errors, direct all students to record 5 points in Box A of their Point Chart. Criterion is 80 percent of rows and columns read without error.)
2. (If the group did not read at least 10 rows and columns without errors, do not award any points for the Word-Attack Skills exercises.)

SELECTION READING

EXERCISE 7

STORY READING

1. (Call on individual students to answer these questions.)
- In the last selection, what new character appears? *A surfer.*
- What happened? (Accept reasonable summaries.)
2. Everybody, touch part 5. ✓
- You're going to read this story.
3. The error limit for this story is 12. If the group reads the story with 12 errors or less, you earn 5 points.

5 **Back on Board**

4. (Call on a student to read the title.) *Back on Board.*
- What do you think this story is about? (Accept reasonable responses.)
5. (Call on individual students. Each is to read two to four sentences.)

To correct word-reading errors:
(As soon as a student misidentifies a word, say:)
a. The word is _____.
b. Touch under that word. ✓
c. What word?
d. Go back to the beginning of the sentence and read that sentence again.

6. (Call on individual students to answer the specified questions during the story reading. Numbers in the story indicate at what point you ask each question.)

To correct comprehension errors:
a. (Call on a student to reread the passage that answers the question.)
b. (Repeat the question for the student who made the error.)
c. (Require that student to give an appropriate answer before proceeding with the story reading.)

Bert was sick. He was hanging on to a surfboard in the middle of the sea. A shark was swimming around and around the surfboard. The surfer didn't seem to mind, but Bert felt faint. ❶

1. Where were Bert and the surfer? (Idea: *In the ocean holding on to a surfboard.*)

He asked the surfer, "How many hours can we survive out here?"

The surfer said, "If that shark gets a hunger pain, you won't have to worry about surviving." ❷

2. What would the shark have done if it got a hunger pain? (Idea: *It would have eaten Bert and the surfer.*)

Bert asked, "What if I make loud sounds? Will it go away then?"

"Sharks dig loud things," the surfer said. "If you do that, sharks will surround us." ❸

3. What would have happened if Bert made loud noises? (Idea: *Sharks would surround them.*)
3. What does **surround** mean? (Idea: *Make a circle around them.*)

At that moment Bert spotted a sailboat bounding over the surf.

"Look, look," Bert shouted. "A craft has come to our aid." ❹

4. What's a craft? *A boat.*
4. What does "come to our aid" mean? (Ideas: *Help us; rescue us.*)

The surfer didn't look up. He simply yawned. "Oh, well," he said, "looks as if our fun is over."

Bert didn't feel that he was having fun. He looked at the sailboat, and he could see somebody perched on the main mast. It was Shirley. ❺

5. Where was Shirley perched? *On the main mast.*

"Ahoy," she wailed. "I see a pair of sick fish on a surfboard."

The boat seemed to move like a snail, but soon it was next to the surfboard. Bert left the surfboard and floundered over to the boat. Then he climbed up over the rail. ❻

6. How do you think Bert looked? (Ideas: *Afraid; uncomfortable; worried.*)
6. What does **floundered** mean? (Idea: *Flopped around.*)

"Oh, that was painful," he said. "We were out there with sharks, and we didn't—"

"Shut up and stop wailing," Shirley said. "Grab a pail and start bailing." ❼

7. What order did Shirley give Bert? (Idea: *Stop wailing and start bailing.*)

The surfer didn't complain. He slipped his surfboard over the rail and climbed up. Then he said, "When do we eat?"

Shirley said, "After you work. Grab a bucket and start bailing."

"Wait," the surfer said. "Let me explain. I don't work. I surf and I eat, but I don't work." ❽

8. What does the surfer usually do? (Idea: *He surfs, and he eats.*)
8. What wouldn't he do? *Work.*

Shirley said, "And I don't serve eats to them that don't work."

"I dig," the surfer said. "I don't feel much hunger, so I'll just sit in a deck chair and take a nap." And that's just what he did.

Bert bailed and bailed. Then he bounded up to the deck and said, "This life at sea is too much strain. Take me back to the sail shop."

"We came out here to fish," Shirley said. "And that's what we're going to do. Drop the anchor chain, and get ready to count the flounder." ❾

9. What did Bert want to do? (Idea: *Go back to shore.*)
9. What did Shirley want them to do? (Idea: *Fish.*)

"I like the ground under my feet," Bert said. "It's plain that I'm no sailor. Take me back."

"Stop your pouting," Shirley said. ❿

10. What does **pouting** mean? (Idea: *Complaining.*)

"There are countless fish out there just waiting for a fish line."

Bert wailed, "I can't stand the smell of fish. I can't stand the sound of the surf. Take me back to my job as a clerk."

The boat bobbed over the waves. Shirley handed Bert a long fishing pole. She slapped Bert on the back. "You'll come around," she said, "after you feel the joy of fishing." ⓫

11. What did Shirley think would change Bert's mind? (Idea: *Fishing.*)

7. (Award points quickly at the end of the story reading.)
8. (If the group makes more than 12 errors, tell them that they earn no points for the story reading. Then do one of the following:)
   a. (If time allows, repeat the story reading immediately. If the group now succeeds, complete the lesson and do the next lesson the following day.)
   b. (If there isn't enough time, repeat the story reading the following day.)

FLUENCY ASSESSMENT

EXERCISE 8

TIMED READING CHECKOUTS

1. (For this part of the lesson, assigned pairs of students work together during the checkouts.)
   - (If one student does not have a checkout partner, arrange another time when you can give the checkout, possibly during the time other students are completing their independent work. Follow the same procedure for students who miss a checkout because they are absent when the checkout is presented.)
2. Now you'll do the timed checkout on the first part of story 4. If you read at least 200 words and make no more than 4 errors, you earn 5 points.
   - While the rest of you are doing your checkout, I'll watch two pairs of students and make sure the checkers are giving good feedback on errors.
3. This is not a race. Just read like you talk.
4. First set of readers, get ready. ✓
   - Go.
   - (After 2 minutes, say:) Stop.
5. (During each timed checkout, observe one pair of students for 2 minutes. Make notes on any mistakes the reader makes. Give the checker feedback on any mistakes that were not caught. Praise checkers who provide good feedback. Praise readers who read accurately.)
6. (Direct checkers to count the number of words read. Students who read at least 200 words and made no more than 4 errors record 5 points in Box C of their Point Chart.)
7. (Direct students to record their reading rate and number of errors on the Individual Reading Progress Chart.)
8. (Repeat steps 4–7 for the second set of readers.)
9. (Record the timed reading checkout performance for each student you observed on the Fluency Assessment Summary form.)

Lesson
4

WORKBOOK EXERCISES

Independent Student Work

Task A

- Open your Workbook to Lesson 4. ✓
- Complete all parts of your Workbook lesson using a pencil. If you make no errors, you will earn 5 points.

Task B

1. (Before presenting Lesson 5, check student Workbooks for Lesson 4.)
   - Now we're going to check the answers you've written. I'll call on individual students to answer each item. You're going to mark any errors using a pen, not a pencil. Put an X next to any item that is wrong.
2. (Call on a student.) Read question 1 and the answer.
3. (Repeat step 2 for the remaining questions in part 1.)
4. (Call on individual students to read the items and answers in part 2.)
5. (Direct the students to count the number of errors and write the number in the Errors box at the top of the Workbook page.)
6. (Award points and direct students to record points in Box D of their Point Chart.)

   0 errors .... 5 points
   1 error .... 3 points
   2 or 3 errors .... 1 point
   more than 3 errors .... 0 points

Point schedule for Lesson 4

Box	Lesson part	Points
A	Word Attack	0 or 5
B	Selection Reading	0 or 5
C	Timed Reading Checkout	0 or 5
D	Workbook	0, 1, 3 or 5
Bonus	(Teacher option)	—

END OF LESSON 4

Lesson
4

Errors

1

1. At the beginning of the story, where were Bert and the surfer? (in the middle of the sea)
2. a. Did the surfer make Bert stop worrying? No.
   b. How do you know? (Accept reasonable responses.)
3. What would the sharks have done if Bert made loud noises? (surrounded them)
4. Who came to the aid of Bert and the surfer? Shirley
5. What kind of craft did Shirley have? a sailboat
6. **Here are some things that happened after Bert spotted Shirley's craft.**
   Number the things 1, 2, 3, and 4 to show the order in which they happened.
   3 Bert wailed about being in the surf.
   4 Bert bailed with a pail.
   1 Shirley wailed, "Ahoy."
   2 Bert climbed over a rail.
7. What would the surfer not do? (work)
8. What did Shirley go to sea to do? (fish)
9. What did Shirley think would change Bert's mind? (the joy of fishing)

6 *Lesson 4* Copyright © SRA/McGraw-Hill. All rights reserved.

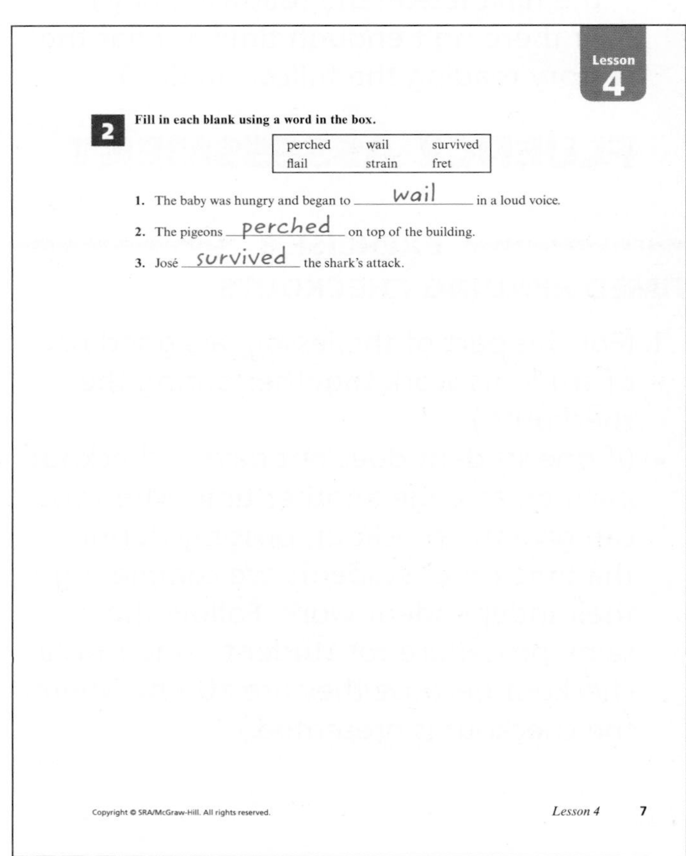

Lesson
4

2 **Fill in each blank using a word in the box.**

perched	wail	survived
flail	strain	fret

1. The baby was hungry and began to wail in a loud voice.
2. The pigeons perched on top of the building.
3. José survived the shark's attack.

Copyright © SRA/McGraw-Hill. All rights reserved. *Lesson 4* 7

WORD-ATTACK SKILLS

To correct word-identification errors:
a. The word is ______.
b. What word? (Signal.)
c. Spell ______. (Signal for each letter.)
- What word? (Signal.)
d. Go back to the first word in the (row/column). ✓
- (Present the words in order.)

Board Work

EXERCISE 1

BUILDUP

1. (Print on the board:)

slid

2. (Point to **slid.** Pause.) What word? (Signal.) *Slid.*
3. (Change the word to:)

slide

- What word now? (Signal.) *Slide.*

4. (Change the word to:)

slider

- What word now? (Signal.) *Slider.*

5. (Change the word to:)

spider

- What word now? (Signal.) *Spider.*

6. (Change to the original word:)

slid

- (Repeat steps 2–5 until firm.)

Student Book

EXERCISE 2

SOUND COMBINATION: ar

Task A

1. Open your Student Book to Lesson 5. ✓

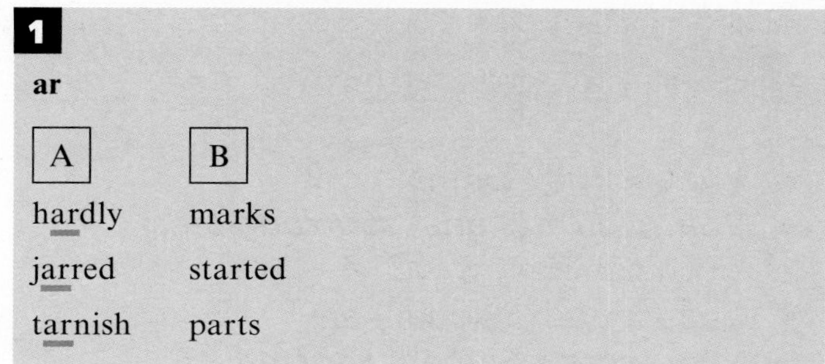

- Touch the letters **A–R** in part 1. ✓
- What sound do the letters **A–R** make? (Signal.) *ar.*

2. You're going to say the sound for the underlined part and then read the word.
3. Touch the first word in column A. ✓
- What sound? (Signal.) *ar.*
- What word? (Signal.) *Hardly.*
4. Touch the next word. ✓
- What sound? (Signal.) *ar.*
- What word? (Signal.) *Jarred.*
5. (Repeat step 4 for **tarnish.**)

Task B

1. Touch the first word in column B. ✓
- What word? (Signal.) *Marks.*
2. Touch the next word. ✓
- What word? (Signal.) *Started.*
3. (Repeat step 2 for **parts.**)
4. (Repeat steps 1–3 until firm.)

EXERCISE 3

WORD PRACTICE

1. Touch the first word in part 2. ✓

2

surrounded spurted hounding sounded
first ground thirst mailed sternly
another mouth jerked tiller around
wailed sputtered ouch survive*

- What sound? (Signal.) *ow.*
- What word? (Signal.) *Surrounded.*

2. Touch the next word. ✓
- What sound? (Signal.) *er.*
- What word? (Signal.) *Spurted.*

3. (Repeat step 2 for each remaining word.)
4. (Repeat each row of words until firm.)
5. What does **survive** mean? (Call on a student.)

EXERCISE 4

VOCABULARY

3

1. serious
2. termites
3. suddenly
4. tiller

1. Touch part 3. ✓
- We're going to talk about what those words mean.

2. Touch word 1. ✓
- What word? (Signal.) *Serious.*
- Something that is **important and not funny** is **serious.** Everybody, what does **serious** mean? (Signal.) *Important and not funny.*

3. Touch word 2. ✓
- What word? (Signal.) *Termites.*
- **Termites** are **bugs that eat wood.** Everybody, what are **termites?** (Signal.) *Bugs that eat wood.*

4. Touch word 3. ✓
- What word? (Signal.) *Suddenly.*
- Who knows what **suddenly** means? (Call on a student.) (Idea: *Something happens all at once.*)

5. Everybody, touch word 4. ✓
- What word? (Signal.) *Tiller.*
- The **tiller** is **the handle that steers a boat.** Everybody, what is a **tiller?** (Signal.) *The handle that steers a boat.*

EXERCISE 5

WORD PRACTICE

1. Touch the first word in part 4. ✓

4

line slump sawdust crack tossed
dropping rolled pulled tugged
splash fooling handle swam swing
splat races morning reach clowning
really you've hasn't we're
haven't weren't I'll shouldn't
didn't I've wouldn't doesn't
couldn't don't I'm you'll

- What word? (Signal.) *Line.*

2. Next word. ✓
- What word? (Signal.) *Slump.*

3. (Repeat step 2 for each remaining word.)
4. (Repeat each row of words until firm.)

EXERCISE 6

WORD-ATTACK SKILLS: Individual tests

1. (Call on individual students. Each student reads a row or column. Tally the rows and columns read without error. If the group reads at least 12 rows and columns without making errors, direct all students to record 5 points in Box A of their Point Chart. Criterion is 80 percent of rows and columns read without error.)
2. (If the group did not read at least 12 rows and columns without errors, do not award any points for the Word-Attack Skills exercises.)

SELECTION READING

EXERCISE 7

STORY READING

1. (Call on individual students to answer these questions.)
- What problem did Bert have in the last selection? (Ideas: *He wanted to get out of the water; he wanted to avoid sharks.*)
- How did this problem get solved? (Idea: *Shirley appeared in her boat.*)
- What problem did the characters have with the boat? (Idea: *They had to bail water.*)
2. Everybody, touch part 5. ✓
- You're going to read this story.
3. The error limit for this story is 12. If the group reads the story with 12 errors or less, you earn 5 points.

5 **Thousands of Flounder**

4. (Call on a student to read the title.) *Thousands of Flounder.*
- What do you think this story is about? (Accept reasonable responses.)
5. (Call on individual students. Each is to read two to four sentences.)

To correct word-reading errors:
(As soon as a student misidentifies a word, say:)
a. The word is _____.
b. Touch under that word. ✓
c. What word?
d. Go back to the beginning of the sentence and read that sentence again.

6. (Call on individual students to answer the specified questions during the story reading. Numbers in the story indicate at what point you ask each question.)

To correct comprehension errors:
a. (Call on a student to reread the passage that answers the question.)
b. (Repeat the question for the student who made the error.)
c. (Require that student to give an appropriate answer before proceeding with the story reading.)

Shirley tossed a pail of little fish over the side of the boat. "This bait will get them," she said. Soon big fish surrounded the sailboat. ❶

1. What was the pail of little fish used for? *Bait.*

Shirley dropped her line into the sea. She jerked up and pulled a big flounder over the rail. She dropped the fish on the surfer. The surfer rolled over and said to the fish, "I was here first, fish." ❷

2. What did the surfer say to the fish? *"I was here first, fish."*

Shirley pulled another fish from the sea and then another. Then she shouted, "Come on, Bert, you grouch, it's time to fish."

Bert dropped his line into the sea. He felt a tug. He jerked up the fishing pole. But Bert didn't pull a flounder from the sea. The flounder pulled him into the sea. Splash. "Cut it out," Shirley yelled. "This is no time to fool around."

Water spurted from Bert's mouth. "I'm not fooling," he sputtered. ❸

3. How do you talk when you sputter? (Ideas: *You stop a lot; you spit while you talk.*)
3. What went wrong when Bert jerked up the fishing pole? (Idea: *He was pulled into the sea.*)
3. What did Shirley think Bert was doing in the water? (Idea: *Fooling around.*)

Lesson
5

"That fish is too big to handle."

Bert swam back to the rail of the boat. He tossed his pole over the rail. The surfer grabbed it and said, "Is this work or fun?"

Shirley said, "This is more fun than playing in the rain." ❹

4. What did Shirley say about fishing? (Idea: *It's more fun than playing in the rain.*)

"Then I'll do it," the surfer said. He jerked up on the pole and pulled a stout flounder from the sea. The flounder swung around and hit Bert just as Bert was trying to climb over the rail. Splat. Bert fell on a fish that was on the deck. ❺

5. Why did Bert fall? (Ideas: *He was hit by a flounder; he slid on a fish.*)

He slid across the deck on that fish and went sailing over the other side of the boat. Splash.

"Cut it out," Shirley said sternly. "This is no time to play around."

Again water spurted from Bert's mouth. "I'm not playing," he said.

"I'm playing," the surfer said. "This is about as much fun as surfing."

The surfer and Shirley ate flounder that night. Bert didn't eat. He sat near the main mast and talked to himself.

He was still talking to himself the next morning when Shirley shouted, "Now it's time to go back to port." ❻

6. What did Bert do all night? (Idea: *Talked to himself.*)
6. What is a port? (Idea: *Place on land where boats go.*)

Shirley grabbed the tiller and turned it to one side, but the boat didn't turn. The tiller broke in her hand. Then she yelled, "Men, we've got termites on this ship. They ground the tiller into sawdust. I don't know how long it will take them to eat the rest of this fine ship." ❼

7. How fine was Shirley's boat? (Idea: *Not fine at all.*)

"Oh, not that," Bert wailed. "I'm a clerk. Why didn't I just stay and be a clerk? Why did I—" ❽

8. What do you think Bert was going to say? (Ideas: *"Why did I come fishing?"; "Why did I believe Shirley?"*)

"It's full sail," Shirley said. "We must reach port before the termites have ground this boat into bits."

"This is the life," the surfer said. "I dig races, and I dig termites."

Bert got up to see what the termites did to the tiller. As he walked near the rail, he felt the deck begin to crack under his feet. Slump. A hole formed in the deck, and Bert fell into the hole filled with a thousand flounder. ❾

9. What happened to Bert? (Idea: *He fell in a hole in the deck.*)

"Stop clowning around," Shirley said. "This is serious."

"But," Bert hollered as he floundered around with the flounders, "the termites really know how to eat wood."

"I just hope they don't eat the main mast," Shirley said. ❿

10. What did Shirley hope? (Idea: *That the termites wouldn't eat the main mast.*)

7. (Award points quickly at the end of the story reading.)
8. (If the group makes more than 12 errors, tell them that they earn no points for the story reading. Then do one of the following:)
   a. (If time allows, repeat the story reading immediately. If the group now succeeds, complete the lesson and do the next lesson the following day.)
   b. (If there isn't enough time, repeat the story reading the following day.)

FLUENCY ASSESSMENT

EXERCISE 8

NEW TIMED READING CHECKOUTS

1. (For this part of the lesson, assigned pairs of students work together during the checkouts.)
   - (If one student does not have a checkout partner, arrange another time when you can give the checkout.)
2. (Each student does a 2-minute timed reading. Students earn 5 points by reading at least 200 words and making no more than 4 errors on the first part of story 5. Students record points in Box C of their Point Chart and plot their reading rate and errors on the Individual Reading Progress Chart.)
   - (During each timed checkout, observe one pair of students for 2 minutes. Make notes on any mistakes the reader makes.)
3. (Record the timed reading checkout performance for each student you observed on the Fluency Assessment Summary form.)

WORKBOOK EXERCISES

Lesson 5

Errors

1

1. What was the pail of little fish used for? (bait)
2. What happened to Bert when he jerked on the fishing pole? (He was pulled into the sea.)
3. What did Shirley say fishing was more fun than? (playing in the rain)
4. What did the surfer and Shirley eat that night? flounder
5. What did Bert do all night? (talked to himself)
6. What did the termites eat first? the tiller
7. Why did Bert fall into a hole filled with flounder? (The deck cracked.)
8. What did Shirley hope? (that the termites wouldn't eat the main mast)

2 Fill in each blank using a word in the box.

flounder	serious	termites
suddenly	tiller	perch

1. Libby used the tiller and turned the boat around.
2. Jolene blew the balloon up until it suddenly burst.
3. The termites ate holes in our new porch.

3 Write the parts for each word.

1. surrounding = surround + ing
2. grounded = ground + ed
3. hardness = hard + ness
4. suddenly = sudden + ly

8 *Lesson 5* Copyright © SRA/McGraw-Hill. All rights reserved.

NEW Independent Student Work

Task A

- Open your Workbook to Lesson 5. ✓
- Complete all parts of your Workbook lesson using a pencil. If you make no errors, you will earn 5 points.

Task B

1. (Before presenting Lesson 6, check student Workbooks for Lesson 5.)
   - (Call on individual students to read the items and answers in each part. Students mark errors using a pen.)
2. (Direct the students to count the number of errors and write the number in the Errors box at the top of the Workbook page.)

3. (Award points and direct students to record points in Box D of their Point Chart.)

   0 errors................................5 points
   1 error ....3 points
   2 or 3 errors ....1 point
   more than 3 errors ....0 points

Point schedule for Lesson 5

Box	Lesson part	Points
A	Word Attack	0 or 5
B	Selection Reading	0 or 5
C	Timed Reading Checkout	0 or 5
D	Workbook	0, 1, 3, or 5
Bonus	(Teacher option)	—

NEW **Five-lesson point summary**

- (For **letter grades** based on points for Lessons **1** through **5,** tell students to compute the total for the blue boxes [C, D, and Bonus] and write the number in the Total box at the end of each row in their Point Chart. The Point Chart is in the back of the Workbook. Students then add the totals and write the sum in the green box.)
- (For **rewards** based on points, tell students to compute the total for all boxes [A, B, C, D, and Bonus] and write the number in the Total box at the end of each row. Students then add the totals and write the sum in the green box.)

END OF LESSON 5

Lesson Objectives	LESSON 6	LESSON 7	LESSON 8	LESSON 9	LESSON 10
	Exercise	Exercise	Exercise	Exercise	Exercise
Word Attack					
Decoding and Word Analysis					
Sound Combination: *ge, gi*		3	2		2
Sound Combination: *ce, ci*			3	3	2
Sound Combination: *tion*					4
Sound Combination: *ar*	2				
Multisyllabic Word Strategies	6	7	7	7	7
Visual Discrimination	1	1, 2	1	1, 2	1
Letter Combinations/Letter Sounds	3	4	4	4	3
Word Recognition	1–6	1–7	1–7	1–7	1–7
High-Frequency/Sight Words	6	7	7	7	7
Vocabulary					
Definitions	3–5	4–6	5, 6	4–6	5, 6
Usage	4, 6	5, 7	5, 7	5, 7	5, 7
Assessment					
Ongoing: Individual Tests	7	8	8	8	8
Group Reading					
Decoding and Word Analysis					
Read Decodable Text	8	9	9	9	9
Comprehension					
Access Prior Knowledge		9			
Draw Inferences	8	9	9	9	9
Note Details	8	9	9	9	9
Predict	8	9	9	9	9
Assessment					
Ongoing: Comprehension Check	8	9	9	9	9
Ongoing: Decoding Accuracy	8	9	9	9	9
Fluency Assessment					
Fluency					
Reread Decodable Text	9	10	10	10	10
Assessment					
Ongoing: Teacher-Monitored Fluency	9	10	10	10	10
Ongoing: Peer-Monitored Fluency	9	10	10	10	10
Workbook Exercises					
Decoding and Word Analysis					
Multisyllabic Word Parts		Ind. Work		Ind. Work	
Comprehension					
Note Details	Ind. Work	Ind. Work	Ind. Work	Ind. Work	Ind. Work
Vocabulary					
Usage	Ind. Work	Ind. Work	Ind. Work	Ind. Work	Ind. Work
Assessment					
Ongoing: Workcheck	Workcheck	Workcheck	Workcheck	Workcheck	Workcheck

Lesson 6

WORD-ATTACK SKILLS

Board Work

EXERCISE 1

BUILDUP

1. (Print on the board:)

bit

2. (Point to **bit.** Pause.) What word? (Signal.) *Bit.*
3. (Change the word to:)

bite

- What word now? (Signal.) *Bite.*

4. (Change the word to:)

biter

- What word now? (Signal.) *Biter.*

5. (Change to the original word:)

bit

- (Repeat steps 2–4 until firm.)

Student Book

EXERCISE 2

SOUND COMBINATION: ar

Task A

1. Open your Student Book to Lesson 6. ✓

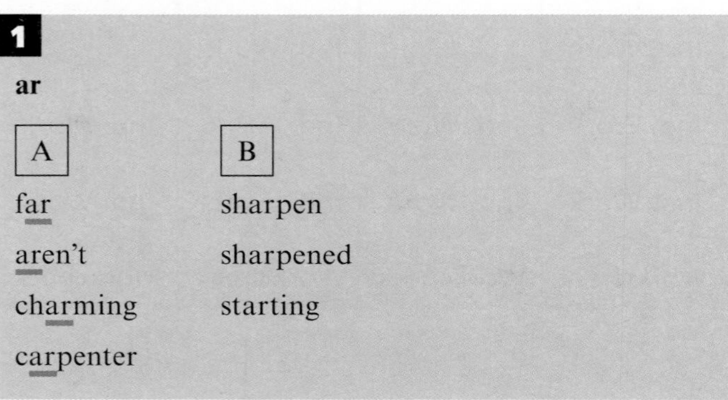

1

ar

A	B
far	sharpen
aren't	sharpened
charming	starting
carpenter	

- Touch the letters **A–R** in part 1. ✓
- What sound do the letters **A–R** make? (Signal.) *ar.*

2. You're going to say the sound for the underlined part and then read the word.
3. Touch the first word in column A. ✓
- What sound? (Signal.) *ar.*
- What word? (Signal.) *Far.*
4. Touch the next word. ✓
- What sound? (Signal.) *ar.*
- What word? (Signal.) *Aren't.*
5. (Repeat step 4 for each remaining word.)

Task B

1. Touch the first word in column B. ✓
- What word? (Signal.) *Sharpen.*
2. Touch the next word. ✓
- What word? (Signal.) *Sharpened.*
3. (Repeat step 2 for **starting.**)
4. (Repeat steps 1–3 until firm.)

EXERCISE 3

WORD PRACTICE

1. Touch the first word in part 2. ✓

2

hour sailor chair south

third pouting tiller* grounded

exclaimed clerked around

- What sound? (Signal.) *ow.*
- What word? (Signal.) *Hour.*
2. Touch the next word. ✓
- What sound? (Signal.) *āāā.*
- What word? (Signal.) *Sailor.*
3. (Repeat step 2 for each remaining word.)
4. (Repeat each row of words until firm.)
5. What does **tiller** mean? (Call on a student.)

EXERCISE 4

VOCABULARY

1. Touch part 3. ✓
   - We're going to talk about what those words mean.

3

1. collapse
2. craft
3. skid

2. Touch word 1. ✓
   - What word? (Signal.) *Collapse.*
   - When something **falls apart,** it **collapses.** Everybody, what's another way of saying "The bed **fell apart** last night"? (Signal.) *The bed collapsed last night.*
3. Touch word 2. ✓
   - What word? (Signal.) *Craft.*
   - A **boat** is sometimes referred to as a **craft.** Everybody, what's another way of saying "They put out a small-**boat** warning"? (Signal.) *They put out a small-craft warning.*
4. Touch word 3. ✓
   - What word? (Signal.) *Skid.*
   - What does something do when it **skids?** (Call on a student.) (Idea: *Slides.*)

EXERCISE 5

WORD PRACTICE

1. Touch the first word in part 4. ✓

4

shouldn't hadn't wasn't suddenly* hasn't
you've isn't weren't what's couldn't that's
into onto unto tottered serious* really
pointed shore rented clowning toward
eaten crafted chewing landed filler front
board casting place raced grabbed during
aground something through passed

   - What word? (Signal.) *Shouldn't.*
2. Next word. ✓
   - What word? (Signal.) *Hadn't.*
3. (Repeat step 2 for each remaining word.)
4. (Repeat each row of words until firm.)
5. What does **suddenly** mean? (Call on a student.)
6. What does **serious** mean? (Call on a student.)

EXERCISE 6

NEW MULTIPART WORDS

Task A

1. Touch part 5. ✓

5

responded generate imagination
1. responded 2. generate 3. imagination

> **Note:** The parts of a word are to be pronounced the same as they are when the word is spoken normally.

2. All of these words have more than one part. The first part and the last part are circled.
3. Touch word 1. ✓
   - Word 1 is **responded.** What word? (Signal.) *Responded.*
4. The parts are **re** (pause) **spond** (pause) **ed.**
   - What's the first part? (Signal.) *re.*
   - The middle part is spelled **S–P–O–N–D.** What does that part say in the word? (Signal.) *spond.*
   - What's the last part? (Signal.) *ed.* (Accept **ed** pronounced as in the word.) Yes, **ed.**
5. Say the whole word. (Signal.) *Responded.*
6. (Repeat steps 3–5 until firm.)
7. Touch word 2. ✓
   - Word 2 is **generate.** What word? (Signal.) *Generate.*
8. The parts are **gen** (pause) **er** (pause) **ate.**
   - What's the first part? (Signal.) *gen.* (Pronounced **jen.**)
   - The middle part is spelled **E–R.** What does that part say in the word? (Signal.) *er.*
   - What's the last part? (Signal.) *ate.*
9. Say the whole word. (Signal.) *Generate.*
10. (Repeat steps 7–9 until firm.)

11. Touch word 3. ✓
 - Word 3 is **imagination.** What word? (Signal.) *Imagination.*
12. The parts are **i** (pause) **magina** (pause) **tion.**
 - What's the first part? (Signal.) *i.* (Accept the sound **i,** not the letter name I.) Yes, **i.**
 - The middle part is spelled **M–A–G–I–N–A.** What does that part say in the word? (Signal.) *magina.*
 - What's the last part? (Signal.) *tion.*
13. Say the whole word. (Signal.) *Imagination.*
14. (Repeat steps 11–13 until firm.)

Task B

1. Touch the sentences below the word list. ✓

> a. She responded to my letter the same day she received it.
>
> b. The dam they are building will generate electricity for the valley.
>
> c. You have to use your imagination to be a good artist.

 - These are sentences that use the words you just read.
2. Raise your hand when you can read sentence A. ✓
3. (Call on a student.) Read sentence A. *She responded to my letter the same day she received it.*
 - That means "She wrote back the same day she got my letter."
4. (Call on a student.) Read sentence B. *The dam they are building will generate electricity for the valley.*
5. (Call on a student.) Read sentence C. *You have to use your imagination to be a good artist.*
 - That means "You have to think of ways that haven't been used before if you want to be a good artist."

EXERCISE 7

NEW **WORD-ATTACK SKILLS: Individual tests**

1. (Call on individual students. Each student reads a row of words, a column of words, or a sentence. **In the Multipart words exercises, the numbered words count as 1 row of words, and each sentence counts as 1 row of words.** Tally the rows, columns, and sentences read without error. If the group reads at least 13 rows and columns without making errors, direct all students to record 5 points in Box A of their Point Chart. Criterion is 80 percent of rows and columns read without error.)
2. (If the group did not read at least 13 rows and columns without errors, do not award any points for the Word-Attack Skills exercises.)

SELECTION READING

EXERCISE 8

STORY READING

1. Everybody, touch part 6. ✓
2. The error limit for this story is 12. If the group reads the story with 12 errors or less, you earn 5 points.

6 **A Race with Termites**

3. (Call on a student to read the title.) *A Race With Termites.*
 - What do you think this story is about? (Accept reasonable responses.)

4. (Call on individual students. Each is to read two to four sentences.)
5. (Call on individual students to answer the specified questions during the story reading.)

It was a race between the termites and the sailboat. The termites had eaten the tiller, and now they were working on the deck. Shirley was saying, "Let out more sail."

Bert was saying, "Why did I ever leave the sail shop?" ❶

1. What was Bert saying? *"Why did I ever leave the sail shop?"*

And the surfer was saying, "This is really fun. I dig it."

Hour after hour dragged by. Then suddenly, the rail on the left side of the boat fell down.

"Look at those termites eat wood," the surfer said.

"Oh, no," Bert said.

"Let out more sail," Shirley said.

An hour later more rail fell down. Bert was sitting in a deck chair talking to himself. "We're not going to make it," he was saying. Suddenly his chair collapsed, and Bert was sitting on the deck. ❷

2. Who was Bert talking to? *Himself.*
2. Why did Bert sit on the deck? (Ideas: *Because his chair had collapsed; because termites had eaten his deck chair.*)

"Stop clowning around," Shirley shouted.

Another hour passed. During that hour the rest of the rail around the boat collapsed. Shirley said, "Men, I think we're too far south to make it back to the dock. We're going to have to turn toward shore before water starts to spout through the bottom of this boat." ❸

3. Why did Shirley want to turn toward shore? (Ideas: *Because there were leaks in the boat; because the boat was too far south.*)

The surfer said, "Why don't you go to my dock? It's over there." He pointed toward the shore.

"Do you rent a dock there?" Shirley asked.

"No," the surfer said. "I own that part of the beach. My uncle left it to me. But I can't stand it because the surf is poor."

"Stop talking and start turning," Bert said. "I want to feel dry ground under my feet." ❹

4. Why didn't the surfer like his beach? (Idea: *It wasn't good for surfing.*)
4. What did Bert want to feel? (Idea: *Dry ground under his feet.*)

So the boat turned toward the shore. Just then the top third of the mast tottered and fell over. The surfer said, "Those termites are something."

The boat came closer and closer to the shore, and the boat got lower and lower in the water. "I think we spouted a leak in the hull," Shirley said. ❺

5. Why did Shirley think there was a leak in the hull? (Idea: *The boat was sinking.*)

"I'll nail some boards over the hole," Bert said. He grabbed a hammer and some boards. He went down the stairs and flailed around in the water with the flounder. But when he tried to use the hammer, the handle broke. The termites had eaten holes in it. Bert was about ready to start pulling out his hair.

"We're going to make it," Shirley shouted from the deck. "I'll just run this craft aground next to the dock." ⑥

6. Why did Bert go downstairs? (Idea: *To repair the hole in the hull.*)
6. What happened to the hammer? (Ideas: *The handle broke; it fell apart.*)
6. How would you run a craft aground? (Idea: *You'd sail the boat into the shore.*)

The old boat was spouting new leaks. It was sinking lower and lower into the water. Bert was chewing his fingernails. He ran up the stairs. And just when he got to the deck, the boat made a loud sound as it came aground next to the dock. The boat stopped so suddenly that Bert skidded on the deck and went sailing over the front of the boat. He landed nose first on the beach. His mouth was filled with sand. "We made it," he yelled. ⑦

7. How did Bert land in the sand? (Ideas: *Face first; nose first.*)
7. What **caused** the boat to sprout leaks? *Termites.*

"Stop clowning around," Shirley said. "Bert, you just don't seem to know when things are serious."

6. (Award points quickly.)
7. (If the group makes more than 12 errors, repeat the reading immediately or on the next day.)

FLUENCY ASSESSMENT

EXERCISE 9

TIMED READING CHECKOUTS

1. (For this part of the lesson, assigned pairs of students work together during the checkouts.)
- (If one student does not have a checkout partner, arrange another time when you can give the checkout.)
2. (Each student does a 2-minute timed reading. Students earn 5 points by reading at least 200 words and making no more than 4 errors on the first part of story 6. Students record points in Box C of their Point Chart and plot their reading rate and errors on the Individual Reading Progress Chart.)
- (During each timed checkout, observe one pair of students for 2 minutes. Make notes on any mistakes the reader makes.)
3. (Record the timed reading checkout performance for each student you observed on the Fluency Assessment Summary form.)

WORKBOOK EXERCISES

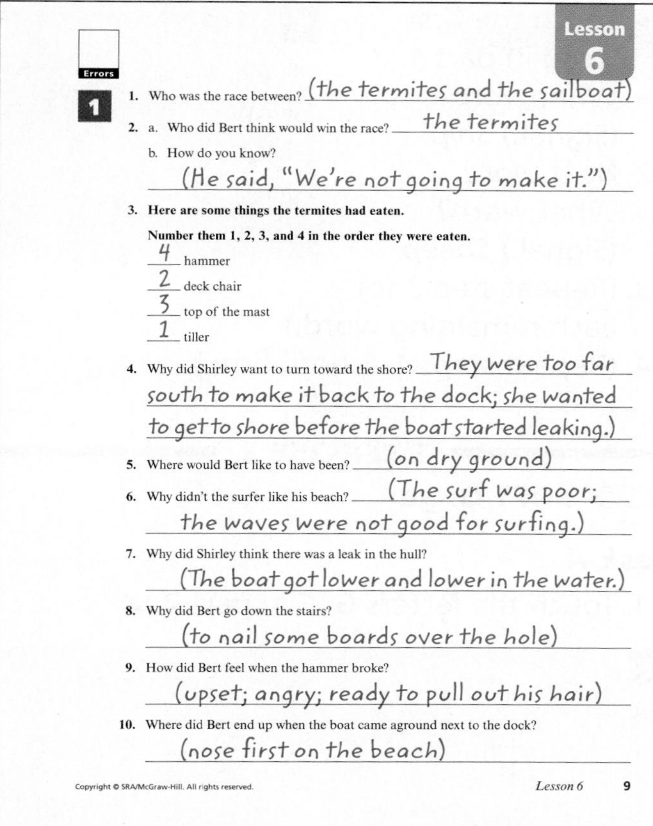

Lesson 6

Errors

1

1. Who was the race between? (the termites and the sailboat)
2. a. Who did Bert think would win the race? the termites

   b. How do you know?

   (He said, "We're not going to make it.")
3. **Here are some things the termites had eaten.**

   Number them 1, 2, 3, and 4 in the order they were eaten.

   4 hammer

   2 deck chair

   3 top of the mast

   1 tiller
4. Why did Shirley want to turn toward the shore? They were too far south to make it back to the dock; she wanted to get to shore before the boat started leaking.)
5. Where would Bert like to have been? (on dry ground)
6. Why didn't the surfer like his beach? (The surf was poor; the waves were not good for surfing.)
7. Why did Shirley think there was a leak in the hull?

   (The boat got lower and lower in the water.)
8. Why did Bert go down the stairs?

   (to nail some boards over the hole)
9. How did Bert feel when the hammer broke?

   (upset; angry; ready to pull out his hair)
10. Where did Bert end up when the boat came aground next to the dock?

    (nose first on the beach)

Copyright © SRA/McGraw-Hill. All rights reserved. Lesson 6 9

Lesson 6

2 **Fill in each blank using a word in the box.**

collapsed	strain	craft
wailed	serious	survived

1. Those termites ate our house until it collapsed.
2. Rosa threw away her raft and built a new craft.
3. The little boy fell down and wailed in pain.

10 Lesson 6 Copyright © SRA/McGraw-Hill. All rights reserved.

Independent Student Work

Task A

- Open your Workbook to Lesson 6. ✓
- Complete all parts of your Workbook lesson using a pencil. If you make no errors, you will earn 5 points.

Task B

1. (Before presenting Lesson 7, check student Workbooks for Lesson 6.)

- (Call on individual students to read the items and answers in each part. Students mark errors using a pen.)

2. (Direct the students to count the number of errors and write the number in the Errors box at the top of the Workbook page.)
3. (Award points and direct students to record points in Box D of their Point Chart.)

0 errors................................5 points
1 error ....3 points
2 or 3 errors ....1 point
more than 3 errors ....0 points

END OF LESSON 6

Lesson 7

WORD-ATTACK SKILLS

Board Work

EXERCISE 1

BUILDUP

1. (Print on the board:)

shi p

2. (Point to **ship.** Pause.) What word? (Signal.) *Ship.*
3. (Change the word to:)

sheep

- What word now? (Signal.) *Sheep.*

4. (Change the word to:)

sharp

- What word now? (Signal.) *Sharp.*

5. (Change the word to:)

shark

- What word now? (Signal.) *Shark.*

6. (Change the word to:)

shake

- What word now? (Signal.) *Shake.*

7. (Change to the original word:)

ship

- (Repeat steps 2–6 until firm.)

Student Book

EXERCISE 2

BUILDUP

1. Open your Student Book to Lesson 7. ✓

- Touch the first word in part 1. ✓
- What word? (Signal.) *Ship.*

2. Next word. ✓

- What word? (Signal.) *Sheep.*

3. (Repeat step 2 for each remaining word.)
4. (Repeat steps 1–3 until firm.)

1

ship
sheep
sharp
shark
shake

EXERCISE 3

NEW **SOFT G: ge**

Task A

1. Touch the letters **G–E** in part 2. ✓

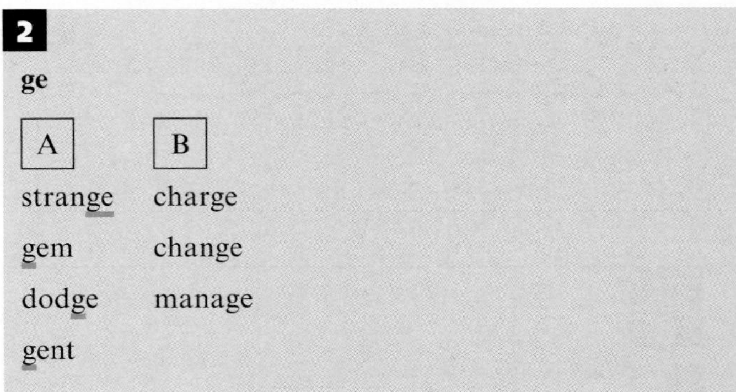

2

ge

A	B
strange	charge
gem	change
dodge	manage
gent	

- When the letter **E** comes after **G,** the **G** makes the sound **j,** as in **gem.** What sound? (Signal.) *j.*

2. You're going to read words that have the sound **j** in them.
3. Touch the first word in column A. ✓

- What sound? (Signal.) *j.*
- What word? (Signal.) *Strange.*

4. Touch the next word. ✓

- What sound? (Signal.) *j.*
- What word? (Signal.) *Gem.*

5. (Repeat step 4 for **dodge, gent.**)

Task B

1. Touch the first word in column B. ✓

- What word? (Signal.) *Charge.*

2. Touch the next word. ✓

- What word? (Signal.) *Change.*

3. (Repeat step 2 for **manage.**)
4. (Repeat steps 1–3 until firm.)

EXERCISE 4

WORD PRACTICE

1. Touch the first word in part 3. ✓

3

lousy started flounder* stairs

fisher sharks sounding parking

around spark repair turned

- What sound? (Signal.) *ow.*
- What word? (Signal.) *Lousy.*

2. Touch the next word. ✓
   - What sound? (Signal.) *ar.*
   - What word? (Signal.) *Started.*
3. (Repeat step 2 for each remaining word.)
4. (Repeat each row of words until firm.)
5. What does **flounder** mean? (Call on a student.)

EXERCISE 5

VOCABULARY

1. Touch part 4. ✓

4

1. business
2. respond
3. exclaim

- We're going to talk about what those words mean.

2. Touch word 1. ✓
   - What word? (Signal.) *Business.*
   - When people **buy and sell things to make money,** we say they are **in business.**
3. Touch word 2. ✓
   - What word? (Signal.) *Respond.*
   - When you **respond** to a question, you **answer** that question. Everybody, what's another way of saying "She **answered** his question"? (Signal.) *She responded to his question.*
4. Touch word 3. ✓
   - What word? (Signal.) *Exclaim.*
   - When you **cry out** about something, you **exclaim.** What's another way of saying, "'It's raining,' she **cried out"?** (Signal.) *"It's raining," she exclaimed.*

EXERCISE 6

WORD PRACTICE

1. Touch the first word in part 5. ✓

5

broken enough responded hey

wouldn't didn't doesn't shouldn't

don't couldn't business picked

holding fishing pulled share poster

loan along across away always replied

right following people period

- What word? (Signal.) *Broken.*

2. Next word. ✓
   - What word? (Signal.) *Enough.*
3. (Repeat step 2 for each remaining word.)
4. (Repeat each row of words until firm.)

EXERCISE 7

MULTIPART WORDS

Task A

1. Touch part 6. ✓

6

tremendous exclamation unbelievable

1. tremendous 2. exclamation 3. unbelievable

> **Note:** The parts of a word are to be pronounced the same as they are when the word is spoken normally.

2. All of these words have more than one part. The first part and the last part are circled.
3. Touch word 1. ✓
   - Word 1 is **tremendous.** What word? (Signal.) *Tremendous.*
4. The parts are **tre** (pause) **mend** (pause) **ous.**
   - What's the first part? (Signal.) *tre.*
   - The middle part is spelled **M–E–N–D.** What does that part say in the word? (Signal.) *mend.*
   - What's the last part? (Signal.) *ous.*
5. Say the whole word. (Signal.) *Tremendous.*

6. (Repeat steps 3–5 until firm.)
7. Touch word 2. ✓
- Word 2 is **exclamation.** What word? (Signal.) *Exclamation.*
8. The parts are **ex** (pause) **clama** (pause) **tion.**
- What's the first part? (Signal.) *ex.*
- The middle part is spelled **C-L-A-M-A.** What does that part say in the word? (Signal.) *clama.*
- What's the last part? (Signal.) *tion.*
9. Say the whole word. (Signal.) *Exclamation.*
10. (Repeat steps 7–9 until firm.)
11. Touch word 3. ✓
- Word 3 is **unbelievable.** What word? (Signal.) *Unbelievable.*
12. The parts are **un** (pause) **believ** (pause) **able.**
- What's the first part? (Signal.) *un.*
- The middle part is spelled **B-E-L-I-E-V.** What does that part say in the word? (Signal.) *believ.*
- What's the last part? (Signal.) *able.*
13. Say the whole word. (Signal.) *Unbelievable.*
14. (Repeat steps 11–13 until firm.)

Task B

1. Touch the sentences below the word list. ✓

a. The lightning was followed by a tremendous explosion of thunder.
b. The exclamation point at the end of a sentence shows what that sentence says is really important!
c. I was shocked to discover that his unbelievable story was true.

- These are sentences that use the words you just read.
2. Raise your hand when you can read sentence A. ✓
3. (Call on a student.) Read sentence A. *The lightning was followed by a tremendous explosion of thunder.*
- That means "The lightning came first, and then a huge boom of thunder followed."
4. (Call on a student.) Read sentence B. *The exclamation point at the end of a sentence shows what that sentence says is really important!*
5. (Call on a student.) Read sentence C. *I was shocked to discover that his unbelievable story was true.*
- That means "The story he told was very hard to believe, but it really happened."

EXERCISE 8

WORD-ATTACK SKILLS: Individual tests

1. (Call on individual students. Each student reads a row of words, a column of words, or a sentence. In the Multipart words exercises, each sentence counts as one row of words. Tally the rows, columns, and sentences read without error. If the group reads at least 14 rows and columns without making errors, direct all students to record 5 points in Box A of their Point Chart. Criterion is 80 percent of rows and columns read without error.)
2. (If the group did not read at least 14 rows and columns without errors, do not award any points for the Word-Attack Skills exercises.)

SELECTION READING

EXERCISE 9

STORY READING

1. (Call on individual students to answer these questions.)
- In the last selection, what caused Shirley's boat to leak so much? (Idea: *Termites ate holes in the boat.*)
- How did Bert try to solve the problem? (Idea: *He wanted to nail boards over the hole in the hull.*)
- What happened? (Accept reasonable summaries.)

2. Everybody, touch part 7. ✓
3. The error limit for this story is 12. If the group reads the story with 12 errors or less, you earn 5 points.

7 What Will Bert Do?

4. (Call on a student to read the title.) *What Will Bert Do?*
• What do you think this story is about? (Accept reasonable responses.)
5. (Call on individual students. Each is to read two to four sentences.)
6. (Call on individual students to answer the specified questions during the story reading.)

Bert was on the beach yelling, "We made it." The boat was grounded next to the dock. ❶

1. What does **grounded** mean? (Idea: *Stuck on the ground.*)

The surfer picked up his surfboard, turned to Shirley, and said, "That trip was a real treat." Just then the front of his surfboard collapsed and fell to the deck. He was left holding a third of his surfboard. "Hey," he said. "That's not fair. How can I go surfing with a broken board?"

Shirley slapped him on the back. "You're born to fish," she shouted. "Stick with me and we'll go after the big flounders." ❷

2. What did Shirley want the surfer to do? (Idea: *To keep fishing with her.*)

Bert got up and spit sand from his mouth. Then he yelled, "I'm not going with you. I'm going back to the sail shop. I'm a clerk, not a sailor."

Shirley said, "How can you go back to that place after you've had the sound of surf in your ears?"

"I dig," the surfer said.

"No, no," Bert yelled. "I like to feel the ground under my feet. I'm sick of the surf, and I can't stand boats with termites." ❸

3. What did Shirley think of Bert's job? (Idea: *It wasn't as good as being a sailor.*)
3. What did Bert like to feel? (Idea: *Ground under his feet.*)

The surfer tossed his broken surfboard on the beach. Then he grabbed a fishing pole and made a long cast along the beach. ❹

4. How do you **cast?** (Idea: *Flick the end of your pole so the fishing line goes out into the water.*)

In an instant he pulled out a big fish. "This fishing is a lot of fun," he said. He swung the fish onto the deck. Then he cast again. He jerked up on the pole and pulled out another fish.

Shirley grabbed the fish and looked at it. "That's a shad," she exclaimed. "Are there always shad around here?"

"Yep," the surfer said as he made another cast. "This water is lousy with shad."

Bert said, "This water is lousy—period. I never want to see any more water. I'm going back to the sail shop." ❺

5. What does "The water is lousy with shad" mean? (Idea: *It's full of shad.*)
5. What did Bert mean when he said, "This water is lousy—period"? (Idea: *He didn't like the sea at all.*)

Shirley said to the surfer, "How much of this beach is yours?"

The surfer said, "About a third of a mile up the beach and about a third of a mile down the beach." ❻

6. How much beach did the surfer own? (Ideas: *Two-thirds of a mile; one-third mile up the beach and one-third mile down the beach.*)

"Wow," Shirley exclaimed.

By now Bert was walking across the beach, away from the boat. "I'm leaving," he said.

"Stop pouting," Shirley said. "First you're clowning around when things are serious, and now you're pouting when things are beautiful." ❼

7. How was Bert feeling? (Ideas: *He was sick of the surf; he wanted to go back to the shop.*)

"What's beautiful?" Bert shouted.

"Well, come on back here and I'll tell you," Shirley responded. "I've got a plan that will make everybody happy. It will make you happy; it will make the surfer happy; and it will make old Shirley happy."

Bert stopped and looked back at the boat. He was thinking. ❽

8. What do you think Shirley's plan was? (Accept reasonable responses.)
7. (Award points quickly.)
8. (If the group makes more than 12 errors, repeat the reading immediately or on the next day.)

FLUENCY ASSESSMENT

EXERCISE 10

TIMED READING CHECKOUTS

1. (For this part of the lesson, assigned pairs of students work together during the checkouts.)
- (If one student does not have a checkout partner, arrange another time when you can give the checkout.)
2. (Each student does a 2-minute timed reading. Students earn 5 points by reading at least 200 words and making no more than 4 errors on the first part of story 7. Students record points in Box C of their Point Chart and plot their reading rate and errors on the Individual Reading Progress Chart.)
- (During each timed checkout, observe one pair of students for 2 minutes. Make notes on any mistakes the reader makes.)
3. (Record the timed reading checkout performance for each student you observed on the Fluency Assessment Summary form.)

Errors

Lesson 7

1

1. a. Was the surfboard made of wood? Yes.
   b. How did it get broken? (The termites ate part of it.)
2. What job did Bert want to have? clerk
3. Did Shirley think Bert's job was fun? No.
4. What kind of fish did the surfer catch? shad
5. Why did Shirley ask the surfer, "Are there always shad around here?"
   Draw a line under the fact that tells why.
   Shirley likes to talk to the surfer.
   Shirley doesn't like shad.
   Shirley has a plan.
6. What does "The water is lousy with shad" mean?
   (There are lots of shad in the water.)
7. What did Bert mean when he said, "This water is lousy—period."
   (He didn't like the water.)
8. Shirley had a plan. Who did she think it would make happy?
   (everybody)
9. What do you think Shirley's plan was?
   (Accept reasonable responses.)

Copyright © SRA/McGraw-Hill. All rights reserved. Lesson 7 11

Lesson 7

2 **Fill in each blank using a word in the box.**

business	surfer	respond
waist	collapse	skid

1. The surfer went down to the beach every day.
2. Bill and Gomez were in the business of selling paper.
3. The red belt is too tight for my waist.

3 **Write the parts for each word.**

1. darkness = dark + ness
2. weekly = week + ly
3. responded = respond + ed
4. hardest = hard + est

12 Lesson 7 Copyright © SRA/McGraw-Hill. All rights reserved.

WORKBOOK EXERCISES

Independent Student Work

Task A

- Open your Workbook to Lesson 7. ✓
- Complete all parts of your Workbook lesson using a pencil. If you make no errors, you will earn 5 points.

Task B

1. (Before presenting Lesson 8, check student Workbooks for Lesson 7.)
   - (Call on individual students to read the items and answers in each part. Students mark errors using a pen.)
2. (Direct the students to count the number of errors and write the number in the Errors box at the top of the Workbook page.)
3. (Award points and direct students to record points in Box D of their Point Chart.)

0 errors................................5 points
1 error.................................3 points
2 or 3 errors.........................1 point
more than 3 errors..............0 points

END OF LESSON 7

Lesson 8

WORD-ATTACK SKILLS

Board Work

EXERCISE 1

BUILDUP

1. (Print on the board:)

bout

2. (Point to **bout.** Pause.) What word? (Signal.) *Bout.*
3. (Change the word to:)

bait

- What word now? (Signal.) *Bait.*

4. (Change the word to:)

bart

- What word now? (Signal.) *Bart.*

5. (Change to the original word:)

bout

- (Repeat steps 2–4 until firm.)

Student Book

EXERCISE 2

SOFT G: ge

Task A

1. Open your Student Book to Lesson 8. ✓

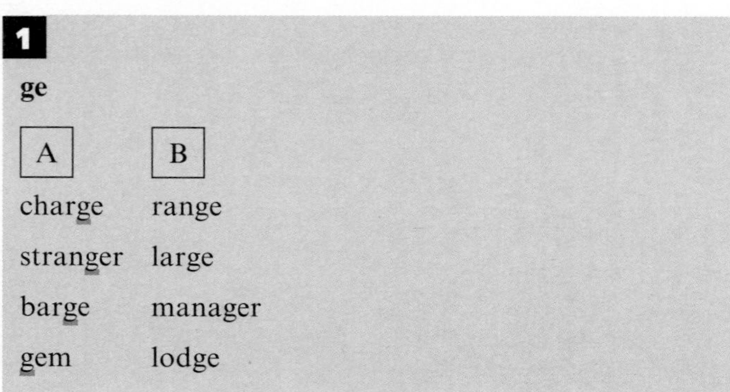

1

ge

A	B
charge	range
stranger	large
barge	manager
gem	lodge

- Touch the letters **G–E** in part 1. ✓
- What sound does the letter **G** make? (Signal.) *j.*

2. You're going to say the sound for the underlined part and then read the word.
3. Touch the first word in column A. ✓
- What sound? (Signal.) *j.*
- What word? (Signal.) *Charge.*

4. Touch the next word. ✓
- What sound? (Signal.) *j.*
- What word? (Signal.) *Stranger.*

5. (Repeat step 4 for **barge, gem.**)

Task B

1. Touch the first word in column B. ✓
- What word? (Signal.) *Range.*

2. Touch the next word. ✓
- What word? (Signal.) *Large.*

3. (Repeat step 2 for **manager, lodge.**)
4. (Repeat steps 1–3 until firm.)

EXERCISE 3

NEW **SOFT C: ce**

Task A

1. Touch the letters **C–E** in part 2. ✓

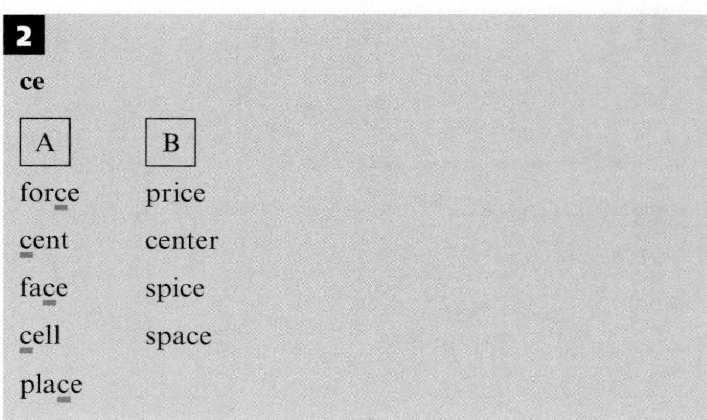

2

ce

A	B
force	price
cent	center
face	spice
cell	space
place	

- When the letter **E** comes after **C,** the **C** makes the sound **sss,** as in **ice.**

2. You're going to read words that have the sound **sss** in them.
3. Touch the first word in column A. ✓
- What sound? (Signal.) *sss.*
- What word? (Signal.) *Force.*

4. Touch the next word. ✓
- What sound? (Signal.) *sss.*
- What word? (Signal.) *Cent.*

5. (Repeat step 4 for **face, cell, place.**)

Task B

1. Touch the first word in column B. ✓
- What word? (Signal.) *Price.*
2. Touch the next word. ✓
- What word? (Signal.) *Center.*
3. (Repeat step 2 for **spice, space.**)
4. (Repeat steps 1–3 until firm.)

EXERCISE 4

WORD PRACTICE

1. Touch the first word in part 3. ✓

3

farmer turning painted third

jar charge plaster aren't

lousy first hailed tarp

- What sound? (Signal.) *ar.*
- What word? (Signal.) *Farmer.*
2. Touch the next word. ✓
- What sound? (Signal.) *er.*
- What word? (Signal.) *Turning.*
3. (Repeat step 2 for each remaining word.)
4. (Repeat each row of words until firm.)

EXERCISE 5

VOCABULARY

1. Touch part 4. ✓

4

1. convert
2. purchase
3. probably
4. reply

- We're going to talk about what those words mean.
2. Touch word 1. ✓
- What word? (Signal.) *Convert.*
- When you **change** something into something else, you **convert** it. Everybody, what's another way of saying "They **changed** the bedroom into a playroom"? (Signal.) *They converted the bedroom into a playroom.*
3. Touch word 2. ✓
- What word? (Signal.) *Purchase.*
- Who knows what **purchase** means? (Call on a student.) (Idea: *Buy.*)
4. Everybody, touch word 3. ✓
- What word? (Signal.) *Probably.*
- When it's **likely** that something will happen, it **probably** will happen. Everybody, what's another way of saying "We will **likely** catch fish here"? (Signal.) *We will probably catch fish here.*
5. Touch word 4. ✓
- What word? (Signal.) *Reply.*
- When you **answer** people, you **reply to** them. Everybody, what's another way of saying "She **answered** his call"? (Signal.) *She replied to his call.*

EXERCISE 6

WORD PRACTICE

1. Touch the first word in part 5. ✓

5

behind ducked alive station chief

posters either business* our shuffling

money replied game booming rubbed

hardly fire fired your neither

gone waist* slowly equipment

- What word? (Signal.) *Behind.*
2. Next word. ✓
- What word? (Signal.) *Ducked.*
3. (Repeat step 2 for each remaining word.)
4. (Repeat each row of words until firm.)
5. What does **business** mean? (Call on a student.)
- (Repeat for **waist.**)

EXERCISE 7

MULTIPART WORDS

Note: The parts of a word are to be pronounced the same as they are when the word is spoken normally. For example, in the word **information, forma** is pronounced **for-may.**

Lesson
8

Task A

1. Touch part 6. ✓

6

information	enlargement	remainder
1. information	2. enlargement	3. remainder

2. All of these words have more than one part. The first part and the last part are circled.
3. Touch word 1. ✓
- Word 1 is **information.** What word? (Signal.) *Information.*
4. The parts are **in** (pause) **forma** (pause) **tion.**
- What's the first part? (Signal.) *in.*
- The middle part is spelled **F–O–R–M–A.** What does that part say in the word? (Signal.) *forma.*
- What's the last part? (Signal.) *tion.*
5. Say the whole word. (Signal.) *Information.*
6. (Repeat steps 3–5 until firm.)
7. Touch word 2. ✓
- Word 2 is **enlargement.** What word? (Signal.) *Enlargement.*
8. The parts are **en** (pause) **large** (pause) **ment.**
- What's the first part? (Signal.) *en.*
- The middle part is spelled **L–A–R–G–E.** What does that part say in the word? (Signal.) *large.*
- What's the last part? (Signal.) *ment.*
9. Say the whole word. (Signal.) *Enlargement.*
10. (Repeat steps 7–9 until firm.)
11. Touch word 3. ✓
- Word 3 is **remainder.** What word? (Signal.) *Remainder.*
12. The parts are **re** (pause) **main** (pause) **der.**
- What's the first part? (Signal.) *re.*
- The middle part is spelled **M–A–I–N.** What does that part say in the word? (Signal.) *main.*
- What's the last part? (Signal.) *der.*
13. Say the whole word. (Signal.) *Remainder.*
14. (Repeat steps 11–13 until firm.)

Task B

1. Touch the sentences below the word list. ✓

a. The information they gave us was not complete.
b. An enlargement of the photo I took hung over the fireplace.
c. We ate the remainder of the chicken salad for lunch.

- These are sentences that use the words you just read.
2. Raise your hand when you can read sentence A. ✓
3. (Call on a student.) Read sentence A. *The information they gave us was not complete.*
- That means "They told us facts, but they didn't tell us enough."
4. (Call on a student.) Read sentence B. *An enlargement of the photo I took hung over the fireplace.*
- That means "A larger version of the photo I took was hanging over the fireplace."
5. (Call on a student.) Read sentence C. *We ate the remainder of the chicken salad for lunch.*
- That means "We ate the leftover chicken salad for lunch."

EXERCISE 8

WORD-ATTACK SKILLS: Individual tests

1. (Call on individual students. Each student reads a row of words, a column of words, or a sentence. In the Multipart words exercises, each sentence counts as one row of words. Tally the rows, columns, and sentences read without error. If the group reads at least 14 rows and columns without making errors, direct all students to record 5 points in Box A of their Point Chart. Criterion is 80 percent of rows and columns read without error.)

2. (If the group did not read at least 14 rows and columns without errors, do not award any points for the Word-Attack Skills exercises.)

SELECTION READING

EXERCISE 9

STORY READING

1. Everybody, touch part 6. ✓
2. The error limit for this story is 12. If the group reads the story with 12 errors or less, you earn 5 points.

6 **A Business on the Beach**

3. (Call on a student to read the title.) *A Business on the Beach.*
   - What do you think this story is about? (Accept reasonable responses.)
4. (Call on individual students. Each is to read two to four sentences.)
5. (Call on individual students to answer the specified questions during the story reading.)

Shirley told the others that she had a plan. Bert was standing on the beach shuffling his feet. The surfer was casting his line into the water. Shirley was waiting for Bert to make up his mind about leaving. ❶

1. What does **shuffling his feet** mean? (Idea: *Moving his feet without going anywhere.*)

Finally Bert shuffled over to Shirley. "Let's hear your plan," he said.

"Here it is," Shirley replied. "The surfer owns this beach. I own this boat. And you, Bert, are a clerk."

"Right," Bert said.

"Cool," the surfer said as he reeled in another shad.

Shirley said, "And this beach is lousy with fish. So what if we opened a business right here on the beach? We could fix up the old boat and convert it into a sail shop. Bert, you could work in the sail shop. We could charge people to fish here. I could be in charge of the fishing. And we would pay the surfer for using his beach." ❷

2. What was Shirley's plan? (Idea: *To set up a shop on the beach.*)
2. What does **convert** mean? (Idea: *To change something into something else.*)
2. What does **be in charge of** mean? (Idea: *To be the boss.*)

"Cool," the surfer said. "I really dig money."

Bert rubbed his chin. "You may have something there," he said slowly. "We could sell sails and bait and anchors and all the other things you would buy in a sail shop."

"Right," Shirley said. "People would get a charge out of coming to our shop. It would be a real boat right here in the water." ❸

3. What does **to get a charge out of something** mean? (Idea: *To feel excited by something.*)

The surfer said, "And I could take the money you give me and buy a new surfboard. And I could fish for free."

"Right," Shirley said. "And I could fish too and sell some fish."

Everybody began talking at the same time. They talked and talked.

On the following morning they began to work. They repaired the old boat. It wasn't in any kind of shape to go back to sea, but it was good enough for resting in water that was waist-deep.

Bert got a loan from the bank and purchased goods for the sail shop. ❹

4. What does **purchase** mean? *Buy.*

Then he made posters. He plastered the posters all around. Some said, "Seashore Sail Shop—Marine supplies, diving equipment, fishing goods." Other posters said, "Fish at Seashore Sail Beach. Pay for the fish you catch. No fish, no pay." ❺

5. What do you think they mean by "no fish, no pay"? (Idea: *If you don't catch some fish, you don't have to pay.*)

That's how the business got started. Hardly a month had gone by before the business was booming. And it's going strong today. Bert and Shirley are pretty rich. You can see them down at Seashore Sail Beach almost any time. But if you go down there, you probably won't see the surfer. You'll probably find him up the beach about five miles, where the waves are good. He comes back to Seashore Sail Beach now and then, either to fish or to pick up his share of the money the business makes. ❻

6. Where can you find Bert and Shirley? *At Seashore Sail Beach.*
6. Where can you probably find the surfer? *About five miles up the beach.*
6. Why does he come back to the Seashore Sail Beach? (Idea: *To pick up money or to fish.*)

So Shirley was right. The business had made everybody happy.

6. (Award points quickly.)
7. (If the group makes more than 12 errors, repeat the reading immediately or on the next day.)

FLUENCY ASSESSMENT

EXERCISE 10

TIMED READING CHECKOUTS

1. (For this part of the lesson, assigned pairs of students work together during the checkouts.)
   - (If one student does not have a checkout partner, arrange another time when you can give the checkout.)
2. (Each student does a 2-minute timed reading. Students earn 5 points by reading at least 200 words and making no more than 4 errors on the first part of story 8. Students record points in Box C of their Point Chart and plot their reading rate and errors on the Individual Reading Progress Chart.)
   - (During each timed checkout, observe one pair of students for 2 minutes. Make notes on any mistakes the reader makes.)
3. (Record the timed reading checkout performance for each student you observed on the Fluency Assessment Summary form.)

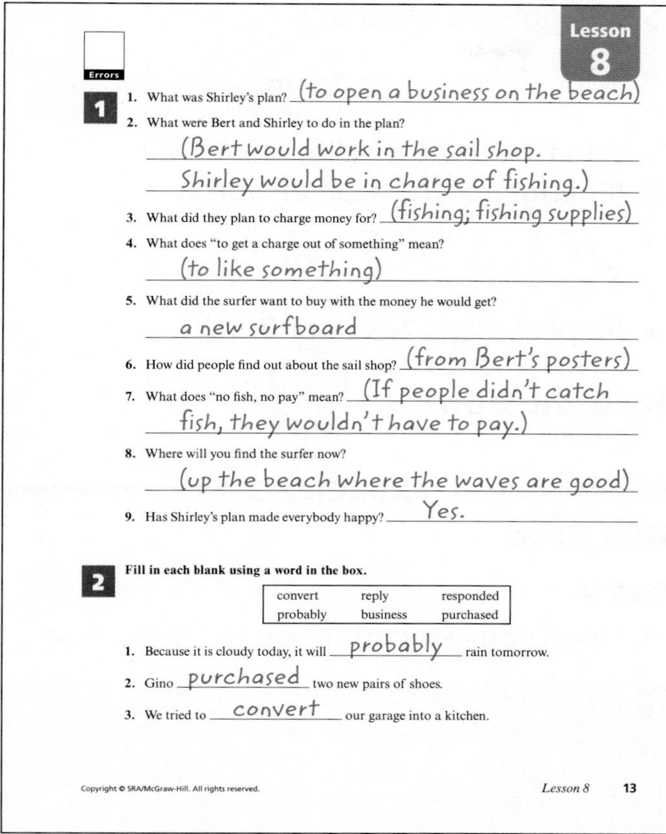
Errors

Lesson 8

1

1. What was Shirley's plan? (to open a business on the beach)
2. What were Bert and Shirley to do in the plan?
(Bert would work in the sail shop.
Shirley would be in charge of fishing.)
3. What did they plan to charge money for? (fishing; fishing supplies)
4. What does "to get a charge out of something" mean?
(to like something)
5. What did the surfer want to buy with the money he would get?
a new surfboard
6. How did people find out about the sail shop? (from Bert's posters)
7. What does "no fish, no pay" mean? (If people didn't catch fish, they wouldn't have to pay.)
8. Where will you find the surfer now?
(up the beach where the waves are good)
9. Has Shirley's plan made everybody happy? Yes.

2 Fill in each blank using a word in the box.

convert	reply	responded
probably	business	purchased

1. Because it is cloudy today, it will probably rain tomorrow.
2. Gino purchased two new pairs of shoes.
3. We tried to convert our garage into a kitchen.

Copyright © SRA/McGraw-Hill. All rights reserved. Lesson 8 13

WORKBOOK EXERCISES

Independent Student Work

Task A

- Open your Workbook to Lesson 8. ✓
- Complete all parts of your Workbook lesson using a pencil. If you make no errors, you will earn 5 points.

Task B

1. (Before presenting Lesson 9, check student Workbooks for Lesson 8.)
- (Call on individual students to read the items and answers in each part. Students mark errors using a pen.)
2. (Direct the students to count the number of errors and write the number in the Errors box at the top of the Workbook page.)
3. (Award points and direct students to record points in Box D of their Point Chart.)

0 errors................................5 points
1 error.................................3 points
2 or 3 errors.........................1 point
more than 3 errors..............0 points

END OF LESSON 8

Lesson 9

WORD-ATTACK SKILLS

Board Work

EXERCISE 1

BUILDUP

1. (Print on the board:)

quit

2. (Point to **quit.** Pause.) What word? (Signal.) *Quit.*
3. (Change the word to:)

quite

- What word now? (Signal.) *Quite.*

4. (Change the word to:)

quiet

- What word now? (Signal.) *Quiet.*

5. (Change to the original word:)

quit

- (Repeat steps 2–4 until firm.)

EXERCISE 2

BUILDUP

1. (Print on the board:)

or

2. (Point to **or.** Pause.) What word? (Signal.) *Or.*
3. (Change the word to:)

for

- What word now? (Signal.) *For.*

4. (Change the word to:)

form

- What word now? (Signal.) *Form.*

5. (Change the word to:)

from

- What word now? (Signal.) *From.*

6. (Change to the original word:)

or

- (Repeat steps 2–5 until firm.)

Student Book

EXERCISE 3

SOFT C: ce

Task A

1. Open your Student Book to Lesson 9. ✓

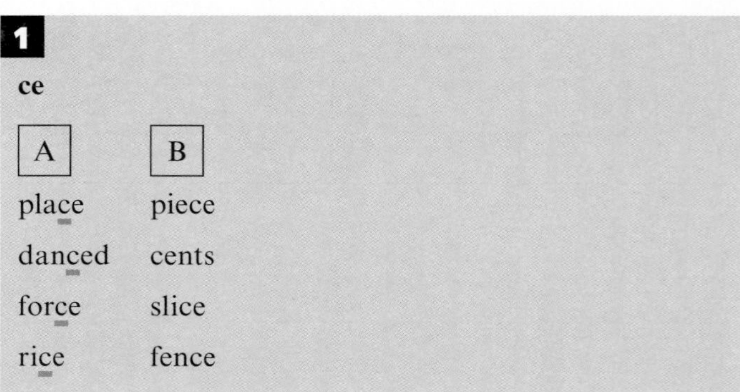

1

ce

A	B
place	piece
danced	cents
force	slice
rice	fence

- Touch the letters **C–E** in part 1. ✓
- What sound does the letter **C** make? (Signal.) *sss.*

2. You're going to say the sound for the underlined part and then read the word.
3. Touch the first word in column A. ✓

- What sound? (Signal.) *sss.*
- What word? (Signal.) *Place.*

4. Touch the next word. ✓

- What sound? (Signal.) *sss.*
- What word? (Signal.) *Danced.*

5. (Repeat step 4 for **force, rice.**)

Task B

1. Touch the first word in column B. ✓

- What word? (Signal.) *Piece.*

2. Touch the next word. ✓

- What word? (Signal.) *Cents.*

3. (Repeat step 2 for **slice, fence.**)
4. (Repeat steps 1–3 until firm.)

EXERCISE 4

WORD PRACTICE

1. Touch the first word in part 2. ✓

2

Kurt jar strange faint* general
counter surge plunger sound*
thirst dodge experts
exclaimed announced departed

- What sound? (Signal.) *er.*
- What word? (Signal.) *Kurt.*

2. Touch the next word. ✓
- What sound? (Signal.) *ar.*
- What word? (Signal.) *Jar.*

3. (Repeat step 2 for each remaining word.)
4. (Repeat each row of words until firm.)
5. What does **faint** mean? (Call on a student.)
- (Repeat for **sound.**)

EXERCISE 5

VOCABULARY

1. Touch part 3. ✓

3

1. several
2. inspect
3. future
4. unusual
5. announce

- We're going to talk about what those words mean.

2. Touch word 1. ✓
- What word? (Signal.) *Several.*
- Who knows what **several** means? (Call on a student.) (Idea: *More than one and less than many.*)

3. Everybody touch word 2. ✓
- What word? (Signal.) *Inspect.*
- When you look something over carefully, you **inspect** it. Everybody, what's another way of saying "She looked the engine over carefully"? (Signal.) *She inspected the engine.*

4. Touch word 3. ✓
- What word? (Signal.) *Future.*
- Who can explain what the **future** is? (Call on a student.) (Idea: *Time that is to come.*)

5. Everybody, touch word 4. ✓
- What word? (Signal.) *Unusual.*
- Who knows what **unusual** means? (Call on a student.) (Ideas: *Uncommon; rare; not usual.*)

6. Everybody, touch word 5. ✓
- What word? (Signal.) *Announce.*
- When you tell something new, you **announce** it. Everybody, what's another way of saying, "He **told** that he was getting married"? (Signal.) *He announced that he was getting married.*

EXERCISE 6

WORD PRACTICE

1. Touch the first word in part 4. ✓

4

I've we're wasn't those what chief station
these touched engines causing arrived examined
stunned different major show glowing mustard
squirt suddenly* disappear done picture minutes
planet instead gone toward slowly fighters
appeared quite glanced circle moving quiet

- What word? (Signal.) *I've.*

2. Next word. ✓
- What word? (Signal.) *We're.*

3. (Repeat step 2 for each remaining word.)
4. (Repeat each row of words until firm.)
5. What does **suddenly** mean? (Call on a student.)

EXERCISE 7

MULTIPART WORDS

Task A

1. Touch part 5. ✓

5

remembering peacefully accidental

1. remembering 2. peacefully 3. accidental

Note: The parts of a word are to be pronounced the same as they are when the word is spoken normally.

2. All of these words have more than one part. The first part and the last part are circled.
3. Touch word 1. ✓
- Word 1 is **remembering.** What word? (Signal.) *Remembering.*
4. The parts are **re** (pause) **member** (pause) **ing.**
- What's the first part? (Signal.) *re.*
- The middle part is spelled **M-E-M-B-E-R.** What does that part say in the word? (Signal.) *member.*
- What's the last part? (Signal.) *ing.*
5. Say the whole word. (Signal.) *Remembering.*
6. (Repeat steps 3–5 until firm.)
7. Touch word 2. ✓
- Word 2 is **peacefully.** What word? (Signal.) *Peacefully.*
8. The parts are **peace** (pause) **ful** (pause) **ly.**
- What's the first part? (Signal.) *peace.*
- The middle part is spelled **F-U-L.** What does that part say in the word? (Signal.) *ful.*
- What's the last part? (Signal.) *ly.*
9. Say the whole word. (Signal.) *Peacefully.*
10. (Repeat steps 7–9 until firm.)
11. Touch word 3. ✓
- Word 3 is **accidental.** What word? (Signal.) *Accidental.*
12. The parts are **ac** (pause) **cident** (pause) **al.**
- What's the first part? (Signal.) *ac.*
- The middle part is spelled **C-I-D-E-N-T.** What does that part say in the word? (Signal.) *cident.*
- What's the last part? (Signal.) *al.*
13. Say the whole word. (Signal.) *Accidental.*
14. (Repeat steps 11–13 until firm.)

Task B

1. Touch the sentences below the word list. ✓

a. I kept remembering what she said.

b. They settled their disagreement peacefully.

c. It was an accidental meeting.

- These are sentences that use the words you just read.
2. Raise your hand when you can read sentence A. ✓
3. (Call on a student.) Read sentence A. *I kept remembering what she said.*
4. (Call on a student.) Read sentence B. *They settled their disagreement peacefully.*
- That means "They came to an agreement without arguing or fighting."
5. (Call on a student.) Read sentence C. *It was an accidental meeting.*
- That means "The meeting happened without anyone knowing it would happen."

EXERCISE 8

WORD-ATTACK SKILLS: Individual tests

1. (Call on individual students. Each student reads a row of words, a column of words, or a sentence. In the Multipart words exercises, each sentence counts as one row of words. Tally the rows, columns, and sentences read without error. If the group reads at least 13 rows and columns without making errors, direct all students to record 5 points in Box A of their Point Chart. Criterion is 80 percent of rows and columns read without error.)
2. (If the group did not read at least 13 rows and columns without errors, do not award any points for the Word-Attack Skills exercises.)

SELECTION READING

EXERCISE 9

STORY READING

1. Everybody, touch part 6. ✓
2. The error limit for this story is 12. If the group reads the story with 12 errors or less, you earn 5 points.

6 **The Mustard Jar**

3. (Call on a student to read the title.) *The Mustard Jar.*
   - What do you think this story is about? (Accept reasonable responses.)
4. (Call on individual students. Each is to read two to four sentences.)
5. (Call on individual students to answer the specified questions during the story reading.)

This is an unusual story in several ways. It is a story that takes place in the future, and it is a story about a mustard jar. ❶

1. What's this story about? *A mustard jar.*

The mustard jar looked a lot like any other mustard jar. It was made of glass, and it had a plunger on the top. ❷

2. What is a plunger? (Idea: *Something you press to make mustard come out of the jar.*)

When you pressed the plunger, yellow mustard squirted out. This mustard jar was on the counter of a snack bar. Every day things were the same for the mustard jar. Every morning Kurt, the man who owned the snack bar, filled the mustard jar. People then came into the snack bar. Some would order a hamburger. They would grab the mustard jar, press the plunger, and squirt mustard onto their hamburgers. Day after day, things didn't change. ❸

3. What did Kurt own? *A snack bar.*
3. Where did people in the snack bar squirt mustard? *Onto their hamburgers.*

But one day was quite unusual. It started out like any other day, with Kurt filling the mustard jar. As usual, people came into the snack bar and squirted mustard on their hamburgers. In the late afternoon the people left the snack bar and Kurt began to clean up. Everything was quiet until suddenly there was a loud sound followed by a strange green light. The snack bar was filled with <u>this</u> green light. Kurt ducked behind the counter and exclaimed, "Oh, no. They've found me." ❹

4. What did Kurt say when he ducked behind the counter? *"Oh, no. They've found me!"*
4. Why was this day unusual? (Idea: *There was a loud sound, and a green light filled the snack bar.*)

Suddenly a strange-looking woman appeared in the middle of the green light. In a husky voice she said, "You must come back to the planet Surge with me." ❺

5. Where did the strange-looking woman want to take Kurt? (Idea: *To the planet Surge.*)

"No, no," Kurt yelled. "I am happy here. I won't go back to that place."

"Then I will have to use force," the strange woman said calmly. She pointed her finger at Kurt and—bong—a path of light danced from her hand into the snack bar as the room rang with a wild sound. Kurt had ducked behind the counter, and the dancing light had not hit him. Instead, it hit the counter, and the counter began to burn. ❻

6. What happened to the counter when the light hit it? (Idea: *The counter began to burn.*)

"You cannot hide," the woman announced. Again she pointed at Kurt, who was dodging this way and that way behind the counter. Bong. The path of light hit the wall behind the counter and made a circle of flame on the wall. Bong. The path hit a picture on the wall, causing the picture to burn. Bong. The path hit the mustard jar, but the mustard jar didn't burn. It began to glow. ❼

7. What happened to the mustard jar when the dancing light hit it? (Idea: *It began to glow.*)

Bong. The path of light hit Kurt and stunned him. He seemed to freeze.

The strange-looking woman jumped over the counter, took Kurt's hand, and led him around the counter. Both of them seemed to disappear in a bright circle of green light. They were gone, and the snack bar was again empty. ❽

8. What happened to Kurt and the strange-looking woman? (Idea: *They seemed to disappear in a bright circle of green light.*)

Within three minutes after the strange woman and Kurt had departed, fire engines arrived at the snack bar. Somebody had seen smoke coming from the shop. Within two minutes after the fire fighters arrived, they had put out the fires. "We're all done here," the chief said. "Take the truck back to the station. I'll stay here and see if I can find out how these little fires got started." ❾

9. Why did the chief stay at the snack bar? (Idea: *To try to find out how the fires got started.*)

The other fire fighters left, and the chief began to inspect the place. She examined the walls and the windows. She examined the floor. ❿

10. How do you examine something? (Idea: *You look at it carefully.*)

As she was inspecting the floor, she glanced to one side and saw the mustard jar. She stopped. "What is this?" she asked herself. "That jar is glowing." Very slowly she moved her hand toward the jar. Then she touched it softly. "It's not hot," she said. "But I think I can feel it moving. It almost seems to be alive." ⓫

11. When the chief touched the jar, how did it feel? (Ideas: *It felt like it was moving; like it was alive.*)
6. (Award points quickly.)
7. (If the group makes more than 12 errors, repeat the reading immediately or on the next day.)

FLUENCY ASSESSMENT

EXERCISE10

TIMED READING CHECKOUTS

1. (For this part of the lesson, assigned pairs of students work together during the checkouts.)
   - (If one student does not have a checkout partner, arrange another time when you can give the checkout.)
2. (Each student does a 2-minute timed reading. Students earn 5 points by reading at least 200 words and making no more than 4 errors on the first part of story 9. Students record points in Box C of their Point Chart and plot their reading rate and errors on the Individual Reading Progress Chart.)
   - (During each timed checkout, observe one pair of students for 2 minutes. Make notes on any mistakes the reader makes.)
3. (Record the timed reading checkout performance for each student you observed on the Fluency Assessment Summary form.)

Lesson 9

Errors

1

1. a. Is this a story about something that really happened? No.
   b. How do you know? (Accept reasonable responses.)
2. What did Kurt own? a snack bar
3. Why was the mustard jar on the counter? (so people could squirt mustard onto their hamburgers)
4. What did Kurt do to the mustard jar every day? (filled it)
5. Where did the strange-looking woman want to take Kurt? (to the planet Surge)
6. What did the dancing light do to the mustard jar? (made it glow)
7. What did the dancing light do to all the other things it hit? (burned them)
8. What happened to Kurt and the strange-looking woman? (They disappeared.)
9. How long did it take for the fire fighters to get to the snack bar and put out the fire? (five minutes)
10. How did the jar feel when the chief touched it? (as if it were moving)

14 Lesson 9 Copyright © SRA/McGraw-Hill. All rights reserved.

Lesson 9

2 Fill in each blank using a word in the box.

several	inspected	future
unusual	convert	exclaimed

1. She inspected the floor to make sure it was clean.
2. "We're cold and hungry!" she exclaimed.
3. Nina had ten cats and several dogs.

3 Write the parts for each word.

1. inspected = inspect + ed
2. appearing = appear + ing
3. smoothness = smooth + ness
4. faintest = faint + est

Copyright © SRA/McGraw-Hill. All rights reserved. Lesson 9 15

WORKBOOK EXERCISES

Independent Student Work

Task A

- Open your Workbook to Lesson 9. ✓
- Complete all parts of your Workbook lesson using a pencil. If you make no errors, you will earn 5 points.

Task B

1. (Before presenting Lesson 10, check student Workbooks for Lesson 9.)
   - (Call on individual students to read the items and answers in each part. Students mark errors using a pen.)
2. (Direct the students to count the number of errors and write the number in the Errors box at the top of the Workbook page.)
3. (Award points and direct students to record points in Box D of their Point Chart.)

0 errors ....5 points
1 error ....3 points
2 or 3 errors ....1 point
more than 3 errors ....0 points

END OF LESSON 9

Lesson 10

WORD-ATTACK SKILLS

Board Work

EXERCISE 1

BUILDUP

1. (Print on the board:)

quiet

2. (Point to **quiet.** Pause.) What word? (Signal.) *Quiet.*
3. (Change the word to:)

quite

- What word now? (Signal.) *Quite.*

4. (Change the word to:)

quit

- What word now? (Signal.) *Quit.*

5. (Change the word to:)

quick

- What word now? (Signal.) *Quick.*

6. (Change to the original word:)

quiet

- (Repeat steps 2–5 until firm.)

Student Book

EXERCISE 2

NEW **SOFT G AND SOFT C: gi, ci**

Task A

1. Open your Student Book to Lesson 10. ✓
- Touch the letters **G–I** in part 1. ✓
- When the letter **I** comes after **G,** the **G** makes the sound **j.**

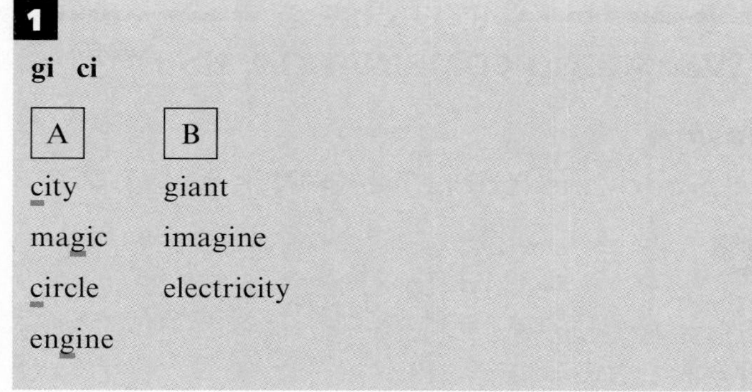

1

gi ci

A	B
city	giant
magic	imagine
circle	electricity
engine	

2. Touch the letters **C–I.** ✓
- When the letter **I** comes after **C,** the **C** makes the sound **sss.**

3. Touch the first word in column A. ✓
- What sound? (Signal.) *sss.*
- What word? (Signal.) *City.*

4. Touch the next word. ✓
- What sound? (Signal.) *j.*
- What word? (Signal.) *Magic.*

5. (Repeat step 4 for **circle, engine.**)

Task B

1. Touch the first word in column B. ✓
- What word? (Signal.) *Giant.*

2. Touch the next word. ✓
- What word? (Signal.) *Imagine.*

3. (Repeat step 2 for **electricity.**)
4. (Repeat steps 1–3 until firm.)

EXERCISE 3

WORD PRACTICE

1. Touch the first word in part 2. ✓

2

mountain plunger dodge
however furnace chance
larger agreed races surge
sparked voice grounded
general sharpener agents
charge discovered several

- What sound? (Signal.) *ow.*
- What word? (Signal.) *Mountain.*

2. Touch the next word. ✓
- What sound? (Signal.) *j.*
- What word? (Signal.) *Plunger.*

3. (Repeat step 2 for each remaining word.)
4. (Repeat each row of words until firm.)

EXERCISE 4

NEW SOUND COMBINATION: tion

Task A

1. Touch the letters **T–I–O–N** in part 3. ✓

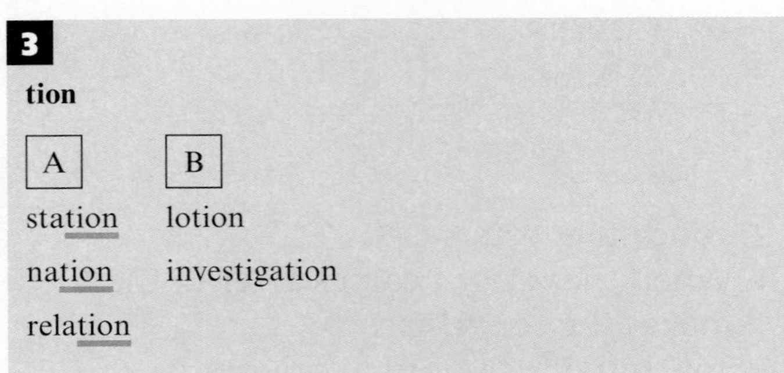

3

tion

A	B
station	lotion
nation	investigation
relation	

- The letters **T–I–O–N** go together and usually make the sound **shun,** as in **station.**

2. You're going to read words that have the sound **shun** in them. You're going to say the sound for the underlined part and then read the word.
3. Touch the first word in column A. ✓
- What sound? (Signal.) *shun.*
- What word? (Signal.) *Station.*
4. Touch the next word. ✓
- What sound? (Signal.) *shun.*
- What word? (Signal.) *Nation.*
5. (Repeat step 4 for **relation**.)

Task B

1. Touch the first word in column B. ✓
- What word? (Signal.) *Lotion.*
2. Touch the next word. ✓
- What word? (Signal.) *Investigation.*
3. (Repeat steps 1 and 2 until firm.)

EXERCISE 5

VOCABULARY

1. Touch part 4. ✓

4

1. beaker
2. device
3. expert
4. investigation
5. laboratory

- We're going to talk about what those words mean.

2. Touch word 1. ✓
- What word? (Signal.) *Beaker.*
- A **beaker** is **a kind of container used in chemistry labs.** Everybody, what is a **beaker?** (Signal.) *A kind of container used in chemistry labs.*
3. Touch word 2. ✓
- What word? (Signal.) *Device.*
- A **device** is **an object made to do something special.** Everybody, what is a **device?** (Signal.) *An object made to do something special.*
4. Touch word 3. ✓
- What word? (Signal.) *Expert.*
- When someone knows a great deal about something, we call that person an **expert.** What's another way of saying "She is a person who knows a great deal about mathematics"? (Call on a student.) (Ideas: *She is an expert about mathematics; she is a mathematics expert; she is an expert in mathematics.*)
5. Touch word 4. ✓
- What word? (Signal.) *Investigation.*
- Who knows what an **investigation** is? (Call on a student.) (Idea: *A close examination of something.*)
6. Everybody, touch word 5. ✓
- What word? (Signal.) *Laboratory.*
- A **laboratory** is a **place where experiments are done.** Everybody, what is a **laboratory?** (Signal.) *A place where experiments are done.*

EXERCISE 6

WORD PRACTICE

1. Touch the first word in part 5. ✓

5

crackled staring increased observed
temperature behind wiggle future
disappear different splashing probably*
metal carefully people secret
fantastic suggested showers might
huge through million move believe

- What word? (Signal.) *Crackled.*
2. Next word. ✓
- What word? (Signal.) *Staring.*
3. (Repeat step 2 for each remaining word.)
4. (Repeat each row of words until firm.)
5. What does **probably** mean? (Call on a student.)

EXERCISE 7

MULTIPART WORDS

Task A

1. Touch part 6. ✓

6

occupation unlimited according
1. occupation 2. unlimited 3. according

> **Note:** The parts of a word are to be pronounced the same as they are when the word is spoken normally. For example, in the word **occupation, cupa** is pronounced **cue-pay.**

2. All of these words have more than one part. The first part and the last part are circled.
3. Touch word 1. ✓
- Word 1 is **occupation.** What word? (Signal.) *Occupation.*
4. The parts are **oc** (pause) **cupa** (pause) **tion.**
- What's the first part? (Signal.) *oc.*
- The middle part is spelled **C–U–P–A.** What does that part say in the word? (Signal.) *cupa.*
- What's the last part? (Signal.) *tion.*
5. Say the whole word. (Signal.) *Occupation.*
6. (Repeat steps 3–5 until firm.)
7. Touch word 2. ✓
- Word 2 is **unlimited.** What word? (Signal.) *Unlimited.*
8. The parts are **un** (pause) **limit** (pause) **ed.**
- What's the first part? (Signal.) *un.*
- The middle part is spelled **L–I–M–I–T.** What does that part say in the word? (Signal.) *limit.*
- What's the last part? (Signal.) *ed.*
9. Say the whole word. (Signal.) *Unlimited.*
10. (Repeat steps 7–9 until firm.)
11. Touch word 3. ✓
- Word 3 is **according.** What word? (Signal.) *According.*
12. The parts are **ac** (pause) **cord** (pause) **ing.**
- What's the first part? (Signal.) *ac.*
- The middle part is spelled **C–O–R–D.** What does that part say in the word? (Signal.) *cord.*
- What's the last part? (Signal.) *ing.*
13. Say the whole word. (Signal.) *According.*
14. (Repeat steps 11–13 until firm.)

Task B

1. Touch the sentences below the word list. ✓

a. For her occupation, she had to travel a lot.
b. It seemed to the others that he had unlimited cash.
c. According to the map, we are a long way from the campsite.

- These are sentences that use the words you just read.
2. Raise your hand when you can read sentence A. ✓
3. (Call on a student.) Read sentence A. *For her occupation, she had to travel a lot.*
- That means "For her job, she had to travel a lot."

4. (Call on a student.) Read sentence B. *It seemed to the others that he had unlimited cash.*
- That means "The others thought that he had endless amounts of money."

5. (Call on a student.) Read sentence C. *According to the map, we are a long way from the campsite.*
- That means "The map shows that we have a long way to go to get to the campsite."

EXERCISE 8

WORD-ATTACK SKILLS: Individual tests

1. (Call on individual students. Each student reads a row of words, a column of words, or a sentence. In the Multipart words exercises, each sentence counts as one row of words. Tally the rows, columns, and sentences read without error. If the group reads at least 16 rows and columns without making errors, direct all students to record 5 points in Box A of their Point Chart. Criterion is 80 percent of rows and columns read without error.)
2. (If the group did not read at least 16 rows and columns without errors, do not award any points for the Word-Attack Skills exercises.)

SELECTION READING

EXERCISE 9

STORY READING

1. Everybody, touch part 7. ✓
2. The error limit for this story is 12. If the group reads the story with 12 errors or less, you earn 5 points.

7 Nothing Changes the Mustard Jar

3. (Call on a student to read the title.) *Nothing Changes the Mustard Jar.*
- What do you think this story is about? (Accept reasonable responses.)

4. (Call on individual students. Each is to read two to four sentences.)
5. (Call on individual students to answer the specified questions during the story reading.)

> The fire chief had discovered the glowing mustard jar in the snack bar. ❶

1. What did the fire chief discover in the snack bar? (Idea: *The glowing mustard jar.*)

> She held it carefully by the plunger and took it to her car. When she got to the fire station, she called the police chief and told the chief about the mustard jar. The police chief called a major in the army. The major called a general, who called somebody in Washington. ❷

2. Who did the general call? (Idea: *Someone in Washington.*)

> While all this calling was going on, the mustard jar was in a glass case in the fire station. All the fire fighters looked at it and shook their heads. "It's almost alive," several of them observed. ❸

3. What did the fire fighters observe? (Idea: *That the jar seemed alive.*)

> Two days after the jar had been discovered in the snack bar, several people from Washington entered the fire station. They were experts on different types of matter. Each looked at the mustard jar, and each observed, "I've never seen anything like this before."
>
> After all the experts had inspected the jar, the one in charge of the experts said, "We don't know anything about this jar. ❹

4. What kind of experts came to the fire station? (Idea: *Experts on different types of matter.*)
4. What does **inspect** mean? (Ideas: *To look at something closely; to examine.*)

We have never seen matter in this form. We must find out what makes it work." The experts returned the mustard jar to the glass case. Then they placed the glass case in a metal box, which they took to a place high in the mountains. A large fence circled this place, and there were many signs on the fence. Each sign said, "Top Secret. Don't talk about your work." 5

5. Where did the experts take the jar? (Ideas: *A place high in the mountains; a top-secret place.*)

The experts went inside to a laboratory, where they removed the mustard jar from the glass case in the metal box. Then they began their investigation. First, they put the mustard jar in a beaker of water. Nothing changed. The jar kept on glowing. Next, the experts put the jar in a freezer. Nothing changed. At last, they put the jar in a furnace, which heated the jar far above the boiling temperature of water. Nothing changed. Still the experts increased the heat to a temperature that would melt glass. Finally, they turned up the heat as high as it would go. The mustard jar glowed just as it had glowed before. The glass didn't melt. 6

6. Name the three things the experts did with the mustard jar. (Idea: *Put it in a beaker of water, put it in the freezer, and put it in a furnace.*)
6. What happened to the jar when the heat was as high as it could get? (Ideas: *The mustard jar glowed as it had before; the glass didn't melt; nothing.*)

"This is fantastic," one of the experts exclaimed. "That jar should have melted."

"I have an idea," another expert suggested. "Let's try electricity."

"Yes," a third expert agreed. "Electricity might work."

So the experts put the mustard jar in a giant device. Then they turned on the electricity. At first, they sent a charge of five thousand volts through the mustard jar. Nothing changed. They increased the charge again and again. "Let's give it all the electricity we can," an expert suggested. "This is our last chance." So the experts sent a charge of three million volts through that jar. Showers of sparks filled the room. The sound of electricity crackled and sparked. First, the jar appeared to wiggle and shake and then to smoke. 7

7. What did the jar do when it got a shock of three million volts? (Idea: *First it wiggled and shook, and then it smoked.*)

"Shut it off," one of the experts yelled. "It's burning up."

Suddenly the room became dark. The experts crowded around the smoking jar. Everybody just stood there, staring at the jar and not speaking. Then one expert yelled, "Am I seeing things, or is that jar getting larger?"

"You're right," another expert agreed as she looked closer. "Look at it grow." 8

8. What happened to the jar after the experts turned off the electricity? (Ideas: *It got larger; it grew.*)

"And I'm alive," a voice said.

The experts looked at each other. "Who said that?" one woman asked. They looked back at the jar, which was now as big as a pop bottle.

The mustard jar said, "I said that. I am alive." ❾

9. Who said, "I'm alive"? (Idea: *The mustard jar.*)
9. How big was the jar when it said that? (Idea: *As big as a pop bottle.*)
9. What **caused** the mustard jar to become alive, grow larger, and be able to talk? (Idea: *A shock of three million volts of electricity.*)

"I'm getting out of this place," one of the experts said. "I don't believe in talking mustard jars." With fast steps, he ran from the room. However, the other experts didn't move. They just stood there with their mouths open, staring at the huge mustard jar.

6. (Award points quickly.)
7. (If the group makes more than 12 errors, repeat the reading immediately or on the next day.)

FLUENCY ASSESSMENT

EXERCISE 10

TIMED READING CHECKOUTS

1. (For this part of the lesson, assigned pairs of students work together during the checkouts.)
   - (If one student does not have a checkout partner, arrange another time when you can give the checkout.)
2. (Each student does a 2-minute timed reading. Students earn 5 points by reading at least 200 words and making no more than 4 errors on the first part of story 10. Students record points in Box C of their Point Chart and plot their reading rate and errors on the Individual Reading Progress Chart.)
   - (During each timed checkout, observe one pair of students for 2 minutes. Make notes on any mistakes the reader makes.)
3. (Record the timed reading checkout performance for each student you observed on the Fluency Assessment Summary form.)

WORKBOOK EXERCISES

Independent Student Work

Task A

- Open your Workbook to Lesson 10. ✓
- Complete all parts of your Workbook lesson using a pencil. If you make no errors, you will earn 5 points.

Task B

1. (Before presenting Lesson 11, check student Workbooks for Lesson 10.)
   - (Call on individual students to read the items and answers in each part. Students mark errors using a pen.)
2. (Direct the students to count the number of errors and write the number in the Errors box at the top of the Workbook page.)
3. (Award points and direct students to record points in Box D of their Point Chart.)

0 errors ....5 points
1 error ....3 points
2 or 3 errors ....1 point
more than 3 errors ....0 points

Point schedule for Lessons 6 through 10

Box	Lesson part	Points
A	Word Attack	0 or 5
B	Selection Reading	0 or 5
C	Timed Reading Checkout	0 or 5
D	Workbook	0, 1, 3, or 5
Bonus	(Teacher option)	—

Five-lesson point summary

- (For **letter grades** based on points for Lessons **6** through **10**, tell students to compute the total for the blue boxes [C, D, and Bonus] and write the number in the Total box at the end of each row in their Point Chart. Students then add the totals and write the sum in the green box.)
- (For **rewards** based on points, tell students to compute the Total for all boxes [A, B, C, D, and Bonus] and write the number in the Total box at the end of each row. Students then add the totals and write the sum in the green box.)

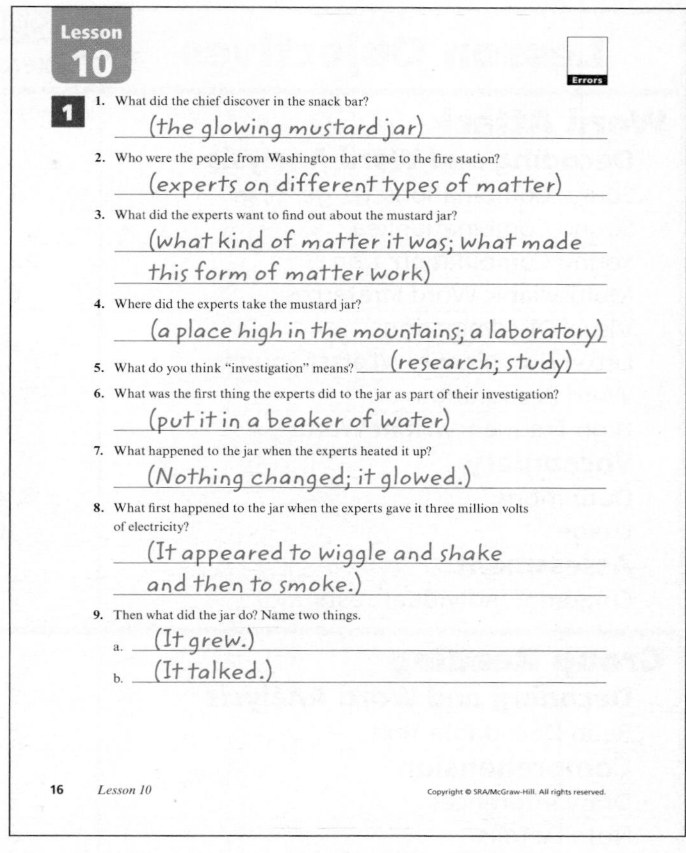

Lesson 10

Errors

1

1. What did the chief discover in the snack bar?
(the glowing mustard jar)
2. Who were the people from Washington that came to the fire station?
(experts on different types of matter)
3. What did the experts want to find out about the mustard jar?
(what kind of matter it was; what made this form of matter work)
4. Where did the experts take the mustard jar?
(a place high in the mountains; a laboratory)
5. What do you think "investigation" means? (research; study)
6. What was the first thing the experts did to the jar as part of their investigation?
(put it in a beaker of water)
7. What happened to the jar when the experts heated it up?
(Nothing changed; it glowed.)
8. What first happened to the jar when the experts gave it three million volts of electricity?
(It appeared to wiggle and shake and then to smoke.)
9. Then what did the jar do? Name two things.
a. (It grew.)
b. (It talked.)

16 *Lesson 10* Copyright © SRA/McGraw-Hill. All rights reserved.

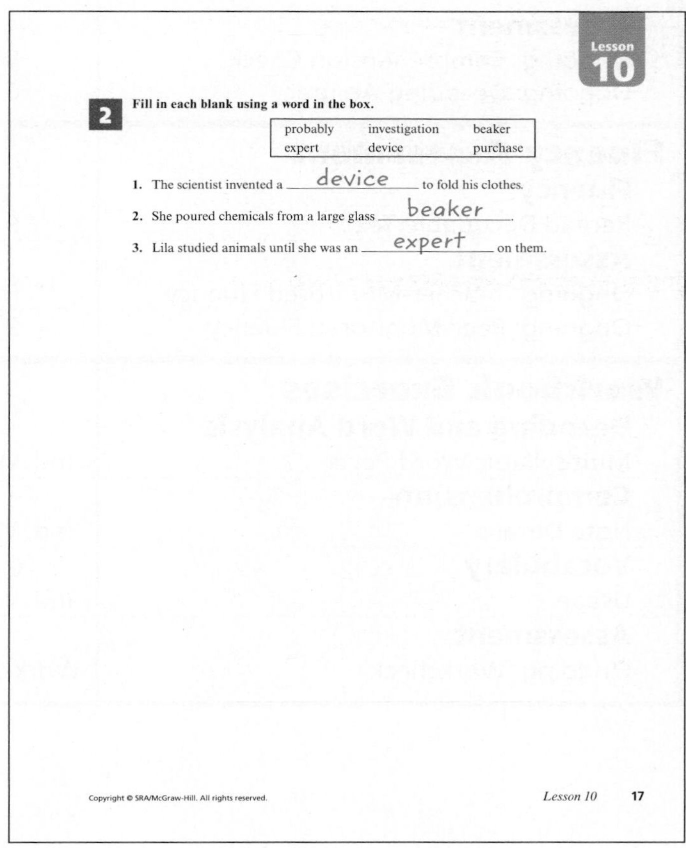

Lesson 10

2 **Fill in each blank using a word in the box.**

probably	investigation	beaker
expert	device	purchase

1. The scientist invented a device to fold his clothes.
2. She poured chemicals from a large glass beaker.
3. Lila studied animals until she was an expert on them.

Copyright © SRA/McGraw-Hill. All rights reserved. *Lesson 10* 17

END OF LESSON 10

Lesson Objectives	LESSON 11 Exercise	LESSON 12 Exercise	LESSON 13 Exercise	LESSON 14 Exercise	LESSON 15 Exercise
Word Attack					
Decoding and Word Analysis					
Sound Combinations: *ce, ge, ci, gi*	1				
Sound Combination: *ea*				2	2
Sound Combination: *tion*	2	2			
Multisyllabic Word Strategies	6	6	5	6	6
Visual Discrimination		1	1	1	1
Letter Combinations/Letter Sounds		3	2	3	3
Word Recognition	1–6	1–6	1–5	1–6	1–6
High-Frequency/Sight Words	6	6	5	6	6
Vocabulary					
Definitions	3, 4	3–5	2–4	3–5	4, 5
Usage	3, 6	4, 6	3, 5	4, 6	5, 6
Assessment					
Ongoing: Individual Tests	7	7	6	7	7
Group Reading					
Decoding and Word Analysis					
Read Decodable Text	8	8	7	8	8
Comprehension					
Draw Inferences	8	8	7	8	8
Note Details	8	8	7	8	8
Predict	8	8	7	8	8
Assessment					
Ongoing: Comprehension Check	8	8	7	8	8
Ongoing: Decoding Accuracy	8	8	7	8	8
Fluency Assessment					
Fluency					
Reread Decodable Text	9	9	8	9	9
Assessment					
Ongoing: Teacher-Monitored Fluency	9	9	8	9	9
Ongoing: Peer-Monitored Fluency	9	9	8	9	9
Workbook Exercises					
Decoding and Word Analysis					
Multisyllabic Word Parts	Ind. Work		Ind. Work		Ind. Work
Comprehension					
Note Details	Ind. Work	Ind. Work	Ind. Work	Ind. Work	Ind. Work
Vocabulary					
Usage	Ind. Work	Ind. Work	Ind. Work	Ind. Work	Ind. Work
Assessment					
Ongoing: Workcheck	Workcheck	Workcheck	Workcheck	Workcheck	Workcheck

WORD-ATTACK SKILLS

Student Book 

EXERCISE 1

SOFT G AND SOFT C: gi, ci

Task A

1. Open your Student Book to Lesson 11. ✓

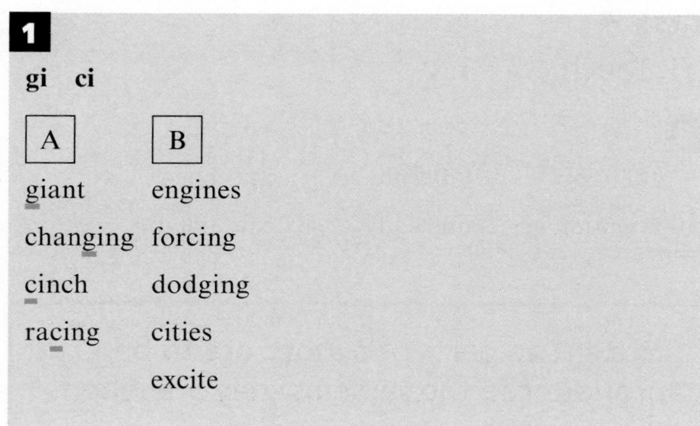

1

gi ci

A	B
giant	engines
changing	forcing
cinch	dodging
racing	cities
	excite

- Touch the letters **G–I** in part 1. ✓
- When the letter **I** comes after **G,** the **G** makes the sound **j.**

2. Touch the letters **C–I** in part 1. ✓
- When the letter **I** comes after **C,** the **C** makes the sound **sss.**
- You're going to say the sound for the underlined part and then read the word.

3. Touch the first word in column A. ✓
- What sound? (Signal.) *j.*
- What word? (Signal.) *Giant.*

4. Touch the next word. ✓
- What sound? (Signal.) *j.*
- What word? (Signal.) *Changing.*

5. (Repeat step 4 for **cinch, racing.**)

Task B

1. Touch the first word in column B. ✓
- What word? (Signal.) *Engines.*

2. Touch the next word. ✓
- What word? (Signal.) *Forcing.*

3. (Repeat step 2 for **dodging, cities, excite.**)
4. (Repeat steps 1–3 until firm.)

EXERCISE 2

SOUND COMBINATION: tion

Task A

1. Touch the letters **T–I–O–N** in part 2. ✓

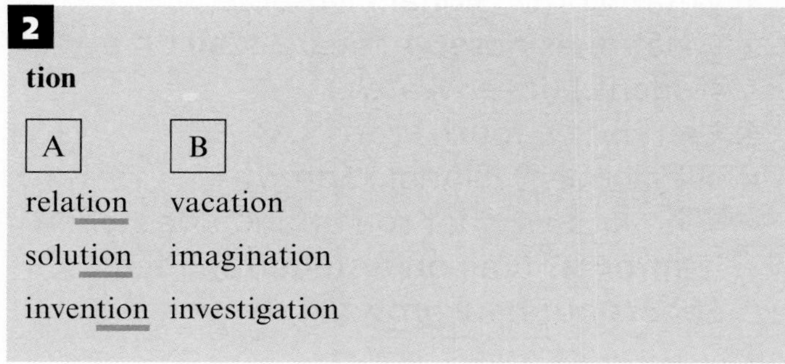

2

tion

A	B
relation	vacation
solution	imagination
invention	investigation

- What sound do the letters **T–I–O–N** make? (Signal.) *shun.*

2. You're going to say the sound for the underlined part and then read the word.
3. Touch the first word in column A. ✓
- What sound? (Signal.) *shun.*
- What word? (Signal.) *Relation.*

4. Touch the next word. ✓
- What sound? (Signal.) *shun.*
- What word? (Signal.) *Solution.*

5. (Repeat step 4 for **invention.**)

Task B

1. Touch the first word in column B. ✓
- What word? (Signal.) *Vacation.*

2. Touch the next word. ✓
- What word? (Signal.) *Imagination.*

3. (Repeat step 2 for **investigation.**)
4. (Repeat steps 1–3 until firm.)

EXERCISE 3

VOCABULARY

1. Touch part 3. ✓

1. crease
2. observe
3. sprout

- We're going to talk about what those words mean.

2. Touch word 1. ✓
- What word? (Signal.) *Crease.*
- A **crease** is **a mark that's left after something has been folded.**

3. Touch word 2. ✓
- What word? (Signal.) *Observe.*
- What does **observe** mean? (Call on a student.) (Idea: *Watch.*)

4. Everybody, touch word 3. ✓
- What word? (Signal.) *Sprout.*
- Who knows what something does when it **sprouts?** (Call on a student.) (Idea: *Shoots out new growth.*)

EXERCISE 4

WORD PRACTICE

1. Touch the first word in part 4. ✓

4

piece sprouted experts* change
darted chance voice spout
spaces huge nerve giant
agents force plunger announced

- What sound? (Signal.) *sss.*
- What word? (Signal.) *Piece.*

2. Touch the next word. ✓
- What sound? (Signal.) *ow.*
- What word? (Signal.) *Sprouted.*

3. (Repeat step 2 for each remaining word.)
4. (Repeat each row of words until firm.)
5. What does **experts** mean? (Call on a student.)

EXERCISE 5

WORD PRACTICE

1. Touch the first word in part 5. ✓

5

flatter quite adventure exactly something
quiet future actually squirt instead touch
wiggled glowing enough replied moved skidded*
flowed minutes stubby tickled second cautioned
laugh eyes lying nobody covered

- What word? (Signal.) *Flatter.*

2. Next word. ✓
- What word? (Signal.) *Quite.*

3. (Repeat step 2 for each remaining word.)
4. (Repeat each row of words until firm.)
5. What does **skidded** mean? (Call on a student.)

EXERCISE 6

NEW MULTIPART WORDS

Task A

1. Touch part 6. ✓

6

attention	unsteady	cautioned
1. attention	2. unsteady	3. cautioned

Note: The parts of a word are to be pronounced the same as they are when the word is spoken normally.

2. All these words have more than one part. The first part and the last part are circled.
3. Touch word 1. ✓
- Word 1 is **attention.** What word? (Signal.) *Attention.*

4. What's the **first** part? (Signal.) *at.*
- What's the **last** part? (Signal.) *tion.*
- The middle part is spelled **T–E–N.** What does that part say in the word? (Signal.) *ten.*

5. So, the parts are **at** (pause) **ten** (pause) **tion.**
- Say the whole word. (Signal.) *Attention.*

6. (Repeat steps 3–5 until firm.)
7. Touch word 2. ✓
- Word 2 is **unsteady.** What word? (Signal.) *Unsteady.*

8. What's the **first** part? (Signal.) *un.*
- What's the **last** part? (Signal.) *y.*
- The middle part is spelled **S–T–E–A–D.** What does that part say in the word? (Signal.) *stead.*

9. So, the parts are **un** (pause) **stead** (pause) **y.**
- Say the whole word. (Signal.) *Unsteady.*

10. (Repeat steps 7–9 until firm.)

11. Touch word 3. ✓
 - Word 3 is **cautioned.** What word? (Signal.) *Cautioned.*
12. What's the first part? (Signal.) *cau.*
 - What's the last part? (Signal.) *ed.* (Accept **ed** pronounced as the sound **d.**)
 - The middle part is spelled **T–I–O–N.** What does that part say in the word? (Signal.) *tion.* (Pronounced **shun.**)
13. So, the parts are **cau** (pause) **tion** (pause) **ed.**
 - Say the whole word. (Signal.) *Cautioned.*
14. (Repeat steps 11–13 until firm.)

Task B

1. Touch the sentences below the word list. ✓

a. He could not keep his attention on the lesson.
b. Her legs were unsteady after she got out of the pool.
c. The doctor cautioned us about eating too much fatty food.

 - These are sentences that use the words you just read.
2. Raise your hand when you can read sentence A. ✓
3. (Call on a student.) Read sentence A. *He could not keep his attention on the lesson.*
 - That means "He couldn't keep thinking about things that were in the lesson."
4. (Call on a student.) Read sentence B. *Her legs were unsteady after she got out of the pool.*
 - That means "Her legs were shaky after she got out of the pool."
5. (Call on a student.) Read sentence C. *The doctor cautioned us about eating too much fatty food.*
 - That means "The doctor told about problems we might have if we ate too much fatty food."

EXERCISE 7

WORD-ATTACK SKILLS: Individual tests

1. (Call on individual students. Each student reads a row of words, a column of words, or a sentence. In the Multipart words exercises, each sentence counts as one row of words. Tally the rows, columns, and sentences read without error. If the group reads at least 14 rows and columns without making errors, direct all students to record 5 points in Box A of their Point Chart. Criterion is 80 percent of rows and columns read without error.)
2. (If the group did not read at least 14 rows and columns without errors, do not award any points for the Word-Attack Skills exercises.)

SELECTION READING

EXERCISE 8

STORY READING

1. Everybody, touch part 7. ✓
2. The error limit for this story is 12. If the group reads the story with 12 errors or less, you earn 5 points.

7 **Glops of Mustard**

3. (Call on a student to read the title.) *Glops of Mustard.*
 - What do you think this story is about? (Accept reasonable responses.)

4. (Call on individual students. Each is to read two to four sentences.)
5. (Call on individual students to answer the specified questions during the story reading.)

Nobody knows exactly how long the experts stood with their mouths open looking at the talking mustard jar. But at last one of them worked up the nerve to talk to the jar. (If you don't think it takes nerve to talk to a mustard jar, try it.) The expert said, "How do you—I mean why are you—I mean what do you—?" ❶

1. Was it easy for the experts to talk to the jar? *No.*

The mustard jar said, "I don't know. I just know that I am alive and I can talk."

"Can you move?" one expert asked.

"I will try." The mustard jar seemed to shake and wiggle. Then it fell over. It shook some more and stood up. "I can move a little bit," the jar said.

"Maybe you can move more if you keep trying," one woman said.

So the jar tried and tried. After trying for a few minutes, the jar said, "I think I can change shape if I really try hard. I will look at something. Then I will change so that I look like that thing." ❷

2. What did the jar say it could do with its shape? (Idea: *That it could change its shape to look like something else.*)

The mustard jar looked at a wall. The experts observed little glass eyes just under the base of its plunger. As the jar looked at the wall, the jar got flatter and flatter. The jar didn't look like a wall, however. It looked like a flat mustard jar. When the jar was quite flat, it fell over. One of the experts began to laugh. "That was funny," he said. ❸

3. What was the jar trying to look like when it got flatter and flatter? *A wall.*
3. Did the jar look like a wall? *No.*
3. What happened? (Idea: *When the mustard jar got flat, it fell over.*)

The jar's eyes darted at the expert. The jar then said, "I will make myself look just like you." As the jar stared at the expert, the jar began to change. It got bigger and bigger and bigger. Then little legs began to sprout from the bottom. And little arms sprouted from the sides of the jar. The mustard jar didn't look like the expert, however. It looked like a huge mustard jar with little stubby legs and arms. All the experts began to laugh. ❹

4. What was the second thing the jar tried to look like? (Idea: *Like one of the experts.*)

"Stop laughing," the jar announced, "or I'll let you have it." But the experts were so tickled that they couldn't stop laughing. Suddenly the plunger on top of the jar went down, and a giant squirt of yellow mustard flowed out of the spout. ❺

5. What's a spout? (Idea: *The place where mustard comes out of the jar.*)

"Take that," the jar said. The experts were covered with glops of mustard.

"My new shirt," one woman said. But as she was talking—squirt—a second shot of yellow mustard hit her in the open mouth. "Ugh," she said. "I can't stand mus—" A third shot hit her in the mouth.

"I'm getting out of here," one expert said, and he began to dash toward the door. When he was about halfway there, however, a huge squirt of mustard landed on the floor in front of him. When he hit the slippery goop, his left foot shot out from under him. His seat landed in the mustard, and he skidded all the way out the door. He left an ugly yellow path on the floor. ❻

6. What happened when one expert tried to talk? (Idea: *Some mustard hit her in the mouth.*)
6. What happened to the other expert who dashed for the door? (Idea: *He slipped on mustard that was on the floor.*)

"Now stop laughing," the mustard jar cautioned. "I look just the way you do."

"Yes, you do," one expert said as she wiped mustard from her face. She was lying, but she felt that she had enough mustard on her face to last her for some time.

Another expert said, "You look fine, just fine."

The mustard jar smiled. You could see a little crease form in the glass when it smiled. Then the jar said, "Now that I look just like a person, I want to do the things that people do." ❼

7. Why did the experts lie about how the mustard jar looked? (Idea: *They didn't want to get squirted with mustard again.*)
7. What could you see when the mustard jar smiled? (Idea: *A little crease in the glass of the jar.*)
7. What **caused** the experts to start laughing at the mustard jar? (Idea: *The mustard jar tried to change shape to look like a wall, but when it became quite flat, it fell over.*)
6. (Award points quickly.)
7. (If the group makes more than 12 errors, repeat the reading immediately or on the next day.)

FLUENCY ASSESSMENT

EXERCISE 9

NEW TIMED READING CHECKOUTS

Note: The rate-accuracy criterion for Lessons 11–20 is 220 words with no more than 4 errors. The 220th word is underlined in the reading selection in the Student Book.

1. (For this part of the lesson, assigned pairs of students work together during the checkouts.)
- (If one student does not have a checkout partner, arrange another time when you can give the checkout.)
2. (Each student does a 2-minute timed reading. Students earn 5 points by reading at least **220 words** and making no more than 4 errors on the first part of story 11. Students record points in Box C of their Point Chart and plot their reading rate and errors on the Individual Reading Progress Chart.)
- (During each timed checkout, observe one pair of students for 2 minutes. Make notes on any mistakes the reader makes.)
3. (Record the timed reading checkout performance for each student you observed on the Fluency Assessment Summary form.)

Lesson 11

Lesson 11

Errors

1

1. Why do you think it took nerve to talk to a mustard jar?
(You'd look silly.)
2. What did the jar say when one expert asked, "Can you move?"
"I will try."
3. What first happened when the mustard jar tried to move?
(It shook and wiggled; it fell over.)
4. What did the mustard jar look like when it tried to change shape into a wall?
(like a flat mustard jar)
5. What happened when the jar was quite flat? (It fell over.)
6. What did the mustard jar sprout when it tried changing shape the second time?
(stubby legs and arms)
7. What happened when the experts couldn't stop laughing?
(They got squirted with mustard.)
8. One expert skidded on the floor. What did he leave behind?
(an ugly yellow path on the floor)
9. Why did one expert say, "You look fine"?
(to keep from getting squirted again)
10. What formed in the glass when the mustard jar smiled?
(a little crease)

 Copyright © SRA/McGraw-Hill. All rights reserved.

Lesson 11

2 Fill in each blank using a word in the box.

laboratory	crease	observed
unusual	future	sprouting

1. The cat carefully observed the mouse.
2. The seeds in our garden are sprouting.
3. The laboratory was filled with beakers and devices for experiments.

3 Write the parts for each word.

1. squirting = squirt + ing
2. stationed = station + ed
3. flatly = flat + ly
4. aliveness = alive + ness

Copyright © SRA/McGraw-Hill. All rights reserved.

WORKBOOK EXERCISES

Independent Student Work

Task A

- Open your Workbook to Lesson 11. ✓
- Complete all parts of your Workbook lesson using a pencil. If you make no errors, you will earn 5 points.

Task B

1. (Before presenting Lesson 12, check student Workbooks for Lesson 11.)
   - (Call on individual students to read the items and answers in each part. Students mark errors using a pen.)
2. (Direct the students to count the number of errors and write the number in the Errors box at the top of the Workbook page.)
3. (Award points and direct students to record points in Box D of their Point Chart.)

0 errors ....5 points
1 error ....3 points
2 or 3 errors ....1 point
more than 3 errors ....0 points

END OF LESSON 11

WORD-ATTACK SKILLS

Board Work

EXERCISE 1

BUILDUP

1. (Print on the board:)

split

2. (Point to **split.** Pause.) What word? (Signal.) *Split.*
3. (Change the word to:)

splits

- What word now? (Signal.) *Splits.*

4. (Change the word to:)

splitting

- What word now? (Signal.) *Splitting.*

5. (Change the word to:)

splitter

- What word now? (Signal.) *Splitter.*

6. (Change the word to:)

splatter

- What word now? (Signal.) *Splatter.*

7. (Change to the original word:)

split

- (Repeat steps 2–6 until firm.)

Student Book

EXERCISE 2

SOUND COMBINATION: tion

1. Open your Student Book to Lesson 12. ✓

1

tion imagina<u>tion</u> inspec<u>tion</u> inven<u>tion</u> direc<u>tion</u>

- Touch the letters **T–I–O–N** in part 1. ✓
- What sound do the letters **T–I–O–N** make? (Signal.) *shun.*

2. You're going to say the sound for the underlined part and then read the word.
3. Touch the first word. ✓

- What sound? (Signal.) *shun.*
- What word? (Signal.) *Imagination.*

4. Touch the next word. ✓

- What sound? (Signal.) *shun.*
- What word? (Signal.) *Inspection.*

5. (Repeat step 4 for **inven<u>tion</u>, direc<u>tion</u>.**)

EXERCISE 3

WORD PRACTICE

1. Touch the first word in part 2. ✓

2

remained chance sparkler imagine

nerves couches germ hardly

largest plunger general surround

fence crouch covered device*

- What sound? (Signal.) *āāā.*
- What word? (Signal.) *Remained.*

2. Touch the next word. ✓

- What sound? (Signal.) *sss.*
- What word? (Signal.) *Chance.*

3. (Repeat step 2 for each remaining word.)
4. (Repeat each row of words until firm.)
5. What does **device** mean? (Call on a student.)

EXERCISE 4

VOCABULARY

1. Touch part 3. ✓

3

1. unfortunate
2. waddle
3. hesitate
4. unbelievable

- We're going to talk about what those words mean.

2. Touch word 1. ✓
- What word? (Signal.) *Unfortunate.*
- Something that is **unfortunate** is **unlucky.** Everybody, what does **unfortunate** mean? (Signal.) *Unlucky.*

3. Touch word 2. ✓
- What word? (Signal.) *Waddle.*
- Who can tell me what **waddle** means? (Call on a student.) (*Idea: Walk in a clumsy manner.*)

4. Everybody, touch word 3. ✓
- What word? (Signal.) *Hesitate.*
- When you **hesitate,** you **pause for a moment.** Everybody, what's another way of saying "The girl **paused for a moment** at the stoplight"? (Signal.) *The girl hesitated at the stoplight.*

5. Touch word 4. ✓
- What word? (Signal.) *Unbelievable.*
- What does **unbelievable** mean? (Call on a student.) (Idea: *Not believable.*)

EXERCISE 5

WORD PRACTICE

1. Touch the first word in part 4. ✓

4

slid slide spit quick suspect
winner behave blanket actually
waddled squirted laboratory* neither
elephant supply crowded pretended
believe built head coughing shoulder
escape before either agreed repair
insisted eyes yellow sniffing unlimited
through disguise clever course

- What word? (Signal.) *Slid.*

2. Next word. ✓
- What word? (Signal.) *Slide.*

3. (Repeat step 2 for each remaining word.)
4. (Repeat each row of words until firm.)
5. What does **laboratory** mean? (Call on a student.)

EXERCISE 6

MULTIPART WORDS

Task A

1. Touch part 5. ✓

5

indication nitrogen immediately

1. indication 2. nitrogen 3. immediately

Note: The parts of a word are to be pronounced the same as they are when the word is spoken normally.

2. All these words have more than one part. The first part and the last part are circled.
3. Touch word 1. ✓
- Word 1 is **indication.** What word? (Signal.) *Indication.*

4. What's the first part? (Signal.) *in.*
- What's the last part? (Signal.) *tion.* (Pronounced **shun.**)
- The middle part is spelled **D–I–C–A.** What does that part say in the word? (Signal.) *dica.*

5. So, the parts are **in** (pause) **dica** (pause) **tion.**
- Say the whole word. (Signal.) *Indication.*

6. (Repeat steps 3–5 until firm.)
7. Touch word 2. ✓
- Word 2 is **nitrogen.** What word? (Signal.) *Nitrogen.*

8. What's the first part? (Signal.) *ni.*
- What's the last part? (Signal.) *gen.*
- The middle part is spelled **T–R–O.** What does that part say in the word? (Signal.) *tro.*

9. So, the parts are **ni** (pause) **tro** (pause) **gen.**
- Say the whole word. (Signal.) *Nitrogen.*

10. (Repeat steps 7–9 until firm.)
11. Touch word 3. ✓
- Word 3 is **immediately.** What word? (Signal.) *Immediately.*

12. What's the first part? (Signal.) *im.*
   - What's the last part? (Signal.) *ly.*
   - The middle part is spelled **M–E–D–I–A–T–E.** What does that part say in the word? (Signal.) *mediate.*
13. So, the parts are **im** (pause) **mediate** (pause) **ly.**
   - Say the whole word. (Signal.) *Immediately.*
14. (Repeat steps 11–13 until firm.)

Task B

1. Touch the sentences below the word list. ✓

> a. The dog gave no indication that it was sick.
>
> b. The divers made sure that there was no nitrogen in the air tanks.
>
> c. When the bell rang, the students immediately left the classroom.

   - These are sentences that use the words you just read.
2. Raise your hand when you can read sentence A. ✓
3. (Call on a student.) Read sentence A. *The dog gave no indication that it was sick.*
   - That means "The dog showed no signs of being sick."
4. (Call on a student.) Read sentence B. *The divers made sure that there was no nitrogen in the air tanks.*
   - Nitrogen is a gas in the air that you breathe.
5. (Call on a student.) Read sentence C. *When the bell rang, the students immediately left the classroom.*
   - That means "When the bell rang, the students did not wait before they left the classroom."

EXERCISE 7

WORD-ATTACK SKILLS: Individual tests

1. (Call on individual students. Each student reads a row of words, a column of words, or a sentence. In the Multipart words exercises, each sentence counts as one row of words. Tally the rows, columns, and sentences read without error.)

   (If the group reads at least 14 rows and columns without making errors, direct all students to record 5 points in Box A of their Point Chart. Criterion is 80 percent of rows and columns read without error.)
2. (If the group did not read at least 14 rows and columns without errors, do not award any points for the Word-Attack Skills exercises.)

SELECTION READING

EXERCISE 8

STORY READING

1. Everybody, touch part 6. ✓
2. The error limit for this story is 12. If the group reads the story with 12 errors or less, you earn 5 points.

> **6**
>
> **The Spy Won't Split**
> **If the Jar Won't Spit**

3. (Call on a student to read the title.) *The Spy Won't Split If the Jar Won't Spit.*
   - What do you think this story is about? (Accept reasonable responses.)
4. (Call on individual students. Each is to read two to four sentences.)
5. (Call on individual students to answer the specified questions during the story reading.)

> When the mustard jar told the experts that it wanted to do the things that people do, the experts agreed. "Yes, that's a fine idea," they insisted. They didn't think the idea was very fine, but they didn't want to get squirted with mustard again. ❶

1. What did the jar want to do? (Idea: *It wanted to do the things people do.*)
1. Why did the experts agree with the mustard jar? (Idea: *Because they didn't want to get squirted with mustard again.*)

So the mustard jar and the experts left the laboratory. The jar, which had made itself about six feet tall, waddled along on its short little legs. Some of the experts started to smile and giggle, but when the jar's eyes darted in their direction, they pretended that they were coughing.

When they were close to the huge fence that circled the top secret laboratory, they saw two people running across the grass. One was yelling, "Stop that man. He is a spy."

The experts looked at each other. They didn't know how to cope with a spy. ❷

2. How do you cope with something? (Ideas: *You do something about it; you take care of something.*)
2. How tall was the jar? *About six feet tall.*

They worked with different kinds of matter, not with fists and guns. But the mustard bottle didn't hesitate. With a quick little waddle the jar moved across the grass. It stopped in front of the spy. The mustard jar remained still for a moment. Then the plunger shot down with unbelievable speed and out came a huge gob of yellow mustard. The unfortunate spy didn't stand a chance when the mustard hit him. It covered him from head to toe like a yellow blanket and gooped up the grass surrounding him. First his left leg went flying. Then his seat hit the grass, and he slid right past the mustard jar, leaving an ugly yellow streak in the grass. ❸

3. How did the mustard jar cope with the spy? (Idea: *It shot mustard at the spy and made the spy fall.*)

"The jar stopped that spy," one of the experts yelled.

Another expert asked, "What chance did he have in the face of the mustard jar?"

The experts ran to the spy. One of them said to the spy, "If you don't behave yourself, I'll tell the jar, and it will splat you good."

The spy said, "I won't split if that jar won't splat me with that stuff." ❹

4. What did the spy mean by "split"? (Idea: *Leave.*)
4. What did one of the experts tell the spy to make him behave? (Idea: *He told the spy to behave or else he would have the mustard jar shoot more mustard.*)

Another expert said, "That's a joke—the spy won't split if the jar won't spit."

The woman who had been chasing the spy ran up to the mustard jar and said, "I don't know what kind of clever device this is, but I'm grateful. What imagination—making a disguise as clever as a mustard bottle. Who would suspect a mustard bottle?" ❺

5. What's a disguise? (Idea: *A change in someone's appearance.*)
5. What did the woman think the jar was disguised as? (Idea: *A mustard jar.*)

The woman patted the mustard jar on the shoulder (the part where the bottle gets wide).

Then she patted the mustard bottle on the other shoulder. "Yes," she said, "we are all grateful."

The mustard jar said, "Everybody loves me so much, it makes me sad." Then just below the mustard jar's eyes, a tear began to form. Of course it was mustard. The tear ran down the mustard jar's cheek. Then the mustard jar wiped the tear away with its stubby little hand. ❻

6. Why did the mustard jar shed a tear? (Idea: *Because everyone loved him so much.*)

One expert said, "There's just one thing that bothers me. If you keep blasting people with mustard, won't you run out of mustard pretty soon?"

"Oh, no," the mustard jar said, wiping another mustard tear from its eye and sniffing through its little nose. "I have an unlimited supply of mustard. Watch this."

The mustard jar squirted out a pile of mustard that was bigger than a cow and almost as big as an elephant. One expert said, "I think I'm going to be sick."

Another expert said, "That's terrible. I've never seen such an unbelievable sight in my life."

The mustard jar said, "Isn't that wonderful? I'm still full of mustard." ⑦

7. What's the jar still full of? *Mustard.*

6. (Award points quickly.)
7. (If the group makes more than 12 errors, repeat the reading immediately or on the next day.)

FLUENCY ASSESSMENT

EXERCISE 9

TIMED READING CHECKOUTS

1. (For this part of the lesson, assigned pairs of students work together during the checkouts.)
   - (If one student does not have a checkout partner, arrange another time when you can give the checkout.)
2. (Each student does a 2-minute timed reading. Students earn 5 points by reading at least 220 words and making no more than 4 errors on the first part of story 12. Students record points in Box C of their Point Chart and plot their reading rate and errors on the Individual Reading Progress Chart.)
   - (During each timed checkout, observe one pair of students for 2 minutes. Make notes on any mistakes the reader makes.)
3. (Record the timed reading checkout performance for each student you observed on the Fluency Assessment Summary form.)

Lesson 12

Lesson 12

Errors

1

1. How tall was the mustard jar? (about six feet tall)
2. What did the experts who were giggling do when the jar looked in their direction? (pretended that they were coughing)
3. How did the mustard jar cope with the spy? (It squirted the spy with mustard.)
4. Did the mustard jar stop the spy? Yes.
5. What did one of the experts say to the spy to make him behave? "If you don't behave yourself, I'll tell the jar and it will splat you good."
6. Who patted the jar on the shoulder? (the woman who had been chasing the spy)
7. What is the shoulder of the mustard jar? (the part where the bottle gets wide)
8. What kind of tears did the mustard jar have? mustard tears
9. When will the mustard jar run out of mustard? (never)
10. How big was the pile of mustard that the jar squirted out? (bigger than a cow; almost as big as an elephant)

20 Lesson 12 Copyright © SRA/McGraw-Hill. All rights reserved.

Lesson 12

2 Fill in each blank using a word in the box.

observe	unfortunate	hesitated
waddled	sprout	crease

1. The unfortunate cat fell down the stairs.
2. Clark hesitated for a moment on the high diving board.
3. The pig was so fat it waddled when it walked.

Copyright © SRA/McGraw-Hill. All rights reserved. Lesson 12 21

WORKBOOK EXERCISES

Independent Student Work

Task A

- Open your Workbook to Lesson 12. ✓
- Complete all parts of your Workbook lesson using a pencil. If you make no errors, you will earn 5 points.

Task B

1. (Before presenting Lesson 13, check student Workbooks for Lesson 12.)
   - (Call on individual students to read the items and answers in each part. Students mark errors using a pen.)
2. (Direct the students to count the number of errors and write the number in the Errors box at the top of the Workbook page.)
3. (Award points and direct students to record points in Box D of their Point Chart.)

0 errors ....5 points
1 error ....3 points
2 or 3 errors ....1 point
more than 3 errors ....0 points

END OF LESSON 12

WORD-ATTACK SKILLS

Board Work

EXERCISE 1

BUILDUP

1. (Print on the board:)

very

2. (Point to **very.** Pause.) What word? (Signal.) *Very.*
3. (Change the word to:)

ever

- What word now? (Signal.) *Ever.*

4. (Change the word to:)

never

- What word now? (Signal.) *Never.*

5. (Change the word to:)

level

- What word now? (Signal.) *Level.*

6. (Change the word to:)

clever

- What word now? (Signal.) *Clever.*

7. (Change to the original word:)

very

- (Repeat steps 2–6 until firm.)

Student Book 

EXERCISE 2

WORD PRACTICE

1. Open your Student Book to Lesson 13. ✓

1

changes chances reflection pardon
grounds starving hailed lousy
investigations gentle department
operated naturally directed scarf
protection apartment device*

- Touch the first word in part 1. ✓
- What sound? (Signal.) *j.*
- What word? (Signal.) *Changes.*

2. Touch the next word. ✓

- What sound? (Signal.) *sss.*
- What word? (Signal.) *Chances.*

3. (Repeat step 2 for each remaining word.)
4. (Repeat each row of words until firm.)
5. What does **device** mean? (Call on a student.)

EXERCISE 3

VOCABULARY

2

1. flinch
2. innocent

1. Touch part 2. ✓

- We're going to talk about what those words mean.

2. Touch word 1. ✓

- What word? (Signal.) *Flinch.*
- When you **flinch,** you **jump as if you are startled.** What are some things that would make you **flinch?** (Call on a student. Accept reasonable responses.)

3. Everybody touch word 2. ✓

- What word? (Signal.) *Innocent.*
- When you're **innocent,** you are **not guilty.** Everybody, what's another way of saying "The man was **not guilty**"? (Signal.) *The man was innocent.*

EXERCISE 4

WORD PRACTICE

1. Touch the first word in part 3. ✓

3

bloop label flowing flinched grown
wag cafeteria built sloshed angrily
sorry waddle* hesitate* business* suspect
demanded either stroked covered proof
wasting laughing breath shower neither
believe poked unusual* barely suggested
peering mound lying certainly
knees ahead tough once spies

- What word? (Signal.) *Bloop.*
2. Next word. ✓
- What word? (Signal.) *Label.*
3. (Repeat step 2 for each remaining word.)
4. (Repeat each row of words until firm.)
5. What does **waddle** mean? (Call on a student.)
- (Repeat for **hesitate, business, unusual.**)

EXERCISE 5

MULTIPART WORDS

Task A

1. Touch part 4. ✓

4

directed	navigation	apartment
1. directed	2. navigation	3. apartment

> **Note:** The parts of a word are to be pronounced the same as they are when the word is spoken normally.

2. All these words have more than one part. The first part and the last part are circled.
3. Touch word 1. ✓
- Word 1 is **directed.** What word? (Signal.) *Directed.*
4. What's the first part? (Signal.) *di.*
- What's the last part? (Signal.) *ed.*
- The middle part is spelled **R–E–C–T.** What does that part say in the word? (Signal.) *rect.*
5. So, the parts are **di** (pause) **rect** (pause) **ed.**
- Say the whole word. (Signal.) *Directed.*
6. (Repeat steps 3–5 until firm.)
7. Touch word 2. ✓
- Word 2 is **navigation.** What word? (Signal.) *Navigation.*
8. What's the first part? (Signal.) *nav.*
- What's the last part? (Signal.) *tion.*
- The middle part is spelled **I–G–A.** What does that part say in the word? (Signal.) *iga.*
9. So, the parts are **nav** (pause) **iga** (pause) **tion.**
- Say the whole word. (Signal.) *Navigation.*
10. (Repeat steps 7–9 until firm.)
11. Touch word 3. ✓
- Word 3 is **apartment.** What word? (Signal.) *Apartment.*
12. What's the first part? (Signal.) *a.*
- What's the last part? (Signal.) *ment.*
- The middle part is spelled **P–A–R–T.** What does that part say in the word? (Signal.) *part.*
13. So, the parts are **a** (pause) **part** (pause) **ment.**
- Say the whole word. (Signal.) *Apartment.*
14. (Repeat steps 11–13 until firm.)

Task B

1. Touch the sentences below the word list. ✓

a. The captain directed the ship's navigation through the channel.

b. The sailors based their navigation on the location of the stars.

c. She directed me to my friend's apartment.

- These are sentences that use the words you just read.

2. Raise your hand when you can read sentence A. ✓
3. (Call on a student.) Read sentence A. *The captain directed the ship's navigation through the channel.*
   - That means "The captain told how to steer the ship through the channel."
4. (Call on a student.) Read sentence B. *The sailors based their navigation on the location of the stars.*
   - That means "The sailors used the stars to figure out where they were."
5. (Call on a student.) Read sentence C. *She directed me to my friend's apartment.*
   - That means "She told me how to find my friend's apartment."

EXERCISE 6

WORD-ATTACK SKILLS: Individual tests

1. (Call on individual students. Each student reads a row of words, a column of words, or a sentence. In the Multipart words exercises, each sentence counts as one row of words. Tally the rows, columns, and sentences read without error. If the group reads at least 14 rows and columns without making errors, direct all students to record 5 points in Box A of their Point Chart. Criterion is 80 percent of rows and columns read without error.)
2. (If the group did not read at least 14 rows and columns without errors, do not award any points for the Word-Attack Skills exercises.)

SELECTION READING

EXERCISE 7

STORY READING

1. Everybody, touch part 5. ✓
2. The error limit for this story is 12. If the group reads the story with 12 errors or less, you earn 5 points.

5 The Mustard Jar Becomes a Spy

3. (Call on a student to read the title.) *The Mustard Jar Becomes a Spy.*
   - What do you think this story is about? (Accept reasonable responses.)
4. (Call on individual students. Each is to read two to four sentences.)
5. (Call on individual students to answer the specified questions during the story reading.)

The mustard jar and the experts were staring at the huge pile of mustard the jar had just squirted onto the ground. The spy chaser said, "Say, I believe I can use this mustard jar on one of my investigations."

The mustard jar said, "Oh, wow, maybe I'll be a spy." ❶

1. What did the spy chaser want to do with the mustard jar? (Idea: *Use it on one of her investigations.*)
1. What did the mustard jar want to be? *A spy.*

The spy chaser stroked her chin with one hand and poked at the jar with the other. This device is a little strange, she observed to herself, but it seems well built.

The jar said, "And I can hide very well. Watch this. I'll make myself look like a dog." The mustard jar got down on its stubby little knees. Then it grew a tail, which began to wag. The spy chaser began to laugh. "What in green hills and valleys is that?" she asked. She was laughing so hard that she almost fell down. "A mustard jar with a tail—I can't believe it." She grabbed her belly and bent over in a big hee-haw laugh. When she stood up to take a breath, she must have seen something very unusual. Imagine looking up in time to see a wall of yellow mustard flying at you so fast that you barely have time to hold your breath and close your eyes. Then that wall of goop hits you—bloop. ❷

2. What did the mustard jar try to look like this time? *A dog.*
2. What did the spy chaser see that was unusual? (Idea: *A wall of mustard flying at her.*)

The spy chaser was on her back. She wasn't laughing any more. Her eyes peered out of the pile of yellow mustard. "What kind of device is this?" she demanded.

"Don't get too loud," one of the experts suggested. "There is a lot more mustard where that came from."

"All right," the spy chaser said angrily. She stood up and sloshed over to the mustard jar. "All right, I'll use you. But we'll have no more of this mustard wasting. Remember there are people in parts of the world who would give a lot for the mustard that you waste. Save that mustard for the—" There was a loud bloop and once more the spy chaser was flat on her back with her eyes peering from a mound of mustard. ❸

3. Is the spy chaser really worried about mustard being wasted? *No.*
3. Why did she say what she did? (Idea: *She wanted to stop the mustard jar from shooting more mustard.*)

About an hour later, the mustard jar and the spy chaser were in the spy chaser's apartment. The spy chaser had taken a shower and was now putting on clean clothes. "Here's the plan," she announced. "I want you to stand in the window of a department store a few blocks from here. That store is operated by spies. We plan to raid the store soon, but we need an insider, and you're it." The spy chaser looked at the mustard jar. "Well, maybe you're not a real person, but you look a lot like one." Naturally she was lying. ❹

4. What was the spy chaser's plan? (Idea: *To have the mustard jar stand in a store and be an insider.*)
4. Did the spy chaser think the mustard jar looked like a person? *No.*

The mustard jar said, "You certainly won't be sorry. I can do a lot of things that the usual spy can't do." The mustard jar pounded itself on the chest. "Nothing can hurt me. Go ahead. Hit me with a hammer."

"Not here in the apartment," the spy chaser said, tying her scarf.

"Oh, go ahead," the mustard jar said. "You have to make sure that I'm tough, don't you? It's for your protection. Go ahead. Get a hammer."

"No, I really—" the spy chaser looked at her clean white shirt, and she remembered how it felt to get hit with a huge mound of yellow mustard. She said, "Well, all right," because she didn't want that to happen again. ❺

5. Why didn't the spy chaser want to hit the jar with a hammer? (Idea: *Because she didn't want the mustard jar to shoot her with mustard.*)

She got a hammer. "Where do you want me to hit you?" she asked.

The mustard jar exclaimed, "It doesn't matter. Just hit me anywhere."

The spy chaser hit the fattest part of the mustard jar's fat body. Then . . . bloop.

The spy chaser was covered with mustard again. The mustard jar said, "I'm sorry. I didn't mean to squirt you that time. When the hammer hit me, I flinched, and I must have pulled in my plunger." Then the mustard jar added, "But at least you know I'm tough." ❻

6. What did the mustard jar do when it was hit by the hammer? (Idea: *It pulled in its plunger and shot more mustard.*)

"I'm really glad I found out," the spy chaser said. She didn't look too happy standing up to her knees in mustard.

6. (Award points quickly.)
7. (If the group makes more than 12 errors, repeat the reading immediately or on the next day.)

FLUENCY ASSESSMENT

EXERCISE 8

TIMED READING CHECKOUTS

1. (For this part of the lesson, assigned pairs of students work together during the checkouts.)
   - (If one student does not have a checkout partner, arrange another time when you can give the checkout.)
2. (Each student does a 2-minute timed reading. Students earn 5 points by reading at least 220 words and making no more than 4 errors on the first part of story 13. Students record points in Box C of their Point Chart and plot their reading rate and errors on the Individual Reading Progress Chart.)
   - (During each timed checkout, observe one pair of students for 2 minutes. Make notes on any mistakes the reader makes.)
3. (Record the timed reading checkout performance for each student you observed on the Fluency Assessment Summary form.)

Lesson 13

Errors

1

1. What did the mustard jar want to be? a spy
2. What did the jar try to do to show that it could hide very well?
   (make itself look like a dog)
3. What happened to the spy when she laughed at the mustard jar?
   (She got squirted with mustard.)
4. Where did the spy chaser take the mustard jar?
   (to her apartment)
5. What was the spy chaser's plan for the mustard jar?
   (for it to stand in the window of a department store; for it to be an insider)
6. Why didn't the spy chaser want to hit the jar with a hammer?
   (because she didn't want the mustard jar to shoot her with mustard)
7. Where did the spy chaser hit the mustard jar with the hammer?
   (the fattest part of the mustard jar's body)
8. What happened to the jar when the spy chaser hit it with the hammer?
   (It flinched and pulled in its plunger.)
9. Was the mustard jar tough? (Yes.)
10. Why do you think the spy chaser didn't look too happy at the end of this story?
   (Accept reasonable responses.)

22 Lesson 13 Copyright © SRA/McGraw-Hill. All rights reserved.

Lesson 13

2 Fill in each blank using a word in the box.

flinched	observe	unbelievable
innocent	hesitate	waddle

1. His story was just too unbelievable to be true.
2. They said that James ate the last cookie, but he was innocent.
3. When the doctor stuck the needle in Tina's arm, she flinched.

3 Write the parts for each word.

1. protected = protect + ed
2. certainly = certain + ly
3. directing = direct + ing
4. gentleness = gentle + ness

Copyright © SRA/McGraw-Hill. All rights reserved. Lesson 13 23

WORKBOOK EXERCISES

Independent Student Work

Task A

- Open your Workbook to Lesson 13. ✓
- Complete all parts of your Workbook lesson using a pencil. If you make no errors, you will earn 5 points.

Task B

1. (Before presenting Lesson 14, check student Workbooks for Lesson 13.)
   - (Call on individual students to read the items and answers in each part. Students mark errors using a pen.)
2. (Direct the students to count the number of errors and write the number in the Errors box at the top of the Workbook page.)
3. (Award points and direct students to record points in Box D of their Point Chart.)

0 errors ....5 points
1 error ....3 points
2 or 3 errors ....1 point
more than 3 errors ....0 points

END OF LESSON 13

WORD-ATTACK SKILLS

Student Book 

EXERCISE 1

BUILDUP

1. Open your Student Book to Lesson 14. ✓
   - Touch the first word in part 1. ✓
   - What word? (Signal.) *My.*
2. Next word. ✓
   - What word? (Signal.) *Sly.*
3. (Repeat step 2 for each remaining word.)
4. (Repeat steps 1–3 until firm.)

1

my
sly
sty
style
styling
spying
spies

EXERCISE 2

NEW **SOUND COMBINATION: ea**

Task A

1. Touch the letters **E–A** in part 2. ✓

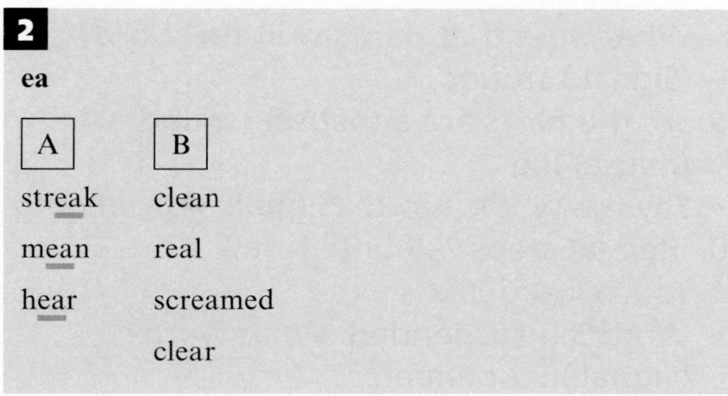

2

ea

A	B
streak	clean
mean	real
hear	screamed
	clear

- The letters **E–A** go together and usually make the sound **ēēē,** as in **eat.** What sound? (Signal.) *ēēē.*
2. You're going to read words that have the sound **ēēē** in them. You're going to say the sound for the underlined part and then read the word.
3. Touch the first word in column A. ✓
   - What sound? (Signal.) *ēēē.*
   - What word? (Signal.) *Streak.*
4. Touch the next word. ✓
   - What sound? (Signal.) *ēēē.*
   - What word? (Signal.) *Mean.*
5. (Repeat step 4 for **hear.**)

Task B

1. Touch the first word in column B. ✓
   - What word? (Signal.) *Clean.*
2. Next word. ✓
   - What word? (Signal.) *Real.*
3. (Repeat step 2 for **screamed, clear.**)
4. (Repeat steps 1–3 until firm.)

EXERCISE 3

WORD PRACTICE

1. Touch the first word in part 3. ✓

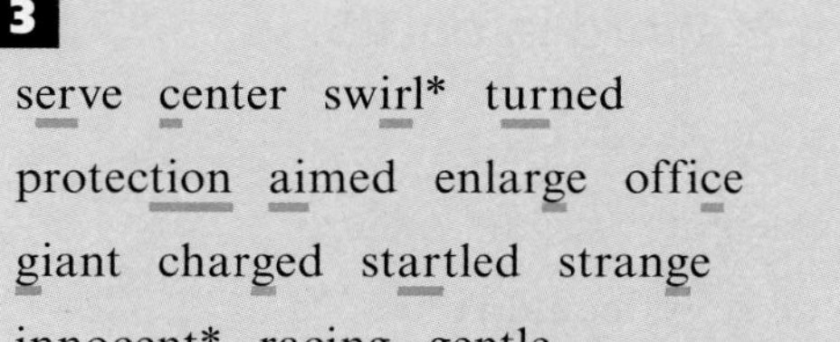

3

serve center swirl* turned
protection aimed enlarge office
giant charged startled strange
innocent* racing gentle

- What sound? (Signal.) *er.*
- What word? (Signal.) *Serve.*
2. Touch the next word. ✓
   - What sound? (Signal.) *sss.*
   - What word? (Signal.) *Center.*
3. (Repeat step 2 for each remaining word.)
4. (Repeat each row of words until firm.)
5. What does **swirl** mean? (Call on a student.)
   - (Repeat for **innocent.**)

EXERCISE 4

VOCABULARY

1. Touch part 4. ✓

4

1. helicopter
2. label
3. tremendous

- We're going to talk about what those words mean.
2. Touch word 1. ✓
   - What word? (Signal.) *Helicopter.*
   - What is a **helicopter?** (Call on a student.) (Idea: *An aircraft that can go straight up and down.*)

3. Everybody, touch word 2. ✓
- What word? (Signal.) *Label.*
- What is a **label?** (Call on a student.) (Idea: *A piece of paper attached to an object that gives information about that object.*)

4. Everybody, touch word 3. ✓
- What word? (Signal.) *Tremendous.*
- What does **tremendous** mean? (Call on a student.) (Ideas: *Very large; great.*)

EXERCISE 5

WORD PRACTICE

1. Touch the first word in part 5. ✓

5

pardon ceiling celebrate strain* quart
direction can't directly couldn't
standing throughout observe* law move
climbing dangling member pressure
secret listened earth department
entirely window briefcase swooped
cafeteria front strolled happening
angrily spies world eight once posing

- What word? (Signal.) *Pardon.*

2. Next word. ✓
- What word? (Signal.) *Ceiling.*

3. (Repeat step 2 for each remaining word.)
4. (Repeat each row of words until firm.)
5. What does **strain** mean? (Call on a student.)
- (Repeat for **observe.**)

EXERCISE 6

MULTIPART WORDS

Task A

1. Touch part 6. ✓

6

impossible astounding suspended
1. impossible 2. astounding 3. suspended

Note: The parts of a word are to be pronounced the same as they are when the word is spoken normally.

2. All these words have more than one part. The first part and the last part are circled.
3. Touch word 1. ✓
- Word 1 is **impossible.** What word? (Signal.) *Impossible.*

4. What's the first part? (Signal.) *im.*
- What's the last part? (Signal.) *ible.*
- The middle part is spelled **P–O–S–S.** What does that part say in the word? (Signal.) *poss.*

5. So, the parts are **im** (pause) **poss** (pause) **ible.**
- Say the whole word. (Signal.) *Impossible.*

6. (Repeat steps 3–5 until firm.)
7. Touch word 2. ✓
- Word 2 is **astounding.** What word? (Signal.) *Astounding.*

8. What's the first part? (Signal.) *a.*
- What's the last part? (Signal.) *ing.*
- The middle part is spelled **S–T–O–U–N–D.** What does that part say in the word? (Signal.) *stound.*

9. So, the parts are **a** (pause) **stound** (pause) **ing.**
- Say the whole word. (Signal.) *Astounding.*

10. (Repeat steps 7–9 until firm.)
11. Touch word 3. ✓
- Word 3 is **suspended.** What word? (Signal.) *Suspended.*

12. What's the first part? (Signal.) *sus.*
- What's the last part? (Signal.) *ed.*
- The middle part is spelled **P–E–N–D.** What does that part say in the word? (Signal.) *pend.*

13. So, the parts are **sus** (pause) **pend** (pause) **ed.**
- Say the whole word. (Signal.) *Suspended.*

14. (Repeat steps 11–13 until firm.)

Task B

1. Touch the sentences below the word list. ✓

a. She found his story to be impossible.
b. The size of the wave was astounding.
c. The ball remained suspended in the air.

- These are sentences that use the words you just read.

2. Raise your hand when you can read sentence A. ✓
3. (Call on a student.) Read sentence A. *She found his story to be impossible.*
- That means "She didn't believe that his story could happen."
4. (Call on a student.) Read sentence B. *The size of the wave was astounding.*
- That means "The size of the wave was amazing."
5. (Call on a student.) Read sentence C. *The ball remained suspended in the air.*
- That means "The ball stayed in the air."

EXERCISE 7

WORD-ATTACK SKILLS: Individual tests

1. (Call on individual students. Each student reads a row of words, a column of words, or a sentence. In the Multipart words exercises, each sentence counts as one row of words. Tally the rows, columns, and sentences read without error. If the group reads at least 16 rows and columns without making errors, direct all students to record 5 points in Box A of their Point Chart. Criterion is 80 percent of rows and columns read without error.)
2. (If the group did not read at least 16 rows and columns without errors, do not award any points for the Word-Attack Skills exercises.)

SELECTION READING

EXERCISE 8

STORY READING

1. Everybody, touch part 7. ✓
2. The error limit for this story is 12. If the group reads the story with 12 errors or less, you earn 5 points.

7 **Ugly Yellow Goop**

3. (Call on a student to read the title.) *Ugly Yellow Goop.*
- What do you think this story is about? (Accept reasonable responses.)
4. (Call on individual students. Each is to read two to four sentences.)
5. (Call on individual students to answer the specified questions during the story reading.)

The next day found the mustard jar standing in a window in a department store with a new label on its front. The label said, "Cafeteria—second floor." The mustard jar didn't like the label very much, but the jar was glad to be a member of the Secret Agents. The jar said to itself, "I'll bet I'm the only mustard jar in the entire world who chases spies." ❶

1. What did the label on the mustard jar say? *Cafeteria—second floor.*
1. Did the jar like the label? (Idea: *No.*)
1. What was the mustard jar glad about? (Idea: *It was glad to be a member of the Secret Agents.*)

Throughout the day people walked past the mustard jar, but not one of them seemed to be a spy. The jar looked and listened, but it didn't observe anything that seemed strange. Once it saw a man start to whisper something to another man, and the jar listened very carefully. But all the first man said was, "Pardon me. Do you know where the men's department is?"

Late that day a woman strolled by with her son. He was about seven years old. When he spotted the mustard jar, he said, "Mother, please buy me that jar."

"No," his mother said, "that jar is much too big for our house." ❷

2. Why didn't the boy's mom want the jar? (Idea: *Because the jar was too big for her house.*)

"I want it," the boy said. "I want that mustard jar."

"Now stop talking so loudly," his mother said. "You must behave yourself."

The boy began to cry. "I want a big mustard jar," he screamed, running from his mother. <u>He</u> ran up to the mustard jar. "I want it," the boy yelled. "Let me have it. Let me have it."

So the mustard jar let him have it with about a quart of mustard that was aimed directly at the center of the boy's mouth. The boy must have been startled indeed, because he stopped crying and stared at the mustard jar. Then he ran back to his mother, who yelled, "How on earth did you get covered with that ugly yellow goop?" ❸

3. What did the boy want? *The mustard jar.*
3. What did he get? (Idea: *Mustard squirted on him.*)
3. Why did he stop crying? (Idea: *Because the shot of mustard surprised him.*)

The mustard jar stood very still, posing as an innocent giant mustard bottle and trying not to smile. But just then there was a huge crash and part of the roof caved in. People screamed and began to run from the store. The mustard jar could see a helicopter through the hole in the roof. At that moment three people ran from an office on the first floor of the department store. A rope dropped from the helicopter, and the three people began climbing the rope. One of them had a briefcase.

Before the mustard jar knew what was happening, eight Secret Agents ran into the department store and charged toward the people who were dangling from the rope. "Stop in the name of the law," they yelled. ❹

4. What was over the store? *A helicopter.*
4. What does **dangling from a rope** mean? (Idea: *Hanging from a rope.*)
4. One of the people who was dangling from the rope was carrying something. What was the person carrying? *A briefcase.*
4. How many agents ran into the store? *Eight.*

But suddenly, the helicopter swooped up in the sky, taking the three spies with it.

"They're gone now," one of the Secret Agents said angrily.

"Yes," another agent said. "We had better call for a plane to follow them."

"I will follow them," the mustard jar said, running toward the Secret Agents. "If I shoot out mustard fast enough, I move in the other direction. I fly. Here I go." ❺

5. How did the secret service agent want to catch the helicopter? (Idea: *By sending a plane after it.*)
5. How was the mustard jar going to fly? (Idea: *By shooting mustard out very quickly.*)

With a tremendous blast of mustard, the mustard jar went flying through the department store. It hit one wall and then another. It hit the floor three times and the ceiling once. Then it sailed through the hole in the roof. The entire department store was a sea of mustard by now. A Secret Agent who had mustard all over her said, "There have to be better ways of catching spies than this." 6

6. How big is a tremendous blast? (Idea: *Very big.*)
6. What did the store look like after the mustard jar went through the hole? (Idea: *It was full of mustard.*)
6. (Award points quickly.)
7. (If the group makes more than 12 errors, repeat the reading immediately or on the next day.)

FLUENCY ASSESSMENT

EXERCISE 9

TIMED READING CHECKOUTS

1. (For this part of the lesson, assigned pairs of students work together during the checkouts.)
   - (If one student does not have a checkout partner, arrange another time when you can give the checkout.)
2. (Each student does a 2-minute timed reading. Students earn 5 points by reading at least 220 words and making no more than 4 errors on the first part of story 14. Students record points in Box C of their Point Chart and plot their reading rate and errors on the Individual Reading Progress Chart.)
   - (During each timed checkout, observe one pair of students for 2 minutes. Make notes on any mistakes the reader makes.)
3. (Record the timed reading checkout performance for each student you observed on the Fluency Assessment Summary form.)

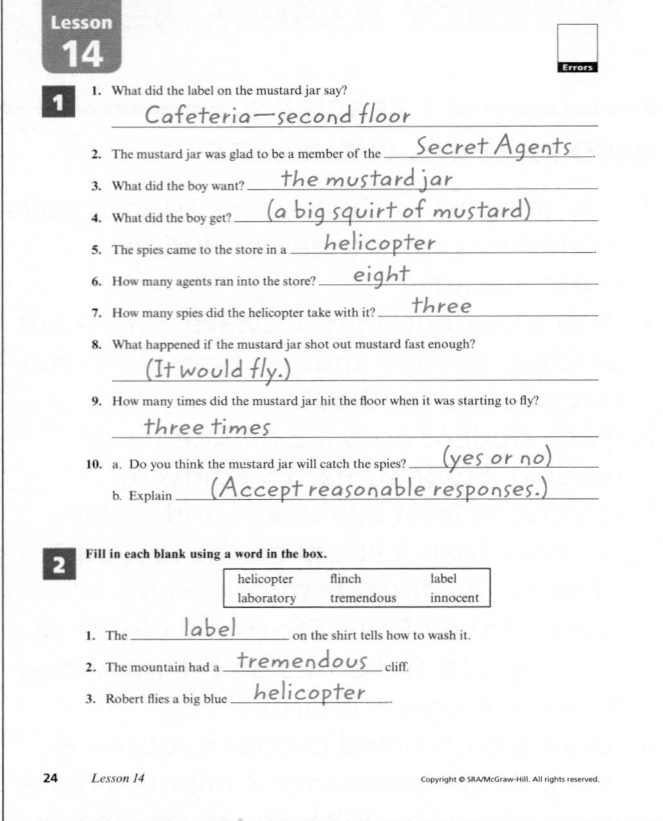

Lesson 14

Errors

1

1. What did the label on the mustard jar say?
Cafeteria—second floor
2. The mustard jar was glad to be a member of the Secret Agents.
3. What did the boy want? the mustard jar
4. What did the boy get? (a big squirt of mustard)
5. The spies came to the store in a helicopter.
6. How many agents ran into the store? eight
7. How many spies did the helicopter take with it? three
8. What happened if the mustard jar shot out mustard fast enough?
(It would fly.)
9. How many times did the mustard jar hit the floor when it was starting to fly?
three times
10. a. Do you think the mustard jar will catch the spies? (yes or no)
b. Explain (Accept reasonable responses.)

2 **Fill in each blank using a word in the box.**

helicopter	flinch	label
laboratory	tremendous	innocent

1. The label on the shirt tells how to wash it.
2. The mountain had a tremendous cliff.
3. Robert flies a big blue helicopter.

24 Lesson 14 Copyright © SRA/McGraw-Hill. All rights reserved.

WORKBOOK EXERCISES

Independent Student Work

Task A

- Open your Workbook to Lesson 14. ✓
- Complete all parts of your Workbook lesson using a pencil. If you make no errors, you will earn 5 points.

Task B

1. (Before presenting Lesson 15, check student Workbooks for Lesson 14.)
- (Call on individual students to read the items and answers in each part. Students mark errors using a pen.)
2. (Direct the students to count the number of errors and write the number in the Errors box at the top of the Workbook page.)
3. (Award points and direct students to record points in Box D of their Point Chart.)

0 errors................................5 points
1 error ....3 points
2 or 3 errors ....1 point
more than 3 errors ....0 points

END OF LESSON 14

WORD-ATTACK SKILLS

Board Work

EXERCISE 1

BUILDUP

1. (Print on the board:)

rip

2. (Point to **rip.** Pause.) What word? (Signal.) *Rip.*
3. (Change the word to:)

trip

- What word now? (Signal.) *Trip.*

4. (Change the word to:)

strip

- What word now? (Signal.) *Strip.*

5. (Change the word to:)

sl ip

- What word now? (Signal.) *Slip.*

6. (Change the word to:)

sl ipper

- What word now? (Signal.) *Slipper.*

7. (Change the word to:)

sl ippery

- What word now? (Signal.) *Slippery.*

8. (Change to the original word:)

rip

- (Repeat steps 2–7 until firm.)

Student Book

EXERCISE 2

SOUND COMBINATION: ea

Task A

1. Open your Student Book to Lesson 15. ✓

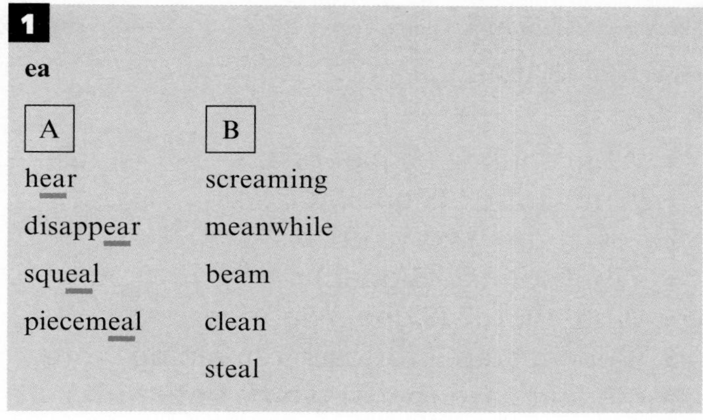

1

ea

A	B
hear	screaming
disappear	meanwhile
squeal	beam
piecemeal	clean
	steal

- Touch the letters **E–A** in part 1. ✓
- What sound do the letters **E–A** make? (Signal.) *ēēē.*

2. You're going to say the sound for the underlined part and then read the word.
3. Touch the first word in column A. ✓
   - What sound? (Signal.) *ēēē.*
   - What word? (Signal.) *Hear.*
4. Touch the next word. ✓
   - What sound? (Signal.) *ēēē.*
   - What word? (Signal.) *Disappear.*
5. (Repeat step 4 for **squeal, piecemeal.**)

Task B

1. Touch the first word in column B. ✓
   - What word? (Signal.) *Screaming.*
2. Next word. ✓
   - What word? (Signal.) *Meanwhile.*
3. (Repeat step 2 for **beam, clean, steal.**)
4. (Repeat steps 1–3 until firm.)

Lesson 15

EXERCISE 3

WORD PRACTICE

1. Touch the first word in part 2. ✓

2

circle sponge office blurt
century imagination ground
straight sharper city disturb
darted celebration generate
location changing

- What sound? (Signal.) *sss.*
- What word? (Signal.) *Circle.*

2. Touch the next word. ✓
- What sound? (Signal.) *j.*
- What word? (Signal.) *Sponge.*

3. (Repeat step 2 for each remaining word.)
4. (Repeat each row of words until firm.)

EXERCISE 4

VOCABULARY

1. Touch part 3. ✓

3

1. situation
2. stunt
3. continue
4. outfit

- We're going to talk about what those words mean.

2. Touch word 1. ✓
- What word? (Signal.) *Situation.*
- A **situation** is what goes on in a place. When strange things go on in a place, you could say it's a strange **situation.** Everybody, what's another way of saying that good things go on in a place? (Signal.) *It's a good situation.*

3. Touch word 2. ✓
- What word? (Signal.) *Stunt.*
- When you do a **stunt,** you do **a hard trick to get attention.** What is a **stunt?** (Call on a student.) (Idea: *A hard trick done to get attention.*)

4. Everybody, touch word 3. ✓
- What word? (Signal.) *Continue.*
- When you **keep** doing the same thing, you **continue** doing it. Everybody, what's another way of saying "The woman **keeps** writing"? (Signal.) *The woman continues writing.*

5. Touch word 4. ✓
- What word? (Signal.) *Outfit.*
- An **outfit** is **a set of clothing.** A waiter's **outfit** is **a set of clothing** the waiter wears.

EXERCISE 5

WORD PRACTICE

1. Touch the first word in part 4. ✓

4

direction swirling* startled
protection squirted huge tremendous*
exclaimed* starting trouble through
helicopter* stunt* throw couple
business* another before skidding
replied landing proof below
glops dive breath observed
unbelievably great company

- What word? (Signal.) *Direction.*

2. Next word. ✓
- What word? (Signal.) *Swirling.*

3. (Repeat step 2 for each remaining word.)
4. (Repeat each row of words until firm.)
5. What does **swirling** mean? (Call on a student.)
- (Repeat for **tremendous, exclaimed, helicopter, stunt, business.**)

EXERCISE 6

MULTIPART WORDS

Task A

1. Touch part 5. ✓

5

arrangements	exceptional	inspired
1. arrangements	2. exceptional	3. inspired
	adventure	
	4. adventure	

Note: The parts of a word are to be pronounced the same as they are when the word is spoken normally. For example, in the word **adventure, ture** is pronounced **chur.**

2. All these words have more than one part. The first part and the last part are circled.
3. Touch word 1. ✓
   - Word 1 is **arrangements.** What word? (Signal.) *Arrangements.*
4. What's the first part? (Signal.) *ar.*
   - What's the last part? (Signal.) *ments.*
   - The middle part is spelled **R–A–N–G–E.** What does that part say in the word? (Signal.) *range.*
5. So, the parts are **ar** (pause) **range** (pause) **ments.**
   - Say the whole word. (Signal.) *Arrangements.*
6. (Repeat steps 3–5 until firm.)
7. Touch word 2. ✓
   - Word 2 is **exceptional.** What word? (Signal.) *Exceptional.*
8. What's the first part? (Signal.) *ex.*
   - What's the last part? (Signal.) *al.*
   - The middle part is spelled **C–E–P–T–I–O–N.** What does that part say in the word? (Signal.) *ception.*
9. So, the parts are **ex** (pause) **ception** (pause) **al.**
   - Say the whole word. (Signal.) *Exceptional.*
10. (Repeat steps 7–9 until firm.)
11. Touch word 3. ✓
    - Word 3 is **inspired.** What word? (Signal.) *Inspired.*
12. What's the first part? (Signal.) *in.*
    - What's the last part? (Signal.) *d.* (Accept *d* pronounced as the sound for the letter **D,** not *dee.*) Yes, **d.**
    - The middle part is spelled **S–P–I–R–E.** What does that part say in the word? (Signal.) *spire.*
13. So, the parts are **in** (pause) **spire** (pause) **d.**
    - Say the whole word. (Signal.) *Inspired.*
14. (Repeat steps 11–13 until firm.)
15. Touch word 4. ✓
    - Word 4 is **adventure.** What word? (Signal.) *Adventure.*
16. What's the first part? (Signal.) *ad.*
    - What's the last part? (Signal.) *ture.* (Accept *ture* pronounced as **chur.**) Yes, **ture.**
    - The middle part is spelled **V–E–N.** What does that part say in the word? (Signal.) *ven.*
17. So, the parts are **ad** (pause) **ven** (pause) **ture.**
    - Say the whole word. (Signal.) *Adventure.*
18. (Repeat steps 15–17 until firm.)

Task B

1. Touch the sentences below the word list. ✓

a. They made exceptional arrangements of flowers.
b. They were inspired by their adventure.
c. We agreed that our adventure was exceptional.
d. She was inspired to write a new musical arrangement.

- These are sentences that use the words you just read.
2. Raise your hand when you can read sentence A. ✓
3. (Call on a student.) Read sentence A. *They made exceptional arrangements of flowers.*
   - That means "The way they arranged flowers was good."

4. (Call on a student.) Read sentence B. *They were inspired by their adventure.*
   - That means "The adventure they had made them feel better about some things."
5. (Call on a student.) Read sentence C. *We agreed that our adventure was exceptional.*
   - That means "We agreed that the adventure was better than most adventures."
6. (Call on a student.) Read sentence D. *She was inspired to write a new musical arrangement.*
   - That means "She was motivated to write a new version of how to sing or play that music."

EXERCISE 7

WORD-ATTACK SKILLS: Individual tests

1. (Call on individual students. Each student reads a row of words, a column of words, or a sentence. In the Multipart words exercises, each sentence counts as one row of words. Tally the rows, columns, and sentences read without error. If the group reads at least 16 rows and columns without making errors, direct all students to record 5 points in Box A of their Point Chart. Criterion is 80 percent of rows and columns read without error.)
2. (If the group did not read at least 16 rows and columns without errors, do not award any points for the Word-Attack Skills exercises.)

SELECTION READING

EXERCISE 8

STORY READING

1. Everybody, touch part 6. ✓
2. The error limit for this story is 12. If the group reads the story with 12 errors or less, you earn 5 points.

6 **The Chase**

3. (Call on a student to read the title.) *The Chase.*
   - What do you think this story is about? (Accept reasonable responses.)
4. (Call on individual students. Each is to read two to four sentences.)
5. (Call on individual students to answer the specified questions during the story reading.)

A great chase was taking place over the city as the mustard jar chased a helicopter. It was a very messy chase. The mustard jar had to squirt mustard out very fast in one direction to make itself move in the other direction. The mustard jar had trouble going in a straight line. So it zigged and zagged and spun around like a pinwheel on the Fourth of July. Sometimes it would dive down, almost to the ground, but then it would turn around, squirt mustard at the ground, and shoot back up in the air. ❶

1. What did the mustard jar have to do to move? (Idea: *Squirt out mustard very fast in the direction opposite to the direction it wanted to travel.*)
1. How well did the mustard jar fly at first? (Ideas: *Not very well; it had trouble flying straight.*)
1. How would the jar shoot back up in the air? (Idea: *By squirting mustard at the ground.*)

The helicopter that was carrying a pilot and three spies zigged and zagged to keep away from the mustard jar. Below, people were standing on the street, watching the great chase across the sky. From time to time, glops of mustard would fall on them. It was a messy situation. One man who got hit on the head with a large glop of yellow mustard said, "What kind of a stunt is this?"

Another man exclaimed, "It looks like mustard."

A woman observed, "It smells like mustard."

A little girl put some of the yellow stuff on her hot dog and said, "It *is* mustard."

Then someone yelled, "It is mustard gas. Run for your life because mustard gas will kill you."

While people were running around or staring into the sky, the chase continued. The helicopter would dart in one direction as the mustard jar chased it. Then the helicopter would stop, and the mustard jar would go flying past it. When the mustard jar passed the helicopter, the helicopter would dart off in another direction. ❷

2. How did the helicopter get away from the mustard jar? **(Idea:** ***By changing its direction.*****)**
2. What happened to people watching the chase? **(Idea:** ***They got hit with globs of mustard.*****)**

As the chase continued, some of the streets below got pretty slippery. You have to remember that for the mustard jar to move, it had to shoot out mustard very fast, and it had to keep on shooting out mustard. As all the mustard was landing on the city, cars were skidding around on the yellow streets. In one part of the city some boys and girls were sliding down a big mustard-covered hill. They sat in inner tubes, and away they went. "This is great," they agreed. "This mustard is a lot better than snow."

A couple of blocks away workers were shoveling the mustard into trucks. These people worked for a mustard company. They were going to load up the mustard, take it to their mustard plant, clean it, and sell it. These people weren't thinking too well. Mustard sales would be unbelievably poor in this city for a long time because people would have had enough mustard to last them for years. ❸

3. What are unbelievably poor sales? **(Idea:** ***When no one buys any of what you're selling.*****)**
3. Some workers were shoveling mustard into trucks. What did the workers plan to do with the mustard? **(Idea:** ***Take it to their mustard company, clean it, and sell it.*****)**
3. Name some other things that were happening in the city. **(Ideas:** ***Cars were skidding; boys and girls were sliding down mustard-covered hills on inner tubes.*****)**

Meanwhile the chase went on over the city. The helicopter stopped, and the mustard jar darted by. The jar made a sharp turn. It was getting better at steering itself. The helicopter kept changing location. The helicopter darted to the left. The mustard jar darted to the left. Suddenly the helicopter stopped, but the mustard jar kept on coming. It was heading right for the helicopter, and it was moving very, very fast. ④

4. What's a location? (Ideas: *Place; position.*)
4. What do you think is going to happen? (Accept reasonable responses.)
6. (Award points quickly.)
7. (If the group makes more than 12 errors, repeat the reading immediately or on the next day.)

FLUENCY ASSESSMENT

EXERCISE 9

TIMED READING CHECKOUTS

1. (For this part of the lesson, assigned pairs of students work together during the checkouts.)
• (If one student does not have a checkout partner, arrange another time when you can give the checkout.)
2. (Each student does a 2-minute timed reading. Students earn 5 points by reading at least 220 words and making no more than 4 errors on the first part of story 15. Students record points in Box C of their Point Chart and plot their reading rate and errors on the Individual Reading Progress Chart.)
• (During each timed checkout, observe one pair of students for 2 minutes. Make notes on any mistakes the reader makes.)
3. (Record the timed reading checkout performance for each student you observed on the Fluency Assessment Summary form.)

WORKBOOK EXERCISES

Independent Student Work

Task A

- Open your Workbook to Lesson 15. ✓
- Complete all parts of your Workbook lesson using a pencil. If you make no errors, you will earn 5 points.

Task B

1. (Before presenting Lesson 16, check student Workbooks for Lesson 15.)
   - (Call on individual students to read the items and answers in each part. Students mark errors using a pen.)
2. (Direct the students to count the number of errors and write the number in the Errors box at the top of the Workbook page.)
3. (Award points and direct students to record points in Box D of their Point Chart.)

   0 errors ....5 points
   1 error ....3 points
   2 or 3 errors ....1 point
   more than 3 errors ....0 points

Point schedule for Lessons 11 through 15

Box	Lesson part	Points
A	Word Attack	0 or 5
B	Selection Reading	0 or 5
C	Timed Reading Checkout	0 or 5
D	Workbook	0, 1, 3, or 5
Bonus	(Teacher option)	—

Five-lesson point summary

- (For **letter grades** based on points for Lessons **11** through **15**, tell students to compute the total for the blue boxes [C, D, and Bonus] and write the number in the Total box at the end of each row in their Point Chart. Students then add the totals and write the sum in the green box.)
- (For **rewards** based on points, tell students to compute the total for all boxes [A, B, C, D, and Bonus] and write the number in the Total box at the end of each row. Students then add the totals and write the sum in the green box.)

Lesson 15

Errors

1

1. How well did the mustard jar fly at first? (Not very well; it had trouble flying straight.)
2. What happened to the people watching the chase? (Glops of mustard fell on them.)
3. What is a stunt? (a trick)
4. What did the cars do? (skidded around)
5. What were the boys and girls doing with the mustard? (sliding down a hill on it)
6. Which did the children think was better for sliding, mustard or snow? mustard
7. Why were the workers shoveling mustard into trucks? (to take it to their mustard plant)
8. After the chase, why would mustard sales be poor? (People would have had enough mustard for years.)
9. Did the mustard jar get better at following the spies? Yes.
10. What was the mustard jar doing at the end of the story? (heading right for the helicopter)

Copyright © SRA/McGraw-Hill. All rights reserved. Lesson 15 25

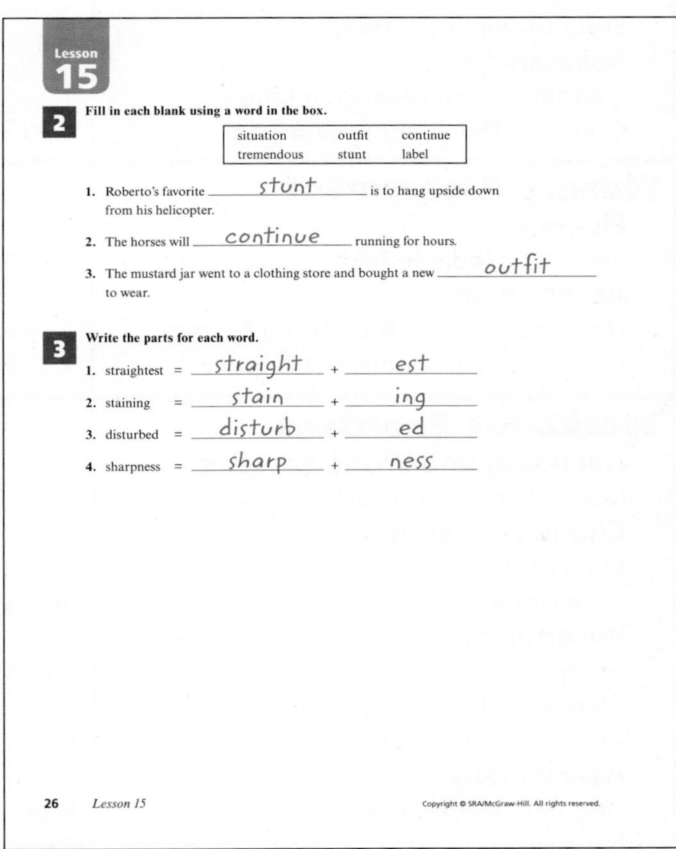
Lesson 15

2 Fill in each blank using a word in the box.

situation	outfit	continue
tremendous	stunt	label

1. Roberto's favorite stunt is to hang upside down from his helicopter.
2. The horses will continue running for hours.
3. The mustard jar went to a clothing store and bought a new outfit to wear.

3 Write the parts for each word.

1. straightest = straight + est
2. staining = stain + ing
3. disturbed = disturb + ed
4. sharpness = sharp + ness

26 Lesson 15 Copyright © SRA/McGraw-Hill. All rights reserved.

END OF LESSON 15

Lesson Objectives	LESSON 16 Exercise	LESSON 17 Exercise	LESSON 18 Exercise	LESSON 19 Exercise	LESSON 20 Exercise
Word Attack					
Decoding and Word Analysis					
Sound Combination: *ee*				2	1
Sound Combination: *ea*	1				
Multisyllabic Word Strategies	5	5	4	6	5
Visual Discrimination		1		1	
Letter Combinations/Letter Sounds	2	2	1	3	2
Word Recognition	1–5	1–5	1–4	1–6	1–5
High-Frequency/Sight Words	5	5	4	6	5
Vocabulary					
Definitions	2–4	3, 4	2, 3	4, 5	3, 4
Usage	3, 5	3, 5	2, 4	4, 6	3, 5
Assessment					
Ongoing: Individual Tests	6	6	5	7	6
Group Reading					
Decoding and Word Analysis					
Read Decodable Text	7	7	6	8	7
Comprehension					
Access Prior Knowledge			6	8	7
Draw Inferences	7	7	6	8	7
Note Details	7	7	6	8	7
Predict	7	7	6	8	7
Story Grammar: Setting					7
Assessment					
Ongoing: Comprehension Check	7	7	6	8	7
Ongoing: Decoding Accuracy	7	7	6	8	7
Fluency Assessment					
Fluency					
Reread Decodable Text	8	8	6	9	8
Assessment					
Ongoing: Teacher-Monitored Fluency	8	8	6	9	8
Ongoing: Peer-Monitored Fluency	8	8	6	9	8
Workbook Exercises					
Decoding and Word Analysis					
Multisyllabic Word Parts				Ind. Work	
Comprehension					
Main Idea		9			
Note Details	Ind. Work	Ind. Work	Ind. Work	Ind. Work	Ind. Work
Vocabulary					
Usage	Ind. Work	Ind. Work	Ind. Work	Ind. Work	Ind. Work
Study Skills					
Writing Mechanics		9			
Assessment					
Ongoing: Workcheck	Workcheck	Workcheck	Workcheck	Workcheck	Workcheck

WORD-ATTACK SKILLS

Student Book 

EXERCISE 1

SOUND COMBINATION: ea

Task A

1. Open your Student Book to Lesson 16. ✓

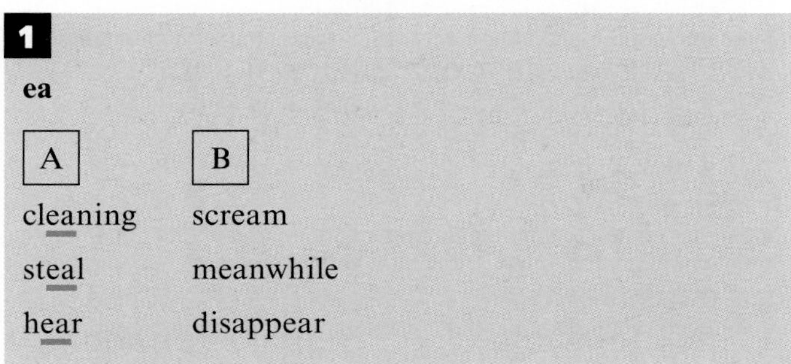

1

ea

A	B
cleaning	scream
steal	meanwhile
hear	disappear

- Touch the letters **E–A** in part 1. ✓
- What sound do the letters **E–A** make? (Signal.) *ēēē.*

2. You're going to say the sound for the underlined part and then read the word.
3. Touch the first word in column A. ✓
   - What sound? (Signal.) *ēēē.*
   - What word? (Signal.) *Cleaning.*
4. Touch the next word. ✓
   - What sound? (Signal.) *ēēē.*
   - What word? (Signal.) *Steal.*
5. (Repeat step 4 for **hear.**)

Task B

1. Touch the first word in column B. ✓
   - What word? (Signal.) *Scream.*
2. Touch the next word. ✓
   - What word? (Signal.) *Meanwhile.*
3. (Repeat step 2 for **disappear.**)
4. (Repeat steps 1–3 until firm.)

EXERCISE 2

WORD PRACTICE

1. Touch the first word in part 2. ✓

2

startled sprain outfit* dangerous
device* instruction enlarger beneath
remain imagine situation*
information strain* complaining
intersection burned range gathered

- What sound? (Signal.) *ar.*
- What word? (Signal.) *Startled.*

2. Touch the next word. ✓
   - What sound? (Signal.) *āāā.*
   - What word? (Signal.) *Sprain.*
3. (Repeat step 2 for each remaining word.)
4. (Repeat each row of words until firm.)
5. What does **outfit** mean? (Call on a student.)
   - (Repeat for each starred word.)

EXERCISE 3

VOCABULARY

1. Touch part 3. ✓

3

1. collide
2. instant
3. deceptive

- We're going to talk about what those words mean.

2. Touch word 1. ✓
   - What word? (Signal.) *Collide.*
   - When things **collide,** they **crash into each other.** Everybody, what's another way of saying "the cars **crashed into each other**"? (Signal.) *The cars collided.*
3. Touch word 2. ✓
   - What word? (Signal.) *Instant.*
   - When something happens **very fast,** it happens **in an instant.** Everybody, what's another way of saying "The frog caught the fly **very fast**"? (Signal.) *The frog caught the fly in an instant.*

4. Touch word 3. ✓
- What word? (Signal.) *Deceptive.*
- Something that is **deceptive** is **misleading.** Everybody, what's another way of saying "The advertising is **misleading**"? (Signal.) *The advertising is deceptive.*

EXERCISE 4

WORD PRACTICE

1. Touch the first word in part 4. ✓

4

celebration thousands giant enough
buildings behind spies chance
changes imagine tremendous* shall
instant treasure waddling pressure
badge nearly pocket

- What word? (Signal.) *Celebration.*
2. Next w ord. ✓
- What word? (Signal.) *Thousands.*
3. (Repeat step 2 for each remaining word.)
4. (Repeat each row of words until firm.)
5. What does **tremendous** mean? (Call on a student.)

EXERCISE 5

MULTIPART WORDS

Task A

1. Touch part 5. ✓

5

continent approaching ordinary
1. continent 2. approaching 3. ordinary
unexpected
4. unexpected

> **Note:** The parts of a word are to be pronounced the same as they are when the word is spoken normally.

2. All these words have more than one part. The first part and the last part are circled.
3. Touch word 1. ✓
- Word 1 is **continent.** What word? (Signal.) *Continent.*
4. What's the first part? (Signal.) *con.*
- What's the last part? (Signal.) *ent.*
- The middle part is spelled **T–I–N.** What does that part say in the word? (Signal.) *tin.*
5. So, the parts are **con** (pause) **tin** (pause) **ent.**
- Say the whole word. (Signal.) *Continent.*
6. (Repeat steps 3–5 until firm.)
7. Touch word 2. ✓
- Word 2 is **approaching.** What word? (Signal.) *Approaching.*
8. What's the first part? (Signal.) *ap.*
- What's the last part? (Signal.) *ing.*
- The middle part is spelled **P–R–O–A–C–H.** What does that part say in the word? (Signal.) *proach.*
9. So, the parts are **ap** (pause) **proach** (pause) **ing.**
- Say the whole word. (Signal.) *Approaching.*
10. (Repeat steps 7–9 until firm.)
11. Touch word 3. ✓
- Word 3 is **ordinary.** What word? (Signal.) *Ordinary.*
12. What's the first part? (Signal.) *or.*
- What's the last part? (Signal.) *ary.*
- The middle part is spelled **D–I–N.** What does that part say in the word? (Signal.) *din.*
13. So, the parts are **or** (pause) **din** (pause) **ary.**
- Say the whole word. (Signal.) *Ordinary.*
14. (Repeat steps 11–13 until firm.)

15. Touch word 4. ✓
- Word 4 is **unexpected.** What word? (Signal.) *Unexpected.*

16. What's the first part? (Signal.) *un.*
- What's the last part? (Signal.) *ed.*
- The middle part is spelled **E–X–P–E–C–T.** What does that part say in the word? (Signal.) *expect.*

17. So, the parts are **un** (pause) **expect** (pause) **ed.**
- Say the whole word. (Signal.) *Unexpected.*

18. (Repeat steps 15–17 until firm.)

Task B

1. Touch the sentences below the word list. ✓

a. The ship is approaching the North American continent.
b. What happened was both not ordinary and unexpected.
c. They found a lot of unexpected things on the continent.
d. The ordinary hound dog was approaching the barn.

- These are sentences that use the words you just read.

2. Raise your hand when you can read sentence A. ✓
3. (Call on a student.) Read sentence A. *The ship is approaching the North American continent.*
- That means "The ship is getting closer to North America."

4. (Call on a student.) Read sentence B. *What happened was both not ordinary and unexpected.*
- That means "What happened was unusual and something that surprised them."

5. (Call on a student.) Read sentence C. *They found a lot of unexpected things on the continent.*
- That means "They were surprised by the things they found on the continent."

6. (Call on a student.) Read sentence D. *The ordinary hound dog was approaching the barn.*
- That means "There was nothing unusual about the hound dog that was going toward the barn."

EXERCISE 6

WORD-ATTACK SKILLS: Individual tests

1. (Call on individual students. Each student reads a row of words, a column of words, or a sentence. In the Multipart words exercises, each sentence counts as one row of words. Tally the rows, columns, and sentences read without error. If the group reads at least 14 rows and columns without making errors, direct all students to record 5 points in Box A of their Point Chart. Criterion is 80 percent of rows and columns read without error.)
2. (If the group did not read at least 14 rows and columns without errors, do not award any points for the Word-Attack Skills exercises.)

SELECTION READING

EXERCISE 7

STORY READING

1. Everybody, touch part 6. ✓
2. The error limit for this story is 12. If the group reads the story with 12 errors or less, you earn 5 points.

6 **A Super Job**

3. (Call on a student to read the title.) *A Super Job.*
- What do you think this story is about? (Accept reasonable responses.)

4. (Call on individual students. Each is to read two to four sentences.)
5. (Call on individual students to answer the specified questions during the story reading.)

Lesson 16

Over a thousand people were standing on the yellow streets below, watching as the mustard jar headed toward the helicopter. It seemed as if the mustard jar would collide with the helicopter. But at the last instant the helicopter dived down, and the jar did not collide with it. Instead, the jar went right over the top of the helicopter. When the jar passed over the helicopter, a great trail of mustard dropped onto the large blades of the helicopter. A helicopter cannot fly if its blades are covered with ice, so you can imagine what happened when they became covered with a load of mustard. Sputter, sputter went the helicopter, and then down it went—zigging and zagging and turning around. ❶

1. How many people were watching the mustard jar and the helicopter? *Over a thousand.*
1. Did the jar collide with the helicopter? *No.*
1. What did it do instead? (Idea: *It went over the top of the helicopter.*)

The helicopter landed in the middle of a street where some girls and boys were sliding on inner tubes. The helicopter, which had landed near the top of the hill, zipped down the hill. It slid further than any of the inner tubes had gone. It slid three blocks to an intersection where a police officer was trying to control traffic. The traffic was a mess because the cars were slipping and sliding around on the mustard. ❷

2. Where's the intersection? (Idea: *Three blocks from the top of the hill.*)
2. Name two things that happened to the helicopter after it landed at the top of the hill. (Idea: *It slid down the hill and slid to an intersection.*)

The police officer had just allowed a long line of cars to creep through the intersection. He was ready to signal the cars going in the other direction when the helicopter came sliding down the street. The police officer got out of the way just in time. He took a big dive into the mustard and slid to the curb. Zip. The helicopter went through the intersection. Then—bang! It hit the back of a bread truck. The police officer got up and ran over to the helicopter. He pointed to his yellow badge and said to the spies inside, "You're under arrest." ❸

3. What did the police officer mean when he said, "You're under arrest"? (Idea: *You have been caught breaking the law.*)

One spy said to another spy, "I didn't know that the police dressed in yellow outfits."

The other spy said, "Oh, shut up."

When the spies were getting out of the helicopter, the mustard jar landed. By now a great crowd had gathered around the helicopter. The mustard jar waddled up to the police officer and said, "I am a member of the Secret Agents. I will take charge of these spies." ❹

4. For whom did the mustard jar work? *The Secret Agents.*
4. Why was the police officer's uniform yellow? (Idea: *From all the mustard that came from the flying mustard jar.*)

The police officer looked at the mustard jar. He was going to say, "What is going on around here?" But he didn't. Instead, he looked at the helicopter in the middle of a city street. He looked at streets and sidewalks and buildings covered with mustard. He looked at a talking mustard jar, as big as a person, waddling around on stubby little legs. When he saw all this, he said to himself, "This is so crazy, it can't really be happening." ❺

5. How did the police officer feel? (Idea: *That everything that had happened was too crazy to be real.*)

He slid his badge into his pocket, smiled at the mustard jar, and said, "I'm always glad to help the Secret Agents."

Later that day so many people called the Secret Agents that they burned out the telephone lines. All these people were complaining. The chief of the Secret Agents called the spy chaser who had hired the mustard jar and complained to her. "That mustard device will cost us thousands and thousands of dollars," the chief said angrily. "Get rid of it. And don't hire any more devices like it."

That evening the spy chaser told the mustard jar, "Well, you did a fine job, but—" The spy chaser didn't want to make the mustard jar mad. "But—" the spy chaser said, "we want you to go undercover from now on. We're going to send you to a quiet place far from this city. We want you to stay there until you hear from us."

The mustard jar smiled and said, "I did a super job, didn't I? I think I'll call myself Super Mustard."

The spy chaser smiled and said, "Yes, you did a super job. Now you must do some undercover work for us."

So the mustard jar went to the quiet place. And what happened there is another story. ❻

6. What is undercover work? *Work that is done in secret.*
6. Why was the mustard jar taken out of spy chasing? (Ideas: *Because it made too much of a mess; it made people angry; it would cost a lot of money to clean up the mess.*)
6. (Award points quickly.)
7. (If the group makes more than 12 errors, repeat the reading immediately or on the next day.)

FLUENCY ASSESSMENT

EXERCISE 8

TIMED READING CHECKOUTS

1. (For this part of the lesson, assigned pairs of students work together during the checkouts.)
- (If one student does not have a checkout partner, arrange another time when you can give the checkout.)
2. (Each student does a 2-minute timed reading. Students earn 5 points by reading at least 220 words and making no more than 4 errors on the first part of story 16. Students record points in Box C of their Point Chart and plot their reading rate and errors on the Individual Reading Progress Chart.)
- (During each timed checkout, observe one pair of students for 2 minutes. Make notes on any mistakes the reader makes.)
3. (Record the timed reading checkout performance for each student you observed on the Fluency Assessment Summary form.)

WORKBOOK EXERCISES

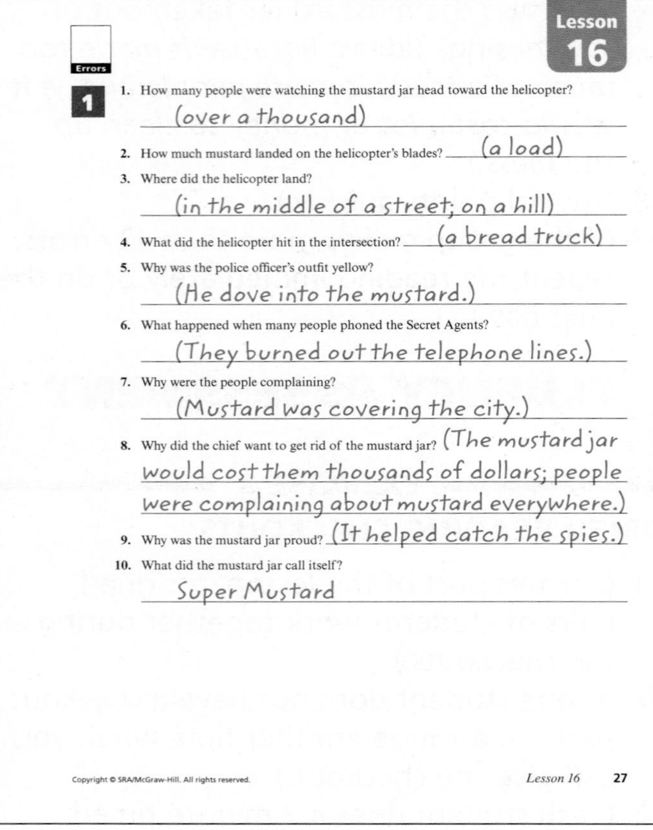

Lesson 16

Errors

1

1. How many people were watching the mustard jar head toward the helicopter? (over a thousand)
2. How much mustard landed on the helicopter's blades? (a load)
3. Where did the helicopter land? (in the middle of a street; on a hill)
4. What did the helicopter hit in the intersection? (a bread truck)
5. Why was the police officer's outfit yellow? (He dove into the mustard.)
6. What happened when many people phoned the Secret Agents? (They burned out the telephone lines.)
7. Why were the people complaining? (Mustard was covering the city.)
8. Why did the chief want to get rid of the mustard jar? (The mustard jar would cost them thousands of dollars; people were complaining about mustard everywhere.)
9. Why was the mustard jar proud? (It helped catch the spies.)
10. What did the mustard jar call itself? Super Mustard

Copyright © SRA/McGraw-Hill. All rights reserved. Lesson 16 27

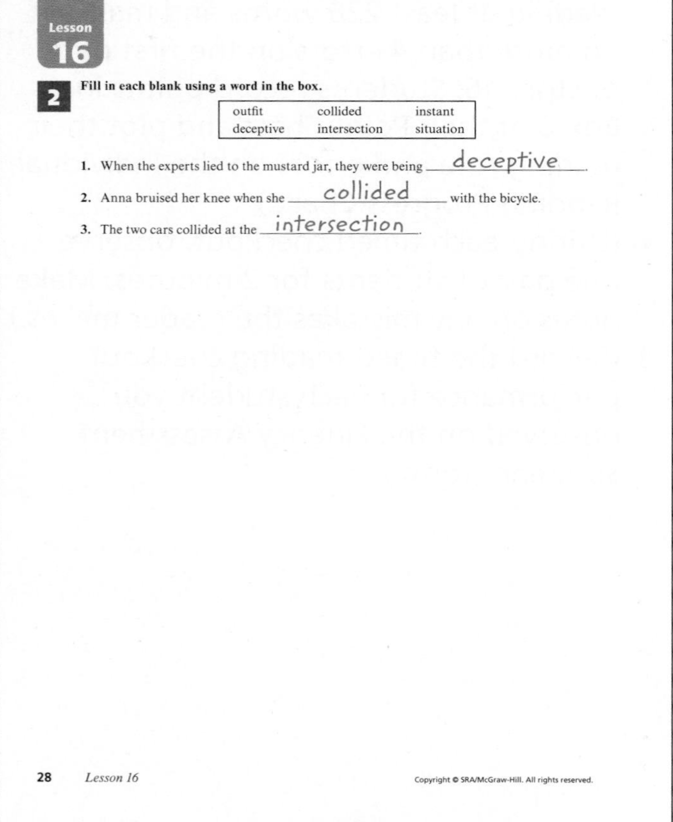

Lesson 16

2 Fill in each blank using a word in the box.

outfit	collided	instant
deceptive	intersection	situation

1. When the experts lied to the mustard jar, they were being deceptive.
2. Anna bruised her knee when she collided with the bicycle.
3. The two cars collided at the intersection.

28 Lesson 16 Copyright © SRA/McGraw-Hill. All rights reserved.

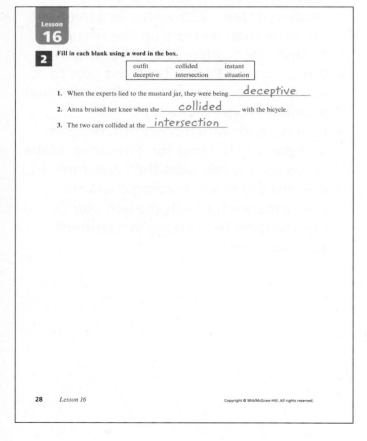

Independent Student Work

Task A

- Open your Workbook to Lesson 16. ✓
- Complete all parts of your Workbook lesson using a pencil. If you make no errors, you will earn 5 points.

Task B

1. (Before presenting Lesson 17, check student Workbooks for Lesson 16.)
   - (Call on individual students to read the items and answers in each part. Students mark errors using a pen.)
2. (Direct the students to count the number of errors and write the number in the Errors box at the top of the Workbook page.)
3. (Award points and direct students to record points in Box D of their Point Chart.)

   0 errors.................................5 points
   1 error ....3 points
   2 or 3 errors ....1 point
   more than 3 errors ....0 points

END OF LESSON 16

WORD-ATTACK SKILLS

Board Work

EXERCISE 1

BUILDUP

1. (Print on the board:)

enough

2. (Point to **enough.** Pause.) What word? (Signal.) *Enough.*
3. (Change the word to:)

t ough

- What word now? (Signal.) *Tough.*

4. (Change the word to:)

t h ought

- What word now? (Signal.) *Thought.*

5. (Change the word to:)

bought

- What word now? (Signal.) *Bought.*

6. (Change the word to:)

ought

- What word now? (Signal.) *Ought.*

7. (Change to the original word:)

enough

- (Repeat steps 2–6 until firm.)

Student Book 

EXERCISE 2

WORD PRACTICE

1. Open your Student Book to Lesson 17. ✓

1

peaceful celebration intersection

sponge rounded dangerous practiced

- Touch the first word in part 1. ✓
- What sound? (Signal.) *ēēē.*
- What word? (Signal.) *Peaceful.*

2. Touch the next word. ✓
- What sound? (Signal.) *shun.*
- What word? (Signal.) *Celebration.*

3. (Repeat step 2 for each remaining word.)
4. (Repeat each row of words until firm.)

EXERCISE 3

VOCABULARY

1. Touch part 2. ✓

2

1. buoy
2. gear
3. occasional
4. gymnastics

- We're going to talk about what those words mean.

2. Touch word 1. ✓
- What word? (Signal.) *Buoy.*
- The **buoy** that is spelled **B–U–O–Y** means **a float that marks something in the water.** Everybody, what is a **buoy?** (Signal.) *A float that marks something in the water.*

3. Touch word 2. ✓
- What word? (Signal.) *Gear.*
- The **equipment** that divers need for diving is called **gear.** Everybody, what's another way of saying "She has a lot of camping **equipment**"? (Signal.) *She has a lot of camping gear.*

4. Touch word 3. ✓
- What word? (Signal.) *Occasional.*
- When rain comes **once in a while,** it is an **occasional** rain. Everybody, what's another way of saying "tests that come **once in a while**"? (Signal.) *Occasional tests.*

5. Touch word 4. ✓
- What word? (Signal.) *Gymnastics.*
- Who knows what **gymnastics** is? (Call on a student.) (Ideas: *Tumbling; stunts on parallel bars; etc.*)

Lesson 17

EXERCISE 4

WORD PRACTICE

1. Touch the first word in part 3. ✓

3

Lopez service ceiling deceptive* Florida
glided Caribbean unbelievably Olympic
scuba warn taught pressure strain*
Dubowski accident treasure woman
classes instructor stripe waddling
women remembering toward coral shadow
great injured during grinder drew
worth coffee knots studied thought

- What word? (Signal.) *Lopez.*

2. Next word. ✓
- What word? (Signal.) *Service.*

3. (Repeat step 2 for each remaining word.)
4. (Repeat each row of words until firm.)
5. What does **deceptive** mean? (Call on a student.)
- (Repeat for **strain.**)

EXERCISE 5

MULTIPART WORDS

Task A

1. Touch part 4. ✓

4

unnatural excellent surrounded
1. unnatural 2. excellent 3. surrounded
continuous protection
4. continuous 5. protection

> **Note:** The parts of a word are to be pronounced the same as they are when the word is spoken normally. For example, in the word **continuous, tinu** is pronounced **tin-you** and **ous** is pronounced **us.**

2. All these words have more than one part. The first part and the last part are circled.
3. Touch word 1. ✓
- Word 1 is **unnatural.** What word? (Signal.) *Unnatural.*

4. What's the first part? (Signal.) *un.*
- What's the last part? (Signal.) *al.*
- The middle part is spelled **N–A–T–U–R.** What does that part say in the word? (Signal.) *natur.*

5. So, the parts are **un** (pause) **natur** (pause) **al.**
- Say the whole word. (Signal.) *Unnatural.*

6. (Repeat steps 3–5 until firm.)
7. Touch word 2. ✓
- Word 2 is **excellent.** What word? (Signal.) *Excellent.*

8. What's the first part? (Signal.) *ex.*
- What's the last part? (Signal.) *ent.*
- The middle part is spelled **C–E–L–L.** What does that part say in the word? (Signal.) *cell.*

9. So, the parts are **ex** (pause) **cell** (pause) **ent.**
- Say the whole word. (Signal.) *Excellent.*

10. (Repeat steps 7–9 until firm.)
11. Touch word 3. ✓
- Word 3 is **surrounded.** What word? (Signal.) *Surrounded.*

12. What's the first part? (Signal.) *sur.*
- What's the last part? (Signal.) *ed.*
- The middle part is spelled **R–O–U–N–D.** What does that part say in the word? (Signal.) *round.*

13. So, the parts are **sur** (pause) **round** (pause) **ed.**
- Say the whole word. (Signal.) *Surrounded.*

14. (Repeat steps 11–13 until firm.)
15. Touch word 4. ✓
- Word 4 is **continuous.** What word? (Signal.) *Continuous.*

16. What's the first part? (Signal.) *con.*
- What's the last part? (Signal.) *ous.*
- The middle part is spelled **T–I–N–U.** What does that part say in the word? (Signal.) *tinu.*

17. So, the parts are **con** (pause) **tinu** (pause) **ous.**
- Say the whole word. (Signal.) *Continuous.*

18. (Repeat steps 15–17 until firm.)

19. Touch word 5. ✓
   - Word 5 is **protection.** What word? (Signal.) *Protection.*
20. What's the first part? (Signal.) *pro.*
   - What's the last part? (Signal.) *tion.*
   - The middle part is spelled **T–E–C.** What does that part say in the word? (Signal.) *tec.*
21. So, the parts are **pro** (pause) **tec** (pause) **tion.**
   - Say the whole word. (Signal.) *Protection.*
22. (Repeat steps 19–21 until firm.)

Task B

1. Touch the sentences below the word list. ✓

a. His coat felt unnatural but gave excellent protection against the cold.

b. A continuous ring of fire surrounded the lake.

c. Her voice sounds loud and unnatural.

d. The bird's only protection against attack was its continuous calling.

   - These are sentences that use the words you just read.
2. Raise your hand when you can read sentence A. ✓
3. (Call on a student.) Read sentence A. *His coat felt unnatural but gave excellent protection against the cold.*
   - That means "The coat was not very comfortable, but it kept him warm."
4. (Call on a student.) Read sentence B. *A continuous ring of fire surrounded the lake.*
   - That means "There were no gaps in the ring of fire all the way around the lake."
5. (Call on a student.) Read sentence C. *Her voice sounds loud and unnatural.*
   - That means "Her voice is too noisy and sounds phony."
6. (Call on a student.) Read sentence D. *The bird's only protection against attack was its continuous calling.*
   - That means "The only way the bird could keep something from attacking it was to keep making bird calls."

EXERCISE 6

WORD-ATTACK SKILLS: Individual tests

1. (Call on individual students. Each student reads a row of words, a column of words, or a sentence. In the Multipart words exercises, each sentence counts as one row of words. Tally the rows, columns, and sentences read without error. If the group reads at least 13 rows and columns without making errors, direct all students to record 5 points in Box A of their Point Chart. Criterion is 80 percent of rows and columns read without error.)
2. (If the group did not read at least 13 rows and columns without errors, do not award any points for the Word-Attack Skills exercises.)

SELECTION READING

EXERCISE 7

STORY READING

1. Everybody, touch part 5. ✓
2. The error limit for this story is 12. If the group reads the story with 12 errors or less, you earn 5 points.

5 **Jane and Doris**

3. (Call on a student to read the title.) *Jane and Doris.*
   - What do you think this story is about? (Accept reasonable responses.)
4. (Call on individual students. Each is to read two to four sentences.)
5. (Call on individual students to answer the specified questions during the story reading.)

Lesson 17

The water looked unbelievably blue to Jane. The sand beneath the water looked blue-white. From time to time a dark shadow of a fish glided over the sand. Everything looked very peaceful. The boat slowly bobbed and dipped over the waves. As Jane looked down to the bottom, she had to remind herself, "Don't be fooled. It is very deceptive down there." ❶

1. What did the water look like? (Idea: *It looked unbelievably blue.*)
1. What did the sand look like? *Blue-white.*
1. What did Jane mean when she told herself, "It is very **deceptive** down there"? (Idea: *It's different from the way it looks.*)

Jane Dubowski was a teacher. She taught gymnastics and swimming. At one time she had wanted to become an Olympic swimmer, but then she injured her leg in an auto accident. She now has a brace on her leg. She liked her teaching job, but for the past year she had been looking forward to her vacation. She wasn't sure when she first got the idea to dive for sunken treasure, and she wasn't sure when the idea became more than an idle dream. But some time during the fall she had asked herself, "Why not? Why not go to the keys off the coast of Florida and dive for treasure?" The Florida Keys are little islands strung out from the tip of Florida into the Caribbean Sea. ❷

2. What kind of work did Jane do? (Idea: *She was a teacher.*)
2. How did Jane injure her leg? (Idea: *In an auto accident.*)
2. What did Jane want to do on her vacation? (Idea: *Dive for sunken treasure.*)

She had told a friend of hers, Doris Lopez, about her idea. Doris, who was also a teacher, liked the idea. Doris and Jane studied maps that showed where people think ships carrying gold had sunk. One ship that had gone down off the Florida Keys was supposed to have carried over fifty million dollars' worth of gold. ❸

3. What kind of work did Doris do? (Idea: *She was a teacher.*)
3. How much was the gold the sunken ship had carried worth? *Over 50 million dollars.*

But Doris and Jane hadn't really thought that they would find the ship. They just thought that the diving would be fun. That winter they had taken scuba diving classes. They had saved their money, and when school was out, they bought airline tickets. They packed their scuba gear and flew to Florida, where they rented a car and drove to one of the keys, named Key West.

When the women arrived at Key West, they rented a boat. It was an old boat, about twenty feet long. It had an engine that sounded like a coffee grinder. The engine pushed the boat along at about four knots—not very fast. On their first two days the teachers took their boat out about a mile and made practice dives under the eye of an instructor. They set out buoys with diving flags. These flags are red with one white stripe cutting across them, and they warn other boats that divers are in the water. ❹

4. What kind of classes had Doris and Jane taken? *Scuba diving classes.*
4. What did the buoys have on them? *Diving flags.*
4. What do the buoys do? (Idea: *They warn other boats that divers are in the water.*)

At first Jane and Doris went down only about thirty feet. The pressure of the water hurt Jane's ears. After she had been underwater for about twenty minutes, however, her ears stopped hurting. But her mask fogged up quite a bit and water kept leaking in around the edges of the mask. She wore a blue wet suit. Doris had a yellow wet suit. When Jane looked at Doris underwater, the suit looked yellow-green, and shadows made by the waves drew little lines over Doris and over the bottom. ⑤

5. How long did Jane's ears hurt? *For twenty minutes.*
5. How did Doris's suit look underwater? (Idea: *It looked yellow-green.*)

"This is great," Jane said to herself. She followed a school of yellow fish along the bottom. She stopped and picked up a sponge from the bottom. She kept telling herself that she was having a good time, but she kept remembering all the things she had heard and read about diving near the reefs, which is where the treasure ships had gone down. She kept thinking about the next day when she would dive near the reefs. And she felt a little afraid. At the same time she kept thinking, "How blue this water is!" ⑥

6. What did Jane follow in the water? (Idea: *A school of yellow fish.*)
6. What is a school of fish? (Idea: *A group of fish.*)
6. (Award points quickly.)
7. (If the group makes more than 12 errors, repeat the reading immediately or on the next day.)

FLUENCY ASSESSMENT

EXERCISE 8

TIMED READING CHECKOUTS

1. (For this part of the lesson, assigned pairs of students work together during the checkouts.)
- (If one student does not have a checkout partner, arrange another time when you can give the checkout.)
2. (Each student does a 2-minute timed reading. Students earn 5 points by reading at least 220 words and making no more than 4 errors on the first part of story 17. Students record points in Box C of their Point Chart and plot their reading rate and errors on the Individual Reading Progress Chart.)
- (During each timed checkout, observe one pair of students for 2 minutes. Make notes on any mistakes the reader makes.)
3. (Record the timed reading checkout performance for each student you observed on the Fluency Assessment Summary form.)

Lesson 17

WORKBOOK EXERCISES

Workbook: Teacher Directed 

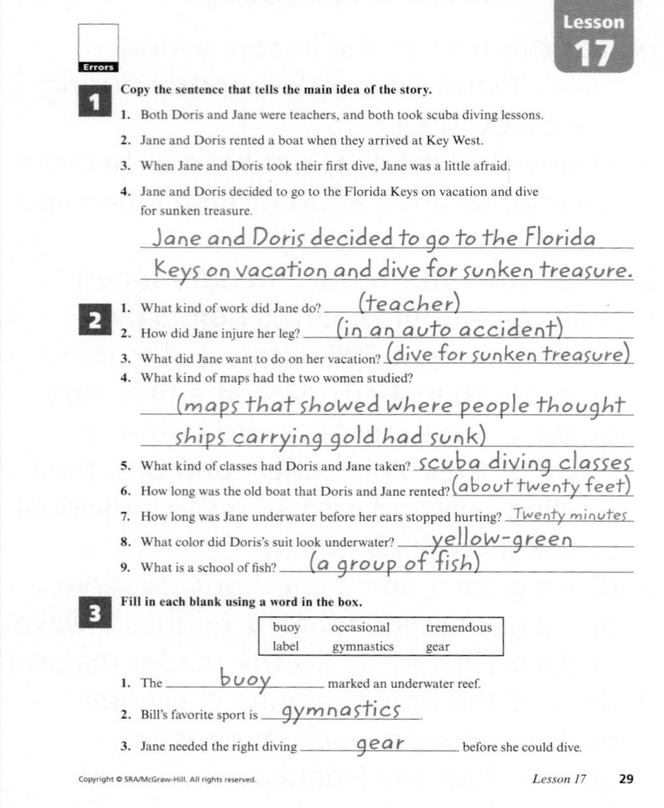

Errors

Lesson 17

1 **Copy the sentence that tells the main idea of the story.**

1. Both Doris and Jane were teachers, and both took scuba diving lessons.
2. Jane and Doris rented a boat when they arrived at Key West.
3. When Jane and Doris took their first dive, Jane was a little afraid.
4. Jane and Doris decided to go to the Florida Keys on vacation and dive for sunken treasure.

Jane and Doris decided to go to the Florida Keys on vacation and dive for sunken treasure.

2

1. What kind of work did Jane do? (teacher)
2. How did Jane injure her leg? (in an auto accident)
3. What did Jane want to do on her vacation? (dive for sunken treasure)
4. What kind of maps had the two women studied? (maps that showed where people thought ships carrying gold had sunk)
5. What kind of classes had Doris and Jane taken? scuba diving classes
6. How long was the old boat that Doris and Jane rented? (about twenty feet)
7. How long was Jane underwater before her ears stopped hurting? Twenty minutes
8. What color did Doris's suit look underwater? yellow-green
9. What is a school of fish? (a group of fish)

3 **Fill in each blank using a word in the box.**

buoy	occasional	tremendous
label	gymnastics	gear

1. The buoy marked an underwater reef.
2. Bill's favorite sport is gymnastics
3. Jane needed the right diving gear before she could dive.

Copyright © SRA/McGraw-Hill. All rights reserved. Lesson 17 29

EXERCISE 9

NEW COPYING MAIN-IDEA SENTENCE

1. Open your Workbook to Lesson 17. ✓
- Touch part 1. ✓
- You're going to copy the sentence that tells the **main idea** of the story. The **main idea** of the story is the **main thing that happened** in the story. One of the four sentences gives the main idea of the story.
2. Touch sentence 1. ✓
- (Call on a student to read sentence 1.) *Both Doris and Jane were teachers, and both took scuba diving lessons.*
- That was not the main thing that happened in the story.
3. Touch sentence 2. ✓
- (Call on a student to read sentence 2.) *Jane and Doris rented a boat when they arrived at Key West.*
- That was not the main thing that happened in the story.
4. Touch sentence 3. ✓
- (Call on a student to read sentence 3.) *When Jane and Doris took their first dive, Jane was a little afraid.*
- Was that the main thing that happened in the story? (Signal.) *No.*
5. Touch sentence 4. ✓
- (Call on a student to read sentence 4.) *Jane and Doris decided to go to the Florida Keys on vacation and dive for sunken treasure.*
- Was that the main thing that happened in the story? (Signal.) *Yes.*
6. Later, you'll copy that sentence on the lines.

Independent Student Work

Task A

- Complete all parts of your Workbook lesson using a pencil. If you make no errors, you will earn 5 points.

Task B

1. (Before presenting Lesson 18, check student Workbooks for Lesson 17.) (Call on individual students to read the items and answers in each part. Students mark errors using a pen.)
2. (Direct the students to count the number of errors and write the number in the Errors box at the top of the Workbook page.)
3. (Award points and direct students to record points in Box D of their Point Chart.)

0 errors.................................5 points
1 error ....3 points
2 or 3 errors ....1 point
more than 3 errors ....0 points

END OF LESSON 17

WORD-ATTACK SKILLS

Student Book 

EXERCISE 1
WORD PRACTICE

1. Open your Student Book to Lesson 18. ✓

1

northeast information giant
markers explained dangerous
carved occupation oxygen
ridge peaceful surface

- Touch the first word in part 1. ✓
- What sound? (Signal.) *ēēē.*
- What word? (Signal.) *Northeast.*

2. Touch the next word. ✓
- What sound? (Signal.) *shun.*
- What word? (Signal.) *Information.*

3. (Repeat step 2 for each remaining word.)
4. (Repeat each row of words until firm.)

EXERCISE 2
VOCABULARY

1. Touch part 2. ✓

2

1. glimpse
2. air pressure
3. prop
4. stranded

- We're going to talk about what those words mean.

2. Touch word 1. ✓
- What word? (Signal.) *Glimpse.*
- A **quick look** at something is a **glimpse.** Everybody, what's another way of saying "She took a **quick look** at the car"? (Signal.) *She took a glimpse at the car.*

3. Touch the words in item 2. ✓
- What words? (Signal.) *Air pressure.*
- The **air pressure** is **how hard the air pushes** against things. If the air pushes harder, is there **more** air pressure or **less** air pressure? (Signal.) *More.*

4. Touch word 3. ✓
- What word? (Signal.) *Prop.*
- **Prop** is a short name for **propeller.** Everybody, what's another word for **prop?** (Signal.) *Propeller.*

5. Touch word 4. ✓
- What word? (Signal.) *Stranded.*
- A person who is **stranded** cannot move from that place. Everybody, what's another way of saying "He could not move from the airport"? (Signal.) *He was stranded at the airport.*

EXERCISE 3
WORD PRACTICE

1. Touch the first word in part 3. ✓

3

large nervous fences patterns sponge
slightly guard weather whistled
sandwich adventure coffee creature
currents coral grinder occasional*
tomorrow ocean spare great worry
replied loaded fruit shifted front
compass toward shadows beautiful
million unlimited escape built cafeteria
briefcase couple bothered expect stretched

- What word? (Signal.) *Large.*

2. Next word. ✓
- What word? (Signal.) *Nervous.*

3. (Repeat step 2 for each remaining word.)
4. (Repeat each row of words until firm.)
5. What does **occasional** mean? (Call on a student.)

Lesson 18

EXERCISE 4

MULTIPART WORDS

Task A

1. Touch part 4. ✓

4

mountainous furniture faithfully

1. mountainous 2. furniture 3. faithfully

conditioner management

4. conditioner 5. management

> **Note:** The parts of a word are to be pronounced the same as they are when the word is spoken normally. For example, in the word **furniture, ture** is pronounced **chur.**

2. All these words have more than one part. The first part and the last part are circled.
3. Touch word 1. ✓
- Word 1 is **mountainous.** What word? (Signal.) *Mountainous.*
4. What's the first part? (Signal.) *mount.*
- What's the last part? (Signal.) *ous.*
- The middle part is spelled **A–I–N.** What does that part say in the word? (Signal.) *ain.*
5. So, the parts are **mount** (pause) **ain** (pause) **ous.**
- Say the whole word. (Signal.) *Mountainous.*
6. (Repeat steps 3–5 until firm.)
7. Touch word 2. ✓
- Word 2 is **furniture.** What word? (Signal.) *Furniture.*
8. What's the first part? (Signal.) *fur.*
- What's the last part? (Signal.) *ture.*
- The middle part is spelled **N–I.** What does that part say in the word? (Signal.) *ni.*
9. So, the parts are **fur** (pause) **ni** (pause) **ture.**
- Say the whole word. (Signal.) *Furniture.*
10. (Repeat steps 7–9 until firm.)
11. Touch word 3. ✓
- Word 3 is **faithfully.** What word? (Signal.) *Faithfully.*
12. What's the first part? (Signal.) *faith.*
- What's the last part? (Signal.) *ly.*
- The middle part is spelled **F–U–L.** What does that part say in the word? (Signal.) *ful.*
13. So, the parts are **faith** (pause) **ful** (pause) **ly.**
- Say the whole word. (Signal.) *Faithfully.*
14. (Repeat steps 11–13 until firm.)
15. Touch word 4. ✓
- Word 4 is **conditioner.** What word? (Signal.) *Conditioner.*
16. What's the first part? (Signal.) *con.*
- What's the last part? (Signal.) *er.*
- The middle part is spelled **D–I–T–I–O–N.** What does that part say in the word? (Signal.) *dition.*
17. So, the parts are **con** (pause) **dition** (pause) **er.**
- Say the whole word. (Signal.) *Conditioner.*
18. (Repeat steps 15–17 until firm.)
19. Touch word 5. ✓
- Word 5 is **management.** What word? (Signal.) *Management.*
20. What's the first part? (Signal.) *man.*
- What's the last part? (Signal.) *ment.*
- The middle part is spelled **A–G–E.** What does that part say in the word? (Signal.) *age.*
21. So, the parts are **man** (pause) **age** (pause) **ment.**
- Say the whole word. (Signal.) *Management.*
22. (Repeat steps 19–21 until firm.)

Task B

1. Touch the sentences below the word list. ✓

a. They bought furniture and an air conditioner.
b. The hikers faithfully followed the park rules for the mountainous area.
c. The management of the furniture company received a lot of money.
d. She used that new skin conditioner very faithfully.

- These are sentences that use the words you just read.
2. Raise your hand when you can read sentence A. ✓
3. (Call on a student.) Read sentence A. *They bought furniture and an air conditioner.*
4. (Call on a student.) Read sentence B. *The hikers faithfully followed the park rules for the mountainous area.*
- That means "The hikers did not break any rules when they were hiking through the mountains in the park."
5. (Call on a student.) Read sentence C. *The management of the furniture company received a lot of money.*
- That means "The people who operated the furniture company received a lot of money."
6. (Call on a student.) Read sentence D. *She used that new skin conditioner very faithfully.*
- That means "She used the skin conditioner exactly the way the directions told her to use it."

EXERCISE 5

WORD-ATTACK SKILLS: Individual tests

1. (Call on individual students. Each student reads a row of words, a column of words, or a sentence. In the Multipart words exercises, each sentence counts as one row of words. Tally the rows, columns, and sentences read without error. If the group reads at least 15 rows and columns without making errors, direct all students to record 5 points in Box A of their Point Chart. Criterion is 80 percent of rows and columns read without error.)
2. (If the group did not read at least 15 rows and columns without errors, do not award any points for the Word-Attack Skills exercises.)

SELECTION READING

EXERCISE 6

STORY READING

1. (Call on individual students to answer these questions.)
- Who were the main characters in the last selection? *Jane and Doris.*
- Where did they work and what did they want to do? (Ideas: *Both women worked as teachers; they wanted to dive for sunken treasure.*)
- What happened? (Accept reasonable summaries.)
2. Everybody, touch part 5. ✓
3. The error limit for this story is 12. If the group reads the story with 12 errors or less, you earn 5 points.

5 **To the Coral Reef**

4. (Call on a student to read the title.) *To the Coral Reef.*
- What do you think this story is about? (Accept reasonable responses.)

5. (Call on individual students. Each is to read two to four sentences.)
6. (Call on individual students to answer the specified questions during the story reading.)

Doris and Jane got up before six the next morning. Doris called the Coast Guard station to get weather information. The person told her that the day should be calm and that small craft should have no trouble. "But we expect a northeast wind to move in by tomorrow. If the air pressure drops today, the wind may come in sooner." A northeast wind was dangerous.

Doris asked, "How long will that wind blow?"

The person told her, "Maybe three or four days."

Doris hung up and shook her head. "We only have a week," she said. "And we may not be able to go out after today for three or four days." ❶

1. How did Doris get weather information? (Idea: *By calling the Coast Guard station.*)
1. What kind of wind was dangerous? *A northeast wind.*
1. Why might Jane and Doris not get to go out after the first day? (Idea: *Because of the northeast wind.*)

"Nuts," Jane said. Jane walked to the window of their motel room and looked out. The sun was coming up over the ocean, and the ocean looked like a sheet of glass that was ruffled by an occasional wind. ❷

2. What's an **occasional** wind? (Idea: *A wind that comes once in a while.*)

"Well, we'll worry about tomorrow later," she said. "Let's get going."

So Doris and Jane took their gear to the pier where their boat was docked. They filled the boat's main gas tank. Then they filled the spare tank. The woman who filled the tanks said, "Where are you going today?"

Jane said, "Out to the coral reef." ❸

3. Where did Jane and Doris take their gear? (Idea: *To the pier where the boat was docked.*)
3. What is **gear?** (Idea: *The equipment they used to scuba dive.*)
3. Where were Jane and Doris going? *Out to the coral reef.*

The woman whistled and shook her head. "That's dangerous," she said. Jane wished the woman hadn't said that. She knew that it was dangerous. She had read about the reef and about the water currents. She had read about how many people had been injured diving near that reef.

The woman explained, "Those currents are bad. They'll suck you down if you don't watch out."

Jane smiled and tried to act as if she wasn't bothered. "We'll be careful," she replied. Inside, she was saying to herself, "Maybe we shouldn't go." ❹

4. Why was the coral reef dangerous? (Idea: *Because of the water currents.*)
4. What did the woman at the dock say that the currents would do? (Idea: *They would suck the women down if they didn't watch out.*)
4. Why was Jane bothered? (Idea: *She was afraid.*)

Before seven o'clock, the boat was loaded. Four air tanks were tied down in the front of the boat. Diving flags and markers were in the boat. On the middle seat was a large cooler filled with fruit, sandwiches, and soft drinks.

Jane started the coffee-grinder engine in the old boat. She shifted it into forward, and the boat began to move away from the dock. "Did you bring the suntan lotion?" Doris called from the front seat.

"Yes," Jane answered. "It's next to the cooler." But Jane wasn't thinking about suntan lotion. She was looking far out over the ocean, trying to get a glimpse of the coral reef. She checked the compass and turned the boat slightly toward the south. ❺

5. What did Doris ask about? (Idea: *About the suntan lotion.*)
5. What was Jane really thinking about? (Ideas: *About the coral reef; about the dangerous conditions.*)
5. What gear was tied down in the front of the boat? *Air tanks.*
5. What was in the cooler? (Idea: *Fruit, sandwiches, soft drinks.*)

Probably fifteen minutes passed before Jane yelled, "There it is." She pointed, and Doris turned around. A large red buoy marked the reef. The reef stretched out for several miles, sticking out of the water in places, very white and very sharp.

Jane steered the boat to a place where the reef was just below the surface of the water. "Watch out," Doris said. "Don't let the prop hit that reef or we'll be stranded out here."

Jane looked at the coral reef below. It was beautiful. It looked like a giant white ridge with a million patterns carved in it. It was a network of sharp knobs and knots and ridges and shadows. Jane could see little caves with fish swimming in and out of them. She said to herself, "It's hard to believe that anything so beautiful could be dangerous." ❻

6. What did the coral reef look life? (Ideas: *It was beautiful; it looked like a giant white ridge with a million patterns carved in it.*)
6. How was the reef marked? (Idea: *With a large red buoy.*)
6. How could Jane and Doris get stranded? (Idea: *If their boat's prop hit the reef.*)
7. (Award points quickly.)
8. (If the group makes more than 12 errors, repeat the reading immediately or on the next day.)

FLUENCY ASSESSMENT

EXERCISE 7

TIMED READING CHECKOUTS

1. (For this part of the lesson, assigned pairs of students work together during the checkouts.)
   - (If one student does not have a checkout partner, arrange another time when you can give the checkout.)
2. (Each student does a 2-minute timed reading. Students earn 5 points by reading at least 220 words and making no more than 4 errors on the first part of story 18. Students record points in Box C of their Point Chart and plot their reading rate and errors on the Individual Reading Progress Chart.)
   - (During each timed checkout, observe one pair of students for 2 minutes. Make notes on any mistakes the reader makes.)
3. (Record the timed reading checkout performance for each student you observed on the Fluency Assessment Summary form.)

Lesson 18

Errors

1

1. How did Doris get weather information? (She called the Coast Guard station.)
2. When did the Coast Guard expect a northeast wind to move in? (by the next day)
3. Where were Jane and Doris going? (to the coral reef)
4. Why was the coral reef dangerous? (because of water currents)
5. What gear was tied down in front of the boat? air tanks
6. Name two other things the women took with them in the boat. (Any two: diving flags; markers; cooler filled with fruit, sandwiches, and soft drinks; suntan lotion)
7. How was the reef marked? (with a large red buoy)
8. How could Jane and Doris get stranded? if the prop hit the reef
9. What did the coral reef look like? a giant white ridge with a million patterns carved in it
10. How do you think Jane felt as she looked down at the coral reef? (excited; afraid)

2 **Fill in each blank using a word in the box.**

pressure	reply	glimpse
prop	stranded	beaker

1. The boat's prop broke on the reef.
2. The old man had been stranded on the island for forty years.
3. The water pressure hurt Sam's ears when he was down fifty feet.

30 *Lesson 18* Copyright © SRA/McGraw-Hill. All rights reserved.

WORKBOOK EXERCISES

Independent Student Work

Task A

- Open your Workbook to Lesson 18. ✓
- Complete all parts of your Workbook lesson using a pencil. If you make no errors, you will earn 5 points.

Task B

1. (Before presenting Lesson 19, check student Workbooks for Lesson 18.)
   - (Call on individual students to read the items and answers in each part. Students mark errors using a pen.)
2. (Direct the students to count the number of errors and write the number in the Errors box at the top of the Workbook page.)
3. (Award points and direct students to record points in Box D of their Point Chart.)

   0 errors.................................5 points
   1 error ....3 points
   2 or 3 errors ....1 point
   more than 3 errors ....0 points

END OF LESSON 18

WORD-ATTACK SKILLS

Board Work

EXERCISE 1

BUILDUP

1. (Print on the board:)

th ough

2. (Point to **though.** Pause.) What word? (Signal.) *Though.*
3. (Change the word to:)

through

- What word now? (Signal.) *Through.*

4. (Change the word to:)

rough

- What word now? (Signal.) *Rough.*

5. (Change the word to:)

tough

- What word now? (Signal.) *Tough.*

6. (Change the word to:)

touch

- What word now? (Signal.) *Touch.*

7. (Change the word to:)

ouch

- What word now? (Signal.) *Ouch.*

8. (Change the word to:)

crouch

- What word now? (Signal.) *Crouch.*

9. (Change to the original word:)

though

- (Repeat steps 2–8 until firm.)

Student Book 

EXERCISE 2

NEW **SOUND COMBINATION: ee**

Task A

1. Open your Student Book to Lesson 19. ✓

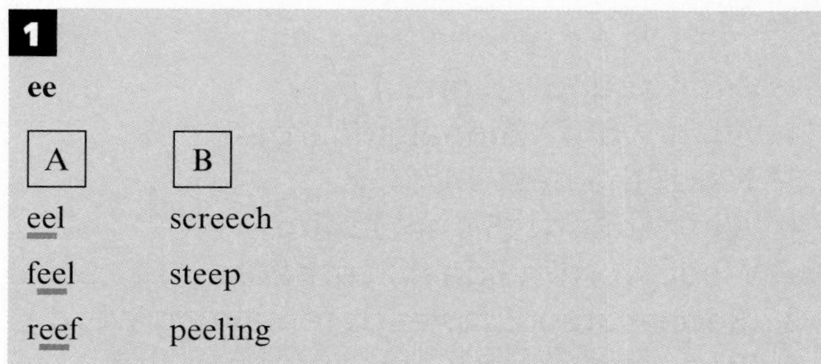

1

ee

A	B
eel	screech
feel	steep
reef	peeling

- Touch the letters **E–E** in part 1. ✓
- What sound do the letters **E–E** make? (Signal.) *ēēē.*

2. You're going to say the sound for the underlined part and then read the word.
3. Touch the first word in column A. ✓
- What sound? (Signal.) *ēēē.*
- What word? (Signal.) *Eel.*

4. Touch the next word. ✓
- What sound? (Signal.) *ēēē.*
- What word? (Signal.) *Feel.*

5. (Repeat step 4 for **reef.**)

Task B

1. Touch the first word in column B. ✓
- What word? (Signal.) *Screech.*

2. Touch the next word. ✓
- What word? (Signal.) *Steep.*

3. (Repeat step 2 for **peeling.**)
4. (Repeat steps 1–3 until firm.)

Lesson 19

EXERCISE 3

WORD PRACTICE

1. Touch the first word in part 2. ✓

2

charges location markers surface

cautioned sharpness sponges

patterns creature mouthpiece

- What sound? (Signal.) *j.*
- What word? (Signal.) *Charges.*

2. Touch the next word. ✓

- What sound? (Signal.) *shun.*
- What word? (Signal.) *Location.*

3. (Repeat step 2 for each remaining word.)
4. (Repeat each row of words until firm.)

EXERCISE 4

VOCABULARY

1. Touch part 3. ✓

3

1. location
2. indicate
3. unsteady

- We're going to talk about what those words mean.

2. Touch word 1. ✓

- What word? (Signal.) *Location.*
- A **location** is a **place.** Everybody, what's another way of saying "She lives in that **place**"? (Signal.) *She lives in that location.*

3. Touch word 2. ✓

- What word? (Signal.) *Indicate.*
- To **indicate** means to **point out** or **signal.** Everybody, what's another way of saying "The clock **signals** that it is time for lunch"? (Signal.) *The clock indicates that it is time for lunch.*

4. Touch word 3. ✓

- What word? (Signal.) *Unsteady.*
- Who knows what **unsteady** means? (Call on a student.) (Ideas: *Shaky; not steady.*)

EXERCISE 5

WORD PRACTICE

1. Touch the first word in part 4. ✓

4

attention surge breathing burst

purchase special unsteady nitrogen

current grumbling swayed glimpse*

watches million worth die razor

anchor twenty smiled backward

bubbles layer sunken adventurous

sunlight purchased according studied

- What word? (Signal.) *Attention.*

2. Next word. ✓

- What word? (Signal.) *Surge.*

3. (Repeat step 2 for each remaining word.)
4. (Repeat each row of words until firm.)
5. What does **glimpse** mean? (Call on a student.)

EXERCISE 6

MULTIPART WORDS

Task A

1. Touch part 5. ✓

5

adjustment preventing exaggerated

1. adjustment 2. preventing 3. exaggerated

production military

4. production 5. military

> **Note:** The parts of a word are to be pronounced the same as they are when the word is spoken normally.

2. All these words have more than one part. The first part and the last part are circled.

3. Touch word 1. ✓
- Word 1 is **adjustment.** What word? (Signal.) *Adjustment.*
4. What's the first part? (Signal.) *ad.*
- What's the last part? (Signal.) *ment.*
- The middle part is spelled **J–U–S–T.** What does that part say in the word? (Signal.) *just.*
5. So, the parts are **ad** (pause) **just** (pause) **ment.**
- Say the whole word. (Signal.) *Adjustment.*
6. (Repeat steps 3–5 until firm.)
7. Touch word 2. ✓
- Word 2 is **preventing.** What word? (Signal.) *Preventing.*
8. What's the first part? (Signal.) *pre.*
- What's the last part? (Signal.) *ing.*
- The middle part is spelled **V–E–N–T.** What does that part say in the word? (Signal.) *vent.*
9. So, the parts are **pre** (pause) **vent** (pause) **ing.**
- Say the whole word. (Signal.) *Preventing.*
10. (Repeat steps 7–9 until firm.)
11. Touch word 3. ✓
- Word 3 is **exaggerated.** What word? (Signal.) *Exaggerated.*
12. What's the first part? (Signal.) *ex.*
- What's the last part? (Signal.) *ated.*
- The middle part is spelled **A–G–G–E–R.** What does that part say in the word? (Signal.) *agger.*
13. So, the parts are **ex** (pause) **agger** (pause) **ated.**
- Say the whole word. (Signal.) *Exaggerated.*
14. (Repeat steps 11–13 until firm.)
15. Touch word 4. ✓
- Word 4 is **production.** What word? (Signal.) *Production.*
16. What's the first part? (Signal.) *pro.*
- What's the last part? (Signal.) *tion.*
- The middle part is spelled **D–U–C.** What does that part say in the word? (Signal.) *duc.*
17. So, the parts are **pro** (pause) **duc** (pause) **tion.**
- Say the whole word. (Signal.) *Production.*
18. (Repeat steps 15–17 until firm.)
19. Touch word 5. ✓
- Word 5 is **military.** What word? (Signal.) *Military.*
20. What's the first part? (Signal.) *mil.*
- What's the last part? (Signal.) *ary.*
- The middle part is spelled **I–T.** What does that part say in the word? (Signal.) *it.*
21. So, the parts are **mil** (pause) **it** (pause) **ary.**
- Say the whole word. (Signal.) *Military.*
22. (Repeat steps 19–21 until firm.)

Task B

1. Touch the sentences below the word list. ✓

a. The president ordered a large adjustment in the size of the military.

b. The report exaggerated the company's production of trucks.

c. The bad weather was preventing military helicopters from landing.

d. Each month they made an adjustment in the production rate of furniture.

- These are sentences that use the words you just read.
2. Raise your hand when you can read sentence A. ✓
3. (Call on a student.) Read sentence A. *The president ordered a large adjustment in the size of the military.*
- That means "The president changed the size of the armed forces."
4. (Call on a student.) Read sentence B. *The report exaggerated the company's production of trucks.*
- That means "The report said that there were more trucks produced than there actually were."
5. (Call on a student.) Read sentence C. *The bad weather was preventing military helicopters from landing.*
- That means "The helicopters could not land, because of the bad weather."

6. (Call on a student.) Read sentence D. *Each month they made an adjustment in the production rate of furniture.*
- That means "Each month they changed how much furniture they made."

EXERCISE 7

WORD-ATTACK SKILLS: Individual tests

1. (Call on individual students. Each student reads a row of words, a column of words, or a sentence. In the Multipart words exercises, each sentence counts as one row of words. Tally the rows, columns, and sentences read without error. If the group reads at least 14 rows and columns without making errors, direct all students to record 5 points in Box A of their Point Chart. Criterion is 80 percent of rows and columns read without error.)
2. (If the group did not read at least 14 rows and columns without errors, do not award any points for the Word-Attack Skills exercises.)

SELECTION READING

EXERCISE 8

STORY READING

1. (Call on individual students to answer these questions.)
- The weather caused one of the problems Jane and Doris had in the last selection. What was that problem? (Idea: *They might not be able to go diving if a dangerous northeast wind came in.*)
- What did they decide to do? (Idea: *They decided to go diving anyway.*)
- What problem did the clerk who filled the boat's gas tanks tell them about? (Idea: *That the currents in the reef could be dangerous.*)
- What happened? (Accept reasonable summaries.)

2. Everybody, touch part 6. ✓
3. The error limit for this story is 12. If the group reads the story with 12 errors or less, you earn 5 points.

6 **Jane and Doris Take a Dive**

4. (Call on a student to read the title.) *Jane and Doris Take a Dive.*
- What do you think this story is about? (Accept reasonable responses.)
5. (Call on individual students. Each is to read two to four sentences.)
6. (Call on individual students to answer the specified questions during the story reading.)

According to a map that Doris and Jane had studied, a ship with more than fifty million dollars' worth of gold had gone down at a location near the middle of the reef. That ship had gone down more than two hundred years ago, and nobody had ever found it. It was hard to say just where the ship went down because the reef changes shape from year to year. The reef is made up of millions of tiny creatures—some living and some dead. The coral shells of these little creatures can be sharp as razors.

"This looks like a good location," Doris said as the boat moved between two lines of coral that stuck up above the water. Doris tossed the anchor over the side. Doris lowered the diving flags into the water. Then Jane slipped her arms into the loops on her air tanks. ❶

1. Where had the ship gone down? (Idea: *Near the middle of the reef.*)
1. How long ago had the ship gone down? *More than 200 years ago.*
1. What is a reef made up of? (Idea: *Millions of tiny creatures.*)
1. How did Jane put on the air tanks? (Idea: *She slipped her arms into the loops on her air tanks.*)

"We'll stay down for one hour," Jane said. "Set your watch." Both Jane and Doris had large diving watches with special markers to indicate how long they had been underwater.

Doris cautioned, "Now don't get too adventurous. Stay on the east side of the reef. And don't go down more than fifty feet."

Jane said, "Right. And don't get too close to the reef. That coral will cut like a razor." ❷

2. What kind of watches did Jane and Doris have? **(Idea:** *Large diving watches.***)**
2. What kind of markers did the watches have? **(Idea:** *Special markers that indicate how long you've been underwater.***)**
2. Why was it dangerous to get close to the reef? **(Idea:** *Because the coral is razor sharp.***)**

Doris put her arm around Jane and patted her on the shoulder. "Good luck," she said. She smiled, but her eyes looked a little unsteady.

Jane sat on the side of the boat with her feet on the boat's floor. Then she fell backward into the water, holding her mask so that water wouldn't leak in. She looked around underwater and could see Doris in a cloud of bubbles. Jane waved. Doris waved. Then the women started to swim along the reef. In some places large plants grew from the reef and swayed slowly in the current of the water, like grass bending in a wind. "Watch those plants," Jane said to herself. "They indicate how the current is flowing." ❸

3. Why did Jane watch the plants? **(Idea:** *Because they indicate how the current is flowing.***)**

Suddenly Jane heard a funny grumbling sound. She looked around and saw that Doris was pointing to something. Jane swam over and looked. Three sponges were stuck to the reef about twenty feet below Doris. Sponges are worth a lot of money. The sponges on the reef were probably worth five dollars each. Jane pointed down, and then she swam down. She pulled two of the sponges from the rock. Doris pulled off the other sponge. Then Jane and Doris returned to the surface. Jane's mask was fogged. She pushed it up and said, "Doris, we may get rich just finding sponges. Who needs a sunken ship?" ❹

4. What did the teachers find attached to the reef? *Sponges.*
4. How much were the sponges worth? **(Idea:** *About five dollars each.***)**

Doris smiled. Jane and Doris swam to the boat and tossed the sponges over the side. Jane explained, "I think I'll go back down there and see if I can find any more sponges."

Jane fixed her mouthpiece in her mouth, put her mask in place, and went underwater about thirty feet. She passed through a school of little silver fish that flashed in the sunlight. She peeked into the caves along the reef. She went down another fifteen feet. She was looking very hard for sponges, but she was not paying attention to the plants and how they were waving in the current. ❺

5. How far down did Jane dive altogether? **(Idea:** *About 45 feet.***)**
5. Did Jane seem to have trouble swimming with a leg brace? **(Idea:** *No.***)**
5. What was Jane looking for? *Sponges.*
5. What should Jane have been watching? **(Idea:** *How the plants were moving in the current.***)**

7. (Award points quickly.)
8. (If the group makes more than 12 errors, repeat the reading immediately or on the next day.)

FLUENCY ASSESSMENT

EXERCISE 9

TIMED READING CHECKOUTS

1. (For this part of the lesson, assigned pairs of students work together during the checkouts.)
   - (If one student does not have a checkout partner, arrange another time when you can give the checkout.)
2. (Each student does a 2-minute timed reading. Students earn 5 points by reading at least 220 words and making no more than 4 errors on the first part of story 19. Students record points in Box C of their Point Chart and plot their reading rate and errors on the Individual Reading Progress Chart.)
   - (During each timed checkout, observe one pair of students for 2 minutes. Make notes on any mistakes the reader makes.)
3. (Record the timed reading checkout performance for each student you observed on the Fluency Assessment Summary form.)

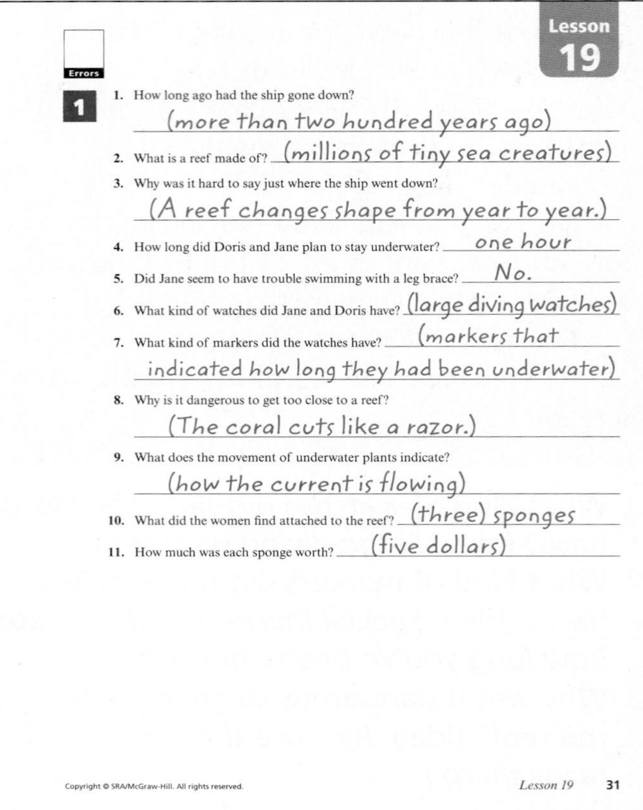

Lesson 19

Errors

1

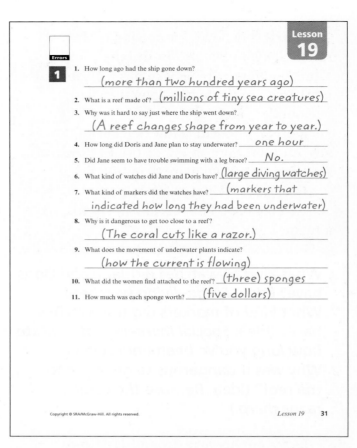

1. How long ago had the ship gone down? (more than two hundred years ago)
2. What is a reef made of? (millions of tiny sea creatures)
3. Why was it hard to say just where the ship went down? (A reef changes shape from year to year.)
4. How long did Doris and Jane plan to stay underwater? one hour
5. Did Jane seem to have trouble swimming with a leg brace? No.
6. What kind of watches did Jane and Doris have? (large diving watches)
7. What kind of markers did the watches have? (markers that indicated how long they had been underwater)
8. Why is it dangerous to get too close to a reef? (The coral cuts like a razor.)
9. What does the movement of underwater plants indicate? (how the current is flowing)
10. What did the women find attached to the reef? (three) sponges
11. How much was each sponge worth? (five dollars)

Copyright © SRA/McGraw-Hill. All rights reserved.

Lesson 19 31

WORKBOOK EXERCISES

Independent Student Work

Task A

- Open your Workbook to Lesson 19. ✓
- Complete all parts of your Workbook lesson using a pencil. If you make no errors, you will earn 5 points.

Task B

1. (Before presenting Lesson 20, check student Workbooks for Lesson 19.)
   - (Call on individual students to read the items and answers in each part. Students mark errors using a pen.)
2. (Direct the students to count the number of errors and write the number in the Errors box at the top of the Workbook page.)
3. (Award points and direct students to record points in Box D of their Point Chart.)

   0 errors................................5 points
   1 error ....3 points
   2 or 3 errors ....1 point
   more than 3 errors ....0 points

END OF LESSON 19

Lesson 19

2 **Fill in each blank using a word in the box.**

current	nitrogen	glimpse
location	unsteady	indicate

1. No one could find the location of the hidden treasure.
2. The skater fell down because he was unsteady.
3. Jane and Doris set up buoys to indicate that divers were in the water.

3 **Write the parts for each word.**

1. meaning = mean + ing
2. screeching = screech + ing
3. steepness = steep + ness
4. roughly = rough + ly

32 *Lesson 19* Copyright © SRA/McGraw-Hill. All rights reserved.

Lesson 20

WORD-ATTACK SKILLS

Student Book 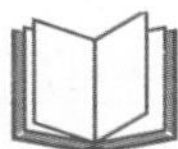

EXERCISE 1

SOUND COMBINATION: ee

Task A

1. Open your Student Book to Lesson 20. ✓

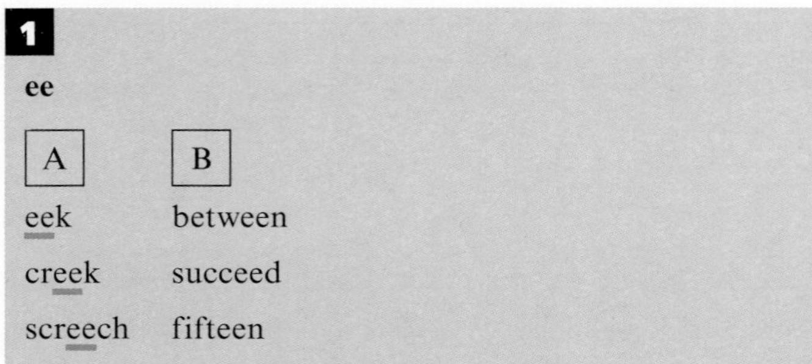

1

ee

A	B
eek	between
creek	succeed
screech	fifteen

- Touch the letters **E–E** in part 1. ✓
- What sound do the letters **E–E** make? (Signal.) *ēēē.*

2. You're going to say the sound for the underlined part and then read the word.
3. Touch the first word in column A. ✓
- What sound? (Signal.) *ēēē.*
- What word? (Signal.) *Eek.*

4. Touch the next word. ✓
- What sound? (Signal.) *ēēē.*
- What word? (Signal.) *Creek.*

5. (Repeat step 4 for **screech**.)

Task B

1. Touch the first word in column B. ✓
- What word? (Signal.) *Between.*

2. Touch the next word. ✓
- What word? (Signal.) *Succeed.*

3. (Repeat step 2 for **fifteen.**)
4. (Repeat steps 1–3 until firm.)

EXERCISE 2

WORD PRACTICE

1. Touch the first word in part 2. ✓

2

breathing hurt pounding barge decide

started about creature grinder except

- What sound? (Signal.) *ēēē.*
- What word? (Signal.) *Breathing.*

2. Touch the next word. ✓
- What sound? (Signal.) *er.*
- What word? (Signal.) *Hurt.*

3. (Repeat step 2 for each remaining word.)
4. (Repeat each row of words until firm.)

EXERCISE 3

VOCABULARY

1. Touch part 3. ✓

1. surface
2. ledge
3. nitrogen

- We're going to talk about what those words mean.

2. Touch word 1. ✓
- What word? (Signal.) *Surface.*
- The **surface** of a highway is the **top** of the highway. Everybody, what's the **surface** of the water? (Signal.) *The top of the water.*

3. Touch word 2. ✓
- What word? (Signal.) *Ledge.*
- A **ledge** is a **narrow shelf.** Everybody, what's another way of saying "The plant was on the **narrow shelf**"? (Signal.) *The plant was on the ledge.*

4. Touch word 3. ✓
- What word? (Signal.) *Nitrogen.*
- **Nitrogen** is **a gas that has no smell or color.** Everybody, what is **nitrogen?** (Signal.) *A gas that has no smell or color.*

EXERCISE 4

WORD PRACTICE

1. Touch the first word in part 4. ✓

4

scream mound burst aloud squint
grumbling farther drifting tilted
continued disk frightened indicate*
tried current moving surge suddenly*
oxygen mouthpiece hidden heart
nobody hundred relax pressing razor
bottle bubbles sunken caught
goose panic cause thought

- What word? (Signal.) *Scream.*
2. Next word. ✓
- What word? (Signal.) *Mound.*
3. (Repeat step 2 for each remaining word.)
4. (Repeat each row of words until firm.)
5. What does **indicate** mean? (Call on a student.)
- (Repeat for **suddenly.**)

EXERCISE 5

MULTIPART WORDS

Task A

1. Touch part 5. ✓

5

occasion selective improvement
1. occasion 2. selective 3. improvement
incapable particular
4. incapable 5. particular

> **Note:** The parts of a word are to be pronounced the same as they are when the word is spoken normally.

2. All these words have more than one part. The first part and the last part are circled.
3. Touch word 1. ✓
- Word 1 is **occasion.** What word? (Signal.) *Occasion.*
4. What's the first part? (Signal.) *oc.*
- What's the last part? (Signal.) *sion.*
- The middle part is spelled **C–A.** What does that part say in the word? (Signal.) *ca.*
5. So, the parts are **oc** (pause) **ca** (pause) **sion.**
- Say the whole word. (Signal.) *Occasion.*
6. (Repeat steps 3–5 until firm.)
7. Touch word 2. ✓
- Word 2 is **selective.** What word? (Signal.) *Selective.*
8. What's the first part? (Signal.) *se.*
- What's the last part? (Signal.) *tive.*
- The middle part is spelled **L–E–C.** What does that part say in the word? (Signal.) *lec.*
9. So, the parts are **se** (pause) **lec** (pause) **tive.**
- Say the whole word. (Signal.) *Selective.*
10. (Repeat steps 7–9 until firm.)
11. Touch word 3. ✓
- Word 3 is **improvement.** What word? (Signal.) *Improvement.*
12. What's the first part? (Signal.) *im.*
- What's the last part? (Signal.) *ment.*
- The middle part is spelled **P–R–O–V–E.** What does that part say in the word? (Signal.) *prove.*
13. So, the parts are **im** (pause) **prove** (pause) **ment.**
- Say the whole word. (Signal.) *Improvement.*
14. (Repeat steps 11–13 until firm.)
15. Touch word 4. ✓
- Word 4 is **incapable.** What word? (Signal.) *Incapable.*
16. What's the first part? (Signal.) *in.*
- What's the last part? (Signal.) *able.*
- The middle part is spelled **C–A–P.** What does that part say in the word? (Signal.) *cape.* Yes, in this word, **C–A–P** is pronounced **cape.**
17. So, the parts are **in** (pause) **cap** (pause) **able.**
- Say the whole word. (Signal.) *Incapable.*
18. (Repeat steps 15–17 until firm.)
19. Touch word 5. ✓

20. Word 5 is **particular.** What word? (Signal.) *Particular.*
21. What's the first part? (Signal.) *par.*
   - What's the last part? (Signal.) *lar.*
   - The middle part is spelled **T–I–C–U.** What does that part say in the word? (Signal.) *ticu.*
22. So, the parts are **par** (pause) **ticu** (pause) **lar.**
   - Say the whole word. (Signal.) *Particular.*
23. (Repeat steps 20–22 until firm.)

Task B

1. Touch the sentences below the word list. ✓

a. The team seemed to be incapable of much improvement.

b. It was snowing on that particular occasion.

c. She was very selective about the people she invited to dinner.

d. We saw great improvement from one occasion to the next.

   - These are sentences that use the words you just read.
2. Raise your hand when you can read sentence A. ✓
3. (Call on a student.) Read sentence A. *The team seemed to be incapable of much improvement.*
   - That means "It looks as if the team can't get much better than it is now."
4. (Call on a student.) Read sentence B. *It was snowing on that particular occasion.*
   - That means "On a certain day, it was snowing."
5. (Call on a student.) Read sentence C. *She was very selective about the people she invited to dinner.*
   - That means "She was particularly choosy about whom she invited to dinner."
6. (Call on a student.) Read sentence D. *We saw great improvement from one occasion to the next.*
   - That means "Things looked better the second time we observed than they did the first time we observed."

EXERCISE 6

WORD-ATTACK SKILLS: Individual tests

1. (Call on individual students. Each student reads a row of words, a column of words, or a sentence. In the Multipart words exercises, each sentence counts as one row of words. Tally the rows, columns, and sentences read without error. If the group reads at least 14 rows and columns without making errors, direct all students to record 5 points in Box A of their Point Chart. Criterion is 80 percent of rows and columns read without error.)
2. (If the group did not read at least 14 rows and columns without errors, do not award any points for the Word-Attack Skills exercises.)

SELECTION READING

EXERCISE 7

STORY READING

1. (Call on individual students to answer these questions.)
   - The **setting** of a story is **where the story takes place.** What was the **setting** for the last selection? (Ideas: *Near a coral reef off the coast of Florida; underwater.*)
   - What did the women hope to find there? *A sunken ship.*
   - What happened? (Accept reasonable summaries.)
2. Everybody, touch part 6. ✓
3. The error limit for this story is 12. If the group reads the story with 12 errors or less, you earn 5 points.

6 **Caught in the Current**

4. (Call on a student to read the title.) *Caught in the Current.*
   - What do you think this story is about? (Accept reasonable responses.)
5. (Call on individual students. Each is to read two to four sentences.)

6. (Call on individual students to answer the specified questions during the story reading.)

Jane was about 45 feet below the surface, swimming next to the reef and looking for sponges. Suddenly she felt something tug at her. It was the current. Her legs were pulled by the current that sped through a break in the reef. Jane could hear herself breathing very hard. She kicked and tried to swim up, but she could not move up. She was slowly drifting down. She kicked again and pulled with her arms as hard as she could, but now she was moving down even faster. She reached out and grabbed a ledge of coral. She felt something cut through her rubber glove. She let go and slid down. ❶

1. What was pulling at Jane? *The current.*
1. Why couldn't Jane swim up? (Idea: *The current was too strong.*)
1. Why did Jane let go of the coral? (Ideas: *Because it was sharp; it cut through her glove.*)

The current pulled Jane down about ten feet. Then it began to move her east through the break in the reef. Jane wanted to scream for help, but she remained silent except for the bubbles that came from her mouth and the pounding of her heart. "I've got to get out of here," she said to herself.

"Relax," she told herself. "Don't panic. Don't panic." The current pulled her through the break in the reef. Then it started to pull her down again, but not as hard. Jane tried to swim up again. She pulled with her arms. She kicked until her legs hurt, but it was no use.

"I'll have to go with the current," she decided. "I just hope that it lets me go pretty soon." The current continued to pull her down, deep into darker water. ❷

2. Why was Jane going with the current? (Ideas: *Because she couldn't fight it; the current was too strong.*)
2. Where was the current pulling Jane? (Idea: *Down.*)
2. Which of Jane's legs would probably hurt the most? (Idea: *The one with the brace.*)

Jane could not see the bottom below her. She could see only darkness. When she looked up, the sun didn't look like a white disk anymore. It looked yellow-green. "Relax," she reminded herself as she drifted with the current.

She looked down again. "I must be sixty feet deep," she said to herself. "I must—what's that?" Jane looked down. The water was pressing Jane's mask against her face so hard that she had to squint to see the dark form that was on the bottom. Was it a mound of coral? Or was it too dark to be coral? What was that long thin line next to it? Jane was almost afraid to say to herself, "It's a ship." But it was. The mast was next to the ship. The hull was tilted with part of it hidden under sand.

"It's a ship," Jane said to herself. "I see a ship." She was all mixed-up. She was frightened. Her heart was beating like the coffee-grinder engine of their boat. She could feel goose bumps forming on her arms. "I am looking at a ship that nobody has seen in over two hundred years. Wow!" At the same time, part of Jane's mind was saying, "I just hope I live to tell somebody about it." ❸

3. Why did Jane feel mixed-up? (Idea: *She was afraid she was going to die, and she was excited to see the underwater ship.*)

The current was pushing her past the ship, but now it seemed to be pushing her up. Again, Jane tried to swim up. This time she began to go up. "Stop," she thought. "If you go up too fast, you'll get the bends."

When somebody gets the bends, bubbles form in the blood. When you open a soft drink bottle, bubbles form because the pressure on the liquid drops when you open the bottle. The same thing happens when divers come up to the surface too fast. As they come up, the pressure on the blood drops. If the pressure drops too fast, bubbles of nitrogen will form in the blood. These nitrogen bubbles can burst blood vessels and cause great pain.

Jane wanted to get to the surface so that she could mark the spot where she saw the sunken ship. She was still drifting farther and farther from the ship. But she had to wait before going up to the surface. She waited and drifted. ④

4. Why did Jane want to get up to the surface? (Idea: *To mark the place where the sunken ship was.*)

4. Why did Jane have to wait before she went to the surface? (Idea: *Because she could get the bends if she came up too fast.*)
4. What happens when someone gets the bends? (Idea: *Bubbles of nitrogen form in the blood.*)
4. What can nitrogen bubbles do? (Idea: *They can burst blood vessels and cause great pain.*)
7. (Award points quickly.)
8. (If the group makes more than 12 errors, repeat the reading immediately or on the next day.)

FLUENCY ASSESSMENT

EXERCISE 8

TIMED READING CHECKOUTS

1. (For this part of the lesson, assigned pairs of students work together during the checkouts.)
- (If one student does not have a checkout partner, arrange another time when you can give the checkout.)
2. (Each student does a 2-minute timed reading. Students earn 5 points by reading at least 220 words and making no more than 4 errors on the first part of story 20. Students record points in Box C of their Point Chart and plot their reading rate and errors on the Individual Reading Progress Chart.)
- (During each timed checkout, observe one pair of students for 2 minutes. Make notes on any mistakes the reader makes.)
3. (Record the timed reading checkout performance for each student you observed on the Fluency Assessment Summary form.)

WORKBOOK EXERCISES

Independent Student Work

Task A

- Open your Workbook to Lesson 20. ✓
- Complete all parts of your Workbook lesson using a pencil. If you make no errors, you will earn 5 points.

Task B

1. (Before presenting Lesson 21, check student Workbooks for Lesson 20.)
   - (Call on individual students to read the items and answers in each part. Students mark errors using a pen.)
2. (Direct the students to count the number of errors and write the number in the Errors box at the top of the Workbook page.)
3. (Award points and direct students to record points in Box D of their Point Chart.)

   0 errors................................5 points
   1 error ....3 points
   2 or 3 errors ....1 point
   more than 3 errors ....0 points

Point schedule for Lessons 16 through 20

Box	Lesson part	Points
A	Word Attack	0 or 5
B	Selection Reading	0 or 5
C	Timed Reading Checkout	0 or 5
D	Workbook	0, 1, 3, or 5
Bonus	(Teacher option)	—

Five-lesson point summary

- (For **letter grades** based on points for Lessons **16** through **20,** tell students to compute the total for the blue boxes [C, D, and Bonus] and write the number in the Total box at the end of each row in their Point Chart. Students then add the totals and write the sum in the green box.)
- (For **rewards** based on points, tell students to compute the total for all boxes [A, B, C, D, and Bonus] and write the number in the Total box at the end of each row. Students then add the totals and write the sum in the green box.)

Lesson 20

Errors

1

1. Why did Jane let go of the coral? (because she felt something cut through her rubber glove)
2. Why was Jane going with the current? (She couldn't fight it.)
3. Why did Jane have to squint to see the dark form below? (The water was pressing the mask against her face so hard.)
4. Where was the ship? (on the bottom)
5. How did Jane feel when she saw the ship? (mixed-up)
6. Jane's heart was beating like the (coffee-grinder engine of their boat)
7. What did Jane feel forming on her arms? goose bumps
8. If a diver comes up too fast, the diver can get the bends
9. What can nitrogen bubbles do to a diver? (burst blood vessels; cause great pain)
10. Why did Jane want to get up to the surface? (so she could mark the spot where she saw the sunken ship)

Copyright © SRA/McGraw-Hill. All rights reserved. Lesson 20 33

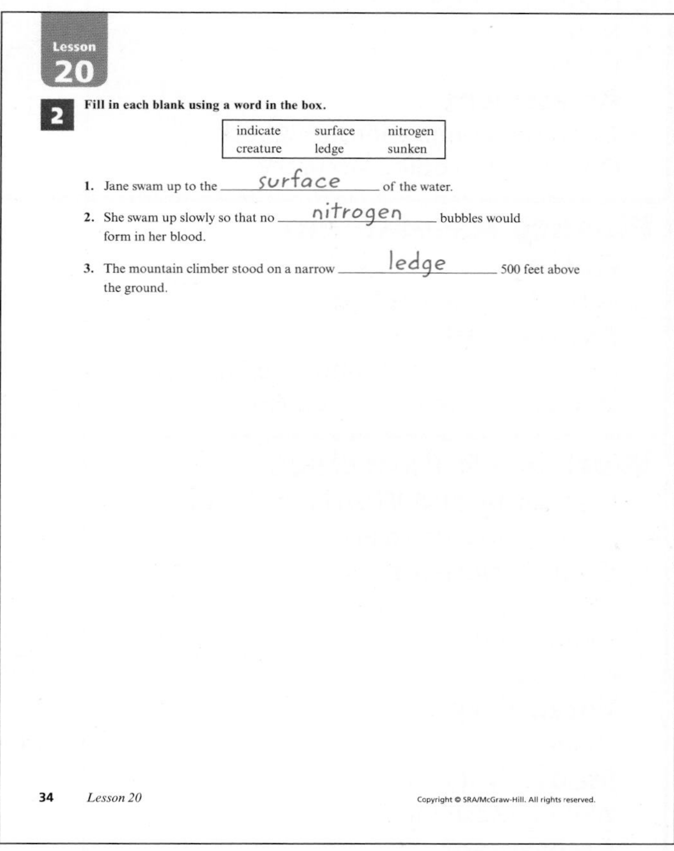
Lesson 20

2 Fill in each blank using a word in the box.

indicate	surface	nitrogen
creature	ledge	sunken

1. Jane swam up to the surface of the water.
2. She swam up slowly so that no nitrogen bubbles would form in her blood.
3. The mountain climber stood on a narrow ledge 500 feet above the ground.

34 Lesson 20 Copyright © SRA/McGraw-Hill. All rights reserved.

END OF LESSON 20

Lesson Objectives	LESSON 21	LESSON 22	LESSON 23	LESSON 24	LESSON 25
	Exercise	Exercise	Exercise	Exercise	Exercise
Word Attack					
Decoding and Word Analysis					
Sound Combinations: *ch, sh, wh*	1				
Sound Combinations: *th, wh*		1			
Sound Combination: *igh*			1		
Sound Combination: *al*				1	
Sound Combination: *oa*					1
Multisyllabic Word Strategies	5	5	5	5	5
Letter Combinations/Letter Sounds	2	2	2	2	2
Word Recognition	1–5	1–5	1–5	1–5	1–5
High-Frequency/Sight Words	5	5	5	5	5
Vocabulary					
Definitions	3, 4	3, 4	2, 4	3, 4	3, 4
Usage	3, 5	3, 5	3, 5	3, 5	3, 5
Assessment					
Ongoing: Individual Tests	6	6	6	6	6
Group Reading					
Decoding and Word Analysis					
Read Decodable Text	7	7	7	7	7
Comprehension					
Access Prior Knowledge	7			7	
Draw Inferences	7	7	7	7	7
Note Details	7	7	7	7	7
Predict	7	7	7	7	7
Assessment					
Ongoing: Comprehension Check	7	7	7	7	7
Ongoing: Decoding Accuracy	7	7	7	7	7
Fluency Assessment					
Fluency					
Reread Decodable Text	8	8	8	8	8
Assessment					
Ongoing: Teacher-Monitored Fluency	8	8	8	8	8
Ongoing: Peer-Monitored Fluency	8	8	8	8	8
Workbook Exercises					
Decoding and Word Analysis					
Multisyllabic Word Parts	Ind. Work		Ind. Work		
Comprehension					
Main Idea			9		9
Sequencing		Ind. Work			
Note Details	Ind. Work	Ind. Work	Ind. Work	Ind. Work	Ind. Work
Vocabulary					
Usage	Ind. Work	Ind. Work	Ind. Work	Ind. Work	Ind. Work
Study Skills					
Writing Mechanics			9		9
Assessment					
Ongoing: Workcheck	Workcheck	Workcheck	Workcheck	Workcheck	Workcheck

WORD-ATTACK SKILLS

Student Book 

EXERCISE 1

NEW SOUND COMBINATIONS: ch, sh, wh

Task A

1. Open your Student Book to Lesson 21. ✓

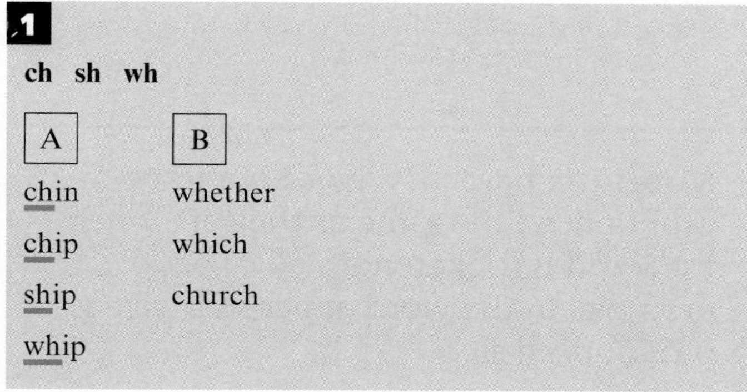

1

ch sh wh

A	B
chin	whether
chip	which
ship	church
whip	

- Touch the letters **C–H** in part 1. ✓
- The letters **C–H** go together and make the sound **ch.** What sound? (Signal.) *ch.*

2. Touch the letters **S–H.** ✓
- The letters **S–H** go together and make the sound **shshsh.** What sound? (Signal.) *shshsh.*

3. Touch the letters **W–H.** ✓
- The letters **W–H** go together and make the sound **www.** What sound? (Signal.) *www.*

4. Your turn. Tell me the sound each combination makes.
- Touch the letters **C–H.** ✓ What sound? (Signal.) *ch.*
- Touch the letters **S–H.** ✓ What sound? (Signal.) *shshsh.*
- Touch the letters **W–H.** ✓ What sound? (Signal.) *www.*

5. (Repeat step 4 until firm.)

Task B

1. You're going to say the sound for the underlined part and then read the word.
2. Touch the first word in column A. ✓
- What sound? (Signal.) *ch.*
- What word? (Signal.) *Chin.*

3. Touch the next word. ✓
- What sound? (Signal.) *ch.*
- What word? (Signal.) *Chip.*

4. (Repeat step 3 for **ship, whip.**)

Task C

- Touch the first word in column B. ✓
- What word? (Signal.) *Whether.*

2. Touch the next word. ✓
- What word? (Signal.) *Which.*

3. (Repeat step 2 for **church.**)
4. (Repeat steps 1–3 until firm.)

EXERCISE 2

WORD PRACTICE

1. Touch the first word in part 2. ✓

2

surfacing succeed remained burnt

speech returned teachers

- What sound? (Signal.) *sss.*
- What word? (Signal.) *Surfacing.*

2. Touch the next word. ✓
- What sound? (Signal.) *ēēē.*
- What word? (Signal.) *Succeed.*

3. (Repeat step 2 for each remaining word.)
4. (Repeat each row of words until firm.)

EXERCISE 3

VOCABULARY

1. Touch part 3. ✓

3

1. decide
2. gasp
3. sprawl
4. immediately

- We're going to talk about what those words mean.

2. Touch word 1. ✓
- What word? (Signal.) *Decide.*
- What do you do when you **decide** something? (Call on a student.) (Idea: *You make up your mind about something.*)

3. Everybody, touch word 2. ✓
- What word? (Signal.) *Gasp.*
- When a person **takes short, fast breaths,** that person **gasps.** Everybody, what's another way of saying "After swimming, she **took short, fast breaths**"? (Signal.) *After swimming, she gasped.*

4. Touch word 3. ✓
- What word? (Signal.) *Sprawl.*
- To **sprawl** is to **stretch out.** Everybody, what's another way of saying "The boy **stretched out** on the floor"? Signal. *The boy sprawled on the floor.*

5. Touch word 4. ✓
- What word? (Signal.) *Immediately.*
- What does **immediately** mean? (Call on a student.) (Idea: *Something happens right away.*)

EXERCISE 4

WORD PRACTICE

1. Touch the first word in part 4. ✓

4

darkness thirty pounding warn

meant warm exclaimed* water

trembling wobbly intended gauge

might indicate* gasped speck

second closer pointed somewhere right

climbed scared caught grinder pressing

wrong trying realized however disk

listen though wrist thought

- What word? (Signal.) *Darkness.*

2. Next word. ✓
- What word? (Signal.) *Thirty.*

3. (Repeat step 2 for each remaining word.)
4. (Repeat each row of words until firm.)
5. What does **exclaimed** mean? (Call on a student.)
- (Repeat for **indicate.**)

EXERCISE 5

MULTIPART WORDS

Task A

1. Touch part 5. ✓

5

expensive responsible approval

1. expensive 2. responsible 3. approval

unfortunate entirely

4. unfortunate 5. entirely

Note: The parts of a word are to be pronounced the same as they are when the word is spoken normally. For example, in the word **expensive, sive** is pronounced **siv.**

2. All these words have more than one part. The first part and the last part are circled.
3. Touch word 1. ✓
- Word 1 is **expensive.** What word? (Signal.) *Expensive.*

4. What's the first part? (Signal.) *ex.*
- What's the last part? (Signal.) *sive.* (Pronounce as **siv,** not **sive.**)
- The middle part is spelled **P–E–N.** What does that part say in the word? (Signal.) *pen.*

5. So, the parts are **ex** (pause) **pen** (pause) **sive.**
- Say the whole word. (Signal.) *Expensive.*

6. (Repeat steps 3–5 until firm.)
7. Touch word 2. ✓
- Word 2 is **responsible.** What word? (Signal.) *Responsible.*

8. What's the first part? (Signal.) *re.*
- What's the last part? (Signal.) *ible.*
- The middle part is spelled **S–P–O–N–S.** What does that part say in the word? (Signal.) *spons.*

9. So, the parts are **re** (pause) **spons** (pause) **ible.**
- Say the whole word. (Signal.) *Responsible.*

10. (Repeat steps 7–9 until firm.)

11. Touch word 3. ✓
   - Word 3 is **approval.** What word? (Signal.) *Approval.*
12. What's the first part? (Signal.) *ap.*
   - What's the last part? (Signal.) *al.*
   - The middle part is spelled **P–R–O–V.** What does that part say in the word? (Signal.) *proov.* Yes, in this word **P–R–O–V** is pronounced **proov.**
13. So, the parts are **ap** (pause) **prov** (pause) **al.**
   - Say the whole word. (Signal.) *Approval.*
14. (Repeat steps 11–13 until firm.)
15. Touch word 4. ✓
   - Word 4 is **unfortunate.** What word? (Signal.) *Unfortunate.*
16. What's the first part? (Signal.) *un.*
   - What's the last part? (Signal.) *ate.*
   - The middle part is spelled **F–O–R–T–U–N.** What does that part say in the word? (Signal.) *fortun.*
17. So, the parts are **un** (pause) **fortun** (pause) **ate.**
   - Say the whole word. (Signal.) *Unfortunate.*
18. (Repeat steps 15–17 until firm.)
19. Touch word 5. ✓
   - Word 5 is **entirely.** What word? (Signal.) *Entirely.*
20. What's the first part? (Signal.) *en.*
   - What's the last part? (Signal.) *ly.*
   - The middle part is spelled **T–I–R–E.** What does that part say in the word? (Signal.) *tire.*
21. So, the parts are **en** (pause) **tire** (pause) **ly.**
   - Say the whole word. (Signal.) *Entirely.*
22. (Repeat steps 19–21 until firm.)

Task B

1. Touch the sentences below the word list. ✓

> a. The shoes were entirely too expensive.
>
> b. They hoped they would get approval from their friends.
>
> c. He was entirely responsible for the unfortunate situation.
>
> d. It's unfortunate that the bike is so expensive.

   - These are sentences that use the words you just read.
2. Raise your hand when you can read sentence A. ✓
3. (Call on a student.) Read sentence A. *The shoes were entirely too expensive.*
   - That means "The shoes cost way too much."
4. (Call on a student.) Read sentence B. *They hoped they would get approval from their friends.*
   - That means "They hoped their friends would support them for what they did."
5. (Call on a student.) Read sentence C. *He was entirely responsible for the unfortunate situation.*
   - That means "He was the one to cause the bad things that happened."
6. (Call on a student.) Read sentence D. *It's unfortunate that the bike is so expensive.*
   - That means "It's too bad the bike costs so much."

EXERCISE 6

WORD-ATTACK SKILLS: Individual tests

1. (Call on individual students. Each student reads a row of words, a column of words, or a sentence. In the Multipart words exercises, each sentence counts as one row of words. Tally the rows, columns, and sentences read without error. If the group reads at least 14 rows and columns without making errors, direct all students to record 5 points in Box A of their Point Chart. Criterion is 80 percent of rows and columns read without error.)
2. (If the group did not read at least 14 rows and columns without errors, do not award any points for the Word-Attack Skills exercises.)

SELECTION READING

EXERCISE 7

STORY READING

1. (Call on individual students to answer these questions.)
- What problem did Jane have in the last selection? (Idea: *She was caught in the current.*)
- The bends can cause serious problems. What kinds of problems? (Idea: *Nitrogen bubbles can form in the blood, bursting blood vessels and causing great pain.*)
2. Everybody, touch part 6. ✓
3. The error limit for this story is 12. If the group reads the story with 12 errors or less, you earn 5 points.

6 **Deep in Dark Water**

4. (Call on a student to read the title.) *Deep in Dark Water.*
- What do you think this story is about? (Accept reasonable responses.)
5. (Call on individual students. Each is to read two to four sentences.)
6. (Call on individual students to answer the specified questions during the story reading.)

Jane remained underwater for another five minutes before surfacing. During that time she tried not to drift too far from the sunken ship. But when she came up, she saw that she was far from the reef, which meant that she was far from the ship. Jane's boat looked as if it were half a mile away. A yellow speck was in the boat. "That's Doris," Jane said aloud. Jane was glad to see Doris, even though Doris was far away. Jane waved and yelled, "Hello." ❶

1. When Jane surfaced, was she close to the reef or far away? (Idea: *Far away.*)

A few seconds passed. Then Doris waved back. Jane put her mask down and started to swim back to the boat. When she was about fifty feet from the boat, she yelled, "I saw a ship. I saw it."

Doris said, "What?"

Jane swam closer. Then she yelled, "I saw a sunken ship."

Doris dove into the water without her mask or air tanks. She swam over to Jane. Out of breath, Doris gasped, "Where is it?" Jane turned around and pointed to a spot on the east side of the reef. "It's right over there, somewhere." ❷

2. Where was Jane pointing? (Idea: *To a spot on the east side of the reef.*)

"Show me," Doris said.

"Let me rest a minute," Jane said. "I got caught in the current and it scared me to death."

Doris said, "Let's sit in the boat a minute, and you can catch your breath."

So the teachers swam back to the boat. They climbed in, and Jane sprawled out in the bottom of the boat. The sun was a white disk directly overhead. It seemed to burn holes into Jane's eyes. Jane rolled over on her side. "I really saw it," she said. "It looked big and dark. I don't know why, but I got very scared when I saw it. I felt like I was seeing something that was trying to hide."

"Oh, I can't wait," Doris exclaimed. "Let's go see it. Right now."

"OK," Jane said. She stood up in the boat. Her hands were trembling, and her knees felt wobbly. She pointed to the east side of the reef. "It's over there, about 150 feet from the other side of the reef." ❸

3. How far is the ship from the reef? (Idea: *About 150 feet from the other side of the reef.*)
3. How had Jane felt when she saw the ship? *Scared.*

Jane decided they should swim to the other side of the reef and then dive down. Jane didn't want to let the currents take them past the ship. Before they went down, Jane said, "I think it's about 100 feet deep or more, but don't go all the way down. We don't have enough air. Don't go below sixty feet."

Down they went through a cloud of bubbles. Down. The water was getting darker. Jane couldn't see the bottom, yet she knew that her eyes would get used to the dark in a minute or so. Down. She could hear her heart pounding, and she could feel the mask pressing against her face. The sound of the bubbles coming from her mouth was very loud—lub–u–glub–u–lub. Down. "Something is wrong," Jane said to herself. Then she realized that more than one thing was wrong. The water was too warm. When she had passed over the ship before, the water was cold. And now there was no current. Were they in the wrong place? ❹

4. How did Jane know that they were in the wrong place? (Ideas: *The water was too warm; there was no current.*)
4. Why couldn't Jane and Doris go below sixty feet? (Idea: *Because they didn't have enough air.*)

Jane peered down. She couldn't see the bottom. She looked at the depth gauge on her wrist. "I've got to see the bottom," she thought. Down. Down. Jane kept looking and swimming. But she wasn't looking at her depth gauge or listening to the sound of her heart. She was now fifty feet down. Doris was above her, trying to signal her, but Jane was looking down and swimming slowly toward the bottom. ❺

5. What was Doris trying to do? (Idea: *Signal Jane.*)

Suddenly Jane stopped. She could see the bottom now. It was very far down. "This can't be the right place," she thought. "I had better go up." When she looked up, she realized that she had gone deeper than she had intended. The sun was green. Doris was a shadow above her. Jane looked at her watch and realized that she did not have enough air to stay underwater very long. If she returned to the surface immediately, however, she might get the bends. ❻

6. How much air did Jane have left? (Idea: *She didn't have enough air to stay underwater very long.*)
6. Why couldn't Jane go to the surface immediately? (Idea: *Because she might get the bends.*)
6. Why do you think that Doris had been signaling Jane? (Idea: *Doris was trying to warn Jane not to go too deep.*)
7. (Award points quickly.)
8. (If the group makes more than 12 errors, repeat the reading immediately or on the next day.)

FLUENCY ASSESSMENT

EXERCISE 8

NEW TIMED READING CHECKOUTS

Note: The rate-accuracy criterion for Lessons 21–50 is 240 words with no more than 5 errors. The 240th word is underlined in the reading selection in the Student Book.

1. (For this part of the lesson, assigned pairs of students work together during the checkouts.)
- (If one student does not have a checkout partner, arrange another time when you can give the checkout.)
2. (Each student does a 2-minute timed reading. Students earn 5 points by reading at least **240 words** and making no more than **5 errors** on the first part of story 21. Students record points in Box C of their Point Chart and plot their reading rate and errors on the Individual Reading Progress Chart.)
- (During each timed checkout, observe one pair of students for 2 minutes. Make notes on any mistakes the reader makes.)
3. (Record the timed reading checkout performance for each student you observed on the Fluency Assessment Summary form.)

WORKBOOK EXERCISES

Independent Student Work

Task A

- Open your Workbook to Lesson 21. ✓
- Complete all parts of your Workbook lesson using a pencil. If you make no errors, you will earn 5 points.

Task B

1. (Before presenting Lesson 22, check student Workbooks for Lesson 21.)
- (Call on individual students to read the items and answers in each part. Students mark errors using a pen.)
2. (Direct the students to count the number of errors and write the number in the Errors box at the top of the Workbook page.)
3. (Award points and direct students to record points in Box D of their Point Chart.)

0 errors.................................5 points
1 error ....3 points
2 or 3 errors ....1 point
more than 3 errors ....0 points

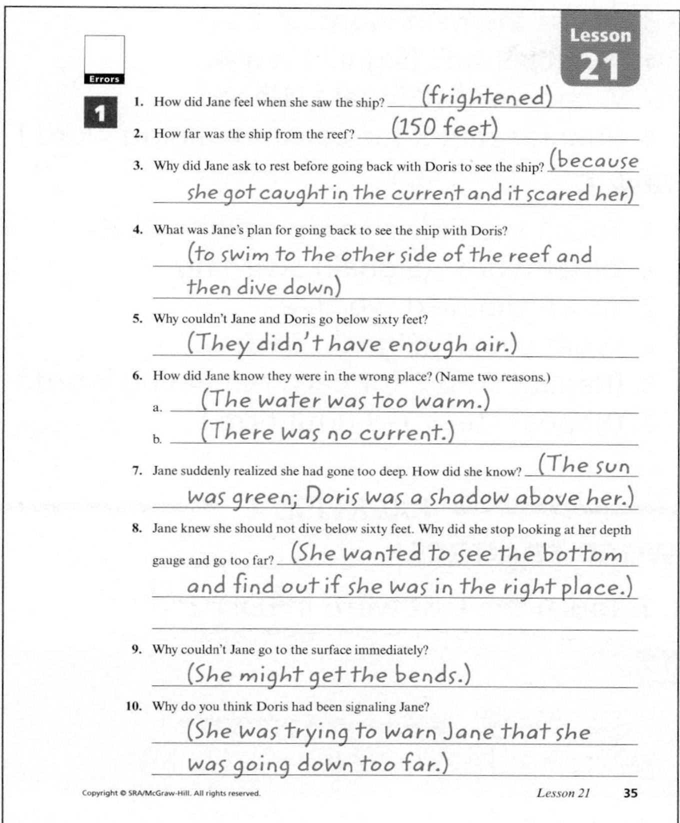

Lesson 21

Errors

1

1. How did Jane feel when she saw the ship? (frightened)
2. How far was the ship from the reef? (150 feet)
3. Why did Jane ask to rest before going back with Doris to see the ship? (because she got caught in the current and it scared her)
4. What was Jane's plan for going back to see the ship with Doris? (to swim to the other side of the reef and then dive down)
5. Why couldn't Jane and Doris go below sixty feet? (They didn't have enough air.)
6. How did Jane know they were in the wrong place? (Name two reasons.)
   a. (The water was too warm.)
   b. (There was no current.)
7. Jane suddenly realized she had gone too deep. How did she know? (The sun was green; Doris was a shadow above her.)
8. Jane knew she should not dive below sixty feet. Why did she stop looking at her depth gauge and go too far? (She wanted to see the bottom and find out if she was in the right place.)
9. Why couldn't Jane go to the surface immediately? (She might get the bends.)
10. Why do you think Doris had been signaling Jane? (She was trying to warn Jane that she was going down too far.)

Copyright © SRA/McGraw-Hill. All rights reserved. Lesson 21 35

Lesson 21

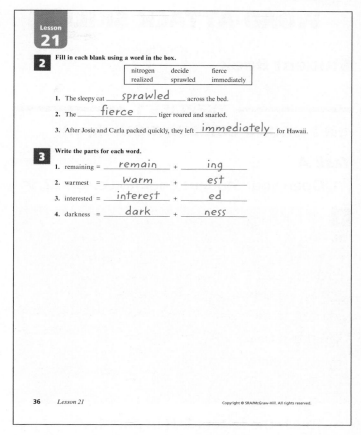

2 **Fill in each blank using a word in the box.**

nitrogen	decide	fierce
realized	sprawled	immediately

1. The sleepy cat sprawled across the bed.
2. The fierce tiger roared and snarled.
3. After Josie and Carla packed quickly, they left immediately for Hawaii.

3 **Write the parts for each word.**

1. remaining = remain + ing
2. warmest = warm + est
3. interested = interest + ed
4. darkness = dark + ness

36 Lesson 21 Copyright © SRA/McGraw-Hill. All rights reserved.

END OF LESSON 21

Lesson 22

WORD-ATTACK SKILLS

Student Book

EXERCISE 1

NEW **SOUND COMBINATION: th, wh**

Task A

1. Open your Student Book to Lesson 22. ✓

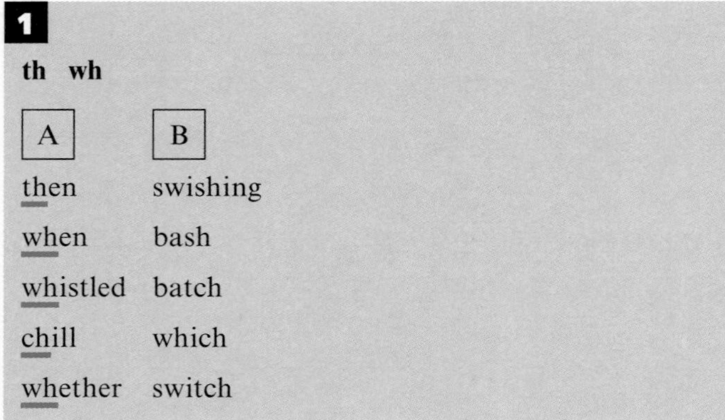

1

th wh

A	B
then	swishing
when	bash
whistled	batch
chill	which
whether	switch

- Touch the letters **T–H** in part 1. ✓
- The letters **T–H** go together and make the sound **ththth.** What sound? (Signal.) *ththth.*

2. Touch the letters **W–H.** ✓
- The letters **W–H** go together and make the sound **www.**
- What sound? (Signal.) *www.*

3. Your turn. Tell me the sound each combination makes. Touch the letters **T–H.** ✓
What sound? (Signal.) *ththth.*
- Touch the letters **W–H.** ✓
What sound? (Signal.) *www.*

4. (Repeat step 3 until firm.)

Task B

1. You're going to say the sound for the underlined part and then read the word.
2. Touch the first word in column A. ✓
- What sound? (Signal.) *ththth.*
- What word? (Signal.) *Then.*

3. Touch the next word. ✓
- What sound? (Signal.) *www.*
- What word? (Signal.) *When.*

4. (Repeat step 3 for each remaining word.)

Task C

1. Touch the first word in column B. ✓
- What word? (Signal.) *Swishing.*

2. Touch the next word. ✓
- What word? (Signal.) *Bash.*

3. (Repeat step 2 for each remaining word.)
4. (Repeat steps 1–3 until firm.)

EXERCISE 2

WORD PRACTICE

1. Touch the first word in part 2. ✓

2

agreed decided hours

northeasters breathe smart

- What sound? (Signal.) *ēēē.*
- What word? (Signal.) *Agreed.*

2. Touch the next word. ✓
- What sound? (Signal.) *sss.*
- What word? (Signal.) *Decided.*

3. (Repeat step 2 for each remaining word.)
4. (Repeat each row of words until firm.)

EXERCISE 3

VOCABULARY

1. Touch part 3. ✓

3

1. fierce
2. pleaded
3. advice
4. nervous

- We're going to talk about what those words mean.

2. Touch word 1. ✓
- What word? (Signal.) *Fierce.*
- A **fierce** wind is a **very violent** wind. Everybody, what's another way of saying "It was a **very violent** storm"? (Signal.) *It was a fierce storm.*

3. Touch word 2. ✓
- What word? (Signal.) *Pleaded.*
- When you **plead,** you **beg** for something. If you **plead** with someone, you try very hard to talk the person into something. Everybody, what's another way of saying "He **begged** for his life?" (Signal.) *He pleaded for his life.*
4. Touch word 3. ✓
- What word? (Signal.) *Advice.*
- When you give your **advice** to someone, you **make a statement of what you think the person should do.**
5. Touch word 4. ✓
- What word? (Signal.) *Nervous.*
- When someone is **edgy** or **jumpy,** that person is **nervous.** Everybody, what's another way of saying "She was a **jumpy** person"? (Signal.) *She was a nervous person.*

EXERCISE 4

WORD PRACTICE

1. Touch the first word in part 4. ✓

4

surround turned distance seafood
mouthpiece meant business* weather
figure wanted valve wasted sprawl*
signaled above worth worry enough
carrying struck warn spare bobbing
television tried spraying morning
report problem goose being knot

- What word? (Signal.) *Surround.*
2. Next word. ✓
- What word? (Signal.) *Turned.*
3. (Repeat step 2 for each remaining word.)
4. (Repeat each row of words until firm.)
5. What does **business** mean? (Call on a student.)
- (Repeat for **sprawl.**)

EXERCISE 5

MULTIPART WORDS

Task A

1. Touch part 5. ✓

5

furthermore difficulty realization
1. furthermore 2. difficulty 3. realization
situation extensive
4. situation 5. extensive

Note: The parts of a word are to be pronounced the same as they are when the word is spoken normally.

2. All these words have more than one part. The first part and the last part are circled.
3. Touch word 1. ✓
- Word 1 is **furthermore.** What word? (Signal.) *Furthermore.*
4. What's the first part? (Signal.) *fur.*
- What's the last part? (Signal.) *more.*
- The middle part is spelled **T–H–E–R.** What does that part say in the word? (Signal.) *ther.*
5. So, the parts are **fur** (pause) **ther** (pause) **more.**
- Say the whole word. (Signal.) *Furthermore.*
6. (Repeat steps 3–5 until firm.)
7. Touch word 2. ✓
- Word 2 is **difficulty.** What word? (Signal.) *Difficulty.*
8. What's the first part? (Signal.) *dif.*
- What's the last part? (Signal.) *y.* (Pronounced **ee.**)
- The middle part is spelled **F–I–C–U–L–T.** What does that part say in the word? (Signal.) *ficult.*
9. So, the parts are **dif** (pause) **ficult** (pause) **y.**
- Say the whole word. (Signal.) *Difficulty.*
10. (Repeat steps 7–9 until firm.)

Lesson

22

11. Touch word 3. ✓
- Word 3 is **realization.** What word? (Signal.) *Realization.*

12. What's the first part? (Signal.) *real.*
- What's the last part? (Signal.) *tion.*
- The middle part is spelled **I–Z–A.** What does that part say in the word? (Signal.) *iz-a.* (Pronounced **iz–ay.**) Yes, in this word **I–Z–A** is pronounced **iz–ay.**

13. So, the parts are **real** (pause) **iza** (pause) **tion.**
- Say the whole word. (Signal.) *Realization.*

14. (Repeat steps 11–13 until firm.)

15. Touch word 4. ✓
- Word 4 is **situation.** What word? (Signal.) *Situation.*

16. What's the first part? (Signal.) *sit.*
- What's the last part? (Signal.) *tion.*
- The middle part is spelled **U–A.** What does that part say in the word? (Signal.) *u-a.* (Pronounced **u–ay.**) Yes, in this word, **U–A** is pronounced just like the letters **U–A.**

17. So, the parts are **sit** (pause) **ua** (pause) **tion.**
- Say the whole word. (Signal.) *Situation.*

18. (Repeat steps 15–17 until firm.)

19. Touch word 5. ✓
- Word 5 is **extensive.** What word? (Signal.) *Extensive.*

20. What's the first part? (Signal.) *ex.*
- What's the last part? (Signal.) *sive.* (Pronounce as **siv,** not **sive.**)
- The middle part is spelled **T–E–N.** What does that part say in the word? (Signal.) *ten.*

21. So, the parts are **ex** (pause) **ten** (pause) **sive.**
- Say the whole word. (Signal.) *Extensive.*

22. (Repeat steps 19–21 until firm.)

Task B

1. Touch the sentences below the word list. ✓

a. The situation created extensive problems.
b. Furthermore, he had the realization that he could succeed.
c. The students were amazed by the difficulty of the assignment.
d. She had a sad realization that her car needed extensive repairs.

- These are sentences that use the words you just read.

2. Raise your hand when you can read sentence A. ✓

3. (Call on a student.) Read sentence A. *The situation created extensive problems.*
- That means "A lot of bad things happened because of some event."

4. (Call on a student.) Read sentence B. *Furthermore, he had the realization that he could succeed.*
- That means "What's more, he knew that he could do it."

5. (Call on a student.) Read sentence C. *The students were amazed by the difficulty of the assignment.*

6. (Call on a student.) Read sentence D. *She had a sad realization that her car needed extensive repairs.*
- That means "She was unhappy because she knew her car needed a lot of fixing up."

EXERCISE 6

WORD-ATTACK SKILLS: Individual tests

1. (Call on individual students. Each student reads a row of words, a column of words, or a sentence. In the Multipart words exercises, each sentence counts as one row of words. Tally the rows, columns, and sentences read without error. If the group reads at least 14 rows and columns without making errors, direct all students to record 5 points in Box A of their Point Chart. Criterion is 80 percent of rows and columns read without error.)
2. (If the group did not read at least 14 rows and columns without errors, do not award any points for the Word-Attack Skills exercises.)

SELECTION READING

EXERCISE 7

STORY READING

1. Everybody, touch part 6. ✓
2. The error limit for this story is 12. If the group reads the story with 12 errors or less, you earn 5 points.

6 **A New Diving Plan**

3. (Call on a student to read the title.) *A New Diving Plan.*
- What do you think this story is about? (Accept reasonable responses.)
4. (Call on individual students. Each is to read two to four sentences.)
5. (Call on individual students to answer the specified questions during the story reading.)

Jane had gone down too deep, and if she returned to the surface too fast, she might get the bends. But she didn't have enough air to go up slowly. She went up until she was about twenty feet below the surface. She signaled to Doris, who was above her. Jane pointed to her tank and shook her head from side to side.

She said, "I'm running out of air," but underwater, what she said sounded like this, "Ibib-rur-n-obobub." ❶

1. How far was Jane from the surface of the water? *About twenty feet.*
1. How did Jane try to signal Doris? (Idea: *By pointing to her tank and shaking her head from side to side.*)
1. What did Jane try to tell Doris? (Idea: *That she was running out of air.*)
1. Why couldn't Doris hear Jane? (Idea: *Because they were underwater.*)

Doris shook her head up and down and gave the OK signal with her right hand as if she understood. Then Doris swam to the surface. Jane waited and waited. She began to get nervous. She had only about a minute's worth of air left. "Where is she?" Jane wondered. Then she saw Doris swimming toward her. Doris had gone back to the boat to get a spare air tank. She was carrying that tank and swimming toward Jane.

Jane took the tank, placed the mouthpiece in her mouth, turned on the air valve, and began to breathe air from the new tank. Jane gave the signal for "thanks," and she meant it. ❷

2. What did Doris bring to Jane? *A spare air tank.*
2. What did Jane do when she got the new air tank? (Idea: *She put the mouthpiece in her mouth, turned on the valve, and breathed from the tank.*)

That evening Jane said, "We're not going at this diving business in a very smart way. When we go back, we'll have to string some spare tanks at the end of the anchor line. When we need them, they'll be there, and we won't be in danger." ❸

3. Why did Jane want to string some spare air tanks on the anchor lines? (Idea: *So they would be there when the divers needed them.*)

Doris agreed. The two women worked out their plan for the next day. They decided that they would go out unless the northeast wind was fierce. Doris said, "If we don't get out there tomorrow, we may never get another chance."

The next morning was gray and cold. The teachers went down to the dock. The boats were bobbing in the waves. The woman at the dock said, "I won't rent a boat to you today. No way."

So the day was wasted. Jane and Doris walked along the beach. They drove to a seafood stand for lunch. They walked along the beach in the afternoon. Then they went back to their motel room and watched television. They didn't talk much. ❹

4. How did Jane and Doris spend their "wasted" day? (Ideas: *They walked on the beach; drove to a seafood stand; watched TV.*)
4. Why wouldn't the woman rent Jane and Doris a boat? (Idea: *Because of the bad weather.*)

Slowly night came, and it was time for bed. But Jane didn't sleep well. The wind whistled through a crack under the door. In the distance waves were breaking on the beach, swishing and spraying.

The next morning was gray and windy. Jane looked out the window and tried to go back to sleep. There would be no diving today. It would be another day of walking around, killing time, and waiting. "Let me see the sun," Jane pleaded. But there was no sun that day.

The next morning was gray, but the wind had stopped. "Get up," Jane yelled. "It's calm. We can go diving."

Jane wanted to get to the reef really fast. In the back of her mind she was afraid that the wind would start blowing again. The woman at the dock said, "I don't know. The weather report says that there may be some more winds today."

"Come on," Doris said. "There's no problem. The water looks smooth as glass, and tomorrow is our last day. We won't sink your boat." ❺

5. What did Jane and Doris want the woman to do? (Idea: *To rent them a boat.*)
5. Why were Jane and Doris nervous about not diving that day? (Ideas: *Because the next day was their last day; because the wind might start blowing again.*)
5. Do you think Jane's leg injury keeps her from doing many things she wants to do? *No.*

"OK," the woman said, "but remember, I warned you. You never know about these northeasters. They can come up in the wink of an eye. My advice to you would be to forget it. Don't go out there, but if you want to go—"

Jane smiled at Doris. Jane felt goose bumps forming on her arms and neck. "This is it," she said. "Today is the day we find that sunken ship."

"Yes," Doris replied. "Today is the day."

An hour later, the boat was near the coral reef again. Jane didn't have any trouble finding the place where she had anchored the boat before. Now all she had to do was figure out where that sunken ship was.

When Doris and Jane went over the side, a line of blue-gray clouds was far to the north. The clouds were moving toward the little boat and the two divers. Those clouds were being pushed by a wind of forty knots. ⑥

6. What was in the sky to the north? (Idea: *A line of blue-gray clouds.*)
6. What could the clouds mean? (Idea: *That the northeast wind/bad weather was coming.*)
6. How much danger do you think that Jane and Doris were in? (Idea: *A lot.*)
6. (Award points quickly.)
7. (If the group makes more than 12 errors, repeat the reading immediately or on the next day.)

FLUENCY ASSESSMENT

EXERCISE 8

TIMED READING CHECKOUTS

1. (For this part of the lesson, assigned pairs of students work together during the checkouts.)
- (If one student does not have a checkout partner, arrange another time when you can give the checkout.)
2. (Each student does a 2-minute timed reading. Students earn 5 points by reading at least 240 words and making no more than 5 errors on the first part of story 22. Students record points in Box C of their Point Chart and plot their reading rate and errors on the Individual Reading Progress Chart.)
- (During each timed checkout, observe one pair of students for 2 minutes. Make notes on any mistakes the reader makes.)
3. (Record the timed reading checkout performance for each student you observed on the Fluency Assessment Summary form.)

Lesson
22

WORKBOOK EXERCISES

Independent Student Work

Task A

- Open your Workbook to Lesson 22. ✓
- Complete all parts of your Workbook lesson using a pencil. If you make no errors, you will earn 5 points.

Task B

1. (Before presenting Lesson 23, check student Workbooks for Lesson 22.)
- (Call on individual students to read the items and answers in each part. Students mark errors using a pen.)
2. (Direct the students to count the number of errors and write the number in the Errors box at the top of the Workbook page.)
3. (Award points and direct students to record points in Box D of their Point Chart.)

0 errors ....5 points
1 error ....3 points
2 or 3 errors ....1 point
more than 3 errors ....0 points

END OF LESSON 22

Lesson 22

Errors

1

1. Doris couldn't understand Jane when she said, "I'm running out of air." So how did Doris know what to do? (Jane pointed to her tank and shook her head from side to side.)
2. What did Jane do when she got the new air tank? (She placed the mouthpiece in her mouth, turned on the air valve, and began to breathe air from the new tank.)
3. Why did Jane want to string some spare tanks on the anchor line? (so she and Doris wouldn't run out of air)
4. Why wouldn't the woman rent Jane and Doris a boat one day? (The weather was bad.)
5. Why were Jane and Doris nervous about not diving once the weather turned bad? (They were afraid they wouldn't get another chance.)
6. **Here are some things Jane and Doris did on their "wasted" day.**
Number them 1, 2, 3, 4, 5, and 6 to show the order in which they happened.
5 They watched television.
4 They walked along the beach again.
6 They went to bed.
3 They ate seafood.
1 They walked along the beach in the morning.
2 They drove to a seafood stand.

Copyright © SRA/McGraw-Hill. All rights reserved.

Lesson 22

7. How long did Jane and Doris kill time? two days
8. On the third day why did Jane want to get to the reef really fast? (She was afraid the wind would start blowing again.)
9. How much danger do you think that Jane and Doris are in at the end of the story? (a lot)
10. a. If the woman at the dock had given you the same advice she gave Jane and Doris, would you have gone out to look for the ship? (Yes or no.)
b. Why? (Accept reasonable responses.)

2 **Fill in each blank using a word in the box.**

pleaded	sprawling	gasping
exclaimed	advice	nervous

1. The runner lay on the ground gasping for breath.
2. Carlos pleaded with his parents to take him to the circus.
3. The scary movie made Melinda nervous and jumpy.

Copyright © SRA/McGraw-Hill. All rights reserved.

WORD-ATTACK SKILLS

Student Book

EXERCISE 1

NEW SOUND COMBINATION: igh

Task A

1. Open your Student Book to Lesson 23. ✓

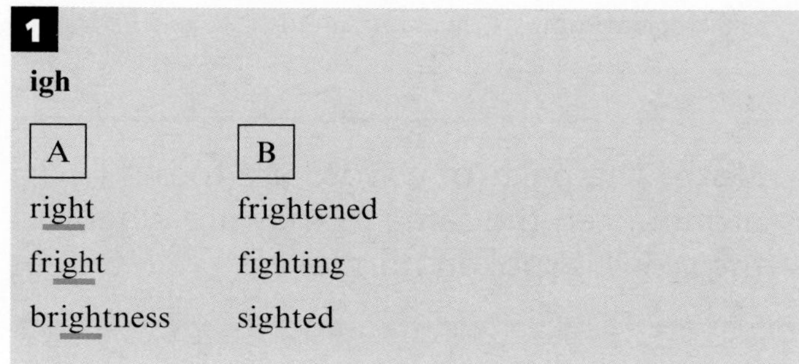

1

igh

A	B
right	frightened
fright	fighting
brightness	sighted

- Touch the letters **I–G–H** in part 1. ✓
- The letters **I–G–H** go together and make the sound **īīī.** What sound? (Signal.) *īīī.*

2. You're going to read words that have the letters **I–G–H** in them. You're going to say the sound for the underlined part and then read the word.
3. Touch the first word in column A. ✓
- What sound? (Signal.) *īīī.*
- What word? (Signal.) *Right.*
4. Touch the next word. ✓
- What sound? (Signal.) *īīī.*
- What word? (Signal.) *Fright.*
5. (Repeat step 4 for **brightness.**)

Task B

1. Touch the first word in column B. ✓
- What word? (Signal.) *Frightened.*
2. Touch the next word. ✓
- What word? (Signal.) *Fighting.*
3. (Repeat step 2 for **sighted.**)
4. (Repeat steps 1–3 until firm.)

EXERCISE 2

WORD PRACTICE

1. Touch the first word in part 2. ✓

2

latch which ouch fresh thrash

through while thought chance

navigation clearly charge motioned

carved investigation* afraid

announced route nearest apart

- What sound? (Signal.) *ch.*
- What word? (Signal.) *Latch.*
2. Touch the next word. ✓
- What sound? (Signal.) *www.*
- What word? (Signal.) *Which.*
3. (Repeat step 2 for each remaining word.)
4. (Repeat each row of words until firm.)
5. What does **investigation** mean? (Call on a student.)

EXERCISE 3

VOCABULARY

1. Touch part 3. ✓

3

1. wispy
2. suspended
3. anchor
4. swayed
5. slime

- We're going to talk about what those words mean.
2. Touch word 1. ✓
- What word? (Signal.) *Wispy.*
- **Wispy** means **very light and dainty.** Everybody, what does **wispy** mean? (Signal.) *Very light and dainty.*

3. Touch word 2. ✓
- What word? (Signal.) *Suspended.*
- When something **hangs in the air,** it is **suspended** in the air. Everybody, what's another way of saying "The kite was **hanging in the air**"? (Signal.) *The kite was suspended in the air.*

4. Touch word 3. ✓
- What word? (Signal.) *Anchor.*
- What is an **anchor?** (Call on a student.) (Idea: *An object used to hold a boat in one place.*)

5. Everybody, touch word 4. ✓
- What word? (Signal.) *Swayed.*
- When something **sways,** it **slowly moves back and forth.** Everybody, what's another way of saying "The weeds **slowly moved back and forth**"? (Signal.) *The weeds swayed.*

6. Touch word 5. ✓
- What word? (Signal.) *Slime.*
- **Slime** is a **slippery coating.** Everybody, what's another way of saying, "The rock was covered with a **slippery coating**?" (Signal.) *The rock was covered with slime.*

EXERCISE 4

WORD PRACTICE

1. Touch the first word in part 4. ✓

4

approached barnacles swirled* glanced
surface* buoys spotted hanging
panic sucking forehead quit
quiet directed peaking staring
caught yanked shadow heavy
lying laying horizon finished

- What word? (Signal.) *Approached.*

2. Next word. ✓
- What word? (Signal.) *Barnacles.*

3. (Repeat step 2 for each remaining word.)
4. (Repeat each row of words until firm.)
5. What does **swirled** mean? (Call on a student.)
- (Repeat for **surface.**)

EXERCISE 5

MULTIPART WORDS

Task A

1. Touch part 5. ✓

5

inflexible temperature remarkable
1. inflexible 2. temperature 3. remarkable
celebration commented
4. celebration 5. commented

> **Note:** The parts of a word are to be pronounced the same as they are when the word is spoken normally.

2. All these words have more than one part. The first part and the last part are circled.
3. Touch word 1. ✓
- Word 1 is **inflexible.** What word? (Signal.) *Inflexible.*

4. What's the first part? (Signal.) *in.*
- What's the last part? (Signal.) *ible.*
- The middle part is spelled **F–L–E–X.** What does that part say in the word? (Signal.) *flex.*

5. So, the parts are **in** (pause) **flex** (pause) **ible.**
- Say the whole word. (Signal.) *Inflexible.*

6. (Repeat steps 3–5 until firm.)
7. Touch word 2. ✓
- Word 2 is **temperature.** What word? (Signal.) *Temperature.*

8. What's the first part? (Signal.) *temp.*
- What's the last part? (Signal.) *ture.*
- The middle part is spelled **E–R–A.** What does that part say in the word? (Signal.) *era.*

9. So, the parts are **temp** (pause) **era** (pause) **ture.**
- Say the whole word. (Signal.) *Temperature.*

10. (Repeat steps 7–9 until firm.)

11. Touch word 3. ✓
   - Word 3 is **remarkable.** What word? (Signal.) *Remarkable.*
12. What's the first part? (Signal.) *re.*
   - What's the last part? (Signal.) *able.*
   - The middle part is spelled **M–A–R–K.** What does that part say in the word? (Signal.) *mark.*
13. So, the parts are **re** (pause) **mark** (pause) **able.**
   - Say the whole word. (Signal.) *Remarkable.*
14. (Repeat steps 11–13 until firm.)
15. Touch word 4. ✓
   - Word 4 is **celebration.** What word? (Signal.) *Celebration.*
16. What's the first part? (Signal.) *cel.*
   - What's the last part? (Signal.) *tion.*
   - The middle part is spelled **E–B–R–A.** What does that part say in the word? (Signal.) *ebra.*
17. So, the parts are **cel** (pause) **ebra** (pause) **tion.**
   - Say the whole word. (Signal.) *Celebration.*
18. (Repeat steps 15–17 until firm.)
19. Touch word 5. ✓
   - Word 5 is **commented.** What word? (Signal.) *Commented.*
20. What's the first part? (Signal.) *com.*
   - What's the last part? (Signal.) *ed.*
   - The middle part is spelled **M–E–N–T.** What does that part say in the word? (Signal.) *ment.*
21. So, the parts are **com** (pause) **ment** (pause) **ed.**
   - Say the whole word. (Signal.) *Commented.*
22. (Repeat steps 19–21 until firm.)

Task B

1. Touch the sentences below the word list. ✓

a. His comments about the team showed how inflexible he was.
b. The family arranged for a remarkable celebration.
c. I commented on the low temperature for today.
d. Her injured arm was totally inflexible.

   - These are sentences that use the words you just read.
2. Raise your hand when you can read sentence A. ✓
3. (Call on a student.) Read sentence A. *His comments about the team showed how inflexible he was.*
   - That means "What he said about the team showed that he wouldn't change his opinion."
4. (Call on a student.) Read sentence B. *The family arranged for a remarkable celebration.*
   - That means "The family made plans for a very good party."
5. (Call on a student.) Read sentence C. *I commented on the low temperature for today.*
   - That means "I said something about the low temperature."
6. (Call on a student.) Read sentence D. *Her injured arm was totally inflexible.*
   - That means "She could not move or bend her arm."

EXERCISE 6

WORD-ATTACK SKILLS: Individual tests

1. (Call on individual students. Each student reads a row of words, a column of words, or a sentence. In the Multipart words exercises, each sentence counts as one row of words. Tally the rows, columns, and sentences read without error. If the group reads at least 15 rows and columns without making errors, direct all students to record 5 points in Box A of their Point Chart. Criterion is 80 percent of rows and columns read without error.)
2. (If the group did not read at least 15 rows and columns without errors, do not award any points for the Word-Attack Skills exercises.)

SELECTION READING

EXERCISE 7

STORY READING

1. Everybody, touch part 6. ✓
2. The error limit for this story is 12. If the group reads the story with 12 errors or less, you earn 5 points.

6

The Gray Ghost Ship

3. (Call on a student to read the title.) *The Gray Ghost Ship.*
- What do you think this story is about? (Accept reasonable responses.)
4. (Call on individual students. Each is to read two to four sentences.)
5. (Call on individual students to answer the specified questions during the story reading.)

Jane and Doris set the diving flags in the water. They hung an air tank on the line leading to the anchor. "Now we should be able to stay down until we find that ship," Jane said when the last flag was in the water.

The plan was for the women to take the route that Jane had taken when she spotted the sunken ship. The women would anchor the boat in the same spot they had before. They would dive there and let the current take them through the gap in the reef and past the ship. One of them would then swim down to the ship while the other went to the anchor line. When the diver who went to the ship finished the investigation, the other diver would swim part way down with a fresh air tank and meet the other diver. ❶

1. Where did Jane and Doris put the extra air tank? (Idea: *They hung it on the line leading to the anchor.*)
1. Which route were Jane and Doris going to take to reach the ship? (Idea: *The same one that Jane had taken before.*)

"Here we go," Jane announced. Both divers were in the water hanging on to the side of the boat. They didn't spot the line of blue-gray clouds to the north. Jane slid her mask over her face. Down she went. Doris was there next to her, moving through a mass of bubbles.

Down they went through the warm water. Down. Then the pull of the current began sucking at their legs. "Don't panic," Jane said to herself. She turned to Doris and smiled, but Doris seemed to slip past her in the current. Down and to the east. Through the gap in the reef. Down, down. Cooler water now, and not as much downward pull. ❷

2. What was pulling Jane and Doris through the water? (Idea: *A strong current.*)

Scan the bottom. Darkness and bubbles. "I wish the sun were out," Jane thought to herself. "It's so dark down here I can't see anything."

"What's that?" A dark line—dark black against the almost-black bottom. The mast. There it is, Jane motioned, but Doris was looking the other way. Jane grabbed Doris's leg. "Look. Look," she exclaimed.

Jane pointed to herself and then pointed down. "I'm going down." And she did. Through the cooler water. Ouch. Her ears hurt, and she felt a sharp pain in the middle of her forehead. The mask seemed to be pushing her face out of shape. Down. ❸

3. What did the mast look like when Jane and Doris first saw it? (Idea: *A dark line.*)
3. What was Jane's mask doing to her face? (Ideas: *Pressing against her face; pushing her face out of shape.*)

Suddenly she could see the ship. It was covered with wispy plants that swayed and swirled in the current. The ship looked like a dark gray ghost. "Maybe I don't want to go down there," Jane thought. She looked up. Doris was a dark figure suspended in the water far above her. "I've come this far," Jane thought, "so I won't quit now." ❹

4. How did the ship look as Jane got closer to it? (Idea: *Like a dark gray ghost.*)
4. What other events in Jane's past let you know that she is not a quitter? (Ideas: *Her recovery after the accident; she doesn't let her injury stop her from doing anything.*)

Down. Jane could now see parts of the ship clearly. There was a rail made of heavy carved timbers, covered with barnacles. There was part of a cabin with a door. The deck seemed to be covered with slime and long strings of seaweed. As Jane approached the door of the cabin, she reached into the pouch in her belt and pulled out an underwater flashlight. She turned it on and directed the beam into the cabin. There were stairs covered with slime. There were some boxes and what looked like a broken chair. And there was a pile of—bones. Part of a skull was peeking through the slime. The eye sockets seemed to be staring at Jane. ❺

5. What was the rail covered with? *Barnacles.*
5. What are barnacles? (Idea: *Small sea creatures that attach themselves to rocks and other solid surfaces.*)
5. What was the deck covered with? (Idea: *Slime and long strings of seaweed.*)
5. Where was the skeleton? *In the ship's cabin.*

She dropped the flashlight and swam. Her arms and legs went as fast as they could go. A string of seaweed caught on one of her arms. She yanked it off. She swam up and up and up. Then she looked back. Below her was the dark shadow of the ship with the even darker mast lying next to it. She stopped and began to talk to herself. "Be calm. It was only a skull, only some bones." She began to swim fast again.

Doris met her about fifty feet from the surface. Doris gave her a fresh tank of air. Jane stayed there for five minutes. From time to time she glanced down at the ship below, but she could no longer see it because the sky was getting darker and darker.

When they reached the surface, Jane told Doris, "I'm not going back down there." ❻

6. Why didn't Jane want to go back down? (Idea: *Because the skull frightened her.*)

Doris pointed to the horizon and said, "Jane, look." Jane looked at the sky.

6. (Award points quickly.)
7. (If the group makes more than 12 errors, repeat the reading immediately or on the next day.)

FLUENCY ASSESSMENT

EXERCISE 8

TIMED READING CHECKOUTS

1. (For this part of the lesson, assigned pairs of students work together during the checkouts.)
   - (If one student does not have a checkout partner, arrange another time when you can give the checkout.)
2. (Each student does a 2-minute timed reading. Students earn 5 points by reading at least 240 words and making no more than 5 errors on the first part of story 23. Students record points in Box C of their Point Chart and plot their reading rate and errors on the Individual Reading Progress Chart.)
   - (During each timed checkout, observe one pair of students for 2 minutes. Make notes on any mistakes the reader makes.)
3. (Record the timed reading checkout performance for each student you observed on the Fluency Assessment Summary form.)

WORKBOOK EXERCISES

Workbook: Teacher Directed 

EXERCISE 9

NEW COPYING MAIN-IDEA SENTENCE

1. Open your Workbook to Lesson 23. ✓
- Touch part 1. ✓
- You're going to copy the sentence that tells the **main idea** of the story. The **main idea** of the story is the **main thing that happened** in the story. One of the four sentences gives the main idea of the story.
2. Touch sentence 1. ✓
- (Call on a student to read sentence 1.) *The sky was gray and became very dark later in the day.*
- Raise your hand if you think sentence 1 gives the main idea.
3. Touch sentence 2. ✓
- (Call on a student to read sentence 2.) *The women anchored their boat in the same spot they had before and dove from that spot.*
- Raise your hand if you think sentence 2 gives the main idea.
4. Touch sentence 3. ✓
- (Call on a student to read sentence 3.) *Jane became frightened after she found a sunken ship where a skull seemed to be staring at her.*
- Raise your hand if you think sentence 3 gives the main idea.
5. Touch sentence 4. ✓
- (Call on a student to read sentence 4.) *The divers carried spare air tanks so they would be able to stay under water longer.*
- Raise your hand if you think sentence 4 gives the main idea.
6. Everybody, which sentence gives the main idea? (Signal.) *Sentence 3.*
7. Later, you'll copy that sentence on the lines.

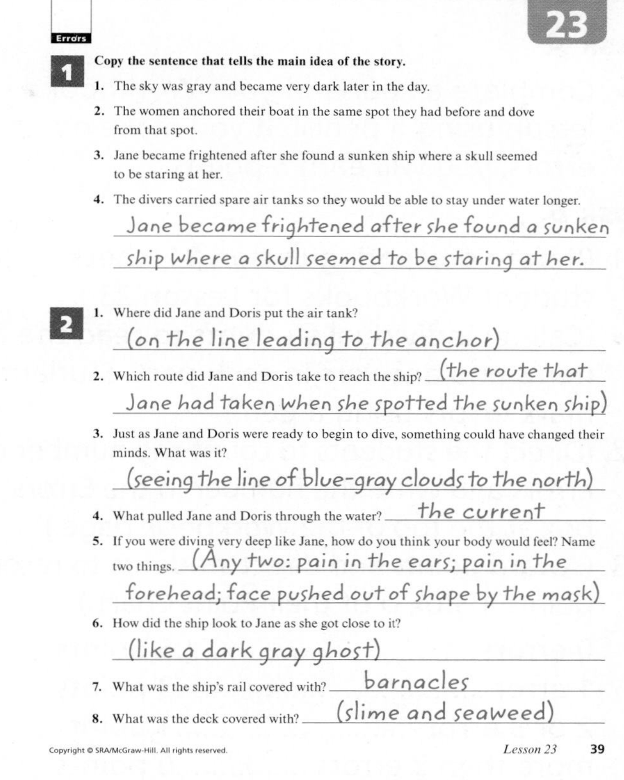

Lesson 23

Errors

1 **Copy the sentence that tells the main idea of the story.**

1. The sky was gray and became very dark later in the day.
2. The women anchored their boat in the same spot they had before and dove from that spot.
3. Jane became frightened after she found a sunken ship where a skull seemed to be staring at her.
4. The divers carried spare air tanks so they would be able to stay under water longer.

Jane became frightened after she found a sunken ship where a skull seemed to be staring at her.

2

1. Where did Jane and Doris put the air tank? (on the line leading to the anchor)
2. Which route did Jane and Doris take to reach the ship? (the route that Jane had taken when she spotted the sunken ship)
3. Just as Jane and Doris were ready to begin to dive, something could have changed their minds. What was it? (seeing the line of blue-gray clouds to the north)
4. What pulled Jane and Doris through the water? the current
5. If you were diving very deep like Jane, how do you think your body would feel? Name two things. (Any two: pain in the ears; pain in the forehead; face pushed out of shape by the mask)
6. How did the ship look to Jane as she got close to it? (like a dark gray ghost)
7. What was the ship's rail covered with? barnacles
8. What was the deck covered with? (slime and seaweed)

Copyright © SRA/McGraw-Hill. All rights reserved. *Lesson 23* 39

Lesson 23

9. Why didn't Jane want to go back down to the ship? (The skull had frightened her.)
10. When Jane was fifty feet from the surface she could no longer see the ship. Why? **Underline the best answer.**
    - Jane's mask was cloudy, so the sky looked dark.
    - It was late, and the sun was going down.
    - Storm clouds made the sky very dark.

3 **Fill in each blank using a word in the box.**

announced	investigation	wispy
gymnastics	suspended	anchor

1. Bill's father announced that the family was moving to New York.
2. The anchor stopped the boat from floating away.
3. The punching bag was suspended from the ceiling by a rope.

4 **Write the parts for each word.**

1. brightest = bright + est
2. freshly = fresh + ly
3. sheltered = shelter + ed
4. modeling = model + ing

40 *Lesson 23* Copyright © SRA/McGraw-Hill. All rights reserved.

Lesson 23

Independent Student Work

Task A

- Complete all parts of your Workbook lesson using a pencil. If you make no errors, you will earn 5 points.

Task B

1. (Before presenting Lesson 24, check student Workbooks for Lesson 23.)
- (Call on individual students to read the items and answers in each part. Students mark errors using a pen.)
2. (Direct the students to count the number of errors and write the number in the Errors box at the top of the Workbook page.)
3. (Award points and direct students to record points in Box D of their Point Chart.)

0 errors.................................5 points
1 error..................................3 points
2 or 3 errors.........................1 point
more than 3 errors ....0 points

END OF LESSON 23

WORD-ATTACK SKILLS

Student Book

EXERCISE 1

NEW **SOUND COMBINATION: al**

Task A

1. Open your Student Book to Lesson 24. ✓

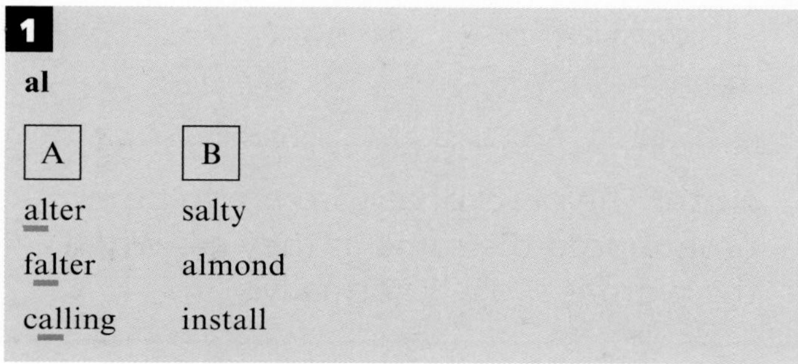

1

al

A	B
alter	salty
falter	almond
calling	install

- Touch the letters **A–L** in part 1. ✓
- The letters **A–L** go together and make the sound **all.** What sound? (Signal.) *all.*

2. You're going to read words that have the letters **A–L** in them. You're going to say the sound for the underlined part and then read the word.
3. Touch the first word in column A. ✓
   - What sound? (Signal.) *all.*
   - What word? (Signal.) *Alter.*
4. Touch the next word. ✓
   - What sound? (Signal.) *all.*
   - What word? (Signal.) *Falter.*
5. (Repeat step 3 for **calling.**)

Task B

1. Touch the first word in column B. ✓
   - What word? (Signal.) *Salty.*
2. Touch the next word. ✓
   - What word? (Signal.) *Almond.*
3. (Repeat step 2 for **install.**)
4. (Repeat steps 1–3 until firm.)

EXERCISE 2

WORD PRACTICE

1. Touch the first word in part 2. ✓

2

while weather whether thrash

slightly bright tightly wheeling

together faintly agreed faster

seemingly feast cloudy first

gently emerging placed salvage

- What sound? (Signal.) *www.*
- What word? (Signal.) *While.*

2. Touch the next word. ✓
   - What sound? (Signal.) *ththth.*
   - What word? (Signal.) *Weather.*
3. (Repeat step 2 for each remaining word.)
4. (Repeat each row of words until firm.)

EXERCISE 3

VOCABULARY

1. Touch part 3. ✓

3

1. protection
2. suggest
3. glance
4. breaker
5. venture
6. emerge

- We're going to talk about what those words mean.

2. Touch word 1. ✓
   - What word? (Signal.) *Protection.*
   - **Something that guards** is a **protection.** Everybody, what's another way of saying "The high wall is **something that guards**"? (Signal.) *The high wall is a protection.*
3. Touch word 2. ✓
   - What word? (Signal.) *Suggest.*
   - Something that **gives a hint suggests.** Everybody, what's another way of saying "His hands **give a hint** that he is a farmer"? (Signal.) *His hands suggest that he is a farmer.*

Lesson
24

4. Touch word 3. ✓
- What word? (Signal.) *Glance.*
- What does **glance** mean? (Call on a student.) (Idea: *Look at something quickly.*)

5. Everybody, touch word 4. ✓
- What word? (Signal.) *Breaker.*
- A **breaker** is a **big wave.** What is a **breaker?** (Signal.) *A big wave.*

6. Touch word 5. ✓
- What word? (Signal.) *Venture.*
- When you **venture,** you **do something daring.** If you go into a dangerous storm, you **venture** into the storm.

7. Touch word 6. ✓
- What word? (Signal.) *Emerge.*
- When you **emerge from** a place, you **come out of** that place. Everybody, what's another way of saying "The woman **came out of** the office"? (Signal.) *The woman emerged from the office.*

EXERCISE 4

WORD PRACTICE

1. Touch the first word in part 4. ✓

4

afternoon patterns flounder* mound
huge hours inspection jerking worse
jagged ruffled horizon plumes
wilder towing aboard spare bluff
responded* rolled forming continued*
gallons whistled designs during flight
impossible whipped evening believe
neither slime* already storm yards

- What word? (Signal.) *Afternoon.*

2. Next word. ✓
- What word? (Signal.) *Patterns.*

3. (Repeat step 2 for each remaining word.)
4. (Repeat each row of words until firm.)
5. What does **flounder** mean? (Call on a student.)
- (Repeat for **responded, continued, slime.**)

EXERCISE 5

MULTIPART WORDS

Task A

1. Touch part 5. ✓

5

injury announcement investigation
1. injury 2. announcement 3. investigation
procedures consistent
4. procedures 5. consistent

Note: The parts of a word are to be pronounced the same as they are when the word is spoken normally.

2. All these words have more than one part. The first part and the last part are circled.
3. Touch word 1. ✓
- Word 1 is **injury.** What word? (Signal.) *Injury.*

4. What's the first part? (Signal.) *in.*
- What's the last part? (Signal.) *y.* (Pronounced **ee.**)
- The middle part is spelled **J–U–R.** What does that part say in the word? (Signal.) *jur.*

5. So, the parts are **in** (pause) **jur** (pause) **y.**
- Say the whole word. (Signal.) *Injury.*

6. (Repeat steps 3–5 until firm.)
7. Touch word 2. ✓
- Word 2 is **announcement.** What word? (Signal.) *Announcement.*

8. What's the first part? (Signal.) *an.*
- What's the last part? (Signal.) *ment.*
- The middle part is spelled **N–O–U–N–C–E.** What does that part say in the word? (Signal.) *nounce.*

9. So, the parts are **an** (pause) **nounce** (pause) **ment.**
- Say the whole word. (Signal.) *Announcement.*

10. (Repeat steps 7–9 until firm.)

11. Touch word 3. ✓
   - Word 3 is **investigation.** What word? (Signal.) *Investigation.*
12. What's the first part? (Signal.) *in.*
   - What's the last part? (Signal.) *tion.*
   - The middle part is spelled **V–E–S–T–I–G–A.** What does that part say in the word? (Signal.) *vestiga.*
13. So, the parts are **in** (pause) **vestiga** (pause) **tion.**
   - Say the whole word. (Signal.) *Investigation.*
14. (Repeat steps 11–13 until firm.)
15. Touch word 4. ✓
   - Word 4 is **procedures.** What word? (Signal.) *Procedures.*
16. What's the first part? (Signal.) *pro.*
   - What's the last part? (Signal.) *ures.*
   - The middle part is spelled **C–E–D.** What does that part say in the word? (Signal.) *ced.*
17. So, the parts are **pro** (pause) **ced** (pause) **ures.**
   - Say the whole word. (Signal.) *Procedures.*
18. (Repeat steps 15–17 until firm.)
19. Touch word 5. ✓
   - Word 5 is **consistent.** What word? (Signal.) *Consistent.*
20. What's the first part? (Signal.) *con.*
   - What's the last part? (Signal.) *tent.*
   - The middle part is spelled **S–I–S.** What does that part say in the word? (Signal.) *sis.*
21. So, the parts are **con** (pause) **sis** (pause) **tent.**
   - Say the whole word. (Signal.) *Consistent.*
22. (Repeat steps 19–21 until firm.)

Task B

1. Touch the sentences below the word list. ✓

a. The judge gave approval for a police investigation.
b. The announcement about the new procedures was not consistent with the earlier announcement.
c. They ran an investigation on what caused the injury.
d. We were surprised that they hadn't made the announcement yet.
e. Their approval of the plan was consistent with the way they voted earlier.

   - These are sentences that use the words you just read.
2. Raise your hand when you can read sentence A. ✓
3. (Call on a student.) Read sentence A. *The judge gave approval for a police investigation.*
   - That means "The judge said that it was okay to have the police look into the situation."
4. (Call on a student.) Read sentence B. *The announcement about the new procedures was not consistent with the earlier announcement.*
   - That means "What was reported this time about the rules was not the same as what was reported last time."
5. (Call on a student.) Read sentence C. *They ran an investigation on what caused the injury.*
   - That means "They examined things to find out what caused the injury."
6. (Call on a student.) Read sentence D. *We were surprised that they hadn't made the announcement yet.*
7. (Call on a student.) Read sentence E. *Their approval of the plan was consistent with the way they voted earlier.*
   - That means "Their support of the plan was what you would expect from the way they voted earlier."

Lesson 24

EXERCISE 6

WORD-ATTACK SKILLS: Individual tests

1. (Call on individual students. Each student reads a row of words, a column of words, or a sentence. In the Multipart words exercises, each sentence counts as one row of words. Tally the rows, columns, and sentences read without error. If the group reads at least 17 rows and columns without making errors, direct all students to record 5 points in Box A of their Point Chart. Criterion is 80 percent of rows and columns read without error.)
2. (If the group did not read at least 17 rows and columns without errors, do not award any points for the Word-Attack Skills exercises.)

SELECTION READING

EXERCISE 7

STORY READING

1. (Call on individual students to answer these questions.)
- What strange object did the women encounter in the last selection? (Idea: *A sunken ship that looked like a dark gray ghost.*)
- Describe the ship. (Accept reasonable responses.)
- What happened? (Accept reasonable summaries.)
2. Everybody, touch part 6. ✓
3. The error limit for this story is 12. If the group reads the story with 12 errors or less, you earn 5 points.

6 **Trapped in the Storm**

4. (Call on a student to read the title.) *Trapped in the Storm.*
- What do you think this story is about? (Accept reasonable responses.)
5. (Call on individual students. Each is to read two to four sentences.)
6. (Call on individual students to answer the specified questions during the story reading.)

There was a line of dark clouds to the north, and there was a line of whitecaps on the horizon under the clouds.

"We're in for it now," Doris exclaimed.

"What are we going to do?" Jane asked. "Those waves are going to hit us in a few minutes."

The women swam back to their boat, towing the spare air tank. They climbed aboard. Jane started the engine, and the boat began to move slowly along the reef. Jane explained, "I don't know where to go. We've got to find some protection from that storm, but I don't see any protection." (1)

1. What were Jane and Doris afraid of now? (Idea: *The bad weather.*)
1. Why would Jane and Doris need protection from the storm? (Ideas: *So the wind and waves would not hit them so hard; so they wouldn't sink.*)

"Let's keep moving along the reef," Doris suggested. "Maybe we can find a place where the reef is high enough to protect the boat."

Jane glanced back. The clouds were closer, and the whitecaps seemed to be bigger and wilder. The old scow continued to move slowly along the west side of the reef. Jane glanced back at the clouds again.

"Look," Doris said. Doris was pointing ahead. "There seems to be a coral bluff ahead."

Jane could barely see it. It looked like a gray-white mound emerging from the sea. The boat was about half a mile from the mound. ❷

2. What did Jane and Doris find to protect the boat? *A coral bluff.*

"I wish this boat would move faster," Jane shouted. Before Doris could respond, however, a gust of cold wind swept past the boat, making ruffled patterns in the water. The boat turned slightly when the wind hit it.

"Here it comes," Doris shouted. Jane could hardly hear Doris's voice above the wind. Already whitecaps were forming on the other side of the reef. The wind was blowing the tops of the waves into a fine spray. Jane felt the side of her face getting wet. She licked her lips. They were salty. ❸

3. Why could Jane hardly hear Doris? (Idea: *Because the wind was so loud.*)

The waves were now starting to roll over the low places along the reef. As the waves rolled under the boat, the boat began to rock from side to side. The rocking, which was gentle at first, became more violent. From time to time one of the waves would splash against the side of the boat and send warm water streaming into the boat. Doris was bailing. The boat was only about a hundred yards from the coral bluff now; however, the boat was moving quite slowly as it climbed over the waves, rolling from side to side. ❹

4. What happened when the waves rolled over the low places along the reef? (Idea: *The boat began to rock from side to side.*)
4. Why was the boat moving slowly? (Idea: *Because of the high waves.*)
4. Why was Doris bailing? (Idea: *Because waves were splashing into the boat.*)

"If it gets any worse," Doris yelled, "we'll have to turn the front of the boat so that it faces into the wind. We're going to flounder if we keep going in this direction."

But the boat continued along the coral and Doris continued to bail. Just before the boat was alongside the coral mound, a huge breaker hit the side of the boat and dumped about twenty gallons of seawater into the boat. "Bail," Jane shouted as she began to splash water from the boat with her hands.

Now the boat was behind the mound. Huge breakers were smashing against the other side of the mound, sending plumes of spray into the air. But the boat was in a protected place. Doris tied a rope around part of the mound. Then she and Jane sat in the front of the boat, close to the coral, as the surf pounded and the wind whistled through the designs in the coral.

The wind blew for more than two hours. During that time the women waited. From time to time they tried to talk, but it was almost impossible to hear what was said above the wind and the surf. ❺

5. How long did the wind blow? *For more than two hours.*
5. Why was it hard for Jane and Doris to talk as the wind blew? (Idea: *Because of the noise of the wind and surf.*)

Then almost as suddenly as the storm had started, the wind died down. Huge waves continued to roll over the reef for another hour, but the waves became smaller and calmer. They were no longer being whipped into jagged shapes by the wind.

At around five o'clock that evening, the waves were small enough for the women to venture back to the dock. Jane said, "I sure won't forget this day for a long, long time." ❻

6. When did Jane and Doris start back to the dock? (Idea: *At around 5:00 that evening.*)
6. Why would Jane and Doris remember that day for a long time? (Idea: *Because it was dangerous/frightening/adventurous.)*
7. (Award points quickly.)
8. (If the group makes more than 12 errors, repeat the reading immediately or on the next day.)

FLUENCY ASSESSMENT

EXERCISE 8

TIMED READING CHECKOUTS

1. (For this part of the lesson, assigned pairs of students work together during the checkouts.)
   - (If one student does not have a checkout partner, arrange another time when you can give the checkout.)
2. (Each student does a 2-minute timed reading. Students earn 5 points by reading at least 240 words and making no more than 5 errors on the first part of story 24. Students record points in Box C of their Point Chart and plot their reading rate and errors on the Individual Reading Progress Chart.)
   - (During each timed checkout, observe one pair of students for 2 minutes. Make notes on any mistakes the reader makes.)
3. (Record the timed reading checkout performance for each student you observed on the Fluency Assessment Summary form.)

WORKBOOK EXERCISES

Independent Student Work

Task A

- Open your Workbook to Lesson 24. ✓
- Complete all parts of your Workbook lesson using a pencil. If you make no errors, you will earn 5 points.

Task B

1. (Before presenting Lesson 25, check student Workbooks for Lesson 24.)
   - (Call on individual students to read the items and answers in each part. Students mark errors using a pen.)
2. (Direct the students to count the number of errors and write the number in the Errors box at the top of the Workbook page.)
3. (Award points and direct students to record points in Box D of their Point Chart.)

   0 errors................................5 points
   1 error ....3 points
   2 or 3 errors ....1 point
   more than 3 errors ....0 points

END OF LESSON 24

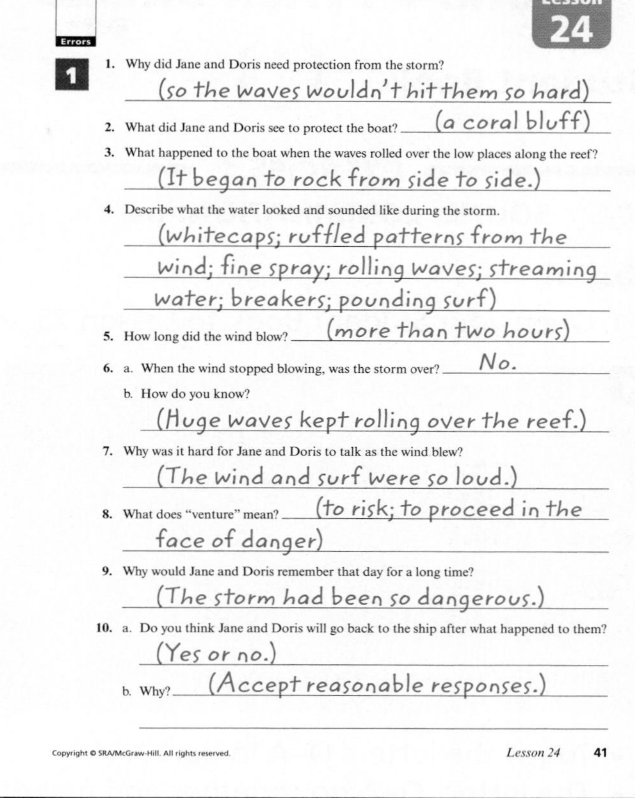

Lesson 24

Errors

1

1. Why did Jane and Doris need protection from the storm?
   (so the waves wouldn't hit them so hard)
2. What did Jane and Doris see to protect the boat? (a coral bluff)
3. What happened to the boat when the waves rolled over the low places along the reef?
   (It began to rock from side to side.)
4. Describe what the water looked and sounded like during the storm.
   (whitecaps; ruffled patterns from the wind; fine spray; rolling waves; streaming water; breakers; pounding surf)
5. How long did the wind blow? (more than two hours)
6. a. When the wind stopped blowing, was the storm over? No.
   b. How do you know?
   (Huge waves kept rolling over the reef.)
7. Why was it hard for Jane and Doris to talk as the wind blew?
   (The wind and surf were so loud.)
8. What does "venture" mean? (to risk; to proceed in the face of danger)
9. Why would Jane and Doris remember that day for a long time?
   (The storm had been so dangerous.)
10. a. Do you think Jane and Doris will go back to the ship after what happened to them?
    (Yes or no.)
    b. Why? (Accept reasonable responses.)

Copyright © SRA/McGraw-Hill. All rights reserved. *Lesson 24* 41

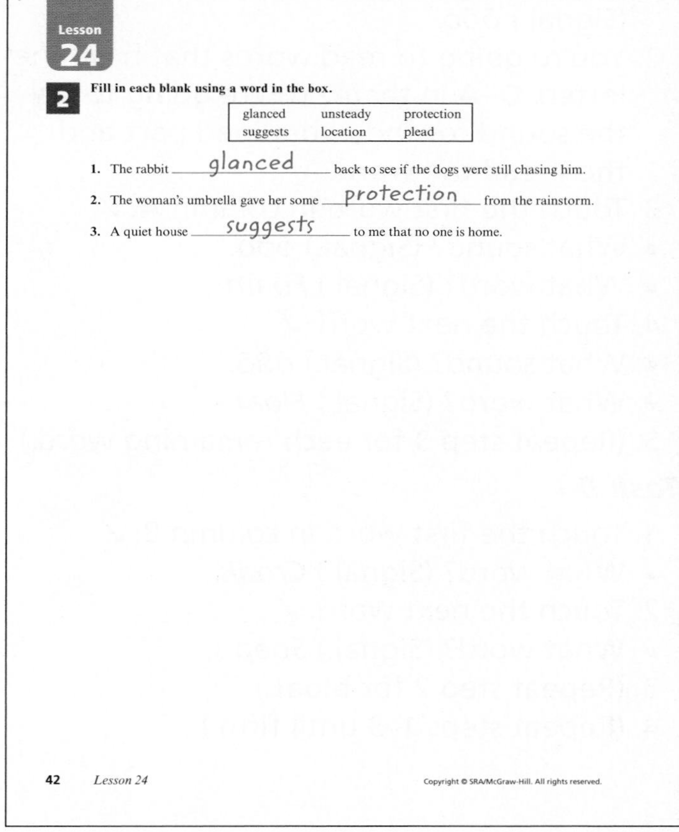

Lesson 24

2 **Fill in each blank using a word in the box.**

glanced	unsteady	protection
suggests	location	plead

1. The rabbit glanced back to see if the dogs were still chasing him.
2. The woman's umbrella gave her some protection from the rainstorm.
3. A quiet house suggests to me that no one is home.

42 *Lesson 24* Copyright © SRA/McGraw-Hill. All rights reserved.

Lesson

25

WORD-ATTACK SKILLS

Student Book 

EXERCISE 1

NEW **SOUND COMBINATION: oa**

Task A

1. Open your Student Book to Lesson 25. ✓

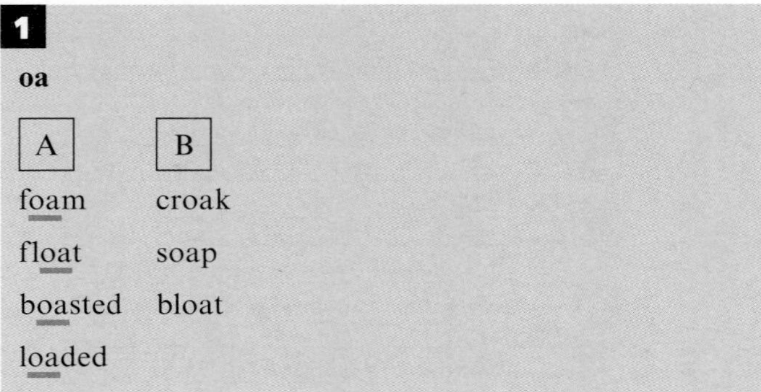

1

oa

A	B
foam	croak
float	soap
boasted	bloat
loaded	

- Touch the letters **O–A** in part 1. ✓
- The letters **O–A** go together and make the sound **ōōō.** What sound? (Signal.) *ōōō.*

2. You're going to read words that have the letters **O–A** in them. You're going to say the sound for the underlined part and then read the word.
3. Touch the first word in column A. ✓
- What sound? (Signal.) *ōōō.*
- What word? (Signal.) *Foam.*

4. Touch the next word. ✓
- What sound? (Signal.) *ōōō.*
- What word? (Signal.) *Float.*

5. (Repeat step 3 for each remaining word.)

Task B

1. Touch the first word in column B. ✓
- What word? (Signal.) *Croak.*

2. Touch the next word. ✓
- What word? (Signal.) *Soap.*

3. (Repeat step 2 for **bloat.**)
4. (Repeat steps 1–3 until firm.)

EXERCISE 2

WORD PRACTICE

1. Touch the first word in part 2. ✓

2

explained changing speedboat

astound carved observed lanterns

already arrangements excited

- What sound? (Signal.) *āāā.*
- What word? (Signal.) *Explained.*

2. Touch the next word. ✓
- What sound? (Signal.) *j.*
- What word? (Signal.) *Changing.*

3. (Repeat step 2 for each remaining word.)
4. (Repeat each row of words until firm.)

EXERCISE 3

VOCABULARY

1. Touch part 3. ✓

3

1. statue
2. figurehead
3. salvage
4. claim
5. marine

- We're going to talk about what those words mean.

2. Touch word 1. ✓
- What word? (Signal.) *Statue.*
- Who knows what a **statue** is? (Call on a student.) (Idea: *A likeness made of stone, wood, or metal.*)

3. Everybody, touch word 2. ✓
- What word? (Signal.) *Figurehead.*
- The **carved figure on the front of a ship** is a **figurehead.**

4. Touch word 3. ✓
- What word? (Signal.) *Salvage.*
- Valuable objects that are saved from the ocean are called **salvage.**

5. Touch word 4. ✓
- What word? (Signal.) *Claim.*
- When you pick up something you own, you **claim** it. Everybody, what's another way of saying "The man picked up the luggage he owns"? (Signal.) *The man claimed his luggage.*

6. Touch word 5. ✓
- What word? (Signal.) *Marine.*
- **Marine** is another word for **sea.** Animals found in the sea are called **marine** animals. Everybody, what are plants that live in the sea called? (Signal.) *Marine plants.*

EXERCISE 4

WORD PRACTICE

1. Touch the first word in part 4. ✓

4

darkness grain better oxygen
placed afraid nearly probably*
believe dead slime* covered
company profits split suggested
proof explore writing important
early guess instruments restaurant

- What word? (Signal.) *Darkness.*

2. Next word. ✓
- What word? (Signal.) *Grain.*

3. (Repeat step 2 for each remaining word.)
4. (Repeat each row of words until firm.)
5. What does **probably** mean? (Call on a student.)
- (Repeat for **slime.**)

EXERCISE 5

MULTIPART WORDS

Task A

1. Touch part 5. ✓

> **Note:** The parts of a word are to be pronounced the same as they are when the word is spoken normally.

5

individual combination obviously
1. individual 2. combination 3. obviously
disagreement participants
4. disagreement 5. participants

2. All these words have more than one part. The first part and the last part are circled.
3. Touch word 1. ✓
- Word 1 is **individual**. What word? (Signal.) *Individual.*

4. What's the first part? (Signal.) *in.*
- What's the last part? (Signal.) *al.*
- The middle part is spelled **D–I–V–I–D–U.** What does that part say in the word? (Signal.) *dividu.*

5. So, the parts are **in** (pause) **dividu** (pause) **al.**
- Say the whole word. (Signal.) *Individual.*

6. (Repeat steps 3–5 until firm.)
7. Touch word 2. ✓
- Word 2 is **combination.** What word? (Signal.) *Combination.*

8. What's the first part? (Signal.) *com.*
- What's the last part? (Signal.) *tion.*
- The middle part is spelled **B–I–N–A.** What does that part say in the word? (Signal.) *bina.*

9. So, the parts are **com** (pause) **bina** (pause) **tion.**
- Say the whole word. (Signal.) *Combination.*

10. (Repeat steps 7–9 until firm.)
11. Touch word 3. ✓
- Word 3 is **obviously.** What word? (Signal.) *Obviously.*

12. What's the first part? (Signal.) *ob.*
- What's the last part? (Signal.) *ly.*
- The middle part is spelled **V–I–O–U–S.** What does that part say in the word? (Signal.) *vious.*

13. So, the parts are **ob** (pause) **vious** (pause) **ly.**
- Say the whole word. (Signal.) *Obviously.*

14. (Repeat steps 11–13 until firm.)

15. Touch word 4. ✓
- Word 4 is **disagreement**. What word? (Signal.) *Disagreement.*

16. What's the first part? (Signal.) *dis.*
- What's the last part? (Signal.) *ment.*
- The middle part is spelled **A–G–R–E–E.** What does that part say in the word? (Signal.) *agree.*

17. So, the parts are **dis** (pause) **agree** (pause) **ment.**
- Say the whole word. (Signal.) *Disagreement.*

18. (Repeat steps 15–17 until firm.)
19. Touch word 5. ✓
- Word 5 is **participants.** What word? (Signal.) *Participants.*

20. What's the first part? (Signal.) *par.*
- What's the last part? (Signal.) *pants.*
- The middle part is spelled **T–I–C–I.** What does that part say in the word? (Signal.) *tici.*

21. So, the parts are **par** (pause) **tici** (pause) **pants.**
- Say the whole word. (Signal.) *Participants.*

22. (Repeat steps 19–21 until firm.)

Task B

1. Touch the sentences below the word list. ✓

a. I am obviously in strong disagreement with that plan.
b. Individual participants went to their different meeting rooms.
c. She obviously had a combination of good looks and a sense of humor.
d. There were only three participants in the final events.
e. Every year some students forget the combination to their locker.

- These are sentences that use the words you just read.

2. Raise your hand when you can read sentence A. ✓
3. (Call on a student.) Read sentence A. *I am obviously in strong disagreement with that plan.*
- That means "It should be very easy to see that I do not agree in any way with that plan."

4. (Call on a student.) Read sentence B. *Individual participants went to their different meeting rooms.*
- That means "Each person who took part went to a particular meeting room."

5. (Call on a student.) Read sentence C. *She obviously had a combination of good looks and a sense of humor.*
- That means "It's easy to see that she had good looks and a sense of humor."

6. (Call on a student.) Read sentence D. *There were only three participants in the final events.*
- That means "Only three individuals took part in the last event."

7. (Call on a student.) Read sentence E. *Every year some students forget the combination to their locker.*

EXERCISE 6

WORD-ATTACK SKILLS: Individual tests

1. (Call on individual students. Each student reads a row of words, a column of words, or a sentence. In the Multipart words exercises, each sentence counts as one row of words. Tally the rows, columns, and sentences read without error. If the group reads at least 14 rows and columns without making errors, direct all students to record 5 points in Box A of their Point Chart. Criterion is 80 percent of rows and columns read without error.)
2. (If the group did not read at least 14 rows and columns without errors, do not award any points for the Word-Attack Skills exercises.)

SELECTION READING

EXERCISE 7

STORY READING

1. Everybody, touch part 6. ✓
2. The error limit for this story is 12. If the group reads the story with 12 errors or less, you earn 5 points.

6

Exploring the Ship

3. (Call on a student to read the title.) *Exploring the Ship.*
- What do you think this story is about? (Accept reasonable responses.)
4. (Call on individual students. Each is to read two to four sentences.)
5. (Call on individual students to answer the specified questions during the story reading.)

Jane and Doris made it home safely from the reef. When the women returned to their motel, Jane was very tired but still excited from her adventures. She and Doris had dinner at the motel restaurant. As they waited to be served, they began to talk. The more they talked, the faster and louder they talked. They made plans about going back to the sunken ship. About a hundred times, Jane said, "There is no way I'm going back inside that ship. I just won't do it." She explained that the storm frightened her, but not nearly as much as that ship had—down in the dark sea, covered with slime and filled with bones. ❶

1. Why didn't Jane want to go back into the ship? (Ideas: *Because it was dark and covered with slime; because of the skeleton.*)
1. What frightened Jane the most? (Idea: *The skull in the ship.*)

"OK," Doris said. "Let's go back early in the morning and put up a salvage-claim flag. Then we'll make a deal with some salvage company to go out there and explore the ship. We'll split the profits with them."

"Hey," Jane said. "That's a good idea. Let's do that."

And they did. The next morning they rented a speedboat—not that old scow that they had been using. The speedboat cost them fifty dollars, which was most of the money they had. The women agreed that it was better to have a fast boat, even if that meant paying more money. ❷

2. What kind of flag were Jane and Doris going to put up? *A salvage-claim flag.*
2. What kind of deal would Jane and Doris make with the salvage company? (Idea: *The salvage company would explore the ship and split the profits with them.*)
2. How much did Jane and Doris pay for the speedboat? *Fifty dollars.*
2. Why did Jane and Doris think that they were better off with the speedboat? (Idea: *Because it was better to have a fast boat.*)

Lesson 25

The ride out was a lot of fun. Doris drove the boat, and Jane sat in the back, feeling the spray made by the boat as it cut a path along the surface of the water. Jane watched the little waves zip by. Then the women placed a red salvage flag along with the diving flags over the spot where the sunken ship was resting.

Jane took a picture of Doris and the salvage flag. "That's just for proof," Jane said. "We have just claimed a sunken treasure. I don't believe it."

"Me neither," Doris agreed.

By noon, the women had made arrangements with a man from a marine salvage outfit. His name was Mike. By two o'clock that afternoon, Mike, Doris, Jane, and two other men were anchored above the sunken ship. They were in a boat that looked like an old tugboat. Mike was in diving gear. He and one of the other men explained that they would go down and explore the ship. ❸

3. Where did Jane and Doris place the salvage flag? (Idea: *Over the spot where the sunken ship was resting.*)
3. Why did Jane take a picture of the flag? (Idea: *For proof that they had found the ship.*)
3. What kind of gear was Mike wearing? *Diving gear.*

By four that afternoon, the divers returned to the surface. Mike's mask bubbled up from the sea. He pushed the mask back and smiled. "Well, you found a sunken ship, all right," he explained. "But I'm afraid there's no gold on this ship."

"Oh, no," Doris said. She turned to Jane, and each woman shook her head.

"But," Mike added, "there are some things on board that are worth some money."

"What?" Jane asked.

"Well, there are a lot of little things. This ship was probably built around 1780. It was probably carrying grain and other supplies. There are some bottles in the hold that are probably worth twenty dollars each. I would guess there are a hundred bottles down there."

Jane and Doris looked at each other and smiled.

"And there are some old navigation instruments. A couple of them seem to be in fair shape. They're probably worth more than two hundred dollars each." Mike listed other things—a statue, a carved figurehead, some writing instruments, some old lanterns. ❹

4. When was the ship built? *Around 1780.*
4. What kinds of treasures were on the ship? (Ideas: *Some old navigation instruments; some old bottles; a statue; a carved figurehead; some writing instruments; some old lanterns.*)

Doris and Jane didn't get rich. Their trip to Florida cost them more than one thousand dollars. But each woman got two thousand dollars for her share of the salvage from the sunken ship. On the flight back home, Jane felt pretty proud. "We may not be rich," she observed, "but we did it. Instead of sitting and thinking about it, we did it. I think that's the most important part." ❺

5. How much did each woman get as her share of the treasure? *Two thousand dollars.*
5. What was most important to Jane? (Idea: *That they did what they wanted to do instead of just sitting and thinking about it.*)
5. What other accomplishments in Jane's life should she be proud of? (Idea: *Overcoming her accident.*)
5. Why do you think that Jane was happy with her trip? (Idea: *Because she had looked for a sunken ship and found it.*)

6. (Award points quickly.)
7. (If the group makes more than 12 errors, repeat the reading immediately or on the next day.)

FLUENCY ASSESSMENT

EXERCISE 8

TIMED READING CHECKOUTS

1. (For this part of the lesson, assigned pairs of students work together during the checkouts.)
- (If one student does not have a checkout partner, arrange another time when you can give the checkout.)
2. (Each student does a 2-minute timed reading. Students earn 5 points by reading at least 240 words and making no more than 5 errors on the first part of story 25. Students record points in Box C of their Point Chart and plot their reading rate and errors on the Individual Reading Progress Chart.)
- (During each timed checkout, observe one pair of students for 2 minutes. Make notes on any mistakes the reader makes.)
3. (Record the timed reading checkout performance for each student you observed on the Fluency Assessment Summary form.)

WORKBOOK EXERCISES

Workbook: Teacher Directed

EXERCISE 9

COPYING MAIN-IDEA SENTENCE

1. Open your Workbook to Lesson 25. ✓

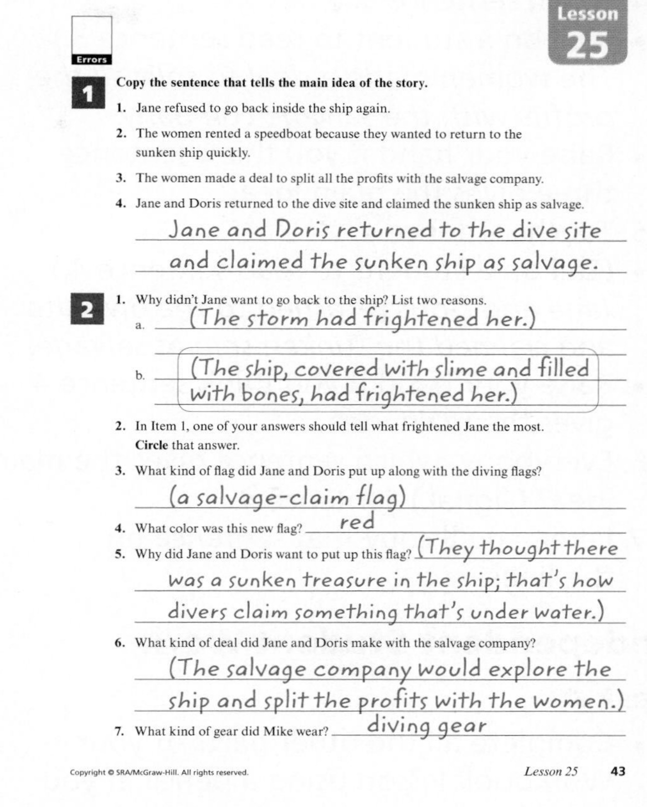

Lesson 25

Errors

1 **Copy the sentence that tells the main idea of the story.**

1. Jane refused to go back inside the ship again.
2. The women rented a speedboat because they wanted to return to the sunken ship quickly.
3. The women made a deal to split all the profits with the salvage company.
4. Jane and Doris returned to the dive site and claimed the sunken ship as salvage.

Jane and Doris returned to the dive site and claimed the sunken ship as salvage.

2

1. Why didn't Jane want to go back to the ship? List two reasons.
   a. (The storm had frightened her.)
   b. (The ship, covered with slime and filled with bones, had frightened her.)
2. In Item 1, one of your answers should tell what frightened Jane the most. **Circle** that answer.
3. What kind of flag did Jane and Doris put up along with the diving flags? (a salvage-claim flag)
4. What color was this new flag? red
5. Why did Jane and Doris want to put up this flag? (They thought there was a sunken treasure in the ship; that's how divers claim something that's under water.)
6. What kind of deal did Jane and Doris make with the salvage company? (The salvage company would explore the ship and split the profits with the women.)
7. What kind of gear did Mike wear? diving gear

Copyright © SRA/McGraw-Hill. All rights reserved. Lesson 25 43

- Touch part 1. ✓
- You're going to copy the sentence that tells the **main idea** of the story. The **main idea** of the story is the **main thing that happened** in the story. One of the four sentences gives the main idea of the story.

2. Touch sentence 1. ✓
- (Call on a student to read sentence 1.) *Jane refused to go back inside the ship again.*
- Raise your hand if you think sentence 1 gives the main idea.
3. Touch sentence 2. ✓
- (Call on a student to read sentence 2.) *The women rented a speedboat because they wanted to return to the sunken ship quickly.*
- Raise your hand if you think sentence 2 gives the main idea.

4. Touch sentence 3. ✓
- (Call on a student to read sentence 3.) *The women made a deal to split all the profits with the salvage company.*
- Raise your hand if you think sentence three gives the main idea.

5. Touch sentence 4. ✓
- (Call on a student to read sentence 4.) *Jane and Doris returned to the dive site and claimed the sunken ship as salvage.*
- Raise your hand if you think sentence 4 gives the main idea.

6. Everybody, which sentence gives the main idea? (Signal.) *Sentence 4.*
7. Later, you'll copy that sentence on the lines.

Independent Student Work

Task A

- Complete all the other parts of your Workbook lesson using a pencil. If you make no errors, you will earn 5 points.

Task B

1. (Before presenting Lesson 26, check student Workbooks for Lesson 25.)
- (Call on individual students to read the items and answers in each part. Students mark errors using a pen.)
2. (Direct the students to count the number of errors and write the number in the Errors box at the top of the Workbook page.)
3. (Award points and direct students to record points in Box D of their Point Chart.)

0 errors .... 5 points
1 error .... 3 points
2 or 3 errors .... 1 point
more than 3 errors .... 0 points

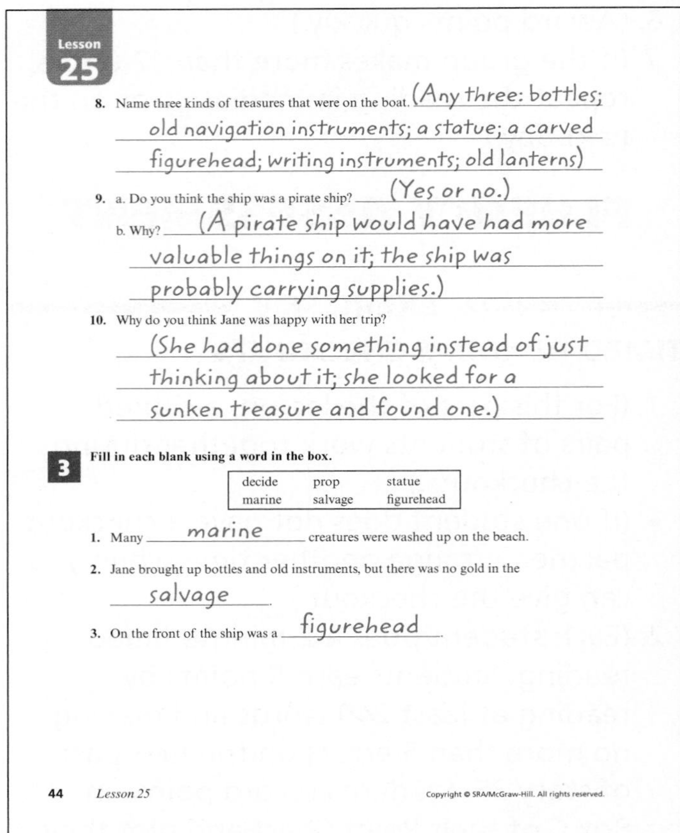
Lesson 25

8. Name three kinds of treasures that were on the boat. (Any three: bottles; old navigation instruments; a statue; a carved figurehead; writing instruments; old lanterns)

9. a. Do you think the ship was a pirate ship? (Yes or no.)
b. Why? (A pirate ship would have had more valuable things on it; the ship was probably carrying supplies.)

10. Why do you think Jane was happy with her trip? (She had done something instead of just thinking about it; she looked for a sunken treasure and found one.)

3 Fill in each blank using a word in the box.

decide	prop	statue
marine	salvage	figurehead

1. Many marine creatures were washed up on the beach.
2. Jane brought up bottles and old instruments, but there was no gold in the salvage.
3. On the front of the ship was a figurehead.

44 *Lesson 25* Copyright © SRA/McGraw-Hill. All rights reserved.

Point schedule for Lessons 21 through 25

Box	Lesson part	Points
A	Word Attack	0 or 5
B	Selection Reading	0 or 5
C	Timed Reading Checkout	0 or 5
D	Workbook	0, 1, 3, or 5
Bonus	(Teacher option)	—

Five-lesson point summary

- (For **letter grades** based on points for Lessons **21** through **25,** tell students to compute the total for the blue boxes [C, D, and Bonus] and write the number in the Total box at the end of each row in their Point Chart. Students then add the totals and write the sum in the green box.)
- (For **rewards** based on points, tell students to compute the total for all boxes [A, B, C, D, and Bonus] and write the number in the Total box at the end of each row. Students then add the totals and write the sum in the green box.)

END OF LESSON 25

Lesson Objectives	LESSON 26 Exercise	LESSON 27 Exercise	LESSON 28 Exercise	LESSON 29 Exercise	LESSON 30 Exercise
Word Attack					
Decoding and Word Analysis					
Sound Combination: *oi*				1	
Sound Combination: *ure*					1
Affix: *ex*	1	1			
Affix: *un*	2	2	1		
Affix: *ly*			2	2	
Letter Combinations/Letter Sounds	3			1	1, 2
Word Recognition	1–5	1–5	1–5	1–5	1–4
Vocabulary					
Morphemic Analysis	1, 2	1, 2	1, 2	2	
Definitions	4, 5	3, 4	3, 4	3–5	3, 4
Usage	4	3	3	3	3
Assessment					
Ongoing: Individual Tests	6	6	6	6	5
Group Reading					
Decoding and Word Analysis					
Read Decodable Text	7	7	7	7	6
Comprehension					
Access Prior Knowledge		7	7	7	
Draw Inferences	7	7	7	7	6
Note Details	7	7	7	7	6
Predict	7	7	7	7	6
Vocabulary: Definitions		7			
Assessment					
Ongoing: Comprehension Check	7	7	7	7	6
Ongoing: Decoding Accuracy	7	7	7	7	6
Formal: Mastery Test					MT 1
Fluency Assessment					
Fluency					
Reread Decodable Text	8	8	8	8	7
Assessment					
Ongoing: Teacher-Monitored Fluency	8	8	8	8	7
Ongoing: Peer-Monitored Fluency	8	8	8	8	7
Workbook Exercises					
Decoding and Word Analysis					
Multisyllabic Word Parts	Ind. Work			Ind. Work	
Comprehension					
Note Details	Ind. Work	Ind. Work	Ind. Work	Ind. Work	Ind. Work
True/False				Ind. Work	
Vocabulary					
Usage	Ind. Work	Ind. Work	Ind. Work	Ind. Work	Ind. Work
Study Skills					
Writing Mechanics					
Assessment					
Ongoing: Workcheck	Workcheck	Workcheck	Workcheck	Workcheck	Workcheck

Lesson 26

WORD-ATTACK SKILLS

Board Work

EXERCISE 1

NEW **AFFIX: ex**

1. (Print in a column on the board:)

tend
cite
ample
plain
pose

2. (Point to **tend.** Pause.) What word? (Signal.) *Tend.*
- (Repeat for **cite, ample, plain, pose.**)
- (Repeat the list until firm.)
3. (Add **ex** to the beginning of each word:)

extend
excite
example
explain
expose

4. (Point to **extend.** Pause.) What word? (Signal.) *Extend.*
- (Repeat for **excite, example, explain, expose.**)
- (Repeat the list until firm.)

Student Book

EXERCISE 2

NEW **AFFIX: un**

1. Open your Student Book to Lesson 26. ✓

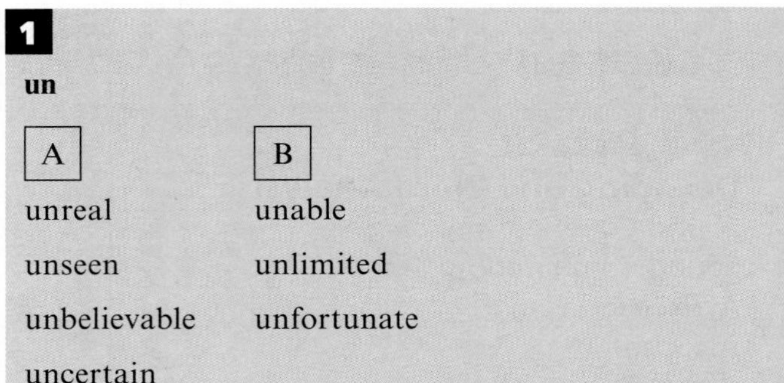

1

un

A	B
unreal	unable
unseen	unlimited
unbelievable	unfortunate
uncertain	

- Touch the letters **U–N** in part 1. ✓
- When those letters appear at the beginning of a word, they usually mean **not.** What does **un** mean? (Signal.) *Not.*
2. Touch the first word in column A. ✓
- What word? (Signal.) *Unreal.*
- What does **unreal** mean? (Signal.) *Not real.*
3. Touch the next word. ✓
- What word? (Signal.) *Unseen.*
- What does **unseen** mean? (Signal.) *Not seen.*
4. (Repeat step 3 for each remaining word.)
5. (Repeat the list until firm.)
6. (Repeat steps 2–5 for the words in column B.)

EXERCISE 3

WORD PRACTICE

1. Touch the first word in part 2. ✓

2

bright easily interesting contained
distance gigantic although falter
fifteenth branches approaches flights
matches floating frightened

- What sound? (Signal.) *īīī.*
- What word? (Signal.) *Bright.*
2. Touch the next word. ✓
- What sound? (Signal.) *ēēē.*
- What word? (Signal.) *Easily.*
3. (Repeat step 2 for each remaining word.)
4. (Repeat each row of words until firm.)

EXERCISE 4

VOCABULARY

1. Touch part 3. ✓

3

1. tunnel
2. fluttered
3. snaked
4. drizzly
5. canopy

- We're going to talk about what those words mean.

2. Touch word 1. ✓
- What word? (Signal.) *Tunnel.*
- Who can tell me what a **tunnel** is? (Call on a student.) (Idea: *A passage through water or mountains.*)
3. Everybody, touch word 2. ✓
- What word? (Signal.) *Fluttered.*
- **Flutter** is another way of saying **move back and forth rapidly.** What's another way of saying "The leaves **moved back and forth rapidly** in the breeze"? (Signal.) *The leaves fluttered in the breeze.*
4. Touch word 3. ✓
- What word? (Signal.) *Snaked.*
- **Snaked** is another way of saying **twisted.** Everybody, what's another way of saying "The road **twisted** between the mountains"? (Signal.) *The road snaked between the mountains.*
5. Touch word 4. ✓
- What word? (Signal.) *Drizzly.*
- Who knows what a **drizzly** rain is like? (Call on a student.) (Idea: *Like a light, quiet rain.*)
6. Everybody, touch word 5. ✓
- What word? (Signal.) *Canopy.*
- A **canopy** is like a **roof** above something. Everybody, what's another way of saying "The branches were a **roof** above the forest"? (Signal.) *The branches were a canopy above the forest.*

EXERCISE 5

WORD PRACTICE

1. Touch the first word in part 4. ✓

4

sequoia foliage building cousin
swirled* darkness drifted develop
survive* through swayed* Pacific
November create covered among
suggested neither extended
constructed parent rapidly

- What word? (Signal.) *Sequoia.*

2. Next word. ✓
- What word? (Signal.) *Foliage.*
3. (Repeat step 2 for each remaining word.)
4. (Repeat each row of words until firm.)
5. What does **swirled** mean? (Call on a student.)
- (Repeat for **survive, swayed.**)

EXERCISE 6

NEW WORD-ATTACK SKILLS: Individual tests

1. (Call on individual students. Each student reads a row or column. Tally the rows and columns read without error. If the group reads at least 10 rows and columns without making errors, direct all students to record 5 points in Box A of their Point Chart. Criterion is 80 percent of rows and columns read without error.)
2. (If the group did not read at least 10 rows and columns without errors, do not award any points for the Word-Attack Skills exercises.)

Lesson
26

SELECTION READING

EXERCISE 7

STORY READING

1. Everybody, touch part 5. ✓
2. The error limit for this story is 12. If the group reads the story with 12 errors or less, you earn 5 points.

5

The Redwood Tree

3. (Call on a student to read the title.) *The Redwood Tree.*
- What do you think this story is about? (Accept reasonable responses.)
4. (Call on individual students. Each is to read two to four sentences.)
5. (Call on individual students to answer the specified questions during the story reading.)

This is the story of a redwood tree that is living today in northern California. That redwood, like many others, has had an interesting life.

Its life began with a seed contained in a cone. A redwood cone is about as big as a quarter. The cone starts to grow in early summer. By late summer it is full-sized and bright green with many seeds inside. The cone is not yet full grown, however. As fall approaches, the cone begins to change color, turning brown. Small flaps on all sides of the cone open, and as they do, the tiny seeds fall out. The seeds are so small that ten of them would easily fit on the end of your finger. If you wanted a pound of these seeds, you would have to collect about 120 thousand of them. ❶

1. How big is a redwood cone? (Idea: *About as big as a quarter.*)
1. How big are the redwood seeds? (Ideas: *Very small; so small that ten could fit on the end of your finger.*)

It seems strange that a seed so small can grow into the world's tallest tree, but it's true. Redwoods are the tallest trees, although a cousin of the redwood—the giant sequoia—has a thicker trunk than the redwood. Some giant sequoias have trunks so thick that people have constructed tunnels through them, and these tunnels are so big that cars can pass through them. The giant sequoia, however, does not grow as tall as the redwood. To get an idea of how tall the bigger redwoods are, imagine what it would be like to climb a flight of stairs as high as these redwoods. Imagine climbing five flights of stairs. Imagine how far down it is when you are five stories high. A big redwood is much taller than a five-story building, however. So imagine going up to the tenth floor, the fifteenth floor, the twentieth floor. From up here you can see a long distance, and it's a long, long way down. However, if you were on the twentieth floor of a building, you would not be near the top of a big redwood. You would probably be tired from climbing twenty flights of stairs; however, to reach the top of a big redwood, you would have to climb another fifteen flights of stairs. That's right. A very tall redwood is about as tall as a thirty-five-story building. A person standing down at the base of the tree would look like an ant. The base of the redwood's trunk is so big that eight people could stand next to each other and hide behind the trunk. And that gigantic tree develops from a seed smaller than a grain of wheat. ❷

2. Which kinds of trees are the tallest? *Redwoods.*
2. Which kinds of trees have the thickest trunks? *Giant sequoias.*
2. How tall is a very tall redwood? (Idea: *About as tall as a thirty-five-story building.*)

It was on a sunny November day that the seed of the redwood tree in this story fluttered from the cone. The parent tree stood on the bank of a small creek that snaked among the giant redwoods. The weather had been cold, and a drizzly rain had been falling for days. During the rain, the flaps of the redwood cone swelled up and closed. But now the sun emerged, and a brisk wind swirled through the tops of the redwoods, bending their tops to the south. As the top of the parent tree swayed in the cool wind, the cones began to dry out, and the flaps began to open. Below, the forest was deeply shaded by the foliage of the giant redwoods, which formed a canopy of green that extended as far as one could see. In the distance was the sound of the Pacific Ocean.

Late that afternoon, a sudden gust of wind pushed through the forest, bending branches of the redwoods. When that wind hit the parent tree, six of the cone's forty seeds fluttered down and drifted down, down, into the dark forest below. One of those seeds would develop into a giant. The others would not survive. ❸

3. When did the seeds from the redwood tree flutter from the cone? (Idea: *On a very sunny November day.*)
3. How many seeds fluttered down? *Six.*
3. How many seeds survived? *One.*
6. (Award points quickly.)
7. (If the group makes more than 12 errors, repeat the reading immediately or on the next day.)

FLUENCY ASSESSMENT

EXERCISE 8

TIMED READING CHECKOUTS

1. (For this part of the lesson, assigned pairs of students work together during the checkouts.)
- (If one student does not have a checkout partner, arrange another time when you can give the checkout.)
2. (Each student does a 2-minute timed reading. Students earn 5 points by reading at least 240 words and making no more than 5 errors on the first part of story 26. Students record points in Box C of their Point Chart and plot their reading rate and errors on the Individual Reading Progress Chart.)
- (During each timed checkout, observe one pair of students for 2 minutes. Make notes on any mistakes the reader makes.)
3. (Record the timed reading checkout performance for each student you observed on the Fluency Assessment Summary form.)

Lesson 26

WORKBOOK EXCERCISES

Errors

Lesson 26

1

1. How does a redwood tree's life begin? (with a seed in a cone)
2. How big is a redwood cone? (about as big as a quarter)
3. How big are redwood seeds? (tiny; so small that ten of them would easily fit on the end of your finger)
4. Which kind of trees have the thickest trunks? giant sequoia
5. How would you describe a giant sequoia trunk to show how thick it is? (Some have had tunnels built in them that were big enough for cars to pass through.)
6. How tall is a very tall redwood? (about as tall as a thirty-five-story building)
7. Which trees are the tallest in the world? redwoods
8. When did the seeds from the redwood tree flutter from the cone? (on a sunny November day)
9. Why didn't the seeds fall from the cone when it was raining? (The flaps of the cone were swelled up and closed.)
10. How many seeds survived? one

Copyright © SRA/McGraw-Hill. All rights reserved.

Lesson 26

2 Fill in each blank using a word in the box.

tunnel	snaked	fluttered
salvage	drizzly	emerged

1. The baby birds fluttered their wings.
2. The door opened, and a tall man emerged.
3. The road snaked around the mountains instead of tunneling through them.

3 Write the parts for each word.

1. untended = un + tend + ed
2. explaining = ex + plain + ing
3. excitement = ex + cite + ment
4. uninteresting = un + interest + ing

Copyright © SRA/McGraw-Hill. All rights reserved.

Independent Student Work

Task A

- Open your Workbook to Lesson 26. ✓
- Complete all the parts of your Workbook lesson using a pencil. If you make no errors, you will earn 5 points.

Task B

1. (Before presenting Lesson 27, check student Workbooks for Lesson 26.)
   - (Call on individual students to read the items and answers in each part. Students mark errors using a pen.)
2. (Direct the students to count the number of errors and write the number in the Errors box at the top of the Workbook page.)
3. (Award points and direct students to record points in Box D of their Point Chart.)

   0 errors ....5 points
   1 error ....3 points
   2 or 3 errors ....1 point
   more than 3 errors ....0 points

END OF LESSON 26

WORD-ATTACK SKILLS

Student Book 

EXERCISE 1

NEW **AFFIX: ex**

1. Open your Student Book to Lesson 27. ✓

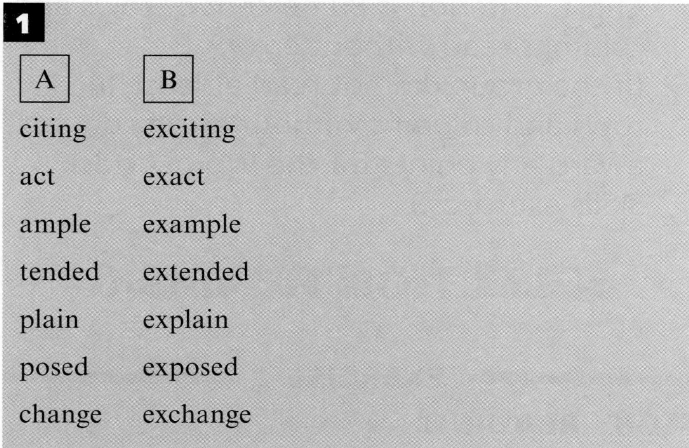

1

A	B
citing	exciting
act	exact
ample	example
tended	extended
plain	explain
posed	exposed
change	exchange

- Touch part 1. ✓
2. Touch the first word in column A. ✓
- What word? (Signal.) *Citing.*
3. Next word. ✓
- What word? (Signal.) *Act.*
4. (Repeat step 3 for **ample, tended, plain, posed, change.**)
5. (Repeat steps 2–4 until firm.)
6. (Repeat steps 2–5 for the words in column B.)

EXERCISE 2

NEW **AFFIX: un**

1. Touch the letters **U–N** in part 2. ✓

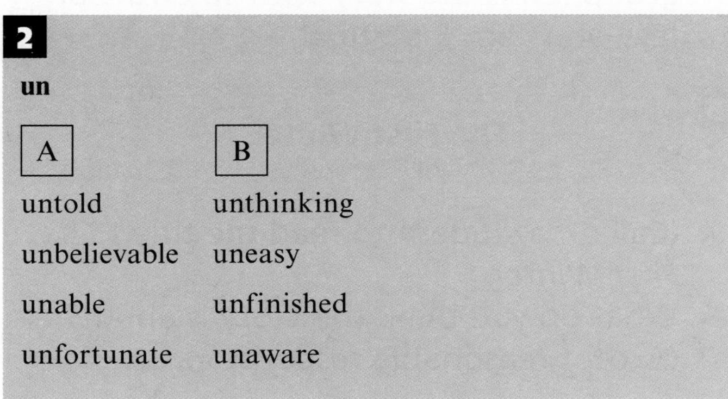

2

un

A	B
untold	unthinking
unbelievable	uneasy
unable	unfinished
unfortunate	unaware

- What does **un** usually mean when it appears at the beginning of a word? (Signal.) *Not.*
2. Touch the first word in column A. ✓
- What word? (Signal.) *Untold.*
- What does **untold** mean? (Signal.) *Not told.*
3. Touch the next word. ✓
- What word? (Signal.) *Unbelievable.*
- What does **unbelievable** mean? (Signal.) *Not believable.*
4. (Repeat step 3 for each remaining word.)
5. (Repeat the list until firm.)
6. (Repeat steps 2–5 for the words in column B.)

EXERCISE 3

VOCABULARY

1. Touch part 3. ✓

3

1. litter
2. mole
3. severe

- We're going to talk about what those words mean.
2. Touch word 1. ✓
- What word? (Signal.) *Litter.*
- Who knows what **litter** is? (Call on a student.) (Idea: *Debris.*)
3. Everybody, touch word 2. ✓
- What word? (Signal.) *Mole.*
- A **mole** is a **small animal that spends most of its life underground.** What is a **mole?** (Call on a student.) *A small animal that spends most of its life underground.*
4. Everybody, touch word 3. ✓
- What word? (Signal.) *Severe.*
- **Severe** is another way of saying **very fierce.** Everybody, what's another way of saying "The storm was **very fierce**"? (Signal.) *The storm was severe.*

Lesson 27

EXERCISE 4

WORD PRACTICE

1. Touch the first word in part 4. ✓

4

slightly boasted crunch installed

astounded alternate cloudy always

seeming inspection alter person

flight white hours exceptionally

produce survive* branches coated

- What sound? (Signal.) *īīī.*
- What word? (Signal.) *Slightly.*

2. Touch the next word. ✓

- What sound? (Signal.) *ōōō.*
- What word? (Signal.) *Boasted.*

3. (Repeat step 2 for each remaining word.)
4. (Repeat each row of words until firm.)
5. What does **survive** mean? (Call on a student.)

EXERCISE 5

WORD PRACTICE

1. Touch the first word in part 5. ✓

5

wrist midst obviously developed

neither fertile receive canopy* event

adventure continued occasionally lodged

quite quiet pinpoints remained

exposed feast contained strength

creating worse jagged ruffled weigh

edge fortunate rattle square

- What word? (Signal.) *Wrist.*

2. Next word. ✓

- What word? (Signal.) *Midst.*

3. (Repeat step 2 for each remaining word.)
4. (Repeat each row of words until firm.)
5. What does **canopy** mean? (Call on a student.)

EXERCISE 6

WORD-ATTACK SKILLS: Individual tests

1. (Call on individual students. Each student reads a row or column. Tally the rows and columns read without error. If the group reads at least 14 rows and columns without making errors, direct all students to record 5 points in Box A of their Point Chart. Criterion is 80 percent of rows and columns read without error.)
2. (If the group did not read at least 14 rows and columns without errors, do not award any points for the Word-Attack Skills exercises.)

SELECTION READING

EXERCISE 7

STORY READING

1. (Call on individual students to answer these questions.)

- What kind of tree is tallest? *The redwood tree.*
- How tall do some of them get? (Idea: *About as tall as a thirty-five-story building.*)
- What kind of tree has the thickest trunk? *The giant sequoia.*
- How thick are the trunks of some giant sequoias? (Idea: *So thick that people have constructed tunnels in the trunks large enough for cars to pass through them.*)

2. Everybody, touch part 6. ✓
3. The error limit for this story is 12. If the group reads the story with 12 errors or less, you earn 5 points.

6 **The First Winter**

4. (Call on a student to read the title.) *The First Winter.*

- What do you think this story is about? (Accept reasonable responses.)

5. (Call on individual students. Each is to read two to four sentences.)
6. (Call on individual students to answer the specified questions during the story reading.)

During a good seed year a large redwood will produce over twelve pounds of seeds, which is nearly a million and a half seeds. And the year that our redwood seed fluttered from the cone was an exceptionally good year. The parent tree produced over fifteen pounds of seeds that year, enough seed to start a forest that would be six square miles in size. However, only a few redwood seeds survived. In fact, only three of the seeds from the parent tree survived their first year, and only one lived beyond the first year. ❶

1. How many pounds of seed did the parent tree produce that year? *Over fifteen pounds.*
1. How many seeds from the parent tree survived beyond the first year? *Only one.*

Obviously, our seed was lucky. It was a fortunate seed because it was fertile. If a seed is not fertile, it cannot grow, and about nine of every ten redwood seeds are not fertile. Our seed was also fortunate because it landed in a place where it could survive. If it had fallen on a part of the forest floor covered with thick, heavy litter, it probably would not have grown. If it had fluttered to a spot that became too dry during the summer, it would have died during that first year. ❷

2. Why was our seed lucky? (Ideas: *Because it was fertile; because it landed on a place where it could survive.*)

Our seed landed in a spot where moles had been digging. They had made small piles of fresh brown dirt, and our seed landed on the edge of the dirt. Later that winter another fortunate event took place. The top fifty feet of a nearby tree broke off during a severe windstorm. When the top, which weighed more than three elephants, crashed to the forest floor, it tore the branches from the trees that were in its path. The fallen top left a large hole in the green canopy that shaded the forest floor. This event was fortunate for our seed because it would receive sunlight. Some trees are capable of growing only in bright sunlight, while other trees survive only in the shade. Redwoods are unusual trees because they can survive in either shade or sunlight; however, they don't grow well in deep shade. ❸

3. What did our seed need to survive? (Idea: *Fresh brown dirt and some sunlight.*)
3. Where did our seed land? (Idea: *In a spot where moles had been digging.*)
3. What happened so that our seed would receive sunlight? (Idea: *A falling treetop made a large hole in the canopy that shaded the forest.*)

To give you an idea of how much faster redwoods grow in the sunlight, let's say that we planted two seeds, one in the deep shade, the other in the sunlight. When we look at the trees fifty years later, we observe that the tree exposed to the full sunlight is over one hundred feet tall. The base of its trunk is almost three feet across. The tree grown in the shade, however, is only about six feet tall, and its trunk is not as big around as your wrist. ❹

4. How much faster would a redwood grow in the sunlight? (Idea: *A lot faster.*)

During the winter that our seed was resting on the mole diggings, the weather was cold and rainy. Most of the rain came in the form of a fine mist that would feel like tiny pinpoints of cold against your face. Occasionally, however, large drops of rain would rattle through the northern California forest, creating tiny streams on the forest floor. Our seed was much smaller than a drop of water, and it was pushed around by the water quite a bit during the first part of the winter. At one time it seemed as if a heavy rain would wash it away from the mole diggings. However, it became lodged in a small crack between two mounds of dirt. And there it remained, ready to grow when days became warmer in the spring. ⑤

5. Where did our seed become lodged? (Idea: *In a crack between two mounds of dirt.*)
5. What does **lodged** mean? (Idea: *Stuck.*)
7. (Award points quickly.)
8. (If the group makes more than 12 errors, repeat the reading immediately or on the next day.)

FLUENCY ASSESSMENT

EXERCISE 8

TIMED READING CHECKOUTS

1. (For this part of the lesson, assigned pairs of students work together during the checkouts.)
- (If one student does not have a checkout partner, arrange another time when you can give the checkout.)
2. (Each student does a 2-minute timed reading. Students earn 5 points by reading at least 240 words and making no more than 5 errors on the first part of story 27. Students record points in Box C of their Point Chart and plot their reading rate and errors on the Individual Reading Progress Chart.)
- (During each timed checkout, observe one pair of students for 2 minutes. Make notes on any mistakes the reader makes.)
3. (Record the timed reading checkout performance for each student you observed on the Fluency Assessment Summary form.)

WORKBOOK EXERCISES

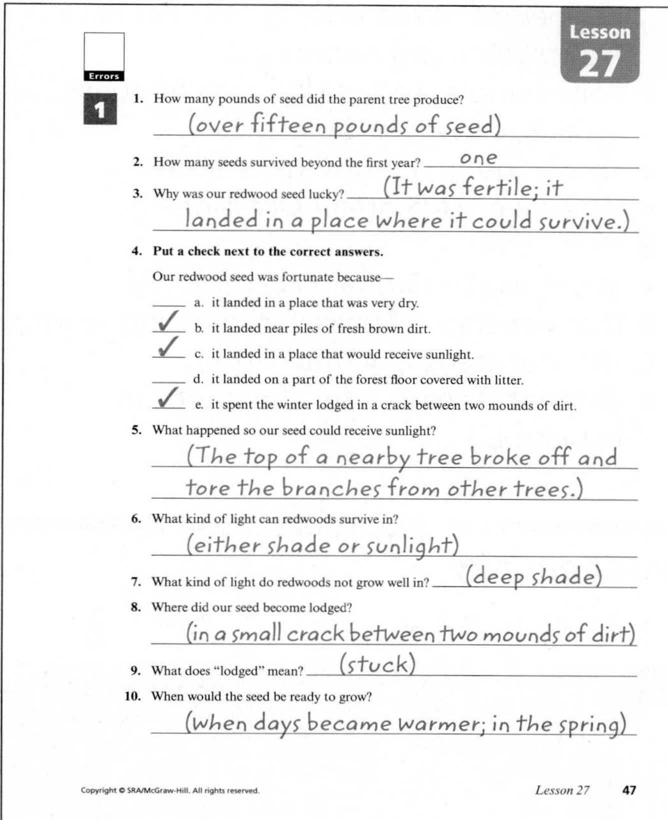

Lesson 27

Errors

1

1. How many pounds of seed did the parent tree produce? (over fifteen pounds of seed)
2. How many seeds survived beyond the first year? one
3. Why was our redwood seed lucky? (It was fertile; it landed in a place where it could survive.)
4. **Put a check next to the correct answers.**

   Our redwood seed was fortunate because—

   ____ a. it landed in a place that was very dry.
   ✓ b. it landed near piles of fresh brown dirt.
   ✓ c. it landed in a place that would receive sunlight.
   ____ d. it landed on a part of the forest floor covered with litter.
   ✓ e. it spent the winter lodged in a crack between two mounds of dirt.
5. What happened so our seed could receive sunlight? (The top of a nearby tree broke off and tore the branches from other trees.)
6. What kind of light can redwoods survive in? (either shade or sunlight)
7. What kind of light do redwoods not grow well in? (deep shade)
8. Where did our seed become lodged? (in a small crack between two mounds of dirt)
9. What does "lodged" mean? (stuck)
10. When would the seed be ready to grow? (when days became warmer; in the spring)

Copyright © SRA/McGraw-Hill. All rights reserved. Lesson 27 47

Lesson 27

2 **Fill in each blank using a word in the box.**

severe	mole	ledge
nervous	slime	location

1. She fell into the muddy pool and emerged covered with slime.
2. The mole lived in a hole in the ground.
3. Everyone found some protection from the severe storm.

48 Lesson 27 Copyright © SRA/McGraw-Hill. All rights reserved.

Independent Student Work

Task A

- Open your Workbook to Lesson 27. ✓
- Complete all the parts of your Workbook lesson using a pencil. If you make no errors, you will earn 5 points.

Task B

1. (Before presenting Lesson 28, check student Workbooks for Lesson 27.)
   - (Call on individual students to read the items and answers in each part. Students mark errors using a pen.)
2. (Direct the students to count the number of errors and write the number in the Errors box at the top of the Workbook page.)
3. (Award points and direct students to record points in Box D of their Point Chart.)

   0 errors ....5 points
   1 error ....3 points
   2 or 3 errors ....1 point
   more than 3 errors ....0 points

END OF LESSON 27

Lesson 28

WORD-ATTACK SKILLS

Student Book 

EXERCISE 1

AFFIX: un

1. Open your Student Book to Lesson 28. ✓

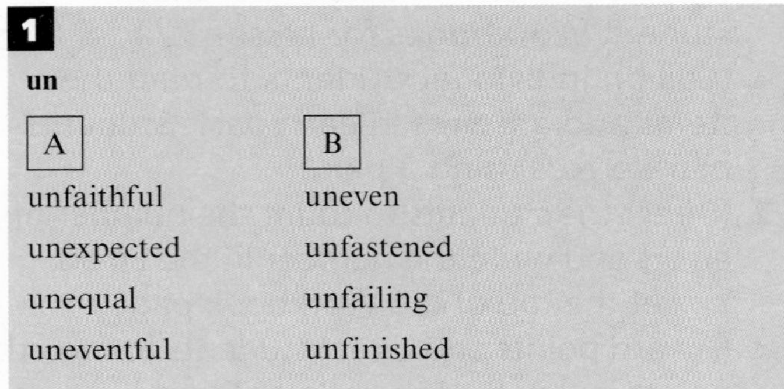

1

un

A	B
unfaithful	uneven
unexpected	unfastened
unequal	unfailing
uneventful	unfinished

- Touch the letters **U–N** in part 1. ✓
- What does **un** usually mean when it appears at the beginning of a word? (Signal.) *Not.*

2. Touch the first word in column A. ✓
- What word? (Signal.) *Unfaithful.*
- What does **unfaithful** mean? (Signal.) *Not faithful.*

3. Touch the next word. ✓
- What word? (Signal.) *Unexpected.*
- What does **unexpected** mean? (Signal.) *Not expected.*

4. (Repeat step 3 for each remaining word.)
5. (Repeat the list until firm.)
6. (Repeat steps 2–5 for the words in column B.)

EXERCISE 2

NEW **AFFIX: ly**

1. Touch the letters **L–Y** in part 2.

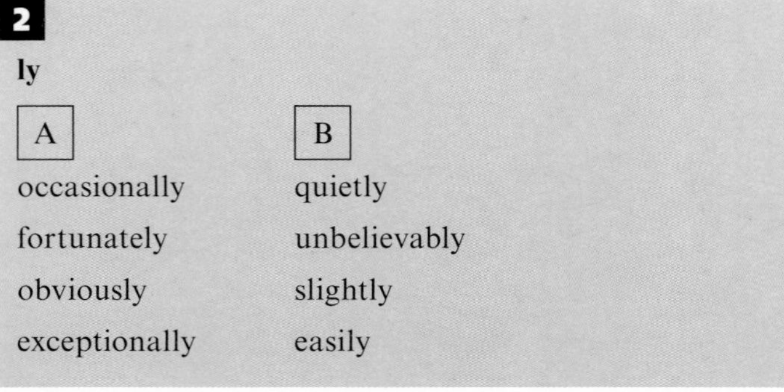

2

ly

A	B
occasionally	quietly
fortunately	unbelievably
obviously	slightly
exceptionally	easily

- When those letters appear at the end of a word, they tell **how something happened.** What does **ly** tell? (Signal.) *How something happened.*
- For example, something may happen quickly, slowly, or quietly.

2. Touch the first word in column A. ✓
- What word? (Signal.) *Occasionally.*

3. Next word. ✓
- What word? (Signal.) *Fortunately.*

4. (Repeat step 3 for each remaining word.)
5. (Repeat steps 2–4 until firm.)
6. (Repeat steps 2–5 for the words in column B.)

EXERCISE 3

VOCABULARY

1. Touch part 3. ✓

3

1. swell
2. torch
3. charred
4. smoldering

- We're going to talk about what those words mean.

2. Touch word 1. ✓
- What word? (Signal.) *Swell.*
- What does something do when it **swells?** (Call on a student.) (Idea: *It gets larger.*)

3. Everybody, touch word 2. ✓
- What word? (Signal.) *Torch.*
- Who can tell me what a **torch** is? (Call on a student.) (Idea: *A big fire on a sticklike object.*)

4. Everybody, touch word 3. ✓
- What word? (Signal.) *Charred.*
- **Charred** is another way of saying **burned and blackened.** Everybody, what's another way of saying "The walls of the house were **burned and blackened?** (Signal.) *The walls of the house were charred.*

5. Touch word 4. ✓
- What word? (Signal.) *Smoldering.*
- **Smoldering** means **burning and smoking without a flame.** Everybody, what's another way of saying "The fire was still **burning and smoking without a flame**"? (Signal.) *The fire was still smoldering.*

EXERCISE 4

WORD PRACTICE

1. Touch the first word in part 4. ✓

4

screech smallest cheap section watch
toasted brightened approached amount
straighten received crushed squirrel
wonder whisper seedling convert*

- What sound? (Signal.) *ēēē.*
- What word? (Signal.) *Screech.*

2. Touch the next word. ✓
- What sound? (Signal.) *all.*
- What word? (Signal.) *Smallest.*

3. (Repeat step 2 for each remaining word.)
4. (Repeat each row of words until firm.)
5. What does **convert** mean? (Call on a student.)

EXERCISE 5

WORD PRACTICE

1. Touch the first word in part 5. ✓

5

visible connected height unfortunate*
ignited exciting motionless thought
impossible celebration pancake strength
stretched changed bounding manufacture
flooding created sapling though
blazed developing emerged* through

- What word? (Signal.) *Visible.*

2. Next word. ✓
- What word? (Signal.) *Connected.*

3. (Repeat step 2 for each remaining word.)
4. (Repeat each row of words until firm.)
5. What does **unfortunate** mean? (Call on a student.)
- (Repeat for **emerged.**)

EXERCISE 6

WORD-ATTACK SKILLS: Individual tests

1. (Call on individual students. Each student reads a row or column. Tally the rows and columns read without error. If the group reads at least 12 rows and columns without making errors, direct all students to record 5 points in Box A of their Point Chart. Criterion is 80 percent of rows and columns read without error.)
2. (If the group did not read at least 12 rows and columns without errors, do not award any points for the Word-Attack Skills exercises.)

SELECTION READING

EXERCISE 7

STORY READING

1. (Call on individual students to answer this question.)
- The last selection told why the redwood seed that survived was lucky. What lucky thing happened? (Accept reasonable summaries that include details about how the seed fell to a spot where it could survive.)

2. Everybody, touch part 6. ✓
3. The error limit for this story is 12. If the group reads the story with 12 errors or less, you earn 5 points.

6 Seedling to Sapling

4. (Call on a student to read the title.) *Seedling to Sapling.*
- What do you think this story is about? (Accept reasonable responses.)

5. (Call on individual students. Each is to read two to four sentences.)
6. (Call on individual students to answer the specified questions during the story reading.)

In April something exciting happened on the floor of the redwood forest, just as it happened every year. Some of the redwood seeds began to develop into baby trees, which are called seedlings. ❶

1. What are baby trees called? *Seedlings.*

The forest floor was soaked by the winter rain, and the rain was still falling; however, the days were becoming warmer. In early April our seed began to change. At first it began to swell slightly as the inside of the seed changed. The hard inside of the seed changed into a white pulp that looks and feels something like pancake batter. Parts of this white blob then began to become harder and take on a form. One end of the blob began to take on the shape of a tiny green plant. The other end became pointed and began to look like a tiny root. The root end pushed out through one end of the seed and began to worm its way down into the soft ground. ❷

2. What was the first change in the seed? (Idea: *It began to swell as the inside changed.*)
2. How did the hard inside of the seed change? (Idea: *It changed into a soft white blob.*)
2. What did the two ends of the blob look like? (Idea: *One end began to look like a plant; the other began to look like a root.*)

When the seedling was less than an inch long, it started to straighten up. The top of the seedling was still inside the seed, and the seed was in the soft mud. The only part of the seedling that was visible above ground was the stem that connected the root to the seed. The seedling looked something like a person bending over in shallow water, with only the person's back above the water. The seedling looked like this:

As the seedling grew a longer root, it had enough strength to pull its top from the seed. The empty seed remained in the mud, and the top slowly began to stand up. It was only about a half inch tall, with two little leaves stretched out to the side like two little green arms. A squirrel could have stepped on that seedling and crushed it. But not far from that unbelievably small seedling was the parent tree, standing over 400 feet tall. ❸

3. When did the seedling pull its top from the seed? (Idea: *When its root grew longer.*)
3. How many leaves did the seedling have? *Two.*

During the seedling's first summer, it grew to a height of about three inches. On sunny days, the sun's rays came through the hole in the forest's canopy and flooded the ground around the seedling with sunlight. Trees, as you know, need sunlight to survive. They take the incoming sunlight and convert it into food. Without sunlight they starve because they can't manufacture food. Our seedling was fortunate because it received a fair amount of sunlight through the hole created by the falling treetop. ❹

4. How tall was the seedling at the end of its first summer? *About three inches tall.*
4. Why did our seedling receive sunlight? (Idea: *Because of the hole created by the falling treetop.*)

Things went well for the seedling for six years. By the end of the sixth year our young redwood was no longer a seedling. It was now what is called a sapling—a young tree. And it was growing quite rapidly. You might think that redwoods are very slow-growing, but they actually grow faster than most trees. At the end of its sixth year, our redwood was nearly twelve feet tall, and it was reaching straight up to the top of the forest, which was still a long, long way above the sapling. But the sapling was now ready to grow nearly three feet a year. ❺

5. What was the seedling called after six years? *A sapling.*
5. How tall was our sapling after six years? *Nearly twelve feet tall.*
5. How much would the sapling grow each year? *Nearly three feet.*

That fall, however, something unfortunate happened. Late one evening lightning struck a nearby tree. A burning branch fell and ignited the litter on the forest floor. Soon a hot, orange fire blazed through the forest. That fire didn't reach even the bottom branches of the bigger trees, because those branches were more than one hundred feet above the forest floor. However, the fire burned the smaller trees to the ground. It swept over our redwood sapling, and within a few seconds, the sapling was a torch. Within a few minutes, the sapling was a charred stick smoldering in the forest. ❻

6. How did the fire begin? (Idea: *Lightning struck a tree.*)
6. Which trees did the fire burn to the ground? (Idea: *The smaller trees.*)
6. What did the sapling look like after the fire swept through the forest? (Idea: *Like a charred stick.*)
7. (Award points quickly.)
8. (If the group makes more than 12 errors, repeat the reading immediately or on the next day.)

FLUENCY ASSESSMENT

EXERCISE 8

TIMED READING CHECKOUTS

1. (For this part of the lesson, assigned pairs of students work together during the checkouts.)
   - (If one student does not have a checkout partner, arrange another time when you can give the checkout.)
2. (Each student does a 2-minute timed reading. Students earn 5 points by reading at least 240 words and making no more than 5 errors on the first part of story 28. Students record points in Box C of their Point Chart and plot their reading rate and errors on the Individual Reading Progress Chart.)
   - (During each timed checkout, observe one pair of students for 2 minutes. Make notes on any mistakes the reader makes.)
3. (Record the timed reading checkout performance for each student you observed on the Fluency Assessment Summary form.)

WORKBOOK EXERCISES

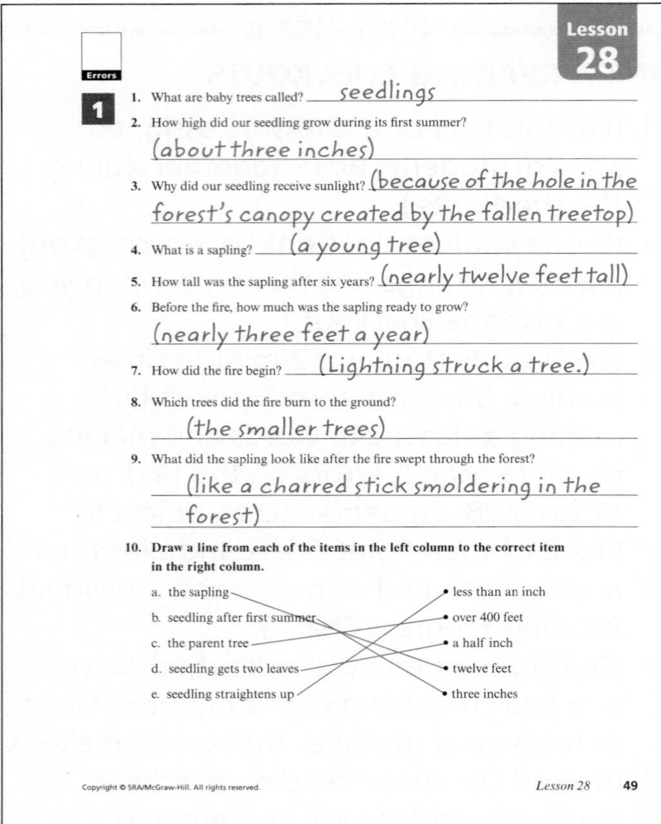
Lesson 28

Errors

1

1. What are baby trees called? seedlings
2. How high did our seedling grow during its first summer? (about three inches)
3. Why did our seedling receive sunlight? (because of the hole in the forest's canopy created by the fallen treetop)
4. What is a sapling? (a young tree)
5. How tall was the sapling after six years? (nearly twelve feet tall)
6. Before the fire, how much was the sapling ready to grow? (nearly three feet a year)
7. How did the fire begin? (Lightning struck a tree.)
8. Which trees did the fire burn to the ground? (the smaller trees)
9. What did the sapling look like after the fire swept through the forest? (like a charred stick smoldering in the forest)
10. **Draw a line from each of the items in the left column to the correct item in the right column.**

a. the sapling • less than an inch
b. seedling after first summer • over 400 feet
c. the parent tree • a half inch
d. seedling gets two leaves • twelve feet
e. seedling straightens up • three inches

Copyright © SRA/McGraw-Hill. All rights reserved. Lesson 28 49

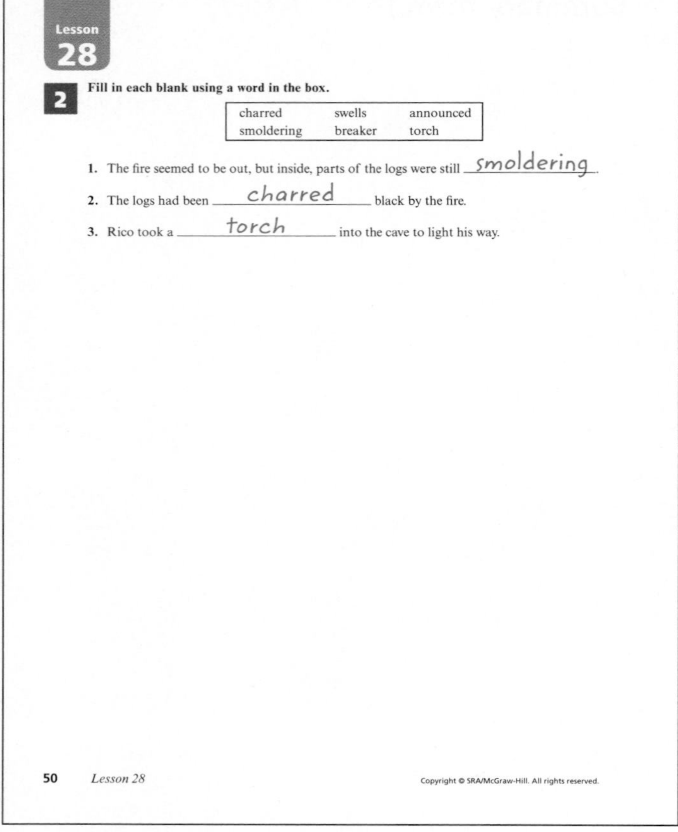
Lesson 28

2 **Fill in each blank using a word in the box.**

charred	swells	announced
smoldering	breaker	torch

1. The fire seemed to be out, but inside, parts of the logs were still smoldering.
2. The logs had been charred black by the fire.
3. Rico took a torch into the cave to light his way.

50 Lesson 28 Copyright © SRA/McGraw-Hill. All rights reserved.

Independent Student Work

Task A

- Open your Workbook to Lesson 28. ✓
- Complete all the parts of your Workbook lesson using a pencil. If you make no errors, you will earn 5 points.

Task B

1. (Before presenting Lesson 29, check student Workbooks for Lesson 28.)
   - (Call on individual students to read the items and answers in each part. Students mark errors using a pen.)
2. (Direct the students to count the number of errors and write the number in the Errors box at the top of the Workbook page.)
3. (Award points and direct students to record points in Box D of their Point Chart.)

   0 errors ....5 points
   1 error ....3 points
   2 or 3 errors ....1 point
   more than 3 errors ....0 points

END OF LESSON 28

WORD-ATTACK SKILLS

Student Book 

EXERCISE 1

NEW SOUND COMBINATION: oi

Task A

1. Open your Student Book to Lesson 29. ✓

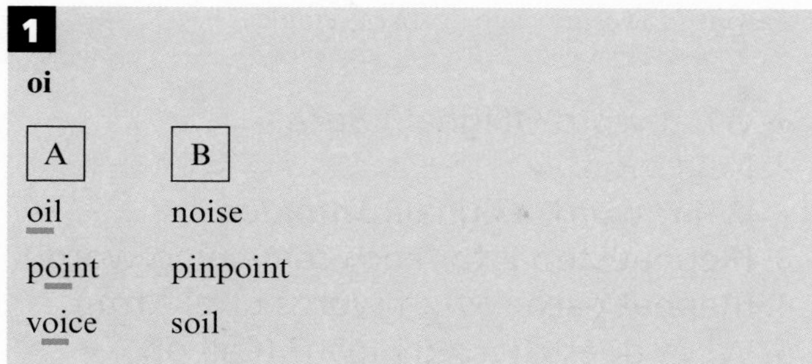

1

oi

A	B
oil	noise
point	pinpoint
voice	soil

- Touch the letters **O–I** in part 1. ✓
- The letters **O–I** go together and make the sound **oy,** as in **oil.** What sound? (Signal.) *oy.*

2. You're going to read words that have the letters **O–I** in them. You're going to say the sound for the underlined part and then read the word.
3. Touch the first word in column A. ✓
   - What sound? (Signal.) *oy.*
   - What word? (Signal.) *Oil.*
4. Touch the next word. ✓
   - What sound? (Signal.) *oy.*
   - What word? (Signal.) *Point.*
5. (Repeat step 4 for **voice.**)

Task B

1. Touch the first word in column B. ✓
   - What word? (Signal.) *Noise.*
2. Next word. ✓
   - What word? (Signal.) *Pinpoint.*
3. (Repeat step 2 for **soil.**)
4. (Repeat steps 1–3 until firm.)

EXERCISE 2

NEW AFFIX: ly

1. Touch the letters **L–Y** in part 2.

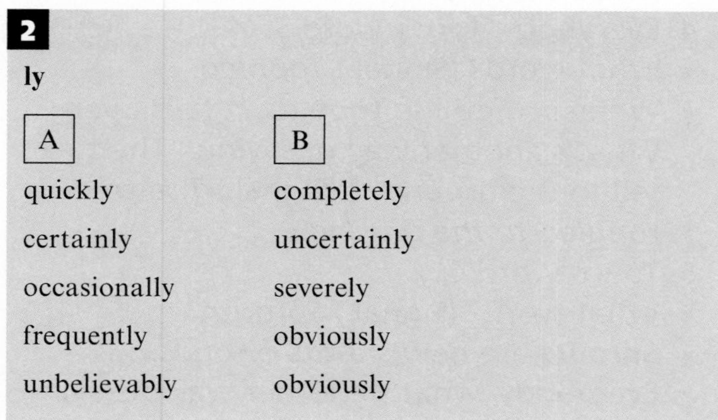

2

ly

A	B
quickly	completely
certainly	uncertainly
occasionally	severely
frequently	obviously
unbelievably	obviously

- What does the ending **ly** tell? (Signal.) *How something happened.*
- Something may happen quickly, slowly, or quietly.

2. Touch the first word in column A. ✓
   - What word? (Signal.) *Quickly.*
3. Next word. ✓
   - What word? (Signal.) *Certainly.*
4. (Repeat step 3 for each remaining word.)
5. (Repeat steps 2–4 until firm.)
6. (Repeat steps 2–5 for the words in column B.)

EXERCISE 3

VOCABULARY

1. Touch part 3. ✓

3

1. original
2. shade
3. toppled
4. sprouts

- We're going to talk about what those words mean.

2. Touch word 1. ✓
   - What word? (Signal.) *Original.*
   - **Original** is another way of saying **first.** The **first** time is the **original** time. Everybody, what's another way of saying "This was the **first** coffeemaker"? (Signal.) *This was the original coffeemaker.*

3. Touch word 2. ✓
- What word? (Signal.) *Shade.*
- Show me what people do when they shade their eyes. (Call on a student.)

4. Everybody, touch word 3. ✓
- What word? (Signal.) *Toppled.*
- When something **topples,** it **falls over.** What's another way of saying "The tree **fell** to the ground"? (Signal.) *The tree toppled to the ground.*

5. Touch word 4. ✓
- What word? (Signal.) *Sprouts.*
- **Sprouts** are **new shoots** or buds. Everybody, what's another way of saying "The tree had **new shoots**"? (Signal.) *The tree had sprouts.*

EXERCISE 4

WORD PRACTICE

1. Touch the first word in part 4. ✓

4

suggestion although investigation*
thousand furthermore cloaked

- What sound? (Signal.) *shun.*
- What word? (Signal.) *Suggestion.*

2. Touch the next word. ✓
- What sound? (Signal.) *all.*
- What word? (Signal.) *Although.*

3. (Repeat step 2 for each remaining word.)
4. (Repeat each row of words until firm.)
5. What does **investigation** mean? (Call on a student.)

EXERCISE 5

WORD PRACTICE

1. Touch the first word in part 5. ✓

burls smolder charred* continued
creating once burnt shaped
disease germs natural original*
survived telephone knotty extended
seasons towering ago causes single

- What word? (Signal.) *Burls.*

2. Next word. ✓
- What word? (Signal.) *Smolder.*

3. (Repeat step 2 for each remaining word.)
4. (Repeat each row of words until firm.)
5. What does **charred** mean? (Call on a student.)
- (Repeat for **original.**)

EXERCISE 6

WORD-ATTACK SKILLS: Individual tests

1. (Call on individual students. Each student reads a row or column. Tally the rows and columns read without error. If the group reads at least 10 rows and columns without making errors, direct all students to record 5 points in Box A of their Point Chart. Criterion is 80 percent of rows and columns read without error.)
2. (If the group did not read at least 10 rows and columns without errors, do not award any points for the Word-Attack Skills exercises.)

SELECTION READING

EXERCISE 7

STORY READING

1. (Call on individual students to answer these questions.)
   - What are baby trees called? *Seedlings.*
   - After they are a few years old, what are young trees called? *Saplings.*
   - How tall was the redwood sapling at the end of six years? (Idea: *About twelve feet tall.*)
   - Before the fire, how much could the redwood tree grow in a year? (Idea: *Nearly three feet a year.*)
2. Everybody, touch part 6. ✓
3. The error limit for this story is 12. If the group reads the story with 12 errors or less, you earn 5 points.

6 **Toward the Towering Green Canopy**

4. (Call on a student to read the title.) *Toward the Towering Green Canopy.*
   - What do you think this story is about? (Accept reasonable responses.)
5. (Call on individual students. Each is to read two to four sentences.)
6. (Call on individual students to answer the specified questions during the story reading.)

No fire fighters came to put out the fire in the redwood forest because that fire took place long ago. In fact, it took place more than two thousand years ago. At that time there were no houses or roads in the area now known as northern California. Nobody put out the fire. So the fire burned. After it flashed through the forest, the flames died away; however, parts of the bigger trees and large fallen branches continued to smolder for nearly a month. A fire smoldered at the base of the redwood's parent tree, creating a charred hole that was big enough for a person to sit in. Many other large trees also had smoldering bases.

But when the heavy rains came in the late fall, the smoldering fires died out and the forest was once more calm with the sound of gentle rain falling on the charred forest floor. ❶

1. Why didn't anyone put out the fire? (Idea: *Because no one was there.*)
1. How long ago did the fire occur? *More than two thousand years ago.*
1. When did the fires die? (Idea: *When the heavy rains came in the late fall.*)

The forest remained calm until the next spring when the trees again began to grow. Our redwood was among the first to start growing. Although it had been burned to the ground, it was not dead. Its roots were alive, and those roots sent up three shoots. These shoots were quite thick and very fast-growing. By the middle of July, the tallest of the three was nearly six feet tall, growing right next to the charred trunk of the tree that had been burnt.

Fires often kill young trees, but fires don't often kill young redwoods because the redwoods simply send up new sprouts. Furthermore, there is no insect or disease that kills redwood saplings. While germs and different kinds of bugs kill other types of trees, no natural enemy kills the redwood. ❷

2. How many shoots did the roots send up? *Three.*
2. How tall was the tallest shoot by mid-July? (Idea: *Nearly six feet tall.*)
2. Why can't a fire kill a young redwood? (Idea: *Because redwoods send up new sprouts.*)
2. Will insects or diseases kill redwood saplings? *No.*
2. Does the redwood have any natural enemies? *No.*

So our redwood continued to grow. Within three years, it was taller than it had been before the fire. By now, one of the original sprouts had become the main trunk and it was growing quite rapidly, while the other sprouts were hardly growing at all. Six years after the fire, the two slow-growing sprouts were dead. Only the main sprout survived. Our sapling was now taller than the roof of a single-story building. Twenty-five years after the fire, our redwood was fifty feet tall, still growing at the rate of about three feet a year. Its trunk was now as big around as a telephone pole, and it had several large burls on it. Redwood burls are knotty growths on the trunk and the branches. They look like big lumps. Smaller burls are as big as your fist. Larger ones may be three feet across and extend a foot out from the tree. These burls are masses of buds. If you take part of a burl and place it in water, the buds will sprout, and a bunch of tiny redwood shoots will begin to grow from the burl. ❸

3. How tall was the sapling after six years? (Idea: *Taller than a single-story building.*)
3. How tall was the sapling after twenty-five years? *Fifty feet tall.*
3. What does a burl look like? (Idea: *Like a big lump.*)

The largest burl on our redwood was right under one of the side branches. It was about as big as two fists held together. By now, our redwood was starting to look like a forest tree. Young redwoods are shaped like Christmas trees. If they grow in a forest, however, the bottom branches don't receive any sun, because the higher branches of the tree block much of the sunlight. This causes the lower branches to die. As the tree continues to grow, the higher branches keep shading the lower branches, and the lower branches keep dying. Soon the trunk of the tree may be free of branches for some distance. When our redwood was fifty feet tall, only the top twenty-five feet of the trunk had living branches. The bottom twenty-five feet of the trunk had either dead branches or no branches.

The seasons followed each other—rain, warmth and sunlight, and more rain. By the time our redwood was eighty years old, it was over 225 feet tall—which is about as tall as an 18-story building. The base of its trunk was six feet across. Its trunk was bare of branches for over ninety feet. And its top was near the green canopy created by the towering older trees. ❹

4. Why was the trunk of the tree soon free of branches at its lower part? (Idea: *Because the higher branches block the sunlight and the lower branches die.*)
4. How tall was the sapling after eighty years? *Over 225 feet tall.*
4. How big was the base of the trunk? *Six feet across.*
7. (Award points quickly.)
8. (If the group makes more than 12 errors, repeat the reading immediately or on the next day.)

FLUENCY ASSESSMENT

EXERCISE 8

TIMED READING CHECKOUTS

1. (For this part of the lesson, assigned pairs of students work together during the checkouts.)
   - (If one student does not have a checkout partner, arrange another time when you can give the checkout.)
2. (Each student does a 2-minute timed reading. Students earn 5 points by reading at least 240 words and making no more than 5 errors on the first part of story 29. Students record points in Box C of their Point Chart and plot their reading rate and errors on the Individual Reading Progress Chart.)
   - (During each timed checkout, observe one pair of students for 2 minutes. Make notes on any mistakes the reader makes.)
3. (Record the timed reading checkout performance for each student you observed on the Fluency Assessment Summary form.)

WORKBOOK EXERCISES

Independent Student Work

Task A

- Open your Workbook to Lesson 29. ✓
- Complete all the parts of your Workbook lesson using a pencil. If you make no errors, you will earn 5 points.

Lesson 29

Errors

1

1. Why didn't anyone put the fire out? (No one was there.)
2. **Fill in the blanks:**

   After the flames died down, bigger trees smoldered for nearly a month. When it rained in late fall, the smoldering fires died out.
3. How many shoots did the roots of the young redwood send up? three
4. Why can't a fire kill a young redwood?

   (The redwoods send up new sprouts.)
5. How tall was the sapling six years after the fire?

   (taller than a single-story building)
6. What does a burl look like? (a big lump)
7. Why do the lower branches on a redwood die?

   (The higher branches block the sunlight.)
8. How tall was the redwood after eighty years?

   (over 225 feet tall; as tall as an 18-story building)
9. How big was the base of the trunk after eighty years?

   (six feet across)
10. Read each item. Circle **True** if you think the item is correct. Circle **False** if you think the item is not correct.
    a. The fire happened more than two thousand years ago. (True) False
    b. The trees began to grow again in the fall after the fire took place. True (False)
    c. Redwood saplings have no natural enemy. (True) False
    d. The roots of the charred redwood were dead. True (False)

Copyright © SRA/McGraw-Hill. All rights reserved.

Lesson 29

2 **Fill in each blank using a word in the box.**

collided	toppled	frequent
ignited	suggest	original

1. The unsteady vase toppled over.
2. The truck and taxicab collided at the intersection.
3. Your original home is the very first one you have.

3 **Write the parts for each word.**

1. uncloaked = un + cloak + ed
2. secondly = second + ly
3. uncertainly = un + certain + ly
4. extended = ex + tend + ed

Copyright © SRA/McGraw-Hill. All rights reserved.

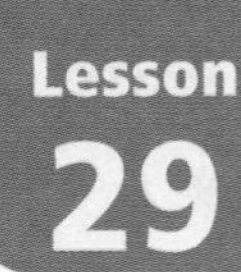

Lesson 29

Task B

1. (Before presenting Lesson 30, check student Workbooks for Lesson 29.)
- (Call on individual students to read the items and answers in each part. Students mark errors using a pen.)
2. (Direct the students to count the number of errors and write the number in the Errors box at the top of the Workbook page.)
3. (Award points and direct students to record points in Box D of their Point Chart.)

0 errors.................................5 points
1 error..................................3 points
2 or 3 errors..........................1 point
more than 3 errors ....0 points

END OF LESSON 29

Note: You will administer Mastery Test 1 after completing this lesson and before beginning Lesson 31.

Photocopy the Mastery Test Group Summary form. You will record each student's score on that form.

WORD-ATTACK SKILLS

Student Book 

EXERCISE 1

NEW **SOUND COMBINATION: ure**

Task A

1. Open your Student Book to Lesson 30. ✓

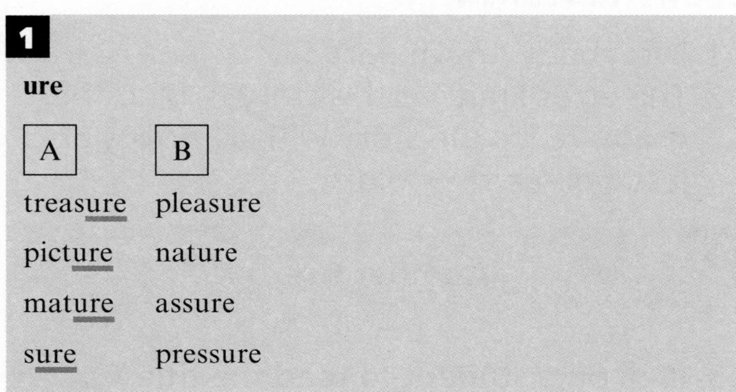
1
ure

A	B
treasure	pleasure
picture	nature
mature	assure
sure	pressure

- Touch the letters **U–R–E** in part 1. ✓
- The letters **U–R–E** go together and make the sound **ure,** as in **picture.** What sound? (Signal.) *ure.*

2. You're going to read words that have the letters **U–R–E** in them. You're going to say the sound for the underlined part and then read the word.
3. Touch the first word in column A. ✓
   - What sound? (Signal.) *ure.*
   - What word? (Signal.) *Treasure.*
4. Touch the next word. ✓
   - What sound? (Signal.) *ure.*
   - What word? (Signal.) *Picture.*
5. (Repeat step 4 for each remaining word.)

Task B

1. Touch the first word in column B. ✓
   - What word? (Signal.) *Pleasure.*
2. Touch the next word. ✓
   - What word? (Signal.) *Nature.*
3. (Repeat step 2 for each remaining word.)
4. (Repeat steps 1–3 until firm.)

EXERCISE 2

NEW **WORD PRACTICE**

Note: In this exercise, you ask, What's the underlined part?, not What sound?

1. Touch the first word in part 2. ✓

2

exceptionally actually noisy installed
severely uncertainly occasionally crouched
foiled unexpectedly emerge* unbelievably
furthermore unfortunately boiling survive*
approaching latches alternate particularly

- What's the underlined part? (Signal.) *ex.*
- What word? (Signal.) *Exceptionally.*

2. Touch the next word. ✓
   - What's the underlined part? (Signal.) *ly.*
   - What word? (Signal.) *Actually.*
3. (Repeat step 2 for each remaining word.)
4. (Repeat each row of words until firm.)
5. What does **emerge** mean? (Call on a student.)
   - (Repeat for **survive.**)

EXERCISE 3

VOCABULARY

1. Touch part 3. ✓

3

1. mature
2. leveled
3. deafening

- We're going to talk about what those words mean.

2. Touch word 1. ✓

- What word? (Signal.) *Mature.*
- **Mature** means **full-grown.** Everybody, what's another way of saying "The plant is **full-grown**"? (Signal.) *The plant is mature.*

3. Touch word 2. ✓
- What word? (Signal.) *Leveled.*
- What do we mean when we say the old house was **leveled**? (Call on a student.) (Idea: *The old house was flattened to the ground.*)

4. Everybody, touch word 3. ✓
- What word? (Signal.) *Deafening.*
- A **very loud** noise is called **deafening.** What's another way of saying **very loud**? (Signal.) *Deafening.*

EXERCISE 4

WORD PRACTICE

1. Touch the first word in part 4. ✓

4

thorough through tough thought
though sugar toppled* producing
producer height reached frightening
flared swirling gigantic toothpicks
including swayed* great burnt
natural towering continuing knotty
change racing parent exchanged

- What word? (Signal.) *Thorough.*

2. Next word. ✓
- What word? (Signal.) *Through.*

3. (Repeat step 2 for each remaining word.)
4. (Repeat each row of words until firm.)
5. What does **toppled** mean? (Call on a student.)
- (Repeat for **swayed.**)

EXERCISE 5

WORD-ATTACK SKILLS: Individual tests

1. (Call on individual students. Each student reads a row or column. Tally the rows and columns read without error. If the group reads at least 12 rows and columns without making errors, direct all students to record 5 points in Box A of their Point Chart. Criterion is 80 percent of rows and columns read without error.)
2. (If the group did not read at least 12 rows and columns without errors, do not award any points for the Word-Attack Skills exercises.)

SELECTION READING

EXERCISE 6

STORY READING

1. Everybody, touch part 5. ✓
2. The error limit for this story is 12. If the group reads the story with 12 errors or less, you earn 5 points.

5 **Another Fire**

3. (Call on a student to read the title.) *Another Fire.*
- What do you think this story is about? (Accept reasonable responses.)

4. (Call on individual students. Each is to read two to four sentences.)
5. (Call on individual students to answer the specified questions during the story reading.)

When our redwood was eighty years old, it was producing seeds; however, less than one of every hundred seeds was fertile. Our redwood did not become a good seed producer until it was over two hundred years old. Then it continued to produce fertile seeds until its death.

After our redwood reached the height of 225 feet, it began to grow more and more slowly. It had become a mature tree. When it was two hundred years old, it was growing only a couple of inches a year, but it was already more than three hundred feet tall. By the time it was four hundred years old, it was growing at the rate of less than an inch a year. ❶

1. How old was our redwood when it became a good seed producer? (Idea: *Over two hundred years old.*)
1. How long did our redwood continue to produce seeds? (Idea: *Until its death.*)
1. How tall was our redwood when it began to grow more slowly? (Idea: *Three hundred feet.*)
1. How fast was our redwood growing when it was four hundred years old? (Idea: *Less than an inch per year.*)

It was during our redwood's 420th year that a terrible fire swept through the forest. This fire was not like the one that had leveled the small trees years before. This was a fire that rolled over the tops of the tallest trees in the forest, sending up flames more than 400 feet into a sky that was dark with smoke. The roar of the fire was deafening. Its speed was frightening. It began in a pile of dry litter near the base of a young tree. The fire flared up in a few seconds. Within a minute it was climbing the smaller trees and then the larger ones. When it reached our redwood, the fire was a rolling, swirling mass that was hot enough to melt metal. With a rush it burned all the green needles from our redwood. It burned the branches and burned the trunk. ❷

2. Where did the fire begin? (Idea: *In a pile of dry litter near the base of a tree.*)
2. Which trees did the fire touch first? *The smaller ones.*
2. Which parts of our redwood burned? (Idea: *The needles, the branches, and the trunk.*)

That fire smoldered for three months. A few trees toppled during the fire, particularly the very old ones. The parent of our redwood was one of those that toppled. The parent tree was more than two thousand years old and had lived through five great fires. But most of the big trees remained standing. They looked like gigantic charred toothpicks sticking up from the black forest floor.

Not all of the trees in the forest were redwoods. Some were sugar pines, and there were a few oaks. The fire swept over all these trees. And when the following spring came, the older oaks were dead and the older sugar pines were dead. But the mature redwoods, including ours, were still alive. ❸

3. How long did the fire smolder? *For three months.*
3. What did the remaining trees look like? (Idea: *Gigantic charred toothpicks.*)
3. Which trees were dead after the fire? (Idea: *The older oaks and the older sugar pines.*)
3. Which trees were alive after the fire? (Idea: *The mature redwoods.*)

The fire never reached the part of the tree trunk that was alive. The living part of a tree trunk is a very thin layer just under the bark. The rest of a tree trunk or a branch is not alive. The wood inside is not alive. It is dead matter with a thin layer of living matter around it. The oaks in the forest were dead because their bark was about an inch thick. The fire burned through their bark and burned the layer of living matter just under the bark. The same thing happened to the sugar pines. But the mature redwoods have very thick bark. The bark on the trunk of our redwood, for example, was about eight inches thick. ❹

4. Where is the living part of the tree trunk? (Idea: *Just under the bark.*)
4. Why were the oaks dead? (Ideas: *Because their bark was too thin; the fire burned through the bark and burned the living part of the tree.*)
4. Why were the sugar pines dead? (Idea: *For the same reason.*)
4. How thick was the bark on the trunk of our redwood? *About eight inches thick.*
6. (Award points quickly.)
7. (If the group makes more than 12 errors, repeat the reading immediately or on the next day.)

FLUENCY ASSESSMENT

EXERCISE 7

TIMED READING CHECKOUTS

1. (For this part of the lesson, assigned pairs of students work together during the checkouts.)
   - (If one student does not have a checkout partner, arrange another time when you can give the checkout.)
2. (Each student does a 2-minute timed reading. Students earn 5 points by reading at least 240 words and making no more than 5 errors on the first part of story 30. Students record points in Box C of their Point Chart and plot their reading rate and errors on the Individual Reading Progress Chart.)
   - (During each timed checkout, observe one pair of students for 2 minutes. Make notes on any mistakes the reader makes.)
3. (Record the timed reading checkout performance for each student you observed on the Fluency Assessment Summary form.)

WORKBOOK EXERCISES

Independent Student Work

Task A

- Open your Workbook to Lesson 30. ✓
- Complete all the parts of your Workbook lesson using a pencil. If you make no errors, you will earn 5 points.

Task B

1. (Before presenting Lesson 31, check student Workbooks for Lesson 30.)
   - (Call on individual students to read the items and answers in each part. Students mark errors using a pen.)
2. (Direct the students to count the number of errors and write the number in the Errors box at the top of the Workbook page.)
3. (Award points and direct students to record points in Box D of their Point Chart.)

   0 errors................................5 points
   1 error ....3 points
   2 or 3 errors ....1 point
   more than 3 errors ....0 points

Point schedule for Lessons 26 through 30

Box	Lesson part	Points
A	Word Attack	0 or 5
B	Selection Reading	0 or 5
C	Timed Reading Checkout	0 or 5
D	Workbook	0, 1, 3, or 5
Bonus	(Teacher option)	—

Lesson 30

Errors

1

1. How old was our redwood tree when it became a good seed producer? (over two hundred years old)
2. How long would our redwood continue to produce seeds? (until its death)
3. What happens to the rate of growth of the redwood when it becomes a mature tree? (It slows down.)
4. Where did the fire begin? (in a pile of dry litter near the base of a young tree)
5. Which trees did the fire touch first? (the smaller trees)
6. How long did the fire smolder? three months
7. After the fire, what did the remaining trees look like? (gigantic charred toothpicks)
8. What part of the tree trunk is the living part? (a thin layer just under the bark)
9. Why did the mature redwoods survive the fire? (Their bark was so thick.)
10. Why did the oaks and sugar pines die in the fire? (Their bark was so thin.)

2 **Fill in each blank using a word in the box.**

mature	snaked	wispy
deafening	leveled	original

1. The wind blew with a deafening roar.
2. When the caterpillar becomes mature, it will be a butterfly.
3. After the forest was leveled, there were only a few tree stumps left.

Copyright © SRA/McGraw-Hill. All rights reserved. Lesson 30 53

Five-lesson point summary

- (For **letter grades** based on points for Lessons **26** through **30,** tell students to compute the total for the blue boxes [C, D, and Bonus] and write the number in the Total box at the end of each row in their Point Chart. Students then add the totals and write the sum in the green box.)
- (For **rewards** based on points, tell students to compute the total for all boxes [A, B, C, D, and Bonus] and write the number in the Total box at the end of each row. Students then add the totals and write the sum in the green box.)

END OF LESSON 30

Administer Mastery Test 1 before you present Lesson 31.

MASTERY TEST 1

AFTER LESSON 30, BEFORE LESSON 31

- (Mastery Test 1 is located at the back of each student's Workbook.)
- (Mastery Test 1 has four parts. Parts 1 and 2 are group tests that test word recognition. Parts 3 and 4 are completed independently by students.)

In Mastery Test 1, you will identify words and word parts. Then you will read a story segment and write answers to comprehension questions.

Part 1 Students identify words

1. Turn to Mastery Test 1 on page 231 of your Workbook. ✓
- Find part 1. ✓
- I'll read a word for each item. You'll fill in the bubble for that word.
2. Item 1. One of the words is **giant.**
- The little boy traveled to the land of the **giant.** Mark **giant.** (Observe, but do not give feedback.)
3. Item 2. One of the words is **chances.**
- His **chances** of winning were good. Mark **chances.** (Observe, but do not give feedback.)
4. (Repeat step 3 for the remaining words:)
- Item 3: **bounding.** The deer was **bounding** across the field. Mark **bounding.**
- Item 4: **tried.** She **tried** and tried until she succeeded. Mark **tried.**
- Item 5: **swirled.** The water **swirled** around the rocks. Mark **swirled.**
- Item 6: **form.** His last dive had very good **form.** Mark **form.**
- Item 7: **pouted.** The children **pouted** because they had to stay inside. Mark **pouted.**
- Item 8: **docked.** The ship **docked** at pier 21. Mark **docked.**
- Item 9: **poked.** They **poked** holes in the snow. Mark **poked.**
- Item 10: **sprained.** I fell and **sprained** my back. Mark **sprained.**
- Item 11: **startled.** The noise **startled** me. Mark **startled.**
- Item 12: **watch.** **Watch** out for falling rocks. Mark **watch.**
- Item 13: **though.** She was fast, even **though** she was very tall. Mark **though.**
- Item 14: **spare.** The car did not have a **spare** tire. Mark **spare.**
- Item 15: **ever.** Will they **ever** learn how to swim? Mark **ever.**
- Item 16: **strip.** He cut a long **strip** of paper. Mark **strip.**
- Item 17: **quite.** That was **quite** a party. Mark **quite.**
- Item 18: **slim.** The dog stopped eating and got very **slim.** Mark **slim.**
- Item 19: **founder.** He was the **founder** of our city. Mark **founder.**
- Item 20: **trunk.** We stuffed all our gear in the **trunk.** Mark **trunk.**
- Item 21: **expect.** Do you **expect** us to eat that food? Mark **expect.**
- Item 22: **listener.** You are a very good **listener.** Mark **listener.**
- Item 23: **fierce.** That dog is **fierce.** Mark **fierce.**
- Item 24: **rear.** We sat near the **rear** of the bus. Mark **rear.**
- Item 25: **boast.** He loves to **boast** about his skills. Mark **boast.**

Part 2 Students identify the middle parts of words

1. Find part 2. ✓
   - The first part and last part of each word are circled. I'll say a middle part for each item. You'll fill in the bubble for the word that has that middle part.
2. Item 1. The middle part is **tinu.** (Pronounce as **tin-you.**)
   - Find the word that has a middle part pronounced **tin-you,** and fill in the bubble for that word. (Observe, but do not give feedback.)
3. Item 2. The middle part is **pen.**
   - Find the word that has the middle part pronounced **pen,** and fill in the bubble for that word. (Observe, but do not give feedback.)
4. Item 3. The middle part is **tion.** (Pronounce as **shun.**)
   - Find the word that has the middle part pronounced **shun,** and fill in the bubble for that word.
5. Item 4. The middle part is **part.**
   - Find the word that has the middle part pronounced **part,** and fill in the bubble for that word.
6. Item 5. The middle part is **tire.**
   - Find the word that has the middle part pronounced **tire,** and fill in the bubble for that word.

Parts 3 and 4 Students read the story selection independently and answer comprehension questions

1. Find part 3. ✓
   - You are going to read this story segment. Then you'll write answers to the questions on the last page.
2. (After students have written answers to the questions, collect tests.)

Scoring the test

1. (Count the number of errors in the whole test. Write that number in the box at the top of the test form.)
2. (Pass criterion: 0–6 errors. Circle **P.**)
   - (Fail criterion: 7 or more errors. Circle **F.**)
3. (Record each student's **P** or **F** score on the Mastery Test Group Summary form under Test 1.)

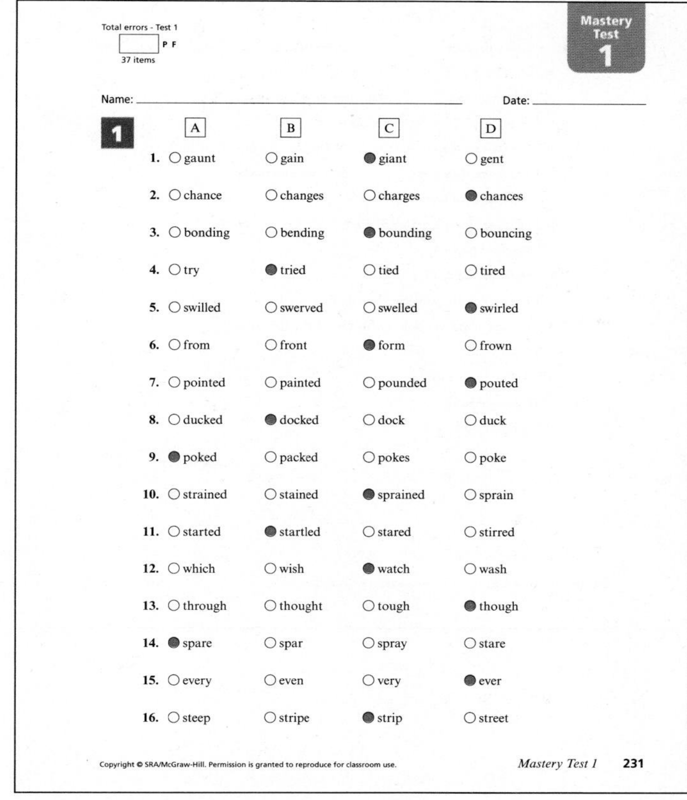

Total errors - Test 1 [ ] P F
37 items

Mastery Test 1

Name: ____________ Date: ____________

1

	A	B	C	D
1.	○ gaunt	○ gain	● giant	○ gent
2.	○ chance	○ changes	○ charges	● chances
3.	○ bonding	○ bending	● bounding	○ bouncing
4.	○ try	● tried	○ tied	○ tired
5.	○ swilled	○ swerved	○ swelled	● swirled
6.	○ from	○ front	● form	○ frown
7.	○ pointed	○ painted	○ pounded	● pouted
8.	○ ducked	● docked	○ dock	○ duck
9.	● poked	○ packed	○ pokes	○ poke
10.	○ strained	○ stained	● sprained	○ sprain
11.	○ started	● startled	○ stared	○ stirred
12.	○ which	○ wish	● watch	○ wash
13.	○ through	○ thought	○ tough	● though
14.	● spare	○ spar	○ spray	○ stare
15.	○ every	○ even	○ very	● ever
16.	○ steep	○ stripe	● strip	○ street

Copyright © SRA/McGraw-Hill. Permission is granted to reproduce for classroom use. *Mastery Test 1* 231

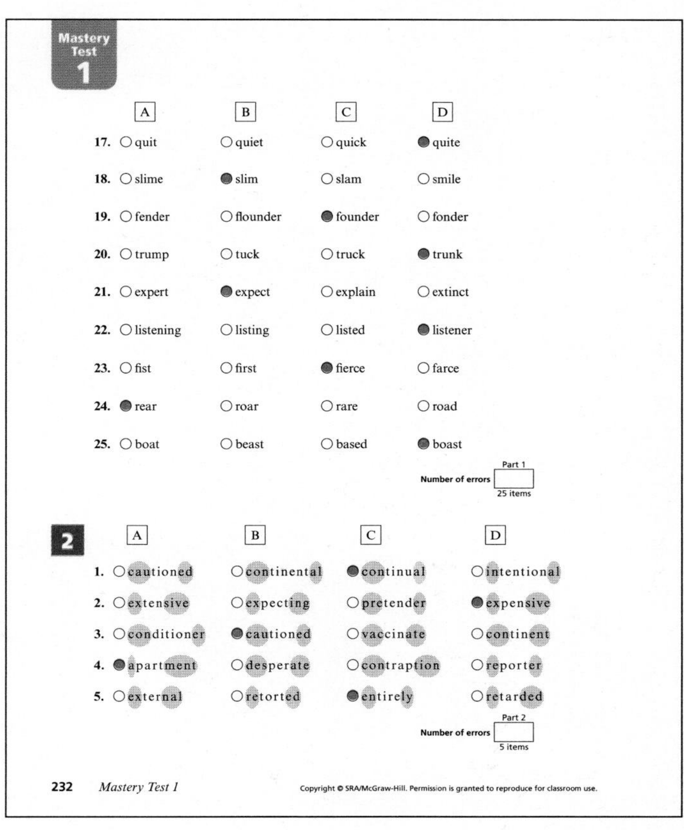

Mastery Test 1

	A	B	C	D
17.	○ quit	○ quiet	○ quick	● quite
18.	○ slime	● slim	○ slam	○ smile
19.	○ fender	○ flounder	● founder	○ fonder
20.	○ trump	○ tuck	○ truck	● trunk
21.	○ expert	● expect	○ explain	○ extinct
22.	○ listening	○ listing	○ listed	● listener
23.	○ fist	○ first	● fierce	○ farce
24.	● rear	○ roar	○ rare	○ road
25.	○ boat	○ beast	○ based	● boast

Part 1 Number of errors [ ] 25 items

2

	A	B	C	D
1.	○ cautioned	○ continental	● continual	○ intentional
2.	○ extensive	○ expecting	○ pretender	● expensive
3.	○ conditioner	● cautioned	○ vaccinate	○ continent
4.	● apartment	○ desperate	○ contraption	○ reporter
5.	○ external	○ retorted	● entirely	○ retarded

Part 2 Number of errors [ ] 5 items

232 *Mastery Test 1* Copyright © SRA/McGraw-Hill. Permission is granted to reproduce for classroom use.

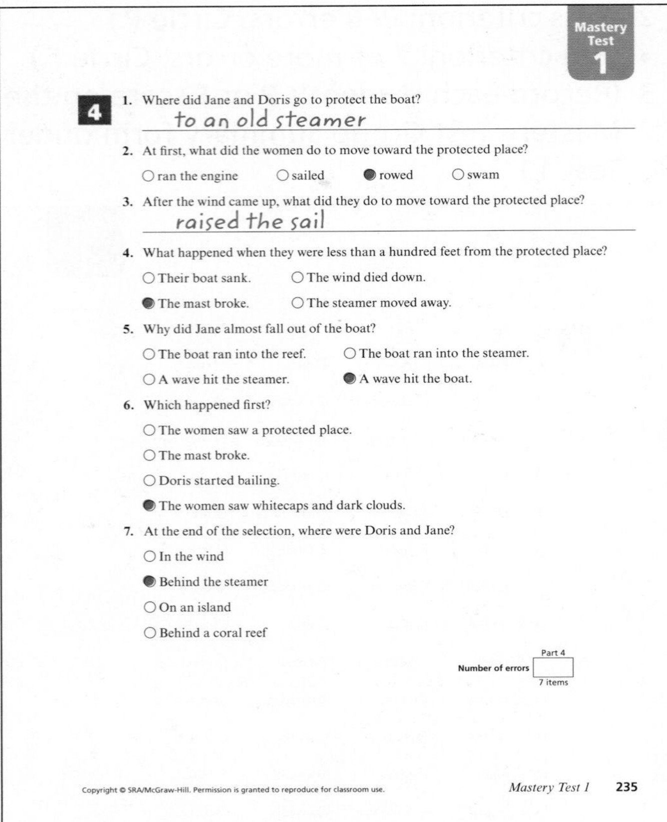

Mastery Test 1

4

1. Where did Jane and Doris go to protect the boat?
   to an old steamer
2. At first, what did the women do to move toward the protected place?
   - ○ ran the engine ○ sailed ● rowed ○ swam
3. After the wind came up, what did they do to move toward the protected place?
   raised the sail
4. What happened when they were less than a hundred feet from the protected place?
   - ○ Their boat sank.
   - ○ The wind died down.
   - ● The mast broke.
   - ○ The steamer moved away.
5. Why did Jane almost fall out of the boat?
   - ○ The boat ran into the reef.
   - ○ The boat ran into the steamer.
   - ○ A wave hit the steamer.
   - ● A wave hit the boat.
6. Which happened first?
   - ○ The women saw a protected place.
   - ○ The mast broke.
   - ○ Doris started bailing.
   - ● The women saw whitecaps and dark clouds.
7. At the end of the selection, where were Doris and Jane?
   - ○ In the wind
   - ● Behind the steamer
   - ○ On an island
   - ○ Behind a coral reef

Part 4
Number of errors ☐
7 items

Copyright © SRA/McGraw-Hill. Permission is granted to reproduce for classroom use.

Mastery Test 1 235

Remedies

1. (If **30 percent or more** of the students fail the test by making **7 or more errors,** present the following firm-up procedure.
   a. Give feedback on Test 1 answers.
   - Read each item.
   - Say the item number and the column letter of the answer—A, B, C, or D.
   - Direct the students to spell the word.

   b. Repeat parts of Lessons 28 through 30:
   - Repeat Word-Attack exercises.
   - Repeat Selection Reading exercises and Fluency Assessment—Individual timed reading checkouts.
   - Present no Workbook tasks.

   c. After students have successfully completed the remedies, retest them on Mastery Test 1. Reproduce the Mastery Test as needed.
2. (If **fewer than 30 percent** of the students fail the test, give these students information on the items they missed.)

Lesson Objectives	LESSON 31	LESSON 32	LESSON 33	LESSON 34	LESSON 35
	Exercise	Exercise	Exercise	Exercise	Exercise
Word Attack					
Decoding and Word Analysis					
Affixes: *un, ly*	1	1			
Affix: *re*				1	
Affixes: *un, ly, re*					1
Visual Discrimination			1		
Letter Combinations/Letter Sounds	2	2	2	2	2
Word Recognition	1–4	1–4	1–4	1–4	1–4
Vocabulary					
Morphemic Analysis	1	1		1	1
Definitions	2–4	2–4	2–4	2, 3	2–4
Usage	3	3	3	3	3
Assessment					
Ongoing: Individual Tests	5	5	5	5	5
Group Reading					
Decoding and Word Analysis					
Read Decodable Text	6	6	6	6	6
Comprehension					
Access Prior Knowledge				6	6
Draw Inferences	6	6	6	6	6
Note Details	6	6	6	6	6
Predict	6	6	6	6	6
Assessment					
Ongoing: Comprehension Check	6	6	6	6	6
Ongoing: Decoding Accuracy	6	6	6	6	6
Fluency Assessment					
Fluency					
Reread Decodable Text	7	7	7	7	7
Assessment					
Ongoing: Teacher-Monitored Fluency	7	7	7	7	7
Ongoing: Peer-Monitored Fluency	7	7	7	7	7
Workbook Exercises					
Decoding and Word Analysis					
Multisyllabic Word Parts		Ind. Work			Ind. Work
Comprehension					
Main Idea			Ind. Work		
Note Details	Ind. Work	Ind. Work	Ind. Work	Ind. Work	Ind. Work
Vocabulary					
Usage	Ind. Work	Ind. Work	Ind. Work	Ind. Work	Ind. Work
Study Skills					
Writing Mechanics			Ind. Work		
Assessment					
Ongoing: Workcheck	Workcheck	Workcheck	Workcheck	Workcheck	Workcheck

Lesson 31

WORD-ATTACK SKILLS

Student Book 

EXERCISE 1

NEW **AFFIX REVIEW**

Task A

1. Open your Student Book to Lesson 31. ✓

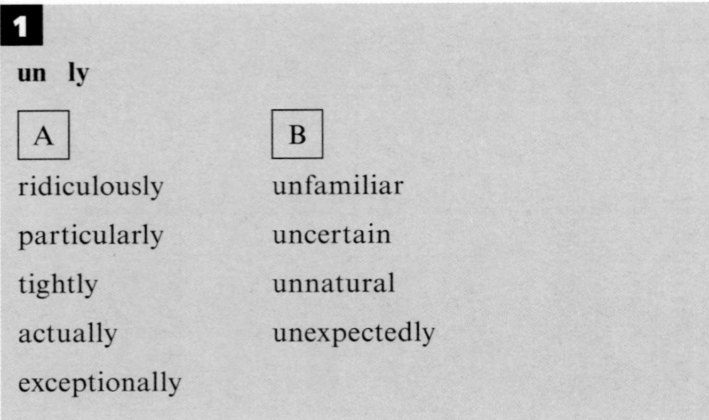

1

un ly

A	B
ridiculously	unfamiliar
particularly	uncertain
tightly	unnatural
actually	unexpectedly
exceptionally	

- Touch the first row in part 1. ✓
- Let's see if you remember a meaning for each of those affixes.

2. Touch the letters **U–N.** ✓
- What's one meaning of **un?** (Signal.) *Not.*

3. Touch the letters **L–Y.** ✓
- What's one meaning of **ly?** (Signal.) *How something happened.*

4. (Repeat steps 2 and 3 until firm.)

Task B

1. Touch the first word in column A. ✓
- What word? (Signal.) *Ridiculously.*

2. Touch the next word. ✓
- What word? (Signal.) *Particularly.*

3. (Repeat step 2 for each remaining word.)
4. (Repeat the list until firm.)
5. (Repeat steps 1–4 for the words in column B.)

EXERCISE 2

WORD PRACTICE

> **Note:** In this exercise, you ask, What's the underlined part? not What sound?

1. Touch the first word in part 2. ✓

2

treasure exaggerate examine sure broil

occasionally probably* stalled situation*

voiced nature boasted moist injure

sprouts mature* brighten insure

- What's the underlined part? (Signal.) *ure.*
- What word? (Signal.) *Treasure.*

2. Touch the next word. ✓
- What's the underlined part? (Signal.) *ex.*
- What word? (Signal.) *Exaggerate.*

3. (Repeat step 2 for each remaining word.)
4. (Repeat each row of words until firm.)
5. What does **probably** mean? (Call on a student.)
- (Repeat for **situation, mature.**)

EXERCISE 3

VOCABULARY

1. Touch part 3. ✓

3

adapt

- We're going to talk about what this word means.

2. Touch the word. ✓
- What word? (Signal.) *Adapt.*
- When you do something to get along in a new situation, you **adapt.** What would you do to **adapt** to the desert? (Call on a student.) (Idea: *Wear different clothes and so on.*)

EXERCISE 4

WORD PRACTICE

1. Touch the first word in part 4. ✓

4

through thought thorough though
tough colony colonies earth canopy*
Atlantic continent realize adopt consider
ordinary continued dense century
terrible surroundings loose danger
destroyed narrower disturbed sugar
endure amazing cause normal possible

- What word? (Signal.) *Through.*

2. Next word. ✓

- What word? (Signal.) *Thought.*

3. (Repeat step 2 for each remaining word.)
4. (Repeat each row of words until firm.)
5. What does **canopy** mean? (Call on a student.)

EXERCISE 5

WORD-ATTACK SKILLS: Individual tests

1. (Call on individual students. Each student reads a row or column. Tally the rows and columns read without error. If the group reads at least 11 rows and columns without making errors, direct all students to record 5 points in Box A of their Point Chart. Criterion is 80 percent of rows and columns read without error.)
2. (If the group did not read at least 11 rows and columns without errors, do not award any points for the Word-Attack Skills exercises.)

SELECTION READING

EXERCISE 6

STORY READING

1. Everybody, touch part 5. ✓
2. The error limit for this story is 12. If the group reads the story with 12 errors or less, you earn 5 points.

5 **A Green Toothpick**

3. (Call on a student to read the title.) *A Green Toothpick.*

- What do you think this story is about? (Accept reasonable responses.)

4. (Call on individual students. Each is to read two to four sentences.)
5. (Call on individual students to answer the specified questions during the story reading.)

To realize how amazing the mature redwoods are, you have to remember that most other older trees become very fixed in their ways and would not adjust to the changes a fire would cause. Most young trees, whether they're redwoods or sugar pines, can adapt well to different situations. If you were to pile up dirt one foot deep around the base of a sugar pine sapling, the tree would adjust and keep on living. However, if you piled up dirt only four inches deep around the base of a mature sugar pine, you would probably kill the tree.

Mature trees often become so set in their ways that they die if the trees next to them are cut down. When these other trees are cut down, sunlight reaches the base of the mature tree, and the tree dies. ❶

1. What does "fixed in their ways" mean? (Idea: *They would not adjust to changes.*)
1. What would happen if you piled up one foot of dirt around a mature sugar pine? (Idea: *The tree would probably die.*)
1. What might happen to a mature tree if a tree next to it is cut down? (Idea: *It might die.*)
1. Why? (Idea: *Because sunlight would reach the base of the tree.*)

Lesson
31

Now consider the mature redwood. Remember, our redwood was 420 years old when the fire burned every needle from it. You would think that a tree so old could not survive. But the redwood is no ordinary tree. And our redwood did survive.

The forest looked very strange the next spring. The charred trees that had looked like black toothpicks now looked like green toothpicks. Little green sprouts shot out from the trunk of every mature redwood—from the ground to the top of every tree. Sprouts also shot out from what was left of the top branches. The trees looked very strange, almost as if somebody had painted the trunks and the remaining branches green.

The shoots grew very fast. By the end of the summer, some of them were almost ten feet long. They continued growing rapidly during the next several years. The shoots near the bottom of the trees became shaded and died off. Those near the top of the trees slowly took the shape of a cone. Within twenty years after the fire, the mature redwoods looked quite normal again, with long, bare trunks and green, full, cone-shaped tops. ❷

2. How did the forest look in the spring after the fire? (Idea: *Very strange.*)
2. Where were the sprouts on the mature redwoods? (Idea: *Everywhere from the ground to the top of the tree.*)
2. How did the trees look with their sprouts? (Idea: *As if someone had painted the trunks and branches green.*)
2. What happened to the shoots near the bottom of the tree? (Idea: *They died.*)
2. Why? (Idea: *Because they were shaded from the sun.*)
2. How long did it take the redwoods to look normal again? *About twenty years.*

Once more a canopy of green shaded the forest floor. The canopy was not as dense as it had been, which meant that some of the younger trees that sprouted from the ground after the fire had a chance to grow more rapidly than young trees did before the great fire.

Century after century went by. When our tree was seventeen hundred years old, it lost its top during a terrible windstorm. This happened the year before Columbus sailed across the Atlantic. The top forty feet of our redwood crashed to the forest floor, tearing branches from the surrounding trees and leaving a large hole in the canopy of green. That hole made it possible for some of the younger redwoods to grow. One seedling that sprouted the next year came from a seed of our redwood. That seedling was growing in the loose dirt dug up when the top of our redwood crashed to the forest floor. The seedling looked ridiculously small next to our huge redwood.

Our redwood did not grow its top back quickly. Over two hundred years passed before the redwood was as tall as it had been before the windstorm. By now, British colonies were being settled on the other side of the continent. ❸

3. When did our tree lose its top? (Ideas: *When it was seventeen hundred years old; the year before Columbus sailed across the Atlantic.*)
3. How long did it take for the redwood to grow as tall as it had been before the storm? *Over two hundred years.*

Things remained peaceful in the redwood forest for the next three hundred years. Three smaller fires swept through the forest, and one left a large hole in the base of our redwood. Over the years a lot of animals used that hole, mostly squirrels and rabbits. It was big enough for three people to sit in, but it didn't really harm the tree. The wood from redwoods doesn't rot even if it is exposed to the rain. Water will rot most other woods. Boards made from pine or fir must be treated if they are to be exposed to the weather. Not so with boards of redwood. ❹

4. How big was the hole in the base of our redwood? (Idea: *Big enough for three people to sit in.*)
4. Why didn't the rain harm the redwood? (Idea: *Because the wood from redwoods doesn't rot when it's exposed to rain.*)
6. (Award points quickly.)
7. (If the group makes more than 12 errors, repeat the reading immediately or on the next day.)

FLUENCY ASSESSMENT

EXERCISE 7

TIMED READING CHECKOUTS

1. (For this part of the lesson, assigned pairs of students work together during the checkouts.)
- (If one student does not have a checkout partner, arrange another time when you can give the checkout.)
2. (Each student does a 2-minute timed reading. Students earn 5 points by reading at least 240 words and making no more than 5 errors on the first part of story 31. Students record points in Box C of their Point Chart and plot their reading rate and errors on the Individual Reading Progress Chart.)
- (During each timed checkout, observe one pair of students for 2 minutes. Make notes on any mistakes the reader makes.)
3. (Record the timed reading checkout performance for each student you observed on the Fluency Assessment Summary form.)

WORKBOOK EXERCISES

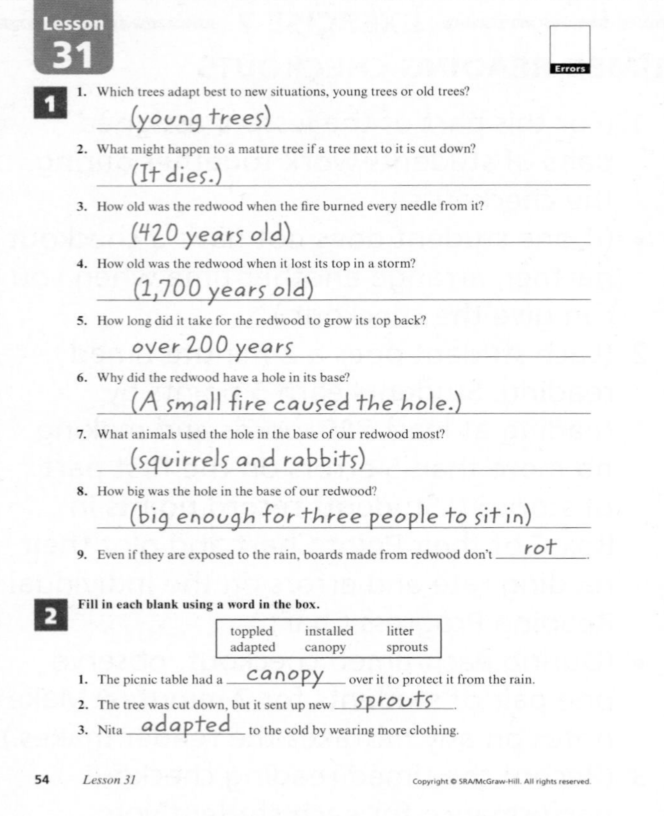

Lesson 31

Errors

1

1. Which trees adapt best to new situations, young trees or old trees?
   (young trees)
2. What might happen to a mature tree if a tree next to it is cut down?
   (It dies.)
3. How old was the redwood when the fire burned every needle from it?
   (420 years old)
4. How old was the redwood when it lost its top in a storm?
   (1,700 years old)
5. How long did it take for the redwood to grow its top back?
   over 200 years
6. Why did the redwood have a hole in its base?
   (A small fire caused the hole.)
7. What animals used the hole in the base of our redwood most?
   (squirrels and rabbits)
8. How big was the hole in the base of our redwood?
   (big enough for three people to sit in)
9. Even if they are exposed to the rain, boards made from redwood don't rot

2 **Fill in each blank using a word in the box.**

toppled	installed	litter
adapted	canopy	sprouts

1. The picnic table had a canopy over it to protect it from the rain.
2. The tree was cut down, but it sent up new sprouts
3. Nita adapted to the cold by wearing more clothing.

54 *Lesson 31* Copyright © SRA/McGraw-Hill. All rights reserved.

Independent Student Work

Task A

- Open your Workbook to Lesson 31. ✓
- Complete all the parts of your Workbook lesson using a pencil. If you make no errors, you will earn 5 points.

Task B

1. (Before presenting Lesson 32, check student Workbooks for Lesson 31.)
   - (Call on individual students to read the items and answers in each part. Students mark errors using a pen.)
2. (Direct the students to count the number of errors and write the number in the Errors box at the top of the Workbook page.)
3. (Award points and direct students to record points in Box D of their Point Chart.)

   0 errors................................5 points
   1 error ....3 points
   2 or 3 errors ....1 point
   more than 3 errors ....0 points

END OF LESSON 31

WORD-ATTACK SKILLS

Student Book 

EXERCISE 1

AFFIX REVIEW

Task A

1. Open your Student Book to Lesson 32. ✓

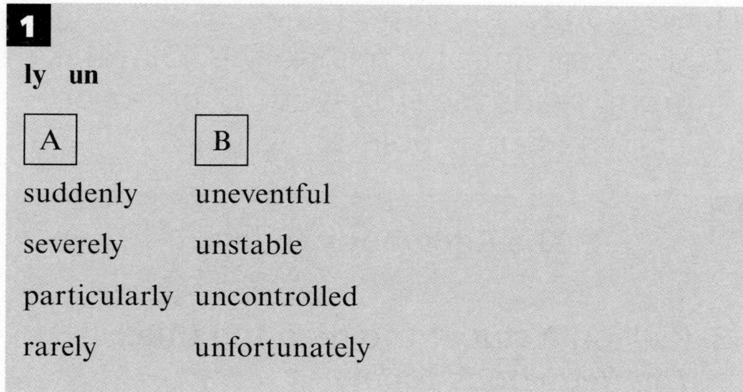

1

ly un

A	B
suddenly	uneventful
severely	unstable
particularly	uncontrolled
rarely	unfortunately

- Touch the first row in part 1. ✓
- Let's see if you remember a meaning for each of those affixes.

2. Touch the letters **L–Y.** ✓
- What's one meaning of **ly?** (Signal.) *How something happened.*

3. Touch the letters **U–N.** ✓
- What's one meaning of **un?** (Signal.) *Not.*

4. (Repeat steps 2 and 3 until firm.)

Task B

1. Touch the first word in column A. ✓
- What word? (Signal.) *Suddenly.*

2. Touch the next word. ✓
- What word? (Signal.) *Severely.*

3. (Repeat step 2 for **particularly, rarely.**)
4. (Repeat the list until firm.)
5. (Repeat steps 1–4 for the words in column B.)

EXERCISE 2

WORD PRACTICE

1. Touch the first word in part 2. ✓

2

exaggerate unfailingly assure jointly
groans exceptionally unexplainable creature
certain hoist lecture surrounding
location* choicest loaning termites*

- What's the underlined part? (Signal.) *ex.*
- What word? (Signal.) *Exaggerate.*

2. Touch the next word. ✓
- What's the underlined part? (Signal.) *ly.*
- What word? (Signal.) *Unfailingly.*

3. (Repeat step 2 for each remaining word.)
4. (Repeat each row of words until firm.)
5. What does **location** mean? (Call on a student.)
- (Repeat for **termites.**)

EXERCISE 3

VOCABULARY

1. Touch part 3. ✓

3

1. polite
2. remarkable
3. outskirts
4. brittle

- We're going to talk about what those words mean.

2. Touch word 1. ✓
- What word? (Signal.) *Polite.*
- What does **polite** mean? (Call on a student.) (Ideas: *Considerate; courteous.*)

3. Everybody, touch word 2. ✓
- What word? (Signal.) *Remarkable.*
- Something that is **remarkable** is **surprising** or **amazing.** Here's another way of saying "an **amazing** story": a **remarkable** story. Everybody, what's another way of saying "an **amazing** tree"? (Signal.) *A remarkable tree.*

4. Touch word 3. ✓
- What word? (Signal.) *Outskirts.*
- The **outskirts** of a town are **the areas on the edge of town.** If you lived on the **edge of town,** you would live on the **outskirts.**

5. Touch word 4. ✓
- What word? (Signal.) *Brittle.*
- Things that are **brittle** don't bend. They break. Ice is **brittle.** Name something else that is **brittle.** (Call on individual students.) (Ideas: *Glass; dried-out twig; etc.*)

EXERCISE 4

WORD PRACTICE

1. Touch the first word in part 4. ✓

4

county country beautiful contains
continues becomes forever
protected gravel narrower edge
mature* destroy contact shallow
furniture excellent fault dangerous
shrink material fences building
square bothered national rarely

- What word? (Signal.) *County.*

2. Next word. ✓
- What word? (Signal.) *Country.*
3. (Repeat step 2 for each remaining word.)
4. (Repeat each row of words until firm.)
5. What does **mature** mean? (Call on a student.)

EXERCISE 5

WORD-ATTACK SKILLS: Individual tests

1. (Call on individual students. Each student reads a row or column. Tally the rows and columns read without error. If the group reads at least 11 rows and columns without making errors, direct all students to record 5 points in Box A of their Point Chart. Criterion is 80 percent of rows and columns read without error.)
2. (If the group did not read at least 11 rows and columns without errors, do not award any points for the Word-Attack Skills exercises.)

SELECTION READING

EXERCISE 6

STORY READING

1. Everybody, touch part 5. ✓
2. The error limit for this story is 12. If the group reads the story with 12 errors or less, you earn 5 points.

5 **The Redwoods Today**

3. (Call on a student to read the title.) *The Redwoods Today.*
- What do you think this story is about? (Accept reasonable responses.)
4. (Call on individual students. Each is to read two to four sentences.)
5. (Call on individual students to answer the specified questions during the story reading.)

As you've seen, redwoods are remarkable. Fire can't destroy them. Even if young trees are cut down, they sprout up again. Redwoods are not bothered by termites or any insect that destroys other trees. The wood from redwoods is as remarkable as the trees. The wood will not rot if it comes in contact with wet earth. Even after the wood has been soaked for years, it won't rot. The wood is soft and easy to work with, so it makes good furniture and excellent siding for houses. ❶

1. What's the most remarkable thing about the wood from redwoods? (Idea: *It doesn't rot.*)

The redwood seems like a perfect tree, except for two faults. The first fault is that the roots of redwoods are very shallow. They rarely go down more than ten feet. The roots fan out to the sides like great hooks or claws that hang on to the soil. When redwoods grow in forests, the roots of one tree lock under the roots of surrounding trees. When no trees surround the mature redwood, however, it becomes unstable. The first strong wind that hits the tree might blow it over. ❷

2. What's the first fault of redwoods? (Idea: *They have shallow roots.*)
2. What might happen to a mature redwood that's standing alone? (Idea: *It might get blown over.*)

Because redwoods have shallow roots, the trees are dangerous near cities. Let's say that a huge redwood—200 feet tall—is growing next to some houses on the outskirts of town. And let's say that there are no surrounding trees. One night there is a great storm, and the redwood comes down.

The second problem is that the wood in older redwoods becomes brittle. It may split or crack. If that happens, parts of the tree may come down during a storm. ❸

3. What's the first problem with redwoods? (Idea: *They have shallow roots.*)
3. What's the second problem with redwoods? (Idea: *The wood of older trees becomes brittle.*)

Because of these two problems, the redwood forests began to shrink up during the past 60 years. The great redwoods came down to make furniture, fences, and other building material. But even as early as 1921, the State of California began giving money so that redwood parks could be formed. The old redwoods within these parks would be protected.

Our redwood does not live in one of these first parks. It lives near Arcata, California, in an area called Redwood Creek. And our redwood was lucky, because in 1968, the whole Redwood Creek area became part of a new park—Redwood National Park. The park contains 172 square miles of mature redwoods. ❹

4. What did the State of California start doing in 1921? (Idea: *Giving money to form redwood parks.*)
4. In which park does our redwood live? *Redwood National Park.*
4. What town is that park near? *Arcata.*

Our redwood is not the tallest tree along Redwood Creek. There is one that is more than four hundred feet tall. But our redwood is one of the biggest trees. It's not easy to find because there is no road that leads to it. To find it, you have to park your car on the gravel county road and walk along the edge of the creek, through the ferns and the soft litter on the forest floor. Look at the bigger trees and you'll see one with a base so big that you could hide three cars behind it. You'll see a cone-shaped hole near the bottom of the tree. And when you look up, the trunk seems to go up forever. But if you look closely, you'll see a place near the top of the tree where the trunk suddenly becomes narrower, marking where the top had broken off long ago. And when you stand there in the silent forest looking at our redwood, you'll probably feel proud. You will be certain of one thing, however—you're looking at one beautiful tree. ❺

5. How can you find our tree? **(Idea:** ***Walk along the edge of the creek and look for the tree with the big base.*****)**
5. How big is the base of our tree? **(Idea:** ***So big that you can hide three cars behind it.*****)**
5. You're going to **compare** redwoods with other larger trees. You'll name some ways redwoods are the same as other large trees and some ways they are different.
- Name some ways redwoods are the **same** as other large trees. **(Ideas:** ***Redwoods and other large trees drop seeds, have cones, keep growing, grow in the summer.*****)**
- Name some ways redwoods are **different** from other large trees. **(Ideas:** ***Redwoods grow naturally in California, are resistant to fire, are not fixed in their ways when they are old.*****)**
- **(Direct students to take out a sheet of paper.)** You're going to write sentences that compare redwoods with other large trees. Write two sentences that tell how redwoods are the **same** as other large trees and two sentences that tell how redwoods are **different.**
- **(Call on several students to read their sentences.)**

6. **(Award points quickly.)**
7. **(If the group makes more than 12 errors, repeat the reading immediately or on the next day.)**

FLUENCY ASSESSMENT

EXERCISE 7

TIMED READING CHECKOUTS

1. **(For this part of the lesson, assigned pairs of students work together during the checkouts.)**
- **(If one student does not have a checkout partner, arrange another time when you can give the checkout.)**

2. **(Each student does a 2-minute timed reading. Students earn 5 points by reading at least 240 words and making no more than 5 errors on the first part of story 32. Students record points in Box C of their Point Chart and plot their reading rate and errors on the Individual Reading Progress Chart.)**
- **(During each timed checkout, observe one pair of students for 2 minutes. Make notes on any mistakes the reader makes.)**

3. **(Record the timed reading checkout performance for each student you observed on the Fluency Assessment Summary form.)**

WORKBOOK EXERCISES

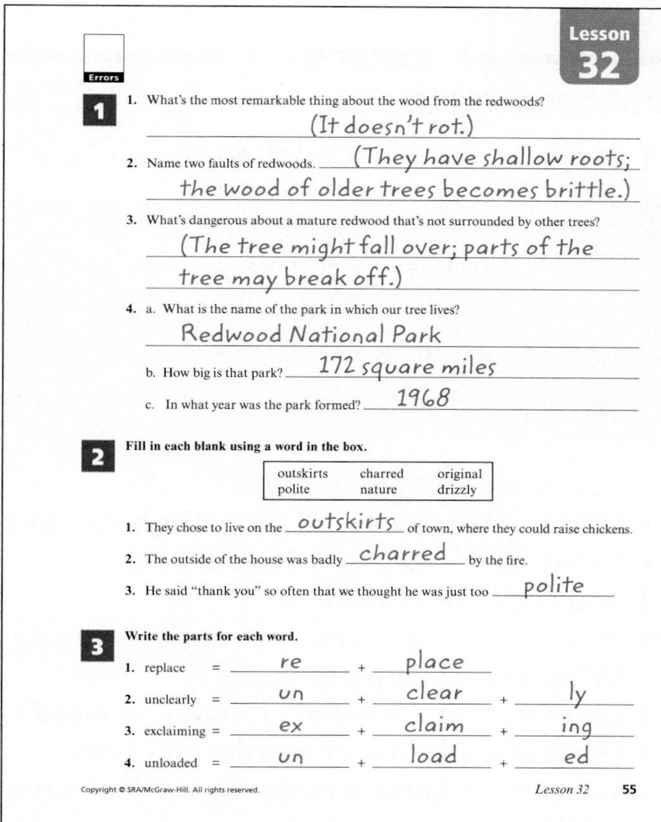

Lesson 32

Errors

1

1. What's the most remarkable thing about the wood from the redwoods?
(It doesn't rot.)
2. Name two faults of redwoods. (They have shallow roots; the wood of older trees becomes brittle.)
3. What's dangerous about a mature redwood that's not surrounded by other trees?
(The tree might fall over; parts of the tree may break off.)
4. a. What is the name of the park in which our tree lives?
Redwood National Park
b. How big is that park? 172 square miles
c. In what year was the park formed? 1968

2 Fill in each blank using a word in the box.

outskirts	charred	original
polite	nature	drizzly

1. They chose to live on the outskirts of town, where they could raise chickens.
2. The outside of the house was badly charred by the fire.
3. He said "thank you" so often that we thought he was just too polite.

3 Write the parts for each word.

1. replace = re + place
2. unclearly = un + clear + ly
3. exclaiming = ex + claim + ing
4. unloaded = un + load + ed

Copyright © SRA/McGraw-Hill. All rights reserved. Lesson 32 55

Independent Student Work

Task A

- Open your Workbook to Lesson 32. ✓
- Complete all the parts of your Workbook lesson using a pencil. If you make no errors, you will earn 5 points.

Task B

1. (Before presenting Lesson 33, check student Workbooks for Lesson 32.)
   - (Call on individual students to read the items and answers in each part. Students mark errors using a pen.)
2. (Direct the students to count the number of errors and write the number in the Errors box at the top of the Workbook page.)
3. (Award points and direct students to record points in Box D of their Point Chart.)

0 errors................................5 points
1 error.................................3 points
2 or 3 errors.........................1 point
more than 3 errors..............0 points

END OF LESSON 32

Lesson 33

WORD-ATTACK SKILLS

Board Work

EXERCISE 1

BUILDUP

1. (Print on the board:)

through

2. (Point to **through.** Pause.) What word? (Signal.) *Through.*
3. (Change the word to:)

th ough

- What word now? (Signal.) *Though.*

4. (Change the word to:)

th ought

- What word now? (Signal.) *Thought.*

5. (Change the word to:)

th ough

- What word now? (Signal.) *Though.*

6. (Change the word to:)

t ough

- What word now? (Signal.) *Tough.*

7. (Change to the original word:)

through

- (Repeat steps 2–6 until firm.)

Student Book

EXERCISE 2

WORD PRACTICE

1. Open your Student Book to Lesson 33. ✓

1

conditioner Bruce office manage
furthermore grouchier occasionally
exceptionally simply curling
unbelievable* pinched choice

- Touch the first word in part 1. ✓
- What's the underlined part? (Signal.) *shun.*
- What word? (Signal.) *Conditioner.*

2. Touch the next word. ✓

- What's the underlined part? (Signal.) *sss.*
- What word? (Signal.) *Bruce.*

3. (Repeat step 2 for each remaining word.)
4. (Repeat each row of words until firm.)
5. What does **unbelievable** mean? (Call on a student.)

EXERCISE 3

VOCABULARY

1. Touch part 2. ✓

2

1. insurance
2. freeway
3. bothersome

- We're going to talk about what those words mean.

2. Touch word 1. ✓

- What word? (Signal.) *Insurance.*
- What is **insurance?** (Call on a student.) (Idea: *Insurance is a guarantee that you won't have to pay for some things that might happen.*)

3. Everybody, touch word 2. ✓

- What word? (Signal.) *Freeway.*
- What is a **freeway?** (Call on a student.) (Idea: *A wide highway that costs no money to travel on and has limited access.*)

4. Everybody, touch word 3. ✓
- What word? (Signal.) *Bothersome.*
- Something that is **bothersome bothers you.** A **bothersome** bug is a bug that **bothers you.** Everybody, what would you call a person who bothers you? (Signal.) *A bothersome person.*

EXERCISE 4

WORD PRACTICE

1. Touch the first word in part 3. ✓

3

sore phony polite* insects world
vice president newspapers freeways
something usually timer everything
oven concrete simple neighbors
peaceful humming ocean groves
bananas coconuts jungle canopy*
wearing pretend sour listen

- What word? (Signal.) *Sore.*
2. Next word. ✓
- What word? (Signal.) *Phony.*
3. (Repeat step 2 for each remaining word.)
4. (Repeat each row of words until firm.)
5. What does **polite** mean? (Call on a student.)
- (Repeat for **canopy.**)

EXERCISE 5

WORD-ATTACK SKILLS: Individual tests

1. (Call on individual students. Each student reads a row or column. Tally the rows and columns read without error. If the group reads at least 10 rows and columns without making errors, direct all students to record 5 points in Box A of their Point Chart. Criterion is 80 percent of rows and columns read without error.)
2. (If the group did not read at least 10 rows and columns without errors, do not award any points for the Word-Attack Skills exercises.)

SELECTION READING

EXERCISE 6

STORY READING

1. Everybody, touch part 4. ✓
2. The error limit for this story is 12. If the group reads the story with 12 errors or less, you earn 5 points.

4

Bruce the Grouch

3. (Call on a student to read the title.) *Bruce the Grouch.*
- What do you think this story is about? (Accept reasonable responses.)
4. (Call on individual students. Each is to read two to four sentences.)
5. (Call on individual students to answer the specified questions during the story reading.)

Bruce Celt had a good job as vice president of an insurance company. Furthermore, he had a nice home. However, he was not happy. He didn't like to drive in his car on the freeways. He didn't like the food that he ate. He read the newspapers only occasionally because everything that happened in the world seemed bad.

Every day Bruce Celt went to work, and every day he worked hard. He worked through the lunch hour because he didn't like eating out. Sometimes he ate an apple or an orange. After work he left the office, but he didn't smile on his way out. He simply drove down the freeway. Honk, honk. Stop and go, and stop again. Honk. Every day it was the same. ❶

1. Name some things Bruce did every day. (Ideas: *Went to work; worked hard; drove on the freeway.*)

Lesson
33

Bruce lived alone. By the time he got home, his eyes were sore, and he had a pain in his head. Usually he parked his car in his garage and went into his house and sat. Occasionally he looked outside and watched what his neighbors were doing. But his neighbors didn't interest him. Sometimes he would sit outside in his yard, but the air was filled with smoke, and somebody was always trying to talk to him. For example, one of his neighbors would say, "Hey, Bruce, have you seen my new car? It's nice. Come on over, and let's go for a spin in it." Bruce would try to be polite, but he couldn't help himself. He was a grouch.

After the sun went down, he would turn on the lights. But he didn't like lights because they seemed phony. They weren't sunlight. Usually he ate a frozen dinner. He took it from the freezer and popped it into the oven. When the timer on the oven went ding, he pulled out the dinner and ate it.

After dinner Bruce would go for a walk. He would try to listen to the sounds of the birds and the insects. All he could hear, however, was the roar of cars on the freeway. Bruce usually walked for an hour. Then he would return to his home and go to bed. ❷

2. Why did Bruce have trouble hearing the birds? (Idea: *Because of the roar of the cars on the freeway.*)
2. How did Bruce feel about his neighbors? (Idea: *He was not interested in them.*)
2. Why did Bruce think lights were phony? (Idea: *Because they weren't sunlight.*)

He was unhappy with his bed. It was too soft and too big. Furthermore, sleeping was not easy for Bruce. He would lie in bed and listen to the sound of the air conditioner. Occasionally he would hear the sound of the motor in the freezer. And as he lay there, Bruce would find himself making the same wish night after night. "I wish I lived a life that was simple. With all my heart I wish that I could live with plants and animals, not with cars and concrete, not with television sets and freezers." ❸

3. What did Bruce wish for? (Idea: *To live a simple life with plants and animals.*)

But then something very strange happened. One night Bruce was sadder and grouchier than he had been for a long time. Things seemed very bad at the office. He couldn't stand another frozen dinner. His neighbors seemed exceptionally bothersome.

And that night he said to himself, "I'm going to wish as hard as I can wish. I'm going to wish myself out of this place. I shouldn't have to spend the rest of my life being so unhappy. I'm going to wish harder than I've ever wished before."

So Bruce pressed his eyes shut as hard as he could and he wished. He made a picture of a place in his mind, and he wished for that place. It was a peaceful place—an island with trees and sand and warm ocean water. "Take me there," he wished. "Please, get me out of here." ❹

4. Describe the place Bruce wished for. (Ideas: *A peaceful place; an island with trees and sand and warm ocean water.*)

Bruce didn't remember falling asleep that night. He only remembered wishing and wishing and wishing. When he woke up the next morning, however, he couldn't believe his eyes. He wasn't sleeping on his soft bed, and he wasn't in his bedroom listening to the humming of the air conditioner. In fact, he wasn't in his house; he was on a sandy beach. Not fifty feet from where he sat was the ocean. Its gentle waves came curling along the beach. In back of him were groves of tall trees. He could see bananas and coconuts beneath the trees. He could hear the sound of jungle birds in the canopy of green. "This is unbelievable," Bruce said to himself. He pinched himself on the arm, but the trees, the sand, the ocean, and the exciting sounds did not go away. "I can't believe it," Bruce said to himself, and he stood up. He was wearing a pair of shorts and nothing more. There were no footprints in the sand. ❺

5. Describe the place where Bruce was. (Ideas: *It was a sandy beach by the ocean; there were trees and fruit and jungle birds.*)
6. (Award points quickly.)
7. (If the group makes more than 12 errors, repeat the reading immediately or on the next day.)

FLUENCY ASSESSMENT

EXERCISE 7

TIMED READING CHECKOUTS

1. (For this part of the lesson, assigned pairs of students work together during the checkouts.)
   - (If one student does not have a checkout partner, arrange another time when you can give the checkout.)
2. (Each student does a 2-minute timed reading. Students earn 5 points by reading at least 240 words and making no more than 5 errors on the first part of story 33. Students record points in Box C of their Point Chart and plot their reading rate and errors on the Individual Reading Progress Chart.)
   - (During each timed checkout, observe one pair of students for 2 minutes. Make notes on any mistakes the reader makes.)
3. (Record the timed reading checkout performance for each student you observed on the Fluency Assessment Summary form.)

Lesson 33

WORKBOOK EXERCISES

Lesson 33

Errors

1

1. What kind of job did Bruce have?
   (vice president of an insurance company)
2. Why did Bruce work through the lunch hour?
   (He didn't like eating out.)
3. What did Bruce usually do first—go for a walk, park his car in the garage, or eat dinner?
   (park his car in the garage)
4. How did Bruce feel about his neighbors?
   (They didn't interest him.)
5. Why didn't Bruce like lights? (They seemed phony.)
6. What would Bruce do after dinner? (go for a walk)
7. Why did Bruce have trouble hearing the birds? (because of the roar of the cars on the freeway)
8. What did Bruce hear while lying in bed?
   (the air conditioner and freezer motor)
9. Describe the place Bruce wished for. (an island with trees, sand, and warm ocean water)
10. Where was Bruce when he woke up? (on a sandy beach)

2 **Fill in each blank using a word in the box.**

insurance	freeway	bothersome
sprouts	torch	mature

1. The bothersome bugs swarmed around her head all night.
2. Joe got in his new car and raced down the freeway.
3. After their house burned down, the people received money from their insurance company.

56 Lesson 33 Copyright © SRA/McGraw-Hill. All rights reserved.

Lesson 33

3 **Copy the sentence that tells the main idea of the story.**

1. Bruce worked hard as vice president of an insurance company but didn't talk much to his neighbors.
2. Every night, Bruce wished for a simple life, and one morning he woke up on a peaceful beach.
3. Every day, Bruce had sore eyes and a pain in his head after he came home from work.
4. Bruce lived alone and realized that he was a grouch.

Every night, Bruce wished for a simple life, and one morning he woke up on a peaceful beach.

Copyright © SRA/McGraw-Hill. All rights reserved. Lesson 33 57

Independent Student Work

Task A

- Open your Workbook to Lesson 33. ✓
- Complete all the parts of your Workbook lesson using a pencil. If you make no errors, you will earn 5 points.

Task B

1. (Before presenting Lesson 34, check student Workbooks for Lesson 33.)
   - (Call on individual students to read the items and answers in each part. Students mark errors using a pen.)
2. (Direct the students to count the number of errors and write the number in the Errors box at the top of the Workbook page.)
3. (Award points and direct students to record points in Box D of their Point Chart.)

   0 errors................................5 points
   1 error ....3 points
   2 or 3 errors ....1 point
   more than 3 errors ....0 points

END OF LESSON 33

WORD-ATTACK SKILLS

Student Book 

EXERCISE 1

NEW **AFFIX: re**

Task A

1. Open your Student Book to Lesson 34. ✓

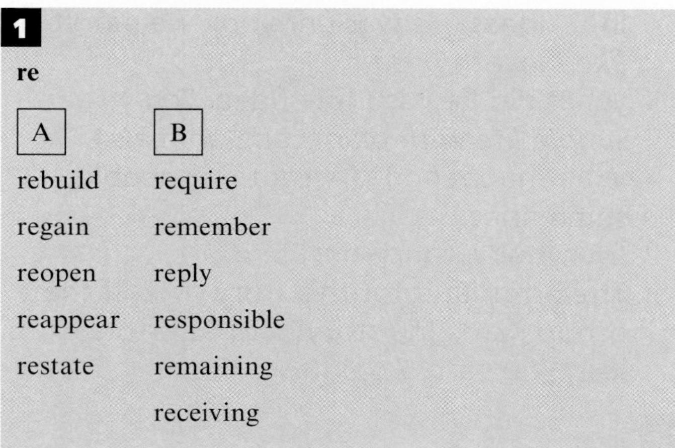

1

re

A	B
rebuild	require
regain	remember
reopen	reply
reappear	responsible
restate	remaining
	receiving

- Touch the letters **R–E** in part 1. ✓
- When those letters appear at the beginning of a word, they sometimes mean **again.** What does **re** mean? (Signal.) *Again.*

2. Touch the first word in column A. ✓
- What word? (Signal.) *Rebuild.*
- What does **rebuild** mean? (Signal.) *Build again.*

3. Touch the next word. ✓
- What word? (Signal.) *Regain.*
- What does **regain** mean? (Signal.) *Gain again.*

4. (Repeat step 3 for each remaining word.)
5. (Repeat the list until firm.)

Task B

1. The words in column B also begin with **re.** The meaning of **re** in those words is not so easy to figure out.
2. Touch the first word in column B. ✓
- What word? (Signal.) *Require.*

3. Next word. ✓
- What word? (Signal.) *Remember.*

4. (Repeat step 3 for each remaining word.)
5. (Repeat the list until firm.)

EXERCISE 2

WORD PRACTICE

1. Touch the first word in part 2. ✓

2

fertile particularly original* especially

swirled* slowly excited survive*

future except thirsty moisture

- What's the underlined part? (Signal.) *er.*
- What word? (Signal.) *Fertile.*

2. Touch the next word. ✓
- What's the underlined part? (Signal.) *ar.*
- What word? (Signal.) *Particularly.*

3. (Repeat step 2 for each remaining word.)
4. (Repeat each row of words until firm.)
5. What does **original** mean? (Call on a student.)
- (Repeat for **swirled, survive.**)

EXERCISE 3

VOCABULARY

1. Touch part 3. ✓

3

1. deserve
2. breadfruit
3. bored

- We're going to talk about what those words mean.

2. Touch word 1. ✓
- What word? (Signal.) *Deserve.*
- You **deserve** something when you **have done something to earn it.** When you do something to earn praise, you **deserve** praise. Everybody, what's another way of saying "He **has done things to earn** our trust"? (Signal.) *He deserves our trust.*

3. Touch word 2. ✓
- What word? (Signal.) *Breadfruit.*
- **Breadfruit** is **a large, tropical fruit.** Everybody, what is a **breadfruit?** (Signal.) *A large, tropical fruit.*

4. Touch word 3. ✓
- What word? (Signal.) *Bored.*
- People feel **bored** when they don't have anything to do.

EXERCISE 4

WORD PRACTICE

1. Touch the first word in part 4. ✓

4

prove approval problems somersaults
earth parrots crickets fourth edge
bubbled fortunate restless wonder
worry tackle unfortunately coconuts
healthy realize although handfuls
shoving among grove single

- What word? (Signal.) *Prove.*

2. Next word. ✓
- What word? (Signal.) *Approval.*

3. (Repeat step 2 for each remaining word.)
4. (Repeat each row of words until firm.)

EXERCISE 5

WORD-ATTACK SKILLS: Individual tests

1. (Call on individual students. Each student reads a row or column. Tally the rows and columns read without error. If the group reads at least 10 rows and columns without making errors, direct all students to record 5 points in Box A of their Point Chart. Criterion is 80 percent of rows and columns read without error.)
2. (If the group did not read at least 10 rows and columns without errors, do not award any points for the Word-Attack Skills exercises.)

SELECTION READING

EXERCISE 6

STORY READING

1. (Call on individual students to answer these questions.)
- What's the name of the character in the last selection? *Bruce Celt.*
- How did he feel about himself and his life? (Ideas: *He was unhappy; he didn't like most things.*)
- What did he wish for? (Idea: *To live a simple life with plants and animals.*)
- What happened? (Accept reasonable summaries.)

2. Everybody, touch part 5. ✓
3. The error limit for this story is 12. If the group reads the story with 12 errors or less, you earn 5 points.

5 **A Dream Come True**

4. (Call on a student to read the title.) *A Dream Come True.*
- What do you think this story is about? (Accept reasonable responses.)

5. (Call on individual students. Each is to read two to four sentences.)
6. (Call on individual students to answer the specified questions during the story reading.)

Bruce walked slowly along the beach, stopping many times to look at the crabs and the seashells. He felt the warm morning breeze in his face. "I hope this is true," he thought. "I hope this is really true." Bruce wanted to jump up and down and yell, "Yippee." He wanted to turn somersaults in the sand. But in the back of his mind he kept thinking, "Maybe this isn't really happening. So don't get your hopes up."

Bruce stopped at the edge of the water and swirled his hand in it. Then he licked his fingers. Salty. The water was salty, so the water was ocean water. ❶

1. How was Bruce feeling now? (Idea: *Happy, but afraid it might not be real.*)
1. How did Bruce know that the water was ocean water? (Idea: *Because it tasted salty.*)

By the evening of his second day on the island, Bruce was getting used to the idea that he was not dreaming. By then he had walked all the way around the island and proved to himself that it was an island. He had eaten coconuts and bananas from the trees. He had also eaten breadfruit and berries. He had fallen asleep in the sun on the beach, and he had a sunburn to prove it. Later he had slept in the shade of a big coconut tree. He had watched parrots and monkeys. He had breathed clean air and listened to the sounds of the waves, the crickets, and the bees. He had gone swimming in the ocean. Fortunately, he had found fresh water near the shore. It came from a refreshing spring. The water bubbled from the rocks and ran down the hill in a little stream. It was the best water Bruce had ever drunk. ❷

2. What's breadfruit? (Idea: *A large, tropical fruit.*)
2. What were some things Bruce did during his first two days on the island? (Ideas: *Walked around the island; ate fruit; slept in the sun; watched parrots and monkeys; breathed clean air; listened to sounds.*)

After his third day on the island, Bruce felt less fortunate and a little more restless. He didn't enjoy watching crabs on the beach as much as he had on the first two days. The parrots in the trees didn't seem as exciting. While the sun seemed a little too hot, the shade seemed too dark. ❸

3. How was Bruce feeling by the end of the third day? (Idea: *He felt less fortunate and more restless.*)
3. Why? (Idea: *Because he was bored.*)

And that evening when the sun was setting, he found himself saying, "I wonder what I'm going to do now?" He didn't want to go to sleep because he wasn't tired. However, there was no television to watch, no books to read, no lights to turn off.

The fourth day was even less exciting than the third. "I wished for this, so I guess I deserve it," he said to himself. "But there is nothing to do here. If only there were some problems in this place. If only there were something to worry about. I wish there were other people on this island—even if I didn't like them." ❹

4. What did Bruce miss? (Ideas: *Other people; things to do; problems.*)
4. What do you think is going to happen? (Idea: *Bruce's wish will come true again.*)

No sooner had Bruce made the wish than he saw a group of women and men walking down the beach. "That's strange," Bruce thought. "I've looked over this island from one end to the other, and I haven't seen a single footprint, except the ones I've made. Where did these people come from?"

"Hello," Bruce called. He waved.

They waved back. Then one of them said in a high voice, "Unk, unk."

Bruce walked over to the people. Bruce pointed to himself. "My name is Bruce," he said. "Bruce."

A tall woman wearing a long robe replied, "Unk," and pointed to her mouth.

"If you're thirsty," Bruce said, "let me give you some water. Follow me." He led the others to the spring in the grove of trees. But when he got to the spot where the water had been bubbling up from the rocks, there was no water. There was no stream.

"Unfortunately, there is no water," Bruce said. "However, we can always drink coconut milk." He looked around for coconuts on the ground. He couldn't see any healthy ones. There had been hundreds of them, but now they all looked rotten. ❺

5. Name two problems that occurred when Bruce wished for something to worry about. (Idea: *The spring dried up, and the food disappeared.*)
7. (Award points quickly.)
8. (If the group makes more than 12 errors, repeat the reading immediately or on the next day.)

FLUENCY ASSESSMENT

EXERCISE 7

TIMED READING CHECKOUTS

1. (For this part of the lesson, assigned pairs of students work together during the checkouts.)
- (If one student does not have a checkout partner, arrange another time when you can give the checkout.)
2. (Each student does a 2-minute timed reading. Students earn 5 points by reading at least 240 words and making no more than 5 errors on the first part of story 34. Students record points in Box C of their Point Chart and plot their reading rate and errors on the Individual Reading Progress Chart.)
- (During each timed checkout, observe one pair of students for 2 minutes. Make notes on any mistakes the reader makes.)
3. (Record the timed reading checkout performance for each student you observed on the Fluency Assessment Summary form.)

WORKBOOK EXERCISES

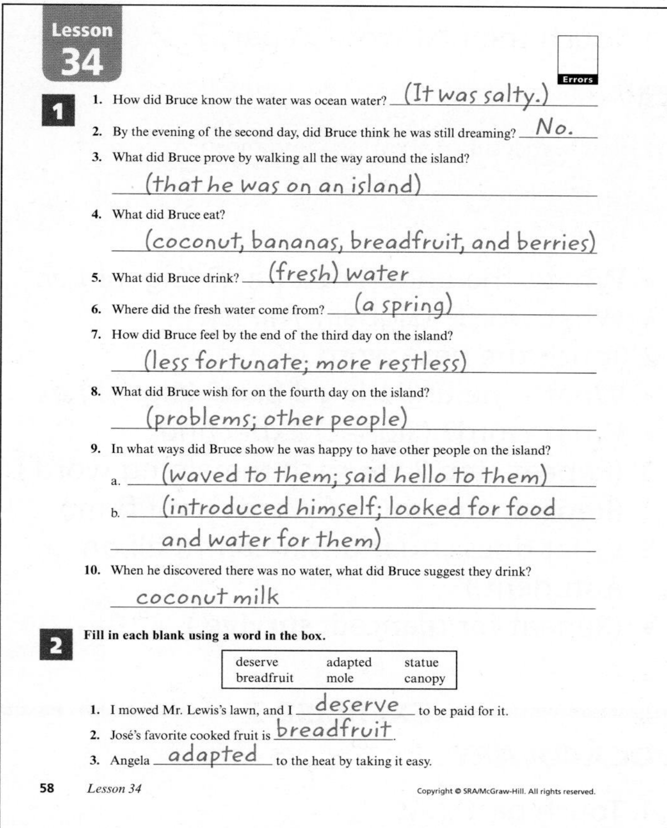
Lesson 34

Errors

1

1. How did Bruce know the water was ocean water? (It was salty.)
2. By the evening of the second day, did Bruce think he was still dreaming? No.
3. What did Bruce prove by walking all the way around the island? (that he was on an island)
4. What did Bruce eat? (coconut, bananas, breadfruit, and berries)
5. What did Bruce drink? (fresh) water
6. Where did the fresh water come from? (a spring)
7. How did Bruce feel by the end of the third day on the island? (less fortunate; more restless)
8. What did Bruce wish for on the fourth day on the island? (problems; other people)
9. In what ways did Bruce show he was happy to have other people on the island?
   a. (waved to them; said hello to them)
   b. (introduced himself; looked for food and water for them)
10. When he discovered there was no water, what did Bruce suggest they drink? coconut milk

2 Fill in each blank using a word in the box.

deserve	adapted	statue
breadfruit	mole	canopy

1. I mowed Mr. Lewis's lawn, and I deserve to be paid for it.
2. José's favorite cooked fruit is breadfruit.
3. Angela adapted to the heat by taking it easy.

58 Lesson 34

Copyright © SRA/McGraw-Hill. All rights reserved.

Independent Student Work

Task A

- Open your Workbook to Lesson 34. ✓
- Complete all the parts of your Workbook lesson using a pencil. If you make no errors, you will earn 5 points.

Task B

1. (Before presenting Lesson 35, check student Workbooks for Lesson 34.)
   - (Call on individual students to read the items and answers in each part. Students mark errors using a pen.)
2. (Direct the students to count the number of errors and write the number in the Errors box at the top of the Workbook page.)
3. (Award points and direct students to record points in Box D of their Point Chart.)

0 errors.................................5 points
1 error ....3 points
2 or 3 errors ....1 point
more than 3 errors ....0 points

END OF LESSON 34

Lesson 35

WORD-ATTACK SKILLS

Student Book 

EXERCISE 1

AFFIX REVIEW

Task A

1. Open your Student Book to Lesson 35. ✓

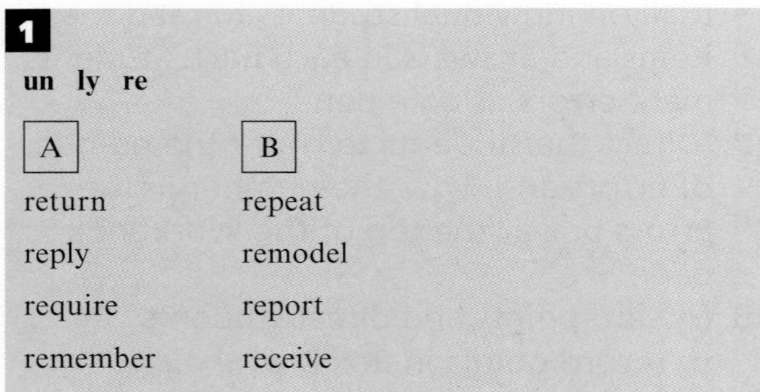

1

un ly re

A	B
return	repeat
reply	remodel
require	report
remember	receive

- Touch part 1. ✓
- The words in columns A and B begin with **re.** The meaning of **re** in those words is not easy to figure out.

2. Touch the affixes in the first row. ✓
- Let's see if you remember a meaning for two of those affixes.

3. Touch the letters **U–N.** ✓
- What's one meaning of **un?** (Signal.) *Not.*

4. Touch the letters **L–Y.** ✓
- What's one meaning of **ly?** (Signal.) *How something happened.*

5. (Repeat steps 3 and 4 until firm.)

Task B

1. Touch the first word in column A. ✓
- What word? (Signal.) *Return.*

2. Touch the next word. ✓
- What word? (Signal.) *Reply.*

3. (Repeat step 2 for **require, remember.**)
4. (Repeat the list until firm.)
5. (Repeat steps 1–4 for the words in column B.)

EXERCISE 2

WORD PRACTICE

1. Touch the first word in part 2. ✓

2

thirsty expecting situations* glanced*
survive* silently except wedged

- What's the underlined part? (Signal.) *er.*
- What word? (Signal.) *Thirsty.*

2. Touch the next word. ✓
- What's the underlined part? (Signal.) *ex.*
- What word? (Signal.) *Expecting.*

3. (Repeat step 2 for each remaining word.)
4. (Repeat each row of words until firm.)
5. What does **situations** mean? (Call on a student.)
- (Repeat for **glanced, survive.**)

EXERCISE 3

VOCABULARY

1. Touch part 3. ✓

3

1. disturbed
2. logical

- We're going to talk about what those words mean.

2. Touch word 1. ✓
- What word? (Signal.) *Disturbed.*
- Another way of saying that somebody is **worried** or **upset** is to say that somebody is **disturbed.** Everybody, what's another way of saying "People are **worried** about the lack of rain"? (Signal.) *People are disturbed about the lack of rain.*

3. Touch word 2. ✓
- What word? (Signal.) *Logical.*
- Something that **makes sense** is **logical.** Everybody, what's another way of saying "It **makes sense** to take this road"? (Signal.) *It is logical to take this road.*
- What's another way of saying "It **makes sense** to stay home"? (Signal.) *It is logical to stay home.*

EXERCISE 4

WORD PRACTICE

1. Touch the first word in part 4. ✓

4

strangely realized immediate solve
fighters although probably* branches
unafraid insurance* extended collecting
decided pry pried forehead
bored* signs ankle among
scoop handfuls shoving tasted

- What word? (Signal.) *Strangely.*

2. Next word. ✓

- What word? (Signal.) *Realized.*

3. (Repeat step 2 for each remaining word.)
4. (Repeat each row of words until firm.)
5. What does **probably** mean? (Call on a student.)

- (Repeat for **insurance, bored.**)

EXERCISE 5

WORD-ATTACK SKILLS: Individual tests

1. (Call on individual students. Each student reads a row or column. Tally the rows and columns read without error. If the group reads at least 10 rows and columns without making errors, direct all students to record 5 points in Box A of their Point Chart. Criterion is 80 percent of rows and columns read without error.)
2. (If the group did not read at least 10 rows and columns without errors, do not award any points for the Word-Attack Skills exercises.)

SELECTION READING

EXERCISE 6

STORY READING

1. (Call on individual students to answer these questions.)

- Compare how Bruce felt the first day on the island to how he felt on day four. (Ideas: *The first day he was happy but afraid it might not be real. By the fourth day, he felt bored and lonely.*)
- What new characters did he encounter? *A group of men and women.*
- Bruce discovers two ways the island had changed after he met the others. What are those ways? (Idea: *The spring had disappeared, and there was no water to drink; the coconuts looked rotten, and they could no longer drink coconut milk.*)

2. Everybody, touch part 5. ✓
3. The error limit for this story is 12. If the group reads the story with 12 errors or less, you earn 5 points.

5 **More Problems to Tackle**

4. (Call on a student to read the title.) *More Problems to Tackle.*

- What do you think this story is about? (Accept reasonable responses.)

5. (Call on individual students. Each is to read two to four sentences.)
6. (Call on individual students to answer the specified questions during the story reading.)

Lesson 35

One man pointed to his mouth and said, "Unk, unk."

Bruce said, "You're probably hungry. Well, we certainly should be able to find some breadfruit or bananas. Follow me." The others followed, but all the trees seemed to be bare. Bruce was becoming disturbed. Where had all the bananas and breadfruit gone? What had happened to the water? And what would happen if he didn't find water pretty soon? Bruce knew that he would probably die within five days without water. He knew that he could go a long time without food. In fact, he had read about people who had gone thirty days without food. However, people can't live very long without water. ❶

1. Why was Bruce becoming disturbed? (Idea: *Because the food and water were gone.*)
1. How long can people usually live without water? *Only five days.*

Bruce turned to the other people, and suddenly he found himself talking to them. He was explaining the situation, even though he knew that they didn't understand what he was saying. "Let's look at our problem," Bruce said slowly. "We have no fresh water. It is impossible for us to drink water from the sea because the water is salty."

Bruce glanced at the strangers. They were standing silently, watching him. Strangely enough, Bruce was unafraid. In fact, he felt excited about solving a problem. For an instant he remembered situations in which he had solved problems for his insurance company. For an instant Bruce realized how much he had missed those problems.

"We don't have to worry so much about food," Bruce said aloud, "because we can survive a long time without food. Our water problem is more immediate." ❷

2. What problem is more immediate? *The water problem.*
2. Why? (Idea: *Because you can live longer without food than you can without water.*)
2. Why is it impossible to drink seawater? (Idea: *Because it is salty.*)
2. What does "for an instant" mean? (Idea: *For a very short time.*)

The strangers stared, and Bruce paced back and forth in front of them. "We can solve this problem if we're logical."

Bruce pointed to the sea. "We could boil seawater and collect the steam, which would turn into fresh water. Or we could dig for water. In either case, we will need tools."

Bruce turned to the strangers. "What do you want to do?"

"Unk." ❸

3. What were two possible ways for solving the water problem? (Idea: *Boiling seawater and collecting the steam, and digging for water.*)
3. What did Bruce mean when he said, "We can solve this problem if we're logical"? (Idea: *If we use our heads, we can find a solution.*)

Bruce decided that it would probably be easier to dig for water than to boil seawater. He and the others walked to the place where the spring had been. Bruce found a rock with a sharp edge that he used to make a point on the end of a stout branch. Then he walked to the pile of rocks where the spring had been. He wedged the point of the stick between two rocks; then he pushed down on the stick and pried a rock loose. Bruce picked up the rock and tossed it aside. "See?" he said. "Use this to dig. Dig." ❹

4. What did Bruce do to make a digging tool? (Idea: *Sharpened the end of a stick with a sharp rock.*)

4. How did he use it? (Idea: *He wedged the stick between rocks and pried them loose.*)

"Unk," one woman said. Soon everybody was working with long, stout branches. Some of the people pried up rocks, while others heaved them aside, making a hole where the stream had been. "If we dig deep enough, we should reach fresh water," Bruce explained as he wiped his hand across his forehead. The work was heavy, and the day seemed exceptionally hot, but Bruce was not bored. He was solving a problem, and that was exciting. ❺

5. What's another way of saying "The day seemed exceptionally hot"? (Idea: *The day seemed hotter than usual.*)
5. Why wasn't Bruce bored? (Idea: *Because he was solving a problem.*)

The hole became deeper and deeper. At first the bottom of the hole was dry. By the time the hole was waist-deep, the rocks were damp, and there were signs of moisture in the hole. When the hole was neck-deep and only two people could work in it at a time, there were more signs of water. The rocks that were being heaved from the hole now were soaking wet. ❻

6. What's moisture? (Idea: *Wetness.*)
6. How did they know they were getting close to water? (Idea: *Because the rocks they dug from the hole were soaking wet.*)

Finally, the two people working in the hole were standing ankle-deep in fresh water, and the hole was beginning to fill. Some of the other people didn't want to wait for the water to reach the level of the ground. They jumped into the hole and began drinking the water, which was still muddy. Bruce was among them. He jumped into the hole and managed to bend over and scoop up handfuls of water. The hole was only about ten feet across, but there were five people in it, shoving, pushing, and trying to drink. But the water tasted great to Bruce. He smiled, laughed, splashed water on the other people, and drank until his sides hurt. He felt unbelievably happy and refreshed. ❼

7. What does "unbelievably happy" mean? (Ideas: *Very happy; full of joy.*)
7. (Award points quickly.)
8. (If the group makes more than 12 errors, repeat the reading immediately or on the next day.)

Lesson
35

FLUENCY ASSESSMENT

EXERCISE 7

TIMED READING CHECKOUTS

1. (For this part of the lesson, assigned pairs of students work together during the checkouts.)
   - (If one student does not have a checkout partner, arrange another time when you can give the checkout.)
2. (Each student does a 2-minute timed reading. Students earn 5 points by reading at least 240 words and making no more than 5 errors on the first part of story 35. Students record points in Box C of their Point Chart and plot their reading rate and errors on the Individual Reading Progress Chart.)
   - (During each timed checkout, observe one pair of students for 2 minutes. Make notes on any mistakes the reader makes.)
3. (Record the timed reading checkout performance for each student you observed on the Fluency Assessment Summary form.)

WORKBOOK EXERCISES

Independent Student Work

Task A

- Open your Workbook to Lesson 35. ✓
- Complete all the parts of your Workbook lesson using a pencil. If you make no errors, you will earn 5 points.

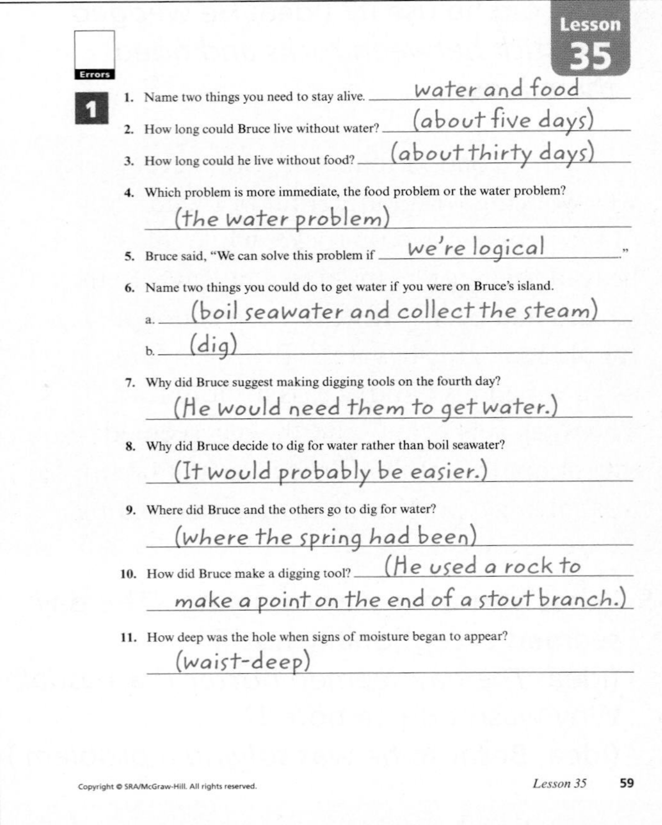

Lesson 35

Errors

1

1. Name two things you need to stay alive. water and food
2. How long could Bruce live without water? (about five days)
3. How long could he live without food? (about thirty days)
4. Which problem is more immediate, the food problem or the water problem? (the water problem)
5. Bruce said, "We can solve this problem if we're logical."
6. Name two things you could do to get water if you were on Bruce's island.
   a. (boil seawater and collect the steam)
   b. (dig)
7. Why did Bruce suggest making digging tools on the fourth day? (He would need them to get water.)
8. Why did Bruce decide to dig for water rather than boil seawater? (It would probably be easier.)
9. Where did Bruce and the others go to dig for water? (where the spring had been)
10. How did Bruce make a digging tool? (He used a rock to make a point on the end of a stout branch.)
11. How deep was the hole when signs of moisture began to appear? (waist-deep)

Copyright © SRA/McGraw-Hill. All rights reserved. Lesson 35 59

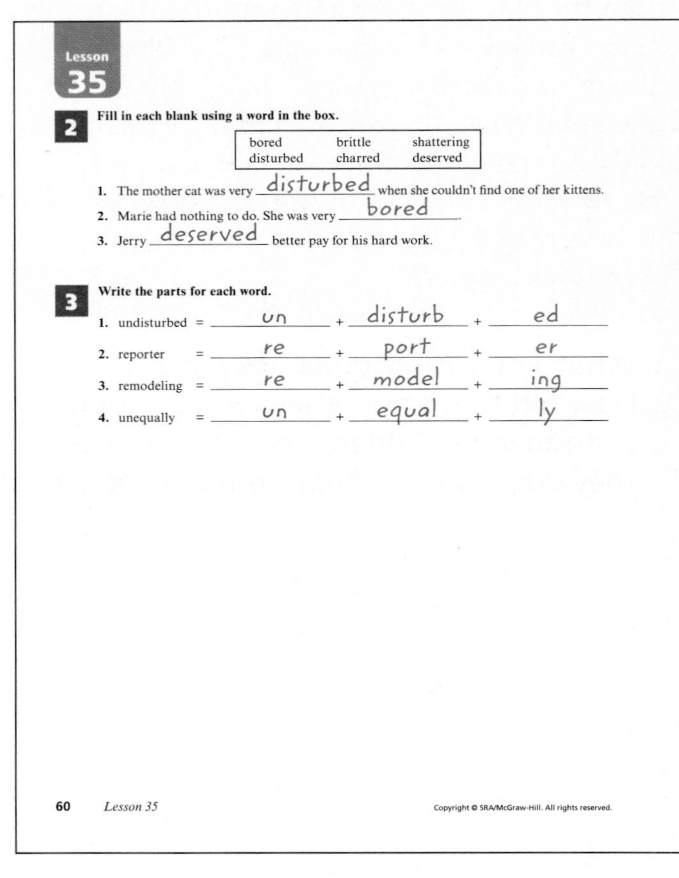

Lesson 35

2 Fill in each blank using a word in the box.

bored	brittle	shattering
disturbed	charred	deserved

1. The mother cat was very disturbed when she couldn't find one of her kittens.
2. Marie had nothing to do. She was very bored.
3. Jerry deserved better pay for his hard work.

3 Write the parts for each word.

1. undisturbed = un + disturb + ed
2. reporter = re + port + er
3. remodeling = re + model + ing
4. unequally = un + equal + ly

60 Lesson 35 Copyright © SRA/McGraw-Hill. All rights reserved.

Task B

1. (Before presenting Lesson 36, check student Workbooks for Lesson 35.)
   - (Call on individual students to read the items and answers in each part. Students mark errors using a pen.)
2. (Direct the students to count the number of errors and write the number in the Errors box at the top of the Workbook page.)
3. (Award points and direct students to record points in Box D of their Point Chart.)

   0 errors................................5 points
   1 error ....3 points
   2 or 3 errors ....1 point
   more than 3 errors ....0 points

Point schedule for Lessons 31 through 35

Box	Lesson part	Points
A	Word Attack	0 or 5
B	Selection Reading	0 or 5
C	Timed Reading Checkout	0 or 5
D	Workbook	0, 1, 3, or 5
Bonus	(Teacher option)	—

Five-lesson point summary

- (For **letter grades** based on points for Lessons **31** through **35,** tell students to compute the total for the blue boxes [C, D, and Bonus] and write the number in the Total box at the end of each row in their Point Chart. Students then add the totals and write the sum in the green box.)
- (For **rewards** based on points, tell students to compute the total for all boxes [A, B, C, D, and Bonus] and write the number in the Total box at the end of each row. Students then add the totals and write the sum in the green box.)

END OF LESSON 35

Lesson Objectives	LESSON 36 Exercise	LESSON 37 Exercise	LESSON 38 Exercise	LESSON 39 Exercise	LESSON 40 Exercise
Word Attack					
Decoding and Word Analysis					
Affix: *dis*			1	2	
Affixes: *un, ly, re*	1				
Affixes: *un, ly, re, dis*					1
Visual Discrimination				1	
Letter Combinations/Letter Sounds	2	1	2		
Word Recognition	1–4	1–3	1–4	1–5	1–3
Vocabulary					
Morphemic Analysis	1		1	2	1
Definitions	2–4	2, 3	1, 3, 4	2–5	2, 3
Usage	3	2	3	4	2
Assessment					
Ongoing: Individual Tests	5	4	5	6	4
Group Reading					
Decoding and Word Analysis					
Read Decodable Text	5	5	6	7	5
Comprehension					
Access Prior Knowledge	5	5			
Draw Inferences	5	5	6	7	5
Note Details	5	5	6	7	5
Predict	5	5	6	7	5
Vocabulary: Definitions	5	5			5
Assessment					
Ongoing: Comprehension Check	5	5	6	7	5
Ongoing: Decoding Accuracy	5	5	6	7	5
Fluency Assessment					
Fluency					
Reread Decodable Text	6	6	7	8	6
Assessment					
Ongoing: Teacher-Monitored Fluency	6	6	7	8	6
Ongoing: Peer-Monitored Fluency	6	6	7	8	6
Workbook Exercises					
Decoding and Word Analysis					
Multisyllabic Word Parts			Ind. Work		
Comprehension					
Note Details	Ind. Work	Ind. Work	Ind. Work		Ind. Work
Vocabulary					
Usage	Ind. Work	Ind. Work	Ind. Work		Ind. Work
Assessment					
Ongoing: Workcheck	Workcheck	Workcheck	Workcheck	Workcheck	Workcheck

WORD-ATTACK SKILLS

Student Book 

EXERCISE 1

AFFIX REVIEW

Task A

1. Open your Student Book to Lesson 36. ✓

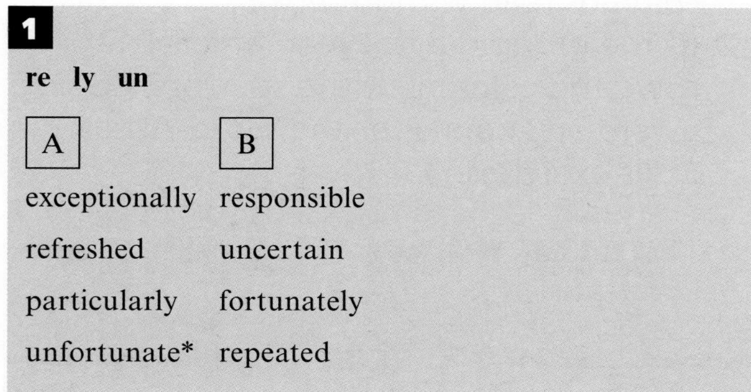

1

re ly un

A	B
exceptionally	responsible
refreshed	uncertain
particularly	fortunately
unfortunate*	repeated

- Touch part 1. ✓

2. Touch the affixes in the first row. ✓
- Let's see if you remember a meaning for each of those affixes.

3. Touch the letters **R–E.** ✓
- What's one meaning of **re?** (Signal.) *Again.*

4. Touch the letters **L–Y.** ✓
- What's one meaning of **ly?** (Signal.) *How something happened.*

5. Touch the letters **U–N.** ✓
- What's one meaning of **un?** (Signal.) *Not.*

6. (Repeat steps 3–5 until firm.)

Task B

1. Touch the first word in column A. ✓
- What word? (Signal.) *Exceptionally.*

2. Touch the next word. ✓
- What word? (Signal.) *Refreshed.*

3. (Repeat step 2 for each remaining word.)
4. (Repeat the list until firm.)
5. (Repeat steps 1–4 for the words in column B.)
6. What does **unfortunate** mean? (Call on a student.)

EXERCISE 2

WORD PRACTICE

1. Touch the first word in part 2. ✓

2

moisture soaking easier sharp

explained replied occasionally

expect painted thirsty

unbelievably stout* injure

- What's the underlined part? (Signal.) *oy.*
- What word? (Signal.) *Moisture.*

2. Touch the next word. ✓
- What's the underlined part? (Signal.) *ōōō.*
- What word? (Signal.) *Soaking.*

3. (Repeat step 2 for each remaining word.)
4. (Repeat each row of words until firm.)
5. What does **stout** mean? (Call on a student.)

EXERCISE 3

VOCABULARY

1. Touch part 3. ✓

3

1. flexible
2. shortage
3. suitable
4. procedure

- We're going to talk about what those words mean.

2. Touch word 1. ✓
- What word? (Signal.) *Flexible.*
- Something that **bends easily** is **flexible.** Everybody, what's another way of saying "That wire **bends easily**"? (Signal.) *That wire is flexible.*

3. Touch word 2. ✓
- What word? (Signal.) *Shortage.*
- There is a **shortage** of something when there is **not enough** of that thing. Everybody, what's another way of saying "There is **not enough** food"? (Signal.) *There is a shortage of food.*

4. Touch word 3. ✓
- What word? (Signal.) *Suitable.*
- Something that is **suitable** is **just right.** Everybody, what's another way of saying "This job is **just right**"? (Signal.) *This job is suitable.*

5. Touch word 4. ✓
- What word? (Signal.) *Procedure.*
- A **procedure** is **a series of steps for doing something.** Everybody, what's another way of saying "What is the **series of steps** for putting the car back together?" (Signal.) *What is the procedure for putting the car back together?*

EXERCISE 4

WORD PRACTICE

1. Touch the first word in part 4. ✓

4

disappeared ordinary surface* stalk
sharpened average constructed serious*
waded waddled severe* branches
solved choice furthermore feathers
probably* practice difficult fitted
instead feast stray rapidly
removed announced* collected
search plenty completed

- What word? (Signal.) *Disappeared.*

2. Next word. ✓
- What word? (Signal.) *Ordinary.*

3. (Repeat step 2 for each remaining word.)
4. (Repeat each row of words until firm.)
5. What does **surface** mean? (Call on a student.)
- (Repeat for each starred word.)

EXERCISE 5

WORD-ATTACK SKILLS: Individual tests

1. (Call on individual students. Each student reads a row or column. Tally the rows and columns read without error. If the group reads at least 12 rows and columns without making errors, direct all students to record 5 points in Box A of their Point Chart. Criterion is 80 percent of rows and columns read without error.)
2. (If the group did not read at least 12 rows and columns without errors, do not award any points for the Word-Attack Skills exercises.)

SELECTION READING

EXERCISE 6

STORY READING

1. (Call on individual students to answer these questions.)
- What were the two serious problems that Bruce and the others faced in the last selection? (Ideas: *The spring dried up, and the healthy coconuts disappeared.*)
- Which problem has to be solved first, and why? (Idea: *Water, because you can live longer without food than you can without water.*)
- How did Bruce and the others solve the water problem? (Idea: *They made tools and dug a hole to find water.*)

2. Everybody, touch part 5. ✓
3. The error limit for this story is 12. If the group reads the story with 12 errors or less, you earn 5 points.

5 **Finding Food**

4. (Call on a student to read the title.) *Finding Food.*
- What do you think this story is about? (Accept reasonable responses.)

5. (Call on individual students. Each is to read two to four sentences.)
6. (Call on individual students to answer the specified questions during the story reading.)

That night, when the well was full of fresh water and the people were no longer thirsty, Bruce thought about the things that had happened. He tried to figure out how his life had changed when the things on the island had changed. Here's what he figured out: To live, you need some things. You need food and water. When the island had plenty of food and water, Bruce didn't have to do anything to stay alive. He didn't have to hunt for food, and he didn't have to hunt for water. But when the food and water disappeared from the island, Bruce had to do something. He had to figure out a way to get water. He dug a well, but before he dug the well, he had to make tools. Bruce hadn't made tools during his first three days on the island because he hadn't needed them to stay alive. ❶

1. What did Bruce do to solve the water problem? (Idea: *He made tools and dug a well.*)

Bruce and the others had solved the water problem. The next problem they faced was the lack of food.

"We can make tools for hunting the animals in the jungle," Bruce said, "or we can make nets for fishing in the sea." He looked at the jungle and then at the sea. "I think we'll start with the tools for hunting birds and rabbits."

The tools were bows and arrows. Bruce made five bows from stout, flexible branches. ❷

2. What are flexible branches? (Idea: *Branches that bend easily.*)
2. What did Bruce plan to do to get food? (Idea: *Make bows and arrows to hunt animals in the jungle.*)

The bowstrings were vines tied to each end of the branches, and the arrows were long, straight sticks, sharpened on one end against a flat rock and fitted on the other end with parrot feathers.

Now it was time to practice shooting with the bows and arrows. After an hour's practice, some of the strangers were quite good. Bruce was probably about average at hitting a target made of grass. ❸

3. What does "Bruce was probably about average" mean? (Idea: *He wasn't poor, and he wasn't great.*)
3. How did Bruce construct bows and arrows? (Idea: *He made bows out of flexible branches, bowstrings out of vines, and arrows out of sticks.*)

Things were far more difficult when they went hunting in the jungle, however. They searched for five hours, and in the end the hunters had killed only two rabbits and one bird.

Even before the hunt was over, Bruce said to himself, "I think that we should try to get food by fishing instead of by hunting." The hunters had spent most of their time trying to find the stray arrows that they had shot. Although the hunters had started out with twenty-one arrows, they had only three left when the hunt was completed. ❹

4. What's another way of saying "When the hunt was completed"? (Idea: *When the hunt was over.*)
4. Why did Bruce decide to try to get food from the sea? (Idea: *Because hunting in the jungle was too difficult.*)

"This won't be a big feast," Bruce announced, "but it will probably be a good one." To cook the dinner, Bruce made a fire. He made it the way the Native Americans would build fires. He looped the bowstring around a stick and twirled the stick back and forth by moving the bow. One end of the stick was pressed against a rock. That end began to get hot as the stick turned rapidly. Small bits of wood placed on the rock next to the hot end of the stick began to smoke. Suddenly, the wood bits burst into flame. The strangers shouted, "Unk, unk," and smiled.

After dinner Bruce was still hungry. Something had to be done about the shortage of food. He said, "We'll probably have better luck fishing than hunting." And he was right. The group made nets from vines collected in the coconut grove. Four people waded into the ocean, tossed the net over a school of fish, pulled the net toward the shore, and caught two fish. They repeated the procedure and caught three more fish. 5

5. What was the fishing procedure? (Idea: *They made nets out of vines and caught fish in the nets.*)

That evening Bruce again thought of the events. "First we solved the water problem, which was the most serious problem," he said to himself. "Now we have solved the food problem." As Bruce lay there near the fire with a long stalk of grass between his teeth, he thought, "I just wish that the other people could speak English. I'm tired of listening to 'unk, unk.' "

At that moment, one woman walked over to Bruce and said, "That was a particularly good fish dinner." 6

6. Why do you think that Bruce might be surprised to hear the woman talk? (Idea: *Because she couldn't speak English before.*)
6. What are events? (Idea: *Things that happen.*)
7. (Award points quickly.)
8. (If the group makes more than 12 errors, repeat the reading immediately or on the next day.)

FLUENCY ASSESSMENT

EXERCISE 7

TIMED READING CHECKOUTS

1. (For this part of the lesson, assigned pairs of students work together during the checkouts.)
   - (If one student does not have a checkout partner, arrange another time when you can give the checkout.)
2. (Each student does a 2-minute timed reading. Students earn 5 points by reading at least 240 words and making no more than 5 errors on the first part of story 36. Students record points in Box C of their Point Chart and plot their reading rate and errors on the Individual Reading Progress Chart.)
   - (During each timed checkout, observe one pair of students for 2 minutes. Make notes on any mistakes the reader makes.)
3. (Record the timed reading checkout performance for each student you observed on the Fluency Assessment Summary form.)

WORKBOOK EXERCISES

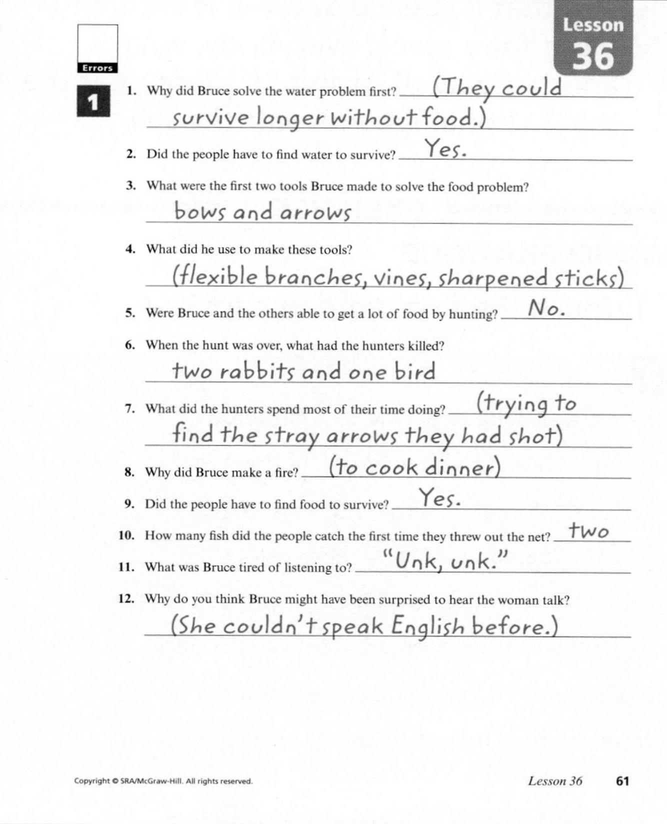
Lesson 36

Errors

1

1. Why did Bruce solve the water problem first? (They could survive longer without food.)
2. Did the people have to find water to survive? Yes.
3. What were the first two tools Bruce made to solve the food problem? bows and arrows
4. What did he use to make these tools? (flexible branches, vines, sharpened sticks)
5. Were Bruce and the others able to get a lot of food by hunting? No.
6. When the hunt was over, what had the hunters killed? two rabbits and one bird
7. What did the hunters spend most of their time doing? (trying to find the stray arrows they had shot)
8. Why did Bruce make a fire? (to cook dinner)
9. Did the people have to find food to survive? Yes.
10. How many fish did the people catch the first time they threw out the net? two
11. What was Bruce tired of listening to? "Unk, unk."
12. Why do you think Bruce might have been surprised to hear the woman talk? (She couldn't speak English before.)

Copyright © SRA/McGraw-Hill. All rights reserved. *Lesson 36* 61

Lesson 36

2 **Fill in each blank using a word in the box.**

shortage	investigation	brittle
fluttered	flexible	waddled

1. The children twisted flexible hangers into different shapes.
2. When the wind blew, leaves fluttered to the ground.
3. The classes had to share books because there was a shortage of them.

62 *Lesson 36* Copyright © SRA/McGraw-Hill. All rights reserved.

Independent Student Work

Task A

- Open your Workbook to Lesson 36. ✓
- Complete all the parts of your Workbook lesson using a pencil. If you make no errors, you will earn 5 points.

Task B

1. (Before presenting Lesson 37, check student Workbooks for Lesson 36.)
   - (Call on individual students to read the items and answers in each part. Students mark errors using a pen.)
2. (Direct the students to count the number of errors and write the number in the Errors box at the top of the Workbook page.)
3. (Award points and direct students to record points in Box D of their Point Chart.)

   0 errors................................5 points
   1 error ....3 points
   2 or 3 errors ....1 point
   more than 3 errors ....0 points

END OF LESSON 36

Lesson 37

WORD-ATTACK SKILLS

Student Book 

EXERCISE 1

WORD PRACTICE

1. Open your Student Book to Lesson 37. ✓

1

returning temperature chattered

remarkable judged unusually

repeated mature* severely celebration

Centa survival extreme

- Touch the first word in part 1. ✓
- What's the underlined part? (Signal.) *re.*
- What word? (Signal.) *Returning.*

2. Touch the next word. ✓
- What's the underlined part? (Signal.) *ure.*
- What word? (Signal.) *Temperature.*

3. (Repeat step 2 for each remaining word.)
4. (Repeat each row of words until firm.)
5. What does **mature** mean? (Call on a student.)

EXERCISE 2

VOCABULARY

1. Touch part 2. ✓

2

1. tingly
2. site

- We're going to talk about what those words mean.

2. Touch word 1. ✓
- What word? (Signal.) *Tingly.*
- **Tingly** is another way of describing **a slightly stinging feeling** of your skin. Everybody, what's another way of saying "My feet felt **a slightly stinging feeling**"? (Signal.) *My feet felt tingly.*

3. Touch word 2. ✓
- What word? (Signal.) *Site.*
- **Site** that is spelled **S–I–T–E** is another word for **a place.** Everybody, what's another way of saying "**A place** near the sea"? (Signal.) *A site near the sea.*

EXERCISE 3

WORD PRACTICE

1. Touch the first word in part 3. ✓

3

breaking delighted shelter gathered

group younger discovered hollowing

serious* huddled covering shivering

already remain blazed bear suitable*

probably* strangers dancing protect

jogged feasting located replies feathers

coals learned reporting particularly

rethink blowing concluded surroundings

- What word? (Signal.) *Breaking.*

2. Next word. ✓
- What word? (Signal.) *Delighted.*

3. (Repeat step 2 for each remaining word.)
4. (Repeat each row of words until firm.)
5. What does **serious** mean? (Call on a student.)
- (Repeat for **suitable, probably.**)

EXERCISE 4

WORD-ATTACK SKILLS: Individual tests

1. (Call on individual students. Each student reads a row or column. Tally the rows and columns read without error. If the group reads at least 10 rows and columns without making errors, direct all students to record 5 points in Box A of their Point Chart. Criterion is 80 percent of rows and columns read without error.)
2. (If the group did not read at least 10 rows and columns without errors, do not award any points for the Word-Attack Skills exercises.)

SELECTION READING

EXERCISE 5

STORY READING

1. (Call on individual students to answer these questions.)
- Bruce and the others tried several ways to solve the food problem. What did they try first? (Idea: *They made bows and arrows, and they hunted for birds and rabbits.*)
- How successful was that plan? (Idea: *Not very successful.*)
- What did they try next? (Idea: *They made nets out of vines and caught fish in nets.*)
- How successful was that plan? (Ideas: *They caught several fish; they were more successful at fishing than they were at hunting.*)
2. Everybody, touch part 4. ✓
3. The error limit for this story is 12. If the group reads the story with 12 errors or less, you earn 5 points.

4 **Fighting the Cold**

4. (Call on a student to read the title.) *Fighting the Cold.*
- What do you think this story is about? (Accept reasonable responses.)
5. (Call on individual students. Each is to read two to four sentences.)
6. (Call on individual students to answer the specified questions during the story reading.)

For some unknown reason all the strangers could speak English. Bruce was delighted. "This is remarkable. It calls for a celebration," he announced. There was a great celebration with racing, dancing, singing, telling stories, and a lot of feasting.

Bruce slept well that night. When he woke up in the morning, he was shivering. ❶

1. What happens when you shiver? (Idea: *You shake all over.*)
1. Why did Bruce call for a celebration? (Idea: *He was delighted that everyone could speak English.*)

It was snowing, and the air was unusually cold. Bruce judged the temperature to be below zero. The ocean was gray. The waves were breaking loudly, and the whitecaps were rolling far up the beach. The trees looked different because they had lost their leaves. Small drifts of snow were starting to build up here and there.

"What's this?" Bruce said. Two people standing near him were shivering, too. One of them was a woman named Centa. Bruce had learned her name the day before.

Centa said, "If we can't find some way to stay warm, I'm afraid we will all die. Already some of us are getting sick." ❷

2. What's the new problem Bruce has to tackle? (Idea: *The cold weather.*)
2. Is staying warm a survival problem? *Yes.*

Bruce thought for a moment. His teeth chattered every time he tried to say something. At last he said, "Let's build up the fire." The people gathered wood and threw it on the fire. The fire blazed up in big, orange flames. Showers of sparks and smoke rose into the air.

"We need a shelter," Bruce said, standing close to the fire and rubbing his hands together. "We'll never survive this cold unless we build a shelter."

"What is shelter?" Centa asked.

Bruce explained, "A shelter is a place that is warm and dry. We could build a place that would protect us from the wind and cold. Maybe we could dig a cave in the side of a hill, or we could construct a shelter out of branches and vines and dry grass." ❸

3. What could they build to solve the cold problem? **(Idea:** ***A shelter.*****)**

Bruce, Centa, and the others jogged off to find a suitable site for the shelter. Centa found a steep hill that faced away from the sea.

"Bring the digging tools over here," Bruce said. "We'll hollow out this part of the hill. After we've made a little cave, we'll cover the front of it with some material that will break the wind."

Three people began hollowing out the side of the hill while Bruce and Centa started to make a covering for the front of the cave. ❹

4. How would you hollow out something? **(Idea:** ***You would take out the insides of the thing and leave the outside shell whole.*****)**

"Let's weave long branches together," Bruce suggested. "Then we can cover them with leaves and grass and whatever else we can find."

One young woman kept the fire going. From time to time people working on the shelter would run over to the fire and warm up. Then they would return to their work. The group worked very fast. Before an hour had gone by, they had hollowed out the side of the hill. By then Bruce and Centa had made a covering for the front of the cave.

Bruce and Centa fitted the "door" they had made over the front of the cave. Then Bruce used a tool to drag hot coals to the shelter. "We don't want a big fire in our shelter," he told the others. "If the fire is too big, it will make a lot of smoke, and we'll have trouble breathing." ❺

5. What did Bruce and the others do to make a shelter? **(Idea:** ***Hollowed out the side of the hill and made a covering for the front of the cave.*****)**
5. Why didn't Bruce want a big fire in the shelter? **(Ideas:** ***Because it would make too much smoke; they would have trouble breathing.*****)**

As everybody huddled together inside the cave, Bruce announced, "The next thing we have to do is make warm clothes. We can use the skins from the rabbits we hunt. Maybe we can also use feathers from the birds."

Unfortunately, the problem with rabbits and birds, as Bruce realized, is that they are small. To make a coat from the hides of rabbits, a person might need as many as twenty or thirty rabbits. The hide of one large animal like a bear, however, would make two or three coats. ❻

6. What's another word for **hide?** *Skin.*
6. How do people huddle together? (Idea: *They stay very close to each other.*)
6. What did Bruce decide to do next about the cold problem?
(Idea: *To make warm clothes.*)

The next morning the wind was blowing particularly hard. As Bruce sat in the shelter waiting for the wind to die down, he began to rethink the things that were happening to him. He concluded, you need some things to stay alive. You need air, warmth, water, and food. Unless you have all of those things, you die. If you don't want to die, you've got to do something. You've got to build something or change your surroundings in some way. ❼

7. What are surroundings? (Idea: *Everything around you.*)
7. What does "he concluded" mean? (Ideas: *He summarized; he put together many facts or ideas.*)

If you don't have enough warmth, you've got to do something so that you can stay warm. If you don't have enough water, you've got to do something that will give you enough water.

7. (Award points quickly.)
8. (If the group makes more than 12 errors, repeat the reading immediately or on the next day.)

FLUENCY ASSESSMENT

EXERCISE 6

TIMED READING CHECKOUTS

1. (For this part of the lesson, assigned pairs of students work together during the checkouts.)
- (If one student does not have a checkout partner, arrange another time when you can give the checkout.)
2. (Each student does a 2-minute timed reading. Students earn 5 points by reading at least 240 words and making no more than 5 errors on the first part of story 37. Students record points in Box C of their Point Chart and plot their reading rate and errors on the Individual Reading Progress Chart.)
- (During each timed checkout, observe one pair of students for 2 minutes. Make notes on any mistakes the reader makes.)
3. (Record the timed reading checkout performance for each student you observed on the Fluency Assessment Summary form.)

WORKBOOK EXERCISES

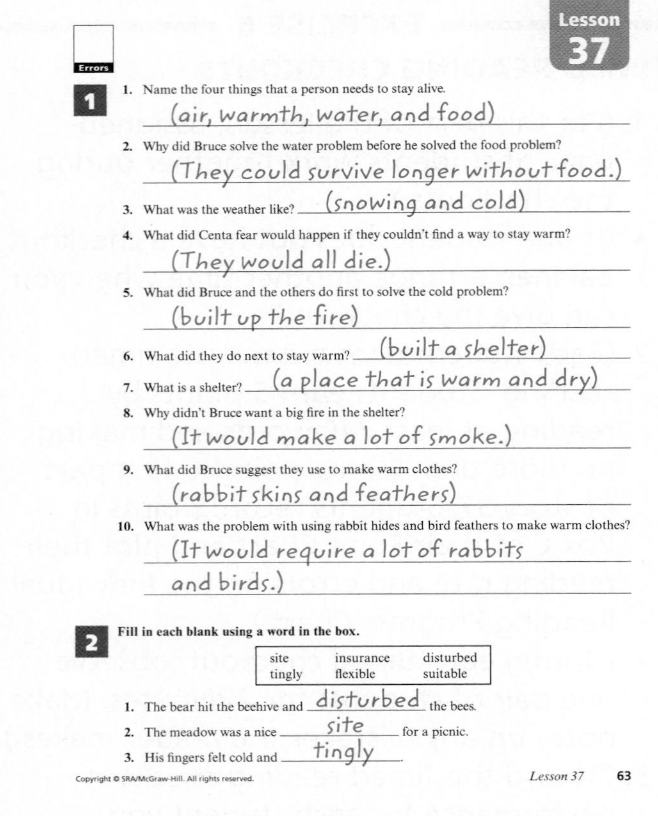

Errors

Lesson 37

1

1. Name the four things that a person needs to stay alive.
   (air, warmth, water, and food)
2. Why did Bruce solve the water problem before he solved the food problem?
   (They could survive longer without food.)
3. What was the weather like? (snowing and cold)
4. What did Centa fear would happen if they couldn't find a way to stay warm?
   (They would all die.)
5. What did Bruce and the others do first to solve the cold problem?
   (built up the fire)
6. What did they do next to stay warm? (built a shelter)
7. What is a shelter? (a place that is warm and dry)
8. Why didn't Bruce want a big fire in the shelter?
   (It would make a lot of smoke.)
9. What did Bruce suggest they use to make warm clothes?
   (rabbit skins and feathers)
10. What was the problem with using rabbit hides and bird feathers to make warm clothes?
    (It would require a lot of rabbits and birds.)

2 Fill in each blank using a word in the box.

site	insurance	disturbed
tingly	flexible	suitable

1. The bear hit the beehive and disturbed the bees.
2. The meadow was a nice site for a picnic.
3. His fingers felt cold and tingly.

Copyright © SRA/McGraw-Hill. All rights reserved. Lesson 37 63

Independent Student Work

Task A

- Open your Workbook to Lesson 37. ✓
- Complete all the parts of your Workbook lesson using a pencil. If you make no errors, you will earn 5 points.

Task B

1. (Before presenting Lesson 38, check student Workbooks for Lesson 37.)
   - (Call on individual students to read the items and answers in each part. Students mark errors using a pen.)
2. (Direct the students to count the number of errors and write the number in the Errors box at the top of the Workbook page.)
3. (Award points and direct students to record points in Box D of their Point Chart.)

   0 errors..................................5 points
   1 error ....3 points
   2 or 3 errors ....1 point
   more than 3 errors ....0 points

END OF LESSON 37

WORD-ATTACK SKILLS

Student Book 

EXERCISE 1

NEW **AFFIX: dis**

Task A

1. Open your Student Book to Lesson 38. ✓

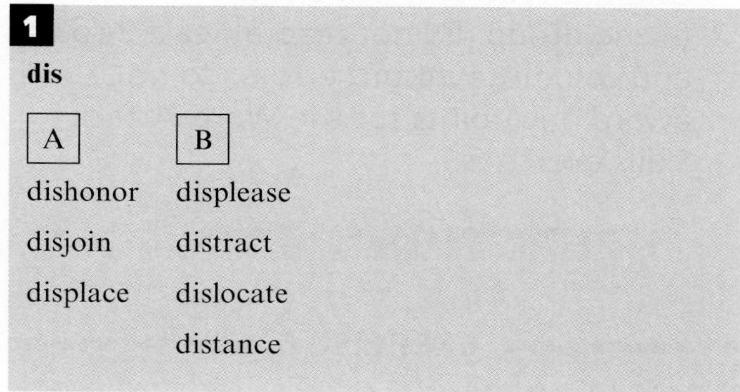

1

dis

A	B
dishonor	displease
disjoin	distract
displace	dislocate
	distance

- Touch the letters **D–I–S** in part 1. ✓
- When those letters appear at the beginning of a word, they usually mean **not** or **the opposite of.** Sometimes **dis** means **away from.**

2. Touch the first word in column A. ✓
- What word? (Signal.) *Dishonor.*
- What does **dishonor** mean? (Call on a student.) (Idea: *The opposite of honor.*) Yes, it means the opposite of honor.

3. Everybody, touch the next word. ✓
- What word? (Signal.) *Disjoin.*
- What does **disjoin** mean? (Call on a student.) (Idea: *The opposite of join.*) Yes, it means the opposite of join.

4. Everybody, touch the next word. ✓
- What word? (Signal.) *Displace.*
- What does **displace** mean? (Call on a student.) (Idea: *To place away from something.*) Yes, it means to place away from something.

5. (Repeat the list until firm.)

Task B

1. Touch the first word in column B. ✓
- What word? (Signal.) *Displease.*

2. Next word. ✓
- What word? (Signal.) *Distract.*

3. (Repeat step 2 for **dislocate, distance.**)
4. (Repeat steps 1–3 until firm.)

EXERCISE 2

WORD PRACTICE

1. Touch the first word in part 2. ✓

choice approached nervously disgusted

- What's the underlined part? (Signal.) *oy.*
- What word? (Signal.) *Choice.*

2. Touch the next word. ✓
- What's the underlined part? (Signal.) *ōōō.*
- What word? (Signal.) *Approached.*

3. (Repeat step 2 for each remaining word.)
4. (Repeat the words until firm.)

EXERCISE 3

VOCABULARY

1. Touch part 3. ✓

3

1. chores
2. comment
3. hoist
4. chimney

- We're going to talk about what those words mean.

2. Touch word 1. ✓
- What word? (Signal.) *Chores.*
- **Chores** are **daily jobs.** Everybody, what's another way of saying "The boy finished his **daily jobs** early"? (Signal.) *The boy finished his chores early.*

3. Touch word 2. ✓
- What word? (Signal.) *Comment.*
- When you **comment,** you **say something** about a situation. Everybody, what's another way of saying "She **said something** about the bad weather"? (Signal.) *She commented about the bad weather.*

4. Touch word 3. ✓
- What word? (Signal.) *Hoist.*
- When you **lift** something, you **hoist** it. Everybody, what's another way of saying "She will **lift** the rock"? (Signal.) *She will hoist the rock.*

5. Touch word 4. ✓
- What word? (Signal.) *Chimney.*
- What does a **chimney** do? (Call on a student.) (Idea: *Carries smoke from a fireplace or furnace.*)

EXERCISE 4

WORD PRACTICE

1. Touch the first word in part 4. ✓

4

whispered sneak spotted squealing calm
hooves thread cloth yarn pounded
braced fan-shaped clothes obviously
remained fibers splitting reported create
howling hollowing pleasantly notice tingly*
surprised gather collected narrow tangles

- What word? (Signal.) *Whispered.*

2. Next word. ✓
- What word? (Signal.) *Sneak.*

3. (Repeat step 2 for each remaining word.)
4. (Repeat each row of words until firm.)
5. What does **tingly** mean? (Call on a student.)

EXERCISE 5

WORD-ATTACK SKILLS: Individual tests

1. (Call on individual students. Each student reads a row or column. Tally the rows and columns read without error. If the group reads at least 8 rows and columns without making errors, direct all students to record 5 points in Box A of their Point Chart. Criterion is 80 percent of rows and columns read without error.)
2. (If the group did not read at least 8 rows and columns without errors, do not award any points for the Word-Attack Skills exercises.)

SELECTION READING

EXERCISE 6

STORY READING

1. (Call on individual students to answer these questions.)
- What is the name of the character introduced in the last selection? *Centa.*
- What did she fear might happen? (Idea: *She was afraid they would all die from the cold weather.*)
- What did Bruce and the others do first to solve the cold problem? (Idea: *They made the fire bigger.*)
- What did they do next? (Idea: *They built a shelter by hollowing out the side of a hill and making a covering for their cave.*)
- What's the last thing they did? (Idea: *They huddled together to help stay warm.*)

2. Everybody, touch part 5. ✓
3. The error limit for this story is 12. If the group reads the story with 12 errors or less, you earn 5 points.

5

Life Problems

4. (Call on a student to read the title.) *Life Problems.*
- What do you think this story is about? (Accept reasonable responses.)
5. (Call on individual students. Each is to read two to four sentences.)
6. (Call on individual students to answer the specified questions during the story reading.)

Bruce looked outside. He could hear the wind howling. It made him shiver just listening to it. He remained in the shelter and began to think again. He thought, "Air, warmth, water, and food are survival problems. If you have more than one survival problem at the same time, the first problem you solve is the problem that would take your life first. If you have a water problem and a food problem, you solve the water problem first, because the water problem will take your life first. If you have a water problem and an air problem, you obviously would solve the air problem first, because the air problem will take your life first." ❶

1. How do you know which life problem to solve first? (Idea: *Solve the problem that would take your life first.*)

Centa went to the door of the shelter and looked outside. "I think the wind is dying down," she reported.

Bruce said, "Good. This is our chance to gather the material that we need to make warm clothes."

Bruce, Centa, and one of the men left the shelter. Bruce braced himself for the cold, and at first he was pleasantly surprised. The air didn't seem as cold as he had thought it would be. However, as he jogged along with the others toward a place where dead vines lay in tangles on the ground, he began to notice the cold. His legs were becoming tingly. The tips of his ears and fingers began to hurt. "Let's keep moving," he said to the others. "It is very cold out here." ❷

2. How do you brace yourself for the cold? (Idea: *You get yourself ready to feel the cold.*)
2. How did Bruce know it was very cold? (Ideas: *His legs became tingly; the tips of his ears and fingers began to hurt.*)

Lesson

38

Bruce collected vines, while Centa picked up the skins of the rabbits they had eaten the day before. The other man peeled bark from some of the trees.

Then they returned to the shelter with their materials. Bruce looked over the materials, and he said, "We can pound the bark with rocks and make cloth out of it." Bruce showed two others how to do it. As they pounded away on the bark, Bruce told another woman, "Pull the fibers from the vines. We can use those fibers as thread or yarn." So the woman began pulling the fibers from the vines.

Bruce said, "I'll use them as thread to lace the rabbit skins together, but first I'll need a needle." ❸

3. What materials did Bruce plan to use for making clothes? (Idea: *Bark, vines, rabbit skins.*)

Centa ran to the beach and found some fan-shaped shells. She took one of the shells and hit it gently with a rock, splitting it into long, narrow pieces that were pointed at one end. "This will work as a needle," she said, handing one of the pieces to Bruce.

Bruce tied the vine fiber around the fat end of the needle and pushed the needle through one of the rabbit skins. As Bruce worked, Centa commented, "We'll need a lot more skins before we can make clothes from these skins. Let's make cloth clothes first; then we'll go hunting for some larger animals."

"Yes," Bruce said. "If we find larger animals, we can make clothes faster." ❹

4. How did Centa make a needle? (Idea: *By splitting shells into long, narrow pieces.*)
4. What did Bruce use for thread? (Idea: *Fibers from vines.*)
4. Why did Bruce want to hunt for larger animals? (Idea: *Because bigger animals have larger skins and they could make clothes faster with larger skins.*)

Early the next day, when the sky was growing light gray, Bruce and two other people went hunting. On the far side of the island, a long distance from their shelter, they found tracks made in the snow by a large animal and examined them. Following the tracks, they soon came to a hill near the beach. A large wild pig and two baby pigs were standing there. "Don't kill the baby pigs," Bruce whispered as he and the other hunters began to sneak up the hill. ❺

5. What kinds of animals were the hunters trying to find? (Idea: *Large animals.*)
5. Why do you think Bruce would say, "Don't kill the baby pigs"? (Ideas: *So they could raise the pigs themselves; so the baby pigs could live to grow larger.*)

The large pig spotted them and began to run away. A woman shot an arrow, hitting the pig in the side. The pig turned around and began to squeal loudly. Bruce shot an arrow that struck the pig in the chest, and the pig fell over.

Bruce felt sick as he walked over to the pig. It disgusted him to kill animals. He wouldn't have killed the pig if he'd had a choice, but what was he to do?

The little pigs ran nervously around the mother pig, squealing loudly. They did not run away when Bruce and the others approached. ❻

6. What does "to approach something" mean? (Idea: *To move closer to it.*)
6. Why did Bruce have to kill the pig? (Idea: *So he and the others could survive.*)

One hunter picked up both of the baby pigs. He held one under each arm. As soon as he picked them up, they stopped squealing, and they seemed to calm down.

Bruce and the others tied the large pig's front hooves together with a vine. They also tied the back hooves together. Then they slid a branch between the pig's legs. They hoisted the branch and carried the pig back to their shelter. ❼

7. How did they carry the pig back to the shelter? (Idea: *By tying its feet together, sliding a branch between its legs, and hoisting the branch.*)
7. (Award points quickly.)
8. (If the group makes more than 12 errors, repeat the reading immediately or on the next day.)

FLUENCY ASSESSMENT

EXERCISE 7

TIMED READING CHECKOUTS

1. (For this part of the lesson, assigned pairs of students work together during the checkouts.)
- (If one student does not have a checkout partner, arrange another time when you can give the checkout.)
2. (Each student does a 2-minute timed reading. Students earn 5 points by reading at least 240 words and making no more than 5 errors on the first part of story 38. Students record points in Box C of their Point Chart and plot their reading rate and errors on the Individual Reading Progress Chart.)
- (During each timed checkout, observe one pair of students for 2 minutes. Make notes on any mistakes the reader makes.)
3. (Record the timed reading checkout performance for each student you observed on the Fluency Assessment Summary form.)

Lesson

38

WORKBOOK EXERCISES

Lesson 38

Errors

1

1. If you had both a water problem and a food problem, which would you solve first?
   the water problem
2. Of which would you die first, a lack of air or of water?
   a lack of air
3. If you had both an air problem and a water problem, which would you solve first?
   the air problem
4. If you had both a food problem and an air problem, which would you solve first?
   the air problem
5. If you had more than one life problem at the same time, which would you solve first?
   the problem that would take your life first
6. Name three things that Bruce and the others did to solve the warmth problem.
   a. (built a fire)
   b. (built a shelter)
   c. (made clothes)
7. What tool did Centa make for sewing clothes? a needle
8. What did Bruce use for thread? (fibers from vines)
9. Name two types of material that Bruce planned to use for making clothes.
   (skins and cloth)
10. How many baby pigs were with the mother pig? two
11. What did Bruce and the others use to carry the pig? a branch

64 Lesson 38 Copyright © SRA/McGraw-Hill. All rights reserved.

Lesson 38

2 Fill in each blank using a word in the box.

hoist	site	chore
breadfruit	provide	commented

1. "What unusually warm weather this is!" the man commented.
2. She tried to hoist the heavy weight.
3. Tony's chore was washing dishes every day.

3 Write the parts for each word.

1. unsheltered = un + shelter + ed
2. remarked = re + mark + ed
3. reconstruct = re + construct
4. discover = dis + cover

Copyright © SRA/McGraw-Hill. All rights reserved. Lesson 38 65

Independent Student Work

Task A

- Open your Workbook to Lesson 38. ✓
- Complete all the parts of your Workbook lesson using a pencil. If you make no errors, you will earn 5 points.

Task B

1. (Before presenting Lesson 39, check student Workbooks for Lesson 38.)
   - (Call on individual students to read the items and answers in each part. Students mark errors using a pen.)
2. (Direct the students to count the number of errors and write the number in the Errors box at the top of the Workbook page.)
3. (Award points and direct students to record points in Box D of their Point Chart.)

   0 errors................................5 points
   1 error.................................3 points
   2 or 3 errors.........................1 point
   more than 3 errors..............0 points

END OF LESSON 38

WORD-ATTACK SKILLS

Board Work

EXERCISE 1

BUILDUP

1. (Print on the board:)

th ough

2. (Point to **though.** Pause.) What word? (Signal.) *Though.*
3. (Change the word to:)

through

- What word now? (Signal.) *Through.*

4. (Change the word to:)

th ough

- What word now? (Signal.) *Though.*

5. (Change the word to:)

th ought

- What word now? (Signal.) *Thought.*

6. (Change to the original word:)

th ough

- (Repeat steps 2–5 until firm.)

Student Book 

EXERCISE 2

AFFIX: dis

Task A

1. Open your Student Book to Lesson 39. ✓

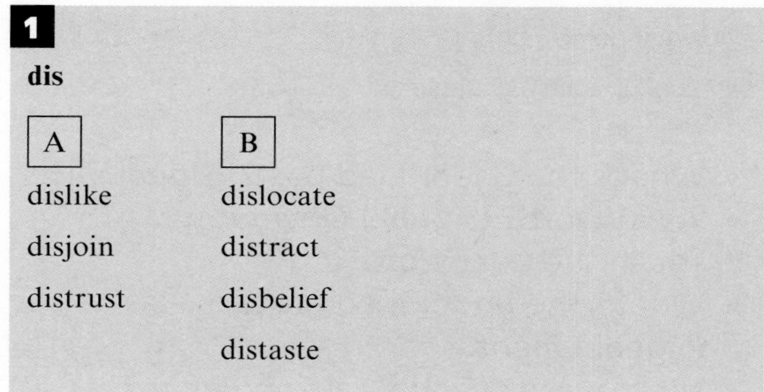

1

dis

A	B
dislike	dislocate
disjoin	distract
distrust	disbelief
	distaste

- Touch the letters **D–I–S** in part 1. ✓
- When those letters appear at the beginning of a word, they usually mean **not** or **the opposite of.** Sometimes **dis** means **away from.**

2. Touch the first word in column A. ✓
- What word? (Signal.) *Dislike.*
- What does **dislike** mean? (Call on a student.) (Idea: *The opposite of like.*) Yes, it means the opposite of like.

3. Everybody, touch the next word. ✓
- What word? (Signal.) *Disjoin.*
- What does **disjoin** mean? (Call on a student.) (Idea: *The opposite of join.*) Yes, it means the opposite of join.

4. Everybody, touch the next word. ✓
- What word? (Signal.) *Distrust.*
- What does **distrust** mean? (Call on a student.) (Idea: *The opposite of trust.*) Yes, it means the opposite of trust.

5. (Repeat the list until firm.)

Task B

1. Touch the first word in column B. ✓
- What word? (Signal.) *Dislocate.*

2. Next word. ✓
- What word? (Signal.) *Distract.*

3. (Repeat step 2 for **disbelief, distaste.**)
4. (Repeat steps 1–3 until firm.)

Lesson 39

EXERCISE 3

WORD PRACTICE

1. Touch the first word in part 2. ✓

2

obviously arrangement chores*
exception unbelievable* piece mounted
occasionally nearly attached specific
chowder investigation* starting
particular charred* relaxed probably*

- What's the underlined part? (Signal.) *ly.*
- What word? (Signal.) *Obviously.*

2. Touch the next word. ✓
- What's the underlined part? (Signal.) *ment.*
- What word? (Signal.) *Arrangement.*
3. (Repeat step 2 for each remaining word.)
4. (Repeat each row of words until firm.)
5. What does **chores** mean? (Call on a student.)
- (Repeat for each starred word.)

EXERCISE 4

VOCABULARY

1. Touch part 3. ✓

3

1. examine
2. chowder
3. husks
4. verses
5. remodel

- We're going to talk about what those words mean.

2. Touch word 1. ✓
- What word? (Signal.) *Examine.*
- When you **examine** something, you **carefully look it over.** What's another way of saying "The hunter **carefully looked over** the animal tracks"? (Signal.) *The hunter examined the animal tracks.*
3. Touch word 2. ✓
- What word? (Signal.) *Chowder.*
- A **chowder** is a **thick soup.** Everybody, what is a **chowder?** (Signal.) *A thick soup.*
4. Touch word 3. ✓
- What word? (Signal.) *Husks.*
- **Husks** are the **dry outer coverings of some fruits** such as coconuts. Everybody, what's another way of saying "The **outer coverings** of the coconuts are brown and stringy"? (Signal.) *The husks of the coconuts are brown and stringy.*
5. Touch word 4. ✓
- What word? (Signal.) *Verses.*
- **Verses** are **the parts of a song that are not sung over and over.** The chorus is the part that is sung over and over.
- Everybody, which parts of a song are not sung over and over? (Signal.) *The verses.*
6. Touch word 5. ✓
- What word? (Signal.) *Remodel.*
- When you **remodel** something, you **change the way it looks.** Everybody, what do you do when you **remodel** something? (Signal.) *You change the way it looks.*

EXERCISE 5

WORD PRACTICE

1. Touch the first word in part 4. ✓

4

chimney* scraped skinned preparing commented*
bowl plenty tackled tusks started
giant caught busy sang chorus
comfortable sense vines solved unfortunately

- What word? (Signal.) *Chimney.*

2. Next word. ✓
- What word? (Signal.) *Scraped.*
3. (Repeat step 2 for each remaining word.)
4. (Repeat each row of words until firm.)
5. What does **chimney** mean? (Call on a student.)
- (Repeat for **commented.**)

EXERCISE 6

WORD-ATTACK SKILLS: Individual tests

1. (Call on individual students. Each student reads a row or column. Tally the rows and columns read without error. If the group reads at least 10 rows and columns without making errors, direct all students to record 5 points in Box A of their Point Chart. Criterion is 80 percent of rows and columns read without error.)
2. (If the group did not read at least 10 rows and columns without errors, do not award any points for the Word-Attack Skills exercises.)

SELECTION READING

EXERCISE 7

STORY READING

1. Everybody, touch part 5. ✓
2. The error limit for this story is 12. If the group reads the story with 12 errors or less, you earn 5 points.

5 **Problems of Comfort**

3. (Call on a student to read the title.) *Problems of Comfort.*
   - What do you think this story is about? (Accept reasonable responses.)
4. (Call on individual students. Each is to read two to four sentences.)
5. (Call on individual students to answer the specified questions during the story reading.)

Bruce said, "We will try to keep the young pigs and raise them. But that means we will have to find food to feed them. And we must build a shelter for them."

For the rest of the day, the people took turns making a shelter for the pigs next to the shelter for the people. There was a pen in front of the pigs' shelter. The pigs could stay in their yard or go inside their shelter.

Bruce and Centa dug up some plants that had survived the snow. They threw the plants inside the pen. "These will give the young pigs something to eat," Bruce commented. ❶

1. Name two jobs that had to be done after Bruce and the others came back with the young pigs. (Idea: *Find food for the baby pigs and build shelter for them.*)

Later that day Bruce and the others were huddled inside the shelter. The large pig was cooking over a small fire. It had been skinned. The skin had been scraped and was hanging on one wall of the shelter.

There was a lot to do—feed the pigs, hunt for food, get water and wood, make clothes, and make the shelter more comfortable. Work would be done faster if each person had a specific job.

Different people were given different jobs. One woman was given the job of preparing the pigskin by pounding it with rocks until it was soft. One man did the chores around the shelter. Other people were given the job of fixing up the shelter. They were to make it bigger and to build a chimney so that the shelter would not be smoky. Bruce and Centa were to take care of the hunting and fishing. They would go out and find food for the others. ❷

2. Why would it be better for each person to have a specific job? (Idea: *Because work could be done faster.*)
2. Why did a chimney have to be built? (Idea: *So that the shelter would not be smoky.*)
2. What job were Bruce and Centa given? *Hunting and fishing.*

Lesson 39

The day after the three pigs were found, Bruce and the others rigged up a way to catch fish without getting wet. They reworked their fishing net so that it looked like a giant bowl that was attached to a long pole. Standing on the shore and holding the pole, Bruce and Centa could move the net along under the water. Fish swam into the open end of the net.

In one day Bruce and Centa caught thirty-six fish. The biggest was nearly three feet long. ❸

3. Why was the new net better than the net the people had used before? (Idea: *Because they could fish without getting wet.*)
3. How many fish did Bruce and Centa catch in one day? *Thirty-six.*

They also made three crab traps. They dug deep holes on the beach, lined the walls of the holes with sticks, and waited. Bruce said, "When the tide comes in, these holes will be underwater. Then the tide will go out. Some crabs should fall into the holes, and they won't be able to get out."

That evening the people had bowls of crab chowder. The bowls were made of coconut husks, and the spoons they used were seashells. There were bits of seaweed and other plants in the crab chowder. After the chowder came fish, and after the fish everybody relaxed.

Bruce looked around at the shelter that the others had made larger. There was a chimney above the fire. The chimney was made of mud and of rocks tied together with vines. ❹

4. What tools did the people use for eating? (Idea: *Coconut husks as bowls and seashells as spoons.*)
4. How did they make a chimney? (Idea: *Out of mud, rocks, and vines.*)

As the people were sitting around, Bruce thought, "Obviously we solved the problems of life first. Those were the problems of water, food, and warmth. After we solved these problems, we started to solve problems of comfort. We didn't have to raise pigs to stay alive; however, raising pigs is easier than hunting for them. We didn't have to make the new nets, but it is much more comfortable to catch fish from the shore with the new net. And we didn't have to remodel the shelter, but the chimney makes it more comfortable in the shelter." ❺

5. Which problems did they solve first, comfort problems or survival problems? *Survival problems.*
5. Why did the chimney make it more comfortable in the shelter? (Idea: *It made the shelter less smoky.*)

Bruce looked at the pigskin mounted on the wall. Then he said to himself, "We solved the life problems first. Then, after we solved the last life problem, we began to solve problems of comfort. That makes a lot of sense. ❻

6. What does it mean when we say something "makes a lot of sense"? (Ideas: *It is easy to understand; it's logical.*)

If we didn't solve all of the life problems first, we wouldn't have to worry about the problems of comfort. Unfortunately, we would be dead."

Just then one young woman said, "Let's sing songs." That sounded like a good idea, so everybody sang. One of the older men made up a song about the shelter. Everybody sang it.

"Oh, the shelter is warm,
the shelter is good.
We've got plenty of food
and plenty of wood.
Our shelter is fine.
Our shelter is fine.
When we're in our shelter,
we have a very good time."

Different people made up verses. Then everybody repeated the chorus of the song. (7)

7. How is a verse different from a chorus? (Idea: *A verse is not sung over and over like a chorus.*)

Late that night Bruce woke up. He hadn't thought about this before, but he realized now that he didn't mind talking to people on the island. He didn't mind his job; in fact, he didn't think about his job much. There were things that had to be done, and Bruce was excited about doing them. There were problems to solve, and he tackled them. He didn't have time to think about whether he was happy or sad. He was too busy to be a grouch. (8)

8. Bruce felt different about some things now than he had when he first came to the island. Name three things he felt different about. (Ideas: *He liked talking to people; he didn't mind his job; his work was exciting; he enjoyed tackling problems.*)

6. (Award points quickly.)
7. (If the group makes more than 12 errors, repeat the reading immediately or on the next day.)

FLUENCY ASSESSMENT

EXERCISE 8

TIMED READING CHECKOUTS

1. (For this part of the lesson, assigned pairs of students work together during the checkouts.)
   - (If one student does not have a checkout partner, arrange another time when you can give the checkout.)
2. (Each student does a 2-minute timed reading. Students earn 5 points by reading at least 240 words and making no more than 5 errors on the first part of story 39. Students record points in Box C of their Point Chart and plot their reading rate and errors on the Individual Reading Progress Chart.)
   - (During each timed checkout, observe one pair of students for 2 minutes. Make notes on any mistakes the reader makes.)
3. (Record the timed reading checkout performance for each student you observed on the Fluency Assessment Summary form.)

Lesson 39

WORKBOOK EXERCISES

Lesson 39

Errors

1

1. Why was the new net better than the net the people had made before? (They could fish without getting wet.)
2. What did the people build to catch crabs? (crab traps; deep holes on the beach lined with sticks)
3. What did the people use for bowls? coconut husks
4. What did the people use for spoons? seashells
5. Write **life** in front of each life problem and **comfort** in front of each comfort problem.
   a. life You have no protection against zero-degree weather.
   b. comfort There's a small hole in the roof.
   c. life You have no water.
   d. life There is no food.
   e. comfort You have to eat bananas every day.
   f. comfort You have no friends.
   g. comfort You have to walk four miles to get water.
   h. life There is no air.
6. The people had a plan for working around the shelter. Did each person do all the different jobs there were to do? No.
7. Name two jobs that had to be done after Bruce and the others came back with the young pigs.
   a. (find food for the pig.)
   b. (build a shelter for the pigs)
8. What were the baby pigs given to eat? plants

66 Lesson 39 Copyright © SRA/McGraw-Hill. All rights reserved.

Lesson 39

2 Fill in each blank using a word in the box.

chimney	hoist	chowder
examined	deserve	procedure

1. They had fish chowder for lunch.
2. Smoke came out of the chimney.
3. He examined his newspaper closely.

Copyright © SRA/McGraw-Hill. All rights reserved. Lesson 39 67

Independent Student Work

Task A

- Open your Workbook to Lesson 39. ✓
- Complete all the parts of your Workbook lesson using a pencil. If you make no errors, you will earn 5 points.

Task B

1. (Before presenting Lesson 40, check student Workbooks for Lesson 39.)
- (Call on individual students to read the items and answers in each part. Students mark errors using a pen.)
2. (Direct the students to count the number of errors and write the number in the Errors box at the top of the Workbook page.)
3. (Award points and direct students to record points in Box D of their Point Chart.)

0 errors ....5 points
1 error ....3 points
2 or 3 errors ....1 point
more than 3 errors ....0 points

END OF LESSON 39

WORD-ATTACK SKILLS

Student Book

EXERCISE 1

AFFIX REVIEW

Task A

1. Open your Student Book to Lesson 40. ✓

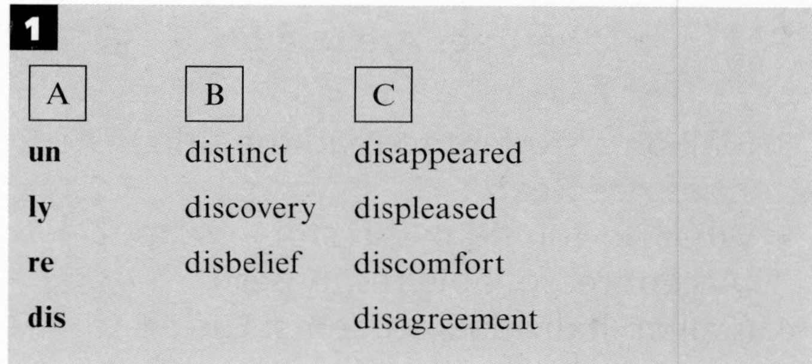

1

A	B	C
un	distinct	disappeared
ly	discovery	displeased
re	disbelief	discomfort
dis		disagreement

- Touch column A in part 1. ✓
- Let's see if you remember a meaning for each of those affixes.

2. Touch the letters **U–N.** ✓
- What's one meaning of **un**? (Signal.) *Not.*

3. Touch the letters **L–Y.** ✓
- What's one meaning of **ly**? (Signal.) *How something happened.*

4. Touch the letters **R–E.** ✓
- What's one meaning of **re**? (Signal.) *Again.*

5. Touch the letters **D–I–S.** ✓
- What's one meaning of **dis?** (Call on a student.) (Accept **not, the opposite of,** or **away from.**)
- What's another meaning of **dis?** (Call on another student.)

6. (Repeat steps 2–5 until firm.)

Task B

1. Touch the first word in column B. ✓
- What word? (Signal.) *Distinct.*

2. Touch the next word. ✓
- What word? (Signal.) *Discovery.*

3. (Repeat step 2 for **disbelief.**)
4. (Repeat the list until firm.)
5. (Repeat steps 1–4 for the words in column C.)

EXERCISE 2

VOCABULARY

1. Touch part 2. ✓

2

1. extension
2. argument
3. deadlocked
4. hammock

- We're going to talk about what those words mean.

2. Touch word 1. ✓
- What word? (Signal.) *Extension.*
- **Something that is added** is an **extension.** Everybody, what's another way of saying "He had an **added part** for his ladder"? (Signal.) *He had an extension for his ladder.*

3. Touch word 2. ✓
- What word? (Signal.) *Argument.*
- What is an **argument?** (Call on a student.) (Idea: *A disagreement.*)

4. Everybody, touch word 3. ✓
- What word? (Signal.) *Deadlocked.*
- When **neither side can win,** the sides are **deadlocked.** Everybody, what's another way of saying "**Neither side can win**"? (Signal.) *The sides are deadlocked.*

5. Touch word 4. ✓
- What word? (Signal.) *Hammock.*
- What is a **hammock?** (Call on a student.) (Idea: *A swinging bed made of net or cloth.*)

EXERCISE 3

WORD PRACTICE

1. Touch the first word in part 3. ✓

3

achieved figure remodeling* completed
loose combination referred original*
rattle consisted thoughtfully kitchen
procedures* particularly warmer
charge collected obviously switched
continued connecting entire leaned
specific occurred examine announced*
arrangement prepared exceptional
unbelievable* agreement individual
caution comfortable unfortunate*
usually decision involved

- What word? (Signal.) *Achieved.*

2. Next word. ✓
- What word? (Signal.) *Figure.*
3. (Repeat step 2 for each remaining word.)
4. (Repeat each row of words until firm.)
5. What does **remodeling** mean? (Call on a student.)
- (Repeat for each starred word.)

EXERCISE 4

WORD-ATTACK SKILLS: Individual tests

1. (Call on individual students. Each student reads a row or column. Tally the rows and columns read without error. If the group reads at least 12 rows and columns without making errors, direct all students to record 5 points in Box A of their Point Chart. Criterion is 80 percent of rows and columns read without error.)
2. (If the group did not read at least 12 rows and columns without errors, do not award any points for the Word-Attack Skills exercises.)

SELECTION READING

EXERCISE 5

STORY READING

1. Everybody, touch part 4. ✓
2. The error limit for this story is 12. If the group reads the story with 12 errors or less, you earn 5 points.

4 **The Trees Are Dead**

3. (Call on a student to read the title.) *The Trees Are Dead.*
- What do you think this story is about? (Accept reasonable responses.)

4. (Call on individual students. Each is to read two to four sentences.)
5. (Call on individual students to answer the specified questions during the story reading.)

The days were cold for about two months. The weather then became obviously warmer. Spring was coming, and by now the shelter had been remodeled three times.

The first remodeling occurred about three weeks after the weather had turned cold. This remodeling was achieved by digging another hole next to the original one and then joining the two holes, forming a shelter that was about twice the size of the original one. The second remodeling began almost as soon as the first had been completed. It consisted of a large extension with a flat roof and a large fireplace. The people referred to this area as the porch. It became the workroom. Animal skins and tools hung on the grass-and-wood walls. The last remodeling consisted of a second story, which was dug out of part of the hill above the original cave and connected with it by a roof and a ladder. ❶

1. What did the people do for the first remodeling? (Idea: *They dug another hole and connected the two holes.*)
1. The story mentions "the original hole." What does that mean? (Idea: *The first hole that was dug in the hillside.*)
1. What did the people do for the second remodeling? (Idea: *They built an extension with a fireplace.*)
1. What's an extension? (Idea: *Something that is added.*)
1. What was the third remodeling? (Idea: *A second story.*)

The second story became the sleeping area, and the entire downstairs became a combination workroom, kitchen, and dining area.

Everyone had specific jobs, but some people had switched jobs with other people. It turned out that one older man was very good at making clothes, so he switched jobs with the man who had been making them. Also, the procedures for taking care of the animals had changed. By now there were four young pigs, two wild dogs, over thirty monkeys, and ten rabbits in a large, open pen. The monkeys were not doing well. They couldn't seem to stand the cold weather. The woman in charge of the animals collected plants and seeds for them to eat, made sure that they had plenty of water, and cleaned the animals' shelter. ❷

2. Did each person do all the different jobs there were to do around the shelter, or did each still do specific jobs? (Idea: *Everyone still had specific jobs.*)
2. What did the woman in charge of the animals have to do? (Idea: *She collected food for them, made sure they had water, and cleaned their shelter.*)

One day, when the weather was particularly warm, Centa and Bruce were out checking their traps. Bruce pointed to the trees. "Unfortunately, I think these trees are dead," he said. He took his ax and chopped through the bark of the tree. He examined the layer that was just beneath the bark. "See," he said. "If this tree were alive, it would have a bright green layer beneath the bark. The layer on this tree is gray, which means that the tree is dead." ❸

3. How could Bruce tell that the trees were dead? (Idea: *Because the layer just below the bark was gray instead of green.*)

Bruce and Centa checked the other trees. All were dead. Finally Bruce said, "We probably won't have coconut, banana, or breadfruit trees this summer. Furthermore, all of the animals that live off the trees will have no food, so they will either die or leave the island."

Centa said, "What are we going to do if we don't have food this summer?"

Bruce said, "We may be able to live off the sea animals. But we will have trouble keeping the land animals if we can't find plants for them." Bruce leaned against a dead tree and continued thoughtfully, "Maybe we should think about building a boat and leaving the island." ❹

4. What would Bruce and the others do for food if the plants and animals on the island died? (Idea: *They might be able to live off sea animals.*)
4. What other choice did Bruce and the others have? (Idea: *They could try to leave the island.*)

That evening Bruce sat on his hammock in the shelter and thought, "When people move from place to place, they do so because they figure that the new place will be better than the old place. The old place probably doesn't give them enough comfort. Things are too hard in the old place. They don't know what things will be like in the new place, but they figure that there is a place where things are better. So they go out to find that place. If the old place gives them the comfort they want, there is no reason for them to move. If the old place doesn't give them the comfort they want, they may think about moving to another place. If the old place has a life problem, they must move from the old place, because if they don't they will die." ⑤

5. When *must* people move from one place to another place? (Idea: *When the old place has a life problem that the people can't solve.*)

The days were getting warmer now. Some grass was beginning to grow, so the group decided to turn the animals loose and let them hunt for their own food. Each animal had a rattle around its neck that was made from little bones and coconut shells. You could hear the animals even if you could not see them. However, most of the animals stayed near the shelter. ⑥

6. Why did the group decide to let the animals hunt for their own food? (Idea: *Because grass was beginning to grow.*)
6. (Award points quickly.)
7. (If the group makes more than 12 errors, repeat the reading immediately or on the next day.)

FLUENCY ASSESSMENT

EXERCISE 6

TIMED READING CHECKOUTS

1. (For this part of the lesson, assigned pairs of students work together during the checkouts.)
- (If one student does not have a checkout partner, arrange another time when you can give the checkout.)
2. (Each student does a 2-minute timed reading. Students earn 5 points by reading at least 240 words and making no more than 5 errors on the first part of story 40. Students record points in Box C of their Point Chart and plot their reading rate and errors on the Individual Reading Progress Chart.)
- (During each timed checkout, observe one pair of students for 2 minutes. Make notes on any mistakes the reader makes.)
3. (Record the timed reading checkout performance for each student you observed on the Fluency Assessment Summary form.)

WORKBOOK EXERCISES

Lesson 40

Errors

1 1. Write **life** in front of each life problem and **comfort** in front of each comfort problem.

a. comfort There is lots of food on the island, but none of it tastes good.
b. life There is no food on the island, and there are no animals in the sea.
c. life There are six people, and there is enough food on the island and in the sea to keep two people alive.
d. comfort There's a small hole in the roof.
e. comfort You have to walk three miles to get water.
f. life You have no water.

2. Did everybody on the island have a specific job? Yes.
3. Who was now in charge of making clothes for the people? (an older man)
4. Name the animals they now had. (pigs, dogs, monkeys, rabbits)
5. Name three jobs the woman in charge of the animals had to do. (collected plants and seeds; made sure they had plenty of water; cleaned the animals' shelter)
6. How did Bruce know that the trees were dead? (The layer just beneath the bark was dead.)
7. Why would some animals die if the trees died? (They would have no food.)
8. How could Bruce and the others get food if all the trees died? (They could live off sea animals.)

68 *Lesson 40* Copyright © SRA/McGraw-Hill. All rights reserved.

Lesson 40

9. When must people move from one place to another? (when the old place has a life problem that can't be solved)

2 **Fill in each blank using a word in the box.**

extension	argument	deadlocked
solved	chore	remodel

1. He added an extension to the end of his fishing pole.
2. The women had an argument about who owned the goat.
3. Neither side could win the fight. The sides were deadlocked

Copyright © SRA/McGraw-Hill. All rights reserved. *Lesson 40* 69

Independent Student Work

Task A

- Open your Workbook to Lesson 40. ✓
- Complete all the parts of your Workbook lesson using a pencil. If you make no errors, you will earn 5 points.

Task B

1. (Before presenting Lesson 41, check student Workbooks for Lesson 40.)
   - (Call on individual students to read the items and answers in each part. Students mark errors using a pen.)
2. (Direct the students to count the number of errors and write the number in the Errors box at the top of the Workbook page.)
3. (Award points and direct students to record points in Box D of their Point Chart.)

   0 errors ....5 points
   1 error ....3 points
   2 or 3 errors ....1 point
   more than 3 errors ....0 points

Point schedule for Lessons 36 through 40

Box	Lesson part	Points
A	Word Attack	0 or 5
B	Selection Reading	0 or 5
C	Timed Reading Checkout	0 or 5
D	Workbook	0, 1, 3, or 5
Bonus	(Teacher option)	—

Five-lesson point summary

- (For **letter grades** based on points for Lessons **36** through **40**, tell students to compute the total for the blue boxes [C, D, and Bonus] and write the number in the Total box at the end of each row in their Point Chart. Students then add the totals and write the sum in the green box.)
- (For **rewards** based on points, tell students to compute the total for all boxes [A, B, C, D, and Bonus] and write the number in the Total box at the end of each row. Students then add the totals and write the sum in the green box.)

END OF LESSON 40

Lesson Objectives	LESSON 41 Exercise	LESSON 42 Exercise	LESSON 43 Exercise	LESSON 44 Exercise	LESSON 45 Exercise
Word Attack					
Decoding and Word Analysis					
Affixes: *un, re, dis*		1		1	
Affixes: *un, ly, re, dis*	2				1
Affixes: *pre*					2
Visual Discrimination	1		1, 2		
Letter Combinations/Letter Sounds			3	2	
Word Recognition	1–5		1–5	1–4	1–5
Vocabulary					
Morphemic Analysis	2	1		1	1, 2
Definitions	2–5	1–4	3–5	3, 4	3–5
Usage	4	3	4	3	4
Assessment					
Ongoing: Individual Tests	6	5	6	5	6
Group Reading					
Decoding and Word Analysis					
Read Decodable Text	7	6	7	6	7
Comprehension					
Access Prior Knowledge					
Draw Inferences	7	6	7	6	7
Note Details	7	6	7	6	7
Predict	7	6	7	6	7
Assessment					
Ongoing: Comprehension Check	7	6	7	6	7
Ongoing: Decoding Accuracy	7	6	7	6	7
Fluency Assessment					
Fluency					
Reread Decodable Text	8	7	8	7	8
Assessment					
Ongoing: Teacher-Monitored Fluency	8	7	8	7	8
Ongoing: Peer-Monitored Fluency	8	7	8	7	8
Workbook Exercises					
Decoding and Word Analysis					
Multisyllabic Word Parts	Ind. Work			Ind. Work	
Comprehension					
Main Idea		Ind. Work			Ind. Work
Sequencing					Ind. Work
Note Details	Ind. Work	Ind. Work	Ind. Work	Ind. Work	Ind. Work
Vocabulary					
Usage	Ind. Work	Ind. Work	Ind. Work	Ind. Work	Ind. Work
Study Skills					
Writing Mechanics		Ind. Work			Ind. Work
Assessment					
Ongoing: Workcheck	Workcheck	Workcheck	Workcheck	Workcheck	Workcheck

WORD-ATTACK SKILLS

Student Book 

EXERCISE 1

BUILDUP

1. Open your Student Book to Lesson 41. ✓

1

agree
agreed
agreement
argue
argument
argued

- Touch the first word in part 1. ✓
- What word? (Signal.) *Agree.*
2. Next word? ✓
- What word? (Signal.) *Agreed.*
3. (Repeat step 2 for each remaining word.)
4. (Repeat steps 1–3 until firm.)

EXERCISE 2

AFFIX REVIEW

Task A

1. Touch the first row in part 2. ✓

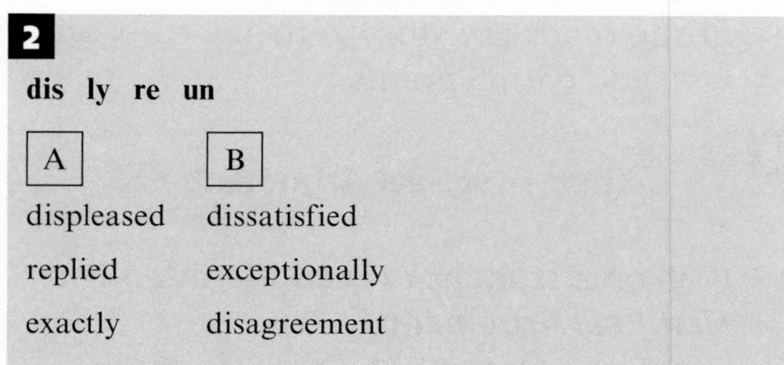

2

dis ly re un

A	B
displeased	dissatisfied
replied	exceptionally
exactly	disagreement

- Let's see if you remember a meaning for each of those affixes.
2. Touch the letters **D–I–S.** ✓
- What's one meaning of **dis?** (Call on a student. Accept **not, the opposite of,** or **away from.**)
- What's another meaning of **dis?** (Call on another student.)
3. Touch the letters **L–Y.** ✓
- Everybody, what's one meaning of **ly?** (Signal.) *How something happened.*
4. Touch the letters **R–E.** ✓
- What's one meaning of **re?** (Signal.) *Again.*
5. Touch the letters **U–N.** ✓
- What's one meaning of **un?** (Signal.) *Not.*
6. (Repeat steps 2–5 until firm.)

Task B

1. Touch the first word in column A. ✓
- What word? (Signal.) *Displeased.*
2. Touch the next word. ✓
- What word? (Signal.) *Replied.*
3. (Repeat step 2 for **exactly.**)
4. (Repeat the list until firm.)
5. (Repeat steps 1–4 for the words in column B.)

EXERCISE 3

WORD PRACTICE

1. Touch the first word in part 3. ✓

3

whether cheered unbelievable* scratched
unusually cautioned announced original*
survived choice maintain future exactly

- What's the underlined part? (Signal.) *www.*
- What word? (Signal.) *Whether.*
2. Touch the next word. ✓
- What's the underlined part? (Signal.) *ch.*
- What word? (Signal.) *Cheered.*
3. (Repeat step 2 for each remaining word.)
4. (Repeat each row of words until firm.)
5. What does **unbelievable** mean? (Call on a student.)
- (Repeat for **original.**)

Lesson
41

EXERCISE 4

VOCABULARY

1. Touch part 4. ✓

4

1. decision
2. solution
3. enforce

- We're going to talk about what those words mean.

2. Touch word 1. ✓
- What word? (Signal.) *Decision.*
- When you **choose** to do something, you **make a decision** to do it. Everybody, what's another way of saying "She **chose** to buy a car"? (Signal.) *She made a decision to buy a car.*

3. Touch word 2. ✓
- What word? (Signal.) *Solution.*
- A **solution** is the **answer** to a problem. An **answer** to the water problem is a **solution** to the water problem. Everybody, what's an **answer** to the pollution problem? (Signal.) *A solution to the pollution problem.*

4. Touch word 3. ✓
- What word? (Signal.) *Enforce.*
- When you **make someone follow rules,** you **enforce** the rules. Everybody, what's another way of saying "The soldier **made them follow** the rules"? (Signal.) *The soldier enforced the rules.*

EXERCISE 5

WORD PRACTICE

1. Touch the first word in part 5. ✓

5

involved deadlocked* possible almost
decided property obviously excited
occasionally meant particularly favor
protected risk exceptionally decisions
individuals agreements unfortunately

- What word? (Signal.) *Involved.*

2. Next word. ✓
- What word? (Signal.) *Deadlocked.*

3. (Repeat step 2 for each remaining word.)
4. (Repeat each row of words until firm.)
5. What does **deadlocked** mean? (Call on a student.)

EXERCISE 6

WORD-ATTACK SKILLS: Individual tests

1. (Call on individual students. Each student reads a row or column. Tally the rows and columns read without error. If the group reads at least 10 rows and columns without making errors, direct all students to record 5 points in Box A of their Point Chart. Criterion is 80 percent of rows and columns read without error.)
2. (If the group did not read at least 10 rows and columns without errors, do not award any points for the Word-Attack Skills exercises.)

SELECTION READING

EXERCISE 7

STORY READING

1. Everybody, touch part 6. ✓
2. The error limit for this story is 12. If the group reads the story with 12 errors or less, you earn 5 points.

6 **Their First Real Argument**

3. (Call on a student to read the title.) *Their First Real Argument.*
- What do you think this story is about? (Accept reasonable responses.)

4. (Call on individual students. Each is to read two to four sentences.)
5. (Call on individual students to answer the specified questions during the story reading.)

The people had their first real argument that spring. The group disagreed about whether they should remain on the island or move. To move, the group would have to build a boat and sail across the sea. Obviously, there was some risk involved in moving. The question was whether there wasn't as much risk in remaining on the island.

Centa didn't want to move. She spoke for the others who agreed with her. She said, "There is some grass on the island, which means that there will be some food for the animals. We will probably discover that we can survive here."

Bruce was in favor of building a boat. He spoke for those who agreed with him. He said, "Even if we don't use the boat, we should be ready to move if we have to. I think we should build the boat and then see what happens." ❶

1. What was the first argument about? (Idea: *Whether the group should leave the island.*)
1. What side did Centa take in the argument? (Idea: *The side that didn't want to move.*)
1. What side did Bruce take in the argument? (Idea: *The side that wanted to build a boat to be ready to move.*)

"No," Centa argued. "Building a boat will take a lot of time. We should use that time for planting seeds and growing crops."

Bruce said, "I don't agree with you. It is possible that most seeds won't grow after the cold winter. Furthermore, some seeds need years and years to grow into plants that will have fruit."

The argument continued for days. At last Centa said, "We've got to figure out some way to settle this argument. Since there is an even number of us, we are deadlocked. Half want to build a boat; half don't. If there were one more person, we could never be deadlocked." ❷

2. Why did Centa not want to build a boat? (Idea: *She thought they should spend their time planting and growing crops.*)
2. Why did Bruce not want to stay on the island? (Ideas: *Because some seeds might not grow after the cold winter; some seeds take years to grow into food.*)
2. Why were the sides deadlocked? (Ideas: *Because there was an even number of people; half were on one side and half were on the other.*)

Then everybody began to argue about how to settle the disagreement. Some people said that Bruce should have two votes. Centa and the people on her side said that Centa should have two votes. But the people on Bruce's side said, "No way."

On the third day of the argument, Bruce stated, "We should figure out a fair way to settle this argument." Everybody agreed, and here's their solution. They found a flat stone and on one side of it scratched an X. They placed the stone inside a coconut shell. Then they shook the shell and turned it over. They had agreed that they would build the boat if the stone landed so that the X was showing. If the other side was showing, they would not build the boat. ❸

3. What was the rule about the stone? (Idea: *They would build the boat if the stone landed with the X showing.*)

> The side without the X showed. Everybody on Centa's side was excited and cheered.
>
> One woman on Bruce's side of the argument was displeased. She said, "I don't care what the stone says. I'm going to build a boat. The rest of you can do anything you want."
>
> Bruce said, "No. We agreed that we would all do whatever the stone said. That means we are all going to do it." ❹

4. Whose side won? (Idea: *Centa's.*)
4. Why wouldn't Bruce let the woman build a boat? (Idea: *Because all the people agreed to do whatever the stone said.*)

> Bruce was thinking there were many laws in the city where he had lived—traffic laws, laws about how to do business, laws that protect people and their property. On the island there were no laws at first. Bruce and the others had just made one—a law about how the group makes decisions. This law told every person that, even though each person has some rights, the group has rights, too. Individuals can not do what they want if it hurts the group.
>
> "I changed my mind," the woman said.
>
> "No," Bruce said. "If we live together, you can't change your mind about some things. What if you decided to kill all of the animals? That would hurt the rest of us, so we couldn't let you do that. What if you decided to take somebody's clothes? That wouldn't be fair to that person. So we can't let you make that choice."
>
> "Who's going to stop me?" the woman asked.
>
> "We will," Bruce said. "The rest of us must enforce the rules." ❺

5. What did Bruce mean by "enforce the rules"? (Idea: *Make sure that people follow the rules.*)
5. Why couldn't individuals do what they wanted? (Ideas: *Because the group has rights, too; individuals could not do what they wanted if it hurt the group.*)
5. What caused the people to have their first real argument? (Ideas: *The group disagreed about whether they should remain on the island or move.*)

> "That's not fair to me," the woman replied.
>
> Bruce said, "Well, it's not fair to us if you break your agreements."
>
> The woman walked away and acted angry for many days. She did her job, but she was pretty dissatisfied and grouchy about it. ❻

6. (Award points quickly.)
7. (If the group makes more than 12 errors, repeat the reading immediately or on the next day.)

FLUENCY ASSESSMENT

EXERCISE 8

TIMED READING CHECKOUTS

1. (For this part of the lesson, assigned pairs of students work together during the checkouts.)
- (If one student does not have a checkout partner, arrange another time when you can give the checkout.)
2. (Each student does a 2-minute timed reading. Students earn 5 points by reading at least 240 words and making no more than 5 errors on the first part of story 41. Students record points in Box C of their Point Chart and plot their reading rate and errors on the Individual Reading Progress Chart.)
- (During each timed checkout, observe one pair of students for 2 minutes. Make notes on any mistakes the reader makes.)

3. (Record the timed reading checkout performance for each student you observed on the Fluency Assessment Summary form.)

WORKBOOK EXERCISES

Independent Student Work

Task A

- Open your Workbook to Lesson 41. ✓
- Complete all the parts of your Workbook lesson using a pencil. If you make no errors, you will earn 5 points.

Task B

1. (Before presenting Lesson 42, check student Workbooks for Lesson 41.)
   - (Call on individual students to read the items and answers in each part. Students mark errors using a pen.)
2. (Direct the students to count the number of errors and write the number in the Errors box at the top of the Workbook page.)
3. (Award points and direct students to record points in Box D of their Point Chart.)

0 errors................................5 points
1 error ....3 points
2 or 3 errors ....1 point
more than 3 errors ....0 points

END OF LESSON 41

Lesson 41

Errors

1

1. What was the first argument about? (whether the group should remain on the island or move)
2. Why didn't Bruce have a lot of faith in planting seeds? (He thought most of the seeds wouldn't grow after the cold winter; it would take too long for the plants that did grow to have fruit.)
3. The people were in a deadlock. What does "deadlock" mean? (The same number of people are on each side of an argument.)
4. Circle the numbers that could lead to a deadlock.
   (4) 5 (6) 7 (8) 9 (10) 11 (12) 13 (14) 15 (16)
5. Why didn't some people want Centa to have two votes? (They knew they would have to stay and grow crops.)
6. What was the rule about the stone? (They would build the boat if the stone landed so that the X was showing.)
7. Whose side won? (Centa's)
8. What was the first law made on the island? (a law about how the group made decisions)

70 *Lesson 41* Copyright © SRA/McGraw-Hill. All rights reserved.

Lesson 41

9. What was the rule about individuals doing what they wanted? (Individuals could not do what they wanted if it hurt the group.)
10. Would it have been all right for individuals to change the agreement if more than half the people decided not to follow it? Yes.

2 **Fill in each blank using a word in the box.**

decision	solution	examine
husks	verses	argument

1. After the argument, Toshi made a decision to move to California.
2. They found a solution to their problem.
3. Sam lost the argument with Cindy.

3 **Write the parts for each word.**

1. explained = ex + plain + ed
2. distracted = dis + tract + ed
3. extend = ex + tend
4. remounted = re + mount + ed

Copyright © SRA/McGraw-Hill. All rights reserved. *Lesson 41* 71

Lesson 42

WORD-ATTACK SKILLS

Student Book 

EXERCISE 1

AFFIX REVIEW

Task A

1. Open your Student Book to Lesson 42. ✓

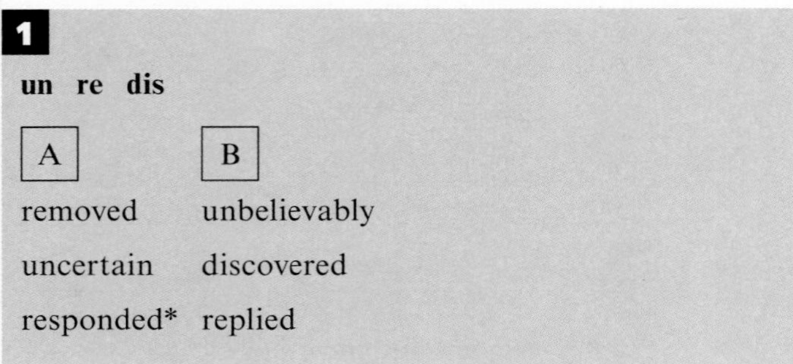

1

un re dis

A	B
removed	unbelievably
uncertain	discovered
responded*	replied

- Touch the first row in part 1. ✓
- Let's see if you remember a meaning for each of those affixes.

2. Touch the letters **U–N.** ✓
- What's one meaning of **un?** (Signal.) *Not.*

3. Touch the letters **R–E.** ✓
- What's one meaning of **re?** (Signal.) *Again.*

4. Touch the letters **D–I–S.** ✓
- What's one meaning of **dis?** (Call on a student. Accept **not, the opposite of,** or **away from.**)
- What's another meaning of **dis?** (Call on another student.)

5. What does **responded** mean? (Call on a student.)

Task B

1. Touch the first word in column A. ✓
- What word? (Signal.) *Removed.*

2. Touch the next word. ✓
- What word? (Signal.) *Uncertain.*

3. (Repeat step 2 for **responded.**)
4. (Repeat the list until firm.)
5. (Repeat steps 1–4 for the words in column B.)

EXERCISE 2

WORD PRACTICE

1. Touch the first word in part 2. ✓

2

excellent surface* thorns

pressure enforce* peacefully

shaped solution* decision* advice*

- What's the underlined part? (Signal.) *ex.*
- What word? (Signal.) *Excellent.*

2. Touch the next word. ✓
- What's the underlined part? (Signal.) *er.*
- What word? (Signal.) *Surface.*

3. (Repeat step 2 for each remaining word.)
4. (Repeat each row of words until firm.)
5. What does **surface** mean? (Call on a student.)
- (Repeat for each starred word.)

EXERCISE 3

VOCABULARY

1. Touch part 3. ✓

3

1. prevented
2. barge
3. minnows
4. evaporate
5. remarked

- We're going to talk about what those words mean.

2. Touch word 1. ✓
- What word? (Signal.) *Prevented.*
- If you **kept something from happening,** you **prevented** it. Everybody, what's another way of saying "She kept a forest fire from happening"? (Signal.) *She prevented a forest fire.*

3. Touch word 2. ✓
- What word? (Signal.) *Barge.*
- A **barge** is **a long, flat-bottomed boat used for carrying things.** Everybody, what is a **barge?** (Signal.) *A long, flat-bottomed boat used for carrying things.*

4. Touch word 3. ✓
- What word? (Signal.) *Minnows.*
- What are **minnows?** (Call on a student.) (Idea: *Small fish frequently used for bait.*)

5. Everybody, touch word 4. ✓
- What word? (Signal.) *Evaporate.*
- When water is heated and goes into the air, it **evaporates.** What happens to water when it is heated and goes into the air? (Signal.) *It evaporates.*

6. Touch word 5. ✓
- What word? (Signal.) *Remarked.*
- **Remarked** means **commented.** Everybody, what's another way of saying "'What a fine day it is,' she **commented**"? (Signal.) *"What a fine day it is," she remarked.*

EXERCISE 4

WORD PRACTICE

1. Touch the first word in part 4. ✓

4

patches paddles smoldering exceptionally
hundred tiller* occasionally narrow
quite cove quiet prevented quit
signaled caught argued piece obviously
stretch attached constructing hooked smiling

- What word? (Signal.) *Patches.*

2. Next word. ✓
- What word? (Signal.) *Paddles.*

3. (Repeat step 2 for each remaining word.)
4. (Repeat each row of words until firm.)
5. What does **tiller** mean? (Call on a student.)

EXERCISE 5

WORD-ATTACK SKILLS: Individual tests

1. (Call on individual students. Each student reads a row or column. Tally the rows and columns read without error. If the group reads at least 9 rows and columns without making errors, direct all students to record 5 points in Box A of their Point Chart. Criterion is 80 percent of rows and columns read without error.)
2. (If the group did not read at least 9 rows and columns without errors, do not award any points for the Word-Attack Skills exercises.)

SELECTION READING

EXERCISE 6

STORY READING

1. Everybody, touch part 5. ✓
2. The error limit for this story is 12. If the group reads the story with 12 errors or less, you earn 5 points.

5 **Visitors**

3. (Call on a student to read the title.) *Visitors.*
- What do you think this story is about? (Accept reasonable responses.)

4. (Call on individual students. Each is to read two to four sentences.)
5. (Call on individual students to answer the specified questions during the story reading.)

As the days got hotter, Bruce and the others planted seeds. First they had to make new tools for plowing up the land. Then they planted the seeds they had found during the winter. After the seeds had been planted, the people waited. Some plants came up, but unfortunately they had bitter stems and bitter roots. Everybody agreed that there would not be a good food crop. The grass on the island grew in little patches; however, these patches were far apart. Between them was bare ground. There were a few bitter plants growing among the dead trees, but there weren't many of them. There were some other plants that grew exceptionally slowly. ①

1. Name three things that went wrong with the plants. (Ideas: *Only some of them came up; the grass grew in patches that were far apart; the plants that did grow were bitter; the plants grew slowly.*)

Then one day one man came running to the shelter. He yelled, "A boat! There's a boat coming to the island!" Bruce and the others ran down to the beach. The boat was over thirty feet long and very narrow. The people on the island jumped into the water and swam out to meet the boat. The people in the boat were smiling and waving their paddles.

When the boat was on the beach and everybody had greeted the people in the boat, a woman from the boat said, "We have come to look for fish—we have no fish near our island." ❷

2. Why had the people in the boat come to the island? (Idea: *To look for fish.*)

"We have lots of fish," Centa said.

The woman said, "We will give you gold for your fish."

Bruce said, "We don't have any need for gold. Do you have anything that we need?"

"All we have with us is a boat full of bananas. That is the only thing that grows on our island."

Bruce and the others smiled.

"Bananas?" Bruce asked. "We will trade for bananas. We will give you one fish for every five bananas." ❸

3. Why didn't Bruce want to take gold for the fish? (Idea: *Because the group had no need for gold.*)
3. Why do you think Bruce wanted five bananas for each fish? (Idea: *Because fish are harder to get than bananas.*)

"That is fair," the woman said as she started to count out five hundred bananas. Bruce counted out one hundred fish, and the trade was made.

When the visitors left the island, they said they would come back within two weeks with at least two thousand bananas. After the boat left, Centa said, "We must start catching fish. We will need four hundred fish for the trade."

"We will need a place to keep those fish alive," Bruce remarked. "If we kill them, they will all be rotten by the time two weeks have passed." That made sense to the others.

Centa said, "I discovered a narrow cove on the north end of the island that will make an excellent sea cage." ❹

4. Why did they decide to keep the fish alive? (Idea: *Because if they killed the fish, the fish would rot before they could be traded.*)

The little cove was shaped like the letter U. "This cove is perfect," Bruce said. "If we stretch a net across the mouth of the cove, the fish will be prevented from swimming away."

After fixing the sea cage, the people began constructing more nets. They made nets for catching small fish that would be used as bait for large fish. The people made fishhooks from the thorns that they removed from dead bushes. They attached minnows to the thorns, and they attached the thorns to a line. A piece of wood attached to the line worked like a bobber; when it went underwater, it signaled that a fish had been hooked. ❺

5. How did the people catch small fish? (Idea: *They made nets.*)
5. What did they do with the small fish? (Idea: *Used them as bait to catch big fish.*)

The people continued to fish night and day; however, after one week had passed, the group had caught only sixty-five fish. Bruce announced, "We've got to figure out how to catch fish at a faster rate. And I think I have an idea. The fish are not near the shore; therefore, they must be out in deep water. We've obviously got to go out and get them."

"How are we going to do that?" one woman asked.

"We'll build a little fishing barge," Bruce replied. "We'll make the barge big enough for two people who will go out and catch fish. They'll store the fish on the barge and return when the barge is loaded with fish." ❻

6. How many fish did they need within two weeks? *Four hundred.*
6. How many did they have at the end of one week? *Sixty-five.*
6. What was the plan for catching more fish? (Idea: *To build a barge so that people could go fishing in deeper water.*)

Two people began to argue. One woman thought that it was a good idea to build a barge. But one man said, "There are more of us than there are of them. When those people come with the bananas, we'll take what we want."

Centa responded, "The people won't want to trade with us after we do that."

Bruce said, "Let's take a vote. And let's give Centa two votes so that we don't have a deadlock." ❼

7. What were the people arguing about now? (Idea: *Whether to catch enough fish for the trade or take the bananas by force.*)
7. Why wouldn't it be a good idea to take what they wanted? (Idea: *Because then the others would not want to trade with them anymore.*)
7. How did giving Centa two votes avoid a deadlock? (Idea: *By making an uneven number of votes.*)

Everybody agreed, and they voted. There were more votes for building the barge. That afternoon they chopped down trees, gathered vines, and tied the tree trunks together with the vines. They worked all night. Occasionally some people would rest for three hours while the other people worked. Then they would switch; those who had been resting would work while the others rested.

6. (Award points quickly.)
7. (If the group makes more than 12 errors, repeat the reading immediately or on the next day.)

FLUENCY ASSESSMENT

EXERCISE 7

TIMED READING CHECKOUTS

1. (For this part of the lesson, assigned pairs of students work together during the checkouts.)
   - (If one student does not have a checkout partner, arrange another time when you can give the checkout.)
2. (Each student does a 2-minute timed reading. Students earn 5 points by reading at least 240 words and making no more than 5 errors on the first part of story 42. Students record points in Box C of their Point Chart and plot their reading rate and errors on the Individual Reading Progress Chart.)
   - (During each timed checkout, observe one pair of students for 2 minutes. Make notes on any mistakes the reader makes.)
3. (Record the timed reading checkout performance for each student you observed on the Fluency Assessment Summary form.)

Lesson 42

WORKBOOK EXERCISES

Lesson 42

Errors

1

1. How much gold did Bruce and the others want for the fish they had? (None.)
2. What did Bruce and the others pay for every five bananas? (one fish)
3. Why did they want to trade for bananas?
   (They didn't have any bananas.)
4. How much would a boatful of bananas have been worth if Bruce's island had had lots of healthy banana trees? (not much)
5. Can you make up a rule about how much things are worth? Think about what makes the price of bananas go up and down. (Things are worth more when they are scarce. Things are worth less when they are plentiful.)
6. To be able to trade four hundred fish for two thousand bananas, the people had to solve some problems. List two problems. (Any two: They needed to catch lots of fish in a short time; they needed a place to keep fish alive; they had to keep the fish from swimming away.)
7. How did the people try to solve the two problems you listed in item 6?
   (They made nets for catching bait; they made fishhooks; they fished all day and all night; they made a sea cage to prevent the fish from swimming away; they built a fishing barge.)
8. How did the people avoid a deadlock on whether they should build a barge?
   (They gave Centa two votes.)

72 Lesson 42 Copyright © SRA/McGraw-Hill. All rights reserved.

Lesson 42

9. a. Do you think this is a fair way to get out of a deadlock? (Yes or no.)
   b. Why? (Accept reasonable responses.)
10. Why did the people need to build a barge?
    to catch the fish in deeper water and store them

2 **Fill in each blank using a word in the box.**

enforces	barge	suitable
prevent	deadlocked	solution

1. The teacher enforces the rules.
2. He held on to his dog to prevent it from running away.
3. The barge carried garbage down the river.

3 **Copy the sentence that tells the main idea of the story.**

1. The people decided to trade fish with people from an island that had lots of bananas.
2. The people on the island were not successful at raising crops.
3. The people decided not to steal the bananas from the people who came to their island.
4. One of the people on the island got two votes so there would not be a deadlock.

The people decided to trade fish with people from an island that had lots of bananas.

Copyright © SRA/McGraw-Hill. All rights reserved. Lesson 42 73

Independent Student Work

Task A

- Open your Workbook to Lesson 42. ✓
- Complete all the parts of your Workbook lesson using a pencil. If you make no errors, you will earn 5 points.

Task B

1. (Before presenting Lesson 43, check student Workbooks for Lesson 42.)
- (Call on individual students to read the items and answers in each part. Students mark errors using a pen.)
2. (Direct the students to count the number of errors and write the number in the Errors box at the top of the Workbook page.)
3. (Award points and direct students to record points in Box D of their Point Chart.)

0 errors..................................5 points
1 error ....3 points
2 or 3 errors ....1 point
more than 3 errors ....0 points

END OF LESSON 42

WORD-ATTACK SKILLS

Board Work

EXERCISE 1

BUILDUP

1. (Print on the board:)

she

2. (Point to **she.** Pause.) What word? (Signal.) *She.*
3. (Change the word to:)

shed

- What word now? (Signal.) *Shed.*

4. (Change the word to:)

shad

- What word now? (Signal.) *Shad.*

5. (Change the word to:)

shade

- What word now? (Signal.) *Shade.*

6. (Change the word to:)

shaded

- What word now? (Signal.) *Shaded.*

7. (Change to the original word:)

she

- (Repeat steps 2–6 until firm.)

Student Book 

EXERCISE 2

BUILDUP

1. Open your Student Book to Lesson 43. ✓

1

thought
through
tough
enough
ought
brought

- Touch the first word in part 1. ✓
- What word? (Signal.) *Thought.*

2. Next word? ✓

- What word? (Signal.) *Through.*

3. (Repeat step 2 for each remaining word.)
4. (Repeat steps 1–3 until firm.)

EXERCISE 3

WORD PRACTICE

1. Touch the first word in part 2. ✓

2

steering returning tiller* regain
probably* displeased unlikely balanced

- What's the underlined part? (Signal.) *ēēē.*
- What word? (Signal.) *Steering.*

2. Touch the next word. ✓

- What's the underlined part? (Signal.) *re.*
- What word? (Signal.) *Returning.*

3. (Repeat step 2 for each remaining word.)
4. (Repeat each row of words until firm.)
5. What does **tiller** mean? (Call on a student.)

- (Repeat for **probably.**)

EXERCISE 4

VOCABULARY

1. Touch part 3. ✓

3

1. shad
2. bargain

- We're going to talk about what those words mean.

2. Touch word 1. ✓
- What word? (Signal.) *Shad.*
- A **shad** is a type of fish. Everybody, what is a **shad?** (Signal.) *A type of fish.*

3. Touch word 2. ✓
- What word? (Signal.) *Bargain.*
- When you **try to buy something at a reduced price,** you **bargain** for it. Everybody, what's another way of saying "Bruce tried to buy smoked fish at a reduced price"? (Signal.) *Bruce bargained for smoked fish.*

EXERCISE 5

WORD PRACTICE

1. Touch the first word in part 4. ✓

4

floated fortunately unfair
remarked* evaporate* smolder*
finally smiling handfuls
spotted cheat branches
pointed argument* weigh weighs
weighed weight attractive

- What word? (Signal.) *Floated.*

2. Next word. ✓
- What word? (Signal.) *Fortunately.*

3. (Repeat step 2 for each remaining word.)
4. (Repeat each row of words until firm.)
5. What does **remarked** mean? (Call on a student.)
- (Repeat for each starred word.)

EXERCISE 6

WORD-ATTACK SKILLS: Individual tests

1. (Call on individual students. Each student reads a row or column. Tally the rows and columns read without error. If the group reads at least 8 rows and columns without making errors, direct all students to record 5 points in Box A of their Point Chart. Criterion is 80 percent of rows and columns read without error.)
2. (If the group did not read at least 8 rows and columns without errors, do not award any points for the Word-Attack Skills exercises.)

SELECTION READING

EXERCISE 7

STORY READING

1. Everybody, touch part 5. ✓
2. The error limit for this story is 12. If the group reads the story with 12 errors or less, you earn 5 points.

5 A Smart Trade

3. (Call on a student to read the title.) *A Smart Trade.*
- What do you think this story is about? (Accept reasonable responses.)

4. (Call on individual students. Each is to read two to four sentences.)
5. (Call on individual students to answer the specified questions during the story reading.)

By noon the next day, they had completed the barge. It wasn't a very attractive barge, but it floated. The bottom of the barge was made up of seven logs tied together. Each log was about twenty-five feet long. In the back of the barge was a tiller for steering. There was a small sail made of grass and vines and bark. And in the middle of the barge was a large box. The box was about twelve feet long, six feet wide, and three feet high. It would hold many, many fish. ❶

1. Describe at least four things about the barge. **(Ideas:** ***It wasn't very attractive; it had a tiller for steering; it had a small sail; it had a large box for holding fish; it was made up of logs.*****)**

Bruce and a man named Jonas went out on the barge with nets and fishing lines. They planned to be gone for as long as a week, returning in time to trade for bananas.

Fortunately, the barge didn't have to go far before the men spotted schools of fish. Most of the fish were more than three feet long. Jonas threw handfuls of small minnows into the water. Just then Bruce had a fish on his line. It pulled so hard that it began to move the barge. "Drop your bait and help me with this fish," Bruce yelled. Jonas pulled in his line and grabbed onto Bruce's line. Finally, the contest was over, and the men had a fish that was ten feet long. It probably weighed more than two hundred pounds. ❷

2. What is a school of fish? **(Idea:** ***A group of fish.*****)**
2. How much did the large fish weigh? ***More than two hundred pounds.***

It was not a shad; it was a big, blue tuna fish.

That was the first tuna fish the men caught, but not the last one. Before the sun went down they had thirty shad and twelve tunas. Most of the tunas were six feet long; however, one was even larger than the first one they had caught.

Finally, the barge box was filled with tuna fish, but Jonas and Bruce did not have hundreds and hundreds of fish. They had only forty-two fish.

Jonas remarked, "We made a deal with the woman to trade one fish for five bananas. But most of these fish must be worth one hundred bananas each. Some of them must be worth five hundred bananas." ❸

3. What kinds of fish did they catch? ***Shad and tuna.***
3. How many fish did they catch? ***Forty-two.***
3. About how many fish did they need in all? ***Four hundred.***
3. Why did Jonas feel some of the fish should be worth more bananas? **(Idea:** ***Because some of the fish were very big.*****)**

A week later the woman and her friends returned to the island. They came in three boats; each boat was loaded with bananas. When Bruce and Centa met them on the shore, Bruce was holding a pan full of minnows. Also in the pan was a fish that was about twelve inches long. This was the size of fish the woman had traded for when she came to the island before.

After Bruce and Centa greeted the woman and the others, Bruce held up the fish that was twelve inches long. ❹

4. How long was the fish Bruce held up? ***Twelve inches.***

Bruce said, "Do you remember what we said we would trade for?"

"Yes," the woman said. "We said that we would give you five bananas for every fish."

"Good," Bruce said. "This fish is worth five bananas. Is that right?"

"Yes," the woman said. She was smiling.

Bruce held up one of the minnows. "And this fish is worth five bananas," he said.

The woman stopped smiling. "Are you trying to cheat us?" she said. "That fish is not even a fish. I won't give you five bananas for that little thing."

"You are right," Bruce said. "We must be fair." Bruce walked over to a scale that he had made from two branches. The branches formed a T. Bruce placed the first fish on one end of the T. Then he placed a rock on the other end, and the scale balanced. Bruce picked up the rock and said, "Why don't we call the weight of this rock one fish?" ❺

5. Why didn't the woman want to give five bananas for a minnow? (Idea: *Because the minnow was so small.*)
5. Why did Bruce pretend that he thought a minnow was worth five bananas? (Ideas: *To show the woman that the size of the fish is very important in making a trade; to show her that they needed to agree on what "one fish" meant.*)
5. What rule did Bruce make up for what they would call "a fish"? (Idea: *They would use the weight of a certain rock to measure the weight of "one fish."*)

"That is fair," the woman said. "So you would have to place many of those tiny fish on the scale to balance the weight of the rock."

"That is right," Bruce said. Then he signaled the others to bring out the largest of the fish from their sea cage. Bruce pointed to the big tuna. He said, "This fish weighs as much as seven hundred of these rocks. So we have to treat this fish as if it were seven hundred fish."

At first the woman looked displeased. Then she smiled and said, "That is fair, and that is a lovely fish."

6. (Award points quickly.)
7. (If the group makes more than 12 errors, repeat the reading immediately or on the next day.)

FLUENCY ASSESSMENT

EXERCISE 8

TIMED READING CHECKOUTS

1. (For this part of the lesson, assigned pairs of students work together during the checkouts.)
   - (If one student does not have a checkout partner, arrange another time when you can give the checkout.)
2. (Each student does a 2-minute timed reading. Students earn 5 points by reading at least 240 words and making no more than 5 errors on the first part of story 43. Students record points in Box C of their Point Chart and plot their reading rate and errors on the Individual Reading Progress Chart.)
   - (During each timed checkout, observe one pair of students for 2 minutes. Make notes on any mistakes the reader makes.)
3. (Record the timed reading checkout performance for each student you observed on the Fluency Assessment Summary form.)

WORKBOOK EXERCISES

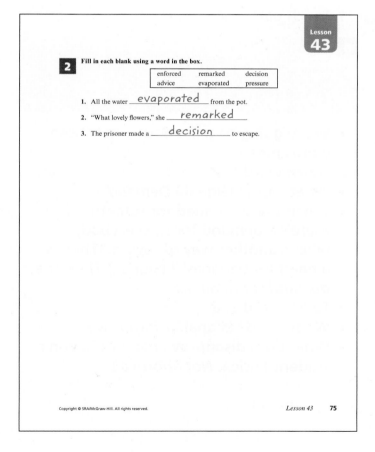

Lesson 43

Errors

1

1. Tell at least three things about the barge. (Any three: it wasn't attractive; it floated; the bottom was made of seven logs; the back had a tiller; there was a small sail; the middle had a box)
2. What is a school of fish? (a group of fish)
3. What did Bruce and Jonas use for bait? minnows
4. What kinds of fish did they catch? shad and tuna
5. How many fish did Bruce and Jonas catch? forty-two
6. Bruce and Jonas caught a large, blue tuna fish. How much did it weigh? two hundred pounds
7. At what point did Jonas realize that some fish should be worth more than five bananas? (when he looked at the size of the fish)
8. How much were most of the fish worth? (one hundred bananas each)
9. If Bruce hadn't shown the woman the minnows, how much would she have said the big fish was worth? (five bananas)
10. Bruce made up a rule about what was worth five bananas. What rule did he make up? (The weight of the rock was worth one fish.)
11. Was the woman displeased about the deal? No.

74 *Lesson 43* Copyright © SRA/McGraw-Hill. All rights reserved.

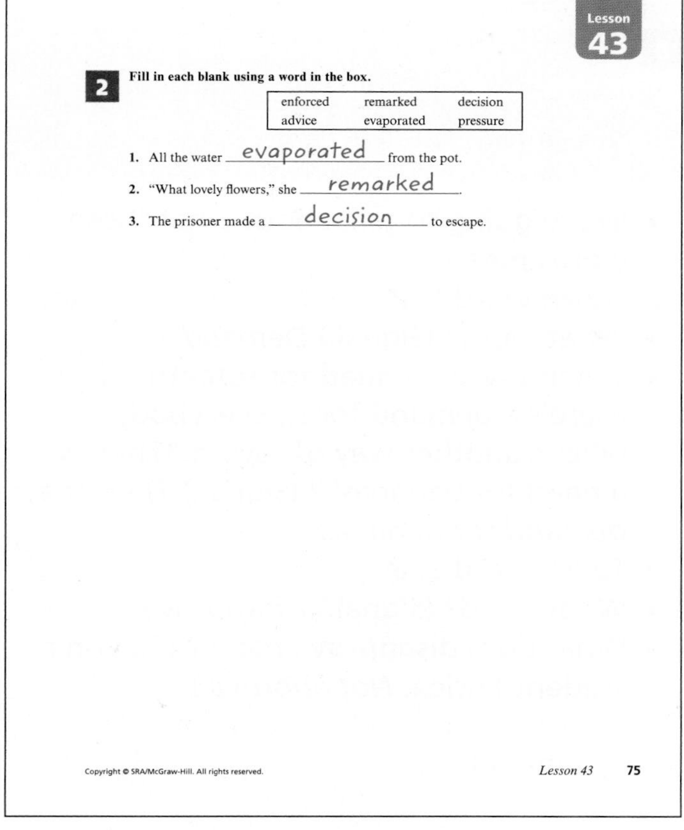

Lesson 43

2 Fill in each blank using a word in the box.

enforced	remarked	decision
advice	evaporated	pressure

1. All the water evaporated from the pot.
2. "What lovely flowers," she remarked
3. The prisoner made a decision to escape.

Copyright © SRA/McGraw-Hill. All rights reserved. *Lesson 43* 75

Independent Student Work

Task A

- Open your Workbook to Lesson 43. ✓
- Complete all the parts of your Workbook lesson using a pencil. If you make no errors, you will earn 5 points.

Task B

1. (Before presenting Lesson 44, check student Workbooks for Lesson 43.)
   - (Call on individual students to read the items and answers in each part. Students mark errors using a pen.)
2. (Direct the students to count the number of errors and write the number in the Errors box at the top of the Workbook page.)
3. (Award points and direct students to record points in Box D of their Point Chart.)

0 errors.................................5 points
1 error ....3 points
2 or 3 errors ....1 point
more than 3 errors ....0 points

END OF LESSON 43

WORD-ATTACK SKILLS

Student Book 

EXERCISE 1

AFFIX REVIEW

Task A

1. Open your Student Book to Lesson 44. ✓

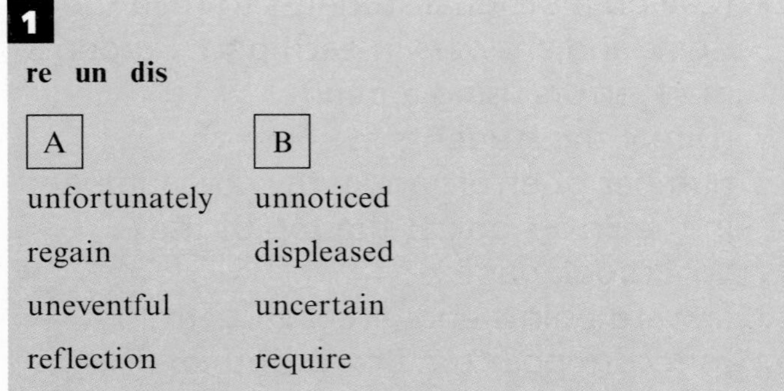

1

re un dis

A	B
unfortunately	unnoticed
regain	displeased
uneventful	uncertain
reflection	require

- Touch the first row in part 1. ✓
- Let's see if you remember a meaning for each of those affixes.

2. Touch the letters **R–E.** ✓
- What's one meaning of **re?** (Signal.) *Again.*

3. Touch the letters **U–N.** ✓
- What's one meaning of **un?** (Signal.) *Not.*

4. Touch the letters **D–I–S.** ✓
- What's one meaning of **dis?** (Call on a student. Accept **not, the opposite of,** or **away from.**)
- What's another meaning of **dis?** (Call on another student.)

Task B

1. Touch the first word in column A. ✓
- What word? (Signal.) *Unfortunately.*

2. Touch the next word. ✓
- What word? (Signal.) *Regain.*

3. (Repeat step 2 for each remaining word.)
4. (Repeat the list until firm.)
5. (Repeat steps 1–4 for the words in column B.)

EXERCISE 2

WORD PRACTICE

1. Touch the first word in part 2. ✓

2

spoil shade amount occasionally

cleaning particularly probably* several*

certainly salted furthermore barges*

- What's the underlined part? (Signal.) *oy.*
- What word? (Signal.) *Spoil.*

2. Touch the next word. ✓
- What's the underlined part? (Signal.) *shshsh.*
- What word? (Signal.) *Shade.*

3. (Repeat step 2 for each remaining word.)
4. (Repeat each row of words until firm.)
5. What does **probably** mean? (Call on a student.)
- (Repeat for **several, barges.**)

EXERCISE 3

VOCABULARY

1. Touch part 3. ✓

3

1. demand
2. disapprove

- We're going to talk about what those words mean.

2. Touch word 1. ✓
- What word? (Signal.) *Demand.*
- When there's a **need** for something, there's a **demand** for it. Everybody, what's another way of saying "There's a **need** for bananas"? (Signal.) *There's a demand for bananas.*

3. Touch word 2. ✓
- What word? (Signal.) *Disapprove.*
- What does **disapprove** mean? (Call on a student.) (Idea: *Not approve.*)

EXERCISE 4

WORD PRACTICE

1. Touch the first word in part 4. ✓

4

shore excellent announced* smolder*
frowned trouble evaporating firewood
demand* fresh stacked pieces bargain*
shad* price severe* simple similar

- What word? (Signal.) *Shore.*

2. Next word. ✓

- What word? (Signal.) *Excellent.*

3. (Repeat step 2 for each remaining word.)
4. (Repeat each row of words until firm.)
5. What does **announced** mean? (Call on a student.)

- (Repeat for each starred word.)

EXERCISE 5

WORD-ATTACK SKILLS: Individual tests

1. (Call on individual students. Each student reads a row or column. Tally the rows and columns read without error. If the group reads at least 8 rows and columns without making errors, direct all students to record 5 points in Box A of their Point Chart. Criterion is 80 percent of rows and columns read without error.)
2. (If the group did not read at least 8 rows and columns without errors, do not award any points for the Word-Attack Skills exercises.)

SELECTION READING

EXERCISE 6

STORY READING

1. Everybody, touch part 5. ✓
2. The error limit for this story is 12. If the group reads the story with 12 errors or less, you earn 5 points.

5 **Another Sharp Trade**

3. (Call on a student to read the title.) *Another Sharp Trade.*

- What do you think this story is about? (Accept reasonable responses.)

4. (Call on individual students. Each is to read two to four sentences.)
5. (Call on individual students to answer the specified questions during the story reading.)

Bruce and the woman decided to trade again. After the three boats left, Centa said, "We should go out for the tuna and shad again. The fish may move away from here, and we won't be able to trade for bananas."

Bruce agreed. Before two people could leave on the fishing trip, everybody helped build a shed for storing the dead fish. They called it the shad shed. One woman said, "We built the shad shed in the shade so that the tuna would not spoil." ❶

1. Why did Bruce and Centa want to do a lot of fishing before the end of the summer? (Idea: *Because the fish might move away from the area.*)
1. What did they build for storing fish? *A shed.*

Jonas and another man went out in the barge for two days. When they returned, they had fifty fish on the barge. Everybody spent most of the day cleaning the fish, removing bones and the insides, and feeding the insides to the pigs and the wild dogs. The people stacked the fish in the shad shed and made a hot fire in the shed. When the fire was blazing hot, they threw wet grass on the fire so that the fire would smolder and produce a great amount of smoke. After smoking the fish for more than twenty-four hours, they rubbed salt all over the fish. They got the salt by evaporating seawater. They smoked the fish again, this time for over a week. The smoke and the salt kept the bugs away from the fish. ❷

2. Why did the people smoke and salt the fish? (Ideas: *To keep bugs away from the fish; to preserve the fish.*)
2. How did they get the salt? (Idea: *By evaporating the seawater.*)

Several days before the boats were to return to the island with bananas, some of the people complained. An old woman said, "We put a lot of work in on this batch of fish. We had to clean them and store them. Then we had to salt them and smoke them so that they would keep. Yet we agreed to trade for the same price we traded for before. That's unfair to us."

Bruce replied, "That's an excellent point. I have a plan, and for this plan we need small shore fish." ❸

3. Why should the price of smoked fish be higher than the price of fresh fish? (Idea: *Because it takes a lot more work to make smoked fish.*)
3. Make up a rule about the amount of work that goes into something and the price of that thing. (Idea: *Something is worth more when it takes more work and worth less when it takes less work.*)

A week later Bruce and Jonas met the boats from the other island. Centa and the others were sitting in the shade near the shad shed eating smoked fish. Next to Bruce were the small shore fish, which were rotting and smelled particularly bad. They were covered with flies and other bugs.

After the boats were on the shore, Bruce announced, "We're ready to trade."

The woman looked at the fish next to Bruce and said, "Those fish are rotten. We certainly won't trade for them."

Jonas said, "Well, the only other fish we have are smoked fish, and I don't think it would be fair to trade those at the fresh fish price." ❹

4. Why did Bruce present the woman with the rotten fish first? (Idea: *So that she would see that smoked fish was better for trading.*)

The woman was displeased and frowned. Bruce called for Centa to bring over some pieces of smoked fish. Centa passed these pieces to the people who had come to trade. "This tastes unusually good," the woman said.

"Yes," Centa said. "And since they are smoked, you certainly don't have to worry about them rotting. They will keep."

The woman frowned again and said, "Yes, some of the fish in the last batch began to rot before we could eat them. However, we wouldn't have that trouble with these fish."

Bruce said, "Do you think it would be fair to trade one smoked fish for nine bananas?" 5

5. Bruce didn't really believe that the smoked fish were worth nine bananas each. Why do you think he set the price at nine bananas? (Idea: *He started higher so that when the woman asked for a lower price, it would still be a good price for Bruce.*)
5. Why are smoked fish better for trading than fresh fish? (Idea: *Because they will keep longer than fresh fish.*)
5. Why is the price higher? (Idea: *Because more work goes into smoked fish than fresh fish.*)

"No, I disapprove," the woman said. "One fish for six bananas."

Centa laughed. "That's not fair," she said.

Centa, Bruce, and the woman bargained for a long time. At last they agreed that one fish for seven and a half bananas was a fair price.

Things were going particularly well on the island. Trading boats came to the island every month during the summer. By the end of the summer there were plenty of bananas for the winter. Life was almost uneventful. 6

6. How would you describe life that's almost uneventful? (Ideas: *Nothing exciting happens; life is easy to predict.*)
6. What's another way of saying "particularly well"? (Ideas: *Unusually well; remarkably well.*)

Centa, Bruce, and Jonas had caught enough fish to last for a long time. These fish were smoked and salted and hung in the shed. Furthermore, during the summer the women and men had found other animals. Now the people on the island had more than fifty animals. Also they had cut down many dead trees, and there was lots of firewood for the winter.

Occasionally, Bruce would think about what had happened. The people on his island could catch fish. There was a demand for fish on the woman's island. The people on her island had lots of bananas. There was a demand for bananas on Bruce's island, so the people traded. The people on Bruce's island got bananas, and the people on the other island got fish. Bruce said to himself, "The price of things goes up when there is a demand for those things. If somebody needs fish, the price goes up. If they have plenty of fish, the price goes down." 7

7. How does the demand for something affect the price? (Idea: *The price of something goes up when there is a demand for it.*)
7. What was there a demand for on Bruce's island? *Bananas.*
6. (Award points quickly.)
7. (If the group makes more than 12 errors, repeat the reading immediately or on the next day.)

FLUENCY ASSESSMENT

EXERCISE 7

TIMED READING CHECKOUTS

1. (For this part of the lesson, assigned pairs of students work together during the checkouts.)
- (If one student does not have a checkout partner, arrange another time when you can give the checkout.)
2. (Each student does a 2-minute timed reading. Students earn 5 points by reading at least 240 words and making no more than 5 errors on the first part of story 44. Students record points in Box C of their Point Chart and plot their reading rate and errors on the Individual Reading Progress Chart.)
- (During each timed checkout, observe one pair of students for 2 minutes. Make notes on any mistakes the reader makes.)
3. (Record the timed reading checkout performance for each student you observed on the Fluency Assessment Summary form.)

Lesson 44

Errors

1

1. Name three things that the people on the island had to do to prepare smoked fish.
(Any three: clean them; remove the bones and the insides; stack them in the shed; make a hot fire; throw wet grass on the fire; rub salt on fish; evaporate seawater)
2. Why did the people go to the trouble of making smoked fish?
(Smoked fish doesn't spoil as fast as fresh fish.)
3. What would happen to the price of fish if fish jumped out of the water and onto the beach?
(The price would go down.)
4. What would happen to the price of fish if the people had to work five hours to catch each fish? (The price would go up.)
5. Make up a rule about the price of fish and the amount of work it takes to catch fish.
(The price of fish goes up when it takes more work to catch them. The price of fish goes down when it takes less work to catch them.)
6. What did Bruce and Centa do to get the woman to trade for smoked fish?
(They started to trade rotten fish.)
7. Bruce didn't really believe that the smoked fish were worth nine bananas each. Why did he set the price at nine bananas when he began bargaining with the woman?
(so that he and the woman could meet each other halfway)

76 *Lesson 44* Copyright © SRA/McGraw-Hill. All rights reserved.

Lesson 44

8. What did Bruce and the woman agree would be a fair price for smoked fish?
$7\frac{1}{2}$ bananas
9. Why would the price of smoked fish be higher than the price of fresh fish?
(Smoked fish take more work.)
10. What do you think would have happened if the woman had not liked the taste of smoked fish?
(She might not have thought a smoked fish was worth $7\frac{1}{2}$ bananas.)
11. Why wasn't there a demand for fish on Bruce's island?
(There were lots of fish there.)
12. Why was there a demand for bananas on Bruce's island?
(Bananas were scarce on the island.)
13. If the demand for something goes up, what will the price do? (go up)

2 **Fill in each blank using a word in the box.**

demand	prevented	minnows
barge	disapproved	remarked

1. There was a much greater demand for ice during the summer.
2. He disapproved of violence.
3. Abby prevented a forest fire by putting out her camp fire.

3 **Write the parts for each word.**

1. disappear = dis + appear
2. unscratched = un + scratch + ed

Copyright © SRA/McGraw-Hill. All rights reserved. *Lesson 44* 77

WORKBOOK EXERCISES

Independent Student Work

Task A

- Open your Workbook to Lesson 44. ✓
- Complete all the parts of your Workbook lesson using a pencil. If you make no errors, you will earn 5 points.

Task B

1. (Before presenting Lesson 45, check student Workbooks for Lesson 44.)
   - (Call on individual students to read the items and answers in each part. Students mark errors using a pen.)
2. (Direct the students to count the number of errors and write the number in the Errors box at the top of the Workbook page.)
3. (Award points and direct students to record points in Box D of their Point Chart.)

0 errors................................5 points
1 error ....3 points
2 or 3 errors ....1 point
more than 3 errors ....0 points

END OF LESSON 44

Lesson 45

WORD-ATTACK SKILLS

Student Book

EXERCISE 1

AFFIX REVIEW

1. Open your Student Book to Lesson 45. ✓

1

un re ly dis

- Touch the first row in part 1. ✓
- Let's see if you remember a meaning for each of those affixes.

2. Touch the letters **U–N.** ✓
- What's one meaning of **un?** (Signal.) *Not.*

3. Touch the letters **R–E.** ✓
- What's one meaning of **re?** (Signal.) *Again.*

4. Touch the letters **L–Y.** ✓
- What's one meaning of **ly?** (Signal.) *How something happened.*

5. (Repeat steps 2–4 until firm.)
6. Touch the letters **D–I–S.** ✓
- What's one meaning of **dis?** (Call on a student. Accept **not, the opposite of,** or **away from.**)
- What's another meaning of **dis?** (Call on another student.)

EXERCISE 2

NEW **AFFIX: pre**

Task A

1. Touch the letters **P–R–E** in part 2. ✓

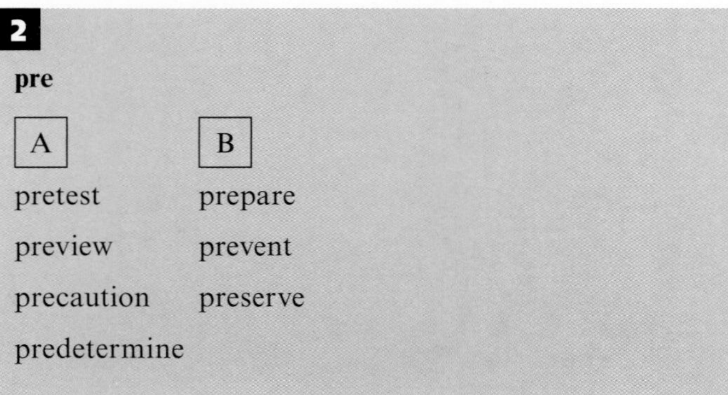

2

pre

A	B
pretest	prepare
preview	prevent
precaution	preserve
predetermine	

- When those letters appear at the beginning of a word, they usually mean **before.** What does **pre** mean? (Signal.) *Before.*

2. Touch the first word in column A. ✓
- What word? (Signal.) *Pretest.*
- What does **pretest** mean? (Call on a student.) (Idea: *A test you take before you study something.*)

3. Everybody, touch the next word. ✓
- What word? (Signal.) *Preview.*
- What does **preview** mean? (Call on a student.) (Idea: *To view before.*)

4. Everybody, touch the next word. ✓
- What word? (Signal.) *Precaution.*
- What does **precaution** mean? (Call on a student.) (Idea: *A caution you take before something happens.*)

5. Everybody, touch the next word. ✓
- What word? (Signal.) *Predetermine.*
- What does **predetermine** mean? (Call on a student.) (Idea: *To determine something beforehand.*)

6. (Repeat the list until firm.)

Task B

1. The words in column B also begin with **pre.** The meaning of **pre** in those words is not so easy to figure out.
2. Touch the first word in column B. ✓
- What word? (Signal.) *Prepare.*

3. Next word. ✓
- What word? (Signal.) *Prevent.*

4. (Repeat step 3 for **preserve.**)
5. (Repeat the list until firm.)

EXERCISE 3

WORD PRACTICE

1. Touch the first word in part 3. ✓

3

salted survival experienced

unusual certainly suddenly*

- What's the underlined part? (Signal.) *all.*
- What word? (Signal.) *Salted.*

2. Touch the next word. ✓

- What's the underlined part? (Signal.) *er.*
- What word? (Signal.) *Survival.*

3. (Repeat step 2 for each remaining word.)
4. (Repeat each row of words until firm.)
5. What does **suddenly** mean? (Call on a student.)

EXERCISE 4

VOCABULARY

1. Touch part 4. ✓

4

1. exceptionally
2. carnivorous

- We're going to talk about what those words mean.

2. Touch word 1. ✓

- What word? (Signal.) *Exceptionally.*
- **Exceptionally** is another word for **unusually.** What's another way of saying "The job is **unusually** easy"? (Signal.) *The job is exceptionally easy.*

3. Touch word 2. ✓

- What word? (Signal.) *Carnivorous.*
- **Carnivorous** animals eat meat. Everybody, what does a **carnivorous** animal eat? (Signal.) *Meat.*

EXERCISE 5

WORD PRACTICE

1. Touch the first word in part 5. ✓

5

particularly company solve

griping hammock* stared realize

started comfortably blankets

warmth glanced though

trimming thought neighbor

- What word? (Signal.) *Particularly.*

2. Next word. ✓

- What word? (Signal.) *Company.*

3. (Repeat step 2 for each remaining word.)
4. (Repeat each row of words until firm.)
5. What does **hammock** mean? (Call on a student.)

EXERCISE 6

WORD-ATTACK SKILLS: Individual tests

1. (Call on individual students. Each student reads a row or column. Tally the rows and columns read without error. If the group reads at least 9 rows and columns without making errors, direct all students to record 5 points in Box A of their Point Chart. Criterion is 80 percent of rows and columns read without error.)
2. (If the group did not read at least 9 rows and columns without errors, do not award any points for the Word-Attack Skills exercises.)

SELECTION READING

EXERCISE 7

STORY READING

1. Everybody, touch part 6. ✓
2. The error limit for this story is 12. If the group reads the story with 12 errors or less, you earn 5 points.

6

A Changed Man

3. (Call on a student to read the title.) *A Changed Man.*
- What do you think this story is about? (Accept reasonable responses.)
4. (Call on individual students. Each is to read two to four sentences.)
5. (Call on individual students to answer the specified questions during the story reading.)

One evening Bruce was lying in his hammock thinking. After he had thought about the island and the things that happened, he began to think about his home in the city and his job. He thought, "People paid me to do my job because there was a demand for insurance. People wanted insurance. They paid for the insurance. But it takes a lot of money to run an insurance company. A lot of people must put in a lot of work to give people insurance. I helped people get insurance, so the people had to pay me for my work." ❶

1. Why did people pay Bruce for his work at the insurance company? (Ideas: *Because there was a demand for insurance; he helped people get insurance.*)
1. Is needing insurance a life problem or a comfort problem? *A comfort problem.*

Bruce thought about his home and his car. He said, "Most of the problems I had to solve were not problems of survival. I had to solve problems of comfort. I had a car, but I didn't need a car to live. I had air conditioning and other things; however, I didn't need those things to live. I needed them to be more comfortable. But you don't think about comfort until your survival problems are solved. All of my problems of survival had been solved. I had enough to eat, I had a house that was warm when the weather got cold, I had warm clothes, and I certainly had good water to drink." ❷

2. What does it mean to solve a survival problem? (Ideas: *To make sure you have what you need to survive; to solve a problem that threatens your life.*)
2. Name two things Bruce had to solve his problems of comfort. *A car and an air conditioner.*
2. Did he have to solve many problems of survival? *No.*

As Bruce lay there in his hammock, he began to wish that he was back in his home. He said to himself, "If I were back there, I would look at things differently. I wouldn't be as grouchy; I would realize that my life was exceptionally easy. I didn't have to work fifteen hours a day. On the island I work fifteen hours a day, and I am happy. Maybe I would be happy in my old home if I worked more. Maybe I wouldn't try as hard to live comfortably. Maybe I would spend more time doing things and less time thinking about how bad things are. I probably made things worse by griping about how bad they were." ❸

3. What's another word for **gripe?** (Idea: *Complain.*)
3. If Bruce went back home again, what things would he do differently? (Ideas: *He wouldn't be as grouchy; he would realize that his life was exceptionally easy; he would spend less time thinking about how bad things are; he would spend more time doing things.*)

The next morning he woke up and rolled over. He ran his hand across his pillow and threw back the blankets before he opened his eyes. Then he noticed the hum of the air conditioner.

He opened his eyes quickly and sat up. He was back in his home. It was quiet and clean. He sat there for a moment trying to figure out what had happened. Then he ran to the telephone, dialed the operator, and asked her the date.

She told him, "August fourteenth."

"What year?" he asked.

She told him the year, and then Bruce knew it was the same day that he had gone to the island. Perhaps the whole thing had been a strange dream. Bruce glanced out of the window. A neighbor woman was trimming her bushes. Bruce waved and smiled; she waved back. ❹

4. Has Bruce changed? *Yes.*
4. How? (Idea: *He waves and smiles at his neighbor now.*)
4. Why did he dial the operator? (Idea: *To find out the date.*)

"It was all a crazy dream," Bruce said to himself. "But I'm glad to be back."

He ran to his dresser and opened it. He was thinking, "I'm going to get dressed and go outside. I'm going to talk to my neighbors and walk around." Suddenly he stopped and stared at something on the dresser. It was an ax made out of a tree branch and a sharp rock. He picked it up and looked at it. It had initials scratched on the handle—B.C.

"Bruce Celt," Bruce said to himself. "This is my ax. I made it on the island."

Bruce felt a little dizzy. Did it really happen, or was it a dream? ❺

5. What made Bruce think it wasn't really a dream? (Idea: *The ax on his dresser.*)

After a minute Bruce said, "I guess I'll never know how it happened, but I'm glad it did happen. I found out a lot of things on that island. I found out a lot about people and why things are the way they are."

And from that day on, Bruce was a changed man. First of all, he didn't hate his job. He always worked to do a better job. And he was no longer a grouch. People who knew him said that he was a good friend. He saw a lot of things about his city that he didn't like. But he didn't gripe about them. Instead he did things to make them better. ❻

6. What did Bruce feel he learned about on the island? (Idea: *About people and why things are the way they are.*)
6. Name some ways that Bruce was different now. (Ideas: *He didn't hate his job; he worked to do a better job; he wasn't a grouch; he didn't gripe about things he didn't like; he tried to change things to make them better.*)

He followed this motto:

We all need each other to solve our problems of life and our problems of comfort.

Bruce knew that people must work together. He knew that everybody has a job and that all jobs are important. Some people bring you food and water, some bring you warmth, and others help you live more comfortably.

6. (Award points quickly.)
7. (If the group makes more than 12 errors, repeat the reading immediately or on the next day.)

FLUENCY ASSESSMENT

EXERCISE 8

TIMED READING CHECKOUTS

1. (For this part of the lesson, assigned pairs of students work together during the checkouts.)
- (If one student does not have a checkout partner, arrange another time when you can give the checkout.)
2. (Each student does a 2-minute timed reading. Students earn 5 points by reading at least 240 words and making no more than 5 errors on the first part of story 45. Students record points in Box C of their Point Chart and plot their reading rate and errors on the Individual Reading Progress Chart.)
- (During each timed checkout, observe one pair of students for 2 minutes. Make notes on any mistakes the reader makes.)
3. (Record the timed reading checkout performance for each student you observed on the Fluency Assessment Summary form.)

WORKBOOK EXERCISES

Lesson 45

Errors

1

1. Is a need for insurance a life problem or a comfort problem?
   a comfort problem
2. Write **survival** in front of each survival problem and **comfort** in front of each comfort problem.
   a. comfort You have to eat bananas and fish every day.
   b. survival There is no air.
   c. comfort You have to walk two miles for food.
   d. comfort You have no friends around.
   e. survival You have only summer clothes to wear in zero-degree weather.
3. Why do you think Bruce wants to go back to the city?
   (He wants a chance to do a better job.)
4. What day did Bruce return to his home in the suburb?
   (the same day he had gone to the island)
5. What made Bruce think that his trip to the island was not a dream?
   (the ax on his dresser)
6. What was Bruce's motto?
   We all need each other to solve our problems of life and our problems of comfort.
7. If there was only a little demand for insurance, would the price of insurance be high or low? low
8. Did Bruce need a car to stay alive? No.

78 *Lesson 45* Copyright © SRA/McGraw-Hill. All rights reserved.

Lesson 45

9. Let's say Bruce dreams himself into another situation and has all these problems at the same time:
   a. 4 It is very cold sometimes.
   b. 1 There is no air.
   c. 3 There is no food.
   d. 2 There is no water.

   List the order in which Bruce should solve these problems. Put a number (1, 2, 3, or 4) in front of each of these problems.

2 **Fill in each blank using a word in the box.**

exceptionally	evaporated	immediately
deceptive	examined	enforced

1. The young flute player was exceptionally talented.
2. All the water in the pan on the stove had evaporated.
3. The police strictly enforced the parking rules.

3 **Copy the sentence that tells the main idea of the story.**

1. Bruce woke up one morning, heard the hum of the air conditioner, and realized that he was back in his home.
2. On Bruce's dresser was the ax that he had made from a tree branch on the island.
3. Island life had changed Bruce and the way he thought about work, other people, and his life.
4. Bruce realized that he worked fifteen hours a day on the island, but he was happy doing that work.

Island life had changed Bruce and the way he thought about work, other people, and his life.

Copyright © SRA/McGraw-Hill. All rights reserved. *Lesson 45* 79

Independent Student Work

Task A

- Open your Workbook to Lesson 45. ✓
- Complete all the parts of your Workbook lesson using a pencil. If you make no errors, you will earn 5 points.

Task B

1. (Before presenting Lesson 46, check student Workbooks for Lesson 45.)
   - (Call on individual students to read the items and answers in each part. Students mark errors using a pen.)
2. (Direct the students to count the number of errors and write the number in the Errors box at the top of the Workbook page.)
3. (Award points and direct students to record points in Box D of their Point Chart.)

   0 errors................................5 points
   1 error ....3 points
   2 or 3 errors ....1 point
   more than 3 errors ....0 points

Point schedule for Lessons 41 through 45

Box	Lesson part	Points
A	Word Attack	0 or 5
B	Selection Reading	0 or 5
C	Timed Reading Checkout	0 or 5
D	Workbook	0, 1, 3, or 5
Bonus	(Teacher option)	—

Five-lesson point summary

- (For **letter grades** based on points for Lessons **41** through **45,** tell students to compute the total for the blue boxes [C, D, and Bonus] and write the number in the Total box at the end of each row in their Point Chart. Students then add the totals and write the sum in the green box.)
- (For **rewards** based on points, tell students to compute the total for all boxes [A, B, C, D, and Bonus] and write the number in the Total box at the end of each row. Students then add the totals and write the sum in the green box.)

END OF LESSON 45

Lesson Objectives	LESSON 46 Exercise	LESSON 47 Exercise	LESSON 48 Exercise	LESSON 49 Exercise	LESSON 50 Exercise
Word Attack					
Decoding and Word Analysis					
Sound Combinations: *aw, au*	1	2	1		
Affix: *tri*	2	1			
Affixes: *re, un, pre, dis*	3				
Affixes: *un, re, pre, tri, dis*				1	
Affixes: *re, ly, tri, pre, dis*					1
Letter Combinations/Letter Sounds	1	2, 3			
Word Recognition	1–6	1–5	1–4	1–4	1–4
High-Frequency Words		5	4		
Vocabulary					
Morphemic Analysis	2, 3	1		1	1
Definitions	2–6	4, 5	2–4	2–4	2–4
Usage	5	4	3	3	3
Assessment					
Ongoing: Individual Tests	7	6	5	5	5
Group Reading					
Decoding and Word Analysis					
Read Decodable Text	8	7	6	6	6
Comprehension					
Access Prior Knowledge	8				
Draw Inferences	8	7	6	6	6
Note Details	8	7	6	6	6
Predict	8	7	6	6	6
Assessment					
Ongoing: Comprehension Check	8	7	6	6	6
Ongoing: Decoding Accuracy	8	7	6	6	6
Fluency Assessment					
Fluency					
Reread Decodable Text	9	8	7	7	7
Assessment					
Ongoing: Teacher-Monitored Fluency	9	8	7	7	7
Ongoing: Peer-Monitored Fluency	9	8	7	7	7
Workbook Exercises					
Decoding and Word Analysis					
Multisyllabic Word Parts		Ind. Work			Ind. Work
Comprehension					
Main Idea		Ind. Work			Ind. Work
Note Details	Ind. Work	Ind. Work	Ind. Work	Ind. Work	Ind. Work
Vocabulary					
Usage	Ind. Work	Ind. Work	Ind. Work	Ind. Work	Ind. Work
Study Skills					
Writing Mechanics		Ind. Work			Ind. Work
Assessment					
Ongoing: Workcheck	Workcheck	Workcheck	Workcheck	Workcheck	Workcheck

WORD-ATTACK SKILLS

Student Book

EXERCISE 1

NEW **SOUND COMBINATIONS: aw, au**

Task A

1. Open your Student Book to Lesson 46. ✓

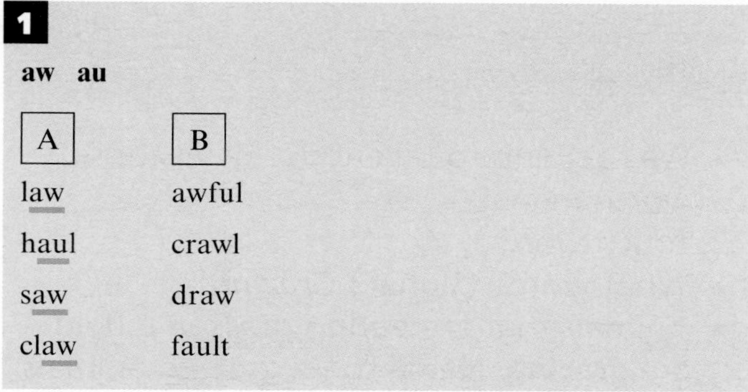

1

aw au

A	B
law	awful
haul	crawl
saw	draw
claw	fault

- Touch the letters **A–W** in part 1. ✓
- The letters **A–W** make the sound **aw,** as in **saw.** What sound? (Signal.) *aw.*

2. Touch the letters **A–U.** ✓
- The letters **A–U** also make the sound **aw.** What sound? (Signal.) *aw.*

3. Your turn. Tell me the sound each combination makes. Touch the letters **A–W.** ✓
- What sound? (Signal.) *aw.*
- Touch the letters **A–U.** ✓
- What sound? (Signal.) *aw.*

4. (Repeat step 3 until firm.)

Task B

1. You're going to say the sound for the underlined part and then read the word.
2. Touch the first word in column A. ✓
- What sound? (Signal.) *aw.*
- What word? (Signal.) *Law.*

3. Touch the next word. ✓
- What sound? (Signal.) *aw.*
- What word? (Signal.) *Haul.*

4. (Repeat step 3 for **saw, claw.**)

Task C

1. Touch the first word in column B. ✓
- What word? (Signal.) *Awful.*

2. Touch the next word. ✓
- What word? (Signal.) *Crawl.*

3. (Repeat step 2 for each remaining word.)
4. (Repeat steps 1–3 until firm.)

EXERCISE 2

NEW **AFFIX: tri**

1. Touch the letters **T–R–I** in part 2. ✓

2

tri

triceratops

tricycle

triangle

- **Tri** means **three.**

2. Touch the first word in the column. ✓
- That word is **triceratops.** (Pronounced **try–SER–a–tops.**) What word? (Signal.) *Triceratops.*
- The prefix **tri** appears in this dinosaur's name because it had three horns.

3. Touch the next word. ✓
- What word? (Signal.) *Tricycle.*
- Why does the prefix **tri** appear in this vehicle's name? (Call on a student.) (Idea: *Because it has three wheels.*)

4. Everybody, touch the next word. ✓
- What word? (Signal.) *Triangle.*
- Why does the prefix **tri** appear in the name of this figure? (Call on a student.) (Idea: *Because it has three sides [or three angles].*)

Lesson
46

EXERCISE 3

AFFIX REVIEW

1. Touch part 3. ✓

3

re un pre dis

- Let's see if you remember a meaning for each of those affixes.
2. Touch the letters **R–E.** ✓
- What's one meaning of **re?** (Signal.) *Again.*
3. Touch the letters **U–N.** ✓
- What's one meaning of **un?** (Signal.) *Not.*
4. Touch the letters **P–R–E.** ✓
- What's one meaning of **pre?** (Signal.) *Before.*
5. (Repeat steps 2–4 until firm.)
6. Touch the letters **D–I–S.** ✓
- What's one meaning of **dis?** (Call on a student. Accept **not, the opposite of,** or **away from.**)
- What's another meaning of **dis?** (Call on another student.)

EXERCISE 4

WORD PRACTICE

1. Touch the first word in part 4. ✓

4

eastern armor prehistoric
snout* carnivorous* emerged*
vegetable extended measure

- What's the underlined part? (Signal.) *ēēē.*
- What word? (Signal.) *Eastern.*
2. Touch the next word. ✓
- What's the underlined part? (Signal.) *ar.*
- What word? (Signal.) *Armor.*
3. (Repeat step 2 for each remaining word.)
4. (Repeat each row of words until firm.)
5. What does **snout** mean? (Call on a student.)
- (Repeat for **carnivorous, emerged.**)

EXERCISE 5

VOCABULARY

1. Touch part 5. ✓

5

1. grazing
2. reptiles
3. mammal
4. thrash
5. herd
6. predator

- We're going to talk about what those words mean.
2. Touch word 1. ✓
- What word? (Signal.) *Grazing.*
- Animals that are **eating grass** in a field are **grazing.** Name some **grazing** animals. (Call on different students.) (Ideas: *Cows, goats, sheep, etc.*)
3. Everybody, touch word 2. ✓
- What word? (Signal.) *Reptiles.*
- Snakes and lizards are **reptiles.**
4. Touch word 3. ✓
- What word? (Signal.) *Mammal.*
- A **mammal** is a **warm-blooded creature that has hair.** Name some **mammals.** (Call on different students.) (Ideas: *Cows, horses, cats, people, etc.*)
5. Everybody, touch word 4. ✓
- What word? (Signal.) *Thrash.*
- **Thrash** means **move about violently.**
6. Touch word 5. ✓
- What word? (Signal.) *Herd.*
- What is a **herd?** (Call on a student.) (Idea: *A group of animals that live together.*)
7. Everybody, touch word 6. ✓
- What word? (Signal.) *Predator.*
- **A predator** is **an animal that kills other animals.** Name some **predators.** (Call on different students.) (Ideas: *Lions, leopards, tigers, etc.*)

EXERCISE 6

WORD PRACTICE

1. Touch the first word in part 6. ✓

6

ornithomimid scene leopard occasional*
rhinoceros territory dinosaur crocodiles
hippopotamus watermelon spine
adulthood shoulders glide buried
incredible fierce* wiggled indicates
unbearable full-grown shield

- That word is **ornithomimid.** (Pronounced **or-NITH-oh-MEE-mid.**) What word? (Signal.) *Ornithomimid.*

2. Next word. ✓
- What word? (Signal.) *Scene.*
3. (Repeat step 2 for each remaining word.)
4. (Repeat each row of words until firm.)
5. What does **occasional** mean? (Call on a student.)
- (Repeat for **fierce.**)

EXERCISE 7

WORD-ATTACK SKILLS: Individual tests

1. (Call on individual students. Each student reads a row or column. Tally the rows and columns read without error. If the group reads at least 11 rows and columns without making errors, direct all students to record 5 points in Box A of their Point Chart. Criterion is 80 percent of rows and columns read without error.)
2. (If the group did not read at least 11 rows and columns without errors, do not award any points for the Word-Attack Skills exercises.)

SELECTION READING

EXERCISE 8

STORY READING

1. (Call on individual students to answer these questions.)
- Compare Bruce before his adventure to Bruce after his adventure. Name some ways that he was the **same** and some ways that he was **different.** (Accept reasonable responses.)
- What was his new motto for understanding life? *We all need each other to solve our problems of life and our problems of comfort.*

2. Everybody, touch part 7. ✓
3. The error limit for this story is 12. If the group reads the story with 12 errors or less, you earn 5 points.

7

A Prehistoric Plain

4. (Call on a student to read the title.) *A Prehistoric Plain.*
- What do you think this story is about? (Accept reasonable responses.)

5. (Call on individual students. Each is to read two to four sentences.)
6. (Call on individual students to answer the specified questions during the story reading.)

Lesson 46

The white-hot sun beat down on the great plain. The plain was covered with grass and occasional trees, and you could see heat waves rising from the ground. The grazing animals, moving slowly across the plain, looked as if they were melting in the heat waves. The heat was almost unbearable, although the animals didn't seem to mind it. The temperature was more than 110 degrees. ❶

1. Describe the great plain. (Ideas: *It was covered with grass; it was very hot; there were a few trees; you could see heat waves rising from the ground; there were grazing animals.*)
1. What was the temperature on the plain? *More than 110 degrees.*

A few of the animals were mammals, but most were reptiles. From time to time, some flying reptiles would glide over the grazing animals looking for a baby or a weak animal they could attack. Everywhere there were insects, some as big as your fist.

If it weren't for the types of animals on the plain, the scene would look quite similar to one you might see in eastern Africa today. Thousands of animals were grazing in herds, each herd moving in its own territory at its own pace. And each herd was taking its turn at the water hole.

Also, like today, there were predators on the plain. The predators today are carnivorous mammals like lions and leopards. But back then the predators on the plain were reptiles, including gigantic dinosaurs. ❷

2. What would the plain look like today? (Idea: *It would look similar, except the animals would be different.*)
2. What predators live on the plain today? (Idea: *Carnivorous animals like lions and leopards.*)
2. What kinds of animals used to live on the plain? (Ideas: *Some mammals; mostly reptiles; many insects.*)

One of the most incredible types of predators lived in a large swamp twenty miles north of the plain. These predators looked like the crocodiles you might see in Africa today. They were different in one respect, however. Though today's crocodiles are only ten feet long, the ones that were in the swamp when our story took place were as long as fifty feet. This means that they were longer than a line of five elephants. Their mouths were so big that a baby hippopotamus could probably fit inside. ❸

3. What did one kind of predator look like? (Idea: *Like a giant crocodile.*)

The ocean north of the great swamp also contained many fierce animals. Some of them were sharks that looked just like sharks you would see today. Others looked like large dinosaurs with flippers instead of legs. Some of the fish you see today were in the ocean back then—the dogfish, the garfish.

Several eggs were buried in the sand near a high cliff at the edge of the plain. One of the eggs was ready to hatch. It didn't look much like a chicken's egg. It was much bigger than any egg you have ever seen. In fact, it was probably bigger than a watermelon, and its shell was about half an inch thick. Suddenly the egg wiggled and moved under the sand as the animal inside tried to get out. The animal's pushing made a crack in the shell, and as it pushed again, the crack became larger. The animal thrashed and kicked for over a minute before its head emerged from the shell. Its head looked like an armor shield, with three horns—one at the end of its snout and two larger horns on its brow, one above each eye. The armor plate of the skull was formed by thick bone, and the plate extended behind the head, covering the upper part of the animal's spine. ❹

4. What did the head of the baby animal look like? (Idea: *Like an armor shield with three horns.*)
4. What was the armor plate of the skull made of? *Thick bone.*

This animal was known as a triceratops. The *tri* in its name indicates that it had three horns. A triceratops was a dinosaur and one of the largest grazing animals on the plain. You could see many full-grown triceratops moving across the plain—they looked like tanks. Of the animals that are alive today, the one that looks most like a triceratops is the rhinoceros; however, a big rhinoceros would look tiny next to a triceratops. ❺

5. What animal living today looks something like a triceratops? *The rhinoceros.*

The triceratops that emerged from the egg already weighed seven pounds. If none of the predators killed it before it reached adulthood, it would grow up to weigh 20,000 pounds—the weight of several elephants—and it would measure more than twenty feet high at the shoulders. As an adult, it would eat more than 2,000 pounds of grass and other forms of vegetable matter each day. But growing up on the plain was not easy, and the chances of our triceratops reaching adulthood were pretty poor. ❻

6. How much would a full-grown triceratops weigh? *20,000 pounds.*
6. How tall would it be? *More than twenty feet at the shoulders.*
6. How much vegetable matter did a triceratops eat each day? *More than 2,000 pounds.*
6. Why were the chances of a baby triceratops reaching adulthood poor? (Idea: *Because growing up on the plain was not easy.*)

7. (Award points quickly.)
8. (If the group makes more than 12 errors, repeat the reading immediately or on the next day.)

FLUENCY ASSESSMENT

EXERCISE 9

TIMED READING CHECKOUTS

1. (For this part of the lesson, assigned pairs of students work together during the checkouts.)
   - (If one student does not have a checkout partner, arrange another time when you can give the checkout.)
2. (Each student does a 2-minute timed reading. Students earn 5 points by reading at least 240 words and making no more than 5 errors on the first part of story 46. Students record points in Box C of their Point Chart and plot their reading rate and errors on the Individual Reading Progress Chart.)
   - (During each timed checkout, observe one pair of students for 2 minutes. Make notes on any mistakes the reader makes.)
3. (Record the timed reading checkout performance for each student you observed on the Fluency Assessment Summary form.)

Lesson 46

WORKBOOK EXERCISES

Independent Student Work

Task A

- Open your Workbook to Lesson 46. ✓
- Complete all the parts of your Workbook lesson using a pencil. If you make no errors, you will earn 5 points.

Task B

1. (Before presenting Lesson 47, check student Workbooks for Lesson 46.)
   - (Call on individual students to read the items and answers in each part. Students mark errors using a pen.)
2. (Direct the students to count the number of errors and write the number in the Errors box at the top of the Workbook page.)
3. (Award points and direct students to record points in Box D of their Point Chart.)

   0 errors.................................5 points
   1 error ....3 points
   2 or 3 errors ....1 point
   more than 3 errors ....0 points

END OF LESSON 46

Lesson 46

Errors

1

1. Describe the great plain. (a large, flat area of ground covered with grass and occasional trees)
2. What kind of animals lived on the plain? (mammals and reptiles)
3. What predators lived on the plain? (reptiles; dinosaurs)
4. How hot was it on the plain? (more than 110 degrees)
5. How many horns did the triceratops have? three
6. What animal living today looks something like a triceratops? rhinoceros
7. How much would a full-grown triceratops weigh? 20,000 pounds
8. A triceratops would weigh as much as several elephants.
9. How tall would a triceratops be? (more than twenty feet)
10. How much did a triceratops eat each day? more than 2,000 pounds of grass and other forms of vegetable matter

2 **Fill in each blank using a word in the box.**

protested	grazing	reptile
mammals	thrashed	herd

1. There was a large herd of cows in the field.
2. The cows were grazing on sweet green grass.
3. Like the snake, the triceratops was a reptile.

80 *Lesson 46*

Copyright © SRA/McGraw-Hill. All rights reserved.

WORD-ATTACK SKILLS

Student Book

EXERCISE 1

AFFIX: tri

1. Open your Student Book to Lesson 47. ✓

1

tri

triangle

triceps

trimester

- Touch the letters **T–R–I** in part 1. ✓
- **Tri** means **three.**

2. Touch the first word in the column. ✓
- That word is **triangle.** What word? (Signal.) *Triangle.*
- Why does the prefix **tri** appear in the name of this figure? (Call on a student.) (Idea: *Because it has three sides [or three angles].*)

3. Touch the next word. ✓
- What word? (Signal.) *Triceps.*
- The prefix **tri** appears in the name of this muscle because it has three heads.

4. Everybody, touch the next word. ✓
- What word? (Signal.) *Trimester.*
- The prefix **tri** appears in this word because it is a period of three months.

EXERCISE 2

NEW **SOUND COMBINATIONS: aw, au**

Task A

1. Touch column A in part 2. ✓

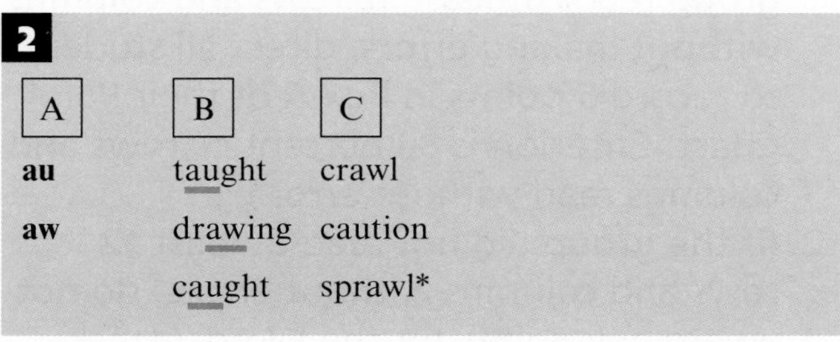

2

A	B	C
au	taught	crawl
aw	drawing	caution
	caught	sprawl*

- Both those sound combinations make the same sound. What sound? (Signal.) *aw.*

2. You're going to say the sound for the underlined part and then read the word.
3. Touch the first word in column B. ✓
- What sound? (Signal.) *aw.*
- What word? (Signal.) *Taught.*

4. Touch the next word. ✓
- What sound? (Signal.) *aw.*
- What word? (Signal.) *Drawing.*

5. (Repeat step 4 for **caught.**)

Task B

1. Touch the first word in column C. ✓
- What word? (Signal.) *Crawl.*

2. Touch the next word. ✓
- What word? (Signal.) *Caution.*

3. (Repeat step 2 for **sprawl.**)
4. (Repeat steps 1–3 until firm.)
5. What does **sprawl** mean? (Call on a student.)

EXERCISE 3

WORD PRACTICE

1. Touch the first word in part 3. ✓

3

differently	attention	rhinoceros
frightened	extinct	instinctively
disturbance	overgrown	motionless

- What's the underlined part? (Signal.) *er.*
- What word? (Signal.) *Differently.*

2. Touch the next word. ✓
- What's the underlined part? (Signal.) *shun.*
- What word? (Signal.) *Attention.*

3. (Repeat step 2 for each remaining word.)
4. (Repeat each row of words until firm.)

EXERCISE 4

VOCABULARY

1. Touch part 4. ✓

4

1. foul-tasting
2. programmed
3. roamed
4. keen
5. taut
6. extinct

- We're going to talk about what those words mean.

2. Touch word 1. ✓
- What word? (Signal.) *Foul-tasting.*
- Something that is **foul-tasting** is **bad tasting.** Everybody, what would you call **bad-tasting water?** (Signal.) *Foul-tasting water.*

3. Touch word 2. ✓
- What word? (Signal.) *Programmed.*
- Something that **always follows the same steps** is **programmed.** Everybody, what's another way of saying "The material in this book **always follows the same steps**"? (Signal.) *The material in this book is programmed.*

4. Touch word 3. ✓
- What word? (Signal.) *Roamed.*
- **Roamed** is another word for **wandered.** Everybody, what's another way of saying "He **wandered** around the parking lot"? (Signal.) *He roamed around the parking lot.*

5. Touch word 4. ✓
- What word? (Signal.) *Keen.*
- **Keen** means **sharp.** Everybody, what does **keen** mean? (Signal.) *Sharp.*

6. Touch word 5. ✓
- What word? (Signal.) *Taut.*
- **Taut** means **stretched tight.** Everybody, what's another way of saying "The sail was **stretched tight**"? (Signal.) *The sail was taut.*

7. Touch word 6. ✓
- What word? (Signal.) *Extinct.*
- An **extinct** animal is one that lived at one time but that is **no longer living** on Earth. Who knows the name of an **extinct** animal? (Call on different students.) (Ideas: *Dinosaur, dodo bird, etc.*)

EXERCISE 5

WORD PRACTICE

1. Touch the first word in part 5. ✓

5

brontosaurs triceratops ornithomimid
tongue galloping Tekla vision
muscles designed straight squirmed
hippopotamus grazing* territory
blazing shoulders ostrich lizard
scrambled predator* successful
shallow caused search inhabited

- That word is **brontosaurs.** (Pronounced **BRON-toe-sores.**) What word? (Signal.) *Brontosaurs.*

2. Next word. ✓
- What word? (Signal.) *Triceratops.*

3. (Repeat step 2 for each remaining word.)
4. (Repeat each row of words until firm.)
5. What do **grazing** animals do? (Call on a student.)
- What does **predator** mean? (Call on a student.)

EXERCISE 6

WORD-ATTACK SKILLS: Individual tests

1. (Call on individual students. Each student reads a row or column. Tally the rows and columns read without error. If the group reads at least 12 rows and columns without making errors, direct all students to record 5 points in Box A of their Point Chart. Criterion is 80 percent of rows and columns read without error.)
2. (If the group did not read at least 12 rows and columns without errors, do not award any points for the Word-Attack Skills exercises.)

SELECTION READING

EXERCISE 7

STORY READING

1. Everybody, touch part 6. ✓
2. The error limit for this story is 12. If the group reads the story with 12 errors or less, you earn 5 points.

6 **Triceratops Meets Ornithomimid**

3. (Call on a student to read the title.) *Triceratops Meets Ornithomimid.*
- What do you think this story is about? (Accept reasonable responses.)
4. (Call on individual students. Each is to read two to four sentences.)
5. (Call on individual students to answer the specified questions during the story reading.)

There were twelve triceratops eggs buried in the sand near the cliff. The first to hatch was Tekla. She squirmed free of the egg, dug her way to the surface, and looked at her world for the first time. She felt warmth and hunger. Her mouth was filled with sand. She moved her tongue, trying to spit out the foul-tasting sand.

Tekla would never know her mother. She didn't have to learn how to walk. Unlike mammals, she was programmed to walk from the moment she was born. She was also programmed to search for food and to fight; she would have no fear of most animals. Only faintly would she realize that she was a triceratops, and not one of the other animals that roamed the plain. She would know only that she felt more comfortable around other triceratops than she did around the other animals. Like most grazing animals, she had a keen sense of smell and sharp vision. ❶

1. Who was the first triceratops to hatch? *Tekla.*
1. What two senses are well developed in most grazing animals? *Smell and vision.*

Still trying to remove the sand from her mouth, she rolled on the hot sand. It felt good on her back. She looked up at the sun, white and blazing. The sun felt good. Suddenly, however, Tekla sensed danger. Instinctively she scrambled to her feet and faced into the wind. Danger, danger, something screamed inside her. Danger. She put her head down and stood motionless with her muscles taut and her heavy, huge feet planted firmly in the sand. ❷

2. How did Tekla know danger was near? (Ideas: *She sensed danger; something screamed inside her.*)

She seemed to be looking straight ahead, but grazing animals are designed differently from predators. Predators have eyes on the front of their heads so they can look straight ahead. They look straight ahead when they attack, and they must attack to survive. Grazing animals, however, have eyes that are on the sides of their heads. A grazing animal like a cow or a horse may seem to be looking only straight ahead, but its right eye can see everything on its right side. And its left eye can see everything on its left. The animal can even see its own back end. ❸

3. How are the eyes of grazing animals different from the eyes of predators? (Idea: *Grazing animals' eyes are on the sides of their head; predators' eyes are at the front of their head.*)

Lesson 47

The eyes are designed to protect the grazing animal from attack. It doesn't have to worry about looking straight ahead as much as it has to worry about predators attacking from behind.

Run, run, something screamed inside Tekla. Instinct was telling Tekla what to do. She had never seen an ornithomimid, the predator who loved to eat dinosaur eggs. She had never smelled an ornithomimid, yet she knew instinctively what to do. She ran from the cliffs toward the other grazing animals on the plain. She could run quite fast, nearly as fast as a horse. ❹

4. What told Tekla to run? *Instinct.*
4. What kind of animal is an ornithomimid? (Idea: *A predator who loved to eat dinosaur eggs.*)

Tekla looked like a fat little rhinoceros, her stubby legs galloping through the heat waves toward the distant line of grazing animals. She was very frightened. Her heart was pounding, but her mind had one thought—escape.

And she did escape. Her brothers and sisters were not as lucky. The ornithomimid sniffed around in the sand. That sand was once a beach, and the cliff had been on the edge of the beach. When the great brontosaurs lived on Earth, Tekla's plain was a large, shallow body of water, and it was inhabited by thousands of brontosaurs. By the time Tekla was born, the great brontosaurs had been extinct for more than sixty million years. ❺

5. What had the plain looked like when the brontosaurs lived on Earth? (Idea: *It was a large, shallow body of water.*)
5. What does **extinct** mean? (Idea: *No longer living on Earth.*)
5. For how long had the brontosaur been extinct when Tekla was born? *More than 60 million years.*

The water had dried up, and all that remained were the cliffs, the great sand beach, the bones of some brontosaurs buried deep under the sand, and the shells of sea animals that once inhabited the plain.

The ornithomimid looked something like an overgrown ostrich with a long lizard tail and sharp teeth. It wasn't usually successful at finding eggs in the sand because they were often buried quite deep. But the disturbance that Tekla caused caught the attention of the ornithomimid. Quickly it ran over to the spot where the pieces of Tekla's shell remained on the sand. The ornithomimid sniffed the shell and then began to dig in the sand. ❻

6. What did an ornithomimid look like? (Idea: *Like an overgrown ostrich with a long lizard tail and sharp teeth.*)
6. What did an ornithomimid like to eat? *Dinosaur eggs.*
6. (Award points quickly.)
7. (If the group makes more than 12 errors, repeat the reading immediately or on the next day.)

FLUENCY ASSESSMENT

EXERCISE 8

TIMED READING CHECKOUTS

1. (For this part of the lesson, assigned pairs of students work together during the checkouts.)
- (If one student does not have a checkout partner, arrange another time when you can give the checkout.)

2. (Each student does a 2-minute timed reading. Students earn 5 points by reading at least 240 words and making no more than 5 errors on the first part of story 47. Students record points in Box C of their Point Chart and plot their reading rate and errors on the Individual Reading Progress Chart.)
- (During each timed checkout, observe one pair of students for 2 minutes. Make notes on any mistakes the reader makes.)

3. (Record the timed reading checkout performance for each student you observed on the Fluency Assessment Summary form.)

WORKBOOK EXERCISES

Independent Student Work

Task A

- Open your Workbook to Lesson 47. ✓
- Complete all the parts of your Workbook lesson using a pencil. If you make no errors, you will earn 5 points.

Task B

1. (Before presenting Lesson 48, check student Workbooks for Lesson 47.)
- (Call on individual students to read the items and answers in each part. Students mark errors using a pen.)

2. (Direct the students to count the number of errors and write the number in the Errors box at the top of the Workbook page.)
3. (Award points and direct students to record points in Box D of their Point Chart.)

0 errors................................5 points
1 error..................................3 points
2 or 3 errors.........................1 point
more than 3 errors..............0 points

END OF LESSON 47

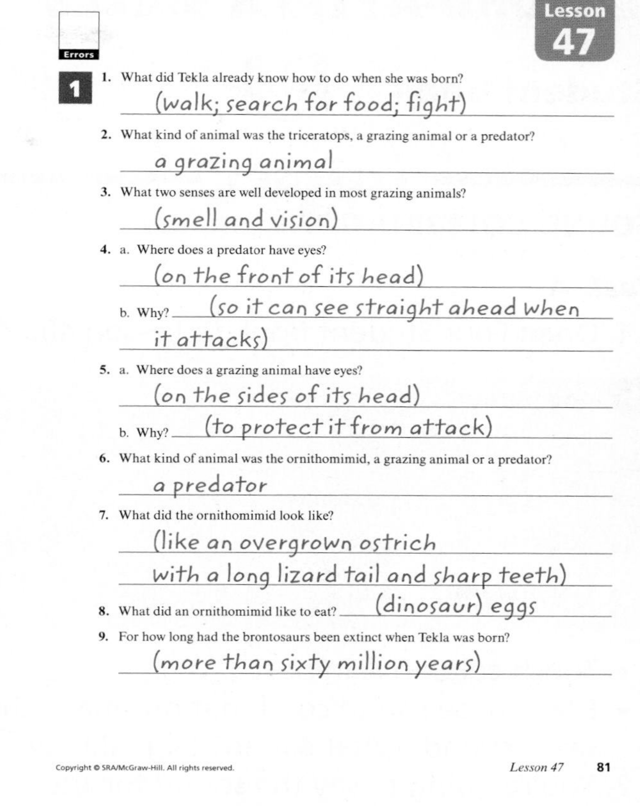

Lesson 47

Errors

1

1. What did Tekla already know how to do when she was born?
(walk; search for food; fight)
2. What kind of animal was the triceratops, a grazing animal or a predator?
a grazing animal
3. What two senses are well developed in most grazing animals?
(smell and vision)
4. a. Where does a predator have eyes?
(on the front of its head)
b. Why? (so it can see straight ahead when it attacks)
5. a. Where does a grazing animal have eyes?
(on the sides of its head)
b. Why? (to protect it from attack)
6. What kind of animal was the ornithomimid, a grazing animal or a predator?
a predator
7. What did the ornithomimid look like?
(like an overgrown ostrich with a long lizard tail and sharp teeth)
8. What did an ornithomimid like to eat? (dinosaur) eggs
9. For how long had the brontosaurs been extinct when Tekla was born?
(more than sixty million years)

Copyright © SRA/McGraw-Hill. All rights reserved.

Lesson 47

2 **Fill in each blank using a word in the box.**

foul-tasting	taut	programmed
roamed	keen	reptiles

1. The pack of wolves roamed through the forest.
2. The wolves' sense of smell was very keen.
3. The rotten cheese was foul-tasting

3 **Copy the sentence that tells the main idea of the story.**

1. Tekla was a grazing animal that had a keen sense of smell and sharp vision.
2. The triceratops eggs were buried in the sand near the edge of a cliff.
3. The animal that ate the triceratops eggs looked like a large ostrich with a lizard tail and very sharp teeth.
4. Tekla was the only baby triceratops in her family that escaped the attack of an ornithomimid.

Tekla was the only baby triceratops in her family that escaped the attack of an ornithomimid.

4 **Write the parts for each word.**

1. previewed = pre + view + ed
2. unlikely = un + like + ly
3. pretender = pre + tend + er
4. disgusting = dis + gust + ing

Copyright © SRA/McGraw-Hill. All rights reserved.

Lesson 48

WORD-ATTACK SKILLS

Student Book 

EXERCISE 1

SOUND COMBINATIONS: au, aw

Task A

1. Open your Student Book to Lesson 48. ✓

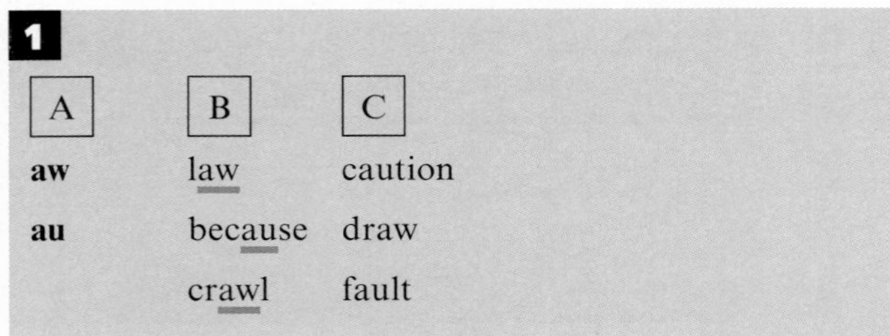

1

A	B	C
aw	law	caution
au	because	draw
	crawl	fault

- Touch column A in part 1. ✓
- Both those sound combinations make the same sound. What sound? (Signal.) *aw.*

2. You're going to say the sound for the underlined part and then read the word.
3. Touch the first word in column B. ✓
- What sound? (Signal.) *aw.*
- What word? (Signal.) *Law.*

4. Touch the next word. ✓
- What sound? (Signal.) *aw.*
- What word? (Signal.) *Because.*

5. (Repeat step 4 for **crawl**.)

Task B

1. Touch the first word in column C. ✓
- What word? (Signal.) *Caution.*

2. Touch the next word. ✓
- What word? (Signal.) *Draw.*

3. (Repeat step 2 for **fault.**)
4. (Repeat steps 1–3 until firm.)

EXERCISE 2

WORD PRACTICE

1. Touch the first word in part 2. ✓

2

exposing thundered emerging* feared
unlike absolutely crunching survived*
screamed silenced several* excite accept

- What's the underlined part? (Signal.) *ex.*
- What word? (Signal.) *Exposing.*

2. Touch the next word. ✓
- What's the underlined part? (Signal.) *er.*
- What word? (Signal.) *Thundered.*

3. (Repeat step 2 for each remaining word.)
4. (Repeat each row of words until firm.)
5. What does **emerging** mean? (Call on a student.)
- (Repeat for **survived, several.**)

EXERCISE 3

VOCABULARY

1. Touch part 3. ✓

3

1. leisurely
2. aroused
3. feast
4. scavengers
5. ignore
6. slither

- We're going to talk about what those words mean.

2. Touch word 1. ✓
- What word? (Signal.) *Leisurely.*
- Something done **leisurely** is done **at a slow and easy pace.** Everybody, how is something done if it is done **leisurely?** (Signal.) *At a slow and easy pace.*

3. Touch word 2. ✓
- What word? (Signal.) *Aroused.*
- When something is **aroused,** it is **awakened** or **stirred up.** Everybody, what's another way of saying "The game **stirred up** his anger"? (Signal.) *The game aroused his anger.*

4. Touch word 3. ✓
- What word? (Signal.) *Feast.*
- What do you do when you **feast?** (Call on a student.) (Idea: *Eat a lot.*)

5. Everybody, touch word 4. ✓
- What word? (Signal.) *Scavengers.*
- **Scavengers** are **animals that eat what other animals leave behind.** Name some animals that are **scavengers.** (Call on different students.) (Ideas: *Crows, vultures, pigs, etc.*)

6. Everybody, touch word 5. ✓
- What word? (Signal.) *Ignore.*
- If you **ignore** something, you do **not pay attention** to it. What's another way of saying "He did **not pay attention** to the stop sign"? (Signal.) *He ignored the stop sign.*

7. Touch word 6. ✓
- What word? (Signal.) *Slither.*
- **Slither** means to **slide along.** Everybody, what does **slither** mean? (Signal.) *To slide along.*

EXERCISE 4

WORD PRACTICE

1. Touch the first word in part 4. ✓

4

tyrannosaur heavy occasional* building predator*
frozen lizard finished instincts distance
constantly instinctively instantly stripped

- That word is **tyrannosaur.** (Pronounced **tie–RAN–oh–sore.**) What word? (Signal.) *Tyrannosaur.*

2. Next word. ✓
- What word? (Signal.) *Heavy.*

3. (Repeat step 2 for each remaining word.)
4. (Repeat each row of words until firm.)
5. What does **occasional** mean? (Call on a student.)
- (Repeat for **predator.**)

EXERCISE 5

WORD-ATTACK SKILLS: Individual tests

1. (Call on individual students. Each student reads a row or column. Tally the rows and columns read without error. If the group reads at least 8 rows and columns without making errors, direct all students to record 5 points in Box A of their Point Chart. Criterion is 80 percent of rows and columns read without error.)
2. (If the group did not read at least 8 rows and columns without errors, do not award any points for the Word-Attack Skills exercises.)

SELECTION READING

EXERCISE 6

STORY READING

1. Everybody, touch part 5. ✓
2. The error limit for this story is 12. If the group reads the story with 12 errors or less, you earn 5 points.

5 **Ornithomimid Meets Tyrannosaur**

3. (Call on a student to read the title.) *Ornithomimid Meets Tyrannosaur.*
- What do you think this story is about? (Accept reasonable responses.)

4. (Call on individual students. Each is to read two to four sentences.)
5. (Call on individual students to answer the specified questions during the story reading.)

The ornithomimid dug in the sand, exposing three eggs. One of Tekla's brothers was emerging from his shell. Snap, went the jaws of the ornithomimid, and Tekla's brother never saw the sun or ate the rich grasses on the plain. The ornithomimid ate three eggs. Suddenly, the ornithomimid stopped and stood up. It looked almost frozen as it sniffed the air. Then it began to run. It ran faster than a horse, but not fast enough.

Another animal thundered behind it—the most feared animal on the plain. It was a tyrannosaur. Like an ornithomimid, it stood on two heavy legs with a long lizard tail behind it. Unlike an ornithomimid, a tyrannosaur was taller than a two-story building. A tyrannosaur was a predator able to kill nearly any other animal on the plain. It was forty feet from the tip of its nose to the end of its tail. Its head was very big. A tyrannosaur looked strange with its tiny front legs that were much smaller than its head. ❶

1. What did a tyrannosaur look like? (Idea: *It stood on two legs, had a long lizard tail, was taller than a two-story building, had a big head, and had small front legs.*)
1. What was a tyrannosaur able to do? (Idea: *Kill almost any other animal on the plain.*)

Although the ornithomimid was swift, the tyrannosaur overtook it after the two animals had run less than fifty feet. The jaws of the tyrannosaur closed on the upper back of the ornithomimid with a crunching sound that could be heard far across the plain. The ornithomimid thrashed and screamed for a moment, but another bite from the tyrannosaur's jaws silenced it.

The tyrannosaur leisurely picked at the dead ornithomimid as several of Tekla's sisters and brothers freed themselves from their eggs. None survived, however. The smell of blood and food had aroused many predators, some large and some small. Some would wait for the scraps left by the larger animals. Others were bigger and bolder. They were ready to steal the kill from other animals—but not from a tyrannosaur. ❷

2. Why wouldn't other predators try to steal from a tyrannosaur? (Idea: *Because it was too dangerous.*)

By the next morning, little remained of Tekla's brothers and sisters except a few pieces of egg shell. And very little remained of the ornithomimid. After the tyrannosaur had finished feasting on the better parts of the ornithomimid, it went off to sleep. Scavengers closed in. Within three hours they had stripped the ornithomimid to the bone. Other scavengers moved in. During the night, they feasted on the bones. And the next morning when the sun rose over the night fog that settled on the plain, all that marked the place where the ornithomimid had fallen were a few large bones and footprints—thousands of them. ❸

3. Why were few ornithomimid bones left the next morning? (Idea: *Because scavengers ate the rest of the ornithomimid remains.*)

That morning found Tekla far from the cliffs. Her instincts had told her to run with the other grazing animals on the plain. So she did. She found herself near a group of about twenty triceratops. They moved slower than most of the other grazing animals, and they ate constantly. They were quite calm—much like a herd of cows on a hot day. From time to time, they lay down. During the hottest part of the day, they slept. Tekla slept with them. They seemed to half ignore and half accept her. After resting with them for about an hour, she began to trot around. Some of them lifted their heads and looked at her for a moment, but then they returned to their afternoon sleep. ❹

4. What had told Tekla to run? *Instinct.*
4. Who did Tekla stay with that day? (Idea: *With a group of about twenty triceratops.*)
4. How did the group of triceratops act? (Ideas: *Quite calm; like a herd of cows.*)

Tekla felt playful, but there wasn't much to play with. She sniffed a snake that was about twenty feet long. The snake slowly began to slither away. Tekla stepped on the snake's tail. Instantly, the snake turned and struck at her. Instinctively, Tekla ducked her head. The snake struck the large plate on Tekla's head. ❺

5. What did the snake hit when it tried to strike Tekla? (Idea: *The large plate on Tekla's head.*)

Before the snake could strike again, Tekla turned and ran back to the sleeping triceratops. She nibbled on grass and strolled around the snoozing animals. She felt content. There were occasional sounds of animals fighting in the distance, but the grazing animals were calm. And so was Tekla.

6. (Award points quickly.)
7. (If the group makes more than 12 errors, repeat the reading immediately or on the next day.)

FLUENCY ASSESSMENT

EXERCISE 7

TIMED READING CHECKOUTS

1. (For this part of the lesson, assigned pairs of students work together during the checkouts.)
- (If one student does not have a checkout partner, arrange another time when you can give the checkout.)
2. (Each student does a 2-minute timed reading. Students earn 5 points by reading at least 240 words and making no more than 5 errors on the first part of story 48. Students record points in Box C of their Point Chart and plot their reading rate and errors on the Individual Reading Progress Chart.)
- (During each timed checkout, observe one pair of students for 2 minutes. Make notes on any mistakes the reader makes.)
3. (Record the timed reading checkout performance for each student you observed on the Fluency Assessment Summary form.)

Errors

1

1. What do grazing animals eat? (plants)
2. What do predators eat? (meat; other animals)
3. Write **grazing animal** or **predator** in front of each animal.
   grazing animal a. triceratops
   predator b. lion
   predator c. tyrannosaur
4. How were the ornithomimid and the tyrannosaur alike? (Each stood on two heavy legs with a long lizard tail.)
5. How tall was the tyrannosaur? (taller than a two-story building)
6. Why did the tyrannosaur look strange? (It had a very big head and tiny front legs.)
7. What attracted the predators? (the smell of blood and food)
8. Why were few ornithomimid bones left the next morning? (Scavengers ate most of them.)
9. Describe the grazing habits of the triceratops. (They moved slowly and ate constantly.)
10. How did Tekla react when the snake struck at her? (She ducked her head.)

Copyright © SRA/McGraw-Hill. All rights reserved.

2

Fill in each blank using a word in the box.

leisurely	aroused	feasting
scavengers	ignored	programmed

1. Mark ignored his dog's whines.
2. The scavengers chewed the bones that the lions left behind.
3. The snail went at a leisurely pace.

Copyright © SRA/McGraw-Hill. All rights reserved.

WORKBOOK EXERCISES

Independent Student Work

Task A

- Open your Workbook to Lesson 48. ✓
- Complete all the parts of your Workbook lesson using a pencil. If you make no errors, you will earn 5 points.

Task B

1. (Before presenting Lesson 49, check student Workbooks for Lesson 48.)
   - (Call on individual students to read the items and answers in each part. Students mark errors using a pen.)
2. (Direct the students to count the number of errors and write the number in the Errors box at the top of the Workbook page.)
3. (Award points and direct students to record points in Box D of their Point Chart.)

   0 errors.................................5 points
   1 error ....3 points
   2 or 3 errors ....1 point
   more than 3 errors ....0 points

END OF LESSON 48

WORD-ATTACK SKILLS

Student Book 

EXERCISE 1

AFFIX REVIEW

1. Open your Student Book to Lesson 49. ✓

1

un re pre tri dis

- Touch part 1. ✓
- Let's see if you remember a meaning for each of those affixes.

2. Touch the letters **U–N.** ✓
- What's one meaning of **un?** (Signal.) *Not.*

3. Touch the letters **R–E.** ✓
- What's one meaning of **re?** (Signal.) *Again.*

4. Touch the letters **P–R–E.** ✓
- What's one meaning of **pre?** (Signal.) *Before.*

5. Touch the letters **T–R–I.** ✓
- What's one meaning of **tri?** (Signal.) *Three.*

6. (Repeat steps 2–5 until firm.)
7. Touch the letters **D–I–S.** ✓
- What's one meaning of **dis?** (Call on a student. Accept **not, the opposite of,** or **away from.**)
- What's another meaning of **dis?** (Call on another student.)

EXERCISE 2

WORD PRACTICE

1. Touch the first word in part 2. ✓

2

beetles related discovery crouched
glancing experiencing carnivores floated
herbivores occasionally extinct* fierce*

- What's the underlined part? (Signal.) *ēēē.*
- What word? (Signal.) *Beetles.*

2. Touch the next word. ✓
- What's the underlined part? (Signal.) *re.*
- What word? (Signal.) *Related.*

3. (Repeat step 2 for each remaining word.)
4. (Repeat each row of words until firm.)
5. What does **extinct** mean? (Call on a student.)
- (Repeat for **fierce.**)

EXERCISE 3

VOCABULARY

1. Touch part 3. ✓

3

1. foliage
2. prance
3. resume
4. unison
5. scramble

- We're going to talk about what those words mean.

2. Touch word 1. ✓
- What word? (Signal.) *Foliage.*
- The **leaves on a bush or a tree** are called **foliage.** Everybody, what are the **leaves on a bush or tree** called? (Signal.) *Foliage.*

3. Touch word 2. ✓
- What word? (Signal.) *Prance.*
- When horses **prance,** they **step high and move around in a frisky way.**

4. Touch word 3. ✓
- What word? (Signal.) *Resume.*
- **Resume** means to **begin again.** Everybody, what's another way of saying "The game will **begin again** after halftime"? (Signal.) *The game will resume after halftime.*

5. Touch word 4. ✓
- What word? (Signal.) *Unison.*
- When people talk in **unison,** they say the same words **at the same time.** Everybody, what would you be doing if you were singing the same words **at the same time?** (Signal.) *Singing in unison.*

6. Touch word 5. ✓
- What word? (Signal.) *Scramble.*
- **Scramble** means **to move quickly.** Everybody, what does **scramble** mean? (Signal.) *To move quickly.*

EXERCISE 4

WORD PRACTICE

1. Touch the first word in part 4. ✓

4

crocodile period metasequoia
dignified ginkgo Cretaceous similar
dragonflies warmth mammal* grove
history ruled inhabit earth
frequently business* realize
flesh listened aware wading

- What word? (Signal.) *Crocodile.*

2. Next word. ✓
- What word? (Signal.) *Period.*

3. (Repeat step 2 for each remaining word.)
4. (Repeat each row of words until firm.)
5. What does **mammal** mean? (Call on a student.)
- (Repeat for **business.**)

EXERCISE 5

WORD-ATTACK SKILLS: Individual tests

1. (Call on individual students. Each student reads a row or column. Tally the rows and columns read without error. If the group reads at least 9 rows and columns without making errors, direct all students to record 5 points in Box A of their Point Chart. Criterion is 80 percent of rows and columns read without error.)
2. (If the group did not read at least 9 rows and columns without errors, do not award any points for the Word-Attack Skills exercises.)

SELECTION READING

EXERCISE 6

STORY READING

1. Everybody, touch part 5. ✓
2. The error limit for this story is 12. If the group reads the story with 12 errors or less, you earn 5 points.

5 **Asleep on the Plain**

3. (Call on a student to read the title.) *Asleep on the Plain.*
- What do you think this story is about? (Accept reasonable responses.)

4. (Call on individual students. Each is to read two to four sentences.)
5. (Call on individual students to answer the specified questions during the story reading.)

The sky became dark as clouds of insects floated over the plain in the late afternoon. Some insects were flies that looked exactly like the flies you see today. Others were dragonflies. Though they were similar to today's dragonflies, they were much bigger. There were butterflies, fleas, and flying ants. There were grasshoppers and flying beetles. Tekla was covered with insects, but they didn't bother her very much. Occasionally, she felt a sharp bite. She would roll over so that some of the insects would fly away. The grass waved in the breeze. ❶

1. What kinds of insects were on the plain? (Ideas: *Flies; dragonflies; butterflies; fleas; flying ants; grasshoppers; flying beetles.*)

In the distance was a grove of trees.

Two types of trees in that grove are alive today. One is related to the redwood. It is called the metasequoia. Its foliage is like that of the redwood, except that its needles fall off in the fall. Until 1946, scientists had thought that the metasequoia had been extinct for over a hundred million years. However, the tree was discovered growing in a remote part of China. The other tree that grows today is the ginkgo. It has leaves shaped like fans, and it makes a good shade tree. Some of the trees in the grove might have looked similar to trees you see today, but they were different and have been extinct for more than a hundred million years. ❷

2. What is the name of the tree on the plain that is related to the redwood? *Metasequoia.*
2. Scientists thought the metasequoia was extinct. What does **extinct** mean? (Idea: *No longer living on Earth.*)
2. What is the other tree that still lives today? *The ginkgo.*

Tekla didn't know anything about her place in the history of the world. She lived in what we call the last part of the dinosaur age. The dinosaurs were on Earth for more than one hundred fifty million years. The last part of the dinosaur age is called the Cretaceous period; the end of the Cretaceous period marked the end of the dinosaurs. ❸

3. For how long did dinosaurs inhabit Earth? (Idea: *More than 150 million years.*)
3. What is the name of the time period in which the last dinosaurs lived? *Cretaceous period.*

Tekla didn't know that there would be humans on Earth eighty million years after the end of the Cretaceous period. She didn't know that the world would be ruled by a mammal, the human, who would control more power than the most fierce tyrannosaur that ever lived. She didn't know that animals like horses, cows, and elephants would someday inhabit Earth. What she did know was that the sun felt good, that the bite of some insects hurt, and that she was thirsty. ❹

4. How long after dinosaurs became extinct did humans inhabit Earth? *Eighty million years.*

The other triceratops were thirsty, too. They awoke, resumed eating, and then began moving slowly toward the water hole that was about three miles away. Tekla tagged along, stopping frequently to look at lizards or other animals. When they reached the water hole, the young triceratops splashed and pranced around in the shallow water. The adults went about the business of drinking in a more dignified way. Experiencing water for the first time, Tekla felt its warmth and listened to the sounds it made as she thrashed about. ❺

5. What did Tekla do at the water hole? (Ideas: *Splashed and pranced around; felt its warmth; listened to the sounds it made.*)
5. What did the adult triceratops do? (Idea: *Drank the water in a more dignified way.*)

The water hole was teeming with animals. Some were wading and drinking. Others crouched along the shore, drinking and glancing about to make sure that no predators were near.

Tekla didn't realize that the different types of animals around her were similar to animals of today. There were those animals that ate the flesh of other animals—the carnivores. And there were those, like Tekla, that ate plants—the herbivores. ❻

6. What do carnivores eat? (Idea: *The flesh of other animals.*)
6. What do herbivores eat? *Plants.*

She wasn't aware that there were carnivores that made their home in the warm water of the water hole. She didn't know that one of those carnivores was about ten feet from her. It was a crocodile hidden under a bed of floating weeds, with only its two eyes and the end of its snout above the surface of the water. Tekla didn't notice that the crocodile's tail was beginning to move, making the animal slide forward in the water. ❼

7. What carnivore was hidden under the weeds? *A crocodile.*
7. What do you think will happen? (Idea: *The crocodile might try to eat Tekla.*)
6. (Award points quickly.)
7. (If the group makes more than 12 errors, repeat the reading immediately or on the next day.)

FLUENCY ASSESSMENT

EXERCISE 7

TIMED READING CHECKOUTS

1. (For this part of the lesson, assigned pairs of students work together during the checkouts.)
- (If one student does not have a checkout partner, arrange another time when you can give the checkout.)
2. (Each student does a 2-minute timed reading. Students earn 5 points by reading at least 240 words and making no more than 5 errors on the first part of story 49. Students record points in Box C of their Point Chart and plot their reading rate and errors on the Individual Reading Progress Chart.)
- (During each timed checkout, observe one pair of students for 2 minutes. Make notes on any mistakes the reader makes.)
3. (Record the timed reading checkout performance for each student you observed on the Fluency Assessment Summary form.)

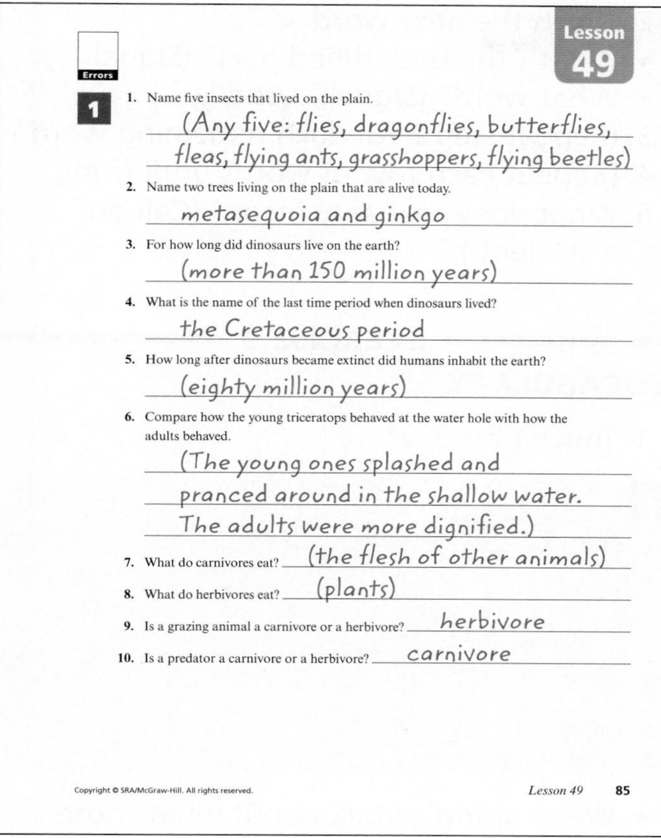

Lesson 49

Errors

1

1. Name five insects that lived on the plain.
(Any five: flies, dragonflies, butterflies, fleas, flying ants, grasshoppers, flying beetles)
2. Name two trees living on the plain that are alive today.
metasequoia and ginkgo
3. For how long did dinosaurs live on the earth?
(more than 150 million years)
4. What is the name of the last time period when dinosaurs lived?
the Cretaceous period
5. How long after dinosaurs became extinct did humans inhabit the earth?
(eighty million years)
6. Compare how the young triceratops behaved at the water hole with how the adults behaved.
(The young ones splashed and pranced around in the shallow water. The adults were more dignified.)
7. What do carnivores eat? (the flesh of other animals)
8. What do herbivores eat? (plants)
9. Is a grazing animal a carnivore or a herbivore? herbivore
10. Is a predator a carnivore or a herbivore? carnivore

Copyright © SRA/McGraw-Hill. All rights reserved. Lesson 49 85

Lesson 49

2 Fill in each blank using a word in the box.

foliage	pranced	resumed
unison	slither	scramble

1. They read the poem in unison
2. The colts pranced across the field.
3. Billy resumed cooking after he got off the phone.

86 Lesson 49 Copyright © SRA/McGraw-Hill. All rights reserved.

WORKBOOK EXERCISES

Independent Student Work

Task A

- Open your Workbook to Lesson 49. ✓
- Complete all the parts of your Workbook lesson using a pencil. If you make no errors, you will earn 5 points.

Task B

1. (Before presenting Lesson 50, check student Workbooks for Lesson 49.)
   - (Call on individual students to read the items and answers in each part. Students mark errors using a pen.)
2. (Direct the students to count the number of errors and write the number in the Errors box at the top of the Workbook page.)
3. (Award points and direct students to record points in Box D of their Point Chart.)

   0 errors ....5 points
   1 error ....3 points
   2 or 3 errors ....1 point
   more than 3 errors ....0 points

END OF LESSON 49

Lesson 50

WORD-ATTACK SKILLS

Student Book

EXERCISE 1

AFFIX REVIEW

1. Open your Student Book to Lesson 50. ✓

1

re ly tri pre dis

- Touch part 1. ✓
- Let's see if you remember a meaning for each of those affixes.

2. Touch the letters **R–E.** ✓
- What's one meaning of **re?** (Signal.) *Again.*

3. Touch the letters **L–Y.** ✓
- What's one meaning of **ly?** (Signal.) *How something happened.*

4. Touch the letters **T–R–I.** ✓
- What's one meaning of **tri?** (Signal.) *Three.*

5. Touch the letters **P–R–E.** ✓
- What's one meaning of **pre?** (Signal.) *Before.*

6. (Repeat steps 2–5 until firm.)
7. Touch the letters **D–I–S.** ✓
- What's one meaning of **dis?** (Call on a student. Accept **not, the opposite of,** or **away from.**)
- What's another meaning of **dis?** (Call on another student.)

EXERCISE 2

WORD PRACTICE

1. Touch the first word in part 2. ✓

2

reopened usually motionless charged
intelligent thundered experience reveal
released probably* bothered measured

- What's the underlined part? (Signal.) *re.*
- What word? (Signal.) *Reopened.*

2. Touch the next word. ✓
- What's the underlined part? (Signal.) *ly.*
- What word? (Signal.) *Usually.*

3. (Repeat step 2 for each remaining word.)
4. (Repeat each row of words until firm.)
5. What does **probably** mean? (Call on a student.)

EXERCISE 3

VOCABULARY

1. Touch part 3. ✓

3

1. alert
2. visible
3. secluded
4. gash
5. daggerlike

- We're going to talk about what those words mean.

2. Touch word 1. ✓
- What word? (Signal.) *Alert.*
- When someone is **alert,** that person is **paying close attention.** Everybody, what's another way of saying "The woman was **paying close attention**"? (Signal.) *The woman was alert.*

3. Touch word 2. ✓
- What word? (Signal.) *Visible.*
- Something that is **visible can be seen.** Everybody, what's another way of saying **visible** objects? (Signal.) *Objects that can be seen.*

4. Touch word 3. ✓
- What word? (Signal.) *Secluded.*
- **Secluded** means **well hidden.** Everybody, what does **secluded** mean? (Signal.) *Well hidden.*

5. Touch word 4. ✓
- What word? (Signal.) *Gash.*
- A **gash** is a **deep cut.** Everybody, what's another way of saying "There was a **deep cut** in the seat"? (Signal.) *There was a gash in the seat.*

6. Touch word 5. ✓
- What word? (Signal.) *Daggerlike.*
- How would you describe a **daggerlike** object? (Call on a student.) (Idea: *An object that is pointed like a dagger.*)

EXERCISE 4

WORD PRACTICE

1. Touch the first word in part 4. ✓

4

movement capable instead unison*
dangerous scramble* crocodile flee
instinctively narrow instincts jaws alert*
shoulder drastic instantly compared

- What word? (Signal.) *Movement.*
2. Next word. ✓
- What word? (Signal.) *Capable.*
3. (Repeat step 2 for each remaining word.)
4. (Repeat each row of words until firm.)
5. What does **unison** mean? (Call on a student.)
- (Repeat for **scramble, alert.**)

EXERCISE 5

WORD-ATTACK SKILLS: Individual tests

1. (Call on individual students. Each student reads a row or column. Tally the rows and columns read without error. If the group reads at least 7 rows and columns without making errors, direct all students to record 5 points in Box A of their Point Chart. Criterion is 80 percent of rows and columns read without error.)
2. (If the group did not read at least 7 rows and columns without errors, do not award any points for the Word-Attack Skills exercises.)

SELECTION READING

EXERCISE 6

STORY READING

1. Everybody, touch part 5. ✓
2. The error limit for this story is 12. If the group reads the story with 12 errors or less, you earn 5 points.

5

A Narrow Escape

3. (Call on a student to read the title.) *A Narrow Escape.*
- What do you think this story is about? (Accept reasonable responses.)
4. (Call on individual students. Each is to read two to four sentences.)
5. (Call on individual students to answer the specified questions during the story reading.)

The movement in the water sent off an instinctive alarm in Tekla. She turned toward the movement and lowered her head. Almost in unison the other triceratops stopped drinking and stood motionless. Some of the younger ones began to back out of the water, still facing Tekla.

Suddenly, a huge open mouth shot from under the water. The mouth was bigger than Tekla. Tekla quickly backed up, almost falling down. The huge crocodile jaws closed on her head. Instantly the jaws reopened. They had closed on Tekla's three horns, and the horns had punched holes in the roof of the crocodile's mouth. ❶

1. How did Tekla know danger was near? (Ideas: *The movement in the water set off an instinctive alarm in her; instinct.*)
1. Why did the crocodile let go of Tekla? (Idea: *Because its jaw had closed on Tekla's horns, and the horns had punched holes in the roof of its mouth.*)

Lesson
50

As soon as the crocodile released her, Tekla scrambled from the water hole. Within a few moments, she was calm again. She didn't feel the blood running from the front of her neck where the crocodile's lower teeth had dug in.

Tekla didn't react very much to the pain because she was a reptile, and pain doesn't serve reptiles the way it serves most intelligent animals. Intelligent animals learn more quickly. Pain helps them learn. When they do something and then feel pain, they soon learn that what they did leads to pain. ❷

2. Why didn't Tekla react much to the pain? (Idea: *Because she was a reptile.*)
2. How does pain serve intelligent animals? (Idea: *Intelligent animals learn from pain.*)

Humans probably react more to pain than any other animal that has lived on Earth. On the other hand, pain didn't help triceratops learn, because they were not capable of learning very much. They had brains that were tiny compared to their overall size, and they were capable of learning very little. But triceratops had instincts that helped them get along in the world. Tekla's instincts told her how to walk, what to eat, when to feel frightened, when to run, when to fight, and when to mate. ❸

3. Why were triceratops not capable of learning very much? (Idea: *Because their brains were tiny.*)
3. What did instincts of triceratops tell them to do? (Ideas: *How to walk; what to eat; when to feel frightened; when to fight; when to run; when to mate.*)

The days went by, and Tekla grew. Every day during her first year, she gained weight. When she was one year old, she was about one-fourth the size of a full-grown triceratops; she weighed about 5,000 pounds. She stood five feet tall and measured seven feet from the tip of her middle horn to the end of her long tail.

That first year went by quickly. Tekla did the same thing day after day. She ate. She became alert if the sound of a tyrannosaur was heard across the plain. She stood shoulder to shoulder with the other triceratops facing a tyrannosaur when one came near the herd. But tyrannosaurs never bothered the herd. ❹

4. How did the triceratops herd defend itself against a tyrannosaur? (Idea: *All the triceratops stood shoulder-to-shoulder and faced the tyrannosaur.*)

Instead, they chose to run down lone dinosaurs as they tried to flee across the plain to the water hole. These attacks were not always successful, especially if the other dinosaur was a large, healthy adult.

Tekla's first year was not marked by drastic changes in seasons. One part of the year was drier than the others. Another part of the year was a little cooler with more rain; however, all seasons were fairly warm and wet with heavy clouds usually visible in the sky.

Shortly after Tekla's first birthday, she left the herd. Four adult female triceratops were going back to the sand near the cliffs to lay their eggs. Tekla tagged along. When the adults got near the cliff, they split up, each going to a secluded spot. Tekla began to follow one of the females. She turned and attacked Tekla. She charged her with her head down. ⑤

5. What caused the female triceratops to attack Tekla? (Idea: *The adult female triceratops was going to lay eggs and wanted to be alone.*)

Tekla tried to get out of the way, but the middle horn caught her hind leg. She turned and began to run. The adult's horn had made a deep gash in her leg, and the leg seemed to drag when she ran.

Suddenly, Tekla sensed something more dangerous than the female triceratops. She stopped and looked around, trying to locate the danger. Then she saw it. Standing above a grove of small trees, it looked like a green mountain. Its mouth was open in a half-smile, revealing two rows of daggerlike teeth. It was the biggest tyrannosaur Tekla had ever seen.

6. (Award points quickly.)
7. (If the group makes more than 12 errors, repeat the reading immediately or on the next day.)

FLUENCY ASSESSMENT

EXERCISE 7

TIMED READING CHECKOUTS

1. (For this part of the lesson, assigned pairs of students work together during the checkouts.)
- (If one student does not have a checkout partner, arrange another time when you can give the checkout.)
2. (Each student does a 2-minute timed reading. Students earn 5 points by reading at least 240 words and making no more than 5 errors on the first part of story 50. Students record points in Box C of their Point Chart and plot their reading rate and errors on the Individual Reading Progress Chart.)
- (During each timed checkout, observe one pair of students for 2 minutes. Make notes on any mistakes the reader makes.)
3. (Record the timed reading checkout performance for each student you observed on the Fluency Assessment Summary form.)

Lesson 50

Errors

1

1. Why did the crocodile let go of Tekla?
(Her horns had punched holes in the roof of the crocodile's mouth.)

2. How does pain serve intelligent animals?
(Pain helps them learn.)

3. What animal probably reacts most to pain? (humans)

4. How did the size of the brain of a triceratops compare with the size of its body?
(The brain was tiny.)

5. Name three things the instincts of a triceratops told it to do.
(Any three: how to walk; what to eat; when to feel frightened; when to run; when to fight; when to mate)

6. Describe the climate of the place where the dinosaurs lived.
(warm and wet)

7. Write **carnivore** or **herbivore** in front of each animal.
carnivore a. lion
herbivore b. triceratops
herbivore c. cow
carnivore d. tyrannosaur

8. How long after the dinosaurs became extinct did humans inhabit the earth?
(eighty million years)

9. Name the two trees living on the plain that are alive today.
(metasequoia and ginkgo)

Copyright © SRA/McGraw-Hill. All rights reserved. Lesson 50 87

Lesson 50

2 **Fill in each blank using a word in the box.**

alert	visible	secluded
daggerlike	gash	unison

1. The tiger smiled, showing her daggerlike teeth.
2. She couldn't find her purse even though it was plainly visible.
3. The thorn left a nasty gash in her arm.

3 **Copy the sentence that tells the main idea of the story.**

1. Tekla weighed over 4,000 pounds but was far from being full-grown.
2. Tekla managed to survive her first year of life.
3. A crocodile attacked Tekla but did not injure her badly.
4. A female triceratops who wanted to lay eggs chased Tekla away.

Tekla managed to survive her first year of life.

4 **Write the parts for each word.**

1. tricycle = tri + cycle
2. unarmed = un + arm + ed
3. extending = ex + tend + ing
4. prehistoric = pre + historic

88 Lesson 50 Copyright © SRA/McGraw-Hill. All rights reserved.

WORKBOOK EXERCISES

Independent Student Work

Task A

- Open your Workbook to Lesson 50. ✓
- Complete all the parts of your Workbook lesson using a pencil. If you make no errors, you will earn 5 points.

Task B

1. (Before presenting Lesson 51, check student Workbooks for Lesson 50.)
   - (Call on individual students to read the items and answers in each part. Students mark errors using a pen.)
2. (Direct the students to count the number of errors and write the number in the Errors box at the top of the Workbook page.)
3. (Award points and direct students to record points in Box D of their Point Chart.)

   0 errors................................5 points
   1 error ....3 points
   2 or 3 errors ....1 point
   more than 3 errors ....0 points

Point schedule for Lessons 46 through 50

Box	Lesson part	Points
A	Word Attack	0 or 5
B	Story Reading	0 or 5
C	Timed Reading Checkout	0 or 5
D	Workbook	0, 1, 3, or 5
Bonus	(Teacher option)	—

Five-lesson point summary

- (For **letter grades** based on points for Lessons **46** through **50,** tell students to compute the total for the blue boxes [C, D, and Bonus] and write the number in the Total box at the end of each row in their Point Chart. Students then add the totals and write the sum in the green box.)
- (For **rewards** based on points, tell students to compute the total for all boxes [A, B, C, D, and Bonus] and write the number in the Total box at the end of each row. Students then add the totals and write the sum in the green box.)

END OF LESSON 50

Lesson Objectives	LESSON 51 Exercise	LESSON 52 Exercise	LESSON 53 Exercise	LESSON 54 Exercise	LESSON 55 Exercise
Word Attack					
Decoding and Word Analysis					
Affix: *sub*		1	1		
Affixes: *pre, re, ly, un, dis, sub*				1	
Letter Combinations/Letter Sounds	1	2	2	2	
Word Recognition	1–3	1–4	1–4	1–4	1, 2
Vocabulary					
Morphemic Analysis		1	1	1	
Definitions	2, 3	1–4	3, 4	1–4	2
Usage	2	3	3	3	2
Assessment					
Ongoing: Individual Tests	4	5	5	5	3
Group Reading					
Decoding and Word Analysis					
Read Decodable Text	5	6	6	6	4
Read Expository Text					4
Comprehension					
Draw Inferences	5	6	6	6	4
Note Details	5	6	6	6	4
Predict	5	6	6	6	4
Author's Purpose					5
Assessment					
Ongoing: Comprehension Check	5	6	6	6	5
Ongoing: Decoding Accuracy	5	6	6	6	5
Fluency Assessment					
Fluency					
Reread Decodable Text	6	7	7	7	6
Assessment					
Ongoing: Teacher-Monitored Fluency	6	7	7	7	6
Ongoing: Peer-Monitored Fluency	6	7	7	7	6
Workbook Exercises					
Decoding and Word Analysis					
Multisyllabic Word Parts			Ind. Work		
Comprehension					
Main Idea		Ind. Work			
Note Details	Ind. Work	Ind. Work	Ind. Work	Ind. Work	Ind. Work
Vocabulary					
Usage	Ind. Work	Ind. Work	Ind. Work	Ind. Work	Ind. Work
Study Skills					
Writing Mechanics		Ind. Work			
Assessment					
Ongoing: Workcheck	Workcheck	Workcheck	Workcheck	Workcheck	Workcheck

WORD-ATTACK SKILLS

Student Book

EXERCISE 1

WORD PRACTICE

1. Open your Student Book to Lesson 51. ✓

1

hesitation pretended differently roamed*
measured prance* blindly instantly

- Touch the first word in part 1. ✓
- What's the underlined part? (Signal.) *shun.*
- What word? (Signal.) *Hesitation.*

2. Touch the next word. ✓
- What's the underlined part? (Signal.) *pre.*
- What word? (Signal.) *Pretended.*

3. (Repeat step 2 for each remaining word.)
4. (Repeat each row of words until firm.)
5. What does **roamed** mean? (Call on a student.)
- (Repeat for **prance.**)

EXERCISE 2

VOCABULARY

1. Touch part 2. ✓

2

1. faked
2. viciously
3. vegetation
4. knee-deep

- We're going to talk about what those words mean.

2. Touch word 1. ✓
- What word? (Signal.) *Faked.*
- If you **faked** something, you **pretended to do it.** Everybody, what's another way of saying "She **pretended to** throw a long pass"? (Signal.) *She faked a long pass.*

3. Touch word 2. ✓
- What word? (Signal.) *Viciously.*
- One meaning for **viciously** is **fiercely.** Everybody, what's another way of saying "The dogs attacked each other **fiercely**"? (Signal.) *The dogs attacked each other viciously.*

4. Touch word 3. ✓
- What word? (Signal.) *Vegetation.*
- **Plant life** is **vegetation.** Everybody, what's another way of saying "The ground was covered with **plant life**"? (Signal.) *The ground was covered with vegetation.*

5. Touch word 4. ✓
- What word? (Signal.) *Knee-deep.*
- What does **knee-deep** mean? (Call on a student.) (Idea: *Up to your knees in something.*)

EXERCISE 3

WORD PRACTICE

1. Touch the first word in part 3. ✓

3

chorus kangaroo tremendous* closest
smiling defend full-grown behave
juvenile grazing* confused butted
though adult predator* plodded
drew herbivore occasion unison*
thundered shoulder bumped

- What word? (Signal.) *Chorus.*

2. Next word. ✓
- What word? (Signal.) *Kangaroo.*

3. (Repeat step 2 for each remaining word.)
4. (Repeat each row of words until firm.)
5. What does **tremendous** mean? (Call on a student.)
- (Repeat for each starred word.)

EXERCISE 4

WORD-ATTACK SKILLS: Individual tests

1. (Call on individual students. Each student reads a row or column. Tally the rows and columns read without error. If the group reads at least 7 rows and columns without making errors, direct all students to record 5 points in Box A of their Point Chart. Criterion is 80 percent of rows and columns read without error.)
2. (If the group did not read at least 7 rows and columns without errors, do not award any points for the Word-Attack Skills exercises.)

SELECTION READING

EXERCISE 5

STORY READING

1. Everybody, touch part 4. ✓
2. The error limit for this story is 12. If the group reads the story with 12 errors or less, you earn 5 points.

4 **Surviving the Attacks**

3. (Call on a student to read the title.) *Surviving the Attacks.*
- What do you think this story is about? (Accept reasonable responses.)
4. (Call on individual students. Each is to read two to four sentences.)
5. (Call on individual students to answer the specified questions during the story reading.)

The huge tyrannosaur hopped forward like a kangaroo. Then it began to walk toward Tekla. Tekla backed up, out of the path of the tyrannosaur. The great dinosaur forgot Tekla. It decided to go after the adult triceratops now in its path.

The tyrannosaur ran around to attack the triceratops from behind, but the triceratops turned around quickly. The tyrannosaur faked with its head several times and then quickly jumped to one side. Again the triceratops turned to face the predator, but as quickly as it turned, the tyrannosaur jumped to the other side. Before the triceratops could turn again, the great smiling jaws of the tyrannosaur came down on its back. The sound of the breaking bones carried across the plain. The tyrannosaur struck again, this time from behind. The triceratops was still on its feet, but it could hardly move. The tyrannosaur moved to the side of the triceratops, butted it viciously until it fell over, and then struck again for the kill.

By now, Tekla was far from the cliffs, running as well as she could across the plain. Her instincts told her to return to the herd. There was safety in the herd. ❶

1. Why did Tekla return to the herd? (Ideas: *Her instincts told her to; there was safety in the herd.*)
1. Why didn't the tyrannosaur attack Tekla? (Idea: *It decided to go after the adult triceratops instead.*)

Five or more triceratops could defend themselves against a tyrannosaur; however, a single triceratops, though it was huge and had great horns, could not hope to survive a battle with a full-grown tyrannosaur.

By the time Tekla reached her fourth birthday, she was full-grown. She didn't behave much differently from the way she had behaved when she was a juvenile. She didn't, however, move around as much now. She plodded along with the herd as it roamed the plain, eating nearly all the time. Now Tekla ate more than 2,000 pounds of vegetation a day. She measured nearly thirty feet from the tip of her nose to the end of her tail. She weighed nearly 20,000 pounds. Every time she stepped on the plain, she left a footprint that was about two inches deep. ❷

2. How did Tekla behave differently when she became an adult? (Idea: *She didn't move around as much.*)

Her size had changed and so had some of her instincts. When Tekla had been a juvenile, her instincts had told her to hide in the face of danger. Now, her instincts told her to fight. When a tyrannosaur drew near the herd, Tekla took her place with the other triceratops, her head down and her large horns pointed at the predator. Perhaps twice a week some large tyrannosaurs would come near, but none ever attacked the herd. Usually the tyrannosaur would prance and jump and make passes at the triceratops. Sometimes it pretended to charge the herd, hoping that one of the herbivores would break away from the group. But on each occasion, the triceratops herd stood its ground, and the tyrannosaur would soon leave to find a meal elsewhere. ❸

3. How did Tekla's instincts change when she became an adult? (Idea: *Her instincts told her to fight instead of run.*)

Shortly after her fourth birthday, Tekla had her first battle with a tyrannosaur. It happened at the water hole. There were many animals along the edge of the hole, most of them grazing animals. Suddenly, a tyrannosaur charged through a grove of trees toward the water hole. In unison, the animals stopped drinking. They stood alert for an instant, and then they ran. The triceratops thundered from the hole. Hundreds of birds took to the air with a chorus of wing flapping that could be heard a mile away. Small reptiles sped from the water hole. ❹

4. Why did all the animals start to flee? (Idea: *Because of the charging tyrannosaur.*)

The animals moved in two waves, one going left and one moving right, leaving a path for the charging tyrannosaur. Tekla and three other triceratops were knee-deep in the water. They were caught in the middle of the confused animals that were all running blindly from the water hole. Before Tekla and the others could leave, they saw they were right in the path of the tyrannosaur.

Instinctively, the four triceratops stood shoulder to shoulder and faced the tyrannosaur. Without hesitation, the huge predator jumped to one side of the group and tried to bite the back of the closest triceratops. All the triceratops tried to turn and face the tyrannosaur, but they just bumped into each other. One of them, a young male, began to run from the water hole. Instantly, the tyrannosaur charged after him. ❺

5. How did the four triceratops defend themselves against the tyrannosaur? (Idea: *They stood shoulder-to-shoulder and faced the tyrannosaur.*)
6. (Award points quickly.)
7. (If the group makes more than 12 errors, repeat the reading immediately or on the next day.)

FLUENCY ASSESSMENT

EXERCISE 6

NEW TIMED READING CHECKOUTS

Note: The rate-accuracy criterion for Lessons 51–54 and 56–59 is 260 words with no more than 5 errors. The 260th word is underlined in the reading selection in the Student Book.

1. (For this part of the lesson, assigned pairs of students work together during the checkouts.)
   - (If one student does not have a checkout partner, arrange another time when you can give the checkout.)
2. (Each student does a 2-minute timed reading. Students earn 5 points by reading at least **260 words** and making no more than 5 errors on the first part of story 51. Students record points in Box C of their Point Chart and plot their reading rate and errors on the Individual Reading Progress Chart.)
   - (During each timed checkout, observe one pair of students for 2 minutes. Make notes on any mistakes the reader makes.)
3. (Record the timed reading checkout performance for each student you observed on the Fluency Assessment Summary form.)

WORKBOOK EXERCISES

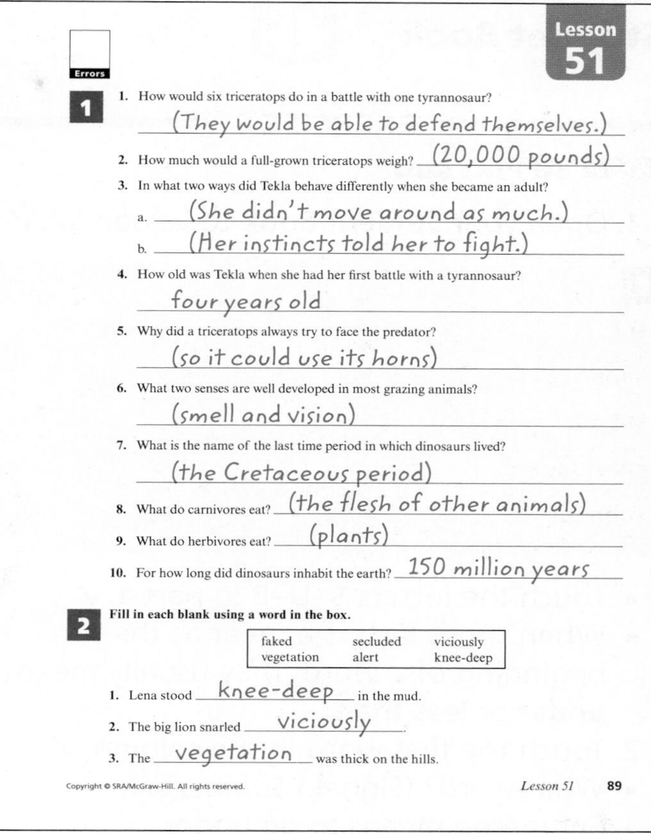

Lesson 51

Errors

1

1. How would six triceratops do in a battle with one tyrannosaur? (They would be able to defend themselves.)
2. How much would a full-grown triceratops weigh? (20,000 pounds)
3. In what two ways did Tekla behave differently when she became an adult?
   a. (She didn't move around as much.)
   b. (Her instincts told her to fight.)
4. How old was Tekla when she had her first battle with a tyrannosaur? four years old
5. Why did a triceratops always try to face the predator? (so it could use its horns)
6. What two senses are well developed in most grazing animals? (smell and vision)
7. What is the name of the last time period in which dinosaurs lived? (the Cretaceous period)
8. What do carnivores eat? (the flesh of other animals)
9. What do herbivores eat? (plants)
10. For how long did dinosaurs inhabit the earth? 150 million years

2 Fill in each blank using a word in the box.

faked	secluded	viciously
vegetation	alert	knee-deep

1. Lena stood knee-deep in the mud.
2. The big lion snarled viciously.
3. The vegetation was thick on the hills.

Copyright © SRA/McGraw-Hill. All rights reserved. Lesson 51 89

Independent Student Work

Task A

- Open your Workbook to Lesson 51. ✓
- Complete all the parts of your Workbook lesson using a pencil. If you make no errors, you will earn 5 points.

Task B

1. (Before presenting Lesson 52, check student Workbooks for Lesson 51.)
   - (Call on individual students to read the items and answers in each part. Students mark errors using a pen.)
2. (Direct the students to count the number of errors and write the number in the Errors box at the top of the Workbook page.)
3. (Award points and direct students to record points in Box D of their Point Chart.)

   0 errors ....5 points
   1 error ....3 points
   2 or 3 errors ....1 point
   more than 3 errors ....0 points

END OF LESSON 51

Lesson 52

WORD-ATTACK SKILLS

Student Book 

EXERCISE 1

NEW **AFFIX: sub**

1. Open your Student Book to Lesson 52. ✓

1

sub
submerge
submit
substandard
subtract

- Touch the letters **S–U–B** in part 1. ✓
- When those letters appear at the beginning of a word, they usually mean **under** or **less than.**

2. Touch the first word in the column. ✓
- What word? (Signal.) *Submerge.*
- **Submerge** means **to go under.**

3. Touch the next word. ✓
- What word? (Signal.) *Submit.*
- **Submit** means **to yield** or **to put yourself under somebody else's will.**

4. Touch the next word. ✓
- What word? (Signal.) *Substandard.*
- **Substandard** means **below standard** or **less than standard.**

5. Touch the next word. ✓
- What word? (Signal.) *Subtract.*
- **Subtract** means to **make the amount less.**

6. (Repeat the list until firm.)

EXERCISE 2

WORD PRACTICE

1. Touch the first word in part 2. ✓

2

moaning semicircle wildly released
thrashing* infection heaving breathed
either leisurely* experienced flail*

- What's the underlined part? (Signal.) *ōōō.*
- What word? (Signal.) *Moaning.*

2. Touch the next word. ✓
- What's the underlined part? (Signal.) *sss.*
- What word? (Signal.) *Semicircle.*

3. (Repeat step 2 for each remaining word.)
4. (Repeat each row of words until firm.)
5. What does **thrashing** mean? (Call on a student.)
- (Repeat for **leisurely, flail.**)

EXERCISE 3

VOCABULARY

1. Touch part 3. ✓

3

1. ribs
2. shrill
3. trample

- We're going to talk about what those words mean.

2. Touch word 1. ✓
- What word? (Signal.) *Ribs.*
- Where are your **ribs?** (Call on a student.) (Idea: *In the chest.*)

3. Everybody, touch word 2. ✓
- What word? (Signal.) *Shrill.*
- A **shrill** sound is a **high-pitched** sound. Everybody, what's another way of saying "The whistle made a **high-pitched** sound"? (Signal.) *The whistle made a shrill sound.*

4. Touch word 3. ✓
- What word? (Signal.) *Trample.*
- When you **trample** something, you **stamp** it **into the ground.** Everybody, what's another way of saying "She **stamped** the grass **into the ground**"? (Signal.) *She trampled the grass.*

EXERCISE 4

WORD PRACTICE

1. Touch the first word in part 4. ✓

4

strength knocked silent injured
struck flicking message normal
lowered powerful locomotive seriously
finished occasionally scavengers*
fallen settled meanwhile

- What word? (Signal.) *Strength.*
2. Next word. ✓
- What word? (Signal.) *Knocked.*
3. (Repeat step 2 for each remaining word.)
4. (Repeat each row of words until firm.)
5. What does **scavengers** mean? (Call on a student.)

EXERCISE 5

WORD-ATTACK SKILLS: Individual tests

1. (Call on individual students. Each student reads a row or column. Tally the rows and columns read without error. If the group reads at least 8 rows and columns without making errors, direct all students to record 5 points in Box A of their Point Chart. Criterion is 80 percent of rows and columns read without error.)
2. (If the group did not read at least 8 rows and columns without errors, do not award any points for the Word-Attack Skills exercises.)

SELECTION READING

EXERCISE 6

STORY READING

1. Everybody, touch part 5. ✓
2. The error limit for this story is 12. If the group reads the story with 12 errors or less, you earn 5 points.

5 **The Tyrannosaur Attacks**

3. (Call on a student to read the title.) *The Tyrannosaur Attacks.*
- What do you think this story is about? (Accept reasonable responses.)
4. (Call on individual students. Each is to read two to four sentences.)
5. (Call on individual students to answer the specified questions during the story reading.)

Fight, Tekla's instincts told her. Fight. Without fear, Tekla charged after the tyrannosaur, who now had its jaws firmly planted in the male's back. The male was trying to turn to face the tyrannosaur, but the tyrannosaur had a firm hold on his back. Tekla lowered her head and charged with all her strength. Like all dinosaurs, her back legs were bigger and more powerful than her front legs, and she pushed so hard against the soft ground near the water hole that she made footprints over a foot deep. ❶

1. How did a dinosaur's back legs differ from its front legs? (Idea: *The back legs were much bigger and stronger than the front legs.*)

She pushed with all her strength. Faster—move faster, her instincts told her.

Her two large horns struck the tyrannosaur in the side. One broke the tyrannosaur's lowest rib. The other entered the side of its belly. Both horns went in their full length.

Tekla had hit the tyrannosaur so hard that the ground shook. The tyrannosaur released its grip on the young male, let out a shrill roar, and fell over, kicking wildly. ❷

2. What did the tyrannosaur do when Tekla hit it? (Ideas: *Released its grip on the male triceratops; let out a shrill roar; fell over.*)

The two other triceratops charged from the water hole. Almost as quickly as the tyrannosaur had fallen over, it stood up again, wildly flailing its tail, and jumping around like a huge kangaroo. Tekla stood her ground with her head down. As the tyrannosaur lowered its head to strike at Tekla's neck, she charged again, this time planting her two large horns in the tyrannosaur's soft belly. At the same time, the two triceratops that had been in the water hole charged forward—one on either side of the tyrannosaur. The tyrannosaur went down as the six horns tore into its sides with the force of a locomotive. Meanwhile, the injured male triceratops stood and watched. It tried to move forward, but it was seriously injured. It would die before the sun set.

The tyrannosaur was on its back, roaring and thrashing its tail from side to side. The tail struck one of the triceratops and knocked it over. One of the other triceratops charged and struck the fallen tyrannosaur in the neck. Another charged and drove its horns into the predator's side.

Just when it seemed as if the tyrannosaur was finished, the giant animal rolled to one side and snapped at Tekla with frightening speed. Its huge jaws caught her front shoulder, right below her armor plate. The tyrannosaur released its grip when the other triceratops charged and struck it in the side of the head.

Suddenly, the plain was silent. The tyrannosaur lay on its back, flicking its tail from time to time. The four triceratops stood in a semicircle facing their fallen enemy. The birds settled along the shore of the water hole, and many dinosaurs returned, acting as if nothing had happened. Some of them walked near the fallen tyrannosaur without even looking at it. It was almost as if a message had gone out to all the animals that the danger had passed and things were back to normal. ❸

3. How did many of the animals act after the battle? (Idea: *As if nothing had happened.*)

The four triceratops stood over the tyrannosaur for about a minute. Then Tekla and two others turned away and returned to the water hole. The injured male didn't follow. It stood there bleeding, its head down and its sides heaving every time it breathed. Long after Tekla and the other triceratops left the water hole and returned to grazing, the injured male stood there. At last it lay down as some of the smaller predators and scavengers moved in for the great feast that night. ❹

4. What kinds of animals eat bones? (Ideas: *Smaller predators; scavengers.*)

The grass around the two fallen dinosaurs had been trampled when the sun came up the next morning. Only a few of the larger bones of the tyrannosaur and the male triceratops marked the spot where the battle had taken place. The animals had forgotten yesterday's battle.

Tekla had several cracked bones and an infection, but she didn't remember the battle. She knew only that she should eat and rest. ⑤

5. What injuries did Tekla have after the battle? (Ideas: *Several cracked bones and an infection.*)
5. Why didn't Tekla remember the battle? (Ideas: *Because the brain of a triceratops is small; triceratops are not very intelligent.*)
6. (Award points quickly.)
7. (If the group makes more than 12 errors, repeat the reading immediately or on the next day.)

FLUENCY ASSESSMENT

EXERCISE 7

TIMED READING CHECKOUTS

1. (For this part of the lesson, assigned pairs of students work together during the checkouts.)
   - (If one student does not have a checkout partner, arrange another time when you can give the checkout.)
2. (Each student does a 2-minute timed reading. Students earn 5 points by reading at least 260 words and making no more than 5 errors on the first part of story 52. Students record points in Box C of their Point Chart and plot their reading rate and errors on the Individual Reading Progress Chart.)
   - (During each timed checkout, observe one pair of students for 2 minutes. Make notes on any mistakes the reader makes.)
3. (Record the timed reading checkout performance for each student you observed on the Fluency Assessment Summary form.)

Lesson 52

Errors

1

1. How were a dinosaur's back legs different from its front legs? (The back legs were bigger and more powerful.)
2. The tyrannosaur jumped around like (a huge) kangaroo
3. How did Tekla get away from the tyrannosaur? (The tyrannosaur released Tekla when the other triceratops struck it in the side of the head.)
4. How did many dinosaurs act after the battle? (as if nothing had happened)
5. Why didn't Tekla remember her battle with the tyrannosaur? (Her brain was not very large; she was not an intelligent animal.)
6. When the battle was over, Tekla knew only that she should eat and rest
7. Name two trees living on the plain that are alive today. metasequoia and ginkgo
8. How long after the dinosaurs became extinct did humans inhabit the earth? eighty million years
9. Write **grazing animal** or **predator** in front of each animal.
   - predator a. tyrannosaur
   - grazing animal b. triceratops
   - grazing animal c. horse
   - predator d. lion
10. What did the ornithomimid like to eat? (dinosaur) eggs

90 *Lesson 52* Copyright © SRA/McGraw-Hill. All rights reserved.

Lesson 52

2 **Fill in each blank using a word in the box.**

faked	ribs	trampled
shrill	submerge	visible

1. The horses trampled the vegetation.
2. The bird song was high and shrill.
3. Your ribs are in your chest.

3 **Copy the sentence that tells the main idea of the story.**

1. After the fight with the tyrannosaur, some triceratops acted as if nothing had happened.
2. When the tyrannosaur was on the ground, one of the triceratops charged and struck it in the side of the head.
3. Tekla received cracked bones and an infection from a battle with a tyrannosaur.
4. When Tekla became an adult, she did not run from predators the way she did as a juvenile.

Tekla received cracked bones and an infection from a battle with a tyrannosaur.

Copyright © SRA/McGraw-Hill. All rights reserved. *Lesson 52* 91

WORKBOOK EXERCISES

Independent Student Work

Task A

- Open your Workbook to Lesson 52. ✓
- Complete all the parts of your Workbook lesson using a pencil. If you make no errors, you will earn 5 points.

Task B

1. (Before presenting Lesson 53, check student Workbooks for Lesson 52.)
- (Call on individual students to read the items and answers in each part. Students mark errors using a pen.)
2. (Direct the students to count the number of errors and write the number in the Errors box at the top of the Workbook page.)
3. (Award points and direct students to record points in Box D of their Point Chart.)

0 errors.................................5 points
1 error ....3 points
2 or 3 errors ....1 point
more than 3 errors ....0 points

END OF LESSON 52

WORD-ATTACK SKILLS

Student Book 

EXERCISE 1

NEW **AFFIX: sub**

1. Open your Student Book to Lesson 53. ✓

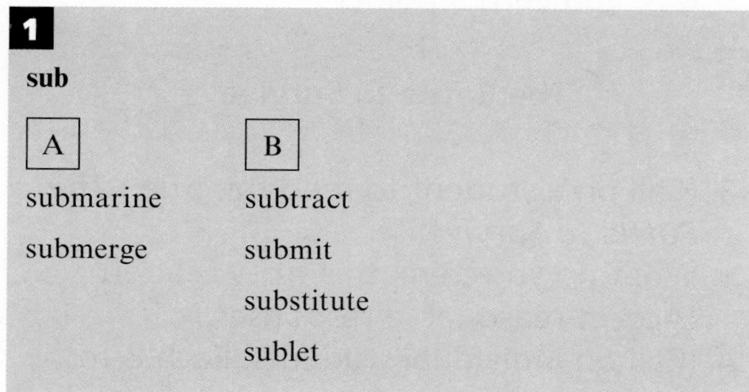

1

sub

A	B
submarine	subtract
submerge	submit
	substitute
	sublet

- Touch the letters **S–U–B** in part 1. ✓
- **Sub** usually means **under** or **less than.**

2. Touch the first word in column A. ✓
- What word? (Signal.) *Submarine.*
- A **submarine** is a ship that can go underwater.

3. Touch the next word. ✓
- What word? (Signal.) *Submerge.*
- What does **submerge** mean? (Call on a student.) (Idea: *Go under.*)

4. Everybody, touch the first word in column B. ✓
- What word? (Signal.) *Subtract.*

5. Next word. ✓
- What word? (Signal.) *Submit.*

6. (Repeat step 5 for **substitute, sublet.**)
7. (Repeat the list until firm.)

EXERCISE 2

WORD PRACTICE

1. Touch the first word in part 2. ✓

2

required interest insurance*
experienced accurately

- What's the underlined part? (Signal.) *re.*
- What word? (Signal.) *Required.*

2. Touch the next word. ✓
- What's the underlined part? (Signal.) *er.*
- What word? (Signal.) *Interest.*

3. (Repeat step 2 for each remaining word.)
4. (Repeat each row of words until firm.)
5. What does **insurance** mean? (Call on a student.)

EXERCISE 3

VOCABULARY

1. Touch part 3. ✓

3

1. stampede
2. offspring
3. urge
4. concealed
5. scent

- We're going to talk about what those words mean.

2. Touch word 1. ✓
- What word? (Signal.) *Stampede.*
- What does a herd of grazing animals do when it **stampedes?** (Call on a student.) (Idea: *Runs together in panic.*)

3. Everybody, touch word 2. ✓
- What word? (Signal.) *Offspring.*
- **Offspring** are **descendants** or **children.** Everybody, what are **offspring?** (Signal.) *Descendants or children.*

4. Touch word 3. ✓
- What word? (Signal.) *Urge.*
- An **urge** is a **desire to do something.** Everybody, what's another way of saying "He had **a desire** to play golf"? (Signal.) *He had an urge to play golf.*

5. Touch word 4. ✓
- What word? (Signal.) *Concealed.*
- Things that are **hidden** are **concealed.** Everybody, what's another way of saying "The house was **hidden**"? (Signal.) *The house was concealed.*

6. Touch word 5. ✓
- What word? (Signal.) *Scent.*
- A **scent** is an **odor.** Everybody, what's another way of saying "The dog followed the rabbit's **odor**"? (Signal.) *The dog followed the rabbit's scent.*

EXERCISE 4

WORD PRACTICE

1. Touch the first word in part 4. ✓

4

focus ancient occurred veered inherit

occasion gallop sprinted tumbled hurry

secluded* mated strongest sixteenth lion

groves electric straight ginkgo buffalo

scrambled* skeleton fought instinctive

- What word? (Signal.) *Focus.*
2. Next word. ✓
- What word? (Signal.) *Ancient.*
3. (Repeat step 2 for each remaining word.)
4. (Repeat each row of words until firm.)
5. What does **secluded** mean? (Call on a student.)
- (Repeat for **scrambled.**)

EXERCISE 5

WORD-ATTACK SKILLS: Individual tests

1. (Call on individual students. Each student reads a row or column. Tally the rows and columns read without error. If the group reads at least 8 rows and columns without making errors, direct all students to record 5 points in Box A of their Point Chart. Criterion is 80 percent of rows and columns read without error.)
2. (If the group did not read at least 8 rows and columns without errors, do not award any points for the Word-Attack Skills exercises.)

SELECTION READING

EXERCISE 6

STORY READING

1. Everybody, touch part 5. ✓
2. The error limit for this story is 12. If the group reads the story with 12 errors or less, you earn 5 points.

5 **The Battle to Survive**

3. (Call on a student to read the title.) *The Battle to Survive.*
- What do you think this story is about? (Accept reasonable responses.)
4. (Call on individual students. Each is to read two to four sentences.)
5. (Call on individual students to answer the specified questions during the story reading.)

When Tekla was five, she mated with a large male triceratops. Three males had fought over her. Their instinctive fighting to see who would mate was insurance that only the strongest would produce offspring, and those offspring would inherit their parents' strength. ❶

1. What led the male triceratops to fight to see who would mate with Tekla? (Idea: *Instincts.*)

In the spring, Tekla experienced some new instincts. She had a strong urge to be alone. If another triceratops drew near her, she would lower her head and move her horns from side to side, a sign that she was ready to attack. The other triceratops kept their distance. A few days after Tekla had experienced the urge to be alone, the urge took on a new focus. Instinct told her, "Go to the cliffs. Go to the cliffs." And so, late one afternoon she left the herd and walked to the ancient beach near the cliffs. Her instincts told her to find a secluded spot and dig a deep hole. She dug the hole with her front feet. Then she walked around the hole three or four times, making sure that she was safe. "Hurry," her instincts told her. It was time to lay eggs. ❷

2. What did Tekla's new instincts tell her to do? (Idea: *Be alone, go to the cliffs, dig a hole, and lay eggs.*)

She laid seven large eggs. Then she covered the hole and returned to the herd. She had done everything that was required of a mother triceratops. She would never know her babies. She would have no interest in them. They were on their own, just as Tekla had been from the day she was born.

Every year for the next twelve years, Tekla returned to the sand beach to lay eggs. Every year after laying the eggs, she returned to the herd. ❸

3. For how many years did Tekla lay eggs? *Twelve.*
3. What did she always do after laying eggs? (Idea: *Returned to the herd.*)

During those twelve years, she had one more fight with a tyrannosaur. She and five other triceratops killed a large female. Tekla left the battle with the tip of her left horn broken off.

Tekla's last fight occurred shortly after her sixteenth birthday. She was grazing on the edge of the herd. The herd made a practice of grazing in the open, far from the groves of trees which could hide the predators. On this occasion, however, the herd had moved close to a grove of ginkgo trees. There was almost no breeze, so Tekla couldn't smell the danger that the grove concealed. ❹

4. Why couldn't Tekla smell the predator? (Idea: *Because there was no breeze.*)

Suddenly, the herd stopped grazing; it was as if an electric shock had been sent through the herd. Then the triceratops began to run. Tekla hadn't caught the scent of the predator, but she caught the panic of the herd. Like stampeding cattle, they began to gallop from the grove of trees. Almost as quickly as they began to stampede, one large tyrannosaur, and then another, sped from the grove. Part of the triceratops herd split, moving off to the right. The rest kept running straight ahead. Tekla also ran straight ahead, but she was far behind the other triceratops. Behind her was one large tyrannosaur that could easily outrun a triceratops.

And it did. As the other tyrannosaur ran after the triceratops that veered to the right, this tyrannosaur sprinted after Tekla, overtaking her about three hundred yards from the grove of ginkgo trees. It tried to break her back with its powerful jaws, but the two animals were moving too fast for the tyrannosaur to direct its jaws accurately. It caught some of Tekla's flesh in its jaws as it fell on her back. Both animals tumbled to the ground with a terrible crash. Tekla scrambled to her feet, began to run away, and then suddenly stopped to face the predator.

Nobody is sure why grazing animals sometimes run from predators and at other times fight. Sometimes water buffalo will run from lions, even though a water buffalo can easily kill a lion. The triceratops herd ran from two tyrannosaurs, although they could easily have killed both of them if they had stood their ground. Tekla had run because the other triceratops had run. Now, however, her instincts told her that she must fight. ❺

5. Why had Tekla stopped running? (Idea: *Her instincts told her to fight.*)
6. (Award points quickly.)
7. (If the group makes more than 12 errors, repeat the reading immediately or on the next day.)

FLUENCY ASSESSMENT

EXERCISE 7

TIMED READING CHECKOUTS

1. (For this part of the lesson, assigned pairs of students work together during the checkouts.)
   - (If one student does not have a checkout partner, arrange another time when you can give the checkout.)
2. (Each student does a 2-minute timed reading. Students earn 5 points by reading at least 260 words and making no more than 5 errors on the first part of story 53. Students record points in Box C of their Point Chart and plot their reading rate and errors on the Individual Reading Progress Chart.)
   - (During each timed checkout, observe one pair of students for 2 minutes. Make notes on any mistakes the reader makes.)
3. (Record the timed reading checkout performance for each student you observed on the Fluency Assessment Summary form.)

Lesson 53

Errors

1

1. It was instinct that led the male triceratops to fight to see who would mate. What did that instinct ensure? (Only the strongest animals would produce offspring.)
2. What did Tekla always do after laying eggs? (She returned to the herd.)
3. Did a mother triceratops raise her young? No.
4. How are human parents different from triceratops parents? (Humans raise their young.)
5. How old was Tekla when she had her last fight? sixteen years old
6. Why did Tekla run from the tyrannosaur at first? (She caught the panic of the herd.)
7. What told Tekla to stop and fight the tyrannosaur? instinct
8. How does pain serve intelligent animals? (They learn from pain.)
9. For how long did dinosaurs inhabit the earth? (more than 150 million years)
10. How much would a full-grown triceratops weigh? 20,000 pounds

92 Lesson 53 Copyright © SRA/McGraw-Hill. All rights reserved.

Lesson 53

2 Fill in each blank using a word in the box.

stampeding	offspring	urge
concealed	faked	trample

1. The black kittens are the offspring of the brown cat.
2. A loud noise frightened the herd into stampeding.
3. Willie fixed dinner because he had an urge to eat.

3 Write the parts for each word.

1. substandard = sub + standard
2. disorderly = dis + order + ly
3. subtracted = sub + tract + ed
4. reminder = re + mind + er

Copyright © SRA/McGraw-Hill. All rights reserved. Lesson 53 93

WORKBOOK EXERCISES

Independent Student Work

Task A

- Open your Workbook to Lesson 53. ✓
- Complete all the parts of your Workbook lesson using a pencil. If you make no errors, you will earn 5 points.

Task B

1. (Before presenting Lesson 54, check student Workbooks for Lesson 53.)
   - (Call on individual students to read the items and answers in each part. Students mark errors using a pen.)
2. (Direct the students to count the number of errors and write the number in the Errors box at the top of the Workbook page.)
3. (Award points and direct students to record points in Box D of their Point Chart.)

0 errors................................5 points
1 error ....3 points
2 or 3 errors ....1 point
more than 3 errors ....0 points

END OF LESSON 53

Lesson 54

WORD-ATTACK SKILLS

Student Book

EXERCISE 1

NEW **AFFIX REVIEW**

Task A

1. Open your Student Book to Lesson 54. ✓

1

pre re ly un dis sub

A	B
reconstruction	submerge
abruptly	remains
unsuccessful	carefully
seriously	removing

- Touch the first row in part 1. ✓
- Let's see if you remember a meaning for each of those affixes.

2. Touch the letters **P–R–E.** ✓
- What's one meaning of **pre?** (Signal.) *Before.*

3. Touch the letters **R–E.** ✓
- What's one meaning of **re?** (Signal.) *Again.*

4. Touch the letters **L–Y.** ✓
- What's one meaning of **ly?** (Signal.) *How something happened.*

5. Touch the letters **U–N.** ✓
- What's one meaning of **un?** (Signal.) *Not.*

6. (Repeat steps 2–5 until firm.)
7. Touch the letters **D–I–S.** ✓
- What's one meaning of **dis?** (Call on a student. Accept **not, the opposite of,** or **away from.**)
- What's another meaning of **dis?** (Call on another student.)

8. Touch the letters **S–U–B.** ✓
- What's one meaning of **sub?** (Call on a student. Accept **under** or **less than.**)
- What's another meaning of **sub?** (Call on another student.)

Task B

1. Touch the first word in column A. ✓
- What word? (Signal.) *Reconstruction.*

2. Touch the next word. ✓
- What word? (Signal.) *Abruptly.*

3. (Repeat step 2 for each remaining word.)
4. (Repeat the list until firm.)
5. (Repeat steps 1–4 for the words in column B.)

EXERCISE 2

WORD PRACTICE

1. Touch the first word in part 2. ✓

2

motionless partner surviving* weakened

- What's the underlined part? (Signal.) *shun.*
- What word? (Signal.) *Motionless.*

2. Touch the next word. ✓
- What's the underlined part? (Signal.) *ar.*
- What word? (Signal.) *Partner.*

3. (Repeat step 2 for each remaining word.)
4. (Repeat the words until firm.)
5. What does **surviving** mean? (Call on a student.)

EXERCISE 3

VOCABULARY

1. Touch part 3. ✓

3

1. pounced
2. preserved
3. silt
4. fossilized
5. buckles
6. paleontologist
7. transform

- We're going to talk about what those words mean.

2. Touch word 1. ✓
- What word? (Signal.) *Pounced.*
- **Pounced** means **jumped on.** Everybody, what's another way of saying "The cat **jumped on** the ball"? (Signal.) *The cat pounced on the ball.*

3. Touch word 2. ✓
- What word? (Signal.) *Preserved.*
- Something that was **preserved** lasted a long time. Everybody, what's another way of saying "The treasure **lasted a long time**"? (Signal.) *The treasure was preserved.*
- What's another way of saying "Mummies **lasted a long time**"? (Signal.) *Mummies were preserved.*

4. Touch word 3. ✓
- What word? (Signal.) *Silt.*
- **Silt** is **a very fine mud.** Everybody, what is **silt?** (Signal.) *A very fine mud.*

5. Touch word 4. ✓
- What word? (Signal.) *Fossilized.*
- A **fossil** is **the remains of a living thing from a past geological age.** Everybody, what is a **fossil?** (Signal.) *The remains of a living thing from a past geological age.*
- When something is **fossilized,** it has become a **fossil.**

6. Touch word 5. ✓
- What word? (Signal.) *Buckles.*
- When something **folds** or **collapses,** it **buckles.** Everybody, what's another way of saying "The roof **collapsed**"? (Signal.) *The roof buckled.*

7. Touch word 6. ✓
- That word is **paleontologist.** What word? (Signal.) *Paleontologist.*
- A **paleontologist** is **a scientist who studies fossils and ancient forms of life.** Everybody, what does a **paleontologist** study? (Signal.) *Fossils and ancient forms of life.*

8. Touch word 7. ✓
- That word is **transform.** What word? (Signal.) *Transform.*
- To **transform** something is to **change** it into something else. Everybody, what's another way of saying "They **changed** electricity into heat"? (Signal.) *They transformed electricity into heat.*

EXERCISE 4

WORD PRACTICE

1. Touch the first word in part 4. ✓

4

paralyzed inflicted Wyoming sun-bleached
chiseling sidestepped locusts seeped
scar wonder skeleton died
agreed replied attempt washed
ringing blinked through respond*
warning limestone wounded

- What word? (Signal.) *Paralyzed.*

2. Next word. ✓
- What word? (Signal.) *Inflicted.*
3. (Repeat step 2 for each remaining word.)
4. (Repeat each row of words until firm.)
5. What does **respond** mean? (Call on a student.)

EXERCISE 5

WORD-ATTACK SKILLS: Individual tests

1. (Call on individual students. Each student reads a row or column. Tally the rows and columns read without error. If the group reads at least 8 rows and columns without making errors, direct all students to record 5 points in Box A of their Point Chart. Criterion is 80 percent of rows and columns read without error.)
2. (If the group did not read at least 8 rows and columns without errors, do not award any points for the Word-Attack Skills exercises.)

Lesson
54

SELECTION READING

EXERCISE 6

STORY READING

1. Everybody, touch part 5. ✓
2. The error limit for this story is 12. If the group reads the story with 12 errors or less, you earn 5 points.

5 **Tekla's Last Battle**

3. (Call on a student to read the title.) *Tekla's Last Battle.*
- What do you think this story is about? (Accept reasonable responses.)
4. (Call on individual students. Each is to read two to four sentences.)
5. (Call on individual students to answer the specified questions during the story reading.)

Tekla fought with all her might. She charged the tyrannosaur and planted her horns in its belly. She lifted her head and tossed the tyrannosaur to the side. The predator, seriously wounded, walked away from her and stood motionless for a moment, as Tekla waited with her head down. The tyrannosaur sidestepped Tekla's next charge and pounced on her back. It was all over for Tekla. She thrashed around, trying to roll over, but the huge carnivore held fast. Its jaws had come down like a mammoth vice on her spine, breaking the bones. Tekla felt dizzy. She tried to move her hind legs, but they wouldn't respond. Her rear half was paralyzed. She turned her head and watched the predator, but she didn't attempt to fight any more. A warm feeling spread over her, as if the sun had become brighter and brighter. Things looked lighter to her. The plain in the distance seemed washed out, almost white. The noises of the plain became faint ringing sounds.

She didn't remember her early years on the plain, the hundreds of times she had roamed through the grass, the water hole. She simply blinked several times. Then she saw no more. She felt very warm as the plain faded farther and farther away. Her huge head dropped to the ground, and she was dead.

The tyrannosaur didn't feed on her. It was bleeding from the deep wounds Tekla had inflicted. ❶

1. What does "the deep wounds Tekla had inflicted" mean? (Idea: *The injuries that the tyrannosaur got when Tekla charged it.*)

It walked around Tekla several times. Then it stood motionless, with its mouth half open. The other tyrannosaur returned from an unsuccessful chase. It caught the smell of blood. Quickly, it hopped around Tekla. Then without any warning, it attacked the wounded tyrannosaur, closing its jaws around the huge animal's throat. Within a few minutes, the weakened tyrannosaur was dead, lying next to Tekla.

Later that afternoon, after the surviving tyrannosaur had eaten its fill and the smaller predators had moved in to finish off the fallen dinosaurs, a strange thing happened. A great cloud of locusts swept over the plain, eating everything in their path. The grazing animals, the scavengers, and even the predators moved quickly to the north, leaving the remains of Tekla and the tyrannosaur to the locusts. If it hadn't been for those locusts, very little might have remained of Tekla. As it turned out, however, her bones and the bones of the tyrannosaur were preserved. They lay sun-bleached on the plain for more than fifty years. ❷

2. Why weren't the bones of Tekla and the tyrannosaur eaten by scavengers? (Idea: *Because a cloud of locusts scared the scavengers away.*)

Then a great flood came, and the place where Tekla had fallen became the bottom of a lake. Each year, more and more silt and sand covered the bones. After thousands of years, a solution of limestone had seeped into the bones, transforming them into solid rock. Tekla's bones were now fossilized.

Eighty million years passed. During that time, the lake dried up, the dinosaurs disappeared from Earth, and the crust of Earth buckled, forming new cliffs and mountains. Tekla's bones were near the edge of one of those cliffs. 3

3. How did the bones become fossilized? (Idea: *They were covered with water and silt, and then a solution of limestone seeped into them and turned them into rock.*)
3. What happened to the crust of the earth during those eighty million years? (Idea: *The crust of the earth buckled.*)

One day over eighty million years after Tekla's death, two paleontologists were digging for fossil remains in northern Wyoming. They were chiseling small bones from the face of a cliff. One of them chiseled around the bones of Tekla's tail. "I think we've found something," the paleontologist said to his partner. It took the paleontologists more than a month to remove the remains of Tekla and the tyrannosaur from the limestone cliff. The paleontologists carefully laid out each bone until they had reconstructed the skeletons of the two animals. They couldn't find the tip of Tekla's left horn.

When they had completed the reconstruction of the two animals, one paleontologist said, "The triceratops has a broken back. It also has an old bone scar. I wonder if the tyrannosaur killed this triceratops." 4

4. What does a paleontologist study? (Idea: *Fossils and ancient life-forms.*)
4. Where were those paleontologists digging for fossils? (Idea: *In the face of a cliff in northern Wyoming.*)

"I don't know," the other paleontologist said. "The tyrannosaur has broken bones in its neck. I don't see how a triceratops could inflict that kind of wound. And there are no signs of horn wounds on the tyrannosaur's skeleton."

"Yes," the first paleontologist said as he looked at a row of fluffy clouds above a nearby mountain. "We'll never know what happened, I guess. But I sure would have liked to have been there and seen just how those animals died."

"Me, too," the other paleontologist agreed. "But I guess we'll never know." 5

5. Where could you go to see the skeleton of a dinosaur? (Idea: *A museum.*)
6. (Award points quickly.)
7. (If the group makes more than 12 errors, repeat the reading immediately or on the next day.)

FLUENCY ASSESSMENT

EXERCISE 7

TIMED READING CHECKOUTS

1. (For this part of the lesson, assigned pairs of students work together during the checkouts.)
- (If one student does not have a checkout partner, arrange another time when you can give the checkout.)
2. (Each student does a 2-minute timed reading. Students earn 5 points by reading at least 260 words and making no more than 5 errors on the first part of story 54. Students record points in Box C of their Point Chart and plot their reading rate and errors on the Individual Reading Progress Chart.)
- (During each timed checkout, observe one pair of students for 2 minutes. Make notes on any mistakes the reader makes.)
3. (Record the timed reading checkout performance for each student you observed on the Fluency Assessment Summary form.)

Lesson 54

Lesson 54

Errors

1

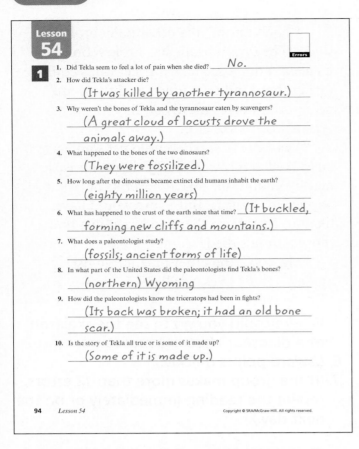

1. Did Tekla seem to feel a lot of pain when she died? No.
2. How did Tekla's attacker die?
(It was killed by another tyrannosaur.)
3. Why weren't the bones of Tekla and the tyrannosaur eaten by scavengers?
(A great cloud of locusts drove the animals away.)
4. What happened to the bones of the two dinosaurs?
(They were fossilized.)
5. How long after the dinosaurs became extinct did humans inhabit the earth?
(eighty million years)
6. What has happened to the crust of the earth since that time? (It buckled, forming new cliffs and mountains.)
7. What does a paleontologist study?
(fossils; ancient forms of life)
8. In what part of the United States did the paleontologists find Tekla's bones?
(northern) Wyoming
9. How did the paleontologists know the triceratops had been in fights?
(Its back was broken; it had an old bone scar.)
10. Is the story of Tekla all true or is some of it made up?
(Some of it is made up.)

94 Lesson 54 Copyright © SRA/McGraw-Hill. All rights reserved.

Lesson 54

2 Fill in each blank using a word in the box.

pounced	preserved	silt
buckled	paleontologist	fossil

1. Silt covered the bottom of the muddy pond.
2. Pepe was a paleontologist who studied dinosaurs.
3. The ancient mummy was well preserved.

Copyright © SRA/McGraw-Hill. All rights reserved. Lesson 54 95

WORKBOOK EXERCISES

Independent Student Work

Task A

- Open your Workbook to Lesson 54. ✓
- Complete all the parts of your Workbook lesson using a pencil. If you make no errors, you will earn 5 points.

Task B

1. (Before presenting Lesson 55, check student Workbooks for Lesson 54.)
   - (Call on individual students to read the items and answers in each part. Students mark errors using a pen.)
2. (Direct the students to count the number of errors and write the number in the Errors box at the top of the Workbook page.)
3. (Award points and direct students to record points in Box D of their Point Chart.)

0 errors ....5 points
1 error ....3 points
2 or 3 errors ....1 point
more than 3 errors ....0 points

END OF LESSON 54

Introduction to new big checkout lesson structure

- From now on, you'll have big checkout lessons and regular lessons. The big checkout lessons will occur every fifth lesson, starting with today's lesson.
- Open your Student Book to Lesson 55 and find part 1. ✓

1

Word-Attack Skills 0	points
Information Passage 5	points
Reading Checkout............ 10	points
Workbook 5	points

- The chart shows how you earn points for a big checkout lesson. You don't get any points for Word-Attack Skills. But you can earn as many as 5 points for reading the information passage.
- You can earn another 10 points for the big reading checkout. You'll read an entire story—one of the last four stories we've read. Then you can earn as many as 5 points if you make no errors in your Workbook.

WORD-ATTACK SKILLS

Student Book

EXERCISE 1

WORD PRACTICE

1. Touch the first word in part 2. ✓

2

fantastic unbelievable* interested world

sorting famous bathtub ounce

authoritative fascinating concerned thrown

- What word? (Signal.) *Fantastic.*

2. Next word. ✓
- What word? (Signal.) *Unbelievable.*
3. (Repeat step 2 for each remaining word.)
4. (Repeat each row of words until firm.)
5. What does **unbelievable** mean? (Call on a student.)

EXERCISE 2

VOCABULARY

1. Touch part 3. ✓

3

1. champion
2. set a record
3. official

- We're going to talk about what those words mean.

2. Touch word 1. ✓
- What word? (Signal.) *Champion.*
- A **champion** is a **person who is the best at something.** What would you call the student who is best in the school at running? (Call on a student.) (Idea: *The champion at running.*)
3. Everybody, touch the words in line 2. ✓
- What words? (Signal.) *Set a record.*
- Who knows what you do when you **set a record?** (Call on a student.) (Idea: *You do something better than anyone else.*)
4. Everybody, touch word 3. ✓
- What word? (Signal.) *Official.*
- An **official** record is one that is **backed by an authority.** What would you call a statement that is **backed by an authority?** (Call on a student.) (Idea: *An official statement.*)

EXERCISE 3

WORD-ATTACK SKILLS: Individual tests

(Call on individual students. Each student reads a row or column.)

Lesson 55

SELECTION READING

EXERCISE 4

NEW INFORMATION-PASSAGE READING

1. Everybody, touch part 4. ✓
2. The error limit for this information passage is **8.** If the group reads the passage with **8 errors** or less, each student earns 5 points.

4 **Setting Records**

3. (Call on a student to read the title.) *Setting Records.*
• What do you think this passage is about? (Accept reasonable responses.)
4. (Call on individual students. Each is to read two to four sentences.)
5. (Call on individual students to answer the specified questions during the passage reading.)

Most people are interested in champions. They want to know who is the best at doing different things. They are interested in the biggest, the oldest, the longest, and the most. They enjoy talking about champions and records, and they sometimes argue about who is the best at doing this or doing that. To settle arguments, people need an official, authoritative list of records. There is just such a list. It is *The Guinness Book of World Records,* a book that set a record of its own. It has become the fastest-selling book in the world. ❶

1. Why do people need an official, authoritative list of records? (Idea: *To settle arguments about champions and records.*)
1. What record has been set by *The Guinness Book of World Records?* (Idea: *The fastest-selling book in the world.*)

The Guinness Book of World Records is fascinating because it lists some of the most fantastic records ever set. Some of these are accidents of nature. Who was the tallest person, what was the largest animal, what was the oldest living thing? These were not records that anyone tried to set. These things just happened.

Some people are apparently so interested in being a champion that they aren't too concerned about what record they set, so long as they set a record or win first prize. ❷

2. Why are some people not too concerned about what record they set? (Idea: *They just want to set a record or win first prize.*)

Some of the records they have set are amazing. The Guinness book records them all.

Take sports—not just ordinary, everyday sports such as swimming, baseball, and track. Here are a few unusual sports records.

Catching a grape in the mouth: longest distance on level ground, grape thrown from 327 feet.

Bathtub racing: 36 miles in one hour, 22 minutes, 27 seconds.

Crawling (at least one knee always on the ground): longest distance, $31\frac{1}{2}$ miles.

Hoop rolling: 600 miles in 18 days.

Pogo-stick jumping: 64,649 jumps in 8 hours, 35 minutes.

Riding on horseback in full armor: 146 miles in 3 days, 3 hours, 40 minutes. ❸

3. Describe an unusual sports record you would like to set. (Accept reasonable responses.)

There are also, if you are interested, records for balancing on one foot, custard-pie throwing, and a record for onion peeling that almost makes you cry!

Some of the records suggest interesting questions. The one for nonstop joke telling, for instance. It was set by someone who cracked jokes for eight hours straight. The question is: How many listeners were still laughing at the end of the eight hours?

6. (If the group reads the passage with no more than **8 errors,** say:) Everybody earns 5 points for this reading. Write 5 in Box B of the Point Chart. ✓
   - (If the group makes more than **8 errors,** tell the students to record 0 points in Box B.)

EXERCISE 5

NEW AUTHOR'S PURPOSE

1. In the selections you've read, the author has more than one **purpose.** One of the author's purposes is to give you **practice reading words** with sounds or combinations you've been taught recently.
   - Name some words that appeared in this selection that did not appear in earlier selections. (Students should identify words such as **apparently, arguments, authoritative, champions, crawling, official, record.**)
2. A second purpose the author has is to give you some **information** you didn't have before.
   - What information about the characters or events did the selection introduce? (Ideas: *Information about interesting and odd records people have set; information about an official authoritative list of records called* The Guinness Book of World Records.)
3. A third purpose the author has is to tell **things that you could find interesting or entertaining.**
   - What are some things that could be interesting or entertaining in the selection you just read? (Accept reasonable responses.)
4. Remember, the selections are designed to give you practice with new words, to give you information about characters or events, and to tell things that you could find interesting or entertaining.

FLUENCY ASSESSMENT

EXERCISE 6

NEW TIMED READING CHECKOUTS

1. (Assigned pairs of students work together during the checkouts.)
   - (If one student does not have a checkout partner, arrange another time when you can give the checkout.)
2. For your **big checkout,** each of you will read all of story _____. (Designate one of the last four stories, 51 through 54. All students read the same story for this checkout.)
3. If you read the story in 5 minutes or less and make no more than 10 errors, you earn 10 points.
4. (Each student does a 5-minute timed reading, starting with the first sentence of the story. Students earn 10 points by reading the whole story and making no more than 10 errors. Students record points in Box C of their Point Chart.)
   - (Observe several pairs of students for about 1 minute each. Praise checkers who provide good feedback. Praise readers who read accurately.)

Note: On big checkout lessons, students do not plot their reading rate and errors on their Individual Reading Progress Chart.

Lesson 55

Lesson 55

Errors

1

1. What is a champion?

(someone who sets a record; someone who does something better than anyone else)

2. Name an official list of records.

The Guinness Book of World Records

3. What kinds of records are people interested in? (the biggest, the oldest, the longest, the most)

4. Why is an authoritative listing of records useful?

(It can be used to find correct answers; it can be used to settle arguments.)

5. What record is held by the Guinness record book?

(It's the fastest-selling book in the world.)

6. Why does the author say the Guinness book is fascinating?

(It lists some of the most fantastic records ever set.)

7. Name three records that could be called accidents of nature.

(the tallest person, the largest animal, the oldest living thing)

8. Why do some people want to set records?

(They want to be champions; they want to show they can do something better than anyone else.)

Copyright © SRA/McGraw-Hill. All rights reserved.

Lesson 55

9. Name three unusual sports in the Guinness book of records. (Any three: catching a grape in the mouth; bathtub racing; crawling; hoop rolling; pogo-stick jumping; riding on horseback in full armor)

10. What interesting question did the joke-telling record suggest?

(How many listeners were still laughing at the end of the eight hours?)

2 Fill in each blank using a word in the box.

champion	pounced	record
fossilized	buckled	official

1. He set a record for the quickest time.
2. The fastest runner was the champion of the contest.
3. The president made an official statement to reporters.

Copyright © SRA/McGraw-Hill. All rights reserved.

WORKBOOK EXERCISES

Independent Student Work

Task A

- Open your Workbook to Lesson 55. ✓
- Complete all the parts of your Workbook lesson using a pencil. If you make no errors, you will earn 5 points.

Task B

1. (Before presenting Lesson 56, check student Workbooks for Lesson 55.)
   - (Call on individual students to read the items and answers in each part. Students mark errors using a pen.)
2. (Direct the students to count the number of errors and write the number in the Errors box at the top of the Workbook page.)
3. (Award points and direct students to record points in Box D of their Point Chart.)

0 errors..................................5 points
1 error ....3 points
2 or 3 errors ....1 point
more than 3 errors ....0 points

Five-lesson point summary

- (For **letter grades** based on points for Lessons **51** through **55,** tell students to compute the total for the blue boxes [C, D, and Bonus] and write the number in the Total box at the end of each row in their Point Chart. Students then add the totals and write the sum in the green box.)
- (For **rewards** based on points, tell students to compute the total for all boxes [A, B, C, D, and Bonus] and write the number in the Total box at the end of each row. Students then add the totals and write the sum in the green box.)

END OF LESSON 55

Lesson Objectives	LESSON 56	LESSON 57	LESSON 58	LESSON 59	LESSON 60
	Exercise	Exercise	Exercise	Exercise	Exercise
Word Attack					
Decoding and Word Analysis					
Sound Combination: *ea*	1	1			
Sound Combination: variant *ea* (*as in* breath)			1	1	
Affixes: *ly, re, dis, sub, tri*	2				
Affixes: *pre, sub, un, re, ly*				2	
Letter Combinations/Letter Sounds	3	2	2	3	
Word Recognition	1–5	1–4	1–4, Info Pass.	1–5	1, 2
Vocabulary					
Morphemic Analysis	2			2	
Definitions	2, 4, 5	3, 4	2–4	2, 4, 5	2
Usage	4	3	3	2, 4	2
Assessment					
Ongoing: Individual Tests	6	5	5	6	3
Group Reading					
Decoding and Word Analysis					
Read Decodable Text	7	6	6	7	4
Read Expository Text			Info Pass.		4
Comprehension					
Access Prior Knowledge		6			
Draw Inferences	7	6	6	7	4
Note Details	7	6	6, Info Pass.	7	4
Predict	7	6	6, Info Pass.	7	
Author's Purpose				8	
Assessment					
Ongoing: Comprehension Check	7	6	6	7	4
Ongoing: Decoding Accuracy	7	6	6	7	4
Formal: Mastery Test					MT 2
Fluency Assessment					
Fluency					
Reread Decodable Text	8	7	7	9	5
Assessment					
Ongoing: Teacher-Monitored Fluency	8	7	7	9	5
Ongoing: Peer-Monitored Fluency	8	7	7	9	5
Workbook Exercises					
Decoding and Word Analysis					
Multisyllabic Word Parts	Ind. Work			Ind. Work	
Comprehension					
Main Idea	Ind. Work				
Note Details	Ind. Work	Ind. Work	Ind. Work	Ind. Work	Ind. Work
Vocabulary					
Usage	Ind. Work	Ind. Work	Ind. Work	Ind. Work	Ind. Work
Study Skills					
Writing Mechanics	Ind. Work				
Assessment					
Ongoing: Workcheck	Workcheck	Workcheck	Workcheck	Workcheck	Workcheck

Lesson 56

Regular lesson structure

- The last lesson was a big checkout lesson. Lessons 56 through 59 are regular lessons. You'll do Word-Attack Skills exercises, Selection Reading, a timed checkout, and Workbook Exercises. You'll earn the same points for each activity as you did in Lesson 54.

WORD-ATTACK SKILLS

Student Book

EXERCISE 1

NEW SOUND COMBINATION: ea

1. Open your Student Book to Lesson 56. ✓

1

ea
head
spread
bread
instead

- Touch the letters **E–A** in part 1. ✓
- Sometimes the letters **E–A** make the sound **ĕĕĕ,** as in **Ed.** You're going to read words that have the sound **ĕĕĕ** in them.

2. Touch the first word in the column. ✓
- What word? (Signal.) *Head.*
3. Touch the next word. ✓
- What word? (Signal.) *Spread.*
4. (Repeat step 3 for each remaining word.)
5. (Repeat steps 2–4 until firm.)

EXERCISE 2

AFFIX REVIEW

1. Touch part 2. ✓

2

ly
re
dis
sub
tri

- Let's see if you remember a meaning for each of those affixes.

2. Touch the letters **L–Y.** ✓
- What's one meaning of **ly?** (Signal.) *How something happened.*
3. Touch the letters **R–E.** ✓
- What's one meaning of **re?** (Signal.) *Again.*
4. Touch the letters **D–I–S.** ✓
- What's one meaning of **dis?** (Call on a student. Accept **not, the opposite of,** or **away from.**)
- What's another meaning of **dis?** (Call on another student.)
5. Everybody, touch the letters **S–U–B.** ✓
- What's one meaning of **sub?** (Call on a student. Accept **under** or **less than.**)
- What's another meaning of **sub?** (Call on another student.)
6. Everybody, touch the letters **T–R–I.** ✓
- What's one meaning of **tri?** (Signal.) *Three.*

EXERCISE 3

WORD PRACTICE

1. Touch the first word in part 3. ✓

3

university intelligent absolutely
replied disgustedly administration

- What's the underlined part? (Signal.) *er.*
- What word? (Signal.) *University.*

2. Touch the next word. ✓
- What's the underlined part? (Signal.) *j.*
- What word? (Signal.) *Intelligent.*

3. (Repeat step 2 for each remaining word.)
4. (Repeat each row of words until firm.)

EXERCISE 4

VOCABULARY

1. Touch part 4. ✓

4

1. physics
2. fault
3. property
4. detect
5. schedule

- We're going to talk about what those words mean.

2. Touch word 1. ✓
- What word? (Signal.) *Physics.*
- **Physics** is the **science of how nonliving things behave.** Everybody, what is **the science of how nonliving things behave?** (Signal.) *Physics.*

3. Touch word 2. ✓
- What word? (Signal.) *Fault.*
- A person who has a **fault** has **something wrong.** A person who **has something wrong with his or her personality** has a **personality fault.**

4. Touch word 3. ✓
- What word? (Signal.) *Property.*
- A **property** of something is a **feature.** Everybody, what's another way of saying "That light had the **feature** of redness"? (Signal.) *That light had the property of redness.*
- What's another way of saying "Some metals have the **feature** of being magnetic"? (Signal.) *Some metals have the property of being magnetic.*

5. Touch word 4. ✓
- What word? (Signal.) *Detect.*
- When you **detect** something, you **find** it. Everybody, what's another way of saying "She **found** a penny in the grass"? (Signal.) *She detected a penny in the grass.*

6. Touch word 5.
- What word? (Signal.) *Schedule.*
- To **schedule** something means to **set up a time** for it. Everybody, what does it mean to **schedule** something? (Signal.) *Set up a time for it.*

EXERCISE 5

WORD PRACTICE

1. Touch the first word in part 5. ✓

5

constantly abruptly producing failure
researchers devices* laboratory*
mathematical laser escalator irritating
focused deliver professors machine
involved clothespins conducted series
detector instruments stranded* locomotive
laugh campus experiment transform

- What word? (Signal.) *Constantly.*

2. Next word. ✓
- What word? (Signal.) *Abruptly.*

3. (Repeat step 2 for each remaining word.)
4. (Repeat each row of words until firm.)
5. What does **devices** mean? (Call on a student.)
- (Repeat for **laboratory, stranded.**)

Lesson
56

EXERCISE 6

WORD-ATTACK SKILLS: Individual tests

1. (Call on individual students. Each student reads a row or column. Tally the rows and columns read without error. If the group reads at least 10 rows and columns without making errors, direct all students to record 5 points in Box A of their Point Chart. Criterion is 80 percent of rows and columns read without error.)
2. (If the group did not read at least 10 rows and columns without errors, do not award any points for the Word-Attack Skills exercises.)

SELECTION READING

EXERCISE 7

STORY READING

1. Everybody, touch part 6. ✓
2. The error limit for this story is 12. If the group reads the story with 12 errors or less, you earn 5 points.

6 **Milly, the Joker**

3. (Call on a student to read the title.) *Milly, the Joker.*
- What do you think this story is about? (Accept reasonable responses.)
4. (Call on individual students. Each is to read two to four sentences.)
5. (Call on individual students to answer the specified questions during the story reading.)

Although Dr. Milly Jacobson was only twenty-eight years old, she was a professor of physics at State University. She was tall, intelligent, and friendly. She was good at playing tennis, at bowling, and at shooting pool. She had one serious fault, however. She constantly played jokes on the other professors. And some of her jokes were very corny and quite irritating to those involved. ❶

1. What was Milly's one serious fault? (Idea: *She constantly played jokes on the other professors.*)

For example, one day she came into her laboratory and said to Dr. Fred Frankle, "Freddy, what's one plus one?"

"Two," Fred Frankle replied.

"And what do the letters *t-o-o* spell?"

"Too," Fred Frankle replied.

"And what's the last name of the person who wrote stories about Tom Sawyer?"

"Twain," Fred replied.

"Good," Milly said. "Now say all of the answers you gave."

Fred thought for a moment. He then said, "Two, too, twain."

"Very good," Milly said and began to laugh. "Tomorrow I'll teach you how to say *locomotive.*"

Fred shook his head and said disgustedly, "Milly, don't you ever get tired of playing those corny jokes on people?"

"I'm sorry," Milly said, walking toward her laser machine. "I just can't help it." She began to laugh again. "Two, too, twain," she said softly to herself. She abruptly stopped smiling and faced Fred. "Oh, by the way. Did you hear about the robbery near campus this morning?"

"No," he said.

"Two clothespins held up a pair of pants," Milly said and began to laugh again.

"Come on, Milly," Fred said. "We've got work to do."

Milly went to her desk and took out a folder containing charts. Next to each chart was a long mathematical formula. For the past year, Milly had been working with laser beams trying to discover some of the basic properties of metals like silver, lead, iron, and gold. ❷

2. What was Milly using to try to discover some of the basic properties of metals? *Laser beams.*

She had conducted hundreds of experiments and had carefully recorded the results of each. For these experiments, she would place a bit of metal on a screen. Then she would turn a laser beam on the metal. Some laser beams are pure red light, and since they are absolutely pure, the beams do not spread out as they move from the laser gun to a nearby target. If a beam is one millimeter wide when it leaves the laser gun, it is one millimeter wide when it strikes the target. And when it strikes the target, it is capable of producing so much heat that it can transform a piece of metal into gas. Milly was using different recording devices to measure how the gas form of silver was different from the gas form of lead. ❸

3. Since a laser beam is absolutely pure, what happens to it when it leaves a laser gun? (Idea: *The light beams do not spread out.*)
3. What can a laser beam do to a piece of metal? (Idea: *Transform the metal into gas.*)

In the last experiments she had run, she had noticed something very strange. She had set the laser gun so it would deliver a series of very short bursts of light and focused it on bits of gold. This experiment had given a strange reading on the metal detector. The reading was unlike readings for lead, zinc, or any other metal.

She prepared another experiment with gold. After placing a bit of gold on the target, she again set the laser gun so it would deliver a series of short bursts. She checked the other recording instruments. Then she turned to Fred Frankle, who was writing notes in a notebook. "Say," Milly said, "did you hear about the power failure in the administration building yesterday?"

"No," Fred replied.

Milly said, "The dean was stranded on the escalator for three hours." Milly began to laugh.

Fred shook his head. "Some day," he said, "you're going to be serious about something, and nobody will believe you. You're like the little child who hollered 'wolf' too many times." ❹

4. What did Fred Frankle mean when he said, "You're like the little child who hollered 'wolf' too many times"? (Idea: *Milly jokes so much that people won't believe her when she tries to be serious.*)

"I know," Milly said. "I should stop joking around, but it makes the day so much more fun."

6. (Award points quickly.)
7. (If the group makes more than 12 errors, repeat the reading immediately or on the next day.)

FLUENCY ASSESSMENT

EXERCISE 8

TIMED READING CHECKOUTS

1. (For this part of the lesson, assigned pairs of students work together during the checkouts.)
   - (If one student does not have a checkout partner, arrange another time when you can give the checkout.)
2. (Each student does a 2-minute timed reading. Students earn 5 points by reading at least 260 words and making no more than 5 errors on the first part of story 56. Students record points in Box C of their Point Chart and plot their reading rate and errors on the Individual Reading Progress Chart.)
   - (During each timed checkout, observe one pair of students for 2 minutes. Make notes on any mistakes the reader makes.)
3. (Record the timed reading checkout performance for each student you observed on the Fluency Assessment Summary form.)

Lesson 56

[Errors]

1

1. What was Milly's job? (professor of physics)
2. What was Milly's one serious fault? (She constantly played jokes on other professors.)
3. What games was Milly good at? tennis, bowling, pool
4. Milly made Fred Frankle say something in baby talk. What did he say? ("Two, too, twain.")
5. What kind of beams was Milly working with? laser (beams)
6. What did Milly do with the results of her experiments? (She carefully recorded them.)
7. What does the heat of a laser beam do to a metal? (Heat transforms it into gas.)
8. Which metal gave a strange reading on the metal detector? gold
9. Why did Fred think Milly should stop telling jokes? (He said that people wouldn't believe her when she was serious.)
10. Why didn't Milly want to stop telling jokes? (It made her day so much fun.)

98 *Lesson 56*

Copyright © SRA/McGraw-Hill. All rights reserved.

Lesson 56

2 **Fill in each blank using a word in the box.**

property	physics	fault
transformed	detect	device

1. Essie couldn't detect the faint odor.
2. The witch transformed the handsome prince into a frog.
3. Arthur has a nice personality except for one fault.

3 **Copy the sentence that tells the main idea of the story.**

1. When Milly Jacobson conducted experiments, she carefully recorded the results.
2. Milly Jacobson was good at playing tennis, bowling, and shooting pool.
3. Milly Jacobson had been experimenting with laser beams, trying to discover some of the basic properties of metals.
4. Milly Jacobson was an intelligent professor of physics who loved to play practical jokes on other professors.

Milly Jacobson was an intelligent professor of physics who loved to play practical jokes on other professors.

4 **Write the parts for each word.**

1. researcher = re + search + er
2. submerge = sub + merge
3. triangle = tri + angle
4. disinterested = dis + interest + ed

Copyright © SRA/McGraw-Hill. All rights reserved.

Lesson 56 99

WORKBOOK EXERCISES

Independent Student Work

Task A

- Open your Workbook to Lesson 56. ✓
- Complete all the parts of your Workbook lesson using a pencil. If you make no errors, you will earn 5 points.

Task B

1. (Before presenting Lesson 57, check student Workbooks for Lesson 56.)
   - (Call on individual students to read the items and answers in each part. Students mark errors using a pen.)
2. (Direct the students to count the number of errors and write the number in the Errors box at the top of the Workbook page.)
3. (Award points and direct students to record points in Box D of their Point Chart.)

0 errors .... 5 points
1 error .... 3 points
2 or 3 errors .... 1 point
more than 3 errors .... 0 points

END OF LESSON 56

Lesson 57

WORD-ATTACK SKILLS

Student Book 

EXERCISE 1

SOUND COMBINATION: ea

1. Open your Student Book to Lesson 57. ✓

1

ea
dealt
instead
wealth
thread
deaf

- Touch the letters **E–A** in part 1. ✓
- Sometimes the letters **E–A** make the sound **ĕĕĕ,** as in **Ed.** You're going to read words that have the sound **ĕĕĕ** in them.

2. Touch the first word in the column. ✓
- What word? (Signal.) *Dealt.*
3. Touch the next word. ✓
- What word? (Signal.) *Instead.*
4. (Repeat step 3 for each remaining word.)
5. (Repeat steps 2–4 until firm.)

EXERCISE 2

WORD PRACTICE

1. Touch the first word in part 2. ✓

2

association expression reservation cigars

- What's the underlined part? (Signal.) *shun.*
- What word? (Signal.) *Association.*

2. Touch the next word. ✓
- What's the underlined part? (Signal.) *ex.*
- What word? (Signal.) *Expression.*
3. (Repeat step 2 for each remaining word.)
4. (Repeat the words until firm.)

EXERCISE 3

VOCABULARY

1. Touch part 3. ✓

3

1. researcher
2. physicist
3. jokester
4. bonds
5. provides

- We're going to talk about what those words mean.

2. Touch word 1. ✓
- What word? (Signal.) *Researcher.*
- A **researcher** is **a person who tries to discover new facts.** What's **a person who tries to discover new facts** about education called? (Call on a student.) (Idea: *An educational researcher.*)
3. Everybody, touch word 2. ✓
- What word? (Signal.) *Physicist.*
- A **physicist** is **a person who works in the field of physics.** Everybody, what is a **person who works in the field of physics** called? (Signal.) *A physicist.*
4. Touch word 3. ✓
- What word? (Signal.) *Jokester.*
- Who knows what a **jokester** is? (Call on a student.) (Idea: *A person who plays a lot of jokes on people.*)
5. Everybody, touch word 4. ✓
- What word? (Signal.) *Bonds.*
- **Forces that hold things together** are called **bonds.** Everybody, what's a **force that holds things together** called? (Signal.) *A bond.*
6. Touch word 5. ✓
- What word? (Signal.) *Provides.*
- When something **provides,** it **gives.** Everybody, what's another way of saying "A well **gives** water"? (Signal.) *A well provides water.*

EXERCISE 4

WORD PRACTICE

1. Touch the first word in part 4. ✓

4

conventions exchange surprised
exploding performing complicated
molecules behavior probably* cue
professors responded* receiving
supposed involved earlier daylights
opportunity accompany buzzer schedule*

- What word? (Signal.) *Conventions.*

2. Next word. ✓
- What word? (Signal.) *Exchange.*

3. (Repeat step 2 for each remaining word.)
4. (Repeat each row of words until firm.)
5. What does **probably** mean? (Call on a student.)
- (Repeat for **responded, schedule.**)

EXERCISE 5

WORD-ATTACK SKILLS: Individual tests

1. (Call on individual students. Each student reads a row or column. Tally the rows and columns read without error. If the group reads at least 7 rows and columns without making errors, direct all students to record 5 points in Box A of their Point Chart. Criterion is 80 percent of rows and columns read without error.)
2. (If the group did not read at least 7 rows and columns without errors, do not award any points for the Word-Attack Skills exercises.)

SELECTION READING

EXERCISE 6

STORY READING

1. (Call on individual students to answer these questions.)
- What are the names of two characters introduced in the last selection? *Milly Jacobson and Fred Frankle.*
- Which one is the main character? *Milly.*
- What did she do for a living? (Idea: *She was a professor of physics.*)
- What was the one serious fault that Milly had? (Idea: *She liked to play jokes on other professors.*)
- What kind of experiments did she run? (Idea: *Experiments about the effect of laser beams on various metals.*)

2. Everybody, touch part 5. ✓
3. The error limit for this story is 12. If the group reads the story with 12 errors or less, you earn 5 points.

5 **Convention**

4. (Call on a student to read the title.) *Convention.*
- What do you think this story is about? (Accept reasonable responses.)

5. (Call on individual students. Each is to read two to four sentences.)
6. (Call on individual students to answer the specified questions during the story reading.)

Lesson 57

Every year there are several large conventions for people who do research in physics, and every year Dr. Milly Jacobson went to one of those conventions. This year she planned to attend the convention of the International Association of Physicists. This convention allows researchers to exchange information about their latest projects, and provides an opportunity for a researcher in a branch of physics to talk to other researchers in that same branch. Milly's behavior at these conventions probably would surprise you. She played a number of jokes at home at State University, but when she went to a convention, she became a full-time jokester. ❶

1. What goes on at a physicists' convention? (Idea: *Researchers exchange information.*)
1. What happened to Milly when she went to a convention? (Idea: *She became a full-time jokester.*)

Before she left for the convention of the International Association of Physicists, she packed her handshake buzzer and her loaded cigars. She also took along her pride—a pool cue with an exploding tip that she invented herself. She had placed an exploding cap in the tip of the cue, so that when somebody tried to shoot a ball with the cue and the end of the cue would strike the ball—bang! ❷

2. What tricks did Milly pack? (Idea: *A handshake buzzer, loaded cigars, and a pool cue with an exploding end.*)

Milly was scheduled to present a paper on the experiments she had been performing with the laser beam and different metals. She wasn't ready to report on the strange readings she was receiving when she used short bursts of laser light on gold. However, she had prepared a paper on some of the earlier work she had done with the laser beam. The paper was very involved and complicated. It dealt with the kinds of bonds that hold the molecules of metals together and how the bonds of different metals responded to the laser beam. ❸

3. What was Milly scheduled to talk about? (Idea: *The experiments she had been performing with the laser beam and different metals.*)
3. What wasn't Milly ready to talk about? (Idea: *The strange readings she got when she used the laser on gold.*)

The convention of the International Association of Physicists was held in New York City. Fred Frankle was to accompany Milly. She told him, "Don't worry about reservations, Freddy. I've taken care of everything." Indeed she had.

Fred and Milly arrived at the airport; they went to the gate for the New York flight; they stood in line waiting for the agent at the gate to take their tickets and check them in for the flight.

When it was Milly's turn, she handed the agent two tickets, one for herself and one for Fred. The agent looked over the tickets. She then looked up and said, "Which one of you is Dr. Frankle?"

"I am," Fred replied.

"Well, I'm very sorry, sir," the agent said. "But this ticket is not for the New York flight. It's for Bismarck, North Dakota."

"Bismarck!" Fred shouted. "I'm supposed to go to New York."

By now Milly was laughing so hard that tears were forming in her eyes. She reached in her purse and pulled out another ticket. "Here," she said, handing the ticket to the agent. "I think this is the right one." It was Fred's ticket to New York. ❹

4. What trick did Milly play on Fred? (Idea: *She reserved a plane ticket for the wrong place.*)

"Milly," Fred said as he and Milly approached the gate. "One of these days I'm going to get really mad at you. You scared the daylights out of me. I could just see myself going to Bismarck, North Dakota."

"Oh," Milly said, laughing. "You should have seen the expression on your face. I wish I had a picture of it."

"Well, I just hope you behave yourself at the convention. Don't make a fool out of yourself like you did last year." ❺

5. Do you think Milly will follow Fred's advice? *No.*

"I'll be good," Milly replied. She was lying.

7. (Award points quickly.)
8. (If the group makes more than 12 errors, repeat the reading immediately or on the next day.)

FLUENCY ASSESSMENT

EXERCISE 7

TIMED READING CHECKOUTS

1. (For this part of the lesson, assigned pairs of students work together during the checkouts.)
- (If one student does not have a checkout partner, arrange another time when you can give the checkout.)
2. (Each student does a 2-minute timed reading. Students earn 5 points by reading at least 260 words and making no more than 5 errors on the first part of story 57. Students record points in Box C of their Point Chart and plot their reading rate and errors on the Individual Reading Progress Chart.)
- (During each timed checkout, observe one pair of students for 2 minutes. Make notes on any mistakes the reader makes.)
3. (Record the timed reading checkout performance for each student you observed on the Fluency Assessment Summary form.)

WORKBOOK EXERCISES

Independent Student Work

Task A

- Open your Workbook to Lesson 57. ✓
- Complete all the parts of your Workbook lesson using a pencil. If you make no errors, you will earn 5 points.

Task B

1. (Before presenting Lesson 58, check student Workbooks for Lesson 57.)
   - (Call on individual students to read the items and answers in each part. Students mark errors using a pen.)
2. (Direct the students to count the number of errors and write the number in the Errors box at the top of the Workbook page.)
3. (Award points and direct students to record points in Box D of their Point Chart.)

   0 errors.................................5 points
   1 error..................................3 points
   2 or 3 errors.........................1 point
   more than 3 errors ....0 points

END OF LESSON 57

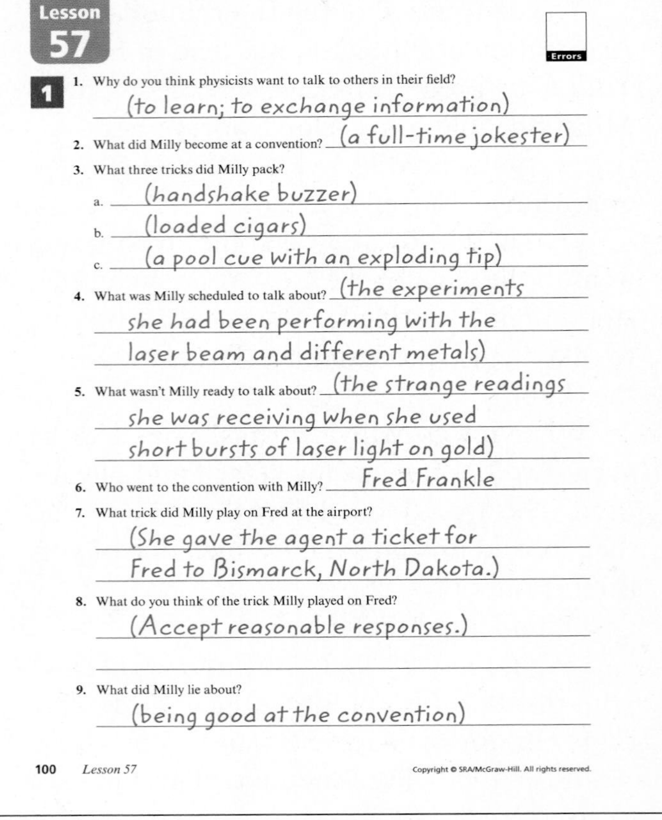

Lesson 57

Errors

1

1. Why do you think physicists want to talk to others in their field?
(to learn; to exchange information)
2. What did Milly become at a convention? (a full-time jokester)
3. What three tricks did Milly pack?
a. (handshake buzzer)
b. (loaded cigars)
c. (a pool cue with an exploding tip)
4. What was Milly scheduled to talk about? (the experiments she had been performing with the laser beam and different metals)
5. What wasn't Milly ready to talk about? (the strange readings she was receiving when she used short bursts of laser light on gold)
6. Who went to the convention with Milly? Fred Frankle
7. What trick did Milly play on Fred at the airport?
(She gave the agent a ticket for Fred to Bismarck, North Dakota.)
8. What do you think of the trick Milly played on Fred?
(Accept reasonable responses.)
9. What did Milly lie about?
(being good at the convention)

100 *Lesson 57* Copyright © SRA/McGraw-Hill. All rights reserved.

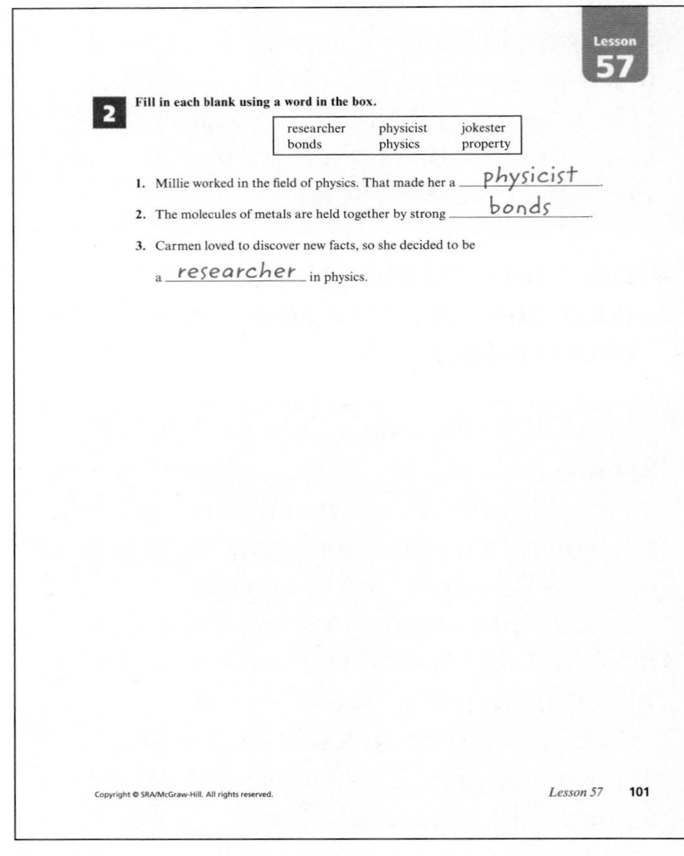

Lesson 57

2 **Fill in each blank using a word in the box.**

researcher	physicist	jokester
bonds	physics	property

1. Millie worked in the field of physics. That made her a physicist.
2. The molecules of metals are held together by strong bonds.
3. Carmen loved to discover new facts, so she decided to be a researcher in physics.

Copyright © SRA/McGraw-Hill. All rights reserved. *Lesson 57* 101

WORD-ATTACK SKILLS

Student Book

EXERCISE 1

NEW SOUND COMBINATION: variant ea

1. Open your Student Book to Lesson 58. ✓

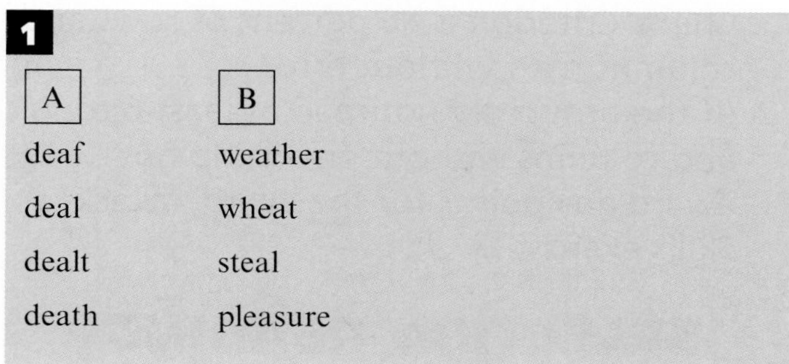

1

A	B
deaf	weather
deal	wheat
dealt	steal
death	pleasure

- Touch part 1. ✓
- In some of those words, the letters **E–A** make the sound **ēēē,** as in **eat.** In some of the words, the letters **E–A** make the sound **ĕĕĕ,** as in **Ed.**

2. Touch the first word in column A. ✓
- What word? (Signal.) *Deaf.*
3. Touch the next word. ✓
- What word? (Signal.) *Deal.*
4. (Repeat step 3 for each remaining word.)
5. (Repeat steps 2–4 for the words in column B.)

To correct word-identification errors:

a. (If students have trouble identifying the variant **ea** words, model reading the words in column A and in column B.)
b. (Then return to step 2 and repeat steps 2–5 until firm.)

EXERCISE 2

WORD PRACTICE

1. Touch the first word in part 2. ✓

2

applauded Virginia physicist* Terrance publication

- What's the underlined part? (Signal.) *aw.*
- What word? (Signal.) *Applauded.*
2. Touch the next word. ✓
- What's the underlined part? (Signal.) *j.*
- What word? (Signal.) *Virginia.*
3. (Repeat step 2 for each remaining word.)
4. (Repeat the words until firm.)
5. What does **physicist** mean? (Call on a student.)

EXERCISE 3

VOCABULARY

1. Touch part 3. ✓

3

1. harmless
2. formal
3. delicately
4. prominent

- We're going to talk about what those words mean.
2. Touch word 1. ✓
- What word? (Signal.) *Harmless.*
- Who knows what **harmless** means? (Call on a student.) (Idea: *Something that will not hurt you.*)
3. Everybody, touch word 2. ✓
- What word? (Signal.) *Formal.*
- When people are very **stiff and polite,** they are **formal.** Everybody, what's another way of saying "Their behavior was very **stiff and polite**"? (Signal.) *Their behavior was very formal.*

4. Touch word 3. ✓
- What word? (Signal.) *Delicately.*
- If you do something **delicately,** you do it **gently and carefully.** Everybody, what's another way of saying "She handled the vase **gently and carefully**"? (Signal.) *She handled the vase delicately.*

5. Touch word 4. ✓
- What word? (Signal.) *Prominent.*
- Someone who is **prominent** is **well known and important.** Everybody, what would you call a **well-known and important** dentist? (Signal.) *A prominent dentist.*
- What would you call a **well-known and important** movie star? (Signal.) *A prominent movie star.*

EXERCISE 4

WORD PRACTICE

1. Touch the first word in part 4. ✓

4

warn restaurant snickered serious* arrived

couple collar effects wonderful lobby

embarrassing association audiences stroked

ushers researchers* gentleman broadly

- What word? (Signal.) *Warn.*

2. Next word. ✓
- What word? (Signal.) *Restaurant.*

3. (Repeat step 2 for each remaining word.)
4. (Repeat each row of words until firm.)
5. What does **serious** mean? (Call on a student.)
- (Repeat for **researchers.**)

EXERCISE 5

WORD-ATTACK SKILLS: Individual tests

1. (Call on individual students. Each student reads a row or column. Tally the rows and columns read without error. If the group reads at least 6 rows and columns without making errors, direct all students to record 5 points in Box A of their Point Chart. Criterion is 80 percent of rows and columns read without error.)
2. (If the group did not read at least 6 rows and columns without errors, do not award any points for the Word-Attack Skills exercises.)

SELECTION READING

EXERCISE 6

STORY READING

1. (Call on individual students to answer this question.)
- In the last selection, Milly went to a convention. What happened? (Accept reasonable summaries.)

2. Everybody, touch part 5. ✓
3. The error limit for this story is 12. If the group reads the story with 12 errors or less, you earn 5 points.

5 **Living It Up**

4. (Call on a student to read the title.) *Living It Up.*
- What do you think this story is about? (Accept reasonable responses.)

5. (Call on individual students. Each is to read two to four sentences.)
6. (Call on individual students to answer the specified questions during the story reading.)

Milly and Fred arrived in New York City shortly after seven in the evening. They took a bus directly to their hotel. In the lobby they met several physicists they knew. One was a very serious man named Dr. Osgood Terrance, who always spoke as if he were in front of a class of students.

"Well," he said, "Dr. Jacobson and Dr. Frankle. It certainly is a pleasure to see you again. I noticed from the program that Dr. Jacobson is delivering another paper. I'm certainly looking forward to it." ❶

1. How did Dr. Osgood Terrance always speak? (Idea: *As if he were in front of a class of students.*)

Milly, who was facing Dr. Terrance, pointed straight ahead and said, "Did you see that? A man picked up somebody else's bag over there." When Dr. Terrance turned around, Milly pinned a large red-and-white button on the back of his collar. The button said KISS ME IN THE DARK.

Fred started to object, but Milly said, "Shhh. It's a harmless joke."

So the very formal Dr. Terrance chatted for a few moments and then walked across the lobby as people turned around and snickered. ❷

2. Why did people snicker at Dr. Terrance? (Idea: *Because of the funny button Milly had put on his back.*)

After going to her room, Milly took her exploding cue stick and went to the hotel's pool room. She beat a couple of physicists and a truck driver in a game of eight ball. Then she secretly loaded the tip of the cue stick with three caps, handed it to one of the physicists, and said, "Here, try this cue stick. I think you'll get a bang out of it."

He did. He was trying to make a very delicate shot. He stroked the stick back and forth several times. Then, very delicately, he hit the cue ball. BOOM. The physicist dropped the cue stick and jumped about a foot off the floor. Everybody laughed, but the physicist who tried to make the shot didn't look very happy.

Before going to bed, Milly shook hands with a very prominent physicist. Of course, she had her handshake buzzer in her hand. She pinned another red-and-white button on the back of a woman from California. Then she went to her room and retired for the night. She was having a wonderful time. ❸

3. What tricks had Milly played so far at the hotel? (Idea: *The exploding cue stick, the handshake buzzer, and funny buttons.*)

The next morning at nine o'clock she gave her talk. About seventy people were in the audience. A professor from Virginia introduced her. "Dr. Jacobson," he began, "is one of the leading laser researchers today." He then listed some of the papers Milly had written for publication and told something about her latest research. ❹

4. What was Milly's latest research about? (Idea: *The effects of laser beams on metals.*)

The people in the audience clapped, and Milly stood up. She said, "I am passing out a paper that summarizes what I have learned about the effects of laser beams on different metals." Three ushers passed out copies of the paper to everyone in the audience. "Please do not open the paper yet," Milly said as the papers were being passed out. "We'll go through it together." The members of the audience held their copies and waited. Printed on the cover of each copy were these words:

EVERYTHING I HAVE LEARNED ABOUT THE EFFECTS OF LASERS, BY DR. MILLY JACOBSON.

"OK," Milly said after all the papers had been passed out. "You can thumb through your copy now." As the members of the audience thumbed through the pages, they began to laugh. Every page was blank. A young physicist from Texas yelled out, "You've learned just as much about lasers as I have." Everybody laughed. Others in the audience made comments.

Then Milly delivered her real paper, and after going through it, she answered questions from the audience. She was very well received. The audience applauded for over a minute, and Milly smiled broadly. ❺

5. How do you know Milly was well received? (Idea: *Because the audience applauded for a long time at the end of her speech.*)

She was having a great time. Just as the audience was getting up to leave, Milly said, "Ladies and gentlemen, I would like to warn you against eating in this hotel's restaurant." Everybody stopped and looked at Milly. "They have some very embarrassing things going on there. Yesterday evening I looked at my table and saw the salad dressing."

"Oh, no," some of the people shouted. "That's corny." But Milly loved it.

7. (Award points quickly.)
8. (If the group makes more than 12 errors, repeat the reading immediately or on the next day.)

FLUENCY ASSESSMENT

EXERCISE 7

TIMED READING CHECKOUTS

1. (For this part of the lesson, assigned pairs of students work together during the checkouts.)
- (If one student does not have a checkout partner, arrange another time when you can give the checkout.)
2. (Each student does a 2-minute timed reading. Students earn 5 points by reading at least 260 words and making no more than 5 errors on the first part of story 58. Students record points in Box C of their Point Chart and plot their reading rate and errors on the Individual Reading Progress Chart.)
- (During each timed checkout, observe one pair of students for 2 minutes. Make notes on any mistakes the reader makes.)
3. (Record the timed reading checkout performance for each student you observed on the Fluency Assessment Summary form.)

WORKBOOK EXERCISES

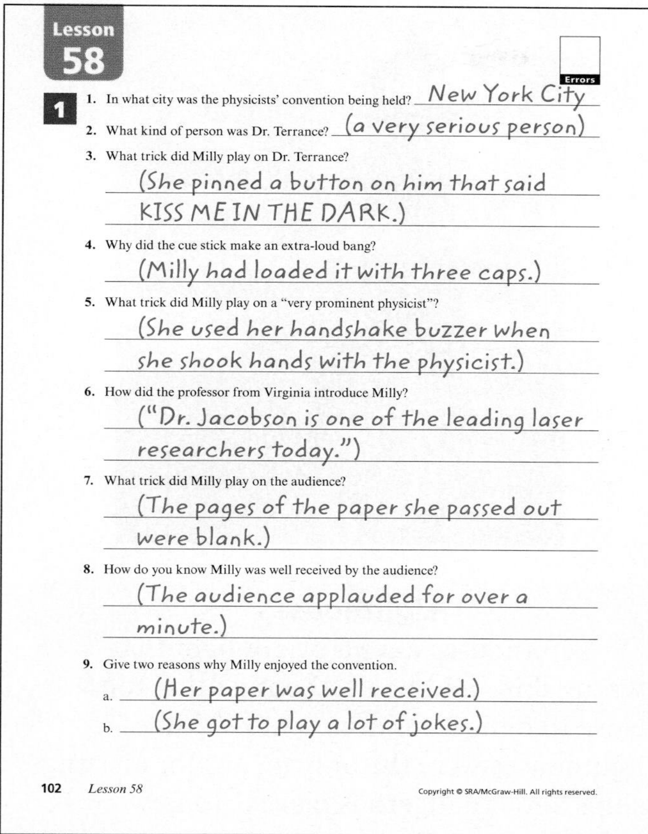

Lesson 58

Errors

1

1. In what city was the physicists' convention being held? New York City
2. What kind of person was Dr. Terrance? (a very serious person)
3. What trick did Milly play on Dr. Terrance?
   (She pinned a button on him that said KISS ME IN THE DARK.)
4. Why did the cue stick make an extra-loud bang?
   (Milly had loaded it with three caps.)
5. What trick did Milly play on a "very prominent physicist"?
   (She used her handshake buzzer when she shook hands with the physicist.)
6. How did the professor from Virginia introduce Milly?
   ("Dr. Jacobson is one of the leading laser researchers today.")
7. What trick did Milly play on the audience?
   (The pages of the paper she passed out were blank.)
8. How do you know Milly was well received by the audience?
   (The audience applauded for over a minute.)
9. Give two reasons why Milly enjoyed the convention.
   a. (Her paper was well received.)
   b. (She got to play a lot of jokes.)

102 Lesson 58 Copyright © SRA/McGraw-Hill. All rights reserved.

Lesson 58

2 Fill in each blank using a word in the box.

harmless	formal	researcher
bonds	prominent	delicately

1. A garter snake isn't poisonous, so it's really harmless.
2. She handled the vase delicately so she wouldn't break it.
3. Wherever the prominent man went, people knew who he was.

Copyright © SRA/McGraw-Hill. All rights reserved. Lesson 58 103

Independent Student Work

Task A

- Open your Workbook to Lesson 58. ✓
- Complete all the parts of your Workbook lesson using a pencil. If you make no errors, you will earn 5 points.

Task B

1. (Before presenting Lesson 59, check student Workbooks for Lesson 58.)
   - (Call on individual students to read the items and answers in each part. Students mark errors using a pen.)
2. (Direct the students to count the number of errors and write the number in the Errors box at the top of the Workbook page.)
3. (Award points and direct students to record points in Box D of their Point Chart.)

0 errors ....5 points
1 error ....3 points
2 or 3 errors ....1 point
more than 3 errors ....0 points

Note: The bonus Information Passage on the next page is not part of the regular 35- to 45-minute lesson activities. Schedule 15 to 20 minutes for presenting the passage.

Lesson 58

INFORMATION PASSAGE

> **Note:** This Information Passage is not part of the regular 35- to 45-minute lesson activities. Schedule 15 to 20 minutes for presenting the passage.

NEW INFORMATION-PASSAGE READING

Task A

1. Turn to page 196 in your Student Book. ✓
- This selection is a bonus information passage. It's something like the information passage you read in Lesson 55, but you don't receive points for reading this passage. The passage is interesting and gives you good practice reading selections that have some difficult words.
- The words in the box are words that you will read in the information passage.

Fresnel	vandals	technology
lenses	columns	engineers

2. Touch the first word. ✓
- That word is a French name, and the English pronunciation is FREZ-nell. What word? (Signal.) *Fresnel.*
3. Next word. ✓
- That word is **vandals.** What word? (Signal.) *Vandals.*
4. (Repeat step 3 for each remaining word.)
5. Go back to the first word. ✓
- What word? (Signal.) *Fresnel.*
6. Next word. ✓
- What word? (Signal.) *Vandals.*
7. (Repeat step 6 for each remaining word.)

Task B

1. (Call on a student to read the title.) *Lighthouses.*
- What is this passage about? (Call on a student.) (Idea: *Lighthouses.*)
2. (Call on individual students. Each is to read two to four sentences.)
3. (Call on individual students to answer comprehension questions during the passage reading.)

Lighthouses

Lighthouses have a bright light that warns ships and boats about getting too close to dangerous areas. At one time, lighthouses were the only means for alerting ships about dangerous places. Today, lighthouses are not necessary because ships have radar and depth finders. Some ships also use messages from Global Positioning System (GPS) to provide information about exactly where the ship is on a map. If the GPS message shows the ship in a particular location, the ship is within 10 to 20 feet of where the message indicates it is. ❶

1. Why are lighthouses located where they are? (Idea: *They were needed in dangerous areas to alert ships.*)
1. Why are lighthouses not necessary today? (Idea: *Ships use radar, depth finders, and GPS for guidance.*)
1. What does GPS stand for? *Global Positioning System.*

The early lighthouses were designed so that they were about 40 miles apart. The light from one lighthouse cannot be seen for more than about 20 miles because Earth is curved, but the light travels in a straight line. If a ship is 20 miles down the coast from one lighthouse, the ship's captain can probably see the light from the next lighthouse.

If the engineers who built lighthouses made them taller, the light would be visible from a greater distance. The problem with making them taller is that fog is common along a coast line. Often there are low clouds not more than 100 feet above the ocean. If the light from a lighthouse came from much more than 100 feet above the ocean, it would often be in the clouds, and the light would not be visible to ships. In some places, lighthouses are only about 30 feet tall. A short lighthouse tells you there are frequent fogs in the area. ❷

2. Why can't the light from a lighthouse be seen for more than 20 miles? (Idea: *Earth is curved, but light travels in a straight line.*)
2. Why aren't lighthouses taller than they are so they could be seen from farther distances? (Idea: *If lighthouses were more than 100 feet above the ocean, the light would often be in clouds and would not be visible to ships.*)
2. What do you know about an area that has a very short lighthouse tower? (Idea: *The area often has fog.*)

The most powerful lenses for lighthouses were built in France and were designed by a man named Fresnel. The Fresnel lens has a very complicated design. It has columns of glass with fins on them. A lighthouse in Oregon had one of the largest Fresnel lenses ever built. This lens, which was over six feet tall, was damaged by vandals in the 1990s. Several experts in glass and lenses decided to make replacements for the columns that were damaged. They worked for three years on this project. Even though they had equipment and technology far more advanced than Fresnel had, they could not make parts as good as those of the original lens. ❸

3. What is the name of the most powerful lighthouse lens? *Fresnel lens.*
3. How long did scientists work on trying to make lenses to replace the damaged Fresnel lenses? *Three years.*
3. Were scientists able to make lenses as effective as the original Fresnel lenses? *No.*

END OF LESSON 58

Lesson 59

WORD-ATTACK SKILLS

Student Book 

EXERCISE 1

SOUND COMBINATION: variant ea

1. Open your Student Book to Lesson 59. ✓

1

A	B
pleasant	deal
please	dealt
dream	instead
health	creature

- Touch part 1. ✓
- In some of those words, the letters **E–A** make the sound **ēēē,** as in **eat.** In some of the words, the letters **E–A** make the sound **ĕĕĕ,** as in **Ed.**

2. Touch the first word in column A. ✓
- What word? (Signal.) *Pleasant.*
3. Touch the next word. ✓
- What word? (Signal.) *Please.*
4. (Repeat step 3 for each remaining word.)
5. (Repeat steps 2–4 for the words in column B.)

To correct word-identification errors:

a. (If students have trouble identifying the variant **ea** words, model reading the words in column A and in column B.)
b. (Then return to step 2 and repeat steps 2–5 until firm.)

EXERCISE 2

AFFIX REVIEW

1. Touch part 2. ✓

2

pre sub un re ly

- Let's see if you remember a meaning for each of those affixes.

2. Touch the letters **P–R–E.** ✓
- What's one meaning of **pre?** (Signal.) *Before.*
3. Touch the letters **S–U–B.** ✓
- What's one meaning of **sub?** (Call on a student. Accept **under** or **less than.**)
- What's another meaning of **sub?** (Call on another student.)
4. Everybody, touch the letters **U–N.** ✓
- What's one meaning of **un?** (Signal.) *Not.*
5. Touch the letters **R–E.** ✓
- What's one meaning of **re?** (Signal.) *Again.*
6. Touch the letters **L–Y.** ✓
- What's one meaning of **ly?** (Signal.) *How something happened.*

EXERCISE 3

WORD PRACTICE

1. Touch the first word in part 3. ✓

3

college taught slightest
seriously pretended acid

- What's the underlined part? (Signal.) *j.*
- What word? (Signal.) *College.*

2. Touch the next word. ✓
- What's the underlined part? (Signal.) *aw.*
- What word? (Signal.) *Taught.*
3. (Repeat step 2 for each remaining word.)
4. (Repeat each row of words until firm.)

EXERCISE 4

VOCABULARY

1. Touch part 4. ✓

4

1. impish
2. undergraduate
3. graduate student
4. doctoral degree
5. related to
6. incurable

- We're going to talk about what those words mean.

2. Touch word 1. ✓
- What word? (Signal.) *Impish.*
- **Impish** means **full of mischief.** Everybody, what's another way of saying "His grin was **full of mischief**"? (Signal.) *His grin was impish.*

3. Touch word 2. ✓
- What word? (Signal.) *Undergraduate.*
- An **undergraduate** is **a student who is studying for a regular college degree.** Everybody, what is **a student working on a regular college degree** called? (Signal.) *An undergraduate.*

4. Touch the words in line 3. ✓
- What words? (Signal.) *Graduate student.*
- A **graduate student** is **someone who has an undergraduate degree and is working on a higher degree.** Everybody, what do we call **a student who has an undergraduate degree and is working on a higher degree?** (Signal.) *A graduate student.*

5. Touch the words in line 4. ✓
- What words? (Signal.) *Doctoral degree.*
- A **doctoral degree** is **the highest degree you can get.** Everybody, what is **the highest degree you can get?** (Signal.) *A doctoral degree.*

6. Touch the words in line 5. ✓
- What words? (Signal.) *Related to.*
- If it **has to do with** another thing, it is **related to** that thing. The theory **had to do** with the universe, so the theory was **related to** the universe. Everybody, what's another way of saying "His behavior **had something to do with** his mood"? (Signal.) *His behavior was related to his mood.*

7. Touch word 6. ✓
- What word? (Signal.) *Incurable.*
- When something is **incurable,** it **can't be cured.** Everybody, what's another way of saying "This disease **can't be cured**"? (Signal.) *This disease is incurable.*
- What's another way of saying "She had an illness that **couldn't be cured**"? (Signal.) *She had an incurable illness.*

EXERCISE 5

WORD PRACTICE

1. Touch the first word in part 5. ✓

5

apologized entertainers respond*
advantage practical wrong
faked conducted striking
attracted professional equals
affect routine clue

- What word? (Signal.) *Apologized.*

2. Next word. ✓
- What word? (Signal.) *Entertainers.*

3. (Repeat step 2 for each remaining word.)
4. (Repeat each row of words until firm.)
5. What does **respond** mean? (Call on a student.)

EXERCISE 6

WORD-ATTACK SKILLS: Individual tests

1. (Call on individual students. Each student reads a row or column. Tally the rows and columns read without error. If the group reads at least 9 rows and columns without making errors, direct all students to record 5 points in Box A of their Point Chart. Criterion is 80 percent of rows and columns read without error.)
2. (If the group did not read at least 9 rows and columns without errors, do not award any points for the Word-Attack Skills exercises.)

SELECTION READING

EXERCISE 7

STORY READING

1. Everybody, touch part 6. ✓
2. The error limit for this story is 12. If the group reads the story with 12 errors or less, you earn 5 points.

6 **The Same Old Routine**

3. (Call on a student to read the title.) *The Same Old Routine.*
- What do you think this story is about? (Accept reasonable responses.)
4. (Call on individual students. Each is to read two to four sentences.)
5. (Call on individual students to answer the specified questions during the story reading.)

Milly had a ball during the remaining two days of the convention of the International Association of Physicists. She attended sessions during the day and was generally very serious, except when she shook hands with her handshake buzzer or pinned one of her red-and-white buttons on another physicist. In the evenings, however, she played one joke after another. By the end of the last evening of the convention, she had attracted a crowd of people who followed her around, waiting to see what her next joke would be. Most of the people in the crowd were physicists, but some were people who found Milly more entertaining than the professional entertainers in the hotel. One reason they found Milly so funny was that, though she had an impish twinkle in her eye, she didn't look like the type of person who would play practical jokes. ❶

1. Why did people find it funny that Milly played practical jokes? (Idea: *Because she didn't look like the type of person who would play practical jokes.*)

For Milly, the convention was more fun than a circus. She had so much fun that she began to plan her tricks for the following year's convention of the International Association of Physicists.

Milly found it a little dull to return to the routine in her laboratory and her classroom. She taught two courses—one for undergraduates who were taking their first college course in physics, and another for graduate students who were studying for their doctoral degree. She was pleasant and entertaining when she taught. She told stories that related to whatever the students were studying.

Milly made it a rule never to play practical jokes on her students. From time to time she would break the rule with her graduate students, but she never joked with undergraduates. She didn't want to take advantage of them because she felt they were not in a position to get even if she played a joke on them. The other physicists, on the other hand, were Milly's equals. They could get mad at her or laugh at her or play a joke on her if they wished. And sometimes they did. ❷

2. What two courses did Milly teach? **(Idea:** *One for undergraduates and one for graduate students.***)**
2. Why wouldn't Milly play jokes on her undergraduate students? **(Idea:** *Because she felt they couldn't get even with her.***)**
2. Why would she play jokes on her fellow physicists? **(Ideas:** *Because they were her equals; because they could get even with her.***)**

For example, after Milly returned from the convention, she had very strange results when she performed a laser experiment on a piece of zinc. The reason was that the piece of zinc was not pure zinc. Fred and one of the other physicists, Dr. Helen Mark, had treated the zinc with acid. As Milly conducted the experiment and recorded the results, Fred watched her, laughing to himself. ❸

3. Why was Fred laughing to himself? **(Idea:** *Because he was playing a joke on Milly.***)**

Milly quickly figured out what was wrong, but she didn't give the slightest clue that she had. Instead, very seriously she performed several other experiments with the treated zinc. For one of these experiments, she placed a piece of the zinc in a box. What Fred didn't know was that Milly had also placed a large rubber snake in the box. The snake was on a large spring, so the snake would pop out of the box when the lid was opened.

Milly placed the box on the laser target and faked an experiment. Then she pretended to open the box and look inside. Finally, she called Fred over and said, "Freddy, I can't understand what's happening with this zinc. Look inside that box; you're not going to believe what you see."

"OK," Fred said, smiling. He opened the box, and the snake flew out, striking him on the chin. He dropped the box lid and jumped in fright. His face turned quite red as he said, "We were just trying to teach you a lesson, but I think you're incurable." ❹

4. Why did Fred say Milly was incurable? **(Idea:** *Because she reacted to his joke by playing another joke on him.***)**

> Milly apologized for her joke; then she returned to her experiments. For some reason, she decided to put a piece of gold in the box and see if the metal detector would still give strange readings. It did. Then she filled the box with dirt and shot a series of short laser bursts at it. The metal detector reacted the same as it had when there was no dirt in the box. Milly began to reason this way: If the box and the dirt don't affect the reading on the metal detector, the laser can be used to detect gold when it is underground. If the beam goes in the direction of gold, the metal detector will respond in that strange way. I can find gold with my laser. ⑤

5. Why did Milly think she could find gold with her laser? (Idea: *Because the dirt and the box didn't affect the readings.*)
6. (Award points quickly.)
7. (If the group makes more than 12 errors, repeat the reading immediately or on the next day.)

EXERCISE 8

NEW **AUTHOR'S PURPOSE**

1. You're going to tell about the **author's purpose** in the selection you just read. Remember, the author has three purposes. The first is to give you practice with new words. The second is to give new information about characters or events. The third is to tell things that you could find interesting or entertaining.
2. Name some new words that appeared in this selection that did not appear in earlier selections. (Students should identify words such as **apologized, college, entertainers, generally, impish, incurable, professional, routine, twinkle, undergraduates.**)
3. What new information about characters or events did the selection present? (Students should provide details about Milly and Fred.)
4. What are some things that could be interesting or entertaining? (Accept reasonable responses.)

FLUENCY ASSESSMENT

EXERCISE 9

TIMED READING CHECKOUTS

1. (For this part of the lesson, assigned pairs of students work together during the checkouts.)
   - (If one student does not have a checkout partner, arrange another time when you can give the checkout.)
2. (Each student does a 2-minute timed reading. Students earn 5 points by reading at least 260 words and making no more than 5 errors on the first part of story 59. Students record points in Box C of their Point Chart and plot their reading rate and errors on the Individual Reading Progress Chart.)
   - (During each timed checkout, observe one pair of students for 2 minutes. Make notes on any mistakes the reader makes.)
3. (Record the timed reading checkout performance for each student you observed on the Fluency Assessment Summary form.)

Lesson 59

1 1. When did Milly play most of her jokes at the convention?
(in the evenings)
2. What was one reason people found Milly so funny?
(She didn't look like the type of person who would play practical jokes.)
3. Why did Milly start planning her tricks for next year's convention?
(She was having so much fun.)
4. Why wouldn't Milly play practical jokes on her students?
(She didn't want to take advantage of them; they were not in a position to get even.)
5. Why did she think it was all right to play jokes on other professors?
(They were her equals; they could play a joke on her if they wished.)
6. What was wrong with the piece of zinc Milly was experimenting with?
(It was treated with acid.)
7. How did Milly turn the tables on Fred over the zinc?
(She put a rubber snake in a box and got Fred to open it.)
8. What did Fred mean when he said Milly was incurable?
(Nothing could stop her from playing practical jokes.)

104 Lesson 59 Copyright © SRA/McGraw-Hill. All rights reserved.

Lesson 59

9. What did Milly put in the box with the gold? dirt
10. Why did Milly think she could find gold with the laser?
(The box and the dirt didn't affect the strange readings on the metal detector.)

2 Fill in each blank using a word in the box.

impish	undergraduate	graduate student
doctoral degree	related to	incurable

1. The work they did was related to the surprise they planned.
2. Hector stayed in school until he finally got his doctoral degree
3. The impish monkey threw a pie in her master's face.

3 Write the parts for each word.

1. preserve = pre + serve
2. subside = sub + side
3. unprofessionally = un + professional + ly
4. rewarmed = re + warm + ed

Copyright © SRA/McGraw-Hill. All rights reserved. Lesson 59 105

WORKBOOK EXERCISES

Independent Student Work

Task A

- Open your Workbook to Lesson 59. ✓
- Complete all the parts of your Workbook lesson using a pencil. If you make no errors, you will earn 5 points.

Task B

1. (Before presenting Lesson 60, check student Workbooks for Lesson 59.)
   - (Call on individual students to read the items and answers in each part. Students mark errors using a pen.)
2. (Direct the students to count the number of errors and write the number in the Errors box at the top of the Workbook page.)
3. (Award points and direct students to record points in Box D of their Point Chart.)

0 errors................................5 points
1 error ....3 points
2 or 3 errors ....1 point
more than 3 errors ....0 points

END OF LESSON 59

Lesson
60

> **Note:** You will administer Mastery Test 2 after completing this lesson and before beginning Lesson 61.
> Record each student's score on the Mastery Test Group Summary form.

Today is a big checkout day. That means that you'll read a short information passage from your book and then do a checkout of an entire story that we've read in the last four lessons.

WORD-ATTACK SKILLS

Student Book

EXERCISE 1

WORD PRACTICE

1. Open your Student Book to Lesson 60. ✓

1

compare scientifically creature designed
greyhound cosmopolitan measuring
cheetah accurate capable distance
spine-tailed falcons maximum marine*
machine difference feats

- Touch the first word in part 1. ✓
- What word? (Signal.) *Compare.*

2. Next word. ✓
- What word? (Signal.) *Scientifically.*

3. (Repeat step 2 for each remaining word.)
4. (Repeat each row of words until firm.)
5. What does **marine** mean? (Call on a student.)

EXERCISE 2

VOCABULARY

1. Touch part 2. ✓

2

1. fascinated
2. attained
3. surpass
4. achieved
5. incredible

- We're going to talk about what those words mean.

2. Touch word 1. ✓
- What word? (Signal.) *Fascinated.*
- You're **fascinated** by something if you're **really interested** in it. Everybody, what's another way of saying "She is **really interested in** arithmetic"? (Signal.) *She is fascinated by arithmetic.*
- What's another way of saying "They were **really interested in** skiing"? (Signal.) *They were fascinated by skiing.*

3. Touch word 2. ✓
- What word? (Signal.) *Attained.*
- When you have **reached** something, you have **attained** it. Everybody, what's another way of saying "She **reached** her goal"? (Signal.) *She attained her goal.*

4. Everybody, touch word 3. ✓
- What word? (Signal.) *Surpass.*
- When you **surpass** something, you **outdo** it. Everybody, what's another way of saying "They **outdid** the old record"? (Signal.) *They surpassed the old record.*
- What's another way of saying "No one can **outdo** her in swimming"? (Signal.) *No one can surpass her in swimming.*

5. Touch word 4. ✓
- What word? (Signal.) *Achieved.*
- When you have **attained** something, you have **achieved** it. Everybody, what's another way of saying "He **attained** a perfect paper"? (Signal.) *He achieved a perfect paper.*
- What's another way of saying "She **attained** her goal"? (Signal.) *She achieved her goal.*

6. Touch word 5. ✓
   - What word? (Signal.) *Incredible.*
   - **Incredible** things are things that are **very hard to believe.** Everybody, what's another way of saying "His story was **very hard to believe**"? (Signal.) *His story was incredible.*

EXERCISE 3

WORD-ATTACK SKILLS: Individual tests

(Call on individual students. Each student reads a row or column.)

SELECTION READING

EXERCISE 4

INFORMATION-PASSAGE READING

1. Everybody, touch part 3. ✓
2. The error limit for this information passage is 8. If the group reads the passage with 8 errors or less, each student earns 5 points.

3

Speed Records

3. (Call on a student to read the title.) *Speed Records.*
   - What do you think this passage is about? (Accept reasonable responses.)
4. (Call on individual students. Each is to read two to four sentences.)
5. (Call on individual students to answer the specified questions during the passage reading.)

For some reason, people are fascinated with records. We like to know the record size of fish that are caught, the record weight of animals, and record feats of strength. The question of record speeds is one of the more popular record topics.

Let's start with human records. The fastest recorded time for a person to run 100 meters (about 328 feet) is 9.77 seconds, which would be an average speed of about 23 miles per hour. ❶

1. What is the fastest recorded time for a human to run 100 meters? *9.77 seconds.*

The human being is much slower in the water. The record time for swimming 100 meters is 47.8 seconds, which is only about 5 miles per hour. This speed is very slow when we compare it with that of the male killer whale, the blue whale. ❷

2. What is the fastest recorded time for a human swimming 100 meters? *47.8 seconds.*

This creature can swim about 30 miles per hour, but it is certainly not the fastest marine animal. The fastest fish to be scientifically clocked was a cosmopolitan sailfish, which attained a speed of 67 miles per hour. At this speed, the sailfish would swim 100 meters in about 3 seconds. ❸

3. How long would it take a sailfish to swim 100 meters? *About 3 seconds.*

Measuring the speed of land animals is much easier than measuring that of creatures in the water. The fastest racehorse achieved an average speed of about 45 miles per hour over a course approximately one-quarter of a mile long. The fastest dog is the greyhound, which has been clocked at 41 miles per hour.

The fastest land animal in the world is probably the cheetah. Experts have not been able to accurately check the top speed of a healthy cheetah. Most agree, however, that it can run over 60 miles per hour over short distances. ❹

4. What is the fastest dog? *The greyhound.*
4. What is the fastest land animal? *The cheetah.*

There are animals that are much faster than the cheetah—these animals fly. The spine-tailed swift has been clocked at about 105 miles per hour. At this speed, the bird could fly about 100 meters in about 2 seconds. There are reports of other birds that can surpass the spine-tailed swift in speed, but none has been proven. Falcons, for example, are supposed to dive at a speed of almost 200 miles per hour. But the maximum speed ever recorded for these birds has been 40 miles per hour. ❺

5. How fast can a spine-tailed swift fly? *About 105 miles per hour.*
5. Which is faster, the diving speed or the flying speed of a falcon? *The diving speed.*

Machines, of course, can go faster than any creature. The fastest car reached a speed of 763 miles per hour; the fastest plane reached a speed of 4,520 miles per hour; and the fastest rocket flew at 158,000 miles per hour.

There is an incredible difference between the speed of the human being and that of some machines. The fastest person could run 100 meters in 9.77 seconds. The fastest airplane can travel that distance in about five-hundredths of a second!

6. (If the group reads the passage with no more than 8 errors, say:) Everybody earns 5 points for this reading. Write 5 in Box B of the Point Chart. ✓
- (If the group makes more than 8 errors, tell the students to record 0 points in Box B.)

FLUENCY ASSESSMENT

EXERCISE 5

NEW TIMED READING CHECKOUTS

1. (Assigned pairs of students work together during the checkouts.)
- (If one student does not have a checkout partner, arrange another time when you can give the checkout.)
2. For your **big checkout,** each of you will read all of story _____. (Designate one of the last four stories, 56 through 59. All students read the same story for this checkout.)
3. (Each student does a 5-minute timed reading, starting with the first sentence of the story. Students earn 10 points by reading the whole story and making no more than 10 errors. Students record points in Box C of their Point Chart.)
- (Observe several pairs of students for about 1 minute each, giving readers and checkers feedback.)

Lesson 60

Errors

1

1. What is one of the more popular record topics?
   (speed records)
2. What is the fastest recorded time for a human to run 100 meters?
   9.77 seconds
3. What is the fastest marine animal to be scientifically clocked?
   cosmopolitan sailfish
4. What is the fastest land animal?
   (probably) the cheetah
5. Is it easier to measure the speed of land animals or the speed of marine animals?
   land animals
6. How fast can a spine-tailed swift fly?
   about 105 miles per hour
7. Which is faster, the diving speed or the flying speed of the falcon?
   diving speed
8. Name two machines that go faster than any creature.
   (Any two: cars, planes, rockets)
9. What is the speed record for the fastest machine in this story?
   158,000 miles per hour

2 **Fill in each blank using a word in the box.**

fascinated	attained	breed
incurable	surpassed	prominent

1. They continued climbing until they attained their goal.
2. Sonia surpassed all other running times to set a new record.
3. Cats are fascinated by mice.

106 *Lesson 60* Copyright © SRA/McGraw-Hill. All rights reserved.

WORKBOOK EXERCISES

Independent Student Work

Task A

- Open your Workbook to Lesson 60. ✓
- Complete all the parts of your Workbook lesson using a pencil. If you make no errors, you will earn 5 points.

Task B

1. (Before presenting Lesson 61, check student Workbooks for Lesson 60.)
   - (Call on individual students to read the items and answers in each part. Students mark errors using a pen.)
2. (Direct the students to count the number of errors and write the number in the Errors box at the top of the Workbook page.)
3. (Award points and direct students to record points in Box D of their Point Chart.)

   0 errors ....5 points
   1 error ....3 points
   2 or 3 errors ....1 point
   more than 3 errors ....0 points

Five-lesson point summary

- (For **letter grades** based on points for Lessons **56** through **60,** tell students to compute the total for the blue boxes [C, D, and Bonus] and write the number in the Total box at the end of each row in their Point Chart. Students then add the totals and write the sum in the green box.)
- (For **rewards** based on points, tell students to compute the total for all boxes [A, B, C, D, and Bonus] and write the number in the Total box at the end of each row. Students then add the totals and write the sum in the green box.)

END OF LESSON 60

Note: Administer Mastery Test 2 before you present Lesson 61.

MASTERY TEST 2

AFTER LESSON 60, BEFORE LESSON 61

- (Mastery Test 2 is located at the back of each student's Workbook.)
- (Mastery Test 2 has three parts. Part 1 is a group test that tests word recognition. Parts 2 and 3 are completed independently by students.)
- In Mastery Test 2, you will identify words. Then you will read a story segment and write answers to comprehension questions.

Part 1 Students identify words

1. Turn to Mastery Test 2 on page 236 of your Workbook. ✓
- Find part 1. ✓
- I'll read a word for each item. You'll fill in the bubble for that word.
2. Item 1. One of the words is **motionless.**
- The air was still, and the leaves were **motionless.** Mark **motionless.** (Observe, but do not give feedback.)
3. Item 2. One of the words is **experiences.**
- She had some interesting **experiences** on her vacation. Mark **experiences.** (Observe, but do not give feedback.)
4. (Repeat step 3 for the remaining words:)
- Item 3: **bothers.** The fly really **bothers** that poor dog. Mark **bothers.**
- Item 4: **measured.** He **measured** the fence with a yard stick. Mark **measured.**
- Item 5: **viciously.** The dog barked **viciously** at the mail carrier. Mark **viciously.**
- Item 6: **unison.** The whole class answered in **unison.** Mark **unison.**
- Item 7: **released.** She **released** her grip and let the rabbit go free. Mark **released.**
- Item 8: **seriously.** Some of the students did not take the test **seriously.** Mark **seriously.**
- Item 9: **incredible.** She performed **incredible** feats of strength. Mark **incredible.**
- Item 10: **inflicted.** The old man was **inflicted** with a terrible disease. Mark **inflicted.**
- Item 11: **seeped.** The water **seeped** through the cracks in the boat. Mark **seeped.**
- Item 12: **wonder.** I **wonder** what I will be doing on Saturday. Mark **wonder.**
- Item 13: **died.** The plant **died** in the hot sun. Mark **died.**
- Item 14: **locusts.** A swarm of **locusts** flew over the plains. Mark **locusts.**
- Item 15: **transformed.** The magician **transformed** a handkerchief into a white bird. Mark **transformed.**
- Item 16: **conducted.** Two teachers **conducted** the meeting. Mark **conducted.**
- Item 17: **director.** The **director** of the band moved her arms this way and that way. Mark **director.**
- Item 18: **physics.** He studied **physics** in college. Mark **physics.**
- Item 19: **ushers.** The **ushers** were dressed in red uniforms. Mark **ushers.**
- Item 20: **couple.** I found one rock, but she found a **couple** of them. Mark **couple.**
- Item 21: **prominent.** She was one of the most **prominent** people in the city. Mark **prominent.**
- Item 22: **locomotive.** You could hear the sound of the **locomotive** miles away. Mark **locomotive.**

- Item 23: **pleasure.**
  It was a great **pleasure** meeting the President of the United States.
  Mark **pleasure.**
- Item 24: **researches.**
  For her job, she **researches** history books.
  Mark **researches.**
- Item 25: **professional.**
  He was a **professional** car driver. Mark **professional.**
- Item 26: **creature.**
  They saw a strange two-legged **creature.**
  Mark **creature.**
- Item 27: **apologize.**
  She tried to **apologize** for the mistake that she made. Mark **apologize.**
- Item 28: **faker.**
  They finally found out that he was not a rich person, just a **faker.** Mark **faker.**

Parts 2 and 3 Students independently read the story selection and answer comprehension questions

1. Find part 2. ✓
   - You are going to read this story segment. Then you'll write answers to the questions on the last page.
2. (After students have written answers to the questions, collect tests.)

Scoring the test

1. (Count the number of errors in the whole test. Write that number in the box at the top of the test form.)
2. (Pass criterion: 0–6 errors. Circle **P.**
   - Fail criterion: 7 or more errors. Circle **F.**)
3. (Record each student's **P** or **F** score on the Mastery Test Group Summary form under Test 2.)

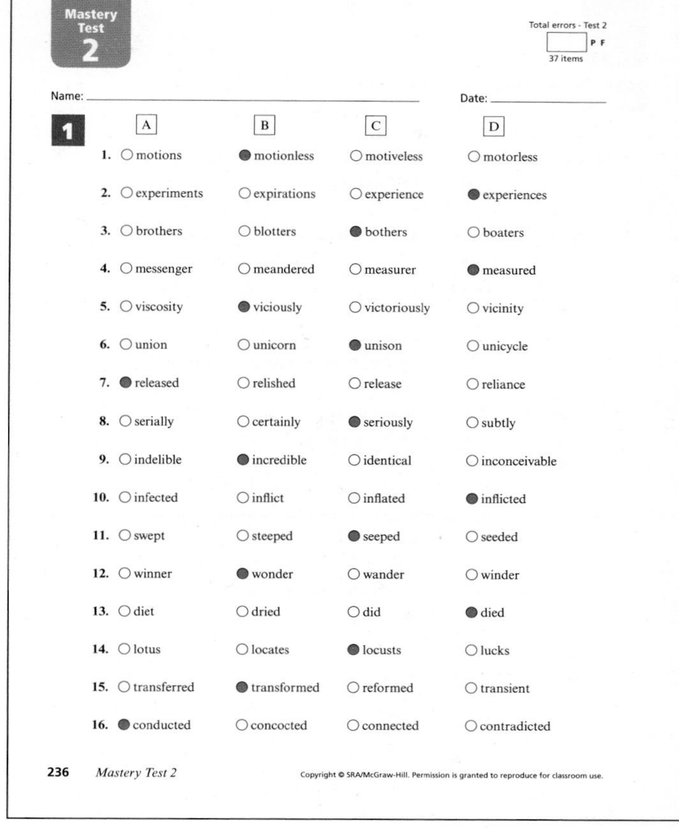

Mastery Test 2

Total errors - Test 2 P F 37 items

Name: Date:

1

	A	B	C	D
1.	○ motions	● motionless	○ motiveless	○ motorless
2.	○ experiments	○ expirations	○ experience	● experiences
3.	○ brothers	○ blotters	● bothers	○ boaters
4.	○ messenger	○ meandered	○ measurer	● measured
5.	○ viscosity	● viciously	○ victoriously	○ vicinity
6.	○ union	○ unicorn	● unison	○ unicycle
7.	● released	○ relished	○ release	○ reliance
8.	○ serially	○ certainly	● seriously	○ subtly
9.	○ indelible	● incredible	○ identical	○ inconceivable
10.	○ infected	○ inflict	○ inflated	● inflicted
11.	○ swept	○ steeped	● seeped	○ seeded
12.	○ winner	● wonder	○ wander	○ winder
13.	○ diet	○ dried	○ did	● died
14.	○ lotus	○ locates	● locusts	○ lucks
15.	○ transferred	● transformed	○ reformed	○ transient
16.	● conducted	○ concocted	○ connected	○ contradicted

236 *Mastery Test 2* Copyright © SRA/McGraw-Hill. Permission is granted to reproduce for classroom use.

Mastery Test 2

	A	B	C	D
17.	○ detector	○ dictator	● director	○ decider
18.	○ physical	○ physiques	○ psychics	● physics
19.	○ users	○ husher	● ushers	○ eskers
20.	● couple	○ capitol	○ capsule	○ copula
21.	○ prominence	● prominent	○ provident	○ promenade
22.	○ locative	○ locomotion	○ lucrative	● locomotive
23.	○ pleasant	○ plunger	● pleasure	○ plumber
24.	● researches	○ researchers	○ resources	○ reserved
25.	○ prospector	● professional	○ processional	○ profitable
26.	○ creator	○ crater	● creature	○ creditor
27.	○ apology	● apologize	○ energize	○ optimize
28.	○ faster	○ facer	● faker	○ factor

Part 1 Number of errors 28 items

Copyright © SRA/McGraw-Hill. Permission is granted to reproduce for classroom use. *Mastery Test 2* 237

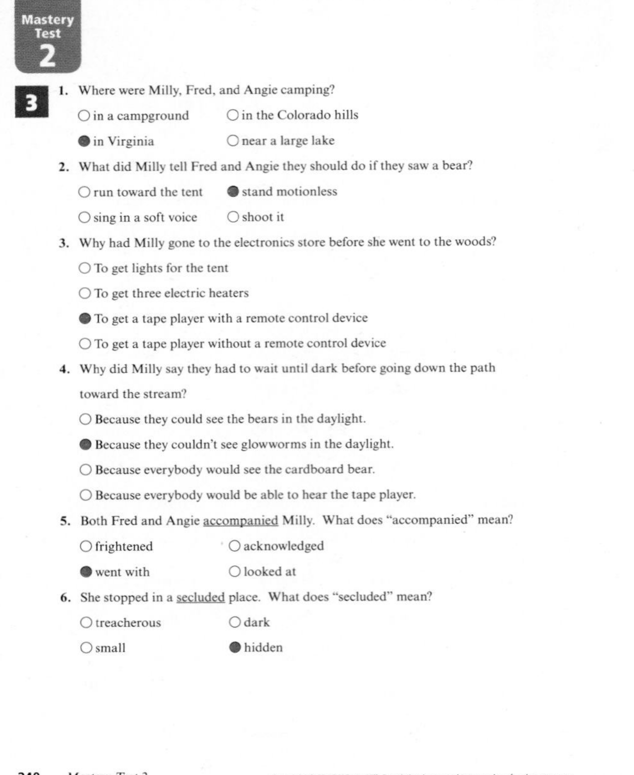
Mastery Test 2

3

1. Where were Milly, Fred, and Angie camping?
   - ○ in a campground
   - ○ in the Colorado hills
   - ● in Virginia
   - ○ near a large lake
2. What did Milly tell Fred and Angie they should do if they saw a bear?
   - ○ run toward the tent
   - ● stand motionless
   - ○ sing in a soft voice
   - ○ shoot it
3. Why had Milly gone to the electronics store before she went to the woods?
   - ○ To get lights for the tent
   - ○ To get three electric heaters
   - ● To get a tape player with a remote control device
   - ○ To get a tape player without a remote control device
4. Why did Milly say they had to wait until dark before going down the path toward the stream?
   - ○ Because they could see the bears in the daylight.
   - ● Because they couldn't see glowworms in the daylight.
   - ○ Because everybody would see the cardboard bear.
   - ○ Because everybody would be able to hear the tape player.
5. Both Fred and Angie accompanied Milly. What does "accompanied" mean?
   - ○ frightened
   - ○ acknowledged
   - ● went with
   - ○ looked at
6. She stopped in a secluded place. What does "secluded" mean?
   - ○ treacherous
   - ○ dark
   - ○ small
   - ● hidden

240 *Mastery Test 2*

Copyright © SRA/McGraw-Hill. Permission is granted to reproduce for classroom use.

Mastery Test 2

7. Why did Milly run toward the tent?
   - ○ Because Angie ran toward the tent.
   - ● Because she saw a cardboard bear.
   - ○ Because Fred was laughing at her.
   - ○ Because there were glowworms in the path.
8. Why did Milly slow down when she was running toward the tent?
   - ○ She was becoming tired.
   - ○ She encountered a bear.
   - ○ Her tape recorder let out a great roar.
   - ● She heard laughter.
9. Which answer tells about the jokes that were played in this selection?
   - ○ Angie's joke and then Milly's joke
   - ○ Fred and Angie's joke and then Milly's joke
   - ● Milly's joke and then Fred and Angie's joke
   - ○ Fred's joke and then Angie's joke

Part 3
Number of errors ☐
9 items

Copyright © SRA/McGraw-Hill. Permission is granted to reproduce for classroom use.

Mastery Test 2 241

Remedies

1. (If **30 percent or more** of the students fail the test by making **7 or more errors,** present the following firm-up procedure.
   a. Give feedback on Test 2 answers.
   - Read each item.
   - Say the item number and the column letter of the answer—A, B, C, or D.
   - Direct the students to spell the word.

   b. Repeat parts of Lessons 58 through 60:
   - Repeat Word-Attack exercises.
   - Repeat Selection Reading exercises and Fluency Assessment—Individual timed reading checkouts.
   - Present no Workbook tasks.

   c. After students have successfully completed the remedies, retest them on Mastery Test 2. Reproduce the Mastery Test as needed.)
2. (If **fewer than 30 percent** of the students fail the test, give these students information on the items they missed.)

Glossary

A

achieved	attained
adapt	do something to get along in a new situation
advice	a statement of what you think a person should do
ail (you)	make you feel bad
air pressure	how hard the air pushes against things
alert	paying close attention
anchor	an object used to hold a boat in one place
announce	tell something new
argument	a disagreement
aroused	awakened, stirred up
attained	reached

B

bargain	try to buy something at a reduced price
barge	a long, flat-bottomed boat used for carrying things
beaker	a container used in chemistry labs
bonds	forces that hold things together
bored	don't have anything to do
bothersome	bothers you
breadfruit	a large, tropical fruit
breaker	a big wave
brittle	breaks, doesn't bend
buckles	folds, collapses
buoy	a float that marks something in the water
business	buy and sell things to make money

C

canopy	a roof
carnivorous	eating mainly meat
champion	a person who is the best at something
charred	burned and blackened
chimney	a tube to carry smoke from a fireplace or furnace
chores	daily jobs
chowder	a thick soup
churned	stirred up very hard
claim	pick up something you own
collapse	fall apart
collide	crash into each other
comment	say something
concealed	hidden
continue	keep doing
convert	change
craft	a boat
crease	a mark that's left after something has been folded

D

daggerlike	pointed like a dagger
deadlocked	when neither side can win
deafening	very loud
deceptive	misleading
decide	make up your mind about something
decision	a choice about what to do
delicately	gently and carefully
demand	a need; insist on
deserve	earn or be worthy of something
detect	find
device	an object made to do something special
disapprove	not approve
disturbed	worried or upset
doctoral degree	the highest degree you can get
drizzly	like a light, quiet rain

E

emerge	come out of
enforce	make someone follow the rules
evaporate	when water is heated and goes into the air
examine	carefully look over

exceptionally	unusually
exclaim	cry out
expert	someone who knows a great deal about something
extension	something that is added
extinct	no longer living

F

faint	very weak
faked	pretended
fascinated	really interested
fault	something wrong
feast	eat a lot
fierce	very violent
figurehead	a carved figure on the front of a ship
flail	swing around like crazy
flexible	bends easily
flinch	jump as if you're startled
flounder	flop around; the name of a fish
fluttered	moved back and forth rapidly
foliage	leaves on a bush or tree
formal	stiff and polite
fossilized	what happens to the remains of a living thing from a past geological age
foul-tasting	bad-tasting
freeway	a wide highway that costs no money to travel on and has limited access
fret	worry
future	time that is to come

G

gash	a deep cut
gasp	take short, fast breaths
gear	equipment
glance	look at something quickly
glimpse	a quick look
graduate student	someone who has an undergraduate degree and is working on a higher degree
grazing	eating grass
gymnastics	tumbling, stunts on parallel bars, etc.

H

hammock	a swinging bed made of net or cloth
harmless	something that will not hurt you
helicopter	an aircraft that can go straight up and down
herd	a group of animals that live together
hesitate	pause for a moment
hoist	lift
hull	body of a ship
husks	the dry outer coverings of some fruits

I

ignore	not pay attention
immediately	something happens right away
impish	full of mischief
incredible	very hard to believe
incurable	can't be cured
indicate	point out; signal
innocent	not guilty
inspect	look over carefully
instant	very fast
insurance	a guarantee that you won't have to pay for some things that might happen
investigation	a close examination of something

J

jokester	a person who plays a lot of jokes on people

K

keen	sharp
knee-deep	up to your knees in something

L

label	a piece of paper attached to an object that gives information about that object
laboratory	a place where experiments are done
ledge	a narrow shelf
leisurely	at a slow and easy pace
leveled	flattened to the ground
litter	debris
location	a place
logical	makes sense

M

mammal	a warm-blooded creature that has hair
marine	living in the sea
mature	full-grown
minnows	small fish frequently used for bait
mole	a small animal that spends most of its life underground

N

nervous	edgy or jumpy
nitrogen	a gas that has no smell or color

O

observe	watch
occasional	once in a while
official	backed by an authority
offspring	descendants, children
original	first
outfit	a set of clothes
outskirts	the areas on the edge of a town

P

paleontologist	a scientist who studies fossils and ancient forms of life
perch	a small fish; to stand on something unsteady or high
physicist	a person who works in the field of physics
physics	the science of how nonliving things behave
pleaded	begged
polite	considerate, courteous
pounced	jumped on
prance	step high and move in a frisky way
predator	an animal that kills other animals
preserved	lasted a long time
prevented	kept something from happening
probably	likely that something will happen
procedure	a series of steps for doing something
programmed	always follows the same steps
prominent	well known and important
prop	short name for **propeller**
property	a feature
protection	something that guards
provides	gives
purchase	buy

R

related to	has to do with
remarkable	surprising or amazing
remarked	commented
remodel	change the way something looks
reply	answer
reptiles	animals like snakes and lizards
researcher	a person who tries to discover new facts
respond	answer
resume	begin again
ribs	bones located in your chest
roamed	wandered

S

salvage	valuable objects saved from someplace
scavengers	animals that eat what other animals leave behind
scent	an odor
schedule	set up a time
scramble	move quickly
secluded	well hidden
serious	important and not funny
set a record	do something better than anyone else
several	more than one and less than many
severe	very fierce
shad	a type of fish
shade	screen from light
shortage	not enough
shrill	high-pitched
silt	very fine mud
site	a place
situation	what goes on
skid	slide
slime	slippery coating
slither	to slide along
smoldering	burning and smoking without a flame
snaked	twisted
snout	the nose of an animal
solution	the answer to a problem
sound	in good condition
sprawl	stretch out
sprout	shoot out new growth
sprouts	new shoots or buds
stampede	run together in panic
statue	a likeness made of stone, wood, or metal
stern	the back end of a boat
stout	strong and heavy
strain	put forth too much effort
stranded	cannot move
stunt	a hard trick done to get attention
suddenly	something happens all at once
suggest	hint
suitable	just right
surface	the top
surfer	a person who rides a surfboard
surpass	outdo
survive	live through
suspended	hanging
swayed	moved slowly back and forth
swell	get larger
swirl	twist around

T

taut	stretched tight
termites	bugs that eat wood
thrash	move about violently
tiller	handle that steers a boat
tingly	a slightly stinging feeling
toppled	fell over
torch	a big fire on a sticklike object
trample	stamp into the ground
transform	change
tremendous	very large, great
tunnel	a passage through water or mountains

U

unbelievable	not believable
undergraduate	a student who is studying for a regular college degree
unfortunate	unlucky
unison	at the same time
unsteady	shaky, not steady
unusual	uncommon, rare, not usual
urge	a desire to do something

V

vegetation plant life

venture do something daring

verses the parts of a song that are not sung over and over

viciously fiercely

visible can be seen

W

waddle walk in a clumsy manner

wail cry out in pain

waist around the middle of the body

wispy very light and dainty